EUROPEAN HISTORICAL DICTIONARIES
Edited by Jon Woronoff

1. *Portugal,* by Douglas L. Wheeler. 1993. *Out of print. See No. 40.*
2. *Turkey,* by Metin Heper. 1994. *Out of print. See No. 38.*
3. *Poland,* by George Sanford and Adriana Gozdecka-Sanford. 1994. *Out of Print. See No. 41.*
4. *Germany,* by Wayne C. Thompson, Susan L. Thompson, and Juliet S. Thompson. 1994
5. *Greece,* by Thanos M. Veremis and Mark Dragoumis. 1995
6. *Cyprus,* by Stavros Panteli. 1995
7. *Sweden,* by Irene Scobbie. 1995
8. *Finland,* by George Maude. 1995
9. *Croatia,* by Robert Stallaerts and Jeannine Laurens. 1995. *Out of Print. See No. 39.*
10. *Malta,* by Warren G. Berg. 1995
11. *Spain,* by Angel Smith. 1996
12. *Albania,* by Raymond Hutchings. 1996. *Out of Print. See No. 42.*
13. *Slovenia,* by Leopoldina Plut-Pregelj and Carole Rogel. 1996
14. *Luxembourg,* by Harry C. Barteau. 1996
15. *Romania,* by Kurt W. Treptow and Marcel Popa. 1996
16. *Bulgaria,* by Raymond Detrez. 1997
17. *United Kingdom: Volume 1, England and the United Kingdom; Volume 2, Scotland, Wales, and Northern Ireland,* by Kenneth J. Panton and Keith A. Cowlard. 1997; 1998
18. *Hungary,* by Steven Béla Várdy. 1997
19. *Latvia,* by Andrejs Plakans. 1997
20. *Ireland,* by Colin Thomas and Avril Thomas. 1997
21. *Lithuania*, by Saulius Suziedelis. 1997
22. *Macedonia,* by Valentina Georgieva and Sasha Konechni. 1998
23. *The Czech State,* by Jiri Hochman. 1998
24. *Iceland,* by Gumundur Hálfdanarson. 1997
25. *Bosnia and Herzegovina,* by Ante Cuvalo. 1997
26. *Russia*, by Boris Raymond and Paul Duffy. 1998
27. *Gypsies (Romanies),* by Donald Kenrick. 1998
28. *Belarus,* by Jan Zaprudnik. 1998
29. *Federal Republic of Yugoslavia,* by Zeljan Suster. 1999
30. *France,* by Gino Raymond. 1998

31. *Slovakia,* by Stanislav J. Kirschbaum. 1998
32. *Netherlands,* by Arend H. Huussen Jr. 1998
33. *Denmark,* by Alastair H. Thomas and Stewart P. Oakley. 1998
34. *Modern Italy,* by Mark F. Gilbert and K. Robert Nilsson. 1998
35. *Belgium,* by Robert Stallaerts. 1999
36. *Austria,* by Paula Sutter Fichtner. 1999
37. *Republic of Moldova,* by Andrei Brezianu. 2000
38. *Turkey,* 2nd edition, by Metin Heper. 2002
39. *Republic of Croatia,* 2nd edition, by Robert Stallaerts. 2003
40. *Portugal*, by Douglas L. Wheeler. 2002
41. *Poland,* 2nd edition, by George Sanford. 2003
42. *Albania,* by Robert Elsie. 2004
43. *Estonia,* by Toivo Miljan. 2004

Historical Dictionary of Estonia

Toivo Miljan

European Historical Dictionaries, No. 43

The Scarecrow Press, Inc.
Lanham, Maryland, and Oxford
2004

SCARECROW PRESS, INC.

Published in the United States of America
by Scarecrow Press, Inc.
A wholly owned subsidiary of
The Rowman & Littlefield Publishing Group, Inc.
4501 Forbes Boulevard, Suite 200, Lanham, Maryland 20706
www.scarecrowpress.com

PO Box 317
Oxford
OX2 9RU, UK

British Library Cataloguing in Publication Information Available

Library of Congress Cataloging-in-Publication Data

Miljan, Toivo.
Historical dictionary of Estonia / Toivo Miljan.
p. cm.— (European historical dictionaries ; no. 43)
Includes bibliographical references.
ISBN 0-8108-4904-6 (alk. paper)
1. Estonia—History—Dictionaries. I. Title. II. Series.
DK503.37 .M55 2004
947.98′003—dc22 2003019176

∞ ™ The paper used in this publication meets the minimum requirements of American National Standard for Information Sciences—Permanence of Paper for Printed Library Materials, ANSI/NISO Z39.48-1992. Manufactured in the United States of America.

To Aina

Contents

Editor's Foreword

For some countries presented in Scarecrow's *European Historical Dictionaries* series, being strategically located can be a tremendous advantage. For others, alas, it has led to unmitigated disaster throughout most of their history. Estonia is very well located, between Sweden and the rest of Scandinavia, Germany, and Russia—and this has been its undoing. Being openly attacked by rulers who wanted to dominate the region or being "defensively" held to keep other rulers out, the country has suffered countless wars and collateral destruction, to say nothing of periodic nationwide hunger and plagues (at worst) and a relatively benevolent domination (at best). For only three decades of the past seven centuries has the country been free, most recently in the form of a Republic of Estonia, which arose out of the old Soviet Estonia. Yet it has constantly fought for its rights and, indeed, led the parade of former Soviet republics that have become states—a feat both astonishing and awe-inspiring.

Estonia is a very small country, even by European standards, but it boasts many notable past achievements and is at present forging one of the most advanced economies in the region. It is also making impressive progress politically, having shed communism and shifted to democracy. Like other books in this series, the *Historical Dictionary of Estonia* first sheds light on the country's long and tortured history in the chronology. It then goes on to explain how the country emerged (and subsequently reemerged) in the introduction. And further reading is provided in the bibliography. Most insightful, however, is the dictionary, which includes numerous entries on people, places, events, and institutions, as well as the various political, economic, social, and cultural aspects of the country. It is interesting to note just how important this last feature, culture, has been in Estonia's evolution and how significant a factor it remains.

This book was written by an "Estonian abroad" who finally went home. Born in Tallinn, Toivo Miljan moved first to Sweden and then to Canada, being educated in Sweden, Canada, and Great Britain. His main teaching position was in the political science department of Wilfrid Laurier University in Ontario, Canada, but he also taught in Sweden and Finland. Dr. Miljan lectured and wrote about Estonia and visited the country periodically until 1983, at which time he decided to spend nearly all of his time in the region. For the past five years, he served as the founding director of the EuroFaculty established by the Council of Baltic Sea States, where he was charged with restructuring education in various fields, including law and economics, at the University of Tartu in Estonia and at other Baltic universities. This experience enabled him to broaden and deepen his knowledge of his native land and produce this extremely informative book.

Jon Woronoff
Series Editor

Preface

Although it is a country with a small population of under 1.4 million, Estonia's physical size is larger than that of Belgium, the Netherlands, Switzerland, and Denmark; it is about half the size of Portugal. However, because of its location at the historical northern interface of east and west just west of St. Petersburg, its territory and its people, along with those of Latvia, have been the objects of great power rivalries for dominion over the borderlands ever since Christianity reached the north in the 13th century. Foreigners—first Germans, then Danes and Swedes, and for the past 300 years Russians—have held colonial sway over these lands in the past. Only fairly recently, from 1918 to 1940 and from 1991 until now, have these nations and their historic lands of settlement been independent and free from foreign dominion—for only 30 years during the past 800!

During the past decade of regained independent statehood, Estonia has quickly transformed itself from an integral part of the Soviet economy, polity, and society to an integrated member of Western Europe with one of the world's most privatized and open economies, one of the world's most computerized governments, and wireless telephone penetration at the Finnish level of saturation. Yet the country's economy, polity, and society are all conducted in impeccable Estonian! According to former president Lennart Meri, the Estonian culture has survived and even flourished under centuries of mostly inimical colonial yokes due to its "secret weapon": the difficult-to-learn Estonian language, the badge of the Estonian clan code. Indeed, Estonians have never communicated their internal feelings, literature, poetry, conflicts, or even history to the rest of the world. Hence, as the bibliography in this volume demonstrates, little is found even in the main European languages of English and German, and almost nothing in French. That is also why this dictionary contains many entries that approach encyclopedic length—to provide readers with an understanding of the complex history and privations that have nurtured this remarkable nation, and the forces that have been driving it for the past decade to "rejoin Europe."

Naturally, although I have tried to be as objective as possible, any book written by a single author will suffer some peculiarities of interpretation.

Reader's Notes

1. Estonian names consist of one Christian name and a surname. There is no patronymic as in Russian, nor is a middle name used very often, even today when West European (including Finnish, which uses middle names) and American influences are strong in every facet of life.
2. Estonian references normally do not use first names, only the initial; hence first names of some lesser historical figures have been mislaid and are difficult to find, particularly when there is only one such person in a historical category.
3. In Estonian, the concept of nation is rendered as "the People" or *rahvas* and nationalism as *rahvuslus*, meaning "centeredness of The People." Until the National Awakening, Estonians referred to themselves as *maarahvas* (people of the soil or land), *talurahvaas* (literally, people of the farm), and *talupojad* (sons of farmers). The English term "peasants," with the adjective "Estonian," most closely, but not accurately, represents the concept behind these terms. Beginning with the National Awakening, the term *Eesti rahvas* came gradually into use and acquired the meaning "Estonian nation." But the original concept of a special rootedness in the soil is still present in such historical terms as *rahvakool* (literally, the people's school), the national public school system originating in the countryside; and *rahvatants* (literally, people's dance), national folkdance.
4. In the dictionary, Estonian forms of Russian names appear except for well-known names where the standard English spelling is used, for example Yeltsin and not the Estonian Jeltsin.
5. The dictionary uses the order of the Estonian alphabet (*see* ESTONIAN LANGUAGE).
6. Finally, Estonian is a phonetic language; hence letters are sounded

in full as written much as in German. The only letter peculiar to Estonian is õ, invented in the late 19th century by **Otto Wilhelm Masing**. It is pronounced as the vowel in the English *no* or *known.* Two of the other three letters not found in English are, however, found in German. The letter ä is pronounced as the vowel in the English *cat*; and although the vowel ü has no equivalent sound in English, it is pronounced as in the German *Mütze* or the French *nul.* The letter ö, also found in the Nordic languages, is pronounced as the vowel in the English *girl*. Only a few loan words use the letters š and ž, as in *šanss* and *garaaž*, pronounced as in "chance" and "garage," respectively.

Acronyms and Abbreviations

AABS	Association for the Advancement of Baltic Studies
BALTBAT	Baltic Battalion
BALTNET	Baltic Airspace Surveillance Network
BALTRON	Baltic Naval Squadron
BATUN	Baltic Appeal to the United Nations
BDCOL	Baltic Defence College
BMD	Baltic Military District (in USSR)
Comintern	Communist International
CC	Central Committee (e.g., CC CPSU)
CBSS	Council of Baltic Sea States
CP(b)SU	Communist Party (Bolshevik) of the Soviet Union
CPSU	Communist Party of the Soviet Union
CSCE	Conference on Security and Cooperation in Europe
EC	European Community (the forerunner of the EU)
ECP	Estonian Communist Party
EKL	Eesti Korporatsioonide Liit (Union of Estonian Student Fraternities)
EKP	Eesti Kommunistlik Partei (Estonian Communist Party, or ECP)
EL	Europa Liit (European Union)
ENSV	Eesti Nõukogude Sotsialistlik Vabariik (Estonian Soviet Socialist Republic, or ESSR)
EPA	Eesti Põllumajanduse Akadeemia (Estonian Agricultural Academy; now EPMÜ)
EPMÜ	Eesti Põllumajandusülikool (Estonian Agricultural University; formerly EPA)
ERKI	Eesti NSV Riiklik Kunstiinstituut (ESSR State Art Institute; now KA)
ERSO	Eesti Riiklik Sümfooniaorkester (Estonian State Symphony Orchestra)

ESSR	Estonian Soviet Socialist Republic
EU	European Union (the name of the EC since 1993)
EÜS	Eesti Üliõpilaste Selts (Estonian Students Society)
EV	Eesti Vabariik (Republic of Estonia)
Ha.	Hectare (2.5 acres)
IME	Isemajandav Eesti (Economically Self-Managing Estonia; the acronym is also the word "miracle")
KA	Kunstiakadeemia (Academy of Art)
KGB	Komitet Gosudarsvennoye Bezopastnosti (Committee of People's Security, the Soviet secret police; successor to the NKVD)
KK	Keskkomitee (Central Committee, e.g., KK EKP)
Korp! *or* korp!	Korporatisoon (Estonian Student Fraternity, based on the German Studentenverbindungen; the Baltic German form is Corp!)
KP	Kommunistlik partei (Communist Party)
MN	Minstrite Nõukogu (Council of Ministers, government or cabinet in the Soviet system)
NATO	North Atlantic Treaty Organization
NFSV	Nõukogude Fõderatriivne Sotsialistlik Vabariik (Soviet Federal Socialist Republic)
NKVD	Narodny Kommisariat Vnutrennykh Del (Peoples' Commissariat of Internal Affairs, predecessor of the KGB)
NLKP	Nõukogude Liidu Kommunistlik Partei (CPSU)
NSDAP	Natisonal Sotsialistische Deutsche Arbeider Partei (National Socialist Workers' Party, the Nazi Party of Germany 1925–1945)
NSV	Nõukogude Sotsialistlik Vabariik (SSR)
NSVL	Nõukogude Sotsialistlike Vabariikide Liit (USSR)
OMON	Otriad Militsii Osobennogo Naznechenii (Special Task Militia Unit of the Ministry of the Interior of the USSR)
OSCE	Organization of Security and Cooperation in Europe
RFSSR	Russian Federated Soviet Socialist Republic
RL	Rahvasteliit (League of Nations)
RR	Rahvarinne (Peoples' Front)
SA	Sturmabteileung (Stormtroopers, also known as Brownshirts)

SD	Sicherheitsdienst (German Security Service)
SS	Schutzstaffel (Shock Troops, also known as Blackshirts)
SSR	Soviet Socialist Republic
TPI	Tallinna Polütehniline Instituut (Tallinn Polytechnical Institute; now TPÜ)
TPÜ	Tallinna Pedakoogikaülikool (Tallinn Pedagogical University)
TRK	Tallinna Riiklik Konservatoorium (Tallinn State Conservatory; now Tallinn Conservatory)
TRÜ	Tartu Riiklik Ülikool (Tartu State University, now TÜ)
TTÜ	Tallinna Tehnikaülikool (Tallinn Technical University; formerly TPI)
TÜ	Tartu Ülikool (University of Tartu)
UN	United Nations
ÜRO	Ühendatud Rahvaste Organiatsioon (**United Nations**)
USSR	Union of Soviet Socialist Republics
VAT	Value-Added Tax
Waffen SS	Volunteer élite army formed as a subdivision of the SS
WEU	West European Union

FINLAND
SWEDEN
NORWAY
Helsinki
Oslo
Stockholm
St. Petersburg
Tallinn
ESTONIA
RUSSIA
Riga
Gothenburg
LATVIA
DANMARK
LITHUANIA
Copenhagen
Malmö
Kaliningrad
Vilnus
Minsk
Gdańsk
Hamburg
BELARUS
Berlin
Amsterdam
POLAND
GERMANY
Warsaw
UKRAINE
Kiev
0
500 km

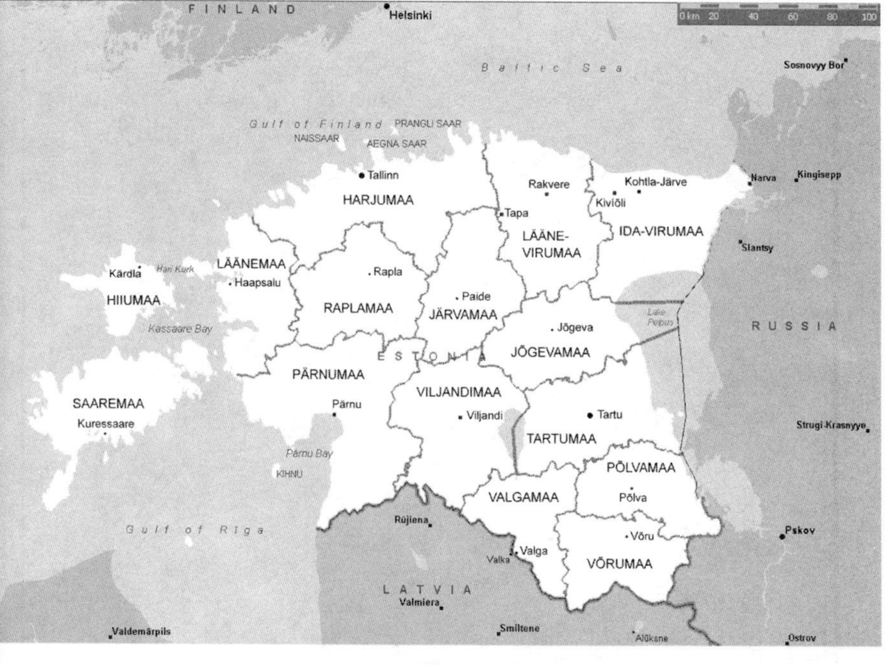

FINLAND
Helsinki
0 km 20 40 60 80 100
Baltic Sea
Sosnovyy Bor
Gulf of Finland
PRANGLI SAAR
NAISSAAR
AEGNA SAAR
Tallinn
HARJUMAA
Rakvere
Kohtla-Järve
Kiviõli
Narva
Kingisepp
Tapa
LÄÄNE-
VIRUMAA
IDA-VIRUMAA
Slantsy
LÄÄNEMAA
Kärdla
Hari Kurk
Haapsalu
HIIUMAA
Rapla
RAPLAMAA
Paide
JÄRVAMAA
Kassaare Bay
Jõgeva
Lake Peipus
RUSSIA
JÕGEVAMAA
ESTONIA
PÄRNUMAA
SAAREMAA
Kuressaare
Pärnu
VILJANDIMAA
Viljandi
Tartu
TARTUMAA
Strugi-Krasnyye
Pärnu Bay
KIHNU
PÕLVAMAA
Põlva
VALGAMAA
Rūjiena
Gulf of Riga
Võru
Pskov
Valga
Valka
VÕRUMAA
LATVIA
Valmiera
Valdemārpils
Smiltene
Alūksne
Ostrov

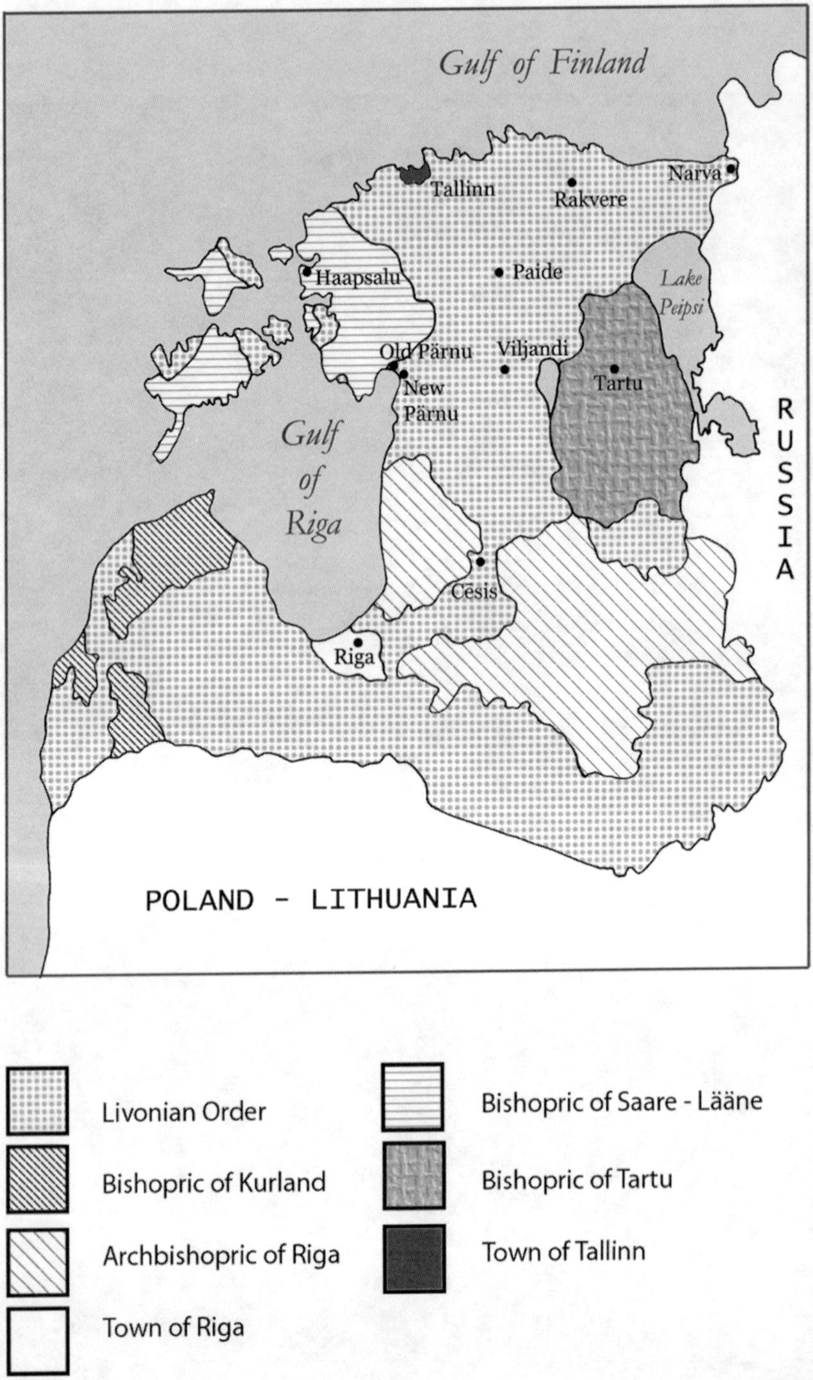

Gulf of Finland
Tallinn
Rakvere
Narva
Haapsalu
Paide
Lake Peipsi
Old Pärnu
Viljandi
New Pärnu
Tartu
Gulf of Riga
RUSSIA
Cēsis
Riga
POLAND - LITHUANIA

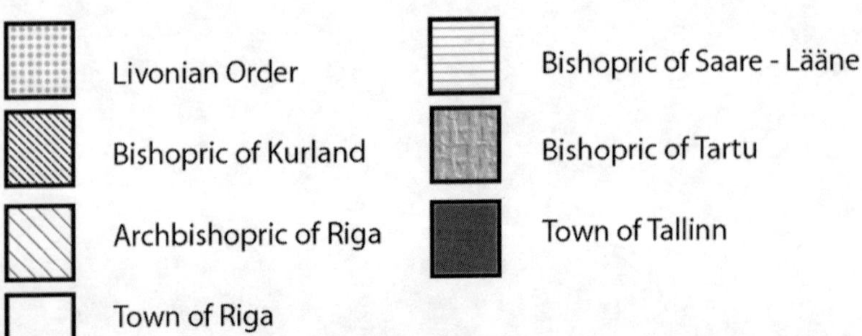

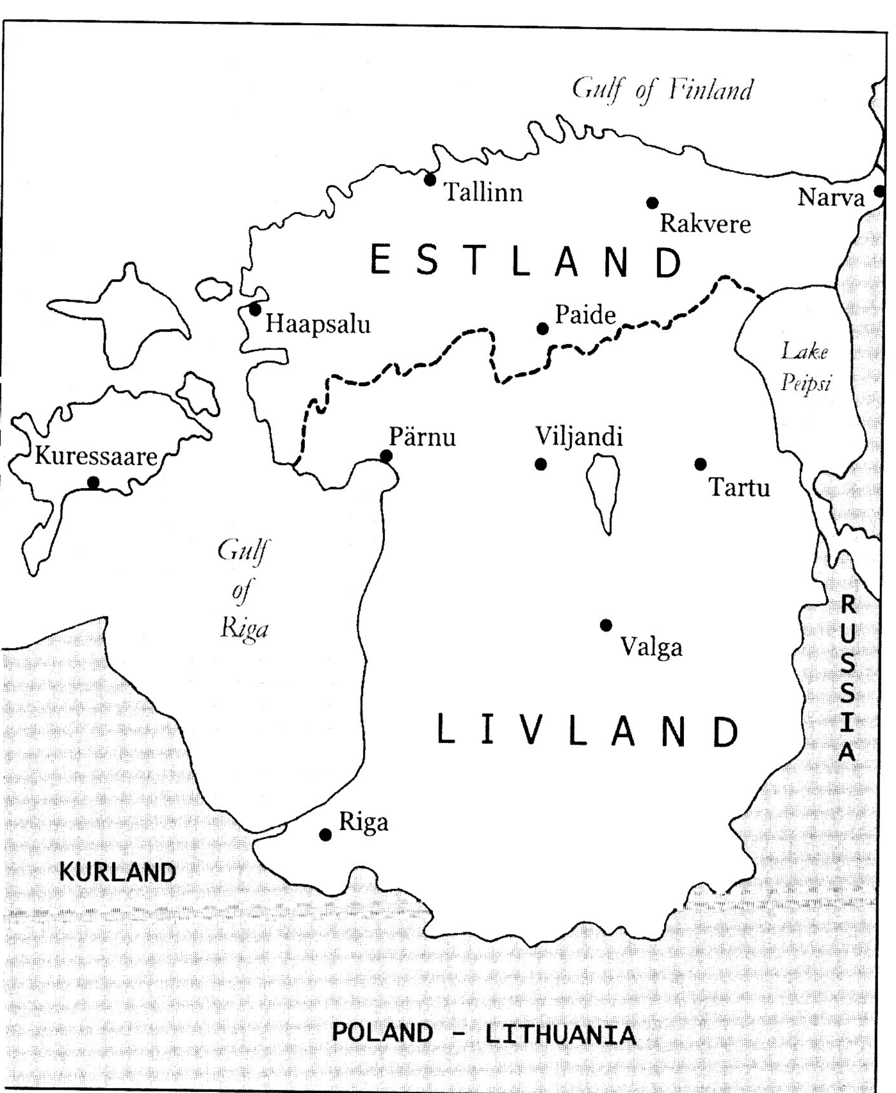
Gulf of Finland
Tallinn
Narva
Rakvere
ESTLAND
Haapsalu
Paide
Lake Peipsi
Pärnu
Viljandi
Kuressaare
Tartu
Gulf of Riga
RUSSIA
Valga
LIVLAND
Riga
KURLAND
POLAND - LITHUANIA

Chronology

Prehistory

1030 Kievan prince Yaroslav (written as Jaroslav in Estonian) the Wise conquers the Tartu (Tarbatu; Jurjev in Russian) fortification, gains control of southeast Estonia, and imposes taxes; possible introduction of Christianity to Estonia; first written reference to Tartu under the name Jurjev.

c. 1050 Estonians begin trading and raiding Viking expeditions across the Baltic Sea to Sweden.

1061 Estonians reconquer the Tartu fort.

c. 1065 The Benedictine monk Fulco is ordained as bishop of Estonia by the archbishop of Lund.

1169 or 1170 Fulco's first mission to Estonia; apparently, there are some Christian congregations already in Estonia.

c. 1177 Fulco's second mission to Estonia.

1202 Pope Innocent III declares crusade to Christianize Old Livonia; the Schwertbrüder Orden (Order of the Brethren of the Sword) is founded.

The Ancient Struggle for Freedom (1208–1227)

1208 The Schwertbrüders' first attack on the county of Ugandi in Estonia together with Christianized Latvians and Livs: burning of Otepää fortification, counterattack by Ugandians and Sakalanians on Latvian territory, and Latvian pillaging attack on Sakala; at year's end, a one-year truce is signed.

1209 The Order and Latvians attack Ugandi.

1210 Russians attack Ugandi; combined forces of the Order, the bishop of Riga, Latvians, and Livs attack Ugandi; the second burning of Otepää; Estonians attack Cēsis (Võnnu in Estonian, Wenden in German); victory at the battle of Ümera (Daugava in Latvian) over the German, Latvian, and Liv force; at year's end, the combined German, Latvian, Liv, and Russian force attacks Soontagana.

1210–11 First recorded plague in Estonia.

1211 Estonian attacks on Latvia; German, Latvian, and Liv attacks in Estonia; siege and conquest of the fortification of Viljandi; baptism of Estonians in Sakala; Estonians besiege Turaida fort in Latvia and are defeated at the battle of Koiva; Russians attack Varbola; Lembitu attacks Pskov.

1212 Three-year truce signed at Turaida between Estonians and Germans.

1213 Lithuanians pillage Sakala.

1215 Germans, Latvians, and Livs pillage Ridala and Sakala and conquer the fort at Leola in the winter; in spring three Estonian *malev* foray into Latvia; in summer Latvians make nine raids into Ugandi and on Valga; battle of the New Harbour in Saaremaa; baptisms at Ugandi and Sakala.

1216 Winter forays by Germans, Latvians, and Livs on Soontagana and Saaremaa; in spring, units from Saaremaa raid northern Latvia; in summer Germans, Latvians, and Livs attack Harju an Revala; in fall Russians attack Ugandi.

1217 In January Germans and Ugandians attack Pskov; in late winter Germans, together with Livs, Latvians, and Ugandians, make a foray into Jervia and Vironia, ending in the capitulation of Jervia; Läänemaa Estonians and Russians encircle Otepää and force its German defenders to retreat; Germans raid northern Latvia; Germans, Latvians, and Livs attack Sakala, resulting in the free Estonian counties joining together and forming a *malev* under the leadership of Lembitu; in the battle of St. Matthew's Day (21 September), the Estonians are defeated and

Lembitu is killed; in consequence, southern and central Estonia counties conclude peace with the Germans and are baptized.

1218 Germans, Latvians, and Livs make a winter excursion into Läänemaa, baptize and impose taxes on them; in spring a Saaremaa *malev* raids northern Latvia; on St. John's Day, Bishop Albert requests the help of Danish King Valdemar II to jointly subdue the Estonians; in fall two German battles with Russians at Väike Emajõgi and the Harrians together with the Russians lay siege to Wenden (Võnnu).

1219 German, Latvian, and Liv forces raid to Harju and Revala during the winter months: Danish naval force lands at Lindanisa fort (site of Tallinn); battle of Lindanisa; Revala capitulates and the people are baptized; in autumn months, Germans, Latvians, and Sakalanians raid Jervia.

1220 In winter Germans, Latvians, and Livs, together with Jervians, Ugandians, and Sakalanians, raid Vironia; thereafter Saaremaa forces pillage christianized Estonians in Jervia; Germans, Latvians, Livs, and baptized Estonians raid Harju and Revala; baptizing of Vironians; agitated by Danes, Harju forces make nine raids into Jervia attempting to force them to renege their commitments to the Germans; during the summer, a Swedish force attacks Läänemaa, captures Lihula fort, and baptizes the people; in August a Saaremaa force recaptures the fort.

1221 In April a combined Saaremaa and North Estonian force fails to recapture Tallinn from the Danes; Danes and Germans agree on establishing spheres of influence; Estonians begin to adopt public symbols and rites of Christianity.

1222 During the summer, a Danish force lands in Saaremaa and builds a stone fort; Saare forces capture the fort after King Voldemar leaves and agitate the Harju, Lääne, Vironia, and Jervia populations into opposing the Germans.

1223 At the end of January, Sakalanias revolt in Viljandi, followed by Ugandian revolt in February, the subsequent encircling of Tallinn, and the capture of German forts; Tallinn remains in Danish hands; attacks and counterattacks in the south of the country; Estonians lose the second Battle of Ümera (Daugava); Germans retake Viljandi in August; a

Russian force raids Germans strongholds throughout Estonia as ally of the Estonians.

1224 In January Germans attack Harju; in August they lay siege to the fort of Tarbatu (Tartu); the whole of the mainland capitulates to the Germans and reaccepts Christianity.

1227 In February a combined force of Germans, Latvians, Livs, and mainland Estonians captures the Muhu (island) fortress; the Valjala fort is destroyed; Saaremaa capitulates and its people are baptized. Thus, the independence of Ancient Estonians ends.

The First Century of Foreign Domination (1227–1340)

1227 The Order of the Brethren of the Sword (Schwertbrüder Orden) consolidates its control over Tallinn and the rest of Estonia; Tallinn receives a town charter from Riga.

1237 The Order of the Brethren of the Sword (Schwertbrüder Orden) join the Deutsche Orden (Teutonic Order) to form the Livonian Order.

1237–41 Saaremaa rises up against the foreign overlords.

1238 The Steinsby Treaty restores Tallinn and northern Estonia to Denmark.

1239 The *Liber Census Daniae* is compiled: it includes the first recorded data on northern Estonia.

1248 Tallinn receives town charter from Lübeck.

1249 The Cloister of Cistercian Order of Nuns is founded in Tallinn.

1251 First record of a school in Estonia (the Cathedral School at Pärnu).

1260–61 Second Saaremaa uprising against the foreign overlords.

1263 Lithuanians raid and burn Old Pärnu; the bishop of Saare-Lääne moves his seat from Pärnu to Haapsalu.

1279 Haapsalu receives town charter.

1283 First reference to Viljandi as a town; during the next few years Tallinn, Tartu, Pärnu, and Haapsalu became members of the Hanseatic League.

1291 Paide receives town charter.

1297–98 Civil war between the Livonian Order and Riga against the bishops.

c. 1300 Three-field system of crop rotation is adopted.

1302 Rakvere receives town charter.

1305 The Cistercians found the Padise Cloister.

1315 Starvation in Livonia as a result of several years of drought.

1328–30 The second Livonian Civil War.

1340 First reference to Tallinn City Hall.

St. George's Night Uprising (1243–1245)

1343 **23 Apr:** Burning of manors, churches, and Padise cloister and the widespread killing of Germans in Harju; Estonians lay siege to Tallinn; the election of four kings. **c. 25 Apr:** Revolt spreads to Läänemaa. **4 May:** Negotiations resulting in the betrayal and murder of the four Estonian kings at Paide. **11 May:** Battle of Kimmola and Kanavere between the Estonian force besieging Tallinn and a Livonian Order relief force. **14 May:** The main Estonian siege force is defeated at the Battle of Sõjamäe. **18 May:** A naval force led by the Swedish Bailiff of Viipuri arrives to assist the Estonians. **26 May:** The Pskov force attacks the Bishopric of Tartu. **24 July:** Saaremaa rises up against the Germans; Põide fortification is captured by Estonians. **End of year:** A large force of the Order arrives in Harju to punish the Estonians.

1244 **Feb:** The Order attacks Saaremaa for the first time.

1245 The second attack on Saaremaa ends in its total subjugation by the Order. Thus ends the last attempt by Estonians to free themselves from foreign rulers by force until 1918.

Old Livonia (1345–1357)

1345 Narva receives town charter.

1346 Danish king sells northern Estonia to the Teutonic Order for 19,000 marks.

1372 First town school built in Tallinn (on Pikk Street).

1396 Bishop Theodoricius of Tartu makes war on the Teutonic Order.

1397 Teutonic Order pillages Tartu in June–July.

1407 Monastery of the Augustinian Order is built at Pirita in Tallinn.

1422 The Diet of Old Livonia gathers for its initial meeting (in Valga), consisting of members of the Livonian Order, their estate-owning vassals, and representatives of the church and burghers; subsequently the Diet becomes the ruling organ of Old Livonia.

1433 First recorded great fire in Tallinn.

1464 Plague kills two thirds of the population of Tallinn.

1474 The Cathedral is completed in Tallinn.

1480–81 First war between Old Livonia and Muscovite Russia.

1492 Russia builds Ivangorod fortress on the right bank of the River Narva opposite the town of Narva.

1500 Estonian population passes a quarter million.

1500–02 Second Livonian-Russian war.

1504–05 Plague ravages Estonia.

1507 Peasants are forbidden to possess weapons in Old Livonia.

1515–20 Several waves of plague sweep over Estonia.

1523 The Reformation comes to Estonia.

1524 **14 Sep:** Catholic churches are pillaged in Tallinn.

1525 **7 and 10 Jan:** Tartu churches are ravaged; Dominican monks are driven from Tallinn during January. **1 Nov:** Catholic churches are pillaged in Viljandi.

1526 On 15 March the Catholic churches are pillaged in New Pärnu.

1552 First library is founded in Tallinn.

1553 Delegates of Old Livonia attempt to extend the peace treaty with Tsar Ivan IV in return for payment of tribute.

1555–56 War between the bishop of Riga and the Livonian Order.

1556 The tsar's representative arrives in Tartu and demands payment of arrears of promised tribute; the bishop makes deceitful promises.

A Century of War (1558–1629)

1558 **Jan–July:** Tsar Ivan IV (the Terrible) attacks, pillages, and captures the lands of the Bishopric of Tartu, which thus becomes the first Livonian state to be extinguished.

1559 The bishop of Saare-Lääne sells his lands to Danish King Frederick II, who installs his brother Duke Magnus as its ruler.

1560 **2 Aug:** The Battle of Härgmäe, in which the Livonian Order is decisively defeated by the Russian invaders, proves to be the Order's last battle. **22 Aug:** Viljandi is captured by the Russians; a few weeks later, a peasants' revolt against the Order in Harjumaa quickly spreads to Virumaa and Läänemaa; at the end of the year, the Order garrisons several towns with Polish forces in an attempt to hang on to power.

1561 **4–6 June:** The nobles of Harju, Virumaa, and Läänemaa, together with the burghers of Tallinn, transfer their allegiance to Swedish King Erik XIV; the nobles of the remaining parts of Old Livonia, including central and southern Estonia, submit to Polish King Zygmund II August who becomes grand duke of Livonia.

1562 Kuressaare on Saaremaa is granted town charter.

1570–78 Northern Estonia is ruled by Duke Magnus, who, however, is a dependent of the Russian tsar.

1578 Widespread starvation in Estonia.

1580 Plague in Estonia.

1581 **6 Nov:** Sweden captures Narva from Russia.

1583 **10 Aug:** Sweden and Russia agree to a three-year armistice.

1584 Valga acquires town rights.

1585 The Russo-Swedish truce is extended to 1590.

1590–95 Russo-Swedish war.

1591 Plague in Estonia.

1595 On 5 May at the Peace of Täyssina Sweden cedes Ingermanland to Russia.

1600–29 Russo-Swedish war over Livland.

1601–02 Starvation and plague in Estonia.

1628 First glass manufacture founded in Estonia on Hiiumaa; it operates until 1664.

1629 **16 Sep:** Russia cedes all of Estonia to Sweden at the Peace of Altmark.

Swedish Times (1629–1699)

1630 First gymnasium in Estonia established at Tartu; gymnasium in Tallinn (now the Gustav Adolf Gymnasium) founded—the oldest continuously operating secondary school in Estonia; first printing press in Estonia established in Tallinn.

1631–56 The University of Tartu is founded by the Swedish king in 1631 and operates under the name Academia Gustaviana in Tartu until 1656.

1643–45 Danish-Swedish war.

1645 Denmark cedes Saaremaa to Sweden at the Peace of Brömsebro.

1656–61 Russo-Swedish war.

1657–58 Plague sweeps Estonia.

1661 Peace treaty between Russia and Sweden.

1680–1700 Most estates of nobles and vassals of the Livonian Order confiscated by the Swedish state.

1684–88 The Forselius seminary for schoolmasters operates near Tartu.

1687 The beginning of widespread founding of village schools for peasants.

1690–1710 The second period of operation of the University of Tartu (1699–1710 in Pärnu).

1695–97 The Great Hunger in Estonia: one fifth (70,000–75,000) of the population dies.

1699 Tsar Peter I, Polish King (who is also German Archduke) August II, and Danish King Frederick IV form military alliance against Swedish King Charles XII.

The Great Northern War (1700–1721)

1699 **22 Feb:** August II begins the war by unsuccessfully laying siege to Riga but is forced to withdraw in May. **30 Aug:** Russia declares war on Sweden. **3 Oct:** Russian forces arrive at Narva. **15 Nov:** Charles XII arrives with his army at Tallinn. **30 Nov:** Charles XII defeats the Russian force at the Battle of Narva.

1702 **9 Jan:** The Russian force defeats the Swedes at the Battle of Erastvere. **29 July:** They repeat their victory at the Battle of Hummuli.

1703 The Russian force devastates Virumaa, Järvamaa, Viljandimaa, Tartumaa, and Võrumaa—thus laying waste most of Estonia.

1704 **14 May:** Russia defeats Sweden at the Battle of Kastre. **4 July:** They capture Tartu; 20 Aug: They capture Narva.

1709 **8 July:** The Swedish defeat at the Battle of Poltava in Poland signals the end of Swedish supremacy on the eastern shores of the Baltic Sea.

1710–13 The last Great Plague scourging Estonia kills 200,000 or about half the population.

1710 **23 Aug:** Russia conquers Pärnu. **26 Sep:** Kuressaare. **10 Oct:** the burghers of Tallinn and the Ritterschaft of Estland pledge allegiance to the tsar.

1718 Peter the Great begins to construct the Palace of Kadriorg (Katharinenthal) in Tallinn as a summer retreat for his queen.

1721 **10 Sep:** The Treaty of Uusikaupunki (Neustadt in German, Nystad in Swedish) transfers Estland, Livland, and Ingermanland, as well as southeastern Karelia, to Russia.

The First 135 Years in the Russian Empire (1721–1856)

1730 The Hernhutian religious sect arrives in Estonia and begins to propagate reading among the peasantry.

1782 The customs border between Russia and the Baltic Provinces is abolished.

1783 Paldiski is granted town rights.

1784 The Town of Võru is founded.

1788–90 Russo-Swedish War.

1792 First factory producing mirrors in Estonia.

1802 After seven decades, the University of Tartu is reopened.

1812 A defense force is organized in Estonia to counter the threat posed by Napoleon's march on Moscow.

1816 Serfdom is abolished in the Gubernya (Province) of Estland (consisting of the northern half of historic Estonia).

1819 Serfdom is abolished in the Gubernya of Livland (consisting of the southern half of Estonia and the historic Latvia provinces of Vidzeme and Zemgale, with Riga as the capital).

1823 In Tallinn, J. A. Hagen forms the first choir of native Estonians.

1834–38 An agricultural institute operates in Vana-Kuuste.

1838 The Estonian Learned Society is founded.

1839 The Cimze Parish schoolmasters seminary is established at Valmiera (Vollmar), which moves to Valga in 1849.

1843 E. Ahrens publishes his Estonian grammar, which becomes the foundation for written Estonian.

1849 Tsar Nikolai I proclaims the new peasant farm law in the Gubernya of Livland, which enables peasants to purchase their tenant farms as freeholds; hence farm purchases begin in Livland (including the southern half of Estonia).

1850 The founding of the Narva linen mill.

1853 The Estonian Naturalists Association is formed.

1853–55 A combined British-French naval force appears in Estonian waters in connection with the Crimean War.

1854 Aleksander II extends the peasant farm law to the Gubernya of Estland, thus enabling farm purchases to begin in northern Estonia.

National Awakening (1857–1880)

1857 *Perno Postimees*, the first permanent Estonian newspaper, begins publication; Kreenholm Manufaktuur, eventually to become the largest textile mill and most progressive industrial complex in Estonia during the ensuing century, is founded in Narva.

1857–61 The national epic *Kalevipoeg* is published by the Estonian Learned Society.

1854 The Mahtra War (*Mahtra sõda*), the last Estonian uprising of peasants.

1860s The beginning of Estonian indigenous building of sailing ships; migration to urban areas begins.

1861 In search of the promised land, followers of the "Prophet Maltsev" migrate to the Crimea.

1863 Movement organized to raise funds and receive imperial authorization to found the Estonian Aleksander School as the first Estonian-language secondary school.

1864 **21 Nov:** At the instigation of Johan Kõler, personal artist to the tsar, a major Estonian peasants' petition is presented to the Tsar.

1865 The song and theater societies Vanemuine in Tartu, and Estonia in Tallinn, are founded.

1866 The Law on Local Self-government abrogates the historic rights of the noble estate owners to control peasant village life; the right of estate owners to keep a herd on village property is removed; the abrogation of the Guild Law enables Estonians to enter skilled occupations.

1967 Corvée labor is abrogated; the last hunger in Estonia, caused by drought.

1867–70 Three influential patriotic speeches by C. R. Jakobson.

1869 The first national Song Festival takes place on 18–20 June in Tartu.

1870 The first play written originally in Estonian, *Saaremaa Onupoeg* (*The Nephew from Saaremaa*) by Lydia Koidula, is also the first presentation by an Estonian national theater (at Vanemuine in Tartu); **5 Nov:** The first railroad in Estonia opens, connecting Paldiski, Tallinn, and Narva to St. Petersburg.

1870–71 The first agricultural societies are formed at Tartu, Pärnu, and Viljandi.

1872–93 The Society of Estonian Literati becomes the foundation of the Estonian intelligentsia until it is closed by imperial authority.

1875 The song and theater society Endla is formed in Pärnu.

1876 Rail traffic between Tapa and Tartu begins on 11 August.

1880 The novel ***Tasuja*** (***The Avenger***) by E. Bornhöhe induces patriotic fervor in large numbers of readers. **11–13 June:** the Third National Song Festival takes place, for the first time in Tallinn.

Russification (1881–1904)

1880 **13 Mar:** The liberal and progressive Tsar Aleksander II is assassinated and is succeeded by the reactionary Russophile Aleksander III.

1881 Carl Robert Jakobson dies at 41; since Jakob Hurt had moved to St. Petersburg, the Gubernya of Estland is left without prominent nationalist leadership.

1882–83 An imperial governmental review of conditions in the Baltic Provinces determines that the Baltic German nobles' rule should be replaced by direct imperial rule as in the rest of the empire.

1883 **4 June:** The blue-black-white tricolor of the Eesti Üliõpilaste Selts (EÜS, the Estonian Students Society), which subsequently becomes the national flag, is blessed at Otepää church.

1886 Russian is decreed the official language of communication in both urban and rural municipal administrations.

1887 Russian is decreed the language of instruction beginning in grade three in all public schools.

1888 Jakob Hurt initiates the collection of national folkloric poetry; the Estonian Aleksander School opens at Põltsamaa, but as a Russian-language school. **10 Aug:** The first horse-drawn tram route opens in Tallinn, connecting Kadriorg with today's Viru Square.

1889 Tartu is renamed Jurjev; the transition from German to Russian begins at the University; the first temperance society in Estonia is founded at Tori.

1893 The first hydroelectric power plant in Estonia begins operating at Kunda with a capacity of 210 kilowatts.

1896 Jaan Tõnisson becomes editor of the newspaper *Postimees*; the first cinematic presentations in Tartu and Tallinn; the first automobile arrives in Estonia; the first narrow gauge railroad, between Pärnu and Valga, begins operating.

1900 Aleksander Läte forms Estonia's first symphony orchestra in Tartu; the electric motor factory Volta begins production.

1900–03 Economic crisis.

1901 Konstantin Päts founds the newspaper *Teataja* in Tallinn.

1902 The first commercial bank in Estonia is founded in Tartu.

1903 Painter Ants Laikmaa founds the first arts academy in Estonia.

1904 The publishing house Noor Eesti is founded; the Keila-Haapsalu rail line opens; after elections in Tallinn, Konstantin Päts leads an Estonian-Russian takeover of the city council from the Baltic Germans.

Revolution to World War I (1905–1916)

1905 25 Jan: A general strike begins in Tallinn. **27 Oct:** Estonian workers join the pan-Russia strike. **29 Oct:** At the New Market in Tallinn, demonstrators are fired on by imperial troops, who kill 90 and wound 200. **26 Dec:** At Tartu in the Bürgermesse Hall, a pan-Estonian congress of elected representatives meets but splits on a left-right dimension with one group moving to the University's Auditorium. **26 Dec and after:** Approximately 120 nobles' manors are burned and looted by mobs in Estonia.

1906 800 imperial navy sailors arrive in Estonia to quell the rioting and are divided into eight 100-man punishment units; 600–700 people are executed by war tribunals and drumhead courts; Estonian as the language of instruction is allowed in the first two years in all primary schools; private Estonian language schools are authorized; the first fully Estonian-language school, the girls' school, Noorsoo Kasvatus Seltsi Tütarlastegymaansium, opens in Tartu; Vanemuine's new purpose-built theater building opens in Tartu.

1907 First plant in Estonia built to provide power for household electric power comes on stream in Pärnu.

1908 First radio transmission station in Estonia is built at the Russian Imperial Baltic Fleet's Tallinn port—during the War of Independence, it plays an important role in enabling communication with foreign states.

1908–18 Mikhail Rostovstsev operates the Tartu Private University with medical, physics, and mathematics faculties.

1909 The Estonian National Museum is founded in Tartu.

1912 Building of major naval port installations and several naval shipyards, as well as the naval fort envisaged by Peter the Great, begins at Tallinn in preparation for the expected war with Germany; the Viljandi Linen Mill begins operation. **27 Apr:** The first airplane lands in Estonia.

1913 24 Aug: The Estonia Theater and Concert Hall building is inaugurated.

1914 1 Aug: Imperial Germany declares war on imperial Russia. **5 Aug:** Imperial Germany declares war on imperial Austria-Hungary.

1914–17 Approximately 100,000 Estonian men are conscripted into the imperial Russian forces; approximately 10,000 are killed.

1915 The battle front reaches Latvia, causing an influx of refugees to Estonia; shortages of flour, sugar, and meat develop during the autumn. **20 Aug:** Russian forces, fearing a German commando operation, burn the Waldhof pulp mill, then the largest in Europe. **15 Nov:** Steam trams begin operating on the Kopli tram line in Tallinn.

1916 The increasing shortage of imported coal leads to the mining of oil shale for underfiring; toward year-end, urban food shortages increase drastically.

Revolution, Declaration of Independence, and German Occupation (1917–1918)

1917 **14 Mar:** General strike begins in Tallinn. **15 Mar:** Sailors from the Baltic Fleet ships in port join the strikers. **20 Mar:** The Russian provisional (Kerensky) government recalls the Russian governor and appoints Jaan Poska, mayor of Tallinn, as its commissioner of the Gubernya of Estland. **22 Mar:** The Tallinn Estonia Federation, a pan-Estonia association of voluntary societies, is formed. **24–26 Mar:** A meeting of representatives of all counties of Estonia demands the union of all Estonian settlement areas into one province. **8 Apr:** 40,000 Estonians demonstrate in St. Petersburg in support of the counties' meeting demand for a united Province of Estonia. **12 Apr:** A Russian provisional government decree establishes the united Province of Estonia (Estland and the northern part of Livland), grants it autonomy with Jaan Poska as governor, and provides for an elected Provincial Council (Maanõukogu). **Apr:** The Estonian Soldiers' Bureau, led by Konstantin Päts and Johan Pitka, begins coordinating the patriation of Estonian soldiers in the imperial army. **5 June:** Election of the Maanõukogu. **1–4 July:** First Estonian Soldiers' Congress, meeting in Tallinn, elects the Estonian Soldiers' Supreme Committee. **14 July:** Maanõukogu convenes at Toompea. **15 July:** A congress of all elected local government representatives, the National Congress (Rahvakongress), meets at the Estonia Theater; left-wing delegates leave the hall under protest. **16–17 July:** Rahvakongress meets. **2–3 Aug:** Maanõukogu meets and elects a government (Maavalitsus) led by Jaan Raamot (later replaced by Päts).

12–21 Oct: German marine units occupy the islands of Saaremaa, Muhu, and Hiiumaa. **9 Nov:** The Bolsheviks in Tallinn remove Jaan Poska as governor and seize power. **14 Nov:** All noncommunist newspapers are closed. **28 Nov:** Maanõukogu declares itself the sovereign power on Estonian territory and resolves to call a Constituent Assembly to regularize sovereign authority in Estonia.

1918 6 Jan: The Council of Elders of the Maanõukogu resolves to declare Estonia a sovereign independent state. **14 Feb:** The Gregorian calendar replaces the Julian (thus 1 Feb. becomes 14 Feb.). **19 Feb:** The Executive Committee of the Maanõukogu, together with its Council of Elders, approves the Manifesto on the Declaration of Independence and elects a three-man Rescue Committee (Konstantin Päts, Jüri Vilms, and Konstantin Konik). **20–21 Feb:** German forces land on the mainland from the islands and cross the border from Latvia in the south. **24 Feb:** Declaration of Independence; provisional government is formed with Päts as prime minister a few hours before the German armed forces reach Tallinn. **25 Feb:** Russian imperial fleet abandons Tallinn naval port as German forces occupy it. **4 Mar:** German forces reach Narva, thereby bringing all of Estonia under German occupation. **Apr:** Estonian national units of the Russian imperial army are disbanded by the Germans; Jüri Vilms, on his way to Finland on provisional government assignment, is captured and executed in Helsinki by German forces. **11 Nov:** First public session of the provisional government; Kaitseliit (Estonian Defense League), is founded. **20 Nov:** The provisional government resigns. **21 Nov:** Mobilization into Estonian national armed forces begins. **22 Nov:** German forces repulse Red army attack on Narva. **24 Nov:** Conscription to Estonian national forces begins in Viru County. **27 Nov:** Päts forms the second provisional government.

War of Independence (1918–1920)

1918 28 Nov: Red Army units, together with Estonian Bolshevik units, capture Narva. **29 Nov:** The Estonian Workers' Commune (Estonian Bolsheviks' puppet government) is formed; the Päts government orders general conscription. **8 Dec:** Red Army conquers Võru; Juhan Laidoner arrives in Estonia. **12 Dec:** A Royal Navy squadron arrives in Tallinn and donates arms for the Estonian national forces. **15–24 Dec:**

Red Army conquers Rakvere, Tartu, and Tapa, thus occupying half of Estonia's territory. **22 Dec:** Col. Laidoner is appointed commander-in-chief of the Estonian Armed Forces. **30 Dec:** The first contingent of Finnish volunteers arrives in Estonia.

1919 7–18 Jan: Estonian Armed Forces under the command of Laidoner roll back the Red Army, freeing Tapa, Rakvere, Tartu, and Narva. **31 Jan:** Victory at the Battle of Paju opens the road to Valga, which, along with Võru, is retaken on 1 February. **5 Feb:** Estonian forces arrive at Petseri (Pechora). **16–24 May:** Red Army attempts repeatedly to breach and push back the battlefront, but is repulsed by Estonian forces; the line is stabilized. **5–7 Apr:** Elections to the Constituent Assembly. **23 Apr:** Constituent Assembly convenes. **9 May:** The provisional government resigns and is replaced by the Strandman cabinet as approved by the Constituent Assembly. **13 May:** The Russian Whites' attack on Petrograd begins. **15 May:** Estonian and Ingrian forces begin campaign to free Ingermanland. **25 May:** Estonian forces conquer Pihkva (Pskov). **27 May:** Estonian forces open campaign on southern front toward Jebkabpils in Latvia. **30 May:** Estonian Bolshevik units are disbanded in Russia by the Red Army, which considers them untrustworthy. **5 June:** On the southern front, the Landeswehr War begins with a German attack on Estonian armored trains. **19 June:** Red Army commences a repulsive attack on the Northern Corps of the Whites at Petrograd. **19–20 June:** Indecisive battles of Lemsalu and Roopa between Estonian forces and the Iron Division of Rüdiger von der Golz. **21–23 June:** Estonians defeat the Iron Division and Landeswehr at the Battle of Võnnu (Cēsis, Wenden), commemorated later by 23 June being named Victory Day. **24 June–3 July:** Estonian forces pursue the Germans to Riga. **8 July–29 Aug:** Successful Red Army campaign to reconquer Pskov. **17–18 Sep:** Unsuccessful armistice negotiations with Russians at Pskov. **10 Oct:** Constituent Assembly adopts radical Land Reform bill, which confiscates almost 97 percent of the nobles' estates to be divided among the landless; Russian White Northern Army commences second attack on Petrograd. **10–23 Oct:** Estonian armored trains at Riga battle Landeswehr force led by Bermondt-Avalov. **11 Oct:** Second Estonian attack on Pihkva. **5–7 Nov:** Third Estonian attack on Pihkva. **11 Nov:** Estonian cabinet decides to stop supporting the Russian Whites. **16 Nov:** Disarming of the retreating White Army begins. **16 Nov–30 Dec:** Final battles on the Viru (Northeast Estonia) front to defeat Red Army attempts to improve its position for the peace negotiations. **1 Dec:** The University of Tartu reopens as an Estonian-language institution. **5 Dec:** Peace negotiations begin at Tartu with Jaan Poska leading the Estonian delegation and Adolf Joffe the Bolshevik Russians. **31 Dec:** Armistice is signed.

1920 **3 Jan:** Armistice enters into effect. **2 Feb:** Peace Treaty is signed with Russia at Tartu.

The Republic of Estonia (1920–1939)

1920 **26 Feb:** Demobilization begins. **15 June:** The Constituent Assembly adopts the first Constitution of the Republic of Estonia; during the year, land reform creates 50,000 new farms.

1921 Estonia joins the League of Nations.

1922 **3 May:** Victor Kingissepp, a leader of the Estonian Communist Party, is shot on the orders of a War Tribunal.

1923 First electric railway line (Tallinn-Pääskula) opens.

1924 **1 Dec:** Bolshevik attempted coup is put down in six hours.

1925 **28 Oct:** First electric tram begins operating on Narva Road in Tallinn.

1926 **18 Dec:** Raadio-Ringhääling begins regular radio broadcasts.

1927 **1 Jan:** Currency reform replaces the mark with the kroon; a chemical industry using oil shale is established.

1928 The Estonian Central Federation of Veterans of the War of Independence is formed.

1929–33 Economic Depression in Estonia.

1932 **4 Jan:** A mutual nonaggression pact is signed with the USSR.

1932–37 The Estonian Encyclopedia is published.

1933 **14–16 Oct:** A Referendum approves a new constitution proposed by the Veterans.

1934 **24 Jan:** The new Constitution enters into force. **12 Mar:** Päts and Laidoner lead a preemptive, constitutionally newly sanctioned putsch to prevent a putative coup by the Veterans; Riigikogu meets for the last time in its current form.

1935 Päts and company form the Isamaaliit (Patriotic Union) as a nonpartisan mass movement to support the government.

1936 Tallinn Technical Institute (subsequently Tallinn Polytechnical Institute and later Tallinn Technical University) is founded.

1937 **28 July:** The Rahvuskogu (National Assembly), a special body elected for the purpose, approves the new (third) Constitution.

1938 **1 Jan:** The third Constitution enters into effect. **24 Apr:** Päts is elected president unopposed. Long-delayed local government reform begins with 14 villages given town status; Estonian Academy of Sciences is founded; persons convicted of planning the coup preempted by Päts are released and granted amnesty.

1939 **7 June:** The Estonian-German Mutual Non-Aggression Pact is signed. **23 Aug:** The Molotov-Ribbentrop Pact is signed in Moscow.

World War II

1939 **28 Sep:** The Union of Soviet Socialist Republics (USSR) coerces Estonia into signing the Mutual Assistance Pact, which allows the USSR to establish military bases in Estonia. **18 Oct:** Red Army forces numbering 25,000 soldiers begin moving to bases in Estonia; Baltic German exodus to Germany begins. **30 Nov:** Finnish Winter War begins; Soviet air force units based in Estonia bomb Finland; young Estonian men flee to Finland to volunteer to fight against the Soviet Union.

1940 **13 Mar:** The Finnish Winter War ends. **16 June:** USSR presents an ultimatum to Estonia and Latvia, accuses them of breaking the Mutual Assistance Pact, and demands the right to bring in additional forces and the formation of new governments that would "honor the Pact." **14 June:** A similar note had been handed to Lithuania. **17 June:** Soviet forces with 90,000 men cross the Estonian border; simultaneously the forces already at bases move out and occupy Estonia. **21 June:** The puppet government of Johannes Vares is formed. **14–15**

July: Elections contrary to the constitution are held; all candidates (save one) who are not members of the "Estonian Working Peoples Party" are stricken from candidate lists. **19 July:** General Laidoner is arrested and deported to Russia. **21 July:** The newly appointed puppet government and undemocratically elected Riigikogu proclaim the Estonian Soviet Socialist Republic. **30 July:** President Päts together with his family is deported to Russia. **6 Aug:** The USSR Supreme Soviet "accepts" Estonia into the USSR; nationalization of banks, factories, transport firms, stores, housing, and so on begins; all existing organizations are closed. **Oct:** Land reform expropriates all holdings over 30 hectares and nationalizes all real estate owned by municipalities and religious denominations.

1941 14 June: First major deportation: 10,157 people are arrested at night and deported to Russia in cattle railroad wagons; in response the guerrilla Metsavennad (Forest Brotherhood) resistance movement is organized and begins harassing Soviet occupation forces—which continues into the mid-1950s. **22 June:** Germany attacks the USSR. **4 July–22 Aug:** The 22nd Corps of the Estonian Territorial Red Army, a unit composed primarily of conscripted former members of the Estonian Army, battles German forces at Pskov and Staraja Rossia—4,500 men of the total of 5,500 surrender to the Germans (most cross the battle line voluntarily). **6 Jul–28 Aug:** German forces drive Soviet forces out of the Estonian mainland and conquer Tallinn on 28 August. **8 Sep–3 Dec:** Battle over the Estonian Baltic Sea islands. **15 Sep:** Gen. Franz von Roques, commander of German Army Group Nord, orders establishment of an Estonian Self-Government (Eesti Omavalitsus) with Hjalmar Mäe at its head. **5 Dec:** Hitler orders the transfer of control over Estonia from Army Group Nord to the Reichskommissariat Ostland, with SA Obergruppenfuher Karl-Sigismund Litzmann as Generalkommissar Estland (commissioner-general of Estonia).

1942 28 Aug: Litzmann announces that Germany has authorized the formation of the Estonian Legion.

1943 Late winter: Conscription begins of those born from 1904 to 1924 with choice of labor service, munitions factory work, or the Estonian Legion. **Oct:** Conscription of those born in 1925; beginning of flight of conscriptees to Finland. **Dec:** Formation of the Finnish Army infantry regiment JR 200 (Jalkaväenrykementti 200), composed of Estonians, later known as Soomeposid (the Finland Boys).

1944 **30 Jan:** General mobilization of all those born from 1904 to 1923. **6–8 Mar:** Soviet bombing raids utterly destroy historical center of Narva. **8 Mar:** Intensive Soviet bombing raid on Tallinn (634 dead, 20,000 homeless). **Mar:** Formation of Eesti Vabariigi Rahvuskomitee (National Committee of the Republic of Estonia) composed of all main parties. **Apr:** A large number of the Rahvuskomitee members are arrested by German security agencies. **26 July:** Soviet forces enter Narva. **20 Aug:** Soomepoisid return to Estonia to fight the Red Army to help liberate Estonia. **23 Aug:** The Presidium of the Supreme Soviet of the USSR transfers the Estonian county of Petseri (Petserimaa) to the Russian SSR. **13 Aug–23 Sep:** Red Army drives out the German forces and reoccupies the Estonian mainland. **29 Sep–24 Nov:** Battle over the Estonian Baltic Sea islands.

The Postwar Period, Stalinism, Thaw, and Stagnation (1945–1986)

1945 Arrests; nationalization of industry; and guerrilla warfare with approximately 15,000 men underground and in the forests. **Jan:** Massive migration of Russians and other Soviet peoples into Estonia begins (during six years of war Estonia had lost one quarter, or 282,000, of its population) to rebuild industry and Russify the country.

1946 The Estonian SSR Academy of Sciences is established.

1947 Currency reform in USSR; nationalization of commerce and trade; end of the land reform whereby most rural land is effectively nationalized; the first *kolkhoz* is set up in Estonia.

1949 **25 Mar:** Second Deportation: 20,702 people are deported to Siberia and other faraway regions of the USSR. **Mar:** Massive formation of *kolkhozes* begins.

1950 **Mar:** Estonian Communist Party (ECP) is brought under centralized Moscow control; large numbers of intelligentsia are fired and replaced by "leading workers" imported from the USSR. **1 Oct:** Counties replaced by rural *rayons.*

1951 Estonian Agricultural Academy founded.

1952 Tallinn Pedagogical Institute founded.

1951–53 Estonia reorganized into three *oblasts:* Tallinn, Tartu, and Pärnu.

1953 Mostly successful eradication of the guerilla underground Metsavennad (Forest Brethren), although small groups continue sporadic sabotage.

1955 **19 July:** First TV broadcast from Tallinn.

1957 The system of Ministries of Industry in the USSR, including ESSR, is replaced by the Councils of National Economy.

1961 Currency reform, rubles reissued at ratio of 1:10, effectively confiscating savings.

1961–73 Construction of Õismäe subdivision in Tallinn—the first planned *microrayon* (city subdivision) in Estonia.

1965 The ESSR Council of National Economy is disbanded and ministries of industry reestablished; grain production reaches prewar levels; Tallinn–Helsinki ferry service restored for first time since before World War II.

1966 Baltic Electricity Power Station, using oil shale for underfiring, comes on stream.

1966–67 Gradual introduction of five-day workweek

1970 Introduction of universal secondary education, which results in a rapid decline of quality of education.

1973 Estonian Electricity Power Station, using oil shale, on stream.

1973–78 Construction of Little Õismäe subdivision in Tallinn.

1977 Building begins of Lasnamäe subdivision in Tallinn; Karl Vaino replaces Johannes Käbin as First Secretary of the Central Committee of the ECP. **13 Oct:** The USSR Council of Ministers' decree "On support for the learning and teaching of Russian in federal republics" marks the beginning of Russification of teaching in kindergartens, schools, and places of higher learning.

1980 **20–30 July:** Sailing competitions of the Moscow Olympics take place at the new Olympic Sailing Center in Tallinn. **22 Sep:** Spontaneous youth demonstration at the Kadriorg Stadium in Tallinn. **1 Oct:** Youth demonstrations in Tallinn at A. H. Tammsaare monument, Town Hall Square and Victory Square. **28 Oct:** The "Letter of the Forty" criticizes the Central Committee of the ECP.

1981 **27 Mar:** Freedom fighter Jüri Kukk dies in a Soviet Russian prison.

1982 Construction begins of the new Tallinn grain port at Muuga, mostly built by Finnish firms; Tartu University celebrates its 350th anniversary.

1985 Estonian Song Festival in Tallinn.

1986 Muuga Port complex becomes operational.

The Soviet Occupation Ends (1987–1991)

1987 **Spring:** Demonstrations in Tallinn and various towns against the opening of new phosphorite mines in Kabala-Toolse. **25 May:** The Central Council of the ESSR Creative Arts Associations is established. **23 Aug:** Demonstration meeting in Hirvepark, below the Parliament Building in Tallinn, led by Molotov-Ribbentropi Pakti Avalikustamise Eesti Grupp (the Estonian Group for Making the Molotov-Ribbentrop Pact Public, known by its initials MRP-AEG). **26 Sept:** The Four-Man Proposal to establish territorial economic self-government in Estonia is published in the Tartu newspaper *Edasi*. **Autumn:** Beginning of official revision of history. **12 Dec:** Formation of the Estonian Heritage Society (Eesti Muinsuskaitse Selts)—within a year, it has 100,000 members.

1988 **2 Feb:** Commemoration of the 68th anniversary of the Peace Treaty of Tartu. **24 Feb:** 70th Independence Day; public commemoration in the Estonia Concert Hall and at the A. H. Tammsaare monument. **10 Mar:** The Estonian National Museum reclaims its old name (it had been renamed the ESSR State Ethnographic Museum). **25 Mar:** The Estonian Heritage Society publicly demands the publication of the lists of the deportees. **1–2 Apr:** Plenary Session of the newly formed Creative Arts Associations: demands are voiced and widely published for extending political rights for Estonia within the USSR, for economic and cultural autonomy, restrictions on immigration from the USSR, and the rehabilitation of those repressed by Stalin. **13 Apr:** Edgar Savisaar proposes the formation of a legal opposition in the form of a Peoples' Movement (Rahvarinne) in the TV talk show *Mõtleme Veel* (*Let Us Continue to Think*). **14–15 Apr:** Tartu Heritage Days—the Estonian flag is openly flown for the first time in the ESSR. **29 Apr:** The Estonian Academic War History Association established. **30 Apr:** Declaration forming the Rahvarinne published in Edasi. **4 June:** First Estonian Independent Youth Forum held in Tallinn. **4–14 June:** The "Night Song-festivals" in Tallinn when 100,000 people gather spontaneously in the streets and sing patriotic songs every night. **16 June:** Karl Vaino is recalled by Moscow and replaced by Vaino Väljas as first secretary of the ECP. **17 June:** Rahvarinne organizes a meeting at the Song Festival Grounds in Tallinn with 150,000 participants to send off and support the Estonian delegates to the CPSU XIX Congress in Moscow. **19 June:** First rebuilt War of Independence monument inaugurated at Lalsi. **23 June:** National symbols resurrected by the Presidium of the Estonian Supreme Soviet by the decree "On the State and National Symbols in the ESSR." **13 July:** Freedom fighter Mart Niklus arrives in Tartu after release from prison in Perm. **19 July:** Intermovement (ESSR International Movement) formed by Jevgeni Kogan and J. Rudjak to oppose the Rahvarinne. **23–24 July:** Estonian Christian-Democratic Party organized. **10 Aug:** The Secret Protocol to the Molotov-Ribbentrop Pact is published in *Rahva Hääl*—for the first time in the USSR. **20 Aug:** Estonian National Independence Party formed. **23 Aug:** Commemoration of the Molotov-Ribbentrop Pact anniversary at Hirvepark and Rahvarinne's political meeting on "Stalin's policy toward Estonia." **26–28 Aug:** First Rock Summer at Tallinn Song Festival Grounds. **9–10 Sep:** ECP Central Committee XI plenary at which the party leadership for the first time declares its support for the demands of the people—the result is the official revival of Estonia-centered politics in Estonia. **11 Sep:** Rahvarinne organizes the mass meeting Estonia's Song with 300,000 participants; demands are openly made for reacquiring independent statehood. **24 Sep:** First Estonian Peoples' Congress (with representatives of all nationalities in Estonia) organized by Rahvarinne. **13 Oct:** Estonian Muinsuskaitse Selts (Heritage Society) organizes a mass meeting in defense of the Estonian language at the Tallinn

Linnahall; the ESSR State Library named after Friedrich Reinhold Kreutzwald is renamed the Estonian National Library. **17 Oct:** Freed freedom fighter Enn Tarto publicly greeted in Tartu and Tallinn. **30 Oct:** The first draft of the Language Law making Estonian the state language of the ESSR is published. **Oct–Nov:** 800,000 signatures are collected in Estonia by Rahvarinne to support the proposed USSR Supreme Soviet draft bill "On changes and revisions in the constitution," which would give Estonia autonomy within the USSR. **16 Nov:** Extraordinary session of the Estonian Supreme Soviet: after revising the constitution, it declares the ESSR sovereign, and the Supreme Soviet of the Estonian SSR is declared the highest constitutional organ in Estonia; this marks the beginning of the disintegration of the USSR by elected representatives of its peoples. **26 Nov:** The Presidium of the Supreme Soviet of the USSR passes a decree disallowing the actions of the Estonian Supreme Soviet on 16 Nov. as being in violation of the USSR constitution. **30 Nov:** The proreform Union Council of ESSR Works Collectives (Ülo Nugis, chair) and the opposing (mostly Russian members) Federation of ESSR Works Collectives (S. Petinov, chair) are organized. **5–7 Dec:** ESSR Supreme Soviet IX Session; status of Estonian as the state language adopted; deportations of the Stalinist period declared crimes against human rights. **17 Dec:** Estonian Christian Federation founded. **21 Dec:** Estonian Democratic Party founded. **24 Dec:** Christmas celebrated publicly for first time in the ESSR.

1989 **14 Jan:** The Estonian Olympic Committee reestablished; henceforth, Estonian athletes will compete under the Estonian flag. **18 Jan:** By a vote of 204 to 50, the ESSR Supreme Soviet X Session passed the law making Estonian the official state language. **17 Feb:** The Presidium of the ESSR Supreme Soviet declared 24 Feb "Independence Day." **23 Feb:** The Estonian Drama Theatre reclaimed its old name; the ESSR flag was lowered for the last time from the national flagstaff atop Pikk Hermann on Toompea and placed in a museum. **24 Feb:** 71st Independence Day celebrations led by government and Rahvarinne; the national flag is flown from Pikk Hermann accompanied by the national anthem at sunrise with 100,000 in attendance; the Heritage Society, Estonian Christian Federation, and the Independence Party organize the Citizens' Committees movement (Kodanike Komiteed); the "internationalists" form strike committees. **26 Feb:** Government decrees the return of property and the paying of compensation to all deportees and those repressed by the Soviet regime. **4–5 Mar:** The Interfront holds its first congress. **14 Mar:** The Interfront organizes demonstrations against Estonian aspirations for independence. **20 Mar:** A decree of the Estonian government moves Estonia into the East European time zone (one hour earlier than Moscow/Leningrad time and the same as Finland). **25 Mar:** Commemoration of the 1949 deportation of 20,000; the Estonian Federation of the Illegally Repressed (Eesti Õigusvastaselt Represseeritute Liit) founded. **26 Mar:** Elections to USSR Supreme Soviet—the first postwar elections in which it is possible to choose among candidates; Rahvarinne candidates win. **1 Apr:** The Isemajandav Eesti (Economically Autonomous Estonia, known by the acronym IME) project proposal is published. **13–14 May:** First Baltic Assembly organized in Tallinn by the Rahvarinne, the Latvian Tautas Fronte, and the Lithuanian Sajudis. **18 May:** The XI Session of the ESSR Supreme Soviet, with a vote of 239 to 1 with 1 abstention, adopts the IME General Program. **25 June:** The rebuilt monument of President Päts at his birthplace in Tahkuranna is rededicated. **30 June:** The Estonian Christian Democratic Federation (Eesti Kristlik-Demokraatlik Liit) is founded. **24 July:** The XII Session of the ESSR Supreme Soviet meets to discuss drastic revision of local electoral law, including the requirement of local residency; first strikes organized by the Intermovement. **27 July:** The USSR Supreme Soviet votes approval of the IME program and authorizes the ESSR to override those USSR laws in contravention of IME. **9 Aug:** The XII Session of the ESSR Supreme Soviet concludes by adopting the local elections law limiting the franchise to citizens who have resided in the local municipality for two years, or in Estonia for five years; candidates' limits are five and 10 years, respectively. **10–19 Aug:** The Intermovement organizes strikes at 20 Tallinn enterprises to protest the new electoral law. **23 Aug:** The Baltic Chain, stretching over 600 kilometers from Tallinn to Vilnius with 2 million participants holding hands, commemorates the 50th anniversary of the Molotov-Ribbentrop Pact. **15 Sep:** The solidarity march of the USSR Interfront reaches Tallinn. **5 Oct:** The XII Session of the ESSR Supreme Soviet decides not to implement the new local elections law for the 10 Dec. local elections. **27 Oct:** The Central Committee of the CPSU issues a threatening memorandum, "Conditions in the Baltic Republics." **11 Nov:** The Estonian government decides to establish an independent

Estonian currency; the Estonian Citizens' General Committee (Eesti Kodanike Peakomitee) is established. **12 Nov:** The ESSR Supreme Soviet adopts by a vote of 188 the historical and legal evaluation of developments in 1940 in Estonia; as a consequence, the incorporation of Estonia into the USSR is declared illegal and void; 40 delegates walk out in protest. **17 Nov:** The ESSR Supreme Soviet passes a new law on elections to the Supreme Soviet, which requires 10-year Estonian residency for candidates. **25 Nov:** First postwar regular air traffic with Stockholm inaugurated. **27 Nov:** The USSR Supreme Soviet adopts a law on the economic autonomy of Estonia, Latvia, and Lithuania. **10 Dec:** Local elections won by democratic movements. **15 Dec:** The Bank of Estonia established. **20 Dec:** Estonian Trades Union Congress: unions declared free and independent. **24 Dec:** The Congress of National Delegates of the USSR accepts the existence of the Secret Protocol to the Molotov-Ribbentrop Pact and declares it null and void ab initio.

1990 11–12 Jan: First Estonian Social-Democratic Forum held in Tartu. **20 Jan:** The political association Vaba Eesti founded with Indrek Toome as chair. **21 Jan:** The Estonian Conservative People's Party founded with Enn Tarto as chair. **2 Feb:** A congress composed of ECP members of all governmental councils at all levels in Estonia adopts a declaration approving the independence of the Estonian State and sends a memorandum to the USSR Supreme Soviet requesting negotiations for reestablishing the independent Estonian state. **17 Feb:** The Estonian Kaitseliit (Defense League) is reestablished. **19 Feb:** The Presidium of the ESSR Supreme Soviet passes a law rehabilitating approximately 60,000 deportees and repressed individuals. **23 Feb:** The Supreme Soviet of the ESSR removes the paragraph from the ESSR constitution designating the Communist Party's leadership role. **24 Feb–1 Mar:** 557,613 citizens of the Estonian Republic (as per the prewar rules of citizenship; i.e., 90 percent of those eligible) and 34,345 applicants for citizenship vote for delegates to the Estonian Congress; of the total, 434 delegates are elected from Estonia and 35 by Estonians abroad; they represent 32 parties and organizations: 109 independents, 107 Popular Front, 104 Estonian Heritage Society, 70 Estonian National Independence Party, and 39 Communist Party. **11–12 Mar:** Estonian Congress Session I (first meeting of an assembly representing the Estonian people since the occupation by the USSR in 1940) adopts a declaration announcing to the world the intention of Estonians to reestablish their independent republic; a permanent 78-member Estonian Committee, with Tunne Kelam as chair, is elected. **18 Mar:** The elections to the XII ESSR Supreme Soviet are won by democratic parties and groups that support independence. **23–25 Mar:** XX ECP Congress: the Party splits into an independent Estonian Communist Party and a USSR-affiliated one, largely along language lines; the independent ECP adopts a program of independence for Estonia. **26 Mar:** The USSR-affiliated Communist Party holds a congress to organize itself. **29 Mar:** Arnold Ruutel is elected chair of the ESSR Supreme Soviet. **30 Mar:** The ESSR Supreme Soviet declares Soviet authority on Estonian territory null and void, and declares the beginning of a period of transition to independence, to end with the formation of constitutionally constituted state organs of the Republic of Estonia; the government of Indrek Toome resigns *in corpore*; the Supreme Soviet adopts the resolution "On the cooperation between the ESSR Supreme Soviet and the Estonian Congress." **3 Apr:** Edgar Savisaar becomes prime minister and forms the transition government. **12 Apr:** The Estonian Trade Union Central Federation is founded. **19 Apr:** Arnold Ruutel, Edgaar Savisaar, and Endel Lippmaa meet with Mikhail Gorbachev and Nikolaj Ryshkov; Moscow offers Estonia special status on a confederal basis with the Soviet Union. **8 May:** The ESSR Supreme Soviet declares the name ESSR null and void, reestablishes the Republic of Estonia as the name of the country, reinstitutes national regalia, and changes its own name in English to the Supreme Council of the Republic of Estonia. **12 May:** Meeting of Presidents Landsbergis of Lithuania, Gorbunovs of Latvia, and Ruutel of Estonia in Tallinn: the 1934 Cooperation treaty among the three Baltic states is reestablished and the Baltic Council is reinstated. **14 May:** Gorbachev issues a decree voiding the 30 March declaration by the Estonian Supreme Soviet on Estonian "secession." **15 May:** The Intermovement fails in attempting a coup at the Estonian government and parliament buildings on Toompea. **16 May:** The government establishes the Home Guard. **25 May:** The Second Session of the Estonian Congress. **26 May:** Intermovement holds a congress at Kohtla-Järve. **26–27 May:** Second congress of the People's Front. **13 June:** The Estonian Supreme Council adopts Property Ownership Law. **27 June:** Baltic foreign ministers' proposal on joint talks with the USSR. **30 June–2 July:** National Song and Dance Festival in Tallinn.

2 July: USSR Council of Ministers decrees the establishment of the pan-Soviet association Integral to cover all economic sectors. **7–8 July:** Owing to objections by the Soviet Army, the meeting of Estonian World War II veterans at Tori is cancelled. **1 Aug:** Agreement between Savisaar and USSR Minster of the Interior Vladimir Bakatin grants the Estonian Ministry of the Interior independence from the USSR Ministry. **3 Aug:** Initial discussions on the proposed Federation Treaty held at the Kremlin. **5 Aug:** Meeting among Latvian, Lithuanian, and Estonian prime ministers on common concerns with leaders of the Russian, Belorussian, and Moldavian SSR's governments; the Moscow and Leningrad city councils' leaders; and the Leningrad Oblast leader at Tallinn. **7 Aug:** The Estonian Supreme Council resolves that future relations with the USSR will be based on the Tartu Peace Treaty of 1920, nullifies the decision of the ESSR SS of 16 Nov 1989 on the Federation Treaty, passes the law regulating the state flag and the state coat of arms (the tricolor is again the official flag of Estonia), and stops the application of the USSR Council of Ministers' decree on Integral in Estonia. **15 Aug:** Negotiations between Estonia and the Russian FSSR begin in Moscow. **23 Aug:** Negotiations (labeled "consultations" by the USSR) begin in Moscow between Estonia and the USSR; the Lenin monument in Tartu is removed by the local Defense League unit. **3 Sep:** The Defense League conducts the staff training course "State border." **6 Sep:** "Consultations" between Estonia and the USSR break down. **9 Sep:** Three recently formed left-wing parties unite to establish the Estonian Social Democratic Party with Marju Lauristin as leader. **14 Sep:** Tripartite agreement on cooperation signed in Leningrad among Leningrad City, Leningrad Oblast, and Estonia. **27 Sep:** The Estonian Royalist Party is established with comedian Kalle Kulbok as leader. **2 Oct:** Foreign Minster Lennart Meri meets with Secretary of State James Baker in Washington. **4 Oct:** Estonian Liberal Democratic Party is accepted as observer by the Liberal International. **8 Oct:** Estonian Social Democratic Party accepted as full member by the Socialist International. **12 Oct:** Prime Minister Savisaar meets with President George H. W. Bush in Washington. **15 Oct:** With the removal of all state subventions for agriculture by the Estonian government, a price inflation spiral starts. **16 Oct:** Decree of the Presidium of the Estonian Supreme Council on state holidays: 1 Jan, 24 Feb: Independence Day, Good Friday, 1 May: Workers Solidarity Day, 23 June: Victory Day (commemorating Battle of Võnnu in 1919), 24 June: Midsummer, 25 Dec: Christmas Day, and 26 Dec: Second Day of Christmas; and days of commemoration: 8 March: International Women's Day, Easter Day, 9 May: Peace Day, 2nd Sunday in May: Mothers' Day, 14 June: National Day of Mourning for Stalinist Victims, and 16 Nov: Day of Rebirth of the Republic. **21 Oct:** The remains of President Päts are reburied in the Forest Cemetery in Tallinn. **22 Oct:** The Supreme Council establishes the Estonian Customs Border. **27–28 Oct:** Estonian Congress Session III: new 55-member Estonia Committee (Eesti Komitee) elected with Tunne Kelam as chair. **27 Nov:** Treaty on Cooperation signed with the Republic of Georgia. **29 Nov:** Treaty of Cooperation signed with the Ukrainian SSR. **19 Dec:** USSR Minster of Defense, General Dmitry Yazov, admits that the Soviet Army has destroyed so-called fascist monuments in the Baltic states. **20 Dec:** Treaty of Cooperation with Moldova signed; Baltic Information Center opened in Copenhagen in connection with a joint meeting of Nordic and Baltic foreign ministers.

1991 **12 Jan:** Agreement on political, economic, and cultural cooperation with the Russian FSR signed in Moscow. **13 Jan:** "Bloody Sunday" in Lithuania as Soviet armed forces attack the TV tower in Vilnius, kill 14 demonstrators, and wound hundreds; anti-independence forces fail to topple the Landsbergis government; in this connection, a joint appeal by the Estonian, Latvian, and Lithuanian republics and the Russian FSR to the secretary-general of the United Nations (UN) is signed in Tallinn; the Presidium of the Estonian Supreme Council forms a three-member Emergency Council of Defense. **18 Jan:** Defensive barricades of heavy concrete and large rock boulders built around Toompea Parliament-Government building. **20 Jan:** OMON ("Black Berets"—special interior ministry troops, mostly Russian) attack Interior Ministry Headquarters in Riga, killing four Latvian bystanders; Republic of Estonia Information Center opens in Stockholm. **30 Jan:** Nordic Council of Ministers Information Bureau opens in Tallinn. **11–13 Jan:** International human rights conference in Tallinn. **16 Feb:** First class graduates from the Republic of Estonia Ministry of the Interior Police Academy. **1 Mar:** The "militia" is replaced by police as the Estonian Police Law enters into force. **3 Mar:** The referendum on restoring Estonian state independence is won by a vote of 77.83 percent of those participating. **17 Mar:** All three Baltic states boycott the pan-

Soviet referendum on preservation of the USSR. **22 Mar:** Baltic Council appeals to the member states of the Conference on Security and Cooperation in Europe (CSCE) to call an international conference to assist in initiating realistic negotiations between the Baltic states and the USSR on troop withdrawals. **13–14 Apr:** III Congress of the Popular Front. **25 May:** Appeal by the Baltic Council to all parliaments, governments, and peoples of the world in connection with new Soviet acts of violence in the Baltic states. **12 June:** Estonian Supreme Council passes the law on principles to govern property reform. **1–7 July:** International Bridges of Song festival in Tallinn. **19 Aug:** Beginning of coup in Moscow; Soviet Army units begin to move toward Tallinn; Estonian Supreme Council declaration concerning the attempted coup in Moscow; Estonian Supreme Soviet gives extraordinary powers to the Republic of Estonia Emergency Council of Defense. (1991 continued below.)

Transition to Independence (1991–1992)

1991 20 Aug: Estonian Supreme Council's Declaration on restoration of Estonian independence; a column of Soviet Commando units arrives in Tallinn from Pskov; volunteers form defensive cordons around Toompea, and the radio and TV buildings. **21 Aug:** During the night, the commando units leave the TV tower that they had partially held; first Certificates of Citizenship of the Republic of Estonia issued in Pärnu. **22 Aug:** Iceland is the first state to recognize the independent Republic of Estonia. **22–23 Aug:** The government of Estonia fires the directors of a number of former Soviet military-related enterprises for supporting the failed coup. **23 Aug:** The statue of Lenin is removed in Tallinn; the government of the Republic outlaws the right of parties and movements to organize activities in enterprises; it outlaws the CPSU and its branches on Estonian territory. **24 Aug:** The Russian FSSR recognizes the independent Republic of Estonia. **27 Aug:** The 12 member states of the European Community (EC) extend recognition to the Republic of Estonia. **29 Aug:** Sweden is the first state to open an embassy in Estonia. **30 Aug:** French Foreign Minister Roland Dumas visits Tallinn. **2 Sep:** The United States recognizes the Republic of Estonia. **3 Sep:** The Estonian Supreme Soviet establishes the Estonian Armed Forces. **6 Sep:** The USSR Federation Council recognizes the independence of the Baltic States. **8 Sep:** Song of Freedom festival organized by the Peoples Front at Tallinn Song Festival Grounds. **10 Sep:** Estonia is accepted as member of the CSCE at a meeting in Moscow. **11 Sep:** German Foreign Minster Hans-Dietrich Genscher visits Tallinn; President Bush meets in Washington with representatives of the governments in exile of the Baltic states. **13 Sep:** The Republic of Estonia Constitutional Assembly begins deliberating. **14 Sep:** U.S. Secretary of State James Baker visits Tallinn. **17 Sep:** The UN accepts the three Baltic states as members. **18 Sep:** The Council of Europe grants the three Baltic states status as extraordinary observers; all are accepted as members by the International Olympic Committee. **1 Oct:** First nine postal stamps of the Republic of Estonia issued. **9 Oct:** Diplomatic relations reestablished between the Republic of Estonia and the USSR. **12 Oct:** The Estonian People's Center Party established with Edgar Savisaar as leader. **15 Oct:** Estonia, Latvia, and Lithuania sign the 1975 Final Document of the CSCE. **24 Oct:** Diplomatic relations established between Estonia and the Russian FSR. **26 Oct:** The Party of Those Illegally Repressed formed. **5–6 Nov:** Danish Prime Minister Peter Schluter is first foreign head of government to visit Estonia. **6 Dec:** Estonia, Latvia, and Lithuania sign the Paris Charter of the CSCE. **21 Dec:** The USSR is formally dissolved at Alma-Ata. **26 Dec:** The Russian Duma ratifies the Estonian-Russian Treaty signed on 12 Jan 1991.

1992 **10 Feb:** EuroInfo 92 bureau opens in Tallinn, thus enabling Estonians to be informed of developments in the EU. **20 Feb:** Russia freezes Estonian bank accounts. **21 Feb:** Latvian embassy in Tallinn opens; Estonia decides to recognize the countries of the Commonwealth of Independent States (CIS), except for Georgia because of the unstable situation there. **27 Feb:** The Law on Citizenship is reinstituted as it was on 16 June 1940; the date for eligibility of naturalization is set at 30 March 1990 and requires two years' residency up to that date plus one year of waiting after application. **29 Feb:** The first private radio station, Radio Kuku, is formed; the price of gasoline is increased fivefold, and the price of electricity is increased to 1 ruble per KwH. **1 Mar:** The Baltic Assembly meets in Tallinn and discusses cooperation with the Nordic Council. **3 Mar:** Sweden offers help in patrolling Estonia's maritime borders. **15 June:** The government approves language standards for citizenship applicants: sufficient spoken and written Estonian to be able to understand and make oneself understood in any situation. **20 June:** Currency reform: the Estonian kroon as the sole legal tender in Estonia goes into circulation with an initial issue of 600 million EEK (its international designation). **23 June:** Estonia becomes a member of the World Bank. **26 June:** The Baltic Council meets in Tallinn, issues an appeal to the G-7 governments to help achieve rapid withdrawal of Russian forces, and appeals to the member governments in the Council of Baltic Sea States (CBSS), the CSCE, and UN to assist in cleaning up the toxic wastes dumped in the Baltic Sea by the Soviet forces. **28 June:** The new constitution is adopted by referendum and enters into effect on 3 July 1992: of 66.8 percent of eligible voters participating, 91.3 percent vote in favor. **4–10 July:** ESTO 92, organized by Estonians abroad, takes place in New York. **14–16 Aug:** The International Monetary Fund (IMF) delegation led by its managing director, Michel Camdessus, commends the Estonian currency and extends a US$40 million loan facility as a signal to foreign investors of the economic progress of Estonia. **Sep:** The first modern fiberoptic cable is laid between Tallinn and Helsinki, thus opening up rapid and convenient telephone communications with the world. **5 Sep:** The government estimates that the Estonian Defense Forces would reach 5,000 by 1993, and consist of a 500-member internal defense task force, a 500-member rescue service, a 2,500-member border guard, and 1,500 defense troops. **8 Sep:** Lithuania and Russia sign an agreement establishing a timetable for withdrawal of Russian troops to be completed by 31 Aug 1993; at the same time, Russia contends that it wishes to maintain the naval (nuclear training) facility in Paldiski, Estonia, and the radar facility in Skrunda, Latvia. **20 Sep:** Elections for president by popular vote (subsequent presidents will be elected by Riigikogu) and for Parliament take place. **5 Oct:** The first session of the newly elected Riigikogu meets and on 6 Oct. swears in Lennart Meri as president of the Republic. **7 Oct:** With the restoration of the constitutional authority of the Republic of Estonia established on 24 Feb 1918, Riigikogu declares the transitional period instituted by the Supreme Council in March 1990 ended. (1992 continued below.)

Beginning Rebuilding of Estonia as a Normal Modern European State (1992–1997)

1992 8 Oct: Heinrich Mark, prime minister in exile with powers of the president, officially hands over his powers to President Meri, thus symbolically ending the 50-year period of exile of the de jure Republic of Estonia. **Oct:** U.S. Congress passes legislation tying U.S. aid to Russia to troop withdrawals: unless withdrawals from all three Baltic states are completed by 1 July 1993, up to half of the agreed aid will be halted. **14 Oct:** Grain prices are freed as part of the policy of freeing all prices resulting in threefold increase in bakery product prices. **19 Oct:** Riigikogu authorizes Mart Laar to form a government with a vote of 54 to 30 and 4 abstentions. **29 Oct:** President Boris Yeltsin declares a moratorium on Russian troop withdrawals from the Baltics until agreements are signed providing social guarantees to retiring Russian servicemen in the Baltic states; Western states label this action contrary to the Helsinki (CSCE) Final Agreement. **6 Nov:** The CSCE decides to send representatives to Estonia to assist in reducing tensions between ethnic Russian and Estonians, and to promote stability in the region. **25 Nov:** The UN General Assembly passes a resolution (proposed by the Baltic states) calling for early withdrawal of Russian forces from the Baltics. **Dec:** The Estonian Privatization Agency in its first round of privatization bids receives 103 tenders for 38 large enterprises to be privatized.

1993 **15 Feb:** CSCE and Estonia agree to establish CSCE bureaus in Tallinn, Kohtla-Järve, and Narva to help Estonia accommodate ethnic Russians concerns. **18 Feb**: Estonia asks for assistance from the North Atlantic Treaty Organization (NATO) in developing its security policy and in building its defense forces. **17 Feb:** Latvia and Estonia agree to mark their land border. **24 Feb:** Estonia, Latvia, and Lithuania agree to their first joint training exercise to take place in May. **1 Mar:** According to the commander of the Tallinn garrison, 5,900 Russian soldiers remain in Estonia. **4 Mar:** Estonian Migration Board says that 35,000–40,000 Russians left Estonia in 1992. **9–12 Mar:** Approximately 80 Estonian enterprises participate for the first time since World War II in an international trade fair, the Leipzig Exposition. **29 Mar:** Russia suspends its troop withdrawals from three Baltic states, charging them with obstruction in drawing agreements and alleging discrimination against their Russian minorities. **20 Apr:** Estonia and Latvia sign a free trade agreement. **22 Apr:** Chancellor Helmut Kohl of Germany supports Estonia's eventual accession to the European Community. **22–23 Apr:** Estonians mark the 650th anniversary of the St. George's Night Uprising in 1343. **28 Apr:** The first session of the Joint Committee of Estonia and the EU takes place in Tallinn. **13 May:** Estonia is invited to become a full member by the Parliamentary Assembly of the Council of Europe. **14 May:** Estonia signs the European Human Rights Convention. **20 May:** The West European Union (WEU) issues a communiqué demanding withdrawal of Russian troops from the Baltics. **25 May:** Estonia approves a plan to resettle Russian officers now living in Narva at Kingisepp in the Leningrad Region and allocates 900,000 EEK to construct apartments to house them. **27 May:** The new State (Supreme) Court is inaugurated at a temporary site in Tartu, 180 kilometers distant from the government buildings in Tallinn, to demonstrate its independence. **28 May:** The first joint tactical training of the defense forces of the three Baltic States takes place at Adazi in Latvia. **31 May:** The Estonian Border Guard assumes control over territorial waters around the islands of Saaremaa and Hiiumaa along with radar stations. **3 June:** The heads of state of Estonia, Latvia, and Lithuania urge the EC to begin negotiations with the Baltic states for associate status before the end of the year. **4 June:** Although Estonia formally takes over the last remaining border post at Rahumäe in Tallinn from the Russians, a Russian border guard detachment and a 10-helicopter squadron remain in Rakvere. **22 June:** The Laar cabinet approves rules governing privatization of housing, and sets the price of a square meter at a nominal 300 EEK, with payment periods of 10 to 20 years. **5 July:** On the eve of the first anniversary of the Helsinki document on Russian troop withdrawals, the Baltic states address a joint appeal to the G-7 for their help in getting Russia to proceed with troop withdrawal. **10 July:** President Meri establishes the Round Table with National Minorities and holds its first meeting. **2 Aug:** The United States allocates $6 million for housing and retraining courses for Russian officers to be repatriated from the Baltic States. **10 Sep:** Pope John Paul II visits Estonia and Latvia. **11 Sep:** The new National Library building opens after a decade under construction. **14 Sep:** Between 4,000 and 4,700 Russian troops remain in Estonia. **16 Sep:** The 1992–93 IMF Report ranks Estonia as highly successful in carrying out economic reforms. **27 Sep:** The three Baltic presidents meet with U.S. President Bill Clinton at the White House and receive a declaration of American support for Russian troop withdrawals. **30 Sep:** President Meri's address to the UN General Assembly focuses on troop withdrawals. **17 Oct:** The first local elections since regaining independence are held with 8,700 candidates vying for 3,427 elected offices; of the 870,041 persons entitled to vote, 699,356 are Estonian citizens and 170,685 are alien residents; 53 percent exercise their franchise, with some of the highest participation rates recorded in the Russian-speaking towns in Northeast Estonia. **14 Oct:** The finance minister presents a balanced draft budget at 5.96 billion EEK (US$435 million). **19 Oct:** President Jacques Santer of the EC Commission tells Prime Minister Laar that he sees no major obstacles to Estonian accession to the EC. **27 Oct:** The Ministry of the Environment releases detailed figures on environmental damage caused by the Soviet Army based on a review of 88 of the 570 Soviet bases in Estonia: airfields have caused 9 billion, military warehouses 2.5 billion, and testing sites 2.16 billion EEK in damages for total damages of 327.7 billion EEK. **2 Nov:** Cabinet approves privatization voucher rules: these are limited to buying land, housing, compensation fund bonds, or shares in state companies to be privatized. **20 Nov:** Estonia, Latvia, and Lithuania agree to set up a Baltic Battalion to serve in UN peacekeeping forces. **23 Nov:** Estonia declares its intention to become a full member of the EC by 2000. **29 Nov:** The cabinet allocates 5 million EEK to research and the first stages of cleaning up environmental damage caused by Soviet forces. **1 Dec:** Estonia replaces the letters EW with EST marking cars registered in the country. **9 Dec:** Effective 1 Jan 1994, Riigikogu passes a flat rate income tax of 26 percent for both individuals and legal persons. **15 Dec:** The presidents of the Baltic states, meeting in Tallinn, declare NATO as their main guarantor of security; Riigikogu ratifies the purchase of small arms from Israel, the only country willing to sell arms to Estonia at this time. **22 Dec:** The last remaining public statue of Lenin in Estonia is removed in Narva. **27 Dec:** The Cabinet accepts in principle Russia's proposed deadline of 31 August 1994 for withdrawal of its troops, on the condition that it present a detailed timetable for the 2,400 remaining troops, including the 1,000-member assault unit.

1994 **1 Jan:** In a joint statement, the three Baltic presidents call for international efforts to speed the withdrawal of Russian troops; the Law on Consumer Protection enters into force. **3 Jan:** The Estonian armed forces have 411 officers, of whom under 10 percent rank higher than captain; there is only one general, Major-General Aleksander Einseln, a retired U.S. colonel, appointed Commander of the Defense Forces. **5 Jan:** Estonia calls on NATO members for the Baltic and Central European states to be in the first group of countries to be offered membership. **11 Jan:** The United States announces that because of successful economic and democratic reforms, it will phase out aid to Estonia and the Czech Republic. **11 May:** The United States announces that it will provide financial support to Estonia in resettling retired former Soviet Russian military officers in Russia. **24 May:** Germany announces that, after taking over the presidency of the European Union in July, it will assist Estonia to enable it quick access to the EU. **27 May:** According to Chief Justice Rait Maruste, the chairman of Estonia's Supreme Court, Estonia has passed the incubation period of judicial and court reform. **11 June:** NATO foreign ministers welcome the Russian-Latvian agreement on troop withdrawals and call on Estonia and Russia to sign a similar agreement to facilitate the withdrawal by 31 August. **14 June:** The first 10 Estonian officers graduate from a special two-year program offered by Santahamina Military College in Finland. **27 June:** Delegations at the CSCE Permanent Committee meeting in Vienna reaffirm their demand that Russian troops be withdrawn by 31 August. **1 July:** Swedish Prime Minister Carl Bildt says that there is no justification for the continued presence of Russian troops in Estonia; Riigikogu passes the Law on the National Border, which reaffirms the Estonian-Russian border defined in the Tartu Peace in 1920. **4 July:** The prime ministers of the Nordic countries, meeting in Finland, reiterate their call for the withdrawal of Russian troops from all the Baltic states by 31 August. **6 July:** The Privatization Agency reports that it sold 86 state enterprises in 1993 for 481.8 million EEK; the fifth international privatization round for 49 enterprises in May drew 142 bids. **14 July:** U.S. Senate votes 89 to 8 to require Russian troops to leave the Baltic states by 31 August, as a precondition for U.S. aid. **12 July:** The Baltic Peacekeeping Battalion begins joint training at Palvadre, Lithuania. **11 July:** Three Russian military units are still located in Tallinn or environs, including the Russian naval headquarters company less than 300 meters from the Estonian Parliament Building, as well as the unit servicing the two training nuclear reactors at the Paldiski submarine base. **13 July:** Estonia and the EU initial the Free Trade Agreement to take effect 1 January 1995. **19 July:** The Russian Baltic Fleet's Tallinn naval base will be closed on 27 July. **26 July:** At a historic meeting, Presidents Meri and Yeltsin sign an agreement on the withdrawal of troops and another providing social guarantees for Russian military retirees in Estonia; they also restart negotiations on removal of the two nuclear reactors in Paldiski. **27 July:** The cabinet decides to add an air unit to Estonia's military forces; representatives of Narva City Council, local leaders, and Soviet war veterans hold several ceremonies commemorating the 50th anniversary of Soviet troops occupying Narva in World War II. **30 July:** The agreement to close the nuclear submarine base at Paldiski is signed in Moscow; the nuclear reactors will be dismantled by 30 September 1995. **15 Aug:** Prime Minister Mart Laar lodges a note with the Russian ambassador protesting Russia's unilateral action in marking its border with Estonia, removing Setumaa from Estonia, on a line at variance with the Tartu Peace of 1920. **31 Aug:** With the departure of the last regular Russian troops, ceremonies are held to mark the symbolic end of World War II in Estonia. **8 Sep:** CSCE High Commissioner for National Minorities Max van der Stoel reports that he has not found any of the human rights abuses in Estonia that Moscow constantly raises. **16 Sep:** Several states at the regular meeting of the CSCE Senior Officials Committee criticize Russia for unilaterally marking its border with Estonia. **26 Sep:** Riigikogu passes a vote of nonconfidence in Prime Minister Laar by a vote of 60 to 27 and one abstention. **28 Sep:** The MS *Estonia,* a passenger car ferry en route from Tallinn to Stockholm, sinks in a gale off the coast of Finland with the loss of 852 lives out of 989 aboard. **10 Oct:** The minister of defense informs Riigikogu that in addition to the 10,689 registered military pensioners, there are about 1,000 former Russian military illegally in Estonia; the prime minister informs the Riigikogu that 23 foreign citizens and 31 former exiled Estonians are currently employed in various ministries. **12 Oct:** The Ministry of Culture and Education announces that it has granted operating licenses to eight private higher educational institutions. **13 Oct:** Riigikogu rejects the nomination of Siim Kallas for prime minister by a simple majority of 55 votes to 40. **4 Nov:** President Meri approves the cabinet proposed by Prime Minister Andres Tarand. **28 Nov:** The foreign ministers of the EU pass a decision authorizing negotiations for EU associate status with Estonia, Latvia, and Lithuania. **29 Nov:** The three Baltic states agree to work closely on military matters and to integrate their forces with the European military structure. Former Soviet-era Prime Minister Indrek Toome is arrested for attempting to bribe a police official in connection with illegally obtained passports. **7 Dec:** Estonian and Russian border guards agree to cooperate in the future. **8**

Dec: The cabinet names the delegation for talks with the EU under Foreign Ministry Deputy Under-Secretary Priit Kolbre.

1995 12 Jan: Riigikogu adopts the Law on Universities, which provides the legal foundation for six state universities: Tartu University, Tallinn Technical University, Estonian Music Academy, Tallinn Pedagogical University, Estonian Agriculture University, and Tallinn Arts University; state-financed student places at these universities, the number to be fixed annually by the Ministry of Education, will continue to be tuition-free; others will pay tuition fees to be determined by each university. **20 Jan:** The second round of talks on Association for Estonia and the European Union takes place in Brussels. **19 Jan:** Riigikogu adopts with 52 affirmative votes the Law on Anti-Corruption, which provides the procedures for both preventing corruption and convicting the people involved; it also adopts a new Law on Citizenship, which replaces the 1938 Law and specifies new rules for the acquisition, receipt, restoration, and loss of citizenship. **26 Jan:** The World Bank lends US$18 million to finance a US$34.5 million health system development project, with Estonia providing US$14.5 million, to be implemented in 1995–99. **31 Jan:** Ambassador Ernst Jaakson becomes dean of the New York consular corps, the world's largest. **27 Jan:** The total foreign investment since independence to date amounts to US$400,000, with Sweden and Finland the leading investors, each with about a quarter, followed by Russia, Germany, and the United States. **1 Feb:** The Russian embassy announces that a total of total 61,401 residents of Estonia have obtained Russian citizenship to date. **15 Feb:** An infantry platoon of the Estonian Peacekeeping Company joins a Danish battalion on a peacekeeping mission in Croatia. **17 Feb:** 20,000 Estonian-language atlases, a gift from the Nordic states' Lion clubs to Estonian schools, arrive from Finland. **21 Feb:** Riigikogu adopts a new law on language that declares Estonian the sole state language in Estonia. **22 Feb:** Estonian and the EU successfully conclude association talks after a two-day third round; Estonia, unlike all other applicants, will not require any transition period before receiving associate status, since its transition to a market economy is largely complete and the necessary legal acts have been adopted. **27 Feb:** The Union Bank of Finland is the first foreign bank to open a branch in Estonia. **1 Mar:** A two-year 70,000-ECU PHARE (Poland, Hungary, and Romania) program to bring Estonia's laws in line with the EU begins. **2 Mar:** The birth rate in Estonia is declining: whereas in 1993 there were 15,025 births, in 1994 the corresponding figure was only 14,016, even though the number of abortions declined even more drastically. **5 March:** The elections to the VIII Riigikogu result in the electoral union Coalition Party and Rural Union, led by Tiit Vähi, winning 174,248 votes (32.23 percent) on a turnout of 545,770 people (68.9 percent of the electorate), the Reform Party Liberals come in second with 16.19 percent, and the Center Party third with 14.17 percent, followed by the Pro Patria and Estonian National Independence Party (ENIP) electoral coalition with 7.86 percent, the Moderates with 5.99 percent, Our Home Is Estonia with 5.87 percent, and the Right Wingers with 5 percent of the vote; this results in the Coalition Party and Rural Union electoral union receiving 41 seats in the 101-member Riigikogu, the Reform Party 19, the Center Party 16, the Pro Patria and ENIP Union 8, the Moderates 6, Our Home Is Estonia 6, and the Right Wingers 5. **28 Mar:** Reform Minister Liia Hänni announces that in 1994, 339 purchase contracts for the privatization of smaller state-owned companies were concluded, averaging one agreement per day; these contracts brought in 1.4 billion EEK to the state. **5 Apr:** Prime Minster Tiit Vähi, with 62 votes for, 34 against, and one abstention, gains Riigikogu's support to form a government to consist of Koonderakond ja Maarahva Ühendus (KMÜ) and the Center Party; the coalition will have 57 votes in the 101-member parliament; the KMÜ itself is a coalition of the Coalition Party, Country's People's Party, Farmers' Union, Rural Union, and Association of Pensioners and Families. **12 Apr:** In the course of large- and medium-scale privatization in Estonia from 1993 to 1995, 299 objects changed ownership for a total sale price of 1.94 billion EEK. **28 Apr:** Estonian Internal Affairs Minister Edgar Savisaar announces initial success in his war on criminal gangs—the arrest of the leaders of the "Perm Gang." **4 May:** The Russian embassy announces that 71,000 people living in Estonia have been granted Russian citizenship; the Board of Migration and Citizenship announces that over 184,000 people had submitted their applications for a residence permit by 2 May. **7 May:** Tourist receipts doubled in 1994 and now generate 10 percent of the GNP. **17 May:** The EU allocates 2.4 million ECU as part of a PHARE program to prepare Estonian infrastructure enterprises for privatization. **22 May:** The publishers of the *Hommikuleht, Päevaleht,* and *Rahva Hääl* newspapers agree to merge their newspapers as of 5 June; the name of the new daily is to be *Eesti Päevalent. 1 June*: The Estonian Border Guard announces that Russia has completed its unilateral demarcation of its border with Estonia on Lake Peipsi and has placed 15 buoys in the lake. **5 June:** Apartments are being privatized at an average of 6,000 per month. **6–17 June:** Navies and air forces from 12 countries participate in the military exercise BALTOPS, which Estonia regards as a demonstration of the United States' continuing concern about preserving stability in North Europe. **8 June:** The conflict between Russia and Estonia over the border issue continues; Prime Minster Vähi announces that Estonia is willing to compromise but only if the 1920 Tartu Peace Treaty forms the basis for talks; Russia, however, continues to refuse to recognize the Treaty. **22 June:** Germany agrees to pay 2 million marks (US$1.4 million) in one-off compensation payments to Estonian citizens who suffered at the hands of the Nazis. **1 July:** Visa-free travel for citizens with valid documents among the three Baltic states enters into effect. **12 July:** The first Estonian-Swedish fiberoptic undersea cable, capable of 30,000 simultaneous phone calls, becomes operational. **14 July:** The Citizenship and Migration Board announces that it has received 327,737 residence permit applications by the 12 July deadline, which forms 80–90 percent of the number of foreigners in Estonia. **28 Aug:** Two Swedish minesweepers finish a two-month period of detonating the last of the 470 leftover World War II mines off the northwest coast of Estonia. **30 Aug:** The last Russian specialists who dismantled the nuclear reactors along with the last Russian military leave Estonia as the Paldiski naval site is handed over to Estonia. **12 Sep:** Prime Minister Tiit Vähi and his government resign following the so-called taping scandal involving Minister of the Interior Edgar Savisaar, the leader of the Center Party, one of the government coalition partners. **20 Oct:** The Estonian company of the Baltic Peacekeeping Battalion, consisting of ESTPLA-1 and ESTPLA-2 platoons, which served in peacekeeping operations in Croatia under Danish command, are declared operational. **22 Oct:** A coalition agreement between KMÜ (Coalition Party and Rural Peoples' Union) and Reform Party Liberals (R) is signed by leaders of the parties, acting Prime Minister Tiit Vähi (KMÜ) and Siim Kallas (R), providing for a new coalition cabinet led by Vähi. **26 Oct:** Riigikogu votes to authorizes Tiit Vähi to form a new government by a vote of 55 to 5, with 19 abstentions. **15 Nov:** The Estonian Privatization Agency announces that in 1996, several infrastructural enterprises will be privatized, including Estonian Railways, Estonian Energy, Estonian Oil Shale, Estonian Telekom, Tallinn Ports, and Estonian Air. **24 Nov:** Estonia formally applies for full EU membership. **1 Dec:** 48.1 percent of the apartments to be privatized have been privatized: 75 percent in Hiumaa and 53 percent in Tallinn, but only 22.3 percent in eastern Virumaa where the population is mostly Russian speaking; Estonian Telekom institutes the toll-free 800-number service. **7 Dec:** The European Free Trade Association (EFTA) and Estonian sign a free trade agreement. **9 Dec:** Estonia replies in a strongly worded statement to the Russian claim that the dispute over church buildings between the Russian Orthodox Church, subject to the Patriarchate of Moscow, and the Estonian Apostolic Orthodox Church, which wishes to return to the Ecumenical Patriarchate in Constantinople, may have an adverse effect on Estonian-Russian relations.

1996 26 Jan: The European Commission opens its office in Tallinn, the first in the Baltic states. 27 private radio stations and eight private TV channels operate in Estonia—four private radio stations are noncommercial and three transmit Russian-language programs. **29 Jan:** Estonia begins a regular dialogue with NATO as a delegation attends NATO's regular ambassador-level meeting in Brussels at which NATO introduces the enlargement plan for 1996. **30 Jan:** The Cabinet forms a working group to begin preparations for Estonia's accession to the European Union; the first fiberoptic cable is laid between Estonia and Russia. **22 Feb:** President Meri announces the Tiger Leap program, which will computerize all schools and classrooms and link them to the Internet by 1999. **20 Mar:** The Defense Police indicts Vassili Riis, head of the NKVD in Saaremaa in 1940–41, for crimes against humanity for approving the execution of 340 innocent Estonian civilians in Kuressaare. **1 April:** In compliance with Riigikogu Act of 2 Feb. 1995, about 1,000 individuals have reported their contacts with foreign intelligence services prior to today's deadline; however, the government has estimated the total number of individuals with such links to be closer to 10,000. **31 May:** After a long period of anticipation, Tallinn Stock Exchange begins operations with a listing of shares of five banks and bonds of six compensation funds. **7 June:** The government adopts a strategy paper for Estonia's integration into the EU, the first such detailed concrete plan to be put on paper. **28 June:** Estonian and Latvian officials initial a maritime border agreement, thus bringing the long-running dispute over fisheries in the Gulf of Riga to a close. **4 July:** Of the 21,639 Russian citizens resident in Estonia voting in the second round of the Russian presidential election, 77.1 percent vote for ultranationalist Gennadi Zhuganov and 20.5 percent for winner President Boris Yeltsin. **12 July:** The final deadline for validity of Soviet-era identity documents; they remain valid only for identification pending receipt of new Estonian documents, such as residency permits; during the past year, over 300,000 applications for residency permits by aliens have been approved, with only 59 rejected; 88,748, or about half the eligible resident aliens, have applied; 15,236 retired Russian military officers and their families have been granted residence permits, and 4,077 applications are under further review. **1 Aug:** Since the old Soviet passports are no longer accepted for travel abroad, 98,010, or about half the eligible resident noncitizen aliens, have applied for alien travel passports. **11 Aug:** The seventh Global ESTO, held in Stockholm, concludes in Tallinn. **20 Aug:** The cabinet decides to privatize Estonian Energy and Estonian Oil Shale, two of the most important infrastructural firms in Estonia. **31 Aug:** Riigikogu concludes its three rounds of voting for the president, without any candidate reaching the required 68 votes; the election will now pass to the electoral college. **17 Sep:** Estonia becomes the first East European state to graduate from receiving U.S. aid. **20 Sep:** President Meri is reelected by the electoral college in the second round of voting with 196 votes to 126 for Arnold Rüütel, 44 blank ballots, and 4 spoiled ballots. **29 Oct:** The second elections since renewed independence to elect 254 municipal councils take place with 11,148 candidates vying for 3,453 seats; of the 882,726 eligible voters, including 70,976 resident noncitizens, 52 percent vote.

1997 **7 Jan:** In preparation to abolishing the death penalty, the president promulgates amendments to the criminal code allowing life imprisonment for serious crimes; however, new prison facilities must be built before these can be implemented. **9 Jan:** Russian Foreign Minister Yevgeni Primakov says Russia will not sign the completed border agreement with Estonia since it wishes to pressure Estonia on other issues. **21 Jan:** The cabinet announces that Estonia will open embassies in the Netherlands, Spain, Portugal, Greece, Ireland, and the Czech Republic to strengthen its position during negotiations for accession talks to the European Union; the Council of European Parliamentary Assembly votes to close its monitoring procedure since Estonia has fulfilled all its undertakings for membership. **29 Jan:** Riigikogu ratifies the European Convention on the Suppression of Terrorism. **May:** Visa-free travel enters into force for Estonians to all Nordic countries. **2 June:** 107,000 aliens' passports have been issued to date. **3 June:** The Estonian government, in principle, backs the bill proposed by Riigikogu's Russian-speaking members that state-financed high schools with tuition in the Russian language continue after the year 2000. **4 June:** The Baltic states have the right to become members of NATO, say German Foreign Minister Klaus Kinkel and Defense Minister Volker Rühe. **9 June:** Finland announces that it is now prepared to sell used weapons to Estonia, the first country to make such a declaration. **11 June:** The Russian embassy announces that it has registered 125,000 Estonian residents as Russian citizens by 1 June, but it estimates that about 20,000 of that number have left for Russia without informing the embassy. **25 June:** NATO Air Defense Committee (NADC) and members of the alliance pledge to support Estonia in setting up airspace surveillance and defense systems. **15 July:** The European Commission reports favorably on Estonia's application on accession and recommends that Estonia be included in the first round. **16 July:** The three largest Baltic banks are Estonia's Hansapank, Hoiupank (Savings Bank), and Ühispank (Union Bank). Of the 57 banks in the Baltics, the 14 Estonian banks account for 36.7 percent of their combined assets. **28 July:** Estonia celebrates 75 years of continuous diplomatic relations with the United States, originally established on 28 July 1922. **17 Sep:** Estonia, Latvia, and Lithuania initial a trilateral agreement to abolish nontariff trade restrictions. **5 Oct:** Next year, Estonia will pay 68.5 million EEK (0.5 percent of the budget, including the UN annual assessment of 5.7 million EEK), an increase from 40.2 million EEK this year, in membership fees to international organizations. **17 Oct:** Transit of Russian goods through Estonian ports has increased sevenfold since Independence in 1991. **17 Nov:** Estonia is 17th in Europe in per capita share of Internet users, and it has 94 computers with Internet access per 10,000 residents for a total of 13,612 Internet-connected computers. **4 Dec:** World Heritage Committee of the United Nations Educational, Social and Cultural Organization (UNESCO) adds the historic Old City center of Tallinn to its

World Heritage List. **11 Dec:** Estonia and Latvia complete jointly marking their common land border of 337 kilometers. **13 Dec:** The EU decides to begin full-accession talks with Estonia, Hungary, Poland, the Czech Republic, Slovenia, and Cyprus in April.

Building a Modern European Society in the Atlantic Alliance (1998–2003)

1998 1 Jan: Estonia announces that it will open a permanent mission to NATO headquarters in Brussels. **8 Jan:** 2.7 million tourists visited Estonia in 1997 and spent US$600 million (8.76 billion EEK), an average of US$400 per visitor; the tourism sector accounted for 18 percent of Estonia's total exports last year, and provides employment to more than 100,000 people. **14 Jan:** Hoiupank and Hansapank confirm their merger under the name of the latter; with assets of 20 billion EEK (US$1.4 billion), the new bank will be the largest in the Baltic States. **17 Jan:** Presidents Lennart Meri of Estonia, Guntis Ulmanis of Latvia, and Algirdas Brazauskas of Lithuania join U.S. President Bill Clinton in signing the U.S.-Baltic Charter of Partnership at the White House; President Clinton announces the formation of a US$15-million Baltic Partnership fund. **30 Jan:** The UN Economic Commission for Europe forecasts that Estonia will be the first candidate from Eastern Europe to become a member of the European Union. **5 Feb:** The International Monetary Fund reports that Estonia has come successfully out of the crisis that hit economies around the world last fall. **20 Feb:** Estonia plans to send its troops to participate in 15 different international military exercises during 1998, many of which will be held under the NATO Partnership for Peace (PfP) program. **26 Feb:** To boost savings, Riigikogu exempts from taxation interest paid by credit institutions to individuals. **18 Mar:** Riigikogu votes to abolish the death penalty to bring Estonia into line with the European Convention on Human Rights. **6 Apr:** The major credit ratings agencies report that Estonia's credit rating is the third highest in Eastern Europe; the Statistical Office reports that the average Estonian earned 1,630 EEK (US$110) per month last year, and expenses reached 1,651 EEK (US$112) per month. **8 Apr:** The headquarters of the BALTRON minesweeping squadron opens at the naval base in Tallinn. **21 Apr:** The Cabinet endorses this year's privatization program, which maps the first phase of the privatization of infrastructure companies, including state holdings in Eesti Põlevkivi (Estonian Oil Shale), Eesti Energia (Estonian Energy), Eesti Raudtee (Estonian Railway), and Eesti Telekom (Estonian Telecommunications) as well as the alcohol producer AS Liviko and the Moe Piiritusetehas distillery. **28 Apr:** The Statistical Office reports that Estonia's population is aging faster than those of other transition countries or Western Europe. **13 May:** On President Meri's initiative, Estonia will, in cooperation with the American Jewish Committee, set up an international commission to investigate crimes committed in Estonia under Soviet and Nazi regimes during the period of 1939–1991; Riigikogu passes a Housing Act amendment opening the way to the gradual liberalization of rents. **8 June:** The government announces that it will set up a central server enabling all residents to fill in official documents via the Internet by 1 January 1999; the server will also provide access to information of all government institutions. **26 June:** The Swedish government decides to donate 2.4 million SEK (4.3 million EEK) to an integration program for Estonia's Russian-speaking residents. **28 July:** 294,000 individuals declared their 1997 income this year, 3 percent more than the number of declarations last year; the total income declared by individuals for 1997 was 11.5 billion EEK; 135,452 people declared incomes of between 10,001 to 50,000 EEK, and 22,000 declared incomes between 100,001 and 500,000 EEK. **4 Aug:** The government endorses an anti–money laundering bill aimed at preventing money earned by criminal means from entering into the financial system. **5 Aug:** Estonia will receive a donation 40,500 new M-14 rifles, worth a total of 43.4 million EEK, from the U.S. Defense Department. **13 Aug:** Police announce that 20,000 pirated cassettes and 8,000 CDs have been confiscated in the first seven months of 1998; they comprise about half of the pirated items currently on sale. **19 Aug:** The Russian ruble's devaluation does not affect the kroon's value. **21 Aug:** The UNDP and the Nordic countries jointly agree to support a program to promote the integration of Estonia's Russian-speaking minority. **25 Aug:** The international rating agency Fitch IBCA reiterates that the Baltic States are not in danger of catching the "Russian flu"; the rating agency Moody's ranks Estonia in 31st place, ahead of Finland and all the larger East European states, by the strength of their banking systems. **5 Sep:** Ernst Jaakson, Estonia's ambassador to the UN, who had represented Estonia abroad during the 50-year Soviet occupation, dies in New York at age 93. **21 Sep:** The University of Tartu's Open University program has created an Internet Estonian language course for Russian speakers. **25 Sep:** Transparency International announces that Estonia ranks 26th among 85 countries with a score of 5.7 out of 10, meaning it is perceived to be relatively free of corruption. **6 Oct:** Debit cards issued by commercial banks total 555,526 at the end of September; the number of cellular phone clients has grown to 213,000, with 28,000 clients being added since July. **13 Oct:** The government undertakes to work out a preliminary financial control system by 1 January 2000, at the latest, to guarantee control over EU subsidies. **16 Oct:** The U.S. House of Representatives unanimously passes a resolution supporting the independence of the Baltic States and urges the Clinton administration to ask Russia, as the successor to the Soviet Union, to denounce the Molotov-Ribbentrop Pact. **21 Oct:** Max van der Stoel, the high commissioner on National Minorities of the Organization for Security and Cooperation in Europe (OSCE), says that he is very satisfied with the work done by Estonia so far, and that the OSCE will not make any new demands on Estonia concerning minorities. **4 Nov:** The European Commission's annual report praises Estonia for its good economic growth and the development of its market economy, and generally expresses satisfaction with Estonia's progress in adopting EU policies. **11 Nov:** Estonia begins substantive negotiations for accession with the EU. **25 Nov:** The Russian armed forces, which withdrew from Estonia four years ago, caused extensive damage to Estonia's natural environment, and cleanup costs are estimated reach at least US$5 billion. **3 Dec:** Estonia ranked 18th with an above-average score of 2.15 among the 160 countries included in the Index of Economic Freedom published by the U.S. Heritage Foundation and the *Wall Street Journal*; this places Estonia at the same ranking as Austria, Chile, and the Netherlands. **4 Dec:** Riigikogu unanimously approves a three-way agreement among the Baltic States on the establishment of the BALTNET joint airspace surveillance system to be built with American funding assistance, which will significantly extend NATO's surveillance of Russian airspace.

1999 12 Jan: The government decides to create a 450-hectare free economic zone in the north coast industrial town of Sillamäe. **13 Jan:** Estonia's per capita use of permanent connections to the Internet places it in 15th position among the countries of the world. **27 Jan:** Riigikogu adopts a new, tougher anticorruption law to expose dishonest officials and bring them to justice. **2 Feb:** Estonia has cut the emission of environmentally dangerous gases by 35 percent and now ranks second in the world after Latvia in terms of such reduction. **12 Feb:** The Estonian Telekom IPO has proven to be the most successful international initial public offering of shares of any East Central European country to date. **1 Mar:** Visa-free travel for Estonians to Germany and France enters into force. **5 Mar:** After eight years of difficult negotiations, Estonia and Russia initial agreements on land and sea borders with Estonia ceding 2,000 square kilometers of territory belonging to it under the Tartu Peace Treaty of 1920. **7 Mar:** The electorate today, with a voter turnout of 55.8 percent, down from the 69.2 percent in 1995, elects the center-right coalition of Pro Patria (18 seats), Reform Party (18), and Moderates (17) to power with 53 seats out of the total of 101; the Center Party, the largest in Riigikogu with 28 seats, will form the main opposition; the Coalition and the Country People's parties received 7 mandates each, and the (Russian) United People's Party elects 6 members. **25 Mar:** The Pro Patria, Reform, and Moderates coalition government, with Mart Laar as prime minister, is sworn into office. **14 May:** The Statistical Office's final calculations show that the economy grew by 10.6 percent in 1997, and preliminary figures indicate growth of 4.0 percent in 1998. **22 June:** The government endorses the draft bill on digital signatures, thus placing Estonia ahead of most European Union countries in this technology. **26 June:** The ashes of Estonia's World War II legendary soldier, Colonel Alfons Rebane, who died in Germany in 1976, are brought home and buried in Forest Cemetery in Tallinn. **30 June:** Visa-free travel to all EU countries for Estonian citizens becomes possible today as Belgium drops visa requirements. **7 July:** The government establishes a ministerial commission to coordinate and accelerate Estonia's internal preparations for joining NATO. **12 July:** The latest global index of the United Nations Human Development Report ranks Estonia in 54th place, up 23 positions from its placement in last year's report. **27 July:** The government today implements stricter requirements for proficiency in Estonian for employees in the public sector, authorized by the amended Language Act. **12 Aug:** The first class of army officers fully trained in Estonia completes their training at the Army Joint Training Institute in Tallinn. **16 Aug:** The Baltic Defense

College (BDCOL), commanded by Danish Brigadier General Michael H. Clemmesen, begins its first year with an international mix of cadets and lecturers from the Baltic States and NATO member states. **15 Sep:** The minister of education announces plans to open a school for Russian speakers with Estonian as the language of instruction in Narva to strengthen the Estonian state in the northeast border city. **1 Oct:** Visas are no longer issued at border points; from today on, visas for visitors from counties for which Estonia requires visas are issued only by Estonian consulates abroad. **13 Nov:** After two years of preparations and negotiations, Estonia becomes the 135th member of the World Trade Organization (WTO). **25 Nov:** The Ministry of the Interior announces that it will reduce the police force in Estonia by 655 in order to develop a more professional and better paid force. **15 Dec:** Riigikogu passes a new Income Tax Act, including abolition of the corporate income tax on reinvested profit

2000 **3 Jan:** Large-scale privatization in Estonia has reached its final stages, with only the privatization of large infrastructure enterprises still to be completed; privatization of companies expected to be completed in year 2000 include Eesti Raudtee (Estonian Railway Co), Edelaraudtee (Southwest Railway), and AS Tarmeko. **2 Feb:** Estonia's three mobile phone operators had a total of 400,000 clients at the beginning of this year. **3 Feb:** Estonia pays its contribution to the United Nations' regular budget for 2000 on schedule and substantially reduces arrears on payments to the peace operations budget from previous years, which the UN had assigned to it as its share of the Soviet Union's unpaid peacekeeping debt. **8 Feb:** Tallinn was the second-largest European cruise port in Europe last year, with 190 cruise ships compared to 230 in the largest cruise port Lisbon, and 187 cruise ships visiting St. Petersburg. **25 Feb:** In 1991–99, Estonia received 198.27 million euros in support programs from the EU; it is expected to receive between 890 million and 1.3 billion EEK (US$57.1 to US$83.4 million) annually until it joins the EU, depending on actual EU budget allocations in various support programs from 2001 to 2003. After becoming a member, EU structural assistance funding may reach up to 4 percent of the GNP. **1 Mar:** Estonians are able to submit income tax returns via the Internet as of today. **8 Mar:** Riigikogu adopts the Digital Signature Act; the World Tourism Organization cites Estonia as the fastest growing tourism destination in Europe: the number of overnight visitors grew 15 percent in 1999, to a total of 3.18 million. **23 Mar:** Estonia expects to complete its transformation to the use of information and communications technology (ITC) within two years, with all government databases, digital signatures in business, and other applications becoming client centered. **21 Mar:** A UN study shows that Estonia is among the most rapidly aging European nations, with the current 19 percent of the population over 60 climbing to 38 percent in 2050. **29 Mar:** Estonia will grant citizenship without requiring additional exams to Russian students who graduate from Estonian-language high schools or programs. **31 Mar:** The first population and housing census in newly independent Estonia starts today, to be completed on 9 April. **4 Apr:** Parliament adopts a bill laying down the process of transition of Russian-language schools to Estonian to begin in 2007–08 at the latest, wherein 60 percent of the syllabus must be taught in Estonian. Under previous legislation, all subjects were to be taught in Estonian only by 2007. **19 Apr:** The percentage of pupils attending Russian-language schools in Estonia has dropped from 37 percent at the beginning of the 1990s to 28 percent last year. **16 May:** Estonia and Russia reach an accord on the principal issues of an agreement that would abolish the double tariffs levied by Russia on imports from Estonia. **1 June:** Parliament ratifies all nine chapters of the European Social Charter, two with reservations. **15 June:** To encourage public debate, Cabinet allocates 200,000 EEK to support projects sponsored by Euroskeptics. **22 June:** The Baltic Defense College (BDCOL) graduates its first class of 32 officers from Estonia, Latvia, Lithuania, Denmark, Germany, Hungary, Sweden, and United States. **28 June:** Estonia establishes a modern three-pillar pension system, in which the first is compulsory, the second provides for voluntary contributions of wages of 2 percent by employees and 4 percent by employers, and the third is for tax-deductible contributions to private supplementary pension plans. **1 July:** A liberalized trading regime with expanded access for Estonian agricultural goods entering EU markets goes into effect. **24 July:** 112,163 people have been naturalized in Estonia since the country's citizenship law took effect in 1992; the largest number were naturalized in 1993–1996 (20,370 in 1993, 22,474 in 1994, 16,674 in 1995, and 22,773 in 1996). **25 July:** The compulsory military conscription period is shortened from 12 to 8 months. **7 Aug:** The Cabinet held its first electronic session, with computer monitors replacing stacks of paper in front of each minister—one minister participated via laptop Internet access from Australia; this was made possible by converting all State Chancellery records to electronic files. **4 Sep:** The share of tourism in Estonia's GNP is constantly growing and has already reached 10 percent; high unemployment combined with a shortage of skilled workers are cited by Hansapank as the main problems facing the Estonian economy. **13 Sep:** Transparency International reports that Estonia continues to be the least corrupt country in East and Central Europe, maintaining its 27th position out of 99 countries studied. **9 Oct:** The Estonian navy receives two minesweepers as a gift from Germany. **10 Oct:** The latest integration report of the government indicates that 84 percent of ethnic non-Estonians regard Estonia as their home and 79.3 percent see themselves as loyal to the Estonian state. **11 Oct:** The Ämari national airspace surveillance center opens as part of the joint Baltic system of surveillance (BALTNET). **5 Dec:** Estonia and the EU have provisionally closed 16 chapters out of 31, ranking Estonia among the most advanced candidate countries. **15 Dec:** The law on digital signatures enters into force.

2001 **1 Jan:** Estonia begins around-the-clock surveillance of its air space. **15 Jan:** The Ministry of Foreign Affairs unveils a plaque commemorating 231 former employees repressed during the Soviet and Nazi German occupations. **16 Jan:** Parliament sets up a special committee to probe into how operations of the Soviet KGB secret police were wound up in Estonia in 1991. **1 Mar:** Estonia, with 56,437 young people studying in 47 higher educational institutions, amounting to 14.7 percent of the population, has the largest percentage of students in Europe, ahead of Sweden, Germany, Switzerland, and Austria. **30 Mar:** In EU accession negotiations, Estonia closes the chapters on free movement of services and financial services, with two transition periods in the latter. **10 Apr:** The Estonian government decides to extend by two years the mission of the country's peacekeepers in Bosnia-Herzegovina and Kosovo. **27 Apr:** Estonia announces that it will issue the safest, tamper-proof, electronically produced and readable passports in Europe in 2002, along with electronically readable ID cards for domestic use. **3 May:** Foreign Minister Toomas Henrik Ilves reports that relations between Estonia and Russia may now be characterized as normal. **9 May:** A draft for a new law on local elections allows EU citizens who reside permanently in Estonia to run for seats on local councils on equal terms with Estonian citizens. **12 May:** Estonian duo Tanel Padar and Dave Benton win this year's Eurovision song contest with "Everybody," by composer Ivar Must, in Copenhagen, creating a sensational outpouring of national pride and introducing Estonia to millions of Europeans. **15 May:** Proficiency in Estonian at least on the intermediate level will be required from all employees in the trade and service spheres in the private sector. **16 May:** Riigikogu amends the wage law to require equal salaries to be paid to men and women for equal work. **18 May:** Estonia received approximately 1 billion EEK support from the EU last year and expects to receive a similar sum from the main preaccession support programs of PHARE (infrastructure), SAPARD (agriculture), and ISPA (environment and transport). **1 June:** Estonia is the first of the Baltic states to close the environmental chapter in EU accession talks, but will need four transition periods from 2004 to 2013 to meet EU standards in sewage systems and waste treatment, oil terminals and gasoline stations, and drinking water systems; 75 percent of costs will be met by EU funding. **14 June:** Parliament adopts a law to set up the Estonian Unemployment Fund to provide compulsory insurance for temporary unemployment. **25 June:** The Estonian government's press office launches a website, www.tom.riik.ee, to enable citizens to comment on draft laws and amendments. **3 July:** Cabinet approves a plan to reform the police system from a repressive to an efficient and effective organization to help people, and it divides the country into four regional police districts. **18 July:** Russia's northwestern Pskov region wishes to set up a Euroregion together with adjoining Estonian territories. **21 Sep:** Arnold Rüütel is elected president by a vote of 186 to Toomas Savi's 155 with 2 invalid and 23 blank ballots cast by the 366 members of the electoral college, thus winning by a margin of 3 votes; in the first round on 28 August, Rüütel garnered 114 votes and Toomas Savi 80 votes to Peeter Tulviste's 89 and Peeter Kreitzbergs's 72. **21 Nov:** Parliament abrogates the requirement adopted three years ago that members of Parliament and local councils must prove their command of Estonian. **8 Dec:** A new political party, Res Publica, is formed with Rein Taagepera as interim leader. **13 Dec:** The Organization of Security and Cooperation in Europe (OSCE) Permanent Council decides that the work of its office in Estonia has been completed and that the office will be closed on 31 December. **20 Dec:** Prime Minister Laar announces that he will resign on 8 January following the breakup of the coalition of his party with the Reform Party in the Tallinn City Council. **27 Dec:** Digital signatures will go into effect at the end of January in connection with the issuance of national digital ID cards.

2002 2 Jan: A new unemployment insurance system goes into effect with employees contributing 1 percent of their pay and employers 0.5 percent of their payroll. The unemployment benefit payment will be 50 percent of the employee's pay. **22 Jan:** Riigikogu approves the appointment of Siim Kallas as the new prime minister by a vote of 62 to 31. He will form a cabinet of Reform and Center parties with the support of the Russian-speaking Estonian People's Party. **28 Jan:** The Kallas cabinet is sworn into office. Mart Laar promises his successor 100 days free of criticism. **25 Feb:** The Tallinn Stock Exchange (TSE) is successfully integrated into the trading system of the Helsinki Stock Exchange (HEX). **28 Feb:** Finland authorizes the laying of an undersea power cable between Estonia and Finland. The 100-million-euro Estlink project is to be operational by 2004. **6 Mar:** Foreign Minister Kristiina Ojuland meets with Russian Foreign Minister Igor Ivanov at a foreign ministers' meeting of the Council of the Baltic Sea States in the Svetlogorsk resort in Russia's Kaliningrad Oblast to discuss ways to improve their countries' relations. The last meeting of the foreign ministers of the two countries took place six years before, in November 1996 in Petroskoye, northwestern Russia, at a similar CBSS meeting, where Siim Kallas and Yevgenii Primakov initialed a border agreement that has not yet been signed. **25 Mar:** Parliament agrees to provide state funding for Russian-language secondary school education after 2007. **27 Mar:** Estonia, Great Britain, Finland, Norway, and Sweden conclude a new three-year agreement to support ethnic minority integration projects in Estonia, with the Western partners picking up over half the cost of US$2 million. The total cost of Estonia's integration programs for 2000–2003 is almost US$7 million. **31 Mar:** After a hiatus of two years, Estonia once again switches to daylight savings time in concert with the rest of Europe. **17 May:** The President's Ethnic Minorities Round Table celebrates its 10th anniversary. **26 May:** The 2002 Eurovision Song Contest in Tallinn ends with rave reviews, with Latvia winning the right to hold the next one in 2003. Estonia is the first postcommunist country to host the contest in its 47-year history. **10**

June: Estonian and Russian prime ministers hold a bilateral meeting during the Council of Baltic Sea States (CBSS) meeting in St. Petersburg. Russia agrees to resume cooperation with Estonia on outstanding economic issues, including the removal of double tariffs. **18 June:** Riigikogu adopts a resolution condemning the activities of the Soviet security agencies and other occupation regime institutions in Estonia, and decrees the Communist Party of the Soviet Union and its satellite, the Estonian Communist Party, as the responsible organs; membership in these, however, does not mean individual responsibility for these organs' actions. **24 June:** President Vladimir Putin confirms that Russia will not obstruct Estonia's admission to NATO. **28 June:** Estonia closes the chapter on taxation in negotiations with the EU on the *Acquis Communitaire*, with minor derogations until 2009. Estonia expects to conclude the remaining three chapters in the next few months, and to be ready to accept the invitation to join the EU at the Copenhagen Summit in December. **24 July:** Estonia rose to 42nd place on the United Nations' Human Development Index of countries, up two places from the year before. **26 July:** The Port of Tallinn ranked first among ports situated on the eastern Baltic ports in freight turnover at 19.03 million tons, ahead of St. Petersburg at 18.66 million and Ventspils at 17.18 million tons. **30 July:** Estonia closes the energy chapter with the EU and agrees to a step-by-step opening of its electricity market up to the year 2012, rising from the current 10 percent to 35 percent by 2009; it will open it fully by 31 December 2012. **12 Aug:** Estonian and Finnish border services agree to a common radio communication system designed for both internal and operative communication. **3 Sep:** Riigikogu ratifies the Kyoto Protocol on reduction of greenhouse gas emission, agreeing to reduce emissions of greenhouse gases in Estonia by 8 percent between 2008 and 2012. **5 Sep:** Half of all income-tax returns in 2002 were submitted electronically. **17 Sep:** Estonia was ranked 27th of 75 countries in the latest Global Competitiveness Report by the World Economic Forum; of the European Union's (EU) candidates, Hungary placed one notch higher than Estonia; Latvia placed 42nd, and Lithuania 49th. **18 Sep:** Estonia is keeping its place among the top Central and Eastern European nations in terms of foreign direct investment (FDI) per capita, being second after the Czech Republic. **4 Oct:** The government of Estonia, the Estonian Apostolic Orthodox Church, and the Orthodox Church of the Moscow Patriarchate in Estonia sign two letters of intent to regulate the property relationships between the two churches. **3 Oct:** Estonia ranks 21st in competitiveness in the Lausanne-based Institute of Management Development in the list of 49 countries; it places 42nd among 173 countries in the UN human development index, and 32nd among 190 countries in the UN's list for e-governance. Estonian companies invest more money abroad per capita than other Central and East European countries. **20 Oct:** In local elections, 13 parties (874 party lists) and 121 individual candidates, totaling 15,203 candidates, contested 3,291 places; 535,370 people or 52.5 percent of the eligible electorate voted. The new party Res Publica came first in 21 local governments and placed second in 39. The most popular party was the Center Party, which also won 38.5 percent of the Tallinn Council seats and will form a coalition city government. **23 Oct:** Former Foreign Minister Toomas Hendrik Ilves becomes the first head of an Estonian political party to resign voluntarily, taking responsibility for the failure of the Moderates in local municipal elections. **26 Oct:** Mart Laar, prime minister in 1999–2001, resigns as head of Pro Patria Union because of its poor results in the recently held local government elections. **12 Nov:** Estonia ranks sixth in the world in terms of economic freedom according to a survey by the Heritage Foundation and the *Wall Street Journal*, sharing this spot with Denmark and the United States, whereas Lithuania ranks 29th and Latvia 33rd. Australia and Great Britain come after Estonia in the 2003 economic freedom list. Finland and Sweden are 11th and 12th, and Russia ranks 135th. **13 Nov:** Estonia has climbed three places to rank 26th in the World Economic Forum's (WEF) country competitiveness list. Belgium is one place ahead of Estonia, and Malaysia, Slovenia, Hungary, and France come after Estonia. **21 Nov:** NATO invites Estonia, Latvia, Lithuania, Slovakia, Slovenia, Romania, and Bulgaria to join as members, effective 2004. **6 Dec:** Leaders of Estonia's northeastern customs district and Russia's regional customs authority agree to carry out joint operations next year at customs checkpoints in Narva and the Russian border town of Ivangorod across the river. **5 Dec:** According to the Open Society Institute and the Jaan Tõnisson Institute, Estonia has the lowest level of corruption of the EU candidate countries; corruption is a "relatively limited problem" in Estonia; on Transparency International's corruption index, Estonia currently ranks 28th of 91 countries. **13 Dec:** Estonia and the other nine candidate states complete final issues in their accession talks with the

EU in Copenhagen, opening the way for them to become EU full members on May 1, 2004. **18 Dec:** Riigikogu decides to hold a referendum on EU membership on 14 September 2004; voters will be asked: "Do you support Estonian Republic's accession to the European Union and adoption of a law of amendments to the constitution of the Republic of Estonia?" Riigikogu also passes the European Parliament Election Bill, under which the Estonians will elect six deputies to the European Parliament of 732 members for the first time in the summer of 2004.

2003 3 Jan: Russia's Ambassador to Estonia, Konstantin Provalov, calls 2002 a very beneficial year in developing normal relations between Estonia and Russia. Never during the last 10–12 years have so many Russian members of states and public and cultural figures visited Estonia as in 2002, and bilateral trade showed a year-on-year growth of 26 percent. **6 Feb:** The number of Russian tourists visiting Estonia has doubled in seven years—142,000 Russians visited Estonia in 1996; in 2002 they totaled 281,000; and Russians form the third largest group of tourists in Estonia after Finns and Latvians. **3 Mar:** Elections to Riigikogu X are held: 963 candidates in 11 party lists and 16 independents compete for 101 seats. Only six parties are elected: the new party, Res Publica, and the Center Party each receive 28 seats, Reform receives 19, Coalition 13, and Pro Patria and Moderates 7 and 6, respectively; 58.2 percent of the electorate vote. **4 Mar:** The Estonian government sets up an e-state academy to offer training services to senior public servants in Caucasian, Central Asian, Balkan, and Central European countries via the Internet; the UNDP and the Open Society agree to provide some funding. **31 Mar:** The electrical power companies Eesti Energia (Estonian Energy), Latvenergo of Latvia, and Pohjolan Voima and Helsingin Energia of Finland sign a protocol to build an underwater power cable, the Estlink, between Estonia and Finland. **10 Apr:** The three-party coalition government of Prime Minister Juhan Parts, consisting of Res Publica, Center, and Coalition parties, takes office. **16 Apr:** Estonia signs the European Union Accession Treaty at the EU Council meeting in Athens, effective 1 May 2004. **21 Apr:** Estonia opens the primary radar for airspace control as part of BALTNET, which makes it possible to see flying objects within 450 kilometers and at up to 30 kilometers' altitude, as a prelude to accession to NATO membership. **10 Jun:** The Parts Cabinet drafts a bill that reduces the flat income tax rates from the current 26 percent progressively to 24, 22, and 20 percent in the tax years 2004, 2005, and 2006, respectively. **16 Jun:** The Estonian police announce the consolidation of the 17 existing national police districts into four superdistricts effective 1 January 2004 as a measure of efficiency. **20 Jun:** Two Estonian Army units leave for service in Iraq and Kuwait aboard a U.S. aircraft; Estonians are also stationed as peacekeepers in Afghanistan, Bosnia, Kosovo, Macedonia, and the Middle East. **14 Sep:** Although Estonians vote overwhelmingly in the referendum to join the EU—66.8 to 33.2 percent—only 64 percent of eligible voters cast a ballot. **30 Oct:** The World Economic Forum ranks Estonia 22nd in economic growth competitiveness, ahead of France, Spain, Portugal, Belgium, and Ireland. **31 Oct:** An EMOR poll reports that 85 percent of the Estonian population favors the direct election of the president, with 11 percent opposed and 4 percent undecided; most also want the president to have greater power.

Introduction

The image of Estonia underwent a magic transformation as it moved from being a forgotten component of the authoritarian and economically moribund Soviet Union to a democratic, vibrant, and competitive modern member of the **European Union** (EU) between 1989 and 2004. The road was not easy, and it depended on a combination of the changing international constellation of power and serendipity, but most of all on the stubborn insistence of Estonians on regaining control over their national destiny. To this end, Estonian political elites consistently pursued four principal policy objectives: an independent sovereign Estonian nation-state, internationally and broadly guaranteed military security against foreign threats, full recognition and participation in the family of nations, and the pursuit of a wealthy competitive and modern service-oriented economy. For Estonians, who enjoyed only two decades of independence in eight centuries prior to being occupied again by their eastern neighbor and long-term former imperial colonizer in 1940 for another half century, guaranteed sovereign independence as a state is a historical imperative for national existence.

History has taught Estonians that their tiny ethnic nation, numbering under a million people, cannot survive alone in an uncertain world of competing powers. Nor can a small state without significant resources prosper if it is left unprotected in a world of economic blocs. Luckily, the international constellation changed sufficiently to allow Estonia to become a member of the **North Atlantic Treaty Organization** (NATO) led by the United States, the sole superpower of the 21st century, thus guaranteeing its security. Similarly, at the right time the European Union (EU) decided to expand to include Estonia and the newly enfranchised former socialist states of Central and Eastern Europe in order to secure its own economy and guarantee democratic capitalist systems on its eastern border. At the beginning of the 21st century, for the first time since they lost their independence in the Christianizing Crusades in the 13th century, Estonians have been served well by their neighbors in the West.

This is the story of the Estonians' voyage from the beginnings of Estonian historical time to full membership in the European and international systems.

LAND AND PEOPLE

The Republic of Estonia (Eesti Vabariik) is located in the northeastern corner of Western Europe, south of Finland, and across the Gulf of Finland on the eastern shore of the **Baltic Sea** between 57°30′ and 59°49′ N latitude and 21°46′ and 28°13′ E longitude. The distance from east to west is 350 kilometers, and from north to south 240 kilometers. Estonia has over 1,500 islands in coastal archipelagoes (totaling 4,144 square kilometers) on the Baltic coast and at the mouth of the Gulf of Finland. The largest are Saaremaa (2,673 square kilometers), Hiiumaa (988 square kilometers), Muhu (200 square kilometers), and Vormsi (93 square kilometers). Lakes, of which the Estonian share of **Lake Peipus** (Peipsi järv) is the largest, form 2,015 square kilometers of the 45,215 square kilometers of territory of Estonia. Hence, Estonia is larger than Denmark, the Netherlands, and Switzerland. Estonia's land borders of 294 kilometers with Russia in the east and 339 kilometers with Latvia in the south pale against the 3,794 kilometers of coastline, which enclose Estonia on three sides and makes it a major Baltic Sea coastal state.

Administratively, Estonia is divided into 15 counties containing 247 self-governing municipalities (*see* **LOCAL GOVERNMENT**). **Tallinn**, the capital, is the largest city with a population of 408,000, followed by the university town of **Tartu** with a population of 101,000, the industrial towns of **Narva** and Kohtla-Järve with 73,000 and 51,000 respectively, and the resort town of **Pärnu** with 51,000.

Geologically, Estonia is located on the northwestern part of the East European platform that varies but slightly in elevation. Over 60 percent of the country's territory lies at an absolute height of 0 to 50 meters, and only one 10th has an elevation of over 100 meters above sea level, with the southeast and east higher than the coast of the Baltic Sea. At

318 meters, the highest point is the Great Egg Mountain (Suur Munamägi), found in the southeast. The northern coast contains the Ordovician limestone plateau with cliffs known as the North Estonian Glint rising up to 56 meters above the shore of the Gulf of Finland. Exploitable deposits of oil shale, phosphate, and limestone for cement and construction materials are found in abundance in this plateau. Since Estonia was covered by continental glaciers several times during the ice age, sediments cover the sandstone bedrock thinly in the north but up to 200 meters in the south, where they form a hilly moraine terrain. Owing to abundant precipitation and low runoff, Estonia has 165,000 marshes greater than one hectare in area, of which 132 peatlands are larger than 1,000 hectares. The total area of marshes and swamp forests measures 1,009,101 hectares, or 22.3 percent of the country's territory, and the peat reserves are estimated at 4 billion tons. Only Estonia's northern neighbor, Finland, has a higher percentage (at 31) of peatland.

The climate of Estonia is determined by its flat, low-lying terrain, the vicinity of the Baltic Sea, and the proximity of the Gulf Stream sweeping up the Norwegian coast of the North Atlantic only 600 kilometers to the west. Hence, the prevailing winds in Estonia blow from the southwest and west. Tempests and tornadoes are rare—the last hurricane raged through Estonia in 1969. Thus, summer temperatures are somewhat lower than the average for the latitude, but winter temperatures are considerably warmer. The average temperature of the coldest month, February, is −3.5° to −7° C, and that of the warmest, July, is 16 to 18°C. Apart from the coast and the western islands, which have little or no snow, snow cover lasts from the beginning of January to the end of March. In mild winters, much of Estonia does not have lasting snow cover at all.

Almost half of Estonian territory, or 47.6 percent, is forested. Owing to good forest management due to the importance of the wood industry, the area of forests has more than doubled during the last 50 years and is still growing. Estonia is situated on a border area where the coniferous Euro-Siberian taiga opens to the European zone of deciduous forests. Eighty-seven native and more than 500 introduced tree and bush species grow in Estonia. Scotch pine is the most common tree dominating 41 percent of forests, followed by birches with 28 percent, Norway spruce with 23 percent, and the remaining 10 percent being alders and aspen. The largest forests are found in the northeast and central parts of the country along a zone stretching from the northern coast to the Latvian border.

Although Estonia is not territorially a small country in the European context, at just under 1.4 million people in 2002, its population is one of the smallest in Europe, with ethnic Estonians forming 65.2 percent (a little over 900,000) and Russians 28 percent, the remaining 6.8 percent being made up mostly of Russian-speaking Ukrainian (2.5 percent) and Byelorussian (1.5 percent) immigrants of the ethnic groups brought to Estonia as labor during the half century of Soviet occupation.

HISTORICAL SURVEY

Ancient Estonia

Although Estonia is usually referred to as one of the three Baltic States along with Latvia and Lithuania, linguistically and ethnically Estonians are not related to their southern Baltic ethnolinguistic neighbors, but are related to the Finns and belong to the **Finno-Ugric** ethnolinguistic group. Their origins are debatable, but they are generally thought to have migrated from the forest zone west of the Ural mountain range perhaps around 3000 B.C. or even earlier. However, there is no agreement on exactly when and how the Finno-Ugrians migrated westward and split up, with the Hungarian branch settling in the Balkans and the Estonians and Finns moving north to the shores of the Baltic Sea. According to archaeological evidence, the earliest human settlements in Estonia, known as the Kunda culture (named after the site of the discovery), date to 7500 B.C., but these people are definitely not the ancestors of the Finno-Ugric Estonians. The latter apparently arrived in waves from the Late Stone Age (4000–1500 B.C.) to the Bronze Age (1500–500 B.C.). By 500 B.C., prehistoric Estonians had separated from the other northern Balto-Finns, and by the time of the birth of Christ, they had settled down to primitive two-field farming within their current borders.

Until the Christianizing **Crusades**, Estonians lived in villages as freemen and banded together to protect themselves as well as to carry out raids on enemy tribes. During the first centuries A.D., a nascent political organization began to develop as elected village elders met in conclaves of several at the *kihelkond* (parish) level at a fortified village, and combined into periodic meetings at the regional *maakond* (county) level, initially to plan defense and warfare. By the 13th century, eight counties had formed: Osilia (the island of Saaremaa), Rotalia (Läänemaa), Harria (Harjumaa), Revelia (Rävala), Vironia (Virumaa), Jervia (Järvamaa), Saccala (Sakala), and Ugandia (Ugandi). Although no Estonian state developed and relations among the counties were loose, based mainly on needs to repel raids from Vikings and from Russian and Latvian tribes, and to organize retributory raids, ancient Estonians lived mostly at peace among themselves and did not come under foreign control until the Crusades. Much of what we know about ancient Estonia (as well as about the Crusades and the conquest) is found in three **chronicles**.

Medieval Livonia

During the Middle Ages, as the Roman Empire collapsed in the west, the Germans steadily expanded trade and territorial control east and reached the Baltic littoral around the end of the 13th century. Because their eastward expansion along the Great North German Plain was blocked by organized Lithuanian opposition, they turned northward, swiftly subdued the **Livs** and Letgallian tribes on Latvian territory, and attacked the Estonians. The key figure in the conquest of the territories of both the Latvians and the Estonians was Bishop Albert von Buxhoevden of Bremen. He served as the first bishop of Livonia in 1199–1229 and worked closely with the Order of Knights of Christ (*see* **CRUSADING ORDERS**), and in 1201 he founded Riga, which subsequently became the headquarters of Germanic control over Estonia and Latvia. It took the combined forces of the bishop, the Order, and co-opted Liv and Lettgallian tribes from 1208 to 1227 to finally defeat the Estonians in fierce warfare. The legendary **Lembitu** for a time led a successful resistance by organizing the first major Estonian *malev* or military unit, but he was killed in battle in 1217.

In the meantime, Swedes made an unsuccessful attempt to conquer the western islands, and the Russian princes entered the fray but joined the Estonians conditionally when it looked like the German advance would threaten them as well. Bishop Albert was forced to seek Danish help to divide and weaken Estonian concentrations. The Danes landed in the north in 1219, founded **Tallinn** as their redoubt, and established control over much of northern Estonia within a year while the Germans conquered the south. The Estonians, however, did not give up, and rose again, but were finally subdued in 1227 by the superior numbers and military technology of the invaders and their own lack of unified political and military structures. The two-decade crusade ostensibly to Christianize, but in reality to expand Germanic trade and to colonize, ended the independent and free ancient Estonia and ushered in seven centuries of foreign domination. However, Estonians also were brought into the sphere of West European civilization, and a lasting line was drawn at Estonia's eastern border against Eastern Orthodoxy and Slavic civilization.

The Estonian Middle Ages

The period from the conquest until the outbreak of the wars in the mid-16th century is known as the Estonian Middle Ages, and the conquered territories of Estonia and Latvia are known as Old Livonia (*see* **LIVONIA**). After several partitions, Estonia was divided between the Livonian Order (*see* **CRUSADING ORDERS**), the Bishopric of **Tartu**, and the Bishopric of Saare-Lääne, the latter comprising the island of Saaremaa and the western Estonian mainland. Northern Estonia, including Tallinn, was ruled by Denmark from 1238 to 1346, when the Danish King Valdemar IV sold it to the Teutonic Order. Already the outlines of the administrative division of the Provinces of Estland and Livland (as they were to become in the 16th century) were in place: northern Estonia, later the Province of Estland until 1917, lay north of a line drawn from Pärnu to the top of **Lake Peipus** and included the large Baltic islands; and southern Estonia (lands belonging to the Livonian Order and the Bishopric of Tartu), later to be joined to the present-day provinces of Vidzeme and Zemgale, became the Province of Livland (Livonia in English).

The crusaders settled on lands granted in fief by masters of the Orders, built manor houses, and engaged in primitive **agriculture** using the three-field system to grow the local crops of rye, barley, oats, and wheat, with bullocks or a new breed of horses imported by the knights. The new rulers imposed taxes and the duty of corvée labor for planting, harvesting, and the building of churches and stone fortifications. Conditions became so intolerable that on the night of St. George's Day, 23

April 1346, a general uprising began with the wholesale killing of the German overlords and burning of their manor houses. The revolt spread across northern Estonia and to Saaremaa. It took the Livonian Order two years to put down the insurrection with the help of reinforcements from Prussia. Although local revolts took place sporadically over the following centuries, the **St. George's Night Rebellion** was the last attempt by Estonians to overthrow the German overlords until the battle against the **Landeswehr** in 1919.

The number of seigniorial estates in Estonia reached 500 during the 16th century as the nobility expropriated the peasants' holdings and reduced them to serfs in bondage to the manors. But not all peasants lost their farms during the Old Livonian period, and the conditions in the countryside actually improved as the West European grain market developed and encouraged large-scale production. There was no immigration of German peasants, but the burghers of the nine towns were all imported German artisans and merchants. The economy of the four principal trading towns, Tallinn, Tartu, **Pärnu**, and **Viljandi**, which belonged to the **Hanseatic League**, was based on the transit trade with the Russian hinterland. Thus, a cultural division was perpetuated from the very beginning of the conquest—the peasantry were monolingual Estonians (and Latvians in Latgallia) and the landed nobility were Germans, who learned just enough of the local languages to be able to command the peasantry through their mostly German overseers. The towns, where the nobles tended to spend the winters, became centers of German culture, with schools, congregations, and guilds of artisans, which did not admit locals. Nevertheless, over time, flight from the oppressive estates and the urban manufacturers' demands for labor brought large numbers of peasants into the towns, where they had to learn at least some German to survive, and were thus partially Germanized, as were all the entrepreneurially minded locals.

Because of continuous conflicts among the vassals of the rulers, frequently leading to small wars, Old Livonia never developed into a cohesive state. Moreover, continuous warfare with Lithuania, Novgorod, and Pihkva (Pskov) finally led to a war with the princes of Moscow. When, in 1503, the Order won the battle of Smolina and signed a 50-year armistice with the Russians, a rare peaceful period followed. The Protestant Reformation, which in 1524–25 quickly swept the towns and the majority of the rural nobility, also led to rapid cultural change among the indigenous populations. The peasants converted later in the century when Lutheran services were held in their mother tongue in contrast to the unintelligible Latin of the Roman Church. The Estonian-speaking German Lutheran clergy encouraged reading, and the first Estonian-language books appeared in 1525. The Reformation marked a significant turning point in Estonian cultural history as reading and writing were taught by the local Lutheran churches, with the result that Estonian became a written language, influenced, of course, by the language and culture of the Germans.

The peaceful and prosperous first half of the century, when the Estonian population grew to an unprecedented 250,000–280,000, ended in 1558 when Ivan the Terrible launched an attack on Tartu and unleashed 70 years of the most terrible, devastating warfare to date, which reduced the Estonian population by two thirds, to 100,000. Ivan's objective was to acquire ice-free ports on the Baltic and thus open a window to the West. To reach his goal, he had to defeat not only the weakened Old Livonian statelets but also his rivals. However, it was equally in the interest of the rulers of Poland–Lithuania and the Danish and Swedish kings to gain control of the Baltic lands, the gateways to Russia, and prevent Ivan access to the trade routes of the ice-free Baltic Sea coast. Political intrigue soon led to the division of the Baltic lands by collapsing Old Livonia between Poland and Sweden, and a half century of warfare and military campaigns on Estonian soil exhausted Russia and forced it to cede Estonia to Sweden at the Peace of Altmark in 1629.

The Good Old Swedish Era

Although Sweden had been in de facto control of much of northern Estonia during the great wars of the 16th century, it was a military occupation. Peace, however, quickly led to an administrative integration of Estland and Livland into Sweden and the eventual application of liberal Swedish law. Although Swedish nobles were given estates by the king, the Baltic German nobility as hereditary local rulers in a devastated land were able to gain considerable autonomy during the Swedish period, until the end of the 17th century when the king freed the peasants from being personal property of the estate owner. The Swedish Lutheran clergy, in their eagerness to finish the Protestant Reformation on the eastern shores of the Baltic, pursued a three-pronged strategy of preaching in the local language, recruiting and training local preachers, and printing Estonian-language religious literature. A major effort was the translation of the Bible into a hitherto largely unwritten language, with the New Testament published in 1686. The need to create a copy of Bible-reading Protestant Sweden led to the establishment of the first gymnasia and the Latin-language **University of Tartu** immediately after the Peace of Altmark. The widespread founding of elementary schools in villages for peasants followed later in the century and formed the basis of early Estonian (and Latvian) literacy, a culture of reading, and the thirst for education.

Hindsight labeled the Swedish period as the "Good Old Swedish Times," not least because it represented a time of peace, prosperity, and unprecedented freedom for the peasantry, sandwiched between terrible wars and disasters. The idyll began to unravel with three years of crop failure and famine in the mid-1690s, followed by the two decades of ferocious pillaging and plague during the **Great Northern War** unleashed by Peter the Great in his quest to finish the project that Ivan the Terrible had started more than a century ago. Estonians, who had grown to 350,000 prior to the famine, were again reduced by two thirds, to 135,000, by the time that Estland and Livland were ceded to Russia by the Treaty of Neustadt (Nystad in Swedish, Uusikaupunki in Finnish) in 1721.

In the Russian Empire

The 200-year suzerainty began badly for the Estonians and Latvians as the Baltic German nobility's lost privileges were restored by a tsar grateful to the nobles for perfidiously abandoning their Swedish king early in the war. The **Special Baltic Order** regime granted the Baltic nobility effectively autonomous states within the Russian Empire. The **Diets** of Estland and Lettland, consisting of the aristocratic owners of all manorial estates, had the right of legislative initiative and appointed the judges, the principal police officials, and the secular members of the Lutheran churches' governing bodies; in short, the Diets controlled the legal, political, and economic life of the provinces. German was the language of official business and the peasantry was again reduced to chattels of the local lord. Although the peasants resisted and **Catherine the Great** and a few lords, inspired by Enlightenment ideals, attempted to modernize Russia, reform in the Baltics was slow, resisted, and perverted at every turn by the powerful gentry. Thus it was not until 1816–19 that a gradual freeing of peasants from serfdom began, initially with the abolition of corvée labor, the instituting of peasant-run village administrations, the establishment of local schools, and the initiation of reform of local courts.

Although the University of Tartu was reopened in 1802 and quickly became a leading intellectual and scientific center in the Empire, not least because it was a German-language institution integrated into the German university system, few Estonians were able to study there until late in the century—in fact, native Estonians did not form a majority of the students until the late 1920s. Similarly, although education spread rapidly among the native population sped by the village school movement, it was not until the mid-19th century that the peasantry was allowed to buy land, that rent paid by statute labor was replaced by money rent, and that manorial estates owners lost control of the village governmental bodies. These reforms were undoubtedly partly due to the spreading of the value of civil liberties across Europe by the French Revolution and Napoleon's armies. But equally, rapidly changing economic conditions that forced integration of the insular self-subsistent Baltic manorial farms into a Europe-wide grain market, brought on by the introduction of modern farm machinery and the railroads, made forced serf labor inefficient and costly.

A major transformation of Estonian society took place during the last third of the 19th century, first as agriculture was modernized and commercialized with a consequent integration of Estonia into the Empire economy; and second, with the development of large-scale industrial production in the port cities of Narva and Tallinn as European **industrialization** invaded the Russian periphery. The completion of the transition to factory-based production during the last quarter of the century brought with it large-scale urbanization, bureaucratization, and the need for an educated middle class. The **National Awakening** (1860–80), led by **Johann Voldemar Jannsen**, his newspaper *Eesti Postimees,* his daughter the poetess **Lydia Koidula**, **Jakob Hurt**, and **Carl Robert Jakobson**, among others, awakened ethnic pride in the Estonian language and native peasant culture rooted in the mythology of ancient greatness. This provided both the educational thrust and the intellectual strength to resist the imperial **Russification** pressures of the 1880s and

1890s. Hence, by the turn of the century when the cross-pressures of industrialization and socialism swept across the urban landscape of Europe, a rapidly maturing and vibrant Estonian professional and intellectual class was able to organize Estonians of all classes politically, first to take power from their historical oppressors the Baltic barons, and then to pursue political autonomy for an Estonian Estonia. The slogan of the **Young Estonia** literary group, "Let us remain Estonian, but let us become European," perfectly expressed the thrust of Estonian cultural and political aspirations throughout the 20th century.

Birth of Independence

The stability, prosperity, cultural growth, and political development of the first two decades of the 20th century received the first blow when the abortive revolution of 1905 led to reprisals that not only killed several hundred innocent Estonians (and Latvians), but also drove patriots into exile. Indiscriminate retaliatory corporal punishment of independent Estonian (and Latvian) peasants by the German landowners so fully alienated Estonians from their historic oppressors that 15 years later the "foreign" aristocrats' estates were confiscated and they were rendered politically invisible. In the war-bound, rapidly industrializing empire, Estonia's economy was totally integrated into Russia, and imperial politics and pan-Russian political parties conditioned political activity in Estonia until the revolutionary year of 1917. In the chaotic spring of that year, Estonians finally managed to persuade St. Petersburg to unite the southern half of historic Estonia with the northern half into one semiautonomous province largely under Estonian control. The approximately 900,000-strong Estonians in their historic homeland were joined by up to 200,000 who had earlier emigrated to Russia in search of land and opportunities, with almost half coming from St. Petersburg. The political mobilization of Estonians was dramatically demonstrated when 40,000 joined a march in the imperial capital to demand autonomy for Estonia. The Bolshevik Revolution in November made clear to the politically mobilized Estonian nation that self-rule in an autonomous province within the Empire, symbolized by the **Maapäev** freely elected in the spring of 1917 under the aegis of the liberal imperial government, had become untenable. Hence, the Maapäev declared itself the highest authority in Estonia. Unfortunately, it was quickly dissolved (but continued underground) by the Bolsheviks, who took over the industrial cites of Narva and Tallinn, populated heavily by revolutionary Russian immigrant workers and thus natural allies of the St. Petersburg revolutionaries.

Thereafter, events moved with lightning speed and were mainly determined by great power rivalries of World War I. In the brief power vacuum between the German advance through Estonia and the Bolshevik retreat, on 24 February 1918 the three-member **Estonian Rescue Committee** appointed by the Maapäev (**Konstantin Päts**, **Jüri Vilms**, and Konstantin Konik) proclaimed the independent Republic of Estonia, raised the national flag atop the national flagstaff of Pikk Hermann, and formed the **Estonian Provisional Government**. But already by the next day, it was forced underground again as German forces entered the capital. During the next several months of German occupation—which restored the power of the Baltic aristocracy and attempted to form a Baltic German vassal duchy—the provisional government organized a home guard (*see* DEFENSE LEAGUE) and lobbied for recognition and support from the Western allies and the Scandinavian states. Since Great Britain and France had already recognized Estonia as a de facto independent state in May 1918, the capitulation of Germany in November automatically provided the provisional government international legitimacy as it assumed power. But real statehood had to be postponed for more than a year as a reinvigorated Red Army attacked Estonia only 10 days after the German collapse.

In the ensuing **War of Independence**, led by the provisional government and General **Johan Laidoner**, who quickly organized the tens of thousands of Estonian soldiers who had been recruited into the now defunct imperial army into an effective Estonian defense force, the Estonians defeated both the Baltic German volunteer **Landeswehr** and several Red armies in little over a year of hard fighting. The great victory at the battle of **Võnnu** on 23 June 1919, when an Estonian force of 3,000 defeated the 10,000 strong battle-hardened Stahldivision of Rüdiger von der Goltz, is still celebrated as **Victory Day**. Half a year later, after a final bloody push by the Red armies, the **Peace of Tartu** was signed on 2 February 1920, in which Russia recognized Estonia as an independent state, ceded some land, and gave up in perpetuity any claims on Estonia.

Independence

Even as the armed forces were fighting for Estonian independence, politicians set about creating the constitutional basis for a democratic republic. On 5–7 April 1919, the **Constituent Assembly** was elected with a participation rate of 80 percent. It quickly adopted a temporary constitution, confiscated the estates of the Baltic German landowners on 10 October, set about distributing the land among the landless and the veterans of the War of Independence, ratified the peace treaty, and adopted the first, ultraliberal **Constitution** of Estonia on 15 June 1920. The new Republic of Estonia was a democratic republic, with supreme legislative power vested in the unicameral **Riigikogu** of 100 members elected on universal suffrage by proportional representation, to be supplemented by referenda. The executive power was exercised by a government responsible to and serving at the pleasure of parliament wherein its head, styled state elder, functioned as both head of government and head of state.

Although independent and a member of the League of Nations, Estonia's economy was in shambles as a result of both the war with Russia that had raged in the industrial north and northeast, the war with the Landeswehr in the southeast, and the need to reorient from serving the needs of a vast empire to a small country of just over a million.

The land reform begun during the war led quickly to a radical reorganization of both agriculture and social structure. A commercial but industrializing agricultural economy and a bifurcated society dominated by the hated foreign elite were instantly replaced by newly created small farmers with classical petit bourgeois values of self-preservation. Whereas prior to the land reform Estonia had 1,149 large estates controlling 58 percent of the farm land and 51,640 small farms averaging 34 hectares owning 42 percent, by 1929 there were only 471 farms over 100 hectares, 45,956 under 10 hectares, 59,212 between 10 and 30 hectares, 22,185 between 30 and 50 hectares, and 6,433 between 50 and 100 hectares.

However, the urban-rural population division did not change rapidly. Whereas in 1922 25 percent lived in urban areas, in 1934 the urban share had risen only to 28.3 percent. Clearly, the Estonia of 1920–40 was a countryside-based state whose people, moreover, according to the 1934 census, were 88.2 percent ethnically Estonian. The politics of this small nation-state of 1,126,000 were conducted by unstable coalitions of small parties representing a left-right continuum consisting of rural-based parties of the center and the right, with a quarter of the members of parliament representing urban workers' socialist (including 5–6 percent communist) parties. Estonia was a petit bourgeois nation of newly minted farm owners, urban bureaucrats, and white-collar workers whose interest was to preserve, and increase, the gains that independent Estonia had brought them. The 1920s were good to them as such agricultural products as butter and bacon made inroads on West European markets as quality products and industrial growth accelerated as the existing textile and wood industries modernized, expanded, and sold their goods abroad. In addition, the government assisted the formation of a chemical and oil industry based on oil shale.

Given economic stability, the squabbling politicians might have learned democratic values of tolerance, restraint, and responsible opposition. However, the worldwide Great Depression combined with the specter of fascism in the early 1930s led to the **preemptive coup** that ushered in the seven years of the **Era of Silence,** acquiesced to by virtually all political leaders as well as the citizenry at large in the name of preserving the Republic. Although a new, more functional constitution was approved in 1937 and democratic elections were about to be called, time ran out when the Secret Protocols of the 1939 **Molotov-Ribbentrop Pact** between the Soviet Union and Nazi Germany ceded the Baltic States to Russia. Accordingly, the following year the Union of Soviet Socialist Republics (USSR) invaded Estonia.

Occupations and World War II

The invasion on 17 June 1940 led to an occupation that began with a brutal reign of terror. Thousands of Estonians, including President Konstantin Päts, were imprisoned and deported to the far reaches of the Soviet Union. Estonia was incorporated into the Soviet Union after fraudulent elections rigged by the Communist Party and controlled by the occupying forces. The Republic's political, judicial, and administrative structures were destroyed and replaced by Soviet models; all large industrial plants, transportation companies, as well as banking and commerce were nationalized. That the Soviet occupying forces were able to carry out such wholesale transformation in the short period between June 1940 and the German invasion on 22 June 1941 testifies to long and thorough preparation.

Although the Germans were welcomed as saviors from the Soviet communist occupation, they, in fact, simply kept the new Soviet structures and simply replaced the communists, most of whom had fled to Russia with the retreating Red Army. A puppet government was set up, Estonia was incorporated into the new colony of **Ostland**, and the economy was exploited to support the German war effort. At first, Estonian young men volunteered for the German forces to fight against the Red Army, but when in 1944 a general mobilization was ordered, many fled to fight for Estonia's freedom in Finland. For the second time in a quarter century, Estonians set up an independent government in the brief interregnum between occupying forces. This time the government of **Otto Tief**, appointed by Acting President **Jüri Uluots**, waited six days in vain for Western help before it was disbanded by the reinvading Red Army on 22 September 1944. Uluots and some members of the government were able to flee to the West and were thus able to keep alive the de jure Republic, with the help of the **Stimson Doctrine** by which the United States refused to accept the Soviet occupation of Estonia as legitimate.

The Soviet Period

The ensuing 47 years of the second Soviet occupation, lasting until 1991, began badly for the occupiers as Estonian soldiers fought a guerilla war against the invaders and carried on until crushed in the early 1950s. In 1949 a brutal collectivization of agriculture took place, which was reinforced by a mass **deportation**. Two smaller deportations were also carried out, one in 1945 and the other in 1951. The communists who had fled in 1941 returned to power with a pro-Moscow mentality and, in the infamous VIII Plenary of the **Estonian Communist Party** (ECP) in 1948, they set out to root out all remaining Estonian nationalism from the party and to destroy the small number of the intellectual elites who had not been deported or fled to the West.

By the middle of the 1950s, both Estonians at home and the émigrés abroad had lost any hope that a new war between the West and communism would take place and free them. The Khrushchev Thaw, however, brought Estonians the hope that they could maintain their culture and language and make a life, even under communism and within the Soviet Union. The subsequent freedom allowed Estonian Communist Party politicians to experiment with agricultural forms with the result that, by the 1970s, Estonian farm production had become the most efficient in the Soviet Union, and farm workers were paid good wages. Unfortunately, the Brezhnev era introduced a program of Russification. Nevertheless, Estonians were able to continue their historic **song festivals** every five years and turned them into public declarations of national fervor, with 25,000 singers and musicians on the stage and audiences of 300,000 renewing their pledge of faith in the nation and its culture. Simultaneously, a new generation of intellectuals—writers, painters, and performers of all kinds—arose and practiced their arts to further the national culture. Moreover, during the very time of the latest Russification attempt, the Estonian language made greater progress in grammatical development than even during the brief period of the lost independence.

Access to Finnish television in the capital and northern Estonia allowed Estonians to keep up with such international developments as the Helsinki Accords. Accordingly, in 1974 two groups addressed appeals to the United Nations (UN) asking for withdrawal of Soviet troops (*see* **DISSIDENTS**). In 1979, the Baltic Appeal signed by people from all three Baltic countries focused Western attention on their illegal annexation by the USSR (*see also* **BATUN**).

The Collapse of the Soviet System

The collapse of the Soviet system was the unintended consequence of Mikhail Gorbachev's attempts to renew the moribund and corrupt system. He had hoped to coopt the intelligentsia, and especially journalists, by his policies of **perestroika and glasnost**. The new openness allowed repressed antagonisms to burst out in the open regarding the ecological disasters that Moscow had perpetrated by its massive industrial projects in total disregard of local conditions. Thus Estonians, always conscious of their little land and more than ever drawn to it as their refuge from Muscovite control, reacted massively in the "**Phosphate War**" in 1987. It seemed that every ethnic Estonian joined the protests, with marches by teenagers and adults, musical groups, and **radio and television** personalities as well as a newspaper campaign. In

August 1987, the ecological protests encouraged dissidents who had hitherto operated underground to organize a demonstration demanding the publication of the secret protocols of the infamous Molotov-Ribbentrop Pact of 1939. Although the reactionary leadership of the Estonian Communist Party attempted to shut down protests and dissidence, the Estonian intelligentsia had become sufficiently radicalized that a few months after successfully forcing Moscow to retreat on the phosphate mining project, it took another step and proposed the establishment of a self-managing economy separate from the centrally planned Soviet economic system under the acronym **IME** (Isemajandav Eesti), which coincidentally means "miracle" in Estonian. The IME program very quickly became identified as shorthand for political independence in the eyes of Estonians.

Gorbachev, impressed with the Estonian progressiveness, unwittingly poured oil on the fire of Estonian national renewal by replacing **Karl Vaino**, the Russified and reactionary first secretary of the Estonian Communist Party, with **Vaino Väljas**, a nationalist, who as heir apparent to Karl Vaino had been shunted aside and exiled to Latin America as Soviet ambassador by Leonid Brezhnev a decade before. Väljas's first move was to declare the Estonian language the medium of communication of the Central Committee and bureaucracy of the ECP. This not only endeared him to the Estonian people but also signaled that the ECP would now pursue some form of sovereignty for Estonia. The joint meeting of the Creative Unions on 1–2 April 1988 marked the rebirth of public discussion as leading intellectuals took public stands not only on professional concerns about censorship, subsidies for theaters, and the state monopoly on publishing but also on a wide array of issues close to every Estonian heart, such as the unchecked immigration of Russian-speaking labor, the environmental degradation, the deficit of democracy in the Communist Party, and the limits on Estonian-language use in public life. They concluded that the only way to safeguard Estonia was to change the Soviet constitution to allow for republican sovereignty on cultural and economic matters, including a separate Estonian citizenship. The IME program would provide the fundamental wherewithal to operate an Estonia separated from the Soviet economy and its culture.

April 1988 also saw the creation of the **People's Front** (officially "to Support Perestroika"), which quickly became the mass movement that mobilized all Estonians, including Party members, to a hitherto unimaginably uninhibited expression of long pent-up national awareness. When Gorbachev called for elections to the Supreme Soviet, delegates supported by the Popular Front won all the seats. The 1988 "Hot Summer" of the "**Singing Revolution**" culminated on 11 September with a patriotic mass Song Festival of 300,000 at which demands for independence were openly made. On 16 November, the **Supreme Soviet of the ESSR** declared Estonia sovereign and itself the highest constitutional organ in Estonia. This quickly led to an open confrontation with the Supreme Soviet of the USSR, which disallowed the Estonian action on 26 November. The Estonians, however, continued on the road to independence and on 5–7 December declared Estonian as the state **language** and the deportations of the Stalinist period as crimes against **human rights**. Christmas was celebrated publicly for the first time since the occupation, political parties were formed one after the other, and the Communist Party of Estonia began to fall apart visibly as members resigned. After the raising of the blue, black, and white national **flag** on the national flagstaff by the government on **Independence** Day, 24 February 1989, reactionary forces organized by leaders of centrally managed large enterprises formed the **Interfront** (also known as the Intermovement) and brought out their workers into the streets to protest and harass Estonians' aspirations for independence. But it was to no avail. On 23 August, the fiftieth anniversary of the Molotov-Ribbentrop Pact, the People's Front organized a **Baltic Chain** of 2 million Estonians, Latvians, and Lithuanians holding hands for a stretch of 600 kilometers, from Tallinn to Vilnius. In an attempt to coopt them, on 17 November 1989 the USSR Supreme Soviet adopted a law granting limited economic autonomy to the Baltic Republics.

The Estonian Supreme Soviet, however, continued on its way to independence, established the central **Bank of Estonia** on 15 December, and, on 23 February 1990, abolished the Communist Party's leading role in the **Constitution of 1978 of the ESSR**. At its XX Congress on 23–25 March, the ECP split into an independent and a Soviet-affiliated party, with the former adopting a policy of independence for Estonia. On 18 March, regular **elections** to the XII ESSR Supreme Soviet took place under democratic rules and were won by democratic parties and groups that supported independence. The newly elected **Supreme Soviet** renamed itself the **Supreme Council,** declared Soviet authority null and void on Estonian territory, and formally instituted a period of transition to independence, which would end with the formation of constitutionally established state organs of the Republic of Estonia. **Arnold Rüütel** became chair of the ESSR Supreme Council and **Edgar Savisaar** formed the transition cabinet. A politically difficult and emotionally stressful year and a half followed, during which Gorbachev tried to hold the Union together in the face of concerted political and legislative onslaughts by the Balts at home and international diplomatic moves in the West.

In the meantime, from 24 February to 1 March, former dissidents who felt that the People's Front and the Supreme Soviet were moving too slowly and who wished to restore the prewar Republic in its entirety organized elections by citizens according to prewar rules of eligibility. These were a resounding success, with a turnout of 557,613 citizens, or 90 percent of those eligible to vote. The **Estonian Congress** consisted of 469 members, including 35 Estonians from abroad, and it represented 32 parties and organizations, with 107 from the Popular Front, 104 from the Estonian Heritage Society, 70 from the Estonian National Independence Party, 39 communists, and 109 representing various small factions. Unfortunately, it elected a permanent organ of 78, the **Estonian Committee**, which pursued a rigid policy of restoring the prewar Republic in all its glory, with the result that it lost its popularity as it degenerated into a right-wing rival of the more pragmatic Supreme Council. Since the Congress had no legislative authority or government institutions at its disposal, it was reluctantly forced to cooperate with the Supreme Council with which it also formed the **Constituent Council** to draft the new Constitution.

The transitional Supreme Council moved rapidly to develop policies and pass laws to establish government institutions and programs to transform Estonia into a West European state as quickly as possible. This process, including the drafting of a Western-type income tax, organizing a taxation department, and instituting the self-declaratory income tax system on 1 January 1991, took place against a recalcitrant Gorbachev and a Moscow hierarchy totally opposed to Estonian independence. Moreover, the KGB, Soviet occupying armed forces, and border guard were still keeping a watchful eye on the Estonians. Sporadic negotiations took place with Moscow, including a visit to the Baltics by Gorbachev, who simply could not understand their desire to leave the USSR. The conflict came to a head on Bloody Sunday, 13 January 1991, when Soviet Army tanks attacked the television tower in Vilnius, killed 13 demonstrators, but failed to topple the breakaway republican government of Vytautas Landsbergis. This attack and the **OMON** attack in Riga on the following weekend brought the Russian government of Boris Yeltsin into the Baltic camp resulting in a joint four-government appeal to the secretary-general of the United Nations. Although the Estonians also fortified their Parliament Building, as did the other Baltics, the Soviet military did not attack Estonia at this time. The Supreme Council unerringly continued its march toward independence, replaced the Soviet militia with newly graduated constables from the new Police School, and passed new laws on private property reform.

On 3 March, a referendum called by the Supreme Council on restoring Estonian state independence was won with the votes of 78 percent of those participating, whereas all three Baltic States boycotted Gorbachev's pan-Soviet referendum on a revised federation. Thus, when the Moscow coup plotters ordered commando units to move on Tallinn, the government, parliament, and people were ready. The Soviet Army column was met on the outskirts of the capital and led to barracks, the Supreme Council met and monitored developments, and people formed defensive cordons on the approaches to the Parliament Building on **Toompea** as well as the radio and TV buildings. The next day, 20 August, the Supreme Council declared the Republic of Estonia restored; on 21 August the coup failed, and the Soviet commando units returned to their bases outside Estonia. On 22 August, Iceland recognized the independent Republic of Estonia, followed by the Russian Federal Republic on 24 August, and Sweden opened its embassy in Tallinn on 29 August. After Estonia was accepted as a member of the Conference on Security and Cooperation in Europe (CSCE) at a meeting in Moscow on 10 September, other states quickly recognized the independence of Estonia and sent diplomatic representatives to Tallinn.

The government now moved rapidly to establish both external and internal guarantors of sovereign independence: it reestablished the Estonian army, signed the charter of the CSCE, opened embassies in the capitals of its closest neighbors and the major powers, reinstituted the prewar **Law on Citizenship**, joined the World Bank, and resurrected its own currency, the **kroon**. The new **Constitution** was adopted by referendum with 91.3 percent in July 1992, and the first Riigikogu and the president were elected under the new Constitution on 20 September. On 7 October, the new Riigikogu declared the transition to Independence instituted by the Supreme Council in 1990 ended and the Republic of Estonia, formed 74 years before, restored.

Rebuilding Estonia as a West European State

Estonians began independence focused on rejoining the Western world from which they had been forcefully isolated for two and a half generations. The immediate objective for all was to get rid of all legacies of the Soviet Union and to guarantee that they would never again fall victim to eventual resurgent Russian imperialism. In Estonian minds, the first requirement was to get Russia to withdraw its military forces form Estonia, to demarcate the border as it was fixed in the Peace of Tartu in 1920, and to get rid of the non-Estonian Russian-speaking alien population that had been brought in as labor by Moscow ministries. Membership in NATO was regarded as the natural and ultimate security guarantee.

The innate need to restore their state as the monoethnic enclave that it had been before the Soviet occupation, when its population was 92 percent ethnically Estonian, however, immediately ran into three opposing forces: the unwillingness of the alien population to leave, the propaganda opportunity that Estonians' antipathy to their Russian population provided Moscow, and the lack of sympathy in the West for an ethnically pure Estonian state. At first Estonians could not, or would not, understand why non-Estonians would not want to return to their homelands. When it eventually became clear that no more than the 70,000 (of the alien population of 400,000) who emigrated in 1992–95 would leave, Estonians finally began to seek ways of integrating the non-Estonians into their society. Pressure was applied by the **Organization of Security and Cooperation in Europe's High Commissioner on National Minorities**, the Council of Europe, and the Commissioner on Ethnic Minorities of the **Council of Baltic Sea States** (CBSS), who, in line with West European human rights rules of nondiscrimination, convinced the government to progressively soften the strict language use and naturalization requirements. By 1998 the government introduced the **Integration** program, which envisages a kind of multicultural society in which the Russian community is able to develop as a distinct Russian-Estonian cultural enclave. The educational segment of the program will progressively integrate it into Estonian national society by requiring all Russian-language schools to teach children to speak good Estonian, and eventually to teach 60 percent of the secondary schools curriculum in Estonian.

Much of the liberalization took place after Estonia was accepted in the first cohort of EU enlargement in 1997. By 2001, parliament even removed the language requirement for candidacy to **Riigikogu elections**, in line with the EU voluntary rules that permit any citizen of a EU country to run for parliament in any other member country.

The national security objective became intermingled with the **alien** migrant issue as the Russian armed forces delayed withdrawing from Estonia, while discharging large numbers of younger officers in Estonia, which was regarded by most Estonians as placing a fifth column of trained soldiers for a future takeover. Although the Russian military withdrew in 1994 after concerted pressure from Western powers and the issue of former Soviet military was finally solved, the main security problem remains.

Immediately after achieving independence, Estonia began to develop a two-pronged military security policy—national **defense forces** with appropriate weapons to make an attack expensive for any aggressor and the securing of international guarantees of collective defense from NATO. In fact, Estonians still see the latter as the only realistic guarantee. Until the end of 2001, all Russian governments and the Duma carried on a vehement campaign opposing Baltic membership in NATO and labeled it a provocation. Partly to buttress arguments of their unsuitability and ineligibility of membership, the Russians continuously but baselessly accused Estonia and Latvia of human rights violations against their Russian populations. Broad hints were made periodically that Russia might consequently have a special duty to intervene in Estonia and Latvia. Russia held up ratification of the border agreement for years even after Estonia had conceded the territory acquired under the Peace of Tartu, tying the delay to the alleged discriminations. Thus, it was not until after the accession of Poland, the Czech Republic, and Hungary and concerted diplomatic efforts that the European NATO states slowly began to make careful statements of support for Estonian membership. After **Baltic Battalion (BALTBAT)** peacekeeping participation in Bosnia and the Kosovo air war, technical and financial support by NATO members began seriously to raise the armed forces of Estonia, Latvia, and Lithuania to NATO standards. Finally, the three, along with Bulgaria, Romania, Slovakia, and Slovenia, were judged ready, invited to join in 2002, and will be welcomed as members at NATO's meeting in May 2004.

In the meantime, membership in the European Union was seen as the soft security option as well as rejoining Europe. Estonia began to pursue full membership in all European intergovernmental organizations within days of reacquiring independence, establishing diplomatic relations with EU members already on 27 August, becoming a full member of the CSCE on 10 September 1991, and declaring officially in October 1992 at a NATO seminar that it considered its security residing exclusively in the context of Europe-wide security. Hence, it also acquired observer status at the West European Union (WEU) on 30 November 1993 and full membership in May 1994. Estonia's approach to the EU has been similarly consistent. Already on 11 May 1992, a trade and cooperation agreement was signed with the European Community (renamed European Union in 1993), and was followed by a free trade agreement on 18 June 1993. In December 1995, Estonia became the first postcommunist state to sign an association treaty with the EU without need of any transition period. Thereupon, Estonia immediately began to prepare an application for accession to the EU, which it submitted on 28 November 1995. In December 1997, the European Council of the EU approved Estonia as one of the six candidates, along with Poland, the Czech Republic, Hungary, Slovenia, Malta, and Cyprus, to begin negotiations in May 1998. In December 2002, the EU approved Estonia, Latvia, Lithuania, the Czech Republic, Hungary, Slovenia, Slovakia, Cyprus, and Malta for membership effective 1 May 2004. In a referendum on 14 September 2003, Estonians decided by a vote of 66.8 to 33.2 percent to accept the invitation. That the rate of voter participation (at 64 percent of the electorate) was low and that the yes-side garnered only two thirds of the votes, while Lithuanians voted 91 to 9 percent in favor of the EU with 63.3 of the electorate participating, and even Latvians, long considered the most euroskeptic of the applicant countries, voted 67 versus 32.3 percent for entry with 72.5 of electors participating, shows the general reluctance of Estonians to give up their newly won independence to the new union run from far-off Brussels by the collectivist-oriented French and Germans.

Membership in the EU has not been an economic objective, but a soft security one to bring this geographically peripheral country into the heartland of Western Europe for the first time since the Hanseatic period. It is thus a formal acknowledgement that Estonia has finally "returned" to its home and rightful place as a fully European state. Economically, Estonia may initially suffer a small decline in the rate of growth of its gross national product (GNP) as a result of the deflection of its trade to the protectionist EU. The consistent pursuit of a liberal and open economy initiated by the IME project brought Estonia to 14th place in 2000 in the Heritage Foundation's list of economically free states and to fourth place out of 155 states in 2001, sharing this with Ireland, Luxembourg, Holland, and the United States, with only Hong Kong, Singapore, and New Zealand ahead of it.

This impressive achievement for a state, which in 1991 was still an integral part of the Soviet command economy, was made possible by the total collapse of the command system and the willingness of the political elites to follow up on the radical liberal principle, popularized by Prime Minster Margaret Thatcher, that the government's role is that of facilitator of the free market, as opposed to the belief that the government's role is as its manager, on which the IME project was based. Restructuring of production on free market principles demanded **privatization** of all real property. At the state enterprises level, Estonia successfully used the German Treuhand model while avoiding its mistakes and completed the sale of state firms by 1998, the largest by five international tender rounds. By 2001 it had also completed the sale of most of the infrastructure of the transport, water, power, and sewage systems. That Estonia did not put any limits on foreign ownership of its enterprises or land explains part of its success in attracting productive foreign investment, at a per capita level exceeding by far all other former postcommunist states and even many West European ones. The early currency reform in June 1992 based on the **currency board** system, which tied the Estonian kroon to the deutsche mark, enforced strict responsibility on the central bank and cabinet in managing state finances and provided currency certainty and stability. The almost simultaneous **banking** reform quickly led to a stable financial system so attractive that by 1998 the banking system was majority owned by two Swedish bank groups. These provided guarantees for financial inflows and a platform for outward investments to the other Baltic States and beyond.

Investment in Estonia was made even more attractive by a flat income tax for both individual and corporate taxpayers at 26 percent. The new coalition government formed by **Juhan Parts** after the 2003 elections even agreed to decrease the flat tax to 20 percent by 2006. The low rate, and a tax system based on weekly computerized reporting of the corporate value-added tax (VAT) and other financial flows, also enforced a high rate of tax compliance and helped reduce corruption to a low level just below that of the Nordics and ahead of many EU members. Foreign investment was made even more attractive in 2001 by allowing reinvested profits to escape all tax for both individuals and corporations.

The dismantling of all tariff and nontariff barriers from the very beginning has made Estonia a model free trader, including in agriculture, thus attracting entrepôt trade production enterprises. It also led to Estonia becoming a full member of the World Trade Organization (WTO) on 13 November 1999, four years after it applied for membership.

The economic success, as demonstrated by the size of the financial industry and by the computerization and Internetization of the schools and government, which in 2000 began holding its cabinet meetings using computer communications and which encourages citizens to submit forms online, however, has created a cleavage between the younger people in the 21st century postindustrial economy and the older, mainly rural residents whose skills date from the Soviet command era. The latter, including a large number depending on subsistence agriculture, are unemployed "losers," while modernized industry suffers a shortage of skilled workers. All cabinets and parliaments have catered to the modern segment of the society–economy to build Estonia into a wealthy modern state. The focus on economic growth and state security has taken place at the cost of social equity, leaving a large gap in needed investments to reform the health, pension, and education systems. Moreover, the steady decline in births during the 1990s has reduced the population by 10 percent to just 1.4 million. Through the 1990s, the political elites paid little attention to this problem, which has serious implications in all aspects of the economy, from health and education to the need for labor. Indeed, it was the perceived gap between the rural "losers" and the urban "winners" that led to the election of Arnold Rüütel as president in 2002 by the **electoral college**. It also led to the formation of a new **political party**, Res Publica, which promised a reformed public service orientation and won enough votes to form a center-right urban-rural coalition government. President Rüütel, on his part, initiated a process of national conciliation (rahva lepitus)—a series of meetings among disaffected social groups—to bridge the perceived gap.

The Dictionary

– A –

AAVIK, JOHANNES (1880–1973). Estonian philologist. Aavik was born on 8 December 1880 in Kõiguste parish and died on 18 March 1973 in Stockholm, Sweden. After studies in history at the **University of Tartu** (1901–02) and the University of Nezin (1902–05), he completed his *cand. phil.* degree in 1910 in Romance languages at Helsinki. Aavik participated in the Noor Eesti (**Young Estonia**) movement, taught Estonian and French at Tartu and Kuressaare, served as lecturer in Estonian at Tartu University (1926–33), and was appointed education consultant to the Ministry of Education and inspector of schools in 1934. In 1944, he fled to Sweden and lived in Stockholm until the end of his life. Aavik is the premier modernizer and developer of the Estonian language.

As a Fennophile (an admirer of Finnish language and culture), he was dissatisfied with the Germanic orthography and grammatical structure that earlier German and Estonian writers on the language had given Estonian. His message to Estonians was that they could not fully join Western civilization or "become European," as the Noor Eesti propagators put it, without a developed language. Hence, Aavik set out to restructure the grammar, the orthography, and the vocabulary of Estonian. Since to him language was the carrier of the culture, it was also the prime tool to express the culture. Consequently, his reforms were based on an interpretation of the rich parochial idiomatic usage of the different regions of Estonia to express the esthetics of the Estonian language and culture and to systematize it as such.

That Aavik succeeded is beyond doubt. Estonians everywhere have self-consciously become proud of their language as an esthetic language that not only expresses but also develops the unique Estonian culture. Today to Estonians, the Estonian language itself *is* Estonian culture. Aavik did this by distinguishing Estonian as the root language of Finnish, by introducing the use of the noun in verb form (which has led to constant enriching of the language, not the least of which has been by way of loan words), and by creating short forms of long words and shortening endings of the 14 declensions, while removing one declension. The result is a constantly changing living language that adds new words every year, but only according to Estonian rules of grammar. *See also* ESTONIAN LANGUAGE.

AAVIKSOO, JAAK (1954–). Professor of physics, member of the Estonian Academy of Science, and rector of the **University of Tartu**. Aaviksoo was born on 1 February 1954 in Tartu, graduated from the University of Tartu in 1976, earned a *cand. mat. phys.* degree in 1981, and was appointed professor of optics and spectroscopy in 1992. Two years later he was elected to the Estonian Academy of Sciences while serving as prorector of the University, 1992–95, then was elected rector of the University in 1998 and reelected for a second five-year term in 2003. Aaviksoo also served as minister of education in the **Tiit Vähi** cabinet 1995–97. Early on, he recognized the importance of information technology (IT) and worked with President **Lennart Meri** to initiate the **Tiger Leap** (Tiigri hüppe) program to place a computer in each school classroom in Estonia; thus Estonia is far ahead of most European states in IT penetration and is close behind the leader, Finland. As rector he is vigorously pursuing the modernization and upgrading of teaching and learning to international standards as rapidly as possible, and is committed to raise the University to top rank among European institutions of higher learning, which admittedly will take decades.

ABORTIVE MOSCOW COUP OF 1991. On 19 August 1991, eight Politburo members formed themselves into a State Committee of Emergency and detained President Mikhail Gorbachev at his villa in the Crimea. After declaring in a televised statement that the president had been removed from office owing to illness, the plotters attempted to take control of the government of the Union of Soviet Socialist Republics (USSR). Boris Yeltsin, the newly elected popular president of the Russian Federated Soviet Socialist Republic (RFSSR), and his Parliament immediately denounced the attempt at a coup. Military units with tanks sent to arrest Yeltsin, on finding the Russian Parliament building surrounded by massed demonstrators, refused to fire on the crowd. After two days, they returned to barracks, and after three days of increasing loss of credibility, as they failed to persuade the military and most constituent republics to support them, the coup masters simply gave up on 21 August.

In Estonia on 19 August, Soviet Army commando units landed at Tallinn airport, a column advanced toward the capital from Pskov, and naval ships blockaded Tallinn harbor for a few hours. Prime Minister **Edgar Savisaar** met the military column and led it to a military depot outside Tallinn. On 20 August, volunteers formed protective shields around the Parliament Building and the radio and television buildings, and **Rahvarinne** organized a mass meeting to demand independence for Estonia. At a late night session, the **Supreme Soviet** of the Estonian Soviet Socialist Republic (ESSR) declared Estonia independent of the Soviet Union and the Republic of Estonia restored. On 21 August, the commandos took over the television tower bloodlessly for a few hours and Estonian Television ceased broadcasting. Estonian Radio, however, continued broadcasting without interruption. As the coup failed in Moscow, the commandos left the television tower on the same day and Estonia the following day, on 22 August.

The Soviet military commands and the KGB in Estonia uniformly refused to support the coup, mostly by simply "not picking up the telephone." Even the commando units sent from Russia acted with restraint, mainly because they were confused as to their mission in the peaceful and relatively prosperous Western-looking **Tallinn**. Hence, no fighting took place, no property was destroyed, nor was any blood shed.

The failed coup sent a strong signal to the world that the Soviet Union was finished as a political and military power. Consequently, on 22 August Iceland was the first foreign state to recognize the Republic of Estonia reinstated, followed by Boris Yeltsin's RFSSR. Thereupon, led by the other Nordic states and the European Community, within two weeks most states extended recognition to the independent Republic of Estonia. *See also* DECLARATION OF INDEPENDENCE OF 1991.

ACQUIS COMMUNITAIRE. On joining the **European Union** (EU), applicant countries are expected to accept the existing laws and rules by which the EU operates. These are based on the three treaties of Rome (1957), Maastricht (1992), and Amsterdam (1997). In 1997 the EU consolidated the applicable laws and regulations amounting to about 30,000 pages into 31 chapters for negotiating purposes with the applicant countries. The laws that each country must adopt as the price of membership include free movement of goods, persons, and capital; common laws and regulations governing companies, taxation, finance, and budgetary provisions; energy, transportation, industrial, and competition policy; agriculture and fisheries; statistics; health, social welfare, education, culture, science, and research; environment, justice, and home affairs; and common foreign and security policy of the EU.

The negotiations were carried on between the Commission of the European Union and each applicant state at a pace determined by the latter, and consisted first of a review of the state of the applicant's progress in passing legislation to implement the contents of the Acquis. Since no derogation was possible, negotiations then revolved around time delays that the applicant would need to bring not only its laws but also its compliance with the Acquis up to the EU standards. Estonia was among the leading applicant countries in adopting EU standards, and completed nearly all of the review and negotiations in summer 2002. Nevertheless it needed deferrals in some chapters, most notably in environment, where negotiations led to an agreement in 2001 that the drinking water standards across Estonia could not reach EU levels until 2014, and then only with financial assistance from the EU, amounting to 75 percent of the costs. Estonia was also given until 2016 to bring its **oil shale** underfiring electricity plants up to EU environmental standards (*see also* ENVIRONMENT).

It should be noted that the Acquis is being added to all the time by new EU legislation, regulations, and new treaties, of which the Treaty of Nice (2000) was the latest. Moreover, a European Convention to restructure the organization pending expansion from 15 members to 28 when all 13 applicants become members began meeting in March 2002 and completed its task to produce a draft treaty establishing a constitution for the European Union in July 2003. The draft will undergo further negotiation among the member governments meeting in an intergovernmental conference to establish the final text of the Constitutional Treaty, which will then eventually be submitted for ratification to each member state. Each applicant country was invited to send three delegates, one representing the government and two the legislature, to participate in the Convention. Not only were the applicant countries delegates vastly outnumbered, but they also had no vote in the outcome. The Estonian delegation consisted of **Lennart Meri** representing the government and the two vice speakers, **Tunne Kelam** and Peter Kreitzberg (replaced by Rein Lang after the March 2003 elections), representing the **Riigikogu**.

AGRICULTURE. The Christianizing crusades of the German Brethren of the Sword (*Schwertbrüder*) (*see* CRUSADING ORDERS) led to the settlement of German landowners, the establishment of manorial estates, and the gradual introduction of tenant farming and corvée labor (in effect, **serfdom**) in the settlement areas of the Estonians. Peasants were forced to provide a fixed numbers of days of statutory unpaid labor (using their own implements and draft animals) to the manor from which they held their tenancy. The tenant farmers engaged in subsistence farming on their tenant lands. Even the manorial farms operated on a subsistence basis for centuries. They had few animals and depended mostly on field crops (rye, barley, oats, and wheat), traditional since prehistoric times to Estland and Livland (*see* LIVONIA), as did the indigenous peasantry. The three-field rotation system of cultivation continued to be used until the 19th century.

Modernization and the innovative use of manure to fertilize fields had to await the formation of capitalist grain markets in Europe in the 19th century, which, as they coincided with the rapid spread of **national awakening** across Europe, led to rapid changes in farming, the final disappearance of the corvée in the 1860s, and the purchase of farms by the tenants. Thus, in the last four decades of the century, an Estonian peasant land-owning class developed that became the carrier of a self-conscious nationalist culture and formed the backbone of the Estonian nation, politics, and economy in the 20th century. Technological innovation was fueled by agricultural **education** (the reopened **University of Tartu** had established a chair of agriculture in 1802, and Riga Polytechnical Institute added one in 1862), the spread of journalism, newly formed agricultural societies, as well as economic necessity as prices on both the world and Russian grain markets fell in the last quarter of the 19th century. These factors led to the introduction and rapid spread of agricultural machinery, and more extensive crop rotation with a consequent continuous rise in productivity. Although rye, oats, and barley remained the staple grain crops in the Baltics (as they have into the 21st century), a marked shift to dairy and cattle farming began, along with concentration on commercial potato and flax cultivation.

Despite the demands for land reform raised by the Russian Revolution of 1905, and although no major reforms took place in the decade preceding World War I, Estonian farmers showed rapid growth of output and productivity driven by continuous innovation, technologization, agricultural education, and the cooperative movement. Whereas in 1910 there were 79 agricultural societies, by 1914 there were 135 milk, 138 consumer, and 153 machinery cooperatives as well as 129 credit unions assisting the modernization and productivity growth of farming.

Immediately after **independence**, even before the **Constitution** was passed, the **Constituent Assembly** in 1919 expropriated the large estates and divided the land among tenants, the landless, and the **veterans** of the **War of Independence**. All, except the veterans who were granted land outright, could purchase land on long-term mortgages or rent it on perpetual tenure from the state. The result was an immediate increase in the number of farms from around 50,000 to over 125,000. Agricultural production during the 1920s and 1930s continued along prewar lines with concentration on dairy farming, cattle breeding, and hog, sheep, and poultry production. By the 1937–38 agricultural year, over half of the output was animal products with the remainder being field crops of the traditional grains, potatoes, and flax. During the 1930s Estonian niche products of bacon and butter became established on the German and British markets. Part of the relative stability of Estonian agriculture during the Depression and until World War II may be attributed to substantial state subsidies.

With the Soviet occupation in 1940, a decade of destruction began during which the structure of agriculture painstakingly built over the preceding century was totally destroyed and replaced by a nationalized state-directed system based on the industrial factory model. Apparently to avoid a repetition of the peasant resistance that took place in the Union of Soviet Socialist Republics (USSR) during the original agricultural **collectivization** in 1929–30, the new regime in Estonia nationalized only 24 percent of the land. This included holdings over 30 hectares (1 hectare = 2.5 acres), and land belonging to churches and municipalities. Half of this land was distributed to landless peasants with 24,000 new small farms averaging 11 hectares (27.5 acres) created. Existing farms of "working peasants" up to 30 hectares were declared to be on perpetual tenure from the state. The result was a significant drop in the average size of farms, from 22.7 hectares in 1930 to 16.7 hectares in 1941, with a consequent sharp decline of farms capable of commercial production. However, the allocation of land to small farmers turned out to be a political sham; the shape of the future was signaled by the creation of 100 **sovkhozes**, 25 machine tractor stations, and 238 horse and machinery lending stations. The negative impact of this on farming was shown by sharp declines in livestock holdings from July 1939 to September 1941: sheep by 41 percent, horses by 20–25 percent, and hogs by 29 percent, as farmers slaughtered animals for fear of being branded kulaks (that is, rich capitalist peasants, and thus natural enemies of communism) or of having livestock confiscated.

The **German occupation** from 22 June 1941, when they launched their attack on the Soviet forces, to September–November 1944, when the last German forces left, reduced Estonian agriculture further. As a result of the scorched earth policy of the retreating Red Army, combined with mobilization, **emigration** and **deportation** losses that reduced farm labor by 50,000, and the demands of wartime occupation, livestock holdings declined drastically. Compared to July 1936, the number of sheep by the end of 1944 had declined by 63 percent, cows by 43 percent, and hogs by 38 percent. In addition, land under cultivation had been reduced by 40 percent.

It took two years after reoccupying Estonia at the end of 1944 for Moscow to begin preparations for full collectivization of Estonian agriculture. In May 1947 initial discussions were held in the Communist Party's Politburo in Moscow about Baltic agriculture, and a decision was made to collectivize (*see also* ESTONIAN COMMUNIST PARTY). Resistance was softened by raising farm taxes up to 75 percent of income, and initially only five **kolkhozes** were established. But, by January 1951, 93 percent of all farms had been collectivized. This process created chaos in an already confused farm community suffering from a decade of reorganization and war.

The psychological upheaval of dispossession, the terror of deportations, and the lack of know-how of managing kolkhozes meant initial chaos in agricultural production. During the first years, the kolkhoz members often received little or no income and kept body and soul together from the proceeds of the one-hectare garden plots allocated to each household. Indeed, through the entire life span of the Soviet Union, right to the end, the productivity of these privately and intensively cultivated garden plots far outstripped state production, to such an extent that most of the vegetables and fruit were produced on these plots. This aspect of "peasant capitalist" farming provided the food safety net in the system. In addition, in the postwar years of shortages, city dwellers were officially encouraged to band together in garden cooperatives and produce vegetables and fruits for their own use, which older Estonians continue to do to the present. Thus, collectivization had the unintended consequence of creating a subsistence peasant mentality throughout the Soviet system.

Collectivized agriculture in Estonia made a breakthrough in 1958 when kolkhoz members began receiving regular monthly paychecks, the state raised the prices that it paid for agricultural products, cattle breeding and milk production were encouraged, and the state began to educate and train agricultural experts. The machine and tractor stations were disbanded in 1958 and each kolkhoz and **sovkhoz** established its own machine park. In the 1960s, Estonian collectivist agriculture developed its productivity rapidly as rural electrification became universal, and technology, including fertilizer usage, expanded, aided by the large stream of agricultural specialists produced by the Agricultural Academy. The 1960s also marked a differentiation in agricultural production, as kolkhozes and sovkhozes began to specialize in industrial-scale chicken production, cattle breeding, dairy farming, and hog production. The 1970s saw an increasing tendency to combine smaller kolkhozes and restructure them into sovkhozes, which meant that the status of farm workers increasingly became that of factory workers in the cities. Thus, the mentality of the peasant was replaced with that of the 8 A.M. to 4 P.M., eight-hour-a-day unskilled laborer. The peasantry became a rural proletariat. The productivity of most sovkhozes trailed that of the kolkhozes, and most received state subventions to keep them alive.

The single-minded focus on industrial farming led to the intended consequences: large increases in specialized meat and poultry production and productivity, and even relative quality increases, so that Estonian (along with Lithuanian and Latvian) farm products were directed to supply the elite cites of Moscow and Leningrad. It also led to a total destruction of the historic farming countryside as villages, stores, and schools were closed and scores of three- to four-story apartment buildings were constructed in kolkhoz-sovkhoz centers to house the new rural proletariat. In addition, industrial farming meant the setting up of large factory-type farm installations in the countryside.

Two additional factors played a role in collectivized farming in Estonia. Those kolkhozes that established their own industrial factories (e.g., wineries, sewing, woodworking, production of souvenirs, assembly of electronic components), which many did in the 1970s and 1980s, became better off and even rich. Still, up to the very end, collectivized farming depended extensively on "volunteer" labor by city factory, school, and university students who were forced to volunteer to work in potato picking and grain harvesting each September–October.

The negative aspects of Soviet-style farming became evident in the 1980s—large-scale **environmental** pollution resulting from overuse of fertilizers and concentrations of animal waste in total disregard of groundwater and aquifer capacity, the use of heavy machinery in the thin-soil conditions of Estonia, as well as the careless and unsightly scattering of unkempt and often decaying factory-type buildings across the landscape.

Consequently, even before the restoration of independence, at the end of the 1980s a movement to return Estonia to the farming landscape of the 1930s began, initially in 1987 in the county of Võru where a number of individual farms were restored to their prewar owners. On independence, a political decision was made to liquidate all the kolkhozes and sovkhozes and return the land to prewar owners or their legal heirs who would operate family farms. However, the attempt to turn the clock back 60 years could not succeed; since postindustrial agricultural technology requires large-scale farming, the small family farm of the 1930s is an uneconomic anachronism everywhere in Europe. Hindsight also shows that the land restitution decision—unavoidable at the time, since the desire to return to the prewar republic was universal—created a legal morass of conflicts among legal heirs as well as between them and the new "owners" who had been born and lived on the state estates all their lives. These conflicts were exacerbated by the need to recreate the land registry that had been destroyed because Soviet rule saw no need for it since all land was decreed state-owned.

The overlapping processes of land registration, restitution, and land **privatization** moved very slowly partly because of the complex structure of county- and municipality-based decision processes on which specific units of real estate should be retained in public ownership as being of national or cultural value (e.g., formerly private property now hospitals, museums, and theaters). This usually led to lengthy litigation in **courts** with inexperienced judges. Hence, by 2000 only 260,000 parcels of land, amounting to 53 percent of the 4.3 million hectares of the total land stock of Estonia, had been listed in the 15 county land registers, ranging from a low of 32 percent in the more urbanized to a high of 73 percent in poorer rural counties. Of the registered land, about 1 million hectares had been restituted, and 400,000 hectares had been privatized. The process of registration of private land slowed significantly in the late 1990s and the registration of public lands, mainly state forests, increased. It is optimistically forecasted that both the land registry and the restitution process should be completed around 2006.

The 1990s witnessed the most radically rapid restructuring of agricultural-rural economy-society anywhere ever—whereas in 1989 20.1 percent of the labor force was employed in agriculture, in 1995 it was 8 percent and by 2001 had fallen further to 5.1 percent. At the same time, agricultural production by 1994 had fallen precipitously to under 66 percent of its 1989 level. The decline in agricultural output continued through the rest of the decade so that in 2000 the share of agriculture (including hunting) in Estonia's gross national product (GNP) was reduced to 3.6 percent. Although the crude figures show that Estonian agriculture has become relatively efficient, unemployment among the older unskilled rural inhabitants, unable to switch into skilled trades, is part of the social cost of this transition. However, the simultaneous virtual tripling of private farms from 19,767 in 1996 to 60,895 in 2001 casts doubt on the claim on efficiency. Indeed, since the size of the average private farm is approximately 21 hectares (52 acres), it is questionable how such tiny plots can possibly be economic in today's mechanized agriculture. Part of the answer is found in the enterprise register, which in 1996, for example, had only 11,515 farms registered as working enterprises. Although the numbers of farms in the land registry increased to 34,671 in 1998, farms listed in the enterprise registry declined to 10,268. Moreover, a division of cows and pigs even among all farms, including the "enterprise" farms, shows an average of 3.5 cows and 2 pigs per farm! Clearly, most of the private farms consist either of simply restituted lands or they are anachronistic subsistence farmlets where the "farmer" requires other employment income. According to calculations, the minimum size of an economically sustainable cowherd is 40 and the minimum acreage for economic grain growing is 70 hectares (175 acres).

Hence the commercial farms in Estonia are either cooperatives or large private farms, some operating on leases of nominal state farms. Most are run by former Soviet-era farm managers who organized the restituted lands of the former kolkhoz members into large specialized industrial farms producing milk, beef, or grain. And many sovkhozes were simply taken over by the state, and are operated on a lease basis (note above that prewar Estonia also operated state farms). Although the numbers of these two categories have been declining steadily, from 873 in 1996 to 680 in 2000, but with a slight increase to 709 in 2001, their share in agricultural production has remained steady at just under half. Although the total agricultural production has declined steadily in the second half of the 1990s to only 80 percent of the 1995 figure, and the number of "private farms" tripled, the production ascribed to these in annual official statistics still amounted to over half of the total in 2000. Nevertheless, available data does show that the Estonian agricultural sector as a whole is rationalizing and preparing to compete in the **European Union** (EU).

The forced intensive production by the USSR for mainly the Moscow and Leningrad markets poisoned the thin soil with fertilizers and polluted the groundwater with manure runoffs. The conscious desire to leave the Soviet period behind and the loss of the collapse of the Russian markets forced the initial restructuring. Thus both the numbers of farm animals and sown acreage along with yields dropped drastically between 1990 and 1995: cattle from 757,800 to 370,400; pigs from 959,900 to 448,800; poultry from 6,536,300 to 2,911,300; and sown area of field crops from 1,116,000 hectares to 850,700 hectares. In the same period, yields dropped from 301,500 metric tons of meat to 117,400 metric tons live weight, milk from 1,208,000 to 706,900 tons, and eggs from 547.1 million to 326.7 million. The average yield of milk per cow decreased by 500 kilograms to 3,588 kilograms.

During the ensuing five years, however, as numbers of producing animals and sown fields decreased, yields began to increase. Thus, 307,500 cattle in 1999 produced almost as much meat by live weight, 21,700 metric tons as the larger numbers in 1995. By 2002, the number of cattle had declined to 260,500 but produced 13,200 tons of meat—a 34 percent gain in seven years. The milk yield of 100,000 fewer cows than in 1995 increased by 500 kilograms to 4,171 kilograms per cow in 1999 and further to 5,119 kilograms per cow in 2002. Although egg production totals have been declining steadily, efficiency has been increasing as half a million fewer hens than in 1995 each produced 42 eggs more per year in 1999. The sown area of field crops decreased further steadily from 1995 to 818,700 hectares in 1999 and to 644,200 hectares in 2001. However, the structure of production did not change markedly: in 2000 field crops (grains and potatoes), vegetables and fruits accounted for about 40 percent of agriculture, and animal products (pork, beef, and chicken) accounted for just over 60 percent, of which milk products provided almost a half or 30 percent of total agricultural production.

Impressive as the agricultural rationalization may be, it is still not enough to allow Estonian agriculture to compete in the European markets. Although the milk yield has reached the EU current annual yield per cow of over 5,000 kilograms, more reorganization is in store for Estonian agriculture before it can compete in the EU markets. For example, producer costs only of pig meat and rapeseed of all agricultural products exceed the costs in the EU, which means that Estonian factor costs, especially of labor, are a fraction of the EU costs. And despite the success of the major Estonian dairies in gaining EU import licenses, meat packers have had difficulty in raising their quality and health controls to the EU level. The EU also demands that in addition to meeting these standards, Estonian internal prices must rise to average 80 percent of EU prices. This, of course, means a major increase in labor costs. However, studies in 2002 show that Estonian agribusinesses are rapidly modernizing and that many milk processors output prices are already close to EU levels.

Still, by 2000 a significant part of the food processing industry had met EU standards, and was exporting some of its production to the Nordic counties, mainly because it was Finnish- or Swedish-owned. The plants producing fruit juices, processed condiments, fish conserves, and canned fruit and vegetables also provided much-needed jobs in the countryside.

ALEXANDER I (1777–1825). Russian tsar from 1801 to 1825. Alexander I, son of Tsar Paul I, ascended the throne as a liberal ruler intent on carrying out reforms to modernize the empire. He freed the serfs in the Baltic Provinces of Estland and Livland from their ties to the land, established a system of government ministries and new rules for **educational** institutions, and established several new universities, all in the interests of modernization.

In 1802 Alexander authorized the reopening of the **University of Tartu** with wide-ranging autonomy and sufficient funding to allow it to exercise its independent status. In 1804 he decreed tenant labor rent to be paid to landlords, and instituted a system of local courts in Estland and Livland. In the 1816 Estonian Peasant Farmers Law, he freed the peasants from **serfdom** on the estates of the nobility, forbade the landlords to buy and sell landless peasants, and granted peasants limited rights of movement and the right to conclude labor tenancy contracts. Limited local self-government by peasants at the parish level was also instituted, thus devolving some authority from the Estland **Diet**. In 1819, the tsar passed the Livland Peasant Farmers Law analogous to the Estland one.

However, despite the freeing of the peasants from ties to the land, since the Laws also confirmed the ownership of the estates of the Baltic German nobility, the condition of the peasants worsened. Because economic relations between the peasants-tenants and the estate-owners were now regulated by contracts, the peasant actually lost the historic right to the land that his forefathers had tilled and passed on to him. The peasant was now a mere contractee. The "free" peasant was now at the mercy of the economic demands of the landowner on a legally enforceable contractual basis, and his workload and obligations to the landowner increased considerably to prevent starvation. After all, **agriculture** in the Baltics was subsistence farming until the landowners introduced modernized large-scale grain farming and animal husbandry on estate farms in the mid-19th century. The tenancy reforms were largely responsible for this because they allowed the landowners to increase the demand for contracted labor of the tenants to work the estate farms. This reduced both the time and the intensity for tilling their own small tenant peasant plots, which thus continued at an increased subsistence level. The former land-serf had become an exploited contractual rural labor-serf.

ALIEN PASSPORTS. In 1994, Estonia began to issue temporary travel documents to legal resident **aliens** who had had been citizens of the Soviet Union and who were not, or had not become, citizens of Estonia, Russia, or any other country, or who still had old Soviet passports that were no longer accepted as valid by Estonia and most other states. The first alien passports were valid for a single departure and reentry. From late 1994, alien passports valid for two years have been issued to resident aliens who are stateless, foreign citizens who have not been able to obtain travel documents from their own country of origin or from another state, persons who have filed for Estonian citizenship and have passed the language exam but have not become citizens yet, and stateless aliens who leave Estonia permanently. Owing to demand, Estonia agreed to expand the categories eligible for alien passports in 2000 to include resident aliens who intend to study abroad and former Soviet military personnel who cannot or do not want to take out Russian citizenship. By the end of 1999, 190,190 alien passports had been issued. The backlog was cleared in 2000 when 117,806 passports were issued, bringing the total to 307,996, including reissued two-year passports.

ALIENS. Estonians began to refer to people in Estonia who were not of Estonian ethnicity by the term *muulane* (alien) as a colloquial euphemism for the Russian-speaking labor brought to Estonia during the half century of Soviet occupation. Although it is still used primarily to refer to Russian speakers, it also covers anyone who is not an ethnic Estonian.

In 1993 parliament enacted the Law on Aliens that defines an alien as a person who is not a citizen of Estonia. The law provided a one-year period during which noncitizens, who had come to Estonia prior to 1 July 1990 and had been permanent residents of the former Estonian Soviet Socialist Republic (ESSR), could apply for temporary residence permits as well as for permanent residence at the same time. Following confusion in implementation by an inexperienced bureaucracy (amidst general wishful expectations that the aliens would all leave Estonia) and criticism by international **human rights** observers, the application deadline was extended for one year, to 12 July 1995. Since only 327,737 of the estimated 370,000 aliens had filed applications by that date, the deadline was extended yet again, to 30 April 1996. Because an indeterminate number, ranging from 20,000 to 50,000, still had not registered, in 1997 the government began a campaign to register them while pledging not to take any punitive measures. Only 2,000 had come forward by September 1998. However, subsequently it has become evident that not only were the estimates of population totals exaggerated (as shown by the 2001 census) but so also were the estimates of illegals.

In 1997 **Riigikogu** amended the 1993 Act to allow those who had applied for residence by 12 July 1995 to change temporary for permanent residency permits. The law was implemented in September 1998. During the following two years, nearly all illegals were registered and received permanent residency permits. In 2001, 64 percent (175,000) of the 261,260 aliens with permanent residency permits in Estonia were stateless, and 34 percent were Russian citizens. Note also that as of end of 2000, 113,764 aliens had been naturalized, nearly all of them former Soviet citizens resident in Estonia and the overwhelming majority of them ethnic Russians. According to surveys, the reason given by 60 percent of the stateless for not having applied for Estonian citizenship was the practical factor that until 2001 **alien passport** holders had preferred cheap visa access to Russia to visit relatives, friends, and business partners. The abrogation of these preferences by Russia and the implementation of an active government policy, supported by all parties in the Riigikogu, encouraging **citizenship** application by aliens in 2001 was expected to reduce the alien population radically during the next few years. Note also that virtually all of these aliens have been eligible for Russian citizenship but have not applied for it and are committed to living in Estonia. *See also* INTEGRATION.

ANCIENT ESTONIA. *See* ARCHEOLOGY *and* ARCHITECTURE.

ANVELT, JAAN (1884–1937). Estonian communist revolutionary, politician, lawyer, writer, and journalist. Anvelt was born to an independent farm family on 18 April 1884 in Võisiku parish. After studies at **Tartu** Teachers College, work in an office in St. Petersburg (1903–05), and work as a village teacher in Estonia (1905–07), he joined the Communist Party in 1907 when he began studies in the law faculty at St. Petersburg. As a student he immersed himself in Marxist theory and took part in student revolutionary activities. He was one of the leaders of the left wing of the Estonian Students' Association at St. Petersburg, but was suspended for his revolutionary activities by the University in 1911 and sent back to Estonia, where he participated in the workers' movements in **Tallinn** and **Narva**. After completing his university degree as an external student in 1912, he began work in Narva both as a lawyer and as editor of the workers' newspaper *Kiir*, which he cofounded and published from 1912 to 1914. Apparently during this period, he became convinced of the rightness of the ideology of class struggle and followed its dictates to the end of his life. After the February 1917 revolution, he served briefly as chair of the Narva Workers and Soldiers Council but moved in March 1917 to Tallinn where he again edited the **Bolshevik** daily *Kiir* and became one of the foremost Leninist leaders among Estonian communists.

As a prominent communist leader of the Tallinn Soviet, he participated in the first pan-Russian Workers and Soldiers Soviet and was elected to its executive committee. In October 1917 as chair of the Estonian Soviet's Executive Committee and member of the Estonian War Revolutionary Committee, Anvelt led the communist revolution in Estonia. Land, banks, and large factories and businesses were nationalized, and nobles' estates were plundered in order to set up collective farms. Although in the Russian Constituent Assembly elections in December the Bolsheviks garnered only 40.2 percent of the votes, in Estonia Anvelt was one of eight elected. During the German occupation of Estonia in 1918, Anvelt was the Nationalities Commissioner of the North Commune in St. Petersburg (at the time renamed Petrograd) and served on the Petrograd War Council. When the German armies retreated from Estonia on 28 November 1918, the Red Army attacked. The very next day, the Estonian Workers Commune was proclaimed in Narva with Anvelt as its chair. On 7 December, the Council of Commissars of the Russian Soviet Socialist Republic (RSSR) recognized the Anvelt executive as the Estonian government. However, when the Estonian bourgeois forces drove the Red Army out of Estonia a few months later in the **War of Independence**, the Anvelt Commune fled to Russia and disbanded itself on 5 June 1919.

During the following year, Anvelt continued his career as a Bolshevik leader in Petrograd, serving at various times as a Red Army political commissar, member of the All-Russia Central Soviet, member of the Petrograd Central Soviet, and so on. After the **Peace Treaty of Tartu** in 1920, his lifelong objective was to subvert the bourgeois Republic of Estonia and to bring Estonia into union with Russia. To this end, he became a leading member of the **Estonian Communist Party** (ECP) after its founding and began to work underground in Estonia from 1921 until the failed armed **attempted coup of 1924**. Anvelt fled Estonia, again for the Soviet Union where he continued his communist career serving as the ECP representative to the Executive Committee of the Comintern, and rose to be its executive secretary in 1935–37. On 11 November 1937, he was executed in the Stalinist mass purge of early ideological communists. Anvelt was also a prolific writer and produced a large numbers of essays and short stories dealing with the class struggle.

ARCHAEOLOGY. Interest in archaeology first arose in Estonia toward the end of the 18th century among individuals who collected and preserved old artifacts. By the middle of the 19th century, enthusiasts had organized into societies and had begun to collect, study, and preserve their heritage on a systematic basis. Among the leaders were the **Estonian Learned Society** founded in 1838, the Estonian

Literature Union in Tallinn (Eestimaa Kirjanduse Ühing Tallinnas) founded in 1842, and similar organizations in **Narva**, Paide, Kuressaare, **Viljandi**, and **Pärnu**—each with its own museum. Archaeological excavations were begun during the second half of the century with the first digs undertaken by amateurs, among whom a local schoolmaster, Jaan Jung of Abja parish, was the leader in surveying and registering sites. Jung also organized an Estonia-wide network of amateur archaeologists. Scholarly archaeological work, however, was conducted by foreigners, the German, Swedish, and Finnish researchers Constantin Grewingk, Richard Hausmann, Max Ebert, and Adolf Freidenthal.

After its refounding as an Estonian-language institution in 1919, the **University of Tartu** established its Department of Archaeology in the 1920s with the Finnish archaeologist Aarne M. Tallgren as its first professor. Tallgren founded not only the University's Museum of Archaeology but also placed scientific archaeological research on a firm footing in Estonia. Subsequently his students (Harri Moora, Marta Schmiedelheim, and Richard Indreko) and their students (Artur Vassar, Lembit Jaanits, Vello Lõugas, Mati Mandel, and Jüri Seilrand) not only carried on systematic archaeological research of Estonia but also formed the necessary cross-disciplinary cooperation with geologists, paleontologists, anthropologists, and philologists. Hence, by the end of the 20th century, Estonia's prehistory was thoroughly surveyed.

Accordingly, it was discovered that human settlement in Estonia reaches back to the eighth century B.C. and that the first settlers migrated from the south or southeast. More recently discovered artifacts indicate a mixing of Mongolian and European sources that suggest immigration of the earliest settlers from Asia. The **Finno-Ugric** settlers, the forefathers of present-day Estonians, first reached Estonia during the third millennium B.C. from the Ural mountain range. Toward the end of that millennium, parts of the massive movement of Indo-European tribes also reached Estonian territory and melded together with the Finno-Ugric settlers and adopted their language. The late Stone Age culture of nomadic hunting and fishing was gradually replaced by settlements of domesticated animal husbandry and field tillage during the Bronze Age in the middle of the second millennium B.C. when bronze artifacts reached Estonia from the Urals,

Scandinavia, Prussia, and northern Germany. By the early Iron Age, from 600 to 100 B.C., when iron was melted from local bog ore, **agriculture** and village life had become the dominant form of economic activity.

Archaeological data from the first centuries A.D. shows a peaceful period with household items, tools, and jewelry but few arms. No fortifications have been found from this period. However, beginning with the fifth century A.D., the tribal migrations again affected Estonia and a large number of fortifications were repeatedly built and destroyed. Gravesites are well supplied with arms as well as rich in ornaments. Iron Age finds also show Scandinavian permanent settlements in the coastal areas.

The final prehistoric period, from the ninth to the 13th century, shows rapid economic and cultural development during a long relatively peaceful period in which the population reached around 150,000 in a net of fixed villages across the whole of Estonia. Only on the island of Hiiumaa and in northeastern and southeastern Estonia was settlement sparse. The villages varied in size from around 10 to about 50 "plough-lands," that is, the amount one plough could till, or about eight to 12 hectares. Thus, village sizes varied from 80 to over 500 cultivated hectares. Moreover, larger settlements grew in **Tallinn** and **Tartu**. Although the primary economic activity revolved around the growing of winter rye, wheat, and barley as well as the keeping of cattle, pigs, and sheep, there was also iron working and pottery making of high quality. Trade with both East and West flourished. Toward the end of the prehistoric period, the country was divided into indigenous *kihelkond* (*see* COURTS), translated as "parish," but at this time not to be confused with the notion of church parish, which they later became. These in turn joined into counties (*maakond*), among which the larger and stronger ones were Sakala, Ugandi, Saaremaa, Revala, Harju, Läänemaa, and Järva. The counties were led by elected elders (*maakonnavanem*) who also represented the county at annual pan-Estonian council meetings.

ARCHITECTURE. The earliest prehistoric buildings on Estonian were typical Stone Age circular or four-cornered dwellings with walls of wattle or turf with lattice roofs covered with animal skins. A ring of stones constituted the fireplace, and a hole in the roof provided escape for the smoke. In the middle of the second millennium B.C., there is evidence of dwellings built with vertical logs. At the end of the Bronze Age (around 1,000 B.C.), settlements began to be built on higher ground with timber-framed rectangular dwellings encircled by protective stockades or stonewalls.

Beginning around the first century A.D., settlements were already of the village type consisting mostly of four-cornered iron axe-formed timber dwellings. In the middle of the first millennium A.D., the more important settlements were approximately 1,000 square meters in size and were built on hills and enclosed by high earthen or stone walls. By the beginning of the second millennium, the fortified villages consisted of several hectares enclosed by walls of up to 10 meters high. Settlements at the more important crossroads, such as **Tallinn**, **Tartu**, and Otepää, became commercial markets. Their typical dwelling was still a single-room building with a simple fire hearth and a hole in the roof for smoke.

The Gothic period of architecture (end of 13th to beginning of 16th century) was ushered in by the Christianizing Crusades, which brought late Romanesque and early Gothic church and castle building styles to Estonia. Initially, fortified strongholds were built at Otepää, Paide, and Lihula and new castles for the **Crusading orders** in Tallinn, Kuressare, Põltsamaa, and other places. During the 14th century the Teutonic Order (*Deutsche Orden*), added convent halls in its strongholds and during the 15th century these fortifications were expanded into fortified towns encircled by high walls in Laiuse, Tallinn, Kuressaare, and Haapsalu. In the 16th century there were around 50 forts, two strongly fortified monasteries (Kärkna and Padise), over 20 fortified churches, and six fortified walled towns (Tallinn, Tartu, **Pärnu**, **Narva**, **Viljandi**, and Haapsalu) on Estonian territory.

Churches began to be built in Estonia during the middle of the 13th century and consisted of three types. The earliest were strongly built single-nave rectangular stone buildings without bell-towers but with richly carved interiors of thick walls, small slit window-openings, and vaulted roofs used often as places of refuge during warfare. The second type consisted of large three-aisle buildings with a high bell-tower at the west end. The third type, large northern Gothic perpendicular-style buildings built in the 15th century, are located in northern Estonia. The best examples are St. Olaf's (Oleviste), still with the tallest steeple in northern Europe; St. Nicholas (Niguliste); Holy Ghost (Pühavaimu); and St. Michael's (Mihkli) churches, all in Tallinn.

During the 15th century, wealthy burghers in Tallinn and Tartu also began to build elaborate late Gothic stone houses and guildhalls. Among the most notable preserved ones are Tallinn Town Hall (1404), the Great Guild (1410), and St. Olaf's Guild (1422), marked by monumental simplicity, large walls, and elaborately carved stone doorways. The typical burgher's dwelling was a gabled rectangular building with the end facing the street. Their principal rooms were a front hall with a large fireplace with a carved stone mantel and a smaller living room at the rear heated by hot air flues. This Tallinn Gothic style, as it came to be known, was subsequently exported to Finland, Sweden, and Novgorod.

During the northern Renaissance period (1620s to 1730s), Estonian architecture was influenced by Dutch, Swedish, and Polish styles. Massive earthen bastions were built in Tallinn and Narva, the Tallinn Town Hall acquired a slender tower with a balcony, and a new type of building with the long facade facing the street appeared. The **Blackheads** (Mustpeade, Schwarzenhäupter) House and the Town Hall Apothecary (Raeapteek) in Tallinn, which has remained both in operation and in possession of the same family since it was built, are prime examples.

The Baroque period (1630s to 1780s) is represented mostly by buildings built by the aristocracy and the Russian imperial court. The style is notable for its nature-friendly attempt to fit the buildings into the landscape. Several surviving nobles' estate ensembles and Kadriorg Palace (built by Peter the Great as a summer house for his queen; today a restored museum) exemplify the style. Church building acquired two new floor plans—the hall church and the cross plan with a nave and transepts. City houses were built according to a basic floor plan of a central vestibule with side public rooms opening off it. The second floor was used for bedrooms, windows were enlarged, and doors and ceilings were covered with paintings. The Rococo period style was represented principally in interior decoration and furniture.

The Classical period (1780s to 1840s) in Estonian architecture began with the building of the Provincial Government Building (today the front wing of Toompea Castle in Tallinn). Both Toompea and the lower city in Tallinn received new large buildings with mezzanine floors, while Gothic gabled roofs were replaced by stepped pediments. Tartu City Hall and the buildings surrounding the square, as well as the Tartu Stone Bridge (destroyed during World War II) and a number of buildings in Kuressaare, Haapsalu, and Võru, are excellent examples of the style. In the countryside, parks on aristocratic landed estates were built on classic principles, as were posthouses and county taverns.

The Historicist period (mid-19th century to World War I) is marked by both the Neogothic and a restrained Jugend style. Examples of the former are the Alaskivi and Sangaste estates' mansion buildings, St. Charles' Church (Kaarli), the bank building at 2 Vana Turg, and the Reaalkool (Realschule) building, both in Tallinn. Examples of the latter style are the Luther Factory's club building, the Estonia Theater and Concert Hall building, a number of apartment buildings in Tallinn, as well as the building of the **Eesti Üliõpilaste Selts** (EÜS) and the Girls Gymnasium School building of the Noorsoo Kasvatuse Selts (Youth Education Society) in Tartu. In addition, the Russian-Baltic shipbuilding complex at Kopli in Tallinn includes both office and workshop buildings as well as housing in Jugend-style architecture.

During the two decades of independence from 1920 to 1940, initially late Jugend and neoclassicism, and later functionalism, dominated Estonian architecture. Comprehensive town planning led to the building of "garden suburbs" of detached single-family houses with gardens laid out in rectangular street patterns. Nõmme, Merivälja, Lilleküla, and Tondi in Tallinn; Tammelinn and Tähtvere in Tartu; and Seedri in Pärnu are prime examples and represent both middle-class and working-class housing of the time. Often carved-dolomite, stylized, national-cultural ornaments were used on facades of the structures. In addition to housing, large numbers of school buildings, community halls, hospitals, and sports halls were built during the two decades.

The half century of Soviet occupation left behind the peculiar Soviet architectural legacy that may be seen everywhere within its former hegemony. The 1950s was marked by showy buildings with design excess, and the 1960s by the first bedroom subdivisions (the so-called *microrayons*), consisting of unit-design, prefabricated, concrete-panel apartment buildings in Tallinn and all the larger towns. Mustamäe in Tallinn and Annelinn in Tartu are the main examples. Nevertheless, a few buildings with architectural merit were designed and built, such as the massive but elegant Song Festival Stage capable of holding 25,000 singers, the Emergency Hospital and the Estonian Cooperatives Building in Tallinn, the Vanemuine Theater in Tartu, the Sanatorium Tervis in Pärnu, and the shopping center in Haapsalu, for example.

The 1980s saw more of the same except that now taller, prefabricated concrete-panel, nine- and 15-story buildings dominated both the new and the expanded subdivisions in Tallinn (Lasnamäe) and Tartu (Annelinn).

Restoration of medieval buildings was begun in the 1950s but little was accomplished until the late 1970s, when preparations for the 1980 Moscow Olympics, with the regatta events scheduled for Tallinn, led to a short-lasting orgy of restoration in Tallinn and beyond. Thus the Narva Town Hall destroyed in the war was reconstructed, as was the Kuressaare Bishop's Castle in Saaremaa. In Tallinn the old town walls, St. Nicolas' Church, the Town Hall, as well as a large number of buildings in the medieval Old City were renovated.

The architectural landscape of Estonia since the restoration of independence has taken on both a Nordic upper middle class low-density character of single-family row-housing with gardens, as well as subdivisions of detached villas, and numerous tall (six- to 20-story) glass cubes, rectangles and curved façade triangle-shaped office buildings, most commissioned and built by the commercial banks between 1995 and 1998 in Tallinn and Tartu. At the beginning of the 21st century, contemporary 20-story tall apartment blocs are also being built in central Tallinn.

ARMED FORCES. Estonians have fought foreign invaders in armed formations and served in the forces of their German, Swedish, and Russian conquerors since the Christianizing Crusades in the 13th century (*see* CHRONOLOGY). The first regularly constituted force on Estonian soil was the Cavalry Troop of the Estland Nobility (Eestimaa aadlilipkond), which served from 1350 to 1720. It was officered and maintained by the Baltic nobles but had local peasants serving as soldiers. During the **Great Northern War**, this force consisted of 750 troops in Estland, 500 in Livland, and 80 in Saaremaa. The Guild of **Blackheads** formed a cavalry squadron (*ratsaeskadron*) to defend **Tallinn** in 1399 and maintained it as a 100–200-man unit until 1788 when it was reorganized as Estonia's first volunteer fire brigade. The first purely Estonian armed unit was formed during the Russo-Livonian War (*see* LIVONIAN WARS) to defend Tallinn in 1570 and consisted of 500 peasants who had sought sanctuary behind the city's defensive walls. The 500-man cavalry troop fought a guerilla war behind Russian lines until their leader Ivo Shenkenberg was captured and tortured to death in 1579. At the beginning of the Great Northern War at the end of the **Swedish era**, the 9,000-man Swedish force in Estland was two thirds Estonian in composition. During the war, new regiments were formed so that by 1710 14,000 Estonians served in the Swedish forces. The war against Russia was fought nearly exclusively by Estonian units: in 1710 Tallinn, for example, was defended by 5,000 men in which Swedes formed a 200-man artillery unit and Finns a similar-sized infantry company. During Swedish times, Estonians also first reached officer rank and served as captains in command of companies. After the Russian conquest in 1710, Estonians were excluded from service in the tsar's forces until 1797, when the imperial government began recruiting soldiers, with little success, to fight against the Napoleon's invading army. Nevertheless, between 1797 and 1874, 100,000 were conscripted into the imperial forces, of whom only 20,000 returned alive to their homeland, most as invalids.

In contrast to the negative attitude of the peasantry toward the Russian armed forces, the Baltic German nobility (*see* BALTIC GERMANS) enjoyed a golden era of military service, with over 800 serving as officers during the Napoleonic Wars alone. Among dozens of Baltic German division and corps commanders, the most notable was Prince Barclay de Tolly (whose statue stands in a park in the center of **Tartu** even today), who served as minister of war and commander-in-chief of the imperial forces. At the same time Johan von Michelson, ennobled in 1783, became the first ethnic Estonian to reach the rank of full general.

Between the formation of the Department of Military Science at the newly refounded **University of Tartu** in 1802 and its liquidation in 1830, 18 of its 139 graduates reached the rank of general and Count von Berg the rank of field marshal. When in 1832 the imperial Military Academy was established in St. Petersburg, Lieutenant General von Rennekamp, a Tartu graduate, became its deputy commandant and his classmate General von Mehden became a member of its academic board. In 1874 Russia instituted general conscription in the empire with the result that by the beginning of the 20th century, a sizeable number of Estonians had been educated as military officers.

Over 10,000 Estonians served in the ill-fated Russo-Japanese War of 1904–05, including about a hundred officers. At the outbreak of war in 1914, 140 Estonians served as professional officers in the imperial forces with 160 in the reserve.

World War I saw 100,000 Estonians conscripted into the imperial armed forces, of whom about 10,000 lost their lives—the most to date in any war in Estonian history. However, war service provided military experience to the Estonian male population, and 2,000 Estonians reached officer status in the imperial forces. Thirteen of the 90 officers who organized the Estonian armed forces in the **War of Independence** had been educated at the imperial military academy, 12 were colonels, and 28 were lieutenant colonels. Three had served at divisional command level, seven served as regimental commanders, and 70 had battalion command experience. They had been awarded 333 imperial medals, including 47 St. George medals of courage. Thus the necessary military command preconditions were amply present for the establishment of independent Estonian armed forces; the February revolution of 1917 provided the political preconditions.

On 21 April 1917, permission was obtained from the new imperial government to form Estonian soldiers into an Estonian regiment on their native soil. Ensign **Konstantin Päts** organized the Eesti Söjaväelaste Büroo (Estonian Soldiers Bureau) to this end. On 1–5 July 1917 the first Congress of Estonian Soldiers, consisting of delegates representing 50,000 Estonian soldiers, elected the Eesti Söjaveäaste Ülemkomitee (Supreme Committee of Estonian Soldiers), which in effect became the initial Estonian Ministry of Defense. On the collapse of imperial power during the October Revolution, it established the Estonian Division under the command of Lt. Col. **Johan Laidoner**.

On the **Declaration of Independence** on 24 February 1918, the

Provisional Government named Colonel **Andres Larka** minister of war and declared itself neutral in the war between Russia and Germany. Initially the German forces, which occupied Estonia during February–March, accepted this and allowed the exiting units to keep their arms. The ministry and forces command quickly designed national insignia for the forces, developed an initial Estonian language command terminology, and promoted the first three generals—Larka, Aleksander Tõnisson, and **Ernst Põdder**. During the summer, it became evident that Germany could not win the war against Russia. Since a German defeat would mean an automatic aggression against an undefended Estonia by the Red Army, and since the German occupation forces would not permit the organization of any local defense units except for the 3,000-man Tallinn Defense Guard (Tallinna Omakaitse), the provisional government ordered their formation underground. Accordingly, **Johan Pitka** together with Generals Larka and Põdder established the **Defense League** (Kaitseliit) based on Omakaitse. By 28 November 1918, after the collapse of Germany on 11 November, General Põdder commanded 14,500 men against the attack of the Red Army.

In the meantime, the provisional government had decided to form regular armed forces with General Larka in command. Initially it was to consist of one army division with General Tõnisson as commander. On 29 November, the day after the Red Army attack, the government decreed general conscription. By January 1919, 13,000 men had been conscripted and by February 30,000, which allowed the Estonian Army to drive the Red Army out of Estonia by Independence Day 1919. This was due largely to the appointment of Colonel **Johan Laidoner** as commander-in-chief with wide powers at the end of December. On 23 February, he established his headquarters staff with Colonel Jaan Soots in command. To increase the flexibility of his command, Laidoner reorganized his forces and established the Second Division in South Estonia with Colonel Viktor Puskar in command. On 10 March, the armored trains were formed into a separate single unit under the command of Captain Karl Parts, and expanded into a division on 27 August. On 27 March, the forces on the Latvian border were reformed into the Third Division under the command of General Põdder. At the end of the War of Independence, the regular Estonian Armed Forces consisted of 85,000 men, with

32,000 trained Defense League soldiers as a reserve. In addition, the Defense League had another 70,000 largely untrained men. Thanks to foreign assistance, the forces were well equipped with modern weapons, including 2,000 machine guns, 300 field guns, 10 armored trains, 12 tanks and armored cars, 28 aircraft, 25 warships, as well as some support vessels.

The structure of the armed forces remained basically unchanged during the decade following the War of Independence, and its objective was to become a leading modern West European small-state armed force. To this end, Lt. Gen. Nikolaj Reek, the first Estonian officer to graduate from the French War College, in his capacity as both minister of war and chief of staff of the armed forces, rapidly brought Estonian military education and training to West European standards. In 1921, he formed the Estonian War College, and in 1923 he combined all military training institutions into a single Armed Forces United Training Institution. In 1925 Estonia reduced the two-year conscription service period to one year, and instituted compulsory military training in secondary schools and universities.

During the second decade of independence, the armed forces were restructured to reflect a defense policy based on the principle of territorial defense. In 1930, air defense was reorganized into a separate command structure with three air squadrons and one anti-aircraft artillery group. The maritime defense command consisted of coastal artillery fortifications and a number of vessels, including two minesweeping coastal submarines bought from Great Britain. At the end of the 1930s, the Estonian defense force consisted of 1,500 professional officers, 2,400 noncommissioned officers, and 12,000 conscripts. This force was backed by a reserve of 147,000 men, of whom 47,000 regularly participated in Defense League training maneuvers. The mobilization plan envisaged a called-up trained force of 6,500 officers, 15,000 noncommissioned officers, and 80,000 soldiers. This force was armed with 2,500 machine guns and 500 submachine guns manufactured by Estonian industry, in addition to semi-automatic rifles. Its heavy armament consisted of 250 field artillery pieces and 50 anti-tank and 15 anti-aircraft cannon.

When the Estonian armed forces were disarmed by the Soviet occupation in June 1940, a number of men fled across the Gulf of Finland and joined the Finnish forces to fight against the Soviet Union, eventually being formed into the infantry brigade **JR 200**.

Owing to training received in the Defense League when the German forces began their attack on the Soviet positions in western Estonia in 1941, a large number of Estonian men were able to immediately begin guerilla warfare in the rear of the retreating Soviets. The new Omakaitse (Self-defense) units, organized on the model of the defunct Kaitseliit, became the resuscitator of national defense forces; in December 1941 it numbered 40,000, but progressively lost members as men joined units at the front to fight against Soviet forces. In the beginning, the **German occupation** authorities did not allow the formation of Estonian national forces larger than battalion size. By February 1942, these numbered 20 with 11,500 men. In August permission was given to organize an Estonian Legion and in May 1943 the Estonian Brigade consisting of 7,000 men was formed. In that year, a total of 15,000 Estonian men served in this and independent national units in battle against the Red Army. Omakaitse had 37,000 men.

When the Soviet forces began their major counterattack against the German forces in the northern sector, including in Estonia, a general mobilization was ordered and the Estonian Brigade was expanded into a division. Six Border Defense Regiments were also formed. In April 1944, 52,000 Estonian men fought in various Estonian national units in German armies. On the retreat of the German forces at the end of the summer of 1944, the Estonian units fought desperately and hopelessly alone against the Soviet attack to stop the Soviet reoccupation in an attempt to regain national independence. At the end of 1944, 2,000 battle-hardened veterans of the disbanded JR 200 arrived to fight for Estonia. A total of almost 100,000 men—about the same number as in the War of Independence, 25 years earlier—fought for Estonian independence in 1944–45. Although the battle for independence was lost, the heroic defense enabled Prime Minster **Jüri Uluots**, who had been named acting president (*see* HEADS OF STATE) by President **Konstantin Päts** prior to his own arrest in 1940 by the Soviets, to again declare the Estonian republic and form a government between the German withdrawal and the Soviet reoccupation. His escape with some of his cabinet enabled a government-in-exile to be organized. As a result, the existence of the Republic de jure continued to be recognized by the United States and 32 other governments until the restoration of independence in 1991.

During World War II, over 14,000 men lost their lives in battle for the freedom of their homeland and up to 5,800 lost their lives in the decade-long guerrilla war (*see* BRETHREN OF THE FOREST) that continued in Estonian forests against the Soviets until well into the 1950s. Thus, this unsuccessful battle for independence cost twice as many Estonian lives as the fight for independence at the end of World War I.

During the Soviet occupation, most men were conscripted into the Soviet armed force for two-year periods; very few, however, chose a military career, with the result that, in contrast to 1918, there were few senior or even mid-level officers or noncommissioned officers on the restoration of independence. Moreover, the few were not trusted since they were regarded as Sovietized. In the event, only one officer of colonel rank joined the nascent Estonian defense forces

Even before regaining independence, Estonians began to reconstruct their military forces, initially at the volunteer militia level in various parts of the country. On regaining independence, the government began immediately to establish the armed forces, now known as the **Estonian Defense Forces.** *See also* BALTIC BATTALION; DEFENSE LEAGUE.

ART. *See separate entries for* GRAPHICS, PAINTING, *and* SCULPTURE *for the three categories of Estonian figurative art.*

ASSOCIATION FOR THE ADVANCEMENT OF BALTIC STUDIES (AABS). An international educational and scholarly nonprofit organization, the AABS was established on 1 December 1968 at the concluding general session of the First Conference on Baltic Studies at the University of Maryland, College Park, with the objective of promoting research and education in Baltic Studies while publicizing the political plight of the Baltic States. Its main activity is a biennial international conference held at a university in the United States or Canada (in June 2002, it held its 17th conference at Johns Hopkins University in Baltimore and scheduled the next at the University of Toronto in 2004). Since 1970 it has published the quarterly *Journal of Baltic Studies*, and it communicates with its members through the quarterly *Baltic Studies Newsletter* (from 1976 to 1993 titled *aabs Newsletter*), which is also found online at www.balticstudies-aabs

.lanet.lv. The AABS is a member of the American Council of Learned Societies. Since 1992, it has also operated a Baltic liaison office in Riga, Latvia, and has been active in promoting regional cross-Baltic research in the social sciences and humanities among Estonian, Latvian, and Lithuanian academics and students.

ATTEMPTED COMMUNIST COUP OF 1924. The openly stated objective of the Communist Party of the Soviet Union from its beginnings until World War II, when Stalin decreed a period of "socialism in one country" mainly for diplomatic alliance reasons, was the gradual communization of the world by revolutionary overthrow of governments. After the establishment of the Soviet state, these activities were coordinated by the Comintern (Communist International) established in 1919 in Moscow. Revolutionary cadres were trained in various international military schools in the Soviet Union. The Third International Military School in Petrograd (Leningrad) provided this training to Estonian and Finnish communists between 1921 and 1928.

The Comintern fomented numerous uprisings but was successful in only a few, among them in the briefly independent Caucasian states. Thus, the attempted coup in Estonia was not unique but part of a plan. Although the coup was well planned in Leningrad, it failed miserably because of misinformation provided by the weak **Estonian Communist Party** (ECP) about the likely support from Estonian soldiers and workers, a lack of revolutionary fervor and support for the uprising in the ECP itself, and the fact that the Estonian security police had thoroughly infiltrated the ECP. Although the government was familiar with the planned coup, it did not know the date of implementation. The cabinet apparently calculated that if it permitted the attempt to take place, and then quickly crushed it, it could with one stroke discredit and rid Estonia of the ECP; which is exactly what happened.

In the event, on 1 December 1924, 279 well-armed (with 5 Thompson submachine guns, 55 rifles, 150 handguns, 65 hand grenades, and 8 hand bombs) revolutionaries, mostly from the Soviet Union, gathered in **Tallinn**. At 5:30 in the morning, they attacked the War Ministry, the Tenth Infantry Regiment's staff office, the Signals Battalion office, the Tank Company's garage, a weapons storehouse, the Police

Cavalry Reserve barracks, the pretrial prison housing 149 underground communists awaiting trial, two main railway stations, the post office (which housed the main telephone exchange), and the government buildings on Toompea. All attacks failed, partly because fewer than 10 percent of the ECP members summoned to participate in the attacks showed up, and because the defenders acted resolutely. By noon, the government announced that the revolt had been repulsed. In fact, the attempt had failed within the hour.

Twenty-six loyal Estonians (17 military and police, and 9 civilian bystanders) were killed and 41 injured (27 military and police, and 14 civilians), and 14 rebels were killed with weapons in hand. A few days later, six more were shot as they tried to escape. A drumhead court-martial convened for the purpose by the Supreme Court sentenced 155 to be shot. In addition, 209 enemy agents were sentenced to prison terms, including 155 who got cold feet and did not actually participate in the coup but were turned in by their comrades. **Jaan Anvelt**, the leader of the coup attempt, and 198 others managed to escape to the Soviet Union. The abortive uprising destroyed the ECP: in 1930 not even a single underground cell was left in Estonia, and in 1938 it had a total of 130 members, including those serving prison sentences.

– B –

BALTIC APPEAL TO THE UNITED NATIONS (BATUN). This organization grew out of the Baltic Freedom Rally held at Madison Square Gardens in New York on 13 November 1965 with 15,000 participants. In 1966, BATUN was formed as a continuing pressure group to bring the plight of the three Baltic nations as illegal captive colonies of the Soviet Union to the attention of the member states of the United Nations (UN). BATUN is an independent voluntary organization of approximately 1,000 mainly American Estonians, Latvians, and Lithuanians, and it is supported solely by private donations. It opened an office in New York in 1967 out of which its publicity activities continue to be coordinated and conducted. At the beginning, its activities concentrated on personal contact with diplomatic representatives at the UN and the provision of printed information on the situation in the Baltic States, against considerable harassment from the Soviet Union, but with increasing support from states that found the data provided to be useful in their own criticism of the Soviet Union. Gradually, the UN press corps was also coopted as a channel for the distribution of information about the Baltic States.

In the late 1980s and through 1991, BATUN's activity level increased dramatically as the Baltic States moved toward restoration of independence. The distribution of memoranda and packets of documents to news media, nongovernmental organizations, and foreign ministries were supplemented by lobbying visits to the annual Human Rights Commission meetings at Geneva. In addition, between 1989 and 1991 BATUN assisted political figures from the Baltics to lobbying directly in New York. From 1991 to 1995, BATUN members worked as well on full-time or part-time basis for the new missions of the Baltic States to the UN. Although its activities declined as the Baltic states developed capable diplomatic services, BATUN continues to publish a Baltic chronology and Geneva Human Rights memoranda, makes twice-yearly Geneva visits, still assists the work of the Baltic UN missions in various ways, and sponsors Baltic cultural events and lectures in New York.

BALTIC BATTALION (BALTBAT). Initiated by General **Aleksander Einseln** in 1993 and launched in 1994 with the support of the Nordic countries and Great Britain, later joined by the Netherlands, France, Germany, and the United States, BALTBAT was intended to perform three functions for the three Baltic States: first, to establish a joint training and cooperative military activity for the three military forces to bring them up to Western standards; second, to provide a highly visible peacekeeping force for United Nations deployment as a demonstration of the sovereign responsibility of the Baltic; and finally, to act as a catalyst for the **defense forces** of the three Baltic States to help integrate them into West European military activities and thereby to prepare for eventual NATO membership. The latter objective was underscored in 1998 when BALTBAT's original name, "Baltic Peacekeeping Battalion," was changed to the present one. The renaming was also intended to emphasize the principle that a peacekeeper must first be a good soldier.

BALTBAT consists of trilateral headquarters, a combined logistics and headquarters company, and three infantry companies, one from each of the Baltic States. The personnel size is set at 721, one third from the professional military of each state drawn on a voluntary and contractual basis, and the rest hired professional soldiers from the three states. Although the national contingents are also intended to be part of the national forces, the fact that most of the soldiers (not officers) are purpose-hired professionals means that in practice the BALTBAT units are independent of national command structures. Although the internal language of each company is its national language, the command and communications language of the battalion is English. The command of BALTBAT rotates among the three states. Each national company is subordinated to the national government until joined under the battalion command for a specific mission or exercise.

Up to the end of 2003, the battalion had not yet participated in any mission as a unit, but companies and platoons from each national contingent had been deployed under the command of Nordic missions. Thus the Estonian company was deployed as part of the Norwegian battalion of the United Nations (UN) peacekeeping action in south Lebanon from December 1996 to June 1997, and six Estonian platoons participated on a rotating basis in Croatia and Bosnia from 1995 to 1998, attached to the Danish battalion. From 1997 to 2003, Estonian officers served on the Golan Heights' UN observer mission, and Estonian platoons served with the peacekeeping forces in Bosnia, Kosovo, and Macedonia under NATO (North Atlantic Treaty Organization) command and under U.S. command in Iraq and Afghanistan.

In 2001–02 BALTBAT underwent restructuring into a light infantry battalion with five companies: three national infantry companies, a headquarters and logistics company, and a new support company with a mortar platoon and antitank squads with state-of-the-art weaponry. The objective of the reorganization was to make BALTBAT capable of performing NATO-led Peace Support Operations, thus integrating at least a part of the Baltic forces with NATO well ahead of international political decisions to admit them as members.

BALTIC CHAIN 1989 (Estonian, Balti Kett; also sometimes Baltic Way in English). On 23 August 1989, 2 million Estonians, Latvians, and Lithuanians held hands and formed a human chain stretching 600 kilometers from **Tallinn** through Riga to Vilnius. The demonstration, organized by the Peoples' Fronts in the three states (at the time, still part of the Soviet Union), protested against the **Molotov-Ribbentrop Pact** signed 60 years earlier to the day, which granted the Soviet Union dominion over the Baltic States. The unprecedented, massive popular joint action amounted to a declaration of independence by the liberation movements in the Baltic Soviet Socialist Republics (SSR) and dramatically publicized to the world's media the determination of the Baltic peoples to free themselves form the yoke of Soviet occupation, illegally acquired by collusion between Stalin and Hitler. The protest grew out of the publication of the texts of the secret protocols of the Pact in the previous year and the adamant refusal of the Soviet Union to acknowledge their existence, which infuriated the Baltic people.

The publicity surrounding the Baltic Chain made clear that the Baltic peoples would not stand for the status quo and that they were united in their opposition to control by the Union of Soviet Socialist Republics (USSR). Moreover, the protest had been organized, not by a group of dissident outsiders, but by leading members of the Baltic communist parties who had organized the **Rahvarinne** in the previous year. Moscow refused to recognize these aspirations to freedom, and subsequently instituted economic blockades, fuel embargoes, raids by **OMON** troops, and **Interfront** counterdemonstrations by local Russian communists. Nevertheless, the Baltic Chain showed a commonness of purpose, emotionally strengthened the Balts commitment to be masters in their own home, and impressed all with the might of common popular action. In the event, the Baltic Chain proved to be the catalyst that by 1990 led to further common action and declarations by each Baltic SSR of autonomy in the Soviet Union in their transition to restored independence.

BALTIC COUNCIL (originally Council of Baltic States). In 1934 the Treaty of Understanding and Cooperation among Estonia, Latvia, and Lithuania was concluded at Geneva and signaled the beginnings of regional cooperation among the three Baltic States. However, during the ensuing six years before the Soviet annexations, little more than trilateral meetings of the foreign ministers took place.

In 1990 the transition governments and parliaments and heads of state of the three Baltic States (still within the Soviet Union) established the Council on the basis of the 1934 treaty as a forum of cooperation in their struggle to regain independence. Six decades later, during the first few years of restored independence, the revived Council created three separate fora for mutual cooperation: the Baltic Assembly for the parliaments in 1991; the Baltic Council of Ministers in 1994; and the Summit of the Presidents of Estonian, Latvia, and Lithuania, also in 1994.

The Summit of the Presidents meets once or twice a year (and has met several times in some years during the 1990s). The meetings are private and mostly off-the-record with only brief communiqués issued at the conclusion.

The Baltic Council of Ministers was formally established in its present structure in June 1994. Meetings of the heads of government are scheduled to take place at least once in winter and once in summer each year. The foreign ministers form the Meeting of Ministers for Baltic Cooperation. They meet at least once a year and are responsible for formulating the policy for the Council and assisting the prime ministers. A Baltic Cooperation Committee consisting of representatives from each government is responsible for the overall coordination and support of the Council at both national and the regional level. The secretariat for the Council is provided by the country holding the annually rotating chair. Branch ministers hold meetings on schedules determined by themselves and are based on the current Action Plan of the Baltic Council of Ministers as adopted by the prime ministers.

Once a year, a joint meeting of the Baltic Assembly and the Baltic Council of Ministers takes place under the name of the Baltic Council.

The Council operates a large number of committees, subcommittees, and working groups of senior officials on the whole range of issues of cooperation. The main areas of concern are economic integration, based on free trade and the eventual access to the European Union (the Baltic Free Trade Agreement covering industrial products came into force on 1 April 1994; free trade on agricultural products was added on 1 January 1997); and the integration of security and defense (*see* BALTIC BATTALION, BALTIC DEFENSE, *and* BALTIC DEFENCE COLLEGE). A myriad of other matters, involving taxation, customs, immigration, criminal investigation, social security, and so on, requiring cooperation and harmonization, take up the time of the branch ministers.

BALTIC DEFENCE COLLEGE (BDCOL). The BDCOL, established in 1997 as the joint highest educational institution to train senior military officers in the Baltic States, graduated its first class in June 2000. It functions as the joint defense college for the three states' **armed forces** (*see also* ESTONIAN DEFENSE FORCES). The Senior Staff Course qualifies graduates to perform duties at the level of chief of staff in military regions or infantry brigades, as well as engage in policy making and long-term planning in Central Staffs and Ministries of Defense. The thrust of the program is on international military cooperation and joint action, and it forms a seminal part of preparing the Baltic States for membership in the **North Atlantic Treaty Organization (NATO)**.

The international regional cooperative function of the BDCOL is underlined by its 16-nation contributing and supporting group, which includes, in addition to the three Baltic beneficiaries, Belgium, Denmark, Finland, France, Germany, Iceland, Netherlands, Norway, Poland, Sweden, Switzerland, United Kingdom, and the United States. The College's first commander is Danish Brigadier-General Michael Clemmesen, and the instructional and administrative staff reflects its international character; as does its first graduating class, composed of two thirds of Baltic senior officers but with representatives from Denmark, Germany, Hungary, Sweden, and the United States.

With the addition in 2001 of the Civil Servant Course, the BDCOL has become the equivalent of the national defense colleges of its supporting states. The College's administrative and teaching language is English, and it publishes the semiannual journal *Baltic Defence Review*, available on the Internet.

BALTIC DEFENSE COOPERATION. Shortly after regaining independence, the three Baltic States began to explore ways to cooperate militarily to defend their newfound sovereignty. The experience of 1938 to 1940, when Stalin first demanded forward bases in each for the Soviet Army (*see* SOVIET-ESTONIAN MUTUAL ASSISTANCE TREATY) and used them to invade and finally to annex the

Baltic States to the Soviet Union, had convinced all Balts that the only security lay in membership in the **North Atlantic Treaty Organization (NATO)**. However, their lack of **defense forces** and the opposition of Russia meant that such membership was not imminent. Thus, when General **Aleksander Einseln**, the newly appointed chief of the Estonian defense forces, himself a retired U.S. Army colonel, suggested the establishment of a joint defensive force, the (peacekeeping) **Baltic Battalion**, as a first step to build up defense forces to NATO standards and to develop a cooperative thrust, Baltic defensive cooperation began. This initiative was extended very quickly with extensive administrative, personnel, financial, and matériel assistance by Nordic neighbors of the Baltic States, other northern NATO states, and the United States, which helped to set up additional cooperative defense ventures among the three Baltic States.

Thus the **Baltic Defence College** opened its doors in 1999 in **Tartu** after three years of planning. The Baltic Squadron (BALTON), a combined multinational naval squadron, was started in 1997 with the objective of developing mine countermeasures, control of territorial seas, NATO interoperability, and international exercises and missions. BALTRON is guided by German naval assistance, and its headquarters is located at **Tallinn**. The Baltic Airspace Surveillance Network (BALTNET) is a comprehensive radar network based on the standards of the U.S. Regional Airspace Initiative and was set up with Norwegian and U.S. assistance; it is intended to be integrated with the NATO surveillance system in the future. BALTPERS is a joint Swedish-Baltic project to create a modern military mobilization registration system to enable the three armed forces to rapidly call up qualified service members in the event of an emergency. BALTSEA is a venture to coordinate Western military, security, and political assistance to the three Baltic States. *See also* GEOSTRATEGIC POSITION AND DEFENSE STRATEGY.

BALTIC GERMANS (Baltdeutsche). Until the middle of the 20th century, the commonly used term for Baltic Germans was simply "the Balts." However, since then international usage has lumped the three Baltic States together under the rubric of the "Baltics" and their ethnic nationals collectively as the "Balts." The historic usage has become anachronistic since virtually all of the Baltic German inhabitants of Estonia and Latvia were resettled in Germany in 1941, and have since become melded into the German population, and thus no longer exist as a distinct ethnic grouping.

The Baltic Germans arrived in the Estonian and Latvian regions with the Christianizing crusaders led by the Brethren of the Sword (*see* CRUSADING ORDERS) at the beginning of the 13th century and subdued the Estonian, Latvian, and Livonian tribes as they Christianized them and established the political system known by historians as Old **Livonia**. In this entity, the Germans formed the upper classes in a countryside dominated by manorial estates and in trading towns that were members of the **Hanseatic League**. Although the indigenous Estonian, Latvian, and **Liv** peasant populations were pejoratively referred to as the *Undeutsch* by their masters, the primarily German clergy of the monastic orders of the Catholic Church (Dominicans, Cistercians, Franciscans, and Order of St. Birgitta) preached in the vernacular. Although the countryside was controlled by descendants of the Crusading Knights, the Hanseatic trading towns grew into prosperous handicrafts and trading centers dominated by guilds of immigrant German merchants and artisans.

Beginning in 1520, the burghers of the Estonian trading towns were the first to convert to Lutheranism under the influence of the close ties that they had with Lutheran northern Germany, and they were followed soon by the landed gentry. The impact on the indigenous population was instantaneous as native language religious books were printed and preaching in the vernacular increased. Thus the adage *cuius regio, eius religio* ("he who rules determines the religion of the ruled") was as valid in the Baltic as in Germany proper, and the results are still evident today, as the indigenous populations of both present-day Estonia and Latvia are still nominally **Lutheran**, with but traces of Roman Catholic and Orthodox faiths.

The Baltic nobility emerged from the **Livonian War** and the conquest by Sweden with their privileges confirmed, the German language and law intact, and their councils and guilds as legitimate political bodies in the two new provinces of Estland (the northern half of present-day Estonia) and Livland (the southern half of Estonia, including **Tartu**, and about half of Latvia, consisting of the current provinces of Vidzeme and Zemgale, with Latgale and Kurzeme [Courland, Kurland] remaining in Polish hands), formed from the disintegrated Old Livonia. During the **Swedish era**, Baltic German culture developed rapidly with the founding of the **University of Tartu** (Dorpat) by Swedish King Gustavus Adolphus (Gustaf Adolf) in 1632. The result was a Baltic German intelligentsia of clergymen, university and gymnasium teachers, and government officials. Hence, the prosperous trading centers of **Tallinn** (Reval) and Riga also developed into Baltic German cultural centers, with newspapers published beginning toward the end of the 17th century, and a lively interaction carried on with German and West European intellectuals.

The Great Famine (1694–95) and the immediately following **Great Northern War** (1700–21), which devastated the indigenous **populations** of Estland and Livland, reducing them by two thirds, in contrast, had an even more positive impact on the Baltic nobility than the Swedish conquest of a century and a half earlier. A decade before the end of the war, in 1710, the principal towns of Riga, Tallinn, and **Pärnu** (Pernau) and the nobility of Livland and Estland surrendered voluntarily to Russia. In return, Tsar **Peter the Great** granted the nobility continued possession of all their lands, the right of self-government, and the supremacy of the German language and of the Lutheran church, and, moreover, confirmed existing the rights of the town councils.

The Baltic Germans returned the confidence of the tsars and played a significant role in the administrative, diplomatic, and military services of the Russian empire—no less than 69 Baltic generals served in the wars against Napoleon. Clearly, the mutual loyalty was at the root of the century and half of virtual autonomy of the Baltic provinces.

In 1795, as a result of the third division of Poland, Kurland was annexed by Russia and added as the third **Baltic province** (*gubernya*) to Estland and Livland. Although the political order in the three varied somewhat, all had a **Diet** consisting of the owners of all manorial estates. It had the right of legislative initiative, and it elected the judges and the principal police officials and the secular members of the **Lutheran** churches' governing bodies; in short, the Diets controlled all political life in the provinces. The main difference was that the Diet of the Province of Estland enjoyed the greatest autonomy from imperial interference, as a result of its historically strong independence since Swedish days, followed by Livland, and then Kurland, in which the governor, appointed by the court at St. Petersburg, controlled the local nobles' authority more closely.

Although the trading towns never regained the prosperity of the Hansa period after the disasters of the Great Northern War and the Great Famine, they nevertheless became cultural centers with schools, printing presses, theaters, libraries, bookshops, music societies, and clubs, as well as continuing as entrepôts for trade with Russia. Their cultural activities were encouraged by the closing of the University of Tartu for the whole of the 18th century, which forced the Baltic Germans to send their sons to German universities and thus led to increased interaction with the Western European cultural trends of the Enlightenment. The general **educational** level of the Baltic Germans reached new heights with the reopening of the University of Tartu in 1802, which quickly became not only a mediator between German and Russian cultures but an integral part of the 19th-century German university system. As such, it produced many outstanding scholars with Europe-wide reputations, such as the physicists J. F. Parrot and E. Lentz, the father of Russian astronomy Fr. F. G. Struwe, the chemists Carl Göbel and H. Hess, and many others.

The cultural growth was enabled not only by political autonomy but also by the modernization of manorial **agriculture** and by opening the Russian market behind tariff walls for grain, meat, and alcohol (produced by nearly all manors from potatoes).

This Baltic German cultural, political, and economic idyll where the ideals of the Enlightenment and nascent agrarian liberalism also provided personal freedom to the peasantry at the beginning of the 19th century, and the concomitant introduction of money rent, which enabled the peasants to purchase land, was destabilized by the demands of Russian nationalists to Russify the provinces as early as the 1860s in order to root out the separatist ideals of the Baltic aristocracy. In 1877, Tsar Alexander III began a systematic process of **Russification** of the peripheries of the empire with a law to replace the old city councils with elected ones based on tax rolls, and the appointment of mayors by the Ministry of the Interior. In 1888–89 the policing and judicial functions were taken over by St. Petersburg, and Russian was mandated as the language of all administration and of instruction at all schools, including at the University of Tartu.

Although the national awakening of Estonia and Latvia was led by

Baltic German intellectuals beginning in the 1860s, the majority of the aristocracy did not recognize the importance of nationalist aspirations and held themselves aloof. As a result, the 1905 revolution in Estonia was largely directed against the landed aristocracy by the growing industrial proletariat, which ransacked and burned a large number of manor houses. The harsh indiscriminate reprisals by the imperial gendarmerie and special punishment units on the perpetrators as well as on innocent Estonians contributed to widespread opposition to the Baltic Germans, who were increasingly regarded as foreign oppressors. In addition, a resurgence of Baltic German national consciousness led to the reopening of German private schools and the formation of the Baltic German Constitutional Party.

The confusion of the revolutionary year, 1917, led to an open political conflict between Estonian nationalist activists and the Baltic Germans. The attempt by some aristocrats to create German states out of the Baltic provinces during the **War of Independence** in 1918–19 led to an insurmountable chasm between the victorious Estonian and Latvian politicians and the minority Baltic Germans. In short order, the **Constituent Assembly** of Estonia confiscated the estates of the aristocracy, then divided the land among tenant farmers, war veterans, and ethnic Estonian immigrants from Russia (the so-called *optandid* in Estonian, those who had opted to return to their homeland). The former owners were left with an average of 20 hectares each (out of thousands of hectares), and often had their manor houses confiscated as well, being left with a small former servant's house. Overnight the aristocratic, wealthy, and politically and economically dominating land-owning stratum had become an impoverished historical curiosity in both Estonia and Latvia. Nevertheless, despite the catastrophe most Baltic Germans, now simple citizens, remained loyal to their historic homelands and awaited better times. Large numbers of well-educated Baltic German officials and intellectuals, industrialists, merchants, and managers continued their work and helped build independent Estonia and Latvia.

When the Law on **Cultural Autonomy** was passed in 1925, the Baltic Germans became its main beneficiaries as they expanded and established schools, newspapers, and journals and other cultural activities. The Baltic Germans also maintained a political presence of 5–8 members in the **Riigikogu** up to 1934, and constituted 22 percent of the Lutheran clergy in Estonia even as late as 1939.

The **Molotov-Ribbentrop Pact** in August 1939 brought about the final catastrophe and destroyed totally a people and culture that had developed over 700 years in Estonia and Latvia. With the Pact assigning the Baltic States to the Soviet sphere and the offer of resettlement in Germany made by the then apparently unstoppable Nazi Germany, 80,000 Baltic Germans left Estonia and Latvia in the fall of 1939 and were resettled in the former Polish lands of West Prussia, under the Nazi program of *Umsiedlung*. When the eastern German front collapsed in 1945, they had to flee again to a defeated West Germany, where they have maintained voluntary organizations among themselves but otherwise have melded into German society.

Since the restoration of independence of Estonia and Latvia, no Baltic Germans have reimmigrated, but many have visited the ruins of their former estates as tourists and a few have managed to reacquire some of their city property. All that is left of the once dominant culture in Estonia is the Gesellschaft für Deutsch-baltischen Kultur in Estland with chapters composed of Estonian Germanophile intellectuals in Tallinn and **Tartu**.

BALTIC MILITARY DISTRICT (BMD). In 1945, after the reoccupation of the Baltic States the BMD, which included these states and Kaliningrad Oblast as well as parts of Leningrad Oblast, was formed as a new territorial command unit of the Soviet armed forces. Although its headquarters were in Riga, Latvia, naval commands were subdivided among naval bases in Kaliningrad Oblast, Liepaja, Latvia, and **Tallinn**. At the restoration of independence of the Baltic States, the dismantling of the Soviet army, air, and naval bases and garrisons became protracted as the armed forces' senior commanders were reluctant to give up territory that they had fought for in World War II and viewed as a forward defensive perimeter against Western aggression. The newly expanded over-the-horizon radar system at Skrunda, Latvia (not even fully operational yet), became a major issue, which the Russian successor state's **armed forces** were extremely reluctant to give up. Eventually it was decommissioned and dismantled in 1994 with American assistance. The nuclear submarine training reactor in **Paldiski** similarly required American assistance in decommissioning and decontamination, and this delayed the final departure of the Soviet forces presence in Estonia to 1995. The Soviet forces' legacy in Lithuania continues since Kaliningrad remains the major Russian military outpost in the **Baltic Sea** littoral and requires transit arrangements across Lithuania to supply its garrison, because there is no other land link with Russia.

As the Soviet forces left, they destroyed most of the garrison buildings, and whatever was left was scavenged by local residents. Large and unsightly ruins were left littering the landscape, which will require decades and an enormous financial cost to remove. The environmental damage and soil pollution left behind by the military similarly will require a large financial input and time to heal. The third major legacy of the military occupation, the retired Soviet army personnel, created a major problem for the newly restored Baltic States as the hastily retired officers were regarded as a possible fifth column by the Balts. The problem was particularly acute in Riga, which, as the headquarters of the BMD, had tens of thousands of retired senior ranks. Colonels and higher had the right to retire wherever they wished in the Soviet Union, and many chose Riga because of its relative "Westernness," yet linguistic Russianness, where over 60 percent of the population is still Russian-speaking in the first decade of the third millennium. Although Estonia had a much smaller contingent of military retirees, the negotiations for allowing them resident status and pension payments poisoned relations between Estonia and Russia for much of the decade following the restoration of independence.

BALTIC PROVINCES. The territories of Estonia, Latvia, and Lithuania were known as the Baltic Provinces or *Gubernya* in imperial Russia, or simply as *Pribaltika*. Since achieving independence at the end of World War I, the three have been known as the Baltic States. During the Soviet occupation, they were illegally incorporated in the Union of Soviet Socialist Republics (USSR) as component Soviet Socialist Republics (SSR), such as the Estonian Soviet Socialist Republic (ESSR). Thirty-seven states never recognized this incorporation (*see* NONRECOGNITION OF SOVIET OCCUPATION). Today, many Russians still refer to the Baltic states as *Pribaltika*.

BALTIC SEA. The enclosed branch of the Atlantic bounded by Sweden, Finland, Estonia, Latvia, Lithuania, Russia, Poland, and Germany forms the western and northern boundaries of Estonia. It is connected with the North Sea by a series of narrow winding channels between the Danish islands, Jutland and Sweden, all bridged when the last, the Õresund (known as the Sound in English) bridge between Sweden and Denmark, was opened in 2000. The Baltic Sea covers an area of about 414,400 square kilometers (about 160,000 square miles). The northern extension consists of two large gulfs: the Gulf of Bothnia, between Finland and Sweden, and the Gulf of Finland, between Finland and Estonia. The Gulf of Riga is a prominent feature of the Baltic's Estonian and Latvian coasts.

The Baltic receives the drainage from a large part of northern Europe. As a result of this drainage and of the restricted channels to the North Sea, the surface water of the Baltic contains relatively little salt. Tidal action is apparent only in the southern part of the Baltic, with only about a 30-centimeter (one-foot) rise and fall along the Estonian coasts. Frequent storms often cause severe damage to ships. Navigation in the Gulf of Bothnia between Sweden and Finland is only possible in winter with the help of icebreakers. The eastern and northern coasts of the Gulf of Finland (including the ports of Helsinki and St. Petersburg) also ice over in winter. The last time the Gulf froze over completely was in the winter of 1941. However, the southwestern coast around **Tallinn** is ice-free in most winters, as is the western coast outside archipelagos hugging Estonia's west coast. Nevertheless, ferry service between the mainland and the islands of Saaremaa (and Hiiumaa) depends in winter on ferries with ice-breaking hulls, both because the shallow waters freeze and also because of drifting ice blown about by storms and currents.

For centuries, the Baltic Sea has formed Estonia's commercial and communications link with Western Europe. It is still the primary commercial route to the markets of Western Europe, although road transport through Latvia, Lithuania, and Poland is competing for truckload-size shipments. Because Tallinn's ports are ice-free, rebuilt and efficient Estonia has also managed to garner a significant share of the transit shipping to Russia, especially to the St. Petersburg region. Its main competitors in the Russian transit trade are the ice-free ports of Riga, Ventspils, and Liepaja in Latvia; Klaipeda in Lithuania; and the Russian enclave of Kaliningrad.

BALTIC UNIVERSITY. The Baltic University was established in 1946 in Hamburg in the British zone of occupied Germany by Estonian, Latvian, and Lithuanian refugee academics to enable refugee students to continue their education. In 1947, it was moved 18 kilometers north to Pinneberg in Schleswig-Holstein, where it operated until it was closed in 1949 after nine semesters during which it had granted 50 diplomas. The faculty at its height in 1947 included 53 professors, 50 docents, and 48 lecturers teaching in nine faculties: agriculture, architecture and engineering, art, chemistry, law and economics, mathematics, natural sciences, mechanics, and medicine. The student numbers reflected the emigration of the refugees from Germany: in 1946 there were 996 students, in 1947 1,052, and in 1949 only 468.

BALTIC WAY. *See* BALTIC CHAIN.

BALTS. The term "Balt" up to the 20th century was used to denote **Baltic Germans,** but after their dispossession in Estonia and Latvia in the 1920s and their final dispersal to Germany during World War II, philologists have described Latvian and Lithuanian as belonging to the "Baltic language" group within the Indo-European languages. However, popular usage in English, German, and other West European languages has designated the peoples of Estonia, Latvia, and Lithuania in common as Balts.

BANK OF ESTONIA (Eesti Riigipank). The central bank of Estonia was originally established in 1919, and reorganized in 1928 when Estonia reformed and renamed its currency the **kroon**. Its main functions were to provide short-term financing credit to the economy and to maintain the value of the currency. The bank was reestablished in 1989 and was charged by the transition government after independence in 1992 to leave the ruble zone and reintroduce the national currency, the kroon.

The bank has enjoyed strong public and parliamentary support since its reincarnation, and was given a politically independent status by act of parliament in 1993. The Bank of Estonia allowed several commercial **banks** to fail during the banking crisis of 1992–93 rather than grant them emergency loans, which increased its credibility as an independent nonpolitical entity and helped to strengthen the Estonian banking system. The bank's independence and adherence to stringent financial solvency requirements, as well as an online reporting-controlling system of the commercial banks, led to a rapid consolidation of the Estonian commercial banks. Throughout the 1990s, the central bank acted swiftly in forcing commercial banks to either declare bankruptcy or to amalgamate with more successful banks, although in the aftermath of the world financial crisis after the Russian default in September 1998, the bank did bail out two banks on a temporary basis. Nevertheless, the Bank of Estonia's policies led to such international confidence in the Estonian banking sector that in the crisis-ridden months of late 1998, two Swedish banks purchased major blocs of shares in the two leading Estonian banks (Hansapank and Eesti Ühispank—Estonian Union Bank) at premium prices. *See also* BANKING; CURRENCY BOARD.

BANKING. The rapid reestablishment of a commercial banking industry, followed by its early rationalization, was undoubtedly one of the fundamental reasons for both the growth and stability of the Estonian **economy** in the 1990s.

In 1988, when the central bank in Moscow allowed a limited type of commercial bank to be formed for the first time in Soviet history, the **Tartu** Commercial Bank was quickly formed by local Estonian state-owned enterprises. During the following year, two other such banks were formed, one owned by local state firms and the other a privatized branch of the Soviet State Export Bank. On 28 December 1988, the Estonian **Supreme Soviet** passed the Banking Act to regulate commercial banks, the first such legislation on the territory of the Soviet Union. By the end of 1990, 12 commercial banks had been formed, owned either by enterprises or privatized branches of Soviet state banks located in Estonia. After the restoration of Independence, the pace of bank formation grew rapidly to a total of 41 by the end of 1992. However, since neither the officials of the reestablished Bank of Estonia nor the managers of the commercial banks had banking experience, proper banking legislation was lacking, the Estonian economy and its currency were still part of the collapsing Soviet Union, and the operations of most of the commercial banks were chaotic. Accordingly, to facilitate the move out of the Soviet economic sphere, on 20 June 1992 Estonia established its own currency, the **kroon,** tied to the stable Deutsche mark by a **currency board** arrangement, which immediately caused a deep banking crisis owing to the inadequacy of the banks' reserves and overexposure to risk. Three major banks, among them the Tartu Commercial Bank, became insolvent and were either liquidated or merged into the new state-owned North Estonia Bank. As a result of the narrowly averted crisis of confidence in the banking sector at the beginning of 1993, the central bank set a new higher minimum share capital requirement of 6 million kroons (750,000 DM, equal to 383,000 euro) as the condition of a banking license. This immediately reduced the number of banks to 21, mostly by mergers but also as a result of several bankruptcies.

In addition, in April 1993 the central bank declared a stabilization period for the banking industry, froze the issuing of new licenses, and established more rigid reporting procedures and prudential regulations, including specifying computing principles and a requirement for the enlargement of share and equity capital. Within the year, these measures led to competition among the remaining banks and forced them to shift into retail banking. Consumer loans, leasing (mostly of automobiles), and debit as well as international credit cards were introduced. Retail competition quickly led to cost-cutting measures and electronic banking. In 1994, several Soviet-era banks disappeared because of their inability to adjust to the highly competitive environment. At the same time, confidence in the banking system was demonstrated when three Finnish banks opened branches in Estonia. In 1995, more foreign banks, including the Swedish Handelsbanken, established offices in Estonia. In the same year, the requirement to increase share capital to 50 million kroons (6.25 million DM, or 3.2 million euro) led to several mergers during the following year and the failure of one small bank, while the largest banks began to expand operations abroad. Hansabank's foray into Latvia, where it purchased Deutsch Lettische Bank in 1996, was followed by Ühispank (Unionbank) and Hoiupank, also into Latvia, after which they moved into Lithuania and then opened offices in Russia and Ukraine.

The international credibility of the Estonian banking system was enhanced when the central bank introduced a state rating system, which led Moody's to rate both Hansabank and Hoiupank as Baa2 (the lowest nonspeculative investment grade) in September 1997. In 1997–98, a few additional bankruptcies took place as did major mergers that resulted in two main banks remaining, Hansapank (Hansabank) and Eesti Ühispank (Estonian Unionbank), which together control 80 percent of the Estonian market, with four small banks dividing the remainder.

In 1999 and 2000, controlling majorities of shares (57 percent and 95 percent) of the two banks were purchased by Swebank and SEB (Skandinaviska Enskilda Banken), both of Sweden. The two groups, through their Estonian subsidiaries, are now the dominant retail bans in Latvia and Lithuania as well. The Estonian retail banking system by 2000 had leapt fully into the electronic age, with 80 percent of retail transactions carried on by Internet or telephone banking.

BIBLE. The New Testament was the first part of the Bible to be translated into Estonian and appeared in 1642 in the Tartu, or southern Estonian, dialect. The first northern Estonian version was published in 1715, with the whole Bible appearing in Estonian in 1739, translated by A. Thor Helle and H. Gutsleff.

BLACKHEADS (Mustpead, Schwarzenhäupter). In 1399 unmarried **Baltic German** merchants established the Brotherhood of Blackheads named after St. Mauritius, a black officer of the Roman Thebes legion. Blackhead brotherhoods were also formed in Riga and other Baltic trading ports. After marriage, members usually joined the Great Guild. The young and single men, full of vigor, both partied and warred with gusto. In 1441 they reputedly put up the first Christmas tree in the world in front of City Hall; decorated it in the old pagan Estonian manner; sang, drank, and danced around it; and then burned the tree as the culmination of the feast. During the **Livonian Wars** they formed a brigade to defend the city, and maintained a cavalry troop until 1787 when they reorganized it into the first voluntary fire brigade in Tallinn. It was replaced only in 1862 when the Tallinn Voluntary Fire Company was formed by concerned citizens in the rapidly industrializing city.

By 1895 industrialization and democratization had made the Brotherhood an anachronism in commerce, so they reorganized themselves as the Blackheads Club, which functioned until the Soviet occupation in 1940. Their most valuable legacy is the Blackheads' House on 26 Pikk Street in the Old Town in **Tallinn**, built in 1597 in the contemporary Renaissance style of the Low Countries. The building, full of valuable architectural carvings, bas-reliefs, portraits, and a silver collection from different periods, has survived intact. It was recently completely restored and is now a museum and site for concerts and meetings.

BOLSHEVIKS. The Russian Democratic Workers Party split in 1903 into a majority (Bolsheviks) who propagated violent revolution, and a minority (Mensheviks) who supported a parliamentary road to socialism. In 1912 the Bolshevik wing constituted itself into the Russian Socialist Democratic Workers (Bolsheviks) Party (RSDW[b]P). In March 1918 at its VII Congress, at Vladimir Lenin's insistence the Party changed its name to the Russian Communist (Bolsheviks) Party (RCP[b]) to reflect its objective—the bringing about of communism. At its XIV Congress, the Party renamed itself the Communist Party of the Soviet Union (Bolsheviks) (CPSU[b]) to reflect the new Soviet State. In 1952, the Party was renamed the Communist Party of the Soviet Union (CPSU) since the Mensheviks had long been purged and the term Bolshevik had only a historical meaning for communists. *See also* ESTONIAN COMMUNIST PARTY.

BRETHREN OF THE FOREST (Metsavennad). An anti-Soviet guerrilla movement sprang up in Estonia spontaneously with the rapid retreat of the German forces in 1944, as thousands of men who had been drafted into the German armies, and who had not managed to flee the country, sought refuge in the forests. Their numbers were supplemented by members of the **Defense League** fleeing the threat of arrest by Soviet security forces. The two mobilizations in the fall of 1944 and spring of 1945 by the occupying Soviet army prompted others to join the guerrillas. Later they were joined by still others seeking revenge against the Soviet regime for the mass deportations associated with the collectivization of March 1949.

Although their total numbers probably never exceeded 5,000, in units ranging in size from several hundred to individuals operating alone, and although they never had a coherent organization, the fact that all were veteran soldiers and that they were well equipped with abandoned German arms and later with captured Soviet munitions, and that they were fighting a desperate battle for survival in familiar home forests, meant that they were able to hold out for a decade, into the mid-1950s. The forces of the Metsavennad were concentrated in the thick forests and swamps of the eastern counties of Virumaa and Võrumaa as well as in west-central Pärnumaa. In addition to hit and run guerrilla tactics during the 1940s, in 1946–48 they fought a number of pitched battles with Soviet forces. Gradually attrition due to military casualties, living in primitive conditions hiding in forests, as well as the psychological trauma of hopelessness reduced their forces to ineffectiveness. After 1955, when the Soviet Estonian government granted an amnesty, very few stayed in the woods.

The longevity of the Forest Brethren's guerrilla action is due to the general expectation among Estonians everywhere (at home and in exile alike) during the immediate postwar years and into the 1950s that the West would sooner or later force the Soviet Union to leave Estonia either by good offices or as a result of a war between the Western democracies and the Soviet Union. Estonians just could not believe that the two systems could coexist peacefully side by side. Moreover, they believed that the idealistic West was morally bound to free the nations conquered by Stalin through no fault of their own. Thus, the Metsavennad carried on the struggle to inflict damage on the enemy, and to protect the local population from violence by the occupying forces, in the expectation of holding out until liberation would come from the West. After the forced collectivization and deportation of 1949–50, disillusionment with the West left only personal survival and revenge as the motive for carrying on guerrilla activity.

– C –

CATHERINE THE GREAT (1729–1796). Ruler of the Russian empire from 1762 to 1796. Tsarina Catherine II was born a German princess in Stettin and married Tsar Peter III, whom she succeeded as sovereign after removing him from the throne with the help of the army. She initially attempted to portray herself as an enlightened monarch who kept up a correspondence with Diderot and Voltaire, but soon proved to be a supporter of reactionary aristocratic policies, including stronger control over the peasantry. Catherine added to the empire by annexing part of Ukraine, Byelorussia, Lithuania, Courland (Kurland), and the Crimea after two wars with Turkey, when she also established the Russian Black Sea fleet.

In the Baltic provinces, her impact was mainly felt by the German nobility whose power she attempted to break by increasing central authority. She visited the Baltics in 1764 early in her rule when she made clear to the nobility that the **Baltic Provinces** were an integral part of Russia. Her governor in Riga, George Browne, implemented her experimental Enlightenment-inspired reforms of the rules governing **serfdom** in a positive manner to help the condition of the peasantry. Accordingly, in 1765 while serfs remained under the control of the landowner, they were given rights of ownership over chattels, the right to freely sell all surplus farm produce, and limitations to corvée obligations to the landowner. Upper limits to flogging by the landowner were also set. In 1783 Catherine extended central imperial administrative authority to the Baltic Provinces whereby their status was made similar to all other provinces in the empire. A single governor was appointed to rule over both provinces (Estland and Livland), and the local government organs were restructured. Participation in the **Diets** was extended to nonaristocratic landowners, all town residents were enfranchised to elect city councils, the Province of Estland was divided into four counties (Läänemaa, Harjumaa, Järvamaa, and Virumaa), the Estonian part of Livland was divided into five counties (Viljandimaa, Tartumaa, Võrumaa, Pärnumaa, and Saaremaa), and all centers of the new counties were given town status in addition to the existing ones. Thus the historically ethnic territories of Estonia had 12 towns by 1784: **Tallinn**, **Tartu**, **Narva**, **Pärnu**, Kuressaare, Haapsalu, Paide, Rakvere, **Viljandi**, Valga, Paldiski, and Võru. In addition, Catherine's reforms included the uniform taxation of all "souls" and hence the institution of a periodic census to establish lists of taxable individuals.

Catherine's reforms reducing their authority were so strongly resented by the Baltic nobility and the German burghers that in the 1796, the year of her death, her successor, Tsar Paul II, was persuaded to partially abrogate her reforms.

CHAIR OF ESTONIAN STUDIES. This was established at the University of Toronto as an endowed chair by the Estonian community of Toronto in 1986. The funds for its endowment were provided by the operating profits from the student residence at Tartu College, owned by the Estonian student fraternities and sororities in Toronto. The original objective of the chair was to form a center of studies of Estonia in the free world, and hence in the search for a chair holder the initial visiting professors were two Western historians and a sociologist of Estonian extraction. A lectureship in Estonian language and literature was also arranged in conjunction with the chair. After Estonia regained independence, the focus of the chair shifted toward strengthening the Estonian **language** and **literature** program and developing a Finno-Ugric studies program in cooperation with the endowed chairs of Hungarian and Finnish Studies. With the appointment of Jüri Kivimäe, professor of Estonian History at the **University of Tartu**, as the first permanent holder of the chair in 1999 and the continuing funding resources based on a large endowment, it is likely that the chair will develop into the prime center of Estonian cultural studies abroad. Although the Estonian language is taught in linguistic programs at several universities in Finland and in Hungary as well as occasionally at some places in the United States and France, Toronto is the only place outside Estonia that has the financial resources and community support to develop a comprehensive program of studies of Estonian culture and history.

CHRONICLES. The first written history of the Estonians and Latvians is found in three chronicles covering the 12th to the end of the 17th centuries. The *Chronicle of Hendrik* of Livonia was apparently written by a Latvian who was sent to Germany as a boy to be educated as a priest and then returned in 1203 with the German crusaders. His chronicle was written during 1225–27 when the **crusading orders** finally conquered the Estonian tribes, and it is based on his personal experiences with the crusaders. The *Livonian Rhymed Chronicle* covers much of the same period but extends into the first half century of German Teutonic Order and settler rule, to about 1290. Not much is known about its author or authors. In contrast, the authorship of *The Livonian Chronicle* of **Bathasar Russow** is well documented. His chronicle, which covers the period from the 12th century in Old

Livonia up to publication, sold out immediately when it appeared in 1579 and had to be reissued in an updated second edition in 1584.

CITIZENSHIP. In 1992 **Riigikogu** adopted the 1938 Citizenship Act, which was based exclusively on *jus sanguinis*, the principle that citizenship is passed on by blood relationship and not by *jus solis*, the principle of state of birth. Hence, only children of citizens could obtain citizenship automatically. The 1992 Act added the modification that anyone born after 21 July 1940 (the date of the formation of the Estonian Soviet Socialist Republic) to a parent who was a citizen of the Republic of Estonia in 1940 was a citizen by birth. The parent did not have to be an ethnic Estonian. An estimated 80,000 persons ethnically not Estonian obtained citizenship under this provision. The requirements for naturalization included a two-year residency period, followed by a one-year waiting period, as well as knowledge of the Estonian language. Accordingly, all those who had moved or been moved to Estonia during the Soviet occupation since 1940 became **aliens**.

In 1995 parliament adopted a new Citizenship Act, which revised the 1992 law and combined into a single statute various provisions on citizenship scattered among several pieces of legislation. It extended the residency requirement for naturalization from two to five years, specified detailed language requirements (listening, speaking, reading, and writing capability) and required knowledge of the **Constitution** and of the Citizenship Act. Aliens who had taken up legal residence in the country prior to 1 July 1990 were exempted from the five-year legal residency requirement and the one-year waiting period. The Act also allowed the government to waive the language requirement but not the civic knowledge requirements for applicants who had Estonian language elementary or higher education, or who had performed valuable service to Estonia. In December 1998 Riigikogu added a paragraph to the Citizenship Act that granted citizenship to stateless children born after 26 February 1992 to legally resident stateless parents upon application by their parents or guardians.

On 1 October 1998 the government dropped the annual quota on the issuance of residence permits to those aliens who had settled in the country prior to 1 July 1990 and who had not departed the country subsequently. Henceforth, any alien legally resident in Estonia who meets the requirements of the Act could apply for naturalization without restrictions.

The Act makes the following classes of legally resident aliens ineligible for naturalization: those filing false data or documents; those not abiding by the Estonian Constitution or not abiding by the laws of the country; those who have acted against the state and its security; those who have committed crimes and have been punished with a sentence of more than one year or who have been repeatedly brought to justice for felonies; those who work or have worked in the intelligence or security services of a foreign state; and those who have served as career soldiers in the armed forces of a foreign state, including those discharged into reserves or retired. The last category includes spouses who have come to Estonia in connection with the service member's assignment to a posting, the reserves, or retirement. An exception allows the granting of citizenship to a foreign military retiree who has been married to a native-born citizen for five years, that is, one who was born a citizen by *jus sanguinis* under the 1938 Act.

Between 1992 and the end of 2000, 113,764 persons received citizenship through naturalization. The vast majority of these (87,712) were naturalized by the end of 1996. In 1997 the Russian embassy reported that about 120,000 persons had obtained Russian citizenship; however, the embassy declined to supply the Estonian government with a list. The number of Russian citizens may be lower since the Russian embassy does not appear to keep records of those who die or leave the country. The Citizenship and Migration Board reported that by 1 August 1999, it had issued 144,631 residence permits to foreign nationals as well as 35,816 permanent and 16,180 temporary residence permits to stateless persons and military retirees of Soviet forces, who did not wish to leave Estonia. *See also* ALIEN PASSPORTS.

COAT OF ARMS OF ESTONIA. *See* NATIONAL SYMBOLS.

COLLECTIVIZATION OF FARMING. The original Communist Party objective of farm collectivization, culminating in the campaign of 1929–30 in the Union of Soviet Socialist Republics (USSR), was to destroy the conservative property-valuing mentality of the peasantry and turn them into propertyless industrial workers, instill socialist values, and make them pliable and obedient instruments of the Communist Party.

To reach this objective in Estonia, farm collectivization was carried out between June 1948 and December 1950 when 118,600 individual farms, comprising 93 percent of all farms in Estonia, were forcibly collectivized into 2,213 **kolkhozes**.

Because the **Estonian Communist Party (ECP)** leadership was reluctant to carry out Moscow's orders, it proposed instead that farmers be paid for their expropriated property and that each be left with 0.7 hectares of land for their own use, two cows, 10–15 sheep, and so on. Moscow did not even bother to reply. Moreover, because of the passive resistance of the farmers, the central organs of the Communist Party of the Soviet Union (CPSU) decided to terrorize the Estonian farmers into collective farms. Accordingly, a plan to **deport** 7,500 farm families (22,326 people) was drawn up, with a contingency reserve of 1,906 families in case all in the primary quota group could not be found. On the night of 25–26 March 1949, 20,713 farm dwellers were rounded up and deported to Siberia or Kazakhstan. They formed 2.5 percent of Estonians. The largest numbers were concentrated in the three counties of Tartu (3,392), Pärnu (2,545), and Võru (2,461). The empty buildings and properties were transferred to kolkhozes.

The terror was followed by rapid collectivization—in one and a half years, the number of kolkhozes increased fivefold, from 445 in January 1949 to 2,213 at the end of 1951. At the same time, a movement began to combine smaller kolkhozes into larger ones. By 1970 there were 292 kolkhozes with an average of 205 members, and in 1986, 143 with an average of 371 members. The cultivated areas of the kolkhoz in these two years averaged 1,314 hectares and 2,905 hectares, respectively. In contrast, in the USSR as a whole the corresponding numbers were very much larger: in 1970 33,000 kolkhozes, with average memberships of 506 cultivating 3,003 hectares; and in 1986 26,300 kolkhozes, with average memberships of 3,480 cultivating 3,480 hectares. The average kolkhoz productivity in the Estonian Soviet Socialist Republic (ESSR) rose fourfold between 1970 and 1986, from 620,000 rubles to 2,432,000 rubles per kolkhoz, in contrast to the average USSR kolkhoz, where the income declined from 691,000 rubles to 620,000 rubles per kolkhoz. *See also* AGRICULTURE.

CONSTITUENT ASSEMBLY (Asutav Kogu). This was elected by a secret ballot on 5–7 April 1919, called by the **Estonian provisional government** in the midst of the **War of Independence**, after the Red armies had been driven from Estonia but before the decisive defeat of the German **Landeswehr** by Estonian forces. The Assembly was elected by proportional representation with a participation rate, including soldiers at the front, of 80 percent, high at any time but remarkably so given that the War of Independence was still ongoing. Left and Center parties won the elections as follows:

Party	*% Votes*	*Seats*
Left		
Social Democrats	33.3	41
Independent Socialists	5.8	7
Center		
Labor Party	25.1	30
National Party	20.7	25
Right		
Christian National Party	4.4	5
Agrarian League	6.5	8
Ethnic minorities	3.8	4
Others	0.4	0
Total	100.0%	120

The Constituent Assembly met on 23 April 1919 and elected the Social Democrat **August Rei** as chair. On 9 May 1919, the provisional government resigned and was replaced by a cabinet headed by Labor Party Prime Minister **Otto Strandman**, which won the confidence of the Assembly and thus became the first fully democratically elected government of Estonia. On 15 May, the Assembly by unanimous vote reaffirmed the **Declaration of Independence** (with the Russian and German minority representatives abstaining), aimed primarily at the international community in a bid for recognition of Estonia as an independent state. On 4 June 1919 it adopted a temporary Constitution; on 10 October 1919 it passed the Land Reform Act, by which the property of the **Baltic German** landowners was confiscated and redistributed among the landless; on 13 February 1920 it ratified the **Peace Treaty of Tartu**, which had been signed on 2 February between Estonia and the Russian Soviet Socialist Republic (RSSR); and on 15 June 1920 it adopted the ultraliberal first **Constitution** of Estonia. The Constituent Assembly disbanded itself on 20 December 1920 after the Constitution had entered into effect, and the first **Riigikogu** elections had been held.

CONSTITUTION OF 1920. During the brief period of its first independence of 22 years, Estonia had three Constitutions and six years of constitutional void when an authoritarian regime ruled. These have left a legacy that is still not resolved despite the adoption of the fourth **Constitution in 1992**.

The first Constitution of 1920 could be characterized as populistic since it gave formal sovereignty to the people. It resembled most closely the Swiss and the Weimar Constitutions, although the drafting Constituent Assembly had studied the American and French Constitutions as well. The sovereign power of the people was exercised by a single-chamber parliament styled the **Riigikogu** (literally, State Assembly), a name that continues in use, elected for a fixed three-year period at a single-stage general election by secret ballot using a form of the d'Hondt proportional representation (PR) system to determining the allocation of seats among parties (*see also* RIIGIKOGU ELECTIONS). All citizens at least 20 years of age had the right to vote and stand for election. Twenty-five thousand citizens could demand a referendum on any matter, and 25,000 citizens could also initiate legislation. Constitutional amendments had to be passed by referendum. The executive power resided in a government (*Valitsus*) appointed and responsible to the Riigikogu, led by the prime minister who was styled *Riigivanem* (state elder). The Riigikogu had total power over the government—it could express lack of confidence in the whole government or any of its members and thus force collective or individual resignations. However, the Riigikogu could not dismiss itself and call new elections within its fixed three-year mandate. There was no head of state; its functions were divided among the speaker of Riigikogu, the prime minister, and the government (cabinet) as a whole, with the Riigivanem functioning as the representative of the state externally and for diplomatic purposes. The Constitution granted citizens the usual democratic civil rights, which could be suspended by parliament only when it declared a state of national defensive emergency.

The first Constitution functioned well during the period of economic stability in the 1920s, but when the World Depression hit Estonia shortly after 1930 the economic destabilization caused a sharpening of conflict among social strata and led to political instability, which caused a constitutional crisis, the more so since the original Constitution had been an expression of the idealism and ultraliberal optimism of the political Center and Left represented in the Constituent Assembly in 1919–20.

CONSTITUTION OF 1933. The World Depression reached Estonia in 1929–30, created economic challenges, and led to a protracted political crisis that the fused executive and legislative power of **Riigikogu** created by the ultrademocratic **Constitution of 1920** could not solve. Between 1929 and 1932 there were six governments, and there were four in 1932 alone. According to the Right, a Finnish- or German-type independently elected president with executive powers independent of parliament would solve the problem. Two such proposed amendments were defeated by referenda in 1932 and 1933, owing to the very strong opposition of the political Left, the first being defeated by less than 1 percent of the 90.5 percent of the electorate participating. The second proposal was regarded by the Right as weakening the executive powers and pandering too much to the Left and was defeated by a vote of 67.3 percent to 32.7 percent with the participation of only 66.5 percent of a disillusioned electorate. Within months, however, the League of **Veterans** of the **War of Independence** entered the political arena, proposed a third variant, organized support for it, and won the vote 72.7 percent to 27.3 percent with the participation of 77.9 percent of the electorate.

The amendments to the Constitution of the October 1933 referendum transformed the institution of Riigivanem (however, not titled president as in the first proposal) from being merely the head of government responsible politically and constitutionally to the Riigikogu, to an independent office elected directly by the people for a five-year term, with the authority to appoint and dismiss the prime minister and cabinet. He could also dissolve the Riigikogu, now reduced from 100 to only 50 members, at will and call new elections. The head of state was given suspensive veto powers over acts of the Riigikogu and could also rule by decree in "case of urgent state necessity" when parliament was not in session. The referendum also removed local self-government from the counties and made them creatures of the central government with the appointment of prefects responsible to the national government.

The amended Constitution, now called the Constitution of 1933, was proclaimed and took effect on 24 January 1934. However, the new Constitution did not solve the political crisis but brought about the suspension of democracy instead. *See* PREEMPTIVE COUP.

CONSTITUTION OF 1937. The **preemptive coup** of 1934 did not solve the constitutional crisis in Estonia. The Constitution proclaimed in 1933 did not reflect the reality of political forces in Estonia. Hence, Riigivanem **Konstantin Päts** declared in January 1935 that a new constituent assembly must be called to draft a new Constitution. In January 1936 he proposed calling together a two-chamber National Assembly (Rahvuskogu) to solve the question of the form and substance of the Constitution. In the referendum of 23–25 February 1936, his proposal was carried by a vote of 474,218 to 148,824. Its first or lower chamber was to be elected in nonpartisan elections (political party activities were outlawed) by direct first-past-the-post elections in 80 single-member districts. However, in protest against the restrictions on party activities, the opposition boycotted the elections. As a consequence, in 50 districts there was only one candidate who was acclaimed elected. In the remaining 30 districts, elections took place on 12–14 December 1936. The 40 members of the second or upper chamber were appointed by selection by corporate entities such as chambers of professional bodies, municipal governments, courts, universities, churches, national minorities, and so on, and 10 were appointed by the Riigivanem. Clearly the National Assembly was composed of Päts's supporters. It convened on 18 February 1937 and discussed a proposal drafted according to Päts's directives. A new constitutional draft was adopted on 28 July 1937 by the National

Assembly and was proclaimed by the president on 17 August 1937 when the Assembly also dissolved itself. The new Constitution entered into effect on 1 January 1938.

The new Constitution further reduced the power of the people by removing the right of citizens to initiate legislation (this had remained in the 1933 Constitution). The right to nominate candidates for president (now so named) was restricted to the two chambers of Riigikogu and the 120-member chamber of representatives of municipal governments. If more than one candidate was nominated, he or she was to be elected by the electorate at large, but if there was only one candidate then he or she was to be elected at a joint meeting of the parliament's two chambers together with the chamber of municipalities. The president was to hold office for six years, and his or her powers were extensive: the president had the right to appoint and dismiss the cabinet or any of its members, and to dismiss parliament and call new elections. The president proclaimed bills of parliament into law and had a suspensive veto over them. He or she had the power to issue decrees between sessions of parliament if they were required by "urgent state need." However, parliament had the right to amend or to declare such decrees void.

Parliament (still named **Riigikogu**, literally State Assembly) now consisted of two chambers. The 80-member lower chamber, the Riigivolikogu (Chamber of Deputies), was elected for a five-year period on the majority principle. Citizens who were 22 years of age or older had the right to vote, and 25-year-old citizens had the right to stand for election. The 40-member upper chamber, Riiginõukogu (State Council), was formed for a five-year period and consisted of 10 members appointed by the president, six ex officio members, and 24 selected by various corporate bodies. According to official propaganda at the time, the new Constitution represented a balance of power among the three bodies of president, parliament, and cabinet. At the time of the elections to the new Riigivolikogu, only one party was allowed, the Põhiseaduse Elluviimise Rahvarinne (National Front for the Implementation of the Constitution), organized to support the new Constitution at the elections. Despite restrictions on party activity, the opposition received 26 seats to the Rahvarinne's 54. On 24 April 1938, Konstantin Päts, being the only candidate, was elected president by a joint meeting of the Riigivolikogu, the Riiginõukogu, and the chamber of municipal representatives, according to the provisions of the new Constitution.

CONSTITUTION OF 1940 OF THE ESSR. This Constitution was adopted by the puppet parliament formed by the Soviet occupation forces, which formed the Estonian Soviet Socialist Republic (ESSR), annexed it to the Union of Soviet Socialist Republics (USSR), and imposed the principles of the 1936 Soviet Constitution on Estonia. According to it, Estonia was a workers' and peasants' socialist state; its political foundation rested on the workers' soviets as organs of the dictatorship of the proletariat; and the economic system of the state was to be socialist and the means of production were to be socialist in ownership (state and cooperative). Everything of economic value—land, all natural resources (including bodies of water and forests), larger factories, mines, rail, water and air transport, banks, communications, agricultural enterprises organized by the state (**sovkhozes**, machine and tractor stations, and so on), and communal enterprises, as well as apartment buildings, were all declared to be owned by the state. Only individual peasant homesteads and artisans' individual workshops were allowed in special zones delineated by exceptional laws. Economic activity was to be determined and operated by state planning.

The Constitution implemented Soviet legal norms for the ESSR. Citizens of the ESSR were declared citizens of the USSR. The Constitution acknowledged the leadership role of the Communist Party, and established the single-chamber **Supreme Soviet** of the ESSR as the highest state legislative organ, elected for four-year terms, on the basis of one member per 10,000 citizens. The Council of People's Commissars was to be the highest executive organ in the state. Ministries were disbanded and replaced by People's Commissariats, some with republican jurisdiction and others subsidiary to the All-Union government. Local government was to be handled by county, city, township, and village working people's councils and executive committees. The Constitution formally established citizens' basic rights as they corresponded with workers' interests and as they secured the socialist order. All 18-year-olds had the right to vote. Candidates could be nominated by workers' social organizations, trade unions, cooperatives, and youth and cultural associations. The Constitution also implemented the Soviet symbols as the state symbols of ESSR: the red flag, hammer and sickle, and the five-pointed red star. Although the ESSR formally had status as a sovereign state and even had the right to secede from the USSR, in practice it was an integral part of the centrally ruled USSR with very limited autonomy. Later several amendments were added. In 1953, for example, the declaration of the total and final victory of socialism was included in the ESSR Constitution.

CONSTITUTION OF 1978 OF THE ESSR. The second Constitution of the Estonian Soviet Socialist Republic (ESSR) was adopted by the ESSR Supreme Soviet on 13 April 1978. This Constitution brought the ESSR into line with the new Constitution of the Union of Soviet Socialist Republics (USSR) adopted on 7 October 1977. It contained no fundamental changes, but was primarily an attempt at modernizing some of the language. Thus the authority of the state was to be based on the principle of democratic centralism, and the Communist Party was stated to be the leading force of society and had the function of determining the direction of development of the state. The economic foundation of the ESSR was to be the socialist economic system and the ownership of the means of production was to be based on the principle of socialism. Three forms of ownership were distinguished: state ownership, **kolkhoz**-cooperative ownership, and ownership held by social organizations. The kolkhoz-cooperative was to approximate public ownership, that is, kolkhozes were gradually to become public or state enterprises and, like the **sovkhozes**, to be directly owned by the state instead of by the members as hitherto. Personal or individual ownership was permitted as long as it was the result of income from work. Individual enterprise was permitted in **agriculture**, handicrafts, and services (of a personal nature, such as hairdressing and shoe repair) as long as it was regulated by the state. The basis of the social organization of the ESSR was to be a triadic union of workers, the peasantry, and the intelligentsia. The Constitution propagated the idea of creating a monolithic single-class (and thus classless) society where all would be workers with agricultural work designated merely a branch of industry so that the peasants would become just industrial workers. This, of course, was the long-term objective of Marxist-Leninist ideology, and was now fixed in the Constitutions of the member states of the Soviet Union—barely 13 years before their collapse.

The Constitution laid down the rights and duties of citizens and granted citizens of the ESSR simultaneous citizenship of the USSR. Similarly, all citizens of the USSR living in the ESSR had all the civil rights of ESSR citizens. Hence, Estonian SSR citizenship was in practice meaningless—all were citizens of the USSR. Citizens had all the usual rights and the right to join any social organization or association as long as it was based on the "objective of building communism." The sovereignty of the Estonian SSR was supposedly demonstrated by the constitutional right to secede from the USSR.

The **Supreme Soviet** of the ESSR was now to be elected for five-year terms (four years previously), with the franchise unchanged at 18 years of age. The Supreme Soviet of the ESSR elected its Presidium (which exercised the rights of the SS between its twice-yearly sessions) and the Supreme Court of the ESSR, and it appointed the Council of Ministers of the ESSR. The legal competence of the ESSR Supreme Soviet was to be subordinated to that of the All-Union Supreme Soviet since the laws passed by the latter took precedence.

The Constitutions of the Soviet Union and its subordinate republics were of little importance since they were paid scant heed and in any case could be changed easily by a majority vote. All power was exercised by the Politburo of the Communist Party of the Soviet Union, physically located in the Kremlin, with the constitutional democratic forms mere window dressing. The modernization of the language in the Constitution, for example, meant the expurgation of the term "dictatorship of the proletariat" that had featured prominently in the 1940 Constitution.

CONSTITUTION OF 1992. The fourth Constitution of the independent Republic of Estonia was the legally decisive instrument in the restitution of the Republic with constitutional democratic governing structures and powers. The draft Constitution was prepared by the **Constitutional Assembly** appointed for that purpose jointly by the **Supreme Council** and the **Estonian Congress.** The Supreme Council of the Republic decided on 22 April 1992 to submit it to a referendum and on 13 May adopted a resolution to implement the new

Constitution and submit this also to referendum together with the draft Constitution. In the constitutional referendum on 28 June 1992 the electorate, consisting of all those who had been citizens of Estonia prior to the Soviet annexation and their direct descendants, numbering 669,080, adopted the Constitution with a vote of 407,867 in favor, 36,708 against, and 2,694 spoiled ballots. The new Constitution became effective on 29 June 1992 as determined by the implementation referendum.

The preamble of the Constitution emphasizes the principle of constitutional continuity of the Estonian Republic and establishes itself as the direct successor to the Constitution of 1938. The content of the new Constitution is modeled on both the **1920** and the **1938 Constitutions** and also reflects the contemporary constitutions of Western democracies. This Constitution clearly differs from its predecessors in its almost strident desire to differentiate independent democratic Estonia from the half century of Soviet occupation. Thus article 1 in Chapter I: General Provisions, declares that "Estonia is an independent and sovereign democratic republic wherein the supreme power is held by the people." Furthermore, "Estonian independence and sovereignty is interminable and inalienable." Article 4 establishes the principle of separation and balancing of the powers of parliament, president, and the courts. Article 6 makes Estonian the official **language** of the country.

In Chapter II: Fundamental Rights, Liberties and Duties, pride of place goes to the establishment of Estonian citizenship (article 8), anchored in *jus sanguinis.* The rights chapter runs to 47 articles (articles 8–54) and includes a detailed listing of every conceivable civil right expected in modern democracies. Thus, the Constitution marks a clear break with the Soviet era.

The right of the people of Estonia to exercise their supreme power is to be carried out by those who have the right to vote (aged at least 18 years) by electing the **Riigikogu** and by participating in referenda (articles 56–57).

A 101-member single-chamber parliament (Riigikogu) is to be elected for a four-year period on the principle of proportionality (article 60). The head of state is the president, elected for a five-year period by the Riigikogu. Each candidate for president must be nominated by at least one fifth of the membership of the Riigikogu. The winning candidate must receive a two-thirds majority vote of the Riigikogu in either the first or the second rounds of voting on two successive days. If no candidate receives the required minimum of votes, a third round of voting will take place between the two leading candidates on the second day after the second vote. Should neither candidate still receive the required two-thirds majority, then the speaker of the Riigikogu shall convene an electoral college within one month, consisting of the members of the Riigikogu and representatives of the local governments. The electoral college shall then elect the president by a simple majority (article 79). No person may be elected to the office for more than two consecutive terms (Art 80) (*see also* ELECTION OF THE PRESIDENT).

The president has a 14-day suspensive veto right over legislation. If the Riigikogu then passes the law, the president has the option of proclaiming it or sending it to the Supreme Court asking that it declare the law in conflict with the Constitution (article 107). The president, together with the cosignatures of the speaker and the prime minister, has the right to issue edicts on matters of urgent public interest when Parliament is prevented from convening. Such edicts must be presented to Parliament for ratification when it convenes. The requirement that the prime minister, cabinet, and cabinet ministers individually retain the confidence of Parliament follows the standard Nordic practice.

However, it should be noted that the fundamental constitutional conflict of the form of the government of Estonia has not been settled yet: proposals are perennially raised in parliament that the president be directly elected, thus deviating from the purely parliamentary form of government. That the fundamental issue of an executive versus a largely ceremonial head of state is still of relevance after first being raised in the original **Constituent Assembly** in 1919 is due both to the record of political instability of the whole history of the Estonian state and the immaturity and lack of depth of Estonia's democratic culture.

CONSTITUTIONAL ASSEMBLY OF 1991 (Põhiseduslik Assamblee). The transitional **Supreme Council** of the Republic of Estonia and the **Estonian Congress** agreed to form a representative organ of 60 members divided equally between them with the function of drafting the new Constitution for the newly restored republic, since it was universally agreed that the three prewar Constitutions were dated and therefore unsuitable. To maintain political and legal continuity, the Supreme Council established the rules on 3 September 1991 for the selection of the members, rules of procedure, and the objectives of the Constitutional Assembly. Two days later, on 5 September, it elected 30 of its members to the Constitutional Assembly. On 7 September, the VI Session of the Estonian Congress similarly elected its 30 representatives.

On 13 September, the Constitutional Assembly began its work and completed its first draft Constitution on 21 December. The primary dispute concerned the role of the president and whether to elect him directly by popular vote or indirectly by **Riigikogu**. In the event, the decision was made to follow the pure parliamentary model. Nevertheless, the Assembly presented a revised version to the Supreme Council on 18 February 1992, to which it later added corrections. The draft bill was published on 28 March. After representations by the public, the Constitutional Assembly made additional amendments. On 10 April 1992, the Constitutional Assembly disbanded, and on 20 April the Supreme Council decided to submit the Draft Constitution to a referendum on 28 June 1992. The Constitution was adopted by an overwhelming majority and entered into effect the very next day, on 29 June 1992. *See* CONSTITUTION OF 1992.

CORRUPTION. Although corruption was as endemic in the Estonian Soviet Socialist Republic (ESSR) in 1991 as elsewhere in the Union of Soviet Socialist Republics (USSR), by 1998 when Transparency International first included the Central and Eastern European states in its annual Corruption Perception Index, Estonia had rooted out most corrupt practices. Indeed, Estonia placed ahead of Belgium, Italy, and Greece, and has remained among the 30 least corrupt states (of almost 200) in the world, at about the level of France, Spain, and Portugal. Estonia and Slovenia are the only former Soviet satellites or members of the USSR that place among the least corrupt at the beginning of the 21st century.

As the Soviet state lost authority, those in positions of power in government, **agriculture**, and **industry** used the confusion, the collapse of the economy, and the lack of understanding of the rules that make the market economy work to arrogate (in fact, steal) economic units from the state, first by "renting" them under Mikhail Gorbachev's liberalizing state control of the economy. They then stripped the assets and then acquired the shell for its disposal value, and bought or started other businesses with the ill-gotten gains. In addition, **banks** were founded with state property as assets and then stripped.

All these methods were used in Estonia from 1988 to 1993, when a major shift took place. After receiving the largest number of seats in the **Riigikogu elections of 1992**, **Mart Laar** of the Pro Patria Party formed a cabinet of young politicians without Communist Party pasts. The government, heavily influenced by the liberal market concepts of British Prime Minister Margaret Thatcher and in a hurry to create a wealthy modern economy, set about creating the conditions for it by authorizing the independent **Bank of Estonia** to impose stricter rules and begin to rein in the predatory "Wild West" banking system typical in all of the newly independent countries, thus also quickly eliminating laundering of illegal Russian foreign earnings. The government set up an independent Treuhand-type **privatization** process by which state enterprises were sold to the highest national or international bidder. They also reorganized the **courts**, fired all Soviet-era judges, and began a review of the faulty real property laws passed since 1999. Most important, the youthful Laar cabinet broke the network of the Soviet-era *nomenklatura* by appointing new, untainted, young civil service department heads. The succeeding cabinets of **Tiit Vähi** and **Mart Siiman** followed these initiatives and refined efficiency by requiring online weekly reporting by banks and businesses on transactions, thus ensuring very high rates of tax compliance of the value-added tax (VAT) as well as income and social taxes. Customs controls, usually a major source of corruption, were progressively tightened by requiring import manifests to be cleared by fax prior to arrival at border inspection stations; in any case, Estonia's free-trade regime meant that little apart from VAT payments and health and environmental regulations needed to be approved. Uncorrupted, well-trained customs personnel applying regulations effectively also closed the international Estonian transit corridor between the West and Russia for car theft. Traffic police, another source of petty but socially damaging corruption, was gradually replaced by the central training of new police officers, requiring traffic fines to be paid into banks and all appeals to be handled by mail only, thus radically reducing personal contacts between offenders and individual police.

Two highly visible actions helped to signal the political elites' will to eliminate corruption: the willingness of the Vähi government to continue to prosecute former ESSR Prime Minister **Indrek Toome** for bribery; and the shooting "war" on organized crime, mostly foreign Russian "mafia" groups, that then Minister of the Interior **Edgar Savisaar** successfully waged in 1995. As a result, bribery in the national public service has all but disappeared, and organized international crime is limited to drug running.

However, in 2003 Estonia was still a long way behind Finland and the other Nordic countries, which are at the very top of perceptions of uncorruptedness. The relatively large number of **local governments** with old-line civil servants still provided opportunities for a variety of corruption such as petty bribery, self-serving by-laws, and misuse of public funds. In **Tallinn** and the national governmental levels, influence peddling and conflict-of-interest abuses (e.g., letting contracts secretly to relatives) still arose, and under-the-table "envelope" wage payments in the construction industry continued, albeit at a reduced rate.

In 2003 the cabinet of **Juhan Parts**, filled with new, enthusiastic, first-time reforming politicians, removed the last visible vestiges of power. Henceforth only the president (for state representation purposes) and prime minister (for security demands) would have state-provided cars—the approximately 200 personal cars provided by taxpayers were sold, and ministers and senior public servants were henceforth reimbursed for public service use of own cars. State apartments leased at nominal rents to various public servants were eliminated, and all politicians and public servants had to find their own accommodations and pay for them.

Despite the vast progress toward a corruption-free country, Estonians still criticized their political and economic elites for corruption, partly because the free press publicizes extensively every case of conflict of interest, and a number of sensational cases of bank fraud from the early 1990s slowly worked their way through the courts between 1997 and 2003.

COUNCIL OF BALTIC SEA STATES (CBSS). A consultative organization, the CBSS was formed in March 1992 by the foreign ministers of Estonia, Finland, Latvia, Lithuania, Norway, Poland, Russia, Sweden, and a member of the European Commission at a meeting in Copenhagen called by the Danish and German foreign ministers who wished to obviate the power vacuum in the region resulting from the collapse of the Soviet Union. (Iceland joined in 1996.) The ministers agreed that the Council of the Baltic Sea States should serve as an overall regional forum focusing on the need for intensified cooperation and coordination among the states surrounding the Baltic Sea. The aim of the cooperation should be to achieve democratic development in the Baltic Sea region and a greater unity among the member countries as well as to secure their favorable economic development.

The work of the CBSS is carried on by the Committee of Senior Officials (CSO), composed of representatives from each foreign ministry, between annual meetings of foreign ministers. Since 1998, a secretariat located in Stockholm has assisted the CSO. The presidency of the CBSS rotates annually. Summit meetings of heads of government have also taken place every two years since the first meeting in Visby in 1996.

Since the CBSS is not an intergovernmental organization established by treaty, it cannot make legally binding decisions and performs only a consultative function. Its importance for Estonia has been to provide a forum for developing its regional foreign policy and its diplomatic skills. That Estonia was able to chair the CBSS in its second year, 1993–94, was made possible by the "troika" arrangement whereby both the outgoing and the next chair assist the current chair holder. Thus, Estonia was assisted by Finland, the first chair, and Poland, the next chair. Estonia's successful year, coming only two years after regained independence, did much to build its reputation on the international scene. Subsequently, Estonian policy makers, with Foreign Minister **Toomas Ilves** in the lead, have periodically stated that they would rather be members of the Nordic Council, which is an intergovernmental organization consisting of Denmark, Finland, Iceland, Norway, and Sweden, and which operates as a law-harmonizing body at both parliamentary and ministerial levels.

The CBSS has assisted in coordinating assistance to the Baltic

States in a number of regional activities, such as customs, immigration and border controls, a regional environmental study of the Baltic Sea basin, encouraging tourism, and studying economic development. However, its highest profile activity is that of the "Commissioner on Democratic Institutions and **Human Rights**, including the Rights of Persons Belonging to Minorities." In 1994 Professor Ole Espersen, a former Danish minister of justice, was appointed to the awkwardly titled office to meet Russian as well as Western concerns about the treatment of the Russian-speaking minorities in Estonia and Latvia. Espersen, something of a maverick, in each of his annual reports also criticized the Western members' treatment of their minorities and immigrants. In 2000 the mandate was changed, the title of the office was shortened to "Commissioner of Democratic Development," and Helle Degn, a former Danish government minister, was appointed to succeed Espersen. Denmark has assumed the costs of the office from its inception.

COUNCIL OF MINISTERS (Ministrite Nõukogu). This was the name of the cabinet of the government of the Estonian Soviet Socialist Republic (ESSR). Its prime minister was selected by the first secretary of the **Estonian Communist Party** with the approval of the Party leaders in Moscow, and thus was always a "trusty" of the Politburo. By an act of 16 December 1989, the Estonian **Supreme Council** replaced the Council of Ministers with the "government" (*valitsus*) to differentiate Estonia from the Soviet Union and to conform with Western terminology. Subsequently, "government" is also officially translated into English as the Cabinet. Until the name change, the role of the Council of Ministers was primarily administrative. It had no power. Whatever political power resided in the ESSR was jointly exercised by the Bureau (the ECP equivalent of the Politburo of the Communist Party of the Soviet Union, CPSU) and the Presidium of the Supreme Soviet of the ESSR.

COURTS. The first court in Estonia was the *vakukohus*—a court apparently held in conjunction with the regular meetings of a *vakk* or *vakus* (3–6 villages) in prehistoric ancient Estonia. By the time of the Crusades, the *vanematekohus* (court of elders), consisting of the leaders (*seniores* in Latin) of the *kihelkond,* a historically formed defensive alliance consisting of a number of villages with a fort as its center, where the elders met in council, was institutionalized. Although its primary function was political consultation for defensive purposes, the *vanematekohus* also carried out judicial functions. At the end of the 13th century, there were 45 *kihelkonda* (plural form) in Estonia. The closest early medieval parallel is the Germanic *Gau.* These in turn formed a *maakond* (county). With the coming of Christianity, the historic *kihelkond* was divided among the local churches and thus became smaller as well as coterminous with the church and thus is translated into English as "parish." There were 59 *kihelkonda* at the end of the 13th century, 83 at the end of the 16th, 102 at the end of the 17th, and 107 in 1925, when the civil *kihelkond* was abolished and church administration became confessional.

After the colonization of Livland and Estland, the *vakus* as an administrative unit continued until the 17th century: the farmers in the historic *vakus* of 3–6 villages came together 2–4 times a year to pay their taxes, after which a feast for feudal lords would be held and disputes among farmers would be settled by the *vakukohus* conducted by the bailiff (in areas of freeman farmers) or the noble landlord (on estates with tenant farms) with 3–6 freeman farmers or tenant farmers, respectively, sitting as assessors.

Over time, separate courts developed for the city burghers and for the aristocracy. Courts and court systems were also created and changed depending on suzerain or ruler. **Catherine the Great**, for example, changed the court system in 1783–97, but her successor, Paul III, reversed the structure of the system in the **Baltic Provinces.** The **Lutheran** Church had its own court system. Most of the courts did not affect the indigenous peasant inhabitants, invariably referred to pejoratively as *Undeusch* by the **Baltic German** nobility. Note that the burghers were also nearly all Germans until the industrialization of the late 19th century.

The modern system of courts in Estonia may be traced to the great court reform instituted by **Alexander I** in the Russian empire in 1864. This, however, was only carried out in modified form in the Baltic Provinces in 1889 since it was delayed by the Baltic nobles, owing to the special status known as the **Special Baltic Order**, that they had been given by **Peter the Great** after his conquest of the Swedish Baltic provinces in the **Great Northern War**.

The formation of the *vald* or township, the basic unit of local government equivalent to the modern commune in the Nordic countries, began in different parts of the Baltic Provinces during the late 18th and early 19th centuries and increased after the abolition of land indenture. The estate court (which had gradually replaced the *vakukohus* as the nobles dispossessed the freedmen during the disasters and wars of the 17th century) was replaced by the *vallakohus*, consisting of a panel of 3–6 judges elected from among themselves by the peasants, to handle civil disputes among themselves, as well as local minor breaches of the peace. In the Province of Estland, it was known as the *kogukonnakohus* until 1866 and in reality amounted to little more than an estate court, since the *vald* was liquidated in 1817 and not reestablished until 1866.

The *kihelkonnakohus* was established in 1803 as a court of first instance for peasants' accusations against administrators and noble landlords, and it consisted of a panel of three estate owners. When the *vald* was reestablished uniformly as the basic administrative unit across the Province of Estland in 1866, the *vallakohus* was regularized as the court of first instance for the farmers, and the *kihelkonnakohus* became a court of appeal and consisted of a landed aristocrat as chair with two peasants as assessors. In the Province of Livland, it had operated already as such since 1804 but with three peasant assessors.

The administrative reform of 1889 swept away the system of *kihelkonnakohus*, as well as all feudal courts, including those of the nobility, the burghers, and the Tartu Õuekohus (*see* SUPREME COURT). The new system divided the Estonian area of the Provinces of Estland and Livland (*see* BALTIC PROVINCES) into 34 districts of courts of first instance (*rahukohus*; literally, peace court, magistrates court dealing with breaches of the peace and nonfarm civil disputes, and five courts of first instance and minor appeal *rahukohtu ringkond* or district court), where two, the **Tallinn** Ringkonnakohus and the Riga Ringkonnakohus, also functioned as superior courts of appeal for the Estland and Livland provinces, respectively. Decisions from these could be appealed to the Kohtupalat (court of appeal) at St. Petersburg. In certain cases, final appeals could be made to the Senate, the highest political organ advising the tsar.

As part of the reforms, commissioners were appointed to oversee the administration of the self-governing *vald*, with power to bring action in the courts. However, the institution of the *vallakohus* as a civil court with jurisdiction over disputes among peasants was retained, and a new system of 16 civil courts of appeal from these for the peasantry, the *ülemtalukohus* (superior farm court), for the Estonian parts of the two provinces was established. The language of all courts, except the peasants' civil courts, was Russian.

After the confusion of the Russian Revolution and German occupation in 1917–18, independent Estonia reorganized its courts into a four-tier system based on the inherited structure. At the local level, the *rahukohus*, later renamed the *jaoskonnakohus* (division court), handled minor civil, criminal, and administrative issues. These courts took over the functions of both the *vallakohus* and the *ülemtalukohus*. The *ringkonnakohus* (district court) was both a court of first instance in serious criminal and civil matters and an appeals court from division courts, and it carried on the functions of the tsarist courts of the same name. The new court of appeals (Kohtukoda), divided into civil and criminal chambers, took appeals only from the district courts. It took over the functions formerly performed by imperial court of appeals in St. Petersburg. Final appeals from both the district courts and the court of appeal were handled by the new Supreme Court (Riigikohus, literally state court), which was divided into criminal, civil, and administrative chambers. It replaced the imperial Senate, which in tsarist times handled final appeals. In addition, there was a system of military courts.

The reorganization of the court system was piecemeal; thus, it was not until two years before the Soviet annexation that the Supreme Court's structure was finally fixed by law. The annexation and occupation of the Republic of Estonia in 1940 resulted in the immediate liquidation of the Supreme Court. The Estonian legal order was forcibly replaced by the Soviet, then the Nazi German, and then again by the Soviet legal regime. Until 20 August 1991, under Soviet rule, the functions of the Supreme Court were carried out by the Supreme Court of the Estonian Soviet Socialist Republic (ESSR), located in Tallinn, and created by the ESSR **Supreme Soviet** and based on Soviet law. It was possible to appeal decisions of that court to the Supreme Court of the Union of Soviet Socialist Republics (USSR), just as in tsarist times it was possible to appeal to the imperial Senate.

Lower courts were reorganized to conform to the court system of Soviet Union.

After the restoration of independence, the court system was restructured during 1993–94 by authority of the Courts Act of 16 December 1992, which set up a three-level system of courts with the **Supreme Court** as the final court of appeal. The country was divided into three circuits or districts (the Tallinn, Tartu, and Viru circuits) with a district court (*ringkonnakohus*) as the court of appeal for each circuit. The courts of first instance are called either the *maakohus* or *linnakohus* (country court or city court), depending on their rural or urban location. The Tallinn court district is the largest with eight courts, followed by the Tartu district with six and the Viru district with four courts. The Tallinn district has two administrative courts (in Tallinn and in Pärnu), and the Viru district has one in Narva. In addition, the other courts of first instance also have judges with administrative law competence who hear only administrative cases. In 2000, there were a total of 168 judges handling civil and criminal cases in the courts of first instance and 36 judges who heard first instance administrative law complaints. In the appeals courts, there were 41 judges who heard civil, criminal, and administrative law appeals.

The number of courts of first instance and the number of judges servicing them are not fixed and have already been increased several times as needed by simple amendments to the Courts Act by parliament. Most first-instance civil and administrative cases are heard by a single judge, as are petty criminal cases; in certain cases, as specified by law, a judge with at least two lay assessors must hear civil, administrative, and criminal cases. All serious criminal charges are heard by a panel of three judges. All appeals cases must be heard by panels of at least three judges. All judges of both the courts of first instance and the appeals courts are nominated by the Supreme Court and appointed by the president of the Republic. Individuals who wish to serve as judges must apply to the Supreme Court, which examines them for competence and enters them on a candidacy list.

The structural reform of the court system included a comprehensive reform of the judiciary. All sitting judges were dismissed during 1993–94 and new ones were appointed according to law, after examination by the Supreme Court's competency panel. The result was that only approximately 10 percent of sitting judges were reappointed. However, since the new judges were also all products of the Soviet educational system, the reform merely removed those who had been appointed because of their trustworthiness to the Soviet Party state. Unfortunately, the new judges knew no more contemporary legal procedural law on safeguarding individual rights than the old judges. Nor did they know any more contemporary, commercial, competition-oriented civil law or administrative law designed to protect citizens' rights, enforce efficiency, and prevent corruption.

Western governments, as well as locally organized judicial training programs run by the Estonian Law Center located next to the Supreme Court in Tartu, have provided assistance since 1995 to upgrade judicial efficacy in Estonia. However, it will still take several decades before the standards of Estonian judges as a group will rise to the West European level as new younger judges, trained only in Western legal traditions, enter the system. Nevertheless, the Estonian judiciary is leaner, corruption-free, and much more concerned with safeguarding individual rights than those of former socialist countries that did not radically reform their systems early in the transition to democracy.

CRUSADES. *See* BALTIC GERMANS *and* CRUSADING ORDERS.

CRUSADING ORDERS. Albert von Buxhoevden of Bremen, the bishop of Livland (1199–1229), who founded the city of Riga in 1201 as an anchor for his Christianizing efforts, in 1202 established the Fratres Militiae Christi order of knights (formally sanctioned by Pope Innocent III in 1204) as his military arm to subdue and baptize the heathen populations of the **Liv**, Latvian, and Estonian settlement areas. Very soon the Schwertbrüder (Brethren of the Sword), as they became known for the red cross and sword on their shields, slipped out from the control of the bishop and pursued an independent colonizing policy. In 1208 they began their crusade against the Estonians and subdued the latter in 20 years of warfare. By 1227 they had crushed Estonian opposition and received one third of the conquered territory as their fief from the bishop. In the meantime, the Danes, whose help had been enlisted by Bishop Albert in 1218, had conquered the islands of Saaremaa (Ösel) and Hiiumaa (Dagö), as well as adjacent parts of the mainland. The Danes also built the fort atop Toompea hill in **Tallinn**. By 1235 the Schwertbrüder had built six large forts on its territories and had a combined strength of 110–180 knights, 30–45 priests, 500 vassal soldiers, and 700 mercenaries.

After a major loss in a battle in 1236 in northern Lithuania to a combined force of Lithuanians and Semigallians, the Schwertbrüder joined with the Teutonic Knights (Deutsche Orden, formally Ordo Domus Santae Mariae Teutonicum). This order had been originally organized to fight in the Third Crusade to the Holy Land and been granted its charter by the pope in 1198 but had subsequently become active in fighting pagans in many East European lands. Its grand master had been made a prince and granted the right to lands conquered during crusades by the Holy Roman Emperor Frederick II. Henceforth the Teutonic Order's Baltic branch has become known in history as the Livonian Order. During the 13th century, the "Ordu," as the Estonians have always called it, together with the Church, carved out five small states in the Baltic (the Bishoprics of Riga, Kurland [Courland], Dorpat [Tartu], and Ösel [Saaremaa], and the lands of the Ordu), which are collectively referred to as **Livonia**, or Old Livonia.

The Livonian Order's power began to wane after Poland and Lithuania entered into dynastic alliance in 1386. Its religious connection dissolved when the Teutonic Order was secularized in Prussia in 1525. Its political power disappeared shortly thereafter when, during the **Livonian Wars**, the last Master of the Livonian Order signed a treaty with the Polish king and became his vassal.

The descendants of the Ordu, however, continued to dominate Estonian and Latvian life (*see* BALTIC GERMANS) under Swedish and Russian suzerains until they were finally defeated at the Battle of Vollmar (Võnnu in Estonian, Cēsis in Latvian) by Estonian forces in 1919 (*see* LANDESWEHR), and in 1920 had their lands seized by the newly established independent Estonian and Latvian states and redistributed to the landless.

CULTURAL AUTONOMY. On 12 February 1925, the Cultural Autonomy of Ethnic Minorities Act was passed by the **Riigikogu**. It affirmed the paragraph in the **Constitution** that Estonia respects the right of all ethnic groups to preserve their ethnic identity, culture, and religious convictions. This Act was the first of its kind in the world and was based on the ideas of the Austrian socialist Karl Renner, who had developed it at the turn of the century to ameliorate problems of ethnic tensions in the multinational Austrian empire.

Any ethnic group with at least 3,000 registered members was granted the right to establish cultural self-government to organize, administer, and monitor public and private educational institutions in their native language; and attend to the minority's other cultural needs and administrative institutions and enterprises established for that purpose. In accordance with the Act, the German (*see* BALTIC GERMANS) and Jewish (*see* JEWISH ESTONIANS) communities (numbering 8,300 and 4,600, respectively, in 1922) established cultural autonomy. The much larger Russian and Swedish minorities, numbering 91,100 and 7,900, respectively, in 1922, did not take advantage of the Act. However, since most of them lived in compact communities, the Russians (*see* RUSSIANS IN ESTONIA) along the western shore of Lake Peipsi and the Swedes (*see* SWEDISH ESTONIANS) on islands and villages in the coastal area in the northwest known as Noa-Rootsi were able to operate schools, churches, and other cultural institutions in their native languages as part of the normal activities of their municipalities.

A new Cultural Autonomy Act was passed on 26 October 1993 by the **Riigikogu**. This Act is virtually identical to the old one but restricts some minority rights to citizens. The vast changes in the ethnic composition of the **population** brought about by the deportations, emigration, war losses, and importation of labor during the Soviet period reduced the ethnic Estonian share from a steady state of almost 90 percent (87 percent in 1922 and 89 percent in 1934) to 62 percent in the 1989 census, which meant that the original conditions had to be modified to conform with the new sociological realities.

It is interesting to note that the process that led to the renewal of the Act began already in 1987 as most of the recently immigrated non-Russian ethnic minority groups joined the movement for Estonian national independence from the Soviet Union. In January 1988, a Jewish cultural society was founded, followed by a Swedish one a few weeks later. By the middle of 1988, there were 15 ethnic cultural associations. In September, the first ethnic forum was held that established the permanent Association of Peoples of Estonia (Eestimaa Rahvuste Ühendus) to represent their political, cultural, and social interests. A working group composed mostly of representatives of this body began preparing a new act already in 1989. The delay of its enactment was caused by the necessity of making changes as Estonia was transformed from a Soviet republic to a restored independent republic with a new Constitution, even as the new law was being drafted.

The major change in the new Act removes the right of noncitizens to membership in cultural autonomies, nor do they have the right to either vote or be elected to the leading organs of these autonomies. Thus any ethnic minority of at least 3,000 registered citizens can establish its cultural council by direct and secret ballot. The regulations for the elections are drafted and authorized by the government. Once a cultural council has been successfully elected, it becomes the highest authority of the cultural autonomy and the state has no more role to play in its activities. It goes without saying that the cultural councils are required to operate within Estonian legislation, to which they can add their own by-laws and regulations. The cultural councils are authorized by the Act to form regional cultural boards according to their needs, appoint cultural deputies, and found ethnic cultural institutions, schools, social and health care establishments, publishing houses, and so on. These institutions have all rights of Estonian legal entities—they may own property and are liable for their financial obligations. Their financial resources originate in specific allocations, partly from the state budget and partly from local municipal budgets, as well as from membership dues and donations from enterprises, organizations, and private persons.

The state's role is to provide legal guarantees for cultural preservation in fulfillment of the Constitution but not to interfere in the operation of the cultural autonomies. To date, no cultural autonomies have been established.

CURRENCY BOARD. As part of the new national economic policy of gaining credibility in the world's financial markets and marketizing the economy to ensure rapid growth and thereby strengthen its independence, Estonia established a politically independent central **Bank of Estonia** (Eesti Riigipank), which was split into two divisions, the Issue Department and the Banking Department. The former functions as a currency board, and the latter handles all other central bank functions.

The currency board principle limits the issuing of the national currency to the amount of the central bank's foreign exchange holdings (including gold), and it does not allow any central bank lending to the government or to the commercial banking system. After a year's experiment with the Estonian **kroon** (introduced in June 1992) tied to the German mark on a currency board base, parliament in June 1993 passed without opposition the Bank of Estonia Act that guaranteed its independence.

The currency board principle has allowed Estonia to rapidly develop international financial credibility that assisted in foreign financial inflows into the country and supported the rapid marketized development of the economy by maintaining currency convertibility and a fixed exchange rate that stabilized the economy and integrated Estonia into the world financial and economic systems. It has also enforced strict financial discipline on government (and parliament), which is forced to borrow in the commercial market at commercial rates for domestic financing.

–D–

DECLARATION OF INDEPENDENCE (24 February 1918). In December 1917 and January 1918, the anti-**Bolshevik** forces in Estonia moved toward establishing a democratic Estonian state, independent of both Soviet Russia and occupation by Germany. In the uncompleted elections to the Estonian Constituent Assembly called by the Bolshevik administration of Estonia (which had taken power from the Provisional Diet of the Province of Estonia [**Eestimaa Kubermangu Ajutine Maanõukogu**] on 28 November 1917, shortly after the October Revolution, driving it underground and forcing it to place its authority in the hands of its Council of Elders), the democratic forces supporting independence garnered 60 percent of the votes. The **Estonian Workers' Commune** government stopped the elections when their defeat became evident and declared a state of emergency. On 10 February 1918, the Russian-German peace talks at Brest-Litovsk broke down, and on 18 February the German forces began a major attack on Russia. The Council of Elders found the confusing time of chaos ripe to declare Estonia an independent state.

On 19 February, it adopted the Estonian Manifesto of Independence and formed the **Estonian Rescue (Salvation) Committee**, with **Konstantin Päts** as chair. As the German forces rapidly approached, the Red Army withdrew to Russia and Estonian nationalist units together with Defense Guard (*see also* KAITSELIIT) units took control of the larger cities before the arrival of the German forces. In **Tallinn**, the Estonian patriots took over power on 24 February and immediately issued the "Manifesto to all the Peoples of Estonia," which declared Estonia an independent democratic republic "within its historic ethnographic territorial boundaries." The Manifesto also declared neutrality in wars between third states (intended to prevent a German occupation), and it promised civic rights to all citizens and cultural autonomy to all national minorities. Political authority was to remain with the Provisional Diet, and the Estonian Provisional Government was to be formed by it until the calling of a Constituent Assembly.

On 24 February, the Rescue Committee named the **Estonian Provisional Government** with Konstantin Päts as chair. On 25 February, German armed forces arrived in Tallinn and occupied all of Estonia by the beginning of March. Although the Germans did not recognize the independence of Estonia, the Declaration, nevertheless, permitted the provisional government to raise the Estonian question in the international arena among the Allied powers the neutral states. In consequence, in May 1918 Great Britain, France, and Italy extended de facto recognition to the Republic of Estonia.

DECLARATION OF INDEPENDENCE (1991). On 18 August 1991, the Soviet leadership under the chairmanship of Vice President Gennady Yanayev, Prime Minister Valentin Pavlov, Vice Chair of the Defense Council Oleg Baklanov, and Defense Minister Dmitry Yazov announced that since President Mikhail Gorbachev was unable to carry out his duties owing to health problems, Vice President Yanayev would take over his duties. Together with this televised announcement, a state of emergency was declared and an eight-man Emergency Committee was established. From further declarations by the committee, it became clear that the objective of this putsch was to stop the reforms of Gorbachev and turn the clock back in an attempt to preserve the power of the Soviet empire. Demonstrations of any kind were forbidden, the media was placed under stringent censorship, firearms in the hands of citizens were to be confiscated, and the Committee condemned Gorbachev's reforms and intended to reinstitute the command system in the economy.

On 19 August, a military convoy appeared headed for **Tallinn** from Russia and a commando unit landed at Tallinn airport. At noon the Estonian Emergency Defense Council declared the Moscow coup illegal and asked the Estonian people to remain calm. At the same time the **Estonian Committee** called on the Estonian people to be prepared for any eventuality, including guerilla fighting. In the afternoon, **Arnold Rüütel**, its chairman, spoke in the **Supreme Council of Estonia**, condemned the illegality of the coup, called for support of Russian President Boris Yeltsin, and informed the assembly that the Estonian **Interfront** (Eesti Interliikumine) had come out in support of the coup. That same evening, the Supreme Council of Estonia declared the coup illegal and void by a vote of 69 to 15. It called on the people of Estonia to defend the radio and television buildings. Cordons of heavy trucks and barriers of concrete were quickly drawn around the Toompea parliament and government centers as well as the **radio and television** buildings, and volunteer units were formed to guard them.

The next day, General Melnitchuk arrived from Moscow and attempted during a meeting lasting several hours to convince Arnold Rüütel and **Edgar Savisaar** (the prime minister) to carry out the dictates of the Moscow Emergency Committee, but it was to no avail. Delegates of the Supreme Council and the Estonian Committee met and decided to form a common body to draft both a law to govern elections and a new Estonian **Constitution**. Next day at four in the afternoon, a mass meeting was held on Freedom Square (Vabaduse Väljak) in Tallinn, which demanded independence for Estonia and the formation of a **Constitutional Assembly** to draft a new Constitution.

That same evening, the Supreme Council adopted a motion declaring Estonia an independent state. It also decided to form the Constituent Assembly to draft a Constitution and to carry out parliamentary elections in 1992.

On 21 August, Soviet commando units stormed and took the television tower but failed to take control of the 22nd floor containing the **television** and **radio** sending equipment. Thus, at a crucial time, broadcast connections with the world were maintained. In the same evening after the failure of the Moscow putsch, Prime Minister Savisaar negotiated the withdrawal of the commando units from Estonia.

On 22 August, Iceland and Lithuania were the first states to recognize the independence of Estonia. On 24 August at a meeting of Arnold Rüütel and Boris Yeltsin in Tallinn, the latter signed a document recognizing Estonian independence. On the same day, Denmark also recognized Estonian independence and France indicated its readiness to do so. By 27 August, 28 states had recognized Estonia.

The declaration of 20 August 1991 reestablished the independent Estonian republic that had been occupied in 1940 by the Soviet Union. The popular foundation of this was the sovereign decision of the Estonian people in a vote carried out on 3 March 1991 in which they supported both independence and the reestablishment of the national Republic of Estonia (*see the table in Appendix C*). *See also* ABORTIVE MOSCOW COUP OF 1991.

DECLARATION OF SOVEREIGNTY. On 16 November 1988, the Estonian **Supreme Soviet** adopted the Declaration of the Sovereignty of the Estonian Soviet Socialist Republic (ESSR) by which it declared itself the supreme political authority in Estonia, with the consequence that the laws it passed were to have validity as the highest laws on Estonian territory. On 26 November, the Estonian Supreme Soviet amended the ESSR **Constitution of 1978** stating that all real property within Estonia's territory belonged solely to the ESSR. Henceforth, private property was also restored in Estonia, and any laws of the Union of Soviet Socialist Republics (USSR) in conflict with those of the ESSR were null and void. This was the first defiance of the Moscow-centered party-state by any legislature in the USSR. Thus, the eventual dismantling of the Soviet Union began by a legislative act.

On 17 February 1989, the Presidium of the Supreme Soviet declared 24 February as Estonian Independence Day. On that day, the blue-black-white tricolor flag of the independent Republic of Estonia was flown on the national flag pole atop Pikk Hermann at the joint initiative of the **Rahvarinne** and the Council of Ministers.

On 30 March 1990, the Estonian Supreme Soviet passed the Act on the Status of the Estonian State (Eesti riiklikust staatusest), which declared the laws and powers of the USSR illegal in occupied Estonia retroactively to the moment of occupation in 1940 and announced the beginning of a period of transition to reestablish the Republic of Estonia, to end when the legal organs of the Estonian state and its **Constitution** come into force.

On 8 May 1990, the ESSR Supreme Soviet adopted the Act on the Symbols of Estonia, which declared null and void the name Estonian Soviet Socialist Republic, restored the official name of Estonia as the Republic of Estonia, and changed its own name to Eesti Vabaariigi Ülemnõukogu, translated officially as the "Supreme Council of the Republic of Estonia." On 7 August 1990, an act reinstituted the tricolor **flag** and the three-lion **coat of arms** as the official regalia of the Republic of Estonia.

DEFENSE LEAGUE (Kaitseliit). To maintain order during the **Bolshevik** Revolution, the Omakaitse (Bürgerwehr) or Home Guard was set up in **Tallinn** as the first armed self-defense organization in Estonia. On 11 November 1918, it was replaced by a nationwide voluntary self-defense organization, the Eesti Kaitse Liit, under the leadership of **Johan Pitka** and **Ernst Põdder** responsible to the minister of defense. It was organized on a hierarchical structure with each city and county Defense League command controlling local town, parish, township, and/or village armed units. In January 1919, the **Estonian Provisional Government** decreed membership compulsory for all 18–60-year-old males unfit for conscription into the regular army. Underage schoolboys also formed voluntary Defense League units that performed signal service. During the **War of Independence**, the numbers serving in the Defense League exceeded those in the regular army at the battlefront (*see* ARMED FORCES). It performed policing functions on the home front, engaged in firefights with Bolshevik groups on the home front, performed border guard duties, and guarded communications installations, roads, prisons, factories, state warehouses, and so on against sabotage. With victory, its then 102,000 (32,000 with military training and 70,000 untrained) members were demobilized and membership became voluntary once again, with a consequent drastic decline in membership.

The **attempted communist coup** of 1 December 1924 reignited interest in the Defense League, which was reorganized on the basis of 15 *malev* (ancient Estonian name for an army or military unit of large but undefined size; today the equivalent of a regiment), and each *malev* into units equivalent to regular army ones—battalions, companies, and platoons. Emphasis was placed on training and membership in the Defense League was propagandized as a patriotic duty. In addition to an annual Defense League rally between 1926 and 1940, a women's organization, the Kodukaitse (Home Defense), and two youth organizations, the Noor Kotkad (young eagles) for boys and Kodutütred (literally, "home daughters") for girls, were formed to develop encompassing patriotism and ensure a steady stream of new members. The youth organizations competed for members with the more internationally oriented Boy Scouts and Girl Guides.

Despite the forced liquidation of the Kaitseliit along with the regular armed forces in 1940, many men kept their arms, went underground, and fought a guerilla war against the Soviet occupiers into the 1950s (*see* BRETHREN OF THE FOREST). However, these were individuals and groups—there was no organization or command structure.

On 17 February 1990, a group reestablished the Kaitseliit as a then still illegal organization in the Estonian Soviet Socialist Republic (ESSR). On 4 September 1991, the newly restored Republic rescinded the Soviet act of 1940 that outlawed it, then reestablished the Kaitseliit as a legal organization on the basis of its 1931 charter. However, the individual units re-formed on a voluntary basis in different parts of the country were unruly and ill-disciplined and created problems, not least because they refused to place themselves under the command of the armed forces commander, even after **Riigikogu** proclaimed them part of the **Estonian Defense Forces** on 28 April 1992. Gradually, however, and particularly after the appointment of **Johannes Kert**, at the time head of the Kaitseliit, as chief of the general staff, the organization has been regularized and proper discipline and training imposed, culminating in a modernized charter passed by the Riigikogu on 8 February 1998.

At the beginning of the new millennium, the Defense League prides itself again as the patriotic home guard that it was in the 1930s and has revived all its auxiliary organs (the women's and youth organizations), and in 2000 claimed 15,000 men, 400 women, 3,000 boys, and 1,600 girls as members.

DEPORTATIONS. The first recorded deportations from Estonia took place during the **Livonian Wars** (1558–83) when the German inhabitants of **Tartu** were forcibly removed to Russia. During the **Great Northern War**, the burghers of Tartu and **Narva** were deported together with their families to Russia.

In the 20th century, the Soviets practiced deportation as a matter of course. In 1918, 500 members of the **Baltic German** nobility and a few hundred Estonians were deported to Siberia. During the Stalinist era, deportations were used to remove independent farmers ("*kulaks*") and other undesirable members of the "bourgeois" class to terrorize people and to remove entire ethnic populations, for example the Chechens from their homeland and the Tatars from the Crimea.

The occupation and annexation of Estonia to the Soviet Union in 1940 was followed by a wave of terror and genocide as part of the process of Sovietization of Estonia. Between June 1940 and October 1941, when the German advance forced the Red Army to retreat from Estonia, 1,950 Estonian citizens were executed and 10,500 were deported in sealed rail cattle wagons, among them President **Konstantin Päts**, Commander in Chief of the Armed Forces General **Johan Laidoner**, cabinet ministers, members of parliament, senior officer ranks, clerics, entrepreneurs, and owners of businesses. Over half were women and children. More than half died in inhuman conditions. In March 1949, 20,713 Estonians, amounting to 2.5 percent of the population, were deported to Siberian Gulags—90 percent were women, children, and pensioners. The 14th of June, the date in 1941 when the rounding up of citizens for mass deportation began, is now commemorated as a national day of mourning.

In addition to the two main waves of deportation, two other less extensive deportations were carried out: in the summer of 1945, 342 Baltic Germans who had remained in Estonia were deported; and in 1951, 259 Christian believers were deported.

On 17 December 1988, the **Supreme Soviet** of the Estonian Soviet Socialist Republic (ESSR) declared the deportations inhumane crimes against human rights and rehabilitated all the deportees of the 1940s and 1950s.

DIET (Landtag). The institution of the Diet arose in Old **Livonia** (1419–1516) out of the meetings of the feudal lords and their vassals holding land in fee to resolve common problems of rule over the local peasantry. The Diet was divided into four estates: the first consisted of the archbishop, bishops, and abbots; the second of the ruling prince of the Teutonic Order (*see* CRUSADING ORDERS), the commanders of the chapters, and sometimes representatives of the bailiffs; the third of representatives of the knights-vassals; and the fourth of representatives of the burghers of the towns. The Diets were usually held at Valga (Valka in Latvian) on the call of the prince, the archbishop of Riga, or both. During the Polish suzerainty over Livland, the Diet consisted solely of representatives of the nobility and the burghers. Beginning in the 16th–17th centuries and until 1783, separate Diets in the principalities of Estland, Livland, Saaremaa, and Kurland (Courland) operated as organs of administrative coordination for the nobles' estate administrators. Subsequently, they became legislative organs of the nobility in the imperial Russian Provinces (Gubernya) of Estland, Livland, and Kurland and lasted as such until formally disbanded in independent Latvia in 1918 and Estonia in 1920, after they had become irrelevant as a result of the revolutionary events of 1917–18. *See also* BALTIC GERMANS; EESTIMAA KUBERMANGU AJUTINE MAANÕUKOGU (Provisional Diet of the Province [Gubernya] of Estland).

DISSIDENTS. Influenced by Russian dissidents, a few Estonian dissidents formed the Estonian Popular Movement (Eesti Rahvusrinne) initiated by Kalju Mätik in 1970 and the Estonian Democratic Movement (Eesti Demokraatlik Liikumine) led by Mati Kiirend and Artjom Juškievitš in 1972. Later that year, **Tunne Kelam** drafted the Memorandum to the United Nations on behalf of the two organizations. The memorandum protested the continuing Soviet occupation of Estonia and demanded the restoration of independence. It reached the UN two years later and the following year, in 1975, all four dissidents involved were sentenced to terms in prison. Despite this, or perhaps because of it, cooperation developed among Estonian, Latvian, and Lithuanian opponents of the regime. On 23 August 1979, an open letter, known as the Baltic Appeal, was addressed by nationalist movements in all three countries to the governments of the Union of Soviet Socialist Republics (USSR), the German Federal Republic, and the German Democratic Republic. The letter protested the

Molotov-Ribbentrop Pact's secret protocols, which had been the "legal" foundation of the Soviet occupation. Forty-five people signed the Baltic Appeal, among them four Estonians (Mart Niklus, Endel Ratas, **Enn Tarto**, and Erik Udam).

As a result of the increasing **Russification** policy of the **Estonian Communist Party (ECP)** in the late 1970s and encouraged by the Solidarity trade union movement in Poland, 40 Estonians signed the Letter of the Forty at the end of October 1980. The letter, addressed to the editors of *Pravda, Rahva Hääl*, and *Sovetskaja Estonia*, was the reaction of the intelligentsia to the massive use of force against a spontaneous youth demonstration that had taken place on 22 September after a soccer game when the authorities precipitously canceled a scheduled appearance of the pop group Propeller. The youths, mostly secondary school pupils, had proceeded to march from the stadium toward the city center, amidst shouts of "Pension off Brezhnev" and "Down with Gretškina" (the unpopular Russifying minister of education in Estonia appointed in 1978). The march was broken up by a police attack; some youths were arrested and some were reportedly also beaten. The immediate result was a series of different expressions of protest against Russification in the schools by youths across **Tallinn** and elsewhere in early October. All these demonstrations were suppressed by the use of force. The impact of the use of force against the youths, combined with the 14 October official announcement labeling the protesting youths hooligans, aroused a very strong negative reaction among the Estonian people.

Thus the carefully written Letter of the Forty, which protested the use of force against youths and explained the concern of Estonians about the future of their nation caused by a mistaken nationalities policy. The letter further emphasized the need to carry out a careful and thorough study of the stresses among nationalities in the Soviet Union.

Within days thousands of copies of the letter, distributed by the recipient news organs, circulated and reached abroad by December, where it was widely publicized on both radio and in the press. The letter raised the Estonian people's consciousness and energized them to think and talk about the future of their nation for the first time since the general loss of hope for regaining independence in the late 1950s. The communist authorities typically began to harass the signatories by calling them in for "conversations," including by the KGB, and punished the writers, journalists, artists, and musicians who had signed the letter by excluding them from public appearance on **radio and television** and in the press. Travel abroad was also curtailed, and some lost their jobs. The six ECP members who had signed the letter received internal Party reprimands.

Although none of the 40 were jailed, possibly because of the number and prominence of those involved as well as the careful composition of the letter, during 1981–84 six political **court** cases took place in which nine accused were sentenced to years in jail. Among these was a former member of the Communist Party of the Soviet Union (CPSU), Tartu professor Jüri Kukk, who died in 1981 in a concentration camp shortly after being sentenced. None of these jailed freedom fighters, however, had the impact that the Letter of the Forty had on the Estonian people and the communist authorities.

– E –

ECONOMIC TRANSFORMATION. In 1989, the Estonian economy was wholly integrated in the segregated and inward-looking Soviet economy, but by 1995 it had become internationally oriented and integrated in the West European economy. The rapid transition from a premodern, authoritarian, ideologically conditioned society (akin to the religiously oriented medieval world) to a modern, differentiated, and democratic society based on individual rights was difficult and uneven, and it left administrative and economic decision-making systems aftereffects. The lack of a separate political authority, combined with the fact that existing economic structures were all early industrial and effectively antimodern in their overemphasis on the factors of industrial production, added excessive costs to the transition. Consequently, the expectation that the collapse of the Soviet system would automatically lead to the development of a democratic capitalist society based on competitive markets was an illusion of wishful thinking.

Fortunately for Estonia, close contacts with Finland had taught the need for radical liberalization of the economy, as shown by the **Isemajandav Eesti** (IME, or Economically Autonomous Estonia) project.

However, it was the innate Estonian desire to reestablish the independent democratic prewar Republic that allowed the very rapid transition from premodern authoritarianism to differentiated democratic competition to begin, even before the restoration of independence. It was also the reason for leaders rising to power who were able to apply Western economic rules and liberalize the economy on a sustained basis. Naturally, since they were inexperienced in democratic politics, public administration, and free-market economic management, they made mistakes. Thus, it was something of a miracle that there was not a backlash among the long-suffering public when the dislocations of the loss of Soviet markets led to five years of drastic industrial decline from 1990 to 1994 which reduced the nominal gross national product to 49.6 percent of the 1989 figure, along with an equally drastic decline in the labor market that wiped out almost a quarter of the jobs.

Hence, although the cabinets led by **Edgar Savisaar** (1990–92), **Tiit Vähi** (1992), and **Mart Laar** (1992–94), respectively, must be respected for achieving independence, stabilizing the economy, and implementing crucial economic reforms, their decisions were based ad hoc as much on economic necessity as on the desire to move Estonia toward the West as rapidly as possible. Accordingly, the transformation of the Estonian economy from an industrial producer of mostly primary products (electricity and building materials) and food processing, which along with **agriculture** generated between 75 and 80 percent of GNP during the 1980s, to an economy dominated by the tertiary sector (commerce, finance, transportation, communication, and services), which by 1995 produced 60 percent of GNP, resulted from the twin factors of the loss of markets for the overpriced, outdated, and inferior quality of Soviet industrial goods, including the overpriced fatty meat products of the agricultural sector, and the invasion of cheap Western manufactures and dumped quality food products.

The former demanded a rapid restructuring of production to the only possible markets—West European ones—and the latter naturally brought Western markets, marketing, and quality directly to the consumer. The transformation was spurred by the universal demand of Estonians to "rejoin Europe," which also led to the early policy decision to apply for membership in the **European Union** (EU), which in turn speeded up the reorganization of the economy to Western standards.

Note that even before the restitution of independence, Estonia instituted a Western self-declaratory income tax system on 1 January 1991, and had already begun to privatize **industry**. The inflation (tenfold in 1991) brought about by the shortage of consumer goods and the need to bring the financial and monetary systems in line with Western Europe led to cutting monetary ties with Russia and the ruble bloc, and the introduction of the independent currency in June 1992. The tying of the Estonian **kroon** to the deutsche mark in a **currency board** arrangement demanded fiscal responsibility from politicians, quickly reduced inflation to acceptable levels, and led to investor confidence in the Estonian economy. The internationalization and rapid **privatization** of industry speeded up the transformation as foreigners bought plants and used them to produce goods for export. By 1995, all large enterprises had been sold, and the banking system had been brought under strict regulatory control of the central bank and internationalized. Political stability guaranteed by a center-right party system (*see* POLITICAL PARTIES) and coalition cabinets cooperating closely with the International Monetary Fund (IMF), maintaining prudent budgets, pursuing free trade with no tariffs even on agricultural goods, and working assiduously to prepare for membership in the European Union, stabilized the transformed economy. By 2000, the biggest trade partners were Finland, Sweden, Germany, and Latvia, which received 31.8, 18.8, 10.1, and 9.6 percent of exports, respectively; in imports, Finland led with 28.9 percent and was followed by Germany and Sweden, each with 9.6 percent. Russia, which as late as 1998 had taken 9.6 percent of exports and provided 11.1 percent of imports, in 2000 took only 2.2 percent of exports and supplied 8.8 percent of imports, mainly of natural gas and petroleum. The export trade by 2000 had become stabilized in two sectors, wood and wood products; and re-exports of processed electronic components, machinery, textiles, and clothing amounted to 41 percent of total exports. The economy was wide open to international markets, including financial markets, since the Swedish-led Nordic **banks** Swebank and Skandinaviska Enskilda Banken owned majority shares in the two major banks, controlling 80 percent of the lending market in Estonia. Moreover, the Helsinki

Stock Exchange had taken over control of the Tallinn Stock Exchange.

Although the economy has been restructured to West European standards and is integrated with its closest neighbors, there are two economic problems that have so far been neglected. The first is the long-term problem of a declining and aging **population** shared with the rest of Europe, including Russia. For Estonia, the decade-long absolute halving of births from 25,000 to under 13,000 and the excess of deaths over births of 6,000–7,000 a year means a rapidly aging labor force that will have a major impact around 2010 on economic production and tax resources. As the direct result of Estonian American ethnologist Aino Järvesoo (1910–2003) spending the last decade of her life and her savings on a massive campaign to increase births in Estonia, the new government of Juhan Parts in 2003 promised to establish programs of grants to young families and of parent "salaries."

The second neglected problem is that of unemployment combined with an increasing shortage of skilled workers. The steady annual decline in the economically active population from 842,600 in 1989 (with no unemployment) to 698,300 in 2001 (of whom 99,000, amounting to 14.2 percent, were unemployed) is the result of the radical shift in the structure of the economy, which reduced the labor force in agriculture from 20.1 percent in 1989 to just 5.1 percent in 2001, while the labor force in the tertiary sector grew from 42 percent to over 60 percent in the same period. It is the immobile, unskilled, older rural population that has suffered the most unemployment followed by the older industrial workers who could not easily switch to service jobs. In fact, much of the service sector is actually in the quaternary, or services to services, sector, which requires higher education, languages, and information technology skills, since the very success of Estonia integrating its economy has led to an explosion of jobs in financial institutions, insurance, international sales, and management. However, there is also a shortage of skilled industrial workers and of technicians in the services sector, since the modernization of the economy has led to the use of complex machinery in even such formerly menial jobs as cleaning offices and industrial floors. Unfortunately, the occupational training system in Estonia at the beginning of the 21st century has not been upgraded, with the result that few students of ability enter it. Nor, in sharp contrast to West European models, have any systematic retraining programs been developed.

EDUCATION. The first schools in Estonia were the cathedral and monastery schools in the 13th–14th centuries, which taught in Latin and prepared locals for clerical functions in the church. By late medieval times, cathedral schools functioned at **Tartu**, Haapsalu, and **Tallinn**. University education was available only abroad, at Rostock, Erfurt, or Leipzig in Germany or in Bologna, Prague, Paris, and so on in old Catholic Europe. Of the monastery schools in Estonia, the Dominicans' school in Tallinn and the Cistercians' school at Kärkna are the best known. During the 15th and 16th centuries, secular town schools were also founded. Education was mainly available to the sons of the nobility and the **Baltic German** burghers although some Estonians were enrolled, even in the Jesuit College in Tartu and in its translation seminar.

During the 16th century, the **Lutheran** church began to teach the peasantry reading as well as the basics of Protestant theology based on the New Testament. The first ABC book in the Estonian language appeared in 1575, Tallinn Gymnasium was established in 1631, and the **University of Tartu** opened in 1632. At the end of the 17th century, the country school system was begun in Estonia, when the Livland **Diet** decided in 1687 that the noble landowners had to build a school in each parish and to pay the schoolmaster's salary. At least 41 such schools, mostly in southern Estonia in the Province of Livland, operated at the end of the century. In 1684, the Forselius seminary for schoolmasters and church cantors (*köster*)—a combined occupation at this time—was organized on the estate of the bishop of Tartu. The course lasted two years and emphasized reading, arithmetic, theology, and church music, primarily hymn singing, although German and bookbinding were also taught. During its four years of operation, it graduated 160 schoolmasters.

After the **Great Northern War**, the educational scene was dismal—there were few schools, and the teacher was usually the church cantor who taught mainly popular theology, the catechism, Bible stories, and hymns. Despite this, literacy among Estonian peasants was fairly high as parents taught children to read at home from church hymnals and prayer books. In 1739 the first complete Estonian language **Bible** appeared, and in the latter half of the century secular **literature** began to be printed, mainly in the form of calendars for the country folk containing instructions for farming and health. Some short stories were usually also included. In 1787, southern Estonia had 300 and northern Estonia 242 country schools. In some places, up to two thirds of the peasantry could read.

A comprehensive school system began to form during the first half of the 19th century as gymnasia, elementary, and regional schools (*kreisikool*) were formed in towns. In 1804, the imperial ministry of education established a system of two- to three-year middle schools in the seats of the uniform imperial administrative districts called *kreis* in Estonian, which replaced the historic counties in Estland and Livland. The 11 such imperial ministry schools opened in 1805 in Estonian territory taught in German and were intended to admit pupils from the parish schools (*kihelkonnakool*)—senior to the primary village schools—and prepare them for the gymnasia. After 1820, these schools produced mainly clerks for industry, commerce, and the civil service. Although physics, the natural sciences, and languages (Latin, Russian, and German) were taught, the emphasis was on application of the theoretical subjects to real life.

The town school (*linnakool*) system replaced the imperial *kreisikool* in 1872 and was a higher type of six-year elementary school intended to educate all children (nobles, burghers, and peasants) taught in Russian, and the parish school system remained in place. Many such schools also had a seventh-year class that prepared country village-school schoolmasters. In 1912, these schools were formally renamed "higher elementary schools." The *linnakool* played a central role in national **cultural awakening** and the development of an educated class of Estonians during the last decades of the 19th century.

Back in 1816 and 1818, new laws had again ordered the establishment of schools on every noble estate and in each parish. The movement to Russify the **population** by encouraging them to convert to the Russian Orthodox Church during the 1840s led to the increase in schools as Orthodox churches also established parish schools. Thus by 1884, there were 315 Orthodox and 1297 **Lutheran** parish schools in Estonia (the Province of Estland and the Estonian part of

Livland). The educational requirements for schooling were systematized and regulated by laws in 1851 and 1867, resulting in the 1881 census showing that nearly the whole Estonian rural population could read and that 40 percent could also write.

Teaching at the **University of Tartu** was disrupted by the **Great Northern War** and although the nobility, together with the town councils of **Tartu** and **Pärnu** (where the University had operated for a time), repeatedly petitioned the imperial government to reopen the University, it was not until 1802, over a century later, that it was reopened. New buildings were built—the observatory, the medical teaching building (the Anatomikum), clinics, the library, which was built into the west wing of the ruins of the medieval cathedral destroyed over a century earlier, and an imposing classical-style main building completed in 1809. In contrast to its first incarnation, the language of the University was now German, not Latin.

During the second half of the 19th century, Estonian nationalism arose and grew into a powerful popular cultural movement based on widespread valuation of education. Already in 1860, Jaan Adamson, the local schoolmaster at the Pullerits village school in Holstre *vald,* raised the idea of establishing middle schools for the peasantry equivalent to the *kreisikool.* Since the imperial government was not interested in Estonian-language schools, it was up to Estonian cultural leaders to organize public financial support and establish a private Estonian-language school. The **Estonian Aleksander School** movement found such widespread popular support that by 1874 a school building was purchased at Põltsamaa.

The ascension to the throne of Alexander III in the 1880s brought about a reversal of the Estonianization of education in Estonia, when in 1887 Russian became the obligatory language of instruction at all levels. At the primary level (Vallakool), only religious instruction was allowed in the native language. **Russification** was so draconian that exchanges among pupils had to take place in Russian. At the University, Russian replaced German as the language of instruction; the Baltic German professorate was forced out, and even the name of the University was changed to Imperial Jurjev University. The Aleksander School, the result of the greatest popular expression of Estonian nationalism to date, was forced to open as a Russian-language institution in 1888. However, Russification of education had little negative effect on the nationalist development of Estonians—if anything, it strengthened it. Moreover, all educated Estonians learned to speak and write Russian in addition to Estonian and German.

A comprehensive educational system continued to develop as new elementary schools (*linnakool*), middle schools, especially those with science orientation (*realkool, Realschule*), as well as gymnasia together with colleges to train teachers for these schools, were founded. The best known are **Treffner Gümnasium**, Tallinna Realkool, and Võru, **Viljandi**, and Põltsamaa middle schools. New technical and professional schools and programs were also established, for example, the Tartu Veterinary School, the Kose Agricultural School, the School of Midwifery at the University of Tartu, the Tallinn Railway Technical School, the seamen's schools at Heinaste and Kuressaare, the Home Economics School at Vönnu, commercial courses at Tallinn, Pärnu, and **Narva** middle schools, and so on. In addition to state schools, a large number of new academic and technical private schools were established.

By the new century, Estonia (and Latvia) had substantial numbers of educated natives who operated the bureaucracy of the state; ran commerce, industry, and farm estates; and organized the direction of development of the educational system.

Independent Estonia quickly established a unified school structure with a four-year primary school (soon extended to six years) with all children between eight and 14 years required to attend. Private schools and home schooling were permitted. The secondary level of general schooling was formed by five-year gymnasia, organized into a lower and a higher stage. Instruction was carried out in Estonian, although foreign languages were permitted, as in the French Lycée and the German schools in Tartu and Tallinn. Numerous new schools were established to bring Estonia rapidly to the European level of education: new technical and occupational schools were especially favored as were schools for handicapped and special care schools. In the school year 1938–39, the primary state schools taught 106,944 and the secondary 16,008, plus pupils in private and occupational secondary and middle schools.

Higher education was limited to the University of Tartu and the Tallinn Technical Institute, founded in 1936 to teach engineering, as well as the State Higher Art School formed in 1938 on the basis of the existing School of Handicraft Art, the Pallas Higher Academy of Art in Tartu, and the Tallinn Conservatory, reorganized in 1923 from the Tallinn Higher Music School.

During the Soviet period, a seven-year primary school was made compulsory, and this was later raised to nine years. As a result, the number of schools rose markedly. Various nonacademic reforms were introduced such as "classes on working," later replaced by polytechnical courses on industrial working, as well as the establishment of boarding schools, which in a country as small as Estonia were completely superfluous from a academic point of view. In 1970, compulsory secondary education was introduced, and in 1977 the "courses on productive working skills" that all pupils and students had to take were replaced by "enhanced" trade courses, which in practice meant working for free in an industrial environment, often in a "teaching production unit." Much of the teaching was professionally underweight as shown by over a quarter of secondary school teachers entering university after completing their minimum teaching assignment. All education was highly oriented toward the party-state's communist ideology. Hence also the heavy emphasis in secondary education on trade and agricultural subjects. Primary and secondary school teachers were trained at Tallinn Pedagogical Institute, a Teachers' Pedagogical Institute at the University in Tartu, and lower level teachers' colleges in Tallinn, Tartu, and Rakvere.

Although most of the education in the primary and secondary schools was in Estonian, most textbooks were translated from Russian; very few textbooks were permitted to be printed by Estonian authors. In the 1970s, when **Karl Vaino** was appointed first secretary of the **Estonian Communist Party**, the tendency to Russify education increased markedly in schooling. Russian became compulsory as a subject in first year, and plans were made to introduce it in nursery schools and kindergarten. The number of mixed language schools, for Russian speakers and Estonian speakers, was increased at the expense of Estonian-only schools, and lectures were increasingly conducted in Russian at higher educational institutes. In 1980, the party-state switched to a more sophisticated Russification under the rubric of the "internationalization" of education.

Whatever the negative aspects of education in the Soviet period, the population's educational qualifications increased markedly as shown below:

Percentages with:	*in 1934*	*in 1979*
Higher education	0.8%	7.4%
Partial higher education	1.1	1.6
Secondary education	4.3	30.2 (including trade schools)
Partial secondary education	8.3	23.8
Primary education	52.6	32.6
Partial primary education	26.2	0
No schooling	7.4	0

Radical changes in the whole educational system began even before Estonia regained independence as new private schools at all levels, from kindergarten to university, appeared. The frenetic rejection of all Soviet legacies in schooling created a chaotic atmosphere in Estonian education, which had not been completely regularized by the year 2003. Private secondary schools and "universities" appeared out of nowhere as middle-class students and parents sought Western education to prepare for full participation in the democratic world. The task of de-Sovietizing the primary and secondary systems involved not only a switch to teaching in Estonian, writing new textbooks (a years-long task), retraining and training new teachers, reforming curricula and course syllabi, but also reorganizing the school system (including closing small schools and irrelevant agricultural and industrial schools) and modernizing the buildings and teaching equipment. At the postsecondary level, Estonia by 1996 had embraced the American accreditation system newly adopted by some European countries, to assist it in forming order out of chaos and reaching the international level of credibility for its higher education standards (*see also* EUROFACULTY).

Still, Estonia has built rapidly on its historic love affair with education, which even the Soviet occupation was not able to destroy. The **literacy** level, at 91.2 percent in 1897 (96.1 percent in 1934 and 100 percent in 1970), was high even by European standards.

The right to an education in Estonian is enshrined in the **Constitution of 1992**, although the choice of language of instruction depends on the institution itself. As of 1998, of the 730 schools in Estonia, 111 were Russian and 23 taught in both languages. The 1992 Education Act established four levels: preprimary (under age seven), general, secondary, and higher. Education is compulsory from age seven until students reach 17 or complete their general education. More than 95 percent of general school students proceed to secondary education, either at a gymnasium or secondary vocational school. General and secondary school teaching follows a national curriculum.

Entry to higher education is by competitive examination, based on *numerus clausus* for most publicly funded programs. The Soviet system of degrees has been totally changed to a hybrid Nordic-American model where a bachelor's degree takes four years, a master's two more, and a doctorate an additional six. In preparation for membership in the European Union (EU), the University of Tartu began to shift in 2003 to the so-called Bologna system (recently adopted by West European Ministers of Education) of a five-year standard master's degree. Despite the time and effort required, higher education is becoming more popular, with the number of enrolled students rising from 25,472 in 1980, remaining at 25,899 in 1990, and rising to 57,286 in 2001. The number of universities, applied higher education institutions, and higher vocational institutions grew from six in Soviet times to 22 in 1993 and 37 in 1998, and then dropped to 33 in 2001. Their numbers will decrease further as both the private universities and private higher professional schools (10 of each in 2001) consolidate. Adult education, as a means of acquiring new skills, receives strong state support, including, since 1993, tax relief for both employers funding their workers and the participants themselves. Around a quarter of adults took some form of further training in 2001. But there are still problems in gearing the educational system toward economic transformation, as vocational postsecondary institutions are still in need of major upgrading to the market economy.

Public education is funded by the state and local budgets (note that local budgets are basically funded from state tax resources), although schools are encouraged to resort to private finance through fees and donations for additional study materials. Private education accounted for less than 2 percent of student intake for the first three levels in 2001, whereas private higher educational establishments attracted a quarter of students. Many of these specialize in business studies. The challenge for the educational elites and bureaucracies for the first decade of the 21st century is to raise the content taught to international levels and then to integrate it into the international system. Although the **Tiger Leap** program is opening up pupils' minds to information technology and the world's databases, most teachers are still products of Soviet education, however good Estonian nationalists they may be. The most serious challenge to a small society with a national language population of under a million is to develop a sufficiently competitive system to enable university graduates to compete at the international level. Content demands university staffs with degrees from competitive foreign institutions as well as expensive, up-to-date library and laboratory resources. Such upgrading after 50 years of complete exclusion and 10 years of uneven transition cannot be completed in less than a generation, despite such Western assistance programs as the EuroFaculty, George Soros's Open Society foundations, and foreign aid programs.

After successfully changing the structure of the educational system, the main challenge for Estonian politicians is the cultural one of integrating the Russian schooling into the Estonian system. Finally, after nine years of lost time, in December 1999 a plan was adopted where by 2007 all Russian schools should have qualified teachers of Estonian so that graduates will be able to speak and write proper Estonian and be fully acculturated to Estonia while maintaining their Russian culture. Throughout the 1990s, although all teachers at Russian-language schools were expected to be fluent in Estonian, in reality very few were (*see* INTEGRATION).

EENPALU, KAAREL (Karl-August Einbund to 1935) (1888–1942). Estonian politician and lawyer. Eenpalu was born on 28 May 1888 at Vesner *vald*. While studying law at the **University of Tartu** from 1909 to 1914, he also served as exhibitions secretary for the Farmers' Association of **Tartu** in 1911–12. After passing the state entrance exams to Moscow University for graduate work, war intervened and he was conscripted to serve as an officer in the artillery in 1915. In 1917, he graduated from the Paul I War College in Petrograd, which prepared him to form the 5th Battalion of the Estonian Artillery Brigade in 1917 and the 2nd Artillery Regiment's 7th Battery in 1918, and to serve as commander of both in the **War of Independence**, fighting on the Tartu and the southern fronts. In April 1919, he was elected to the **Constituent Assembly** and named state auditor. A year later, in 1920 he was appointed minister of the interior in **Jaan Tõnisson**'s cabinet, where he brought the police force under central control, and reorganized and professionalized it so that he became known as "the father" of the Estonian police force. He served in the same ministry for six years, with breaks, in subsequent cabinets.

In 1923, Eenpalu joined the Farmers Union (Fatherland Union) party and was elected to all the successive Parliaments under its aegis. In 1926–32 and 1933–34, he served as speaker of parliament and as head of state for two and a half months in 1932. In 1934 he joined **Konstantin Päts** in his **preemptive coup** and served as minister of the interior and deputy prime minister from 1934 to 1938. After the 1938 presidential elections, President Päts appointed him prime minister. However, conflicts with Päts and **Johan Laidoner** soon led to his resignation. Thereafter, until the Soviet occupation he served as director of the national Shale Oil firm, when he was arrested at his farm and held in a **Tallinn** jail for 10 months, and then deported to Kirov oblast, where he died in a concentration camp at Vjatlag on 27 January 1942.

Eenpalu was a strong supporter of guided democracy. Even when it became clear that the preemptive coup of 1934 was a mistake and there was no right-wing conspiracy, he not only supported Päts but also was the author of many of the government's policies. Indeed, he was regarded by many as the *éminence grise* behind the throne. He was undoubtedly a very able administrator, as well as a skilled politician. As minister of the interior of the Päts regime, he was responsible for propagating such nationalist policies as the Estonianization of names (his own included), the popularization of wearing national costumes, and the flying of the national **flag**. He was also the driving force in the formation of the Fatherland Union and the Popular Front.

EESTIMAA KUBERMANGU AJUTINE MAANÕUKOGU (Provisional Diet of the Province of Estland). Also known as Maanõukogu and Maapäev in Estonian history, this Diet (*zemstvo* in Russian) was authorized by a decree of the Russian Provisional Government on 12 April 1917. The first organ of self-government in Estonia, it consisted of representatives elected from towns and counties on the basis of one deputy per 20,000 inhabitants. It met on 14 July 1917 under the leadership of **Otto Strandman** and Ado Birk but was dismissed by the **Estonian Workers' Commune** on 28 November 1917. Just prior to this, it delegated its powers to its Executive Committee and Council of Elders, which continued to operate underground. The Diet reconvened on 20 November 1918 and disbanded on 24 April 1919 when the **Constituent Assembly** met.

EESTI ÜLIÕPILASTE SELTS (EÜS, Estonian University Students Association). The organization known universally by its acronym, EÜS, is the oldest and largest of the Estonian university **student fraternities**. It was formed at the **University of Tartu** in 1870 informally by Estonian-minded students who began to meet to pursue nationalist objectives at the then German-language University of Tartu. In 1883, it was formally organized and its blue-black-white flag, symbolizing the blue sky of Estonia, the black earth, and the white fields of ripe grain, was consecrated in 1884 at Otepää, site of an ancient Estonian fortification. Subsequently, as a result of the identification of the EÜS leaders with the struggle for national recognition, autonomy, and finally independence, their flag became the national symbol of Estonians and was formally adopted as the **national flag** in 1918. Although EÜS was formed by students who had been members of the German fraternities, the Studentenverbindungen, called Korporatsioonid in Estonian, EÜS has always eschewed many of the trappings and the formality of the former. During both the Soviet and Nazi occupations, EÜS and the traditional fraternities were outlawed, but their members continued to meet underground until they were restored at **Tartu** in 1988–89.

During the first period of their activity up to 1940, they contained the elite of Estonia's leaders and operated as clubs of lifelong members where seniors educated juniors in the values of national service and looked after the welfare of juniors in providing jobs and preferment after graduation. Since the restoration of independence, EÜS and the fraternities have largely reverted to their prewar roles, with the exception that the generations who attended university in the Soviet period are missing. Thus, even the graduate membership is relatively young.

EINSELN, ALEKSANDER (1931–). Retired general in the Estonian Army and former chief of the general staff of the **Estonian De-**

fense Forces. Born on 25 October 1931 in **Tallinn**, in 1944 Einseln fled the coming of the second Soviet occupation to Germany and emigrated to the United States in 1949, where he enlisted in the army in 1950. He fought in Korea in 1950–53, and was commissioned lieutenant in 1955. In 1964, he completed the Special Forces officers' course and served with the Green Berets in Viet Nam until 1966. He graduated from George Washington University in 1968 and from the Army Staff College in 1969, and he served again in Viet Nam in 1971–72. In 1975–76, he served at Army Headquarters in staff training. Immediately on graduating from the National Defense College senior course in 1977, he was appointed head of the European and NATO office in the Planning and Policy Division of the Joint Chiefs of Staff during the Polish crisis, where he served until 1982. From 1982 to his retirement in 1985 with the rank of colonel, he served as deputy inspector-general of the U.S. Army's Pacific Command. During his 35-year career in the U.S. Army, he commanded infantry, special forces, paratroopers, as well as training units, and he earned 28 medals.

In May 1993, Einseln was appointed commanding officer of the **Estonian Defense Forces** with the rank of major general by President **Lennart Meri** in his constitutional capacity as commander in chief. The decision drew strong objections from the U.S. Department of State, which feared upsetting Russia by allowing a former U.S. senior officer to serve in a high post on the territory of the former Soviet Union. The United States threatened to revoke Einseln's military pension and even his citizenship. Support for the new Estonian general from several U.S. senators, however, eventually resolved the controversy and he received official permission to remain in his new command.

In Estonia, however, Einseln rapidly found himself in conflict with his senior officers whose former Soviet training, military experience, and mentality contrasted sharply with his own. Moreover, both his colleagues and Einseln came from the largest military establishments of the modern era, with no knowledge or experience in how to establish an effective defensive force for a small state from scratch. The resultant mistrust escalated into an open conflict with Defense Minister Andrus Öövel and led to Einseln's resignation in December 1995. On his retirement, President Meri promoted him to full general. *See also* ESTONIAN DEFENSE FORCES.

ELECTION OF THE PRESIDENT. Except for the election by popular mandate of the first president under the Constitution of 1992, the president is elected by the **Riigikogu**. If the Riigikogu fails to agree, then an electoral college will be called into session.

Election by Riigikogu: Any Estonian citizen by birth who has attained 40 years of age may be nominated as a candidate for president of the Republic. The president will be elected for a term of five years, and may be reelected for a second consecutive term. Any group of one fifth (21) or more members of the Riigikogu (101 members) may nominate a candidate for president, and the candidate who receives a two-thirds majority (68) of votes of the membership of the Riigikogu will be declared elected. If no candidate receives the required majority, a second round of voting will be held on the next day. For the second round of voting, candidates will be nominated anew (the same, as well as new, candidates may be proposed). If no candidate receives the required two-thirds majority in the second round, a third round of voting will be held on the same day. For the third round, the names of the two candidates who receive the greatest number of votes in the second round will be entered on the ballot. If no candidate receives the required two-thirds majority, the speaker of the Riigikogu will convene an electoral college for the election of the president.

Election by Electoral College: The electoral body shall be composed of members of the Riigikogu and representatives of the local government councils. The local government representatives are chosen by each local council on the following bases: one member from each municipality with up to 10,000 voting-age Estonian citizens; two from each with between 10,001 and 50,000 voters; four from each with 50,001 to 100,000 voters; and 10 representatives from each local municipality with more than 100,000 voting-age citizens. As the number of local government units is changing due to the administrative-territorial reform, the number of members of the electoral college changes: in the 1996 elections it was 374 (101 members of the Riigikogu and 273 representatives from the local government councils), and in the 2001 elections it was 367 (101 members of the Riigikogu and 266 local government representatives). The State Electoral Commission is responsible for determining the numbers of local electoral representatives.

For the first round of voting, the names of candidates who participated in the third round of voting in the Riigikogu and any new candidates nominated will be entered on the ballot. The candidate who receives a majority of the votes of members of the electoral college participating in the voting will be declared elected. If no candidate receives the required majority, a second round of voting will take place on the same day. The second round of voting will take place between the two candidates who received the greatest number of votes in the first round of voting, and the candidate who receives the votes of a majority of the members of the electoral college participating in the elections will be declared elected.

If no candidate receives the required majority within 14 days, the election of the president returns to the Riigikogu, and the process begins over again.

ELECTORAL DEMOCRACY. The calling of the elections for the Congress of People's Deputies by Mikhail Gorbachev in 1988 instituted an intense period of electoral activity among Estonians. For the first time since 1938, they had a real possibility to actually affect the outcome of elections. And, although the Congress was still controlled by the **Estonian Communist Party (ECP)**, Estonians made sure that the deputies they were able to elect represented their desire for independence. As the table in appendix 3 shows, participation at 87.1 percent of eligible voters has not been reached since. Nevertheless, the 14 elections in a decade that Estonians engaged in show that, although they may have suffered electoral weariness in the late 1990s, they did express themselves very clearly on independence and on the form of government that they wanted. Moreover, the recent low turnouts are not very different from those in mature democracies, which may reflect both a normalization of sociopolitical life and the increasing irrelevance of government to Estonians' individual and collective private socioeconomic activities. *See* appendix 3, Estonian Participation in Mostly Free and Free Elections, 1989–2003.

ELECTORAL SYSTEMS. During the first period of independence in the five general elections to the 100-seat **Riigikogu**, from 1920 to 1933, the party list system of proportional representation (PR) in multiparty electoral districts was used. Each citizen (of at least one year's standing) and aged at least 21 cast a single vote for a party list. The mandates were then divided among the parties based on the percentages of the vote received in each district. Since there was no minimum threshold vote, there was criticism that the system led to excessive party splintering.

In the **Era of Silence**, the electoral system was changed by referendum in 1936 to the majoritarian single-member district system for elections to the National Assembly to draft the new Constitution. The elections after the adoption of the new **Constitution of 1937** followed this system.

The sham elections in 1940 after the Soviet occupation of Estonia, in which only candidates vetted by the **Estonian Communist Party (ECP)** were allowed to stand for office, continued the first-past-the-post system. The **Constitution of 1940** of the Estonian Soviet Socialist Republic (ESSR) established a single-chamber Supreme Soviet of the ESSR as the highest state legislative organ, elected for four-year terms on a majoritarian basis of one member per 10,000 citizens but again with communist party vetting of candidates.

The electoral system established for the restored Riigikogu in 1992 attempts to eschew the splintering effect of the original electoral system while providing proportional representation to as many partisan groupings as possible. Accordingly, the 101 members of the Riigikogu are elected by a proportional system with a party list in 11 multimember electoral districts ranging in size from seven to 13 members, with a 5 percent threshold applied for "compensation" mandates. Each voter casts a ballot for as many candidates as there are seats in his electoral district.

In the first round of counting, a simple quota is calculated for each electoral district by dividing the number of voters in the electoral region by the number of mandates allocated to the region. Candidates who reach the simple quota of votes in each electoral district are declared elected.

In the second round of counting, all votes are counted to determine which parties received at least 5 percent of the votes cast nationwide. Next, candidates are placed on party lists in each electoral district according to the number of votes cast for them. Parties are then awarded mandates according to the numbers of times that the combined votes for their candidates exceed the simple quota in the district. Candidates who receive at least 10 percent of the simple quota are then declared elected according to their preferred placement on the party lists. In the third round of counting, all votes not so far allocated are divided as "compensation" mandates among national party lists that reach the 5 percent threshold, based on a quota calculated on a modified d'Hondt method using the coefficient 0.9. This method favors larger parties.

The current PR method has reduced the number of parties elected from the European record of 14 in 1923 (not exceeded until the Polish election in 1991): in 1992 and 1995 nine parties were elected, seven were elected in 1999, and only six were in 2003. Part of the reason for the reduced numbers until the new millennium was that some of the "parties" were in fact electoral coalitions.

This method, although complex and ill understood by the electorate, reduces the election of very small or local parties. It also forces the parties to recruit large numbers of "name" candidates to pad their votes and leads to election of many who receive a very small number of votes. In the 1999 elections, only 11 candidates received enough votes to be declared elected in the first round, that is, they received a "personal" mandate, 41 were elected from electoral district party lists, and 46 were elected from nationwide party lists as "compensation" mandates. The number of individual votes cast for the successful candidates ranged from 14,320 to 64.

ELECTRICITY. *See* OIL SHALE; ENERGY.

EMIGRATION. Estonians have emigrated to foreign lands in significant numbers only since the middle of the 19th century. Apart from a trickle of political refugees fleeing the reprisals after the abortive 1905 Revolution, people moved abroad for economic reasons until the displacements of World War II, when the sole reason for emigration became political survival.

Emigration in the 19th Century: Mass emigration of Estonians began in the second half of the 19th century resulting from lack of farming land, restrictions on purchasing of farms from the aristocratic landowners, and the opportunity to earn better income in Russia.

The first wave of emigrants left Estonia in the 1860s when the "prophet" Maltsveti (Juhan Leinberg) called on people to move to the Promised Land. In the spring of 1861, several hundred gathered at the Lasnamäe escarpment overlooking Tallinn Bay to await the Lord's "White Ship" to take them to the promised land of the Crimea. Despite being disappointed in their expectations, hundreds nevertheless emigrated to the Crimea and established several Estonian settlements. Some southern Estonians also resettled closer in Russia, on the eastern shore of Lake Peipus (**Peipsi**). The first wave accounted for 3,600 emigrants.

The famine of 1868 led to a second wave of emigration with northern Caucasus as the preferred destination; 32 Estonian settlements were established there. In the final decades of the century, rural Estonian emigrants formed settlements over a wide area of imperial Russia, especially central Russia and the further reaches of the Caucasus, as well as in northern *gubernyas* of Ter, Mogiljov, Orjol, and Volga-Baskhir. The first Siberian Estonian settlements were formed by forced labor and exiles. They were joined at the end of the century by voluntary emigrants, of whom the majority settled in the Tobolsky and Jenissei *gubernyas*. For urban emigrants, the preferred cities were Moscow, Riga, and Pskov, with St. Petersburg as the favorite destination. At the beginning of the 1890s, 7,431 Estonians lived there, but in 1910 their numbers had reached 14,704 and increased rapidly during the war to over 50,000 by 1917.

According to the imperial census of 1897, the population of Estonians was distributed as follows among the provinces or *gubernyas* of imperial Russia:

Livland	518,594
Estland	365,959
St. Petersburg (including Narva)	64,116
Pskov	25,458
Caucasus	4,281
Siberia	4,202
Novgorod	3,112
Tauria	2,210
Samara	2,029
Tver	1,516
Central Asia	440

Overall, by the end of the 19th century approximately 110,000 Estonians lived outside the historic limits of Estonia; of these, two thirds were farmers. But by 1917 the number of Estonians in Russia had increased to over 200,000 living in 200 settlements with a concentration of 50,000 in St. Petersburg.

Westward Emigration prior to Independence: Emigration westward to North America began at the end of the 19th century initially with Estonian sailors who jumped imperial Russian merchant ships in the United States and settled in New York, San Francisco, Philadelphia, and Chicago. The first Estonian farming community was established in South Dakota in 1892, followed by settlements in Wisconsin and Montana. Six farming settlements were also founded in Alberta, Canada, at the beginning of the 20th century. After the 1905 revolutionary disturbances, a wave of refugees arrived in North America, with most settling in cities. It has been estimated that between 10,000 and 15,000 Estonians lived in North America by the outbreak of the World War I. Small numbers also emigrated to Australia and South America. Around 500 Estonians lived in Australia in 1912.

Emigration during Independence, 1918 to 1940: During the two decades of independence, at least 250,000 Estonians lived abroad. Of these, 195,000 lived in the Soviet Union. As a result of the Tartu Peace Treaty of 1920, 40,000 opted to return to Estonia (universally called optants). In 1926, 254,600 Estonians remained in the Soviet Union, and 139,500 of these spoke Estonian. Most lived in the territory of the Russian Federal Soviet Socialist Republic:

RFSSR	150,378
Siberia	29,890
Ukraine	2,011
Caucasus	1,043
Byelorussia	967
Uzbekistan	216
Turkmenistan	51

The vast majority of these, 119,000, lived in rural areas. At the end of the 1920s, there were 24,000 Estonian farms in the Soviet Union. Most were relatively well off with the result that the owners, mostly small farmers, were labeled *kulaks* (a communist term of opprobrium denoting capitalist farmers who exploited the rural working classes) and their farms forcibly nationalized during Stalin's collectivization drive. As a result of the Stalinist antinationalist policy, Estonian schools, newspapers, libraries, and choirs were also closed. Leading "Estonian nationalists" in the settlements were deported to Siberia, and such prominent Estonian communists in the Soviet Union as **Jaan Anvelt**, Otto Rästas, and Hans Pöögelman were shot as enemies of the people. Ironically, after Stalin's death they were honored in Soviet Estonia with streets and factories named after them. The forced **collectivization** of the farming communities into "collective" farms across the Soviet Union and the repression of Estonian "nationalism" led to a decline of the Estonian population to 143,600 by 1929.

During the period of independence, over 17,000 Estonians emigrated to the western hemisphere, with most leaving during the difficult initial years of building the republic in the 1920s (2,676 left in 1926); in the 1930s, the number leaving fluctuated between 300 and 600 per year. In addition, after the signing of the **Molotov-Ribbentrop Pact** in 1938, 20,000 German Estonians were "called home" by Hitler and left for Germany together with 500 Estonians (*see* BALTIC GERMANS).

World War II and After: World War II ushered in a new wave of emigration. The initial Soviet occupation of 1941 led to 8,000 fleeing west. In 1942–43, many fled to Finland to escape German mobilization. Together with the "repatriation" of the Swedish Estonian population, approximately 3,000 Estonians left for Sweden.

When it became clear in the spring of 1944 that Estonia would probably be occupied by the Soviet Union once again, the last major emigration began. During the summer an evacuation center to assist Estonians was established in Stockholm, and in September regular ship and boat trips were organized to Sweden. A massive evacuation took place from western Estonia, especially from the farming-fishing villages of the coast and the islands, with between 26,000 and 27,000 arriving safely in Sweden by 1945. Many also drowned in the fall and winter storms and in air attacks on the refugee ships and boats.

Simultaneously, large numbers of Estonians also left for Germany under different pretexts. For example, the 3,000 inhabitants of the Sõrve peninsula were forcibly transported to Germany, others pretended that they were Baltic Germans in order to be let out by the German border guards, and soldiers and work battalion draftees were transported by German occupation authorities. Over 4,000 of the Germany-bound refugees died at sea, mostly from Soviet air attacks. At the end of the war, between 45,000 and 50,000 Estonians found themselves in Germany: former soldiers, prisoners of war, forced laborers, and simple refugees. The war-induced emigration in 1944 totaled between 60,000 and 80,000.

The years 1945 to 1952 saw extensive re-emigration of the war refugees. The majority of the 32,000 who found themselves in the displaced persons (DP) camps in Germany re-emigrated to Great Britain, the Americas, Australia, and New Zealand. Large numbers left Sweden for the United States and Canada, as a result of fear created by the Soviet demand for forcible repatriation of those who had fought in the German armies. In the period 1948–52, on the basis of the DP regulations 11,000 refugees emigrated to the United States, 12,000 to Canada, and 4,700 to Australia.

At the collapse of the Soviet Union in 1991, Estonians abroad represented approximately 13 percent of all Estonians and were spread about the globe as follows:

USSR, outside Estonia	66,000
In RFSSR	46,000
In Ukrainian SSR	4,000
In Latvian SSR	3,500
In Kazakhstan	3,300
In Georgian SSR	2,000
In Kazakhstan	3,300
United States	27,000
Sweden	25,000
Canada	20,000
Australia and New Zealand	6,000
South America (Argentina, Brazil, Uruguay)	3,000
United Kingdom	2,700
Germany	2,500

It has been estimated that in all, about 150,000 ethnic Estonians resided abroad at the end of the Soviet era. These figures include children of mixed marriages and those born outside Estonia. At least half of them spoke Estonian. *See also* ESTONIAN CANADIANS.

ENERGY. Estonia's domestic energy resources are limited to small hydroelectric power stations, peat for some small heating plants, large amounts of **oil shale** used mostly for electricity generation and heating plants, and also in the production of heavy oil and chemicals. Wood is used for 75 percent of heating in villages and farms. Estonia is dependent on imports for the rest of its energy requirements: refined petroleum products for transportation and natural gas for 90 percent of its urban district heating. Since the restoration of Independence in 1991, the importation and distribution of gasoline and diesel oil has been totally redirected from Russian sources to Western ones. These are now imported mostly through three oil terminals at **Muuga** port by several competing international retail distributing chains. Natural gas is imported by pipeline from Russia, which is connected to large underground reservoirs in Latvia. Eesti Gaas was fully **privatized** in 1997 and is owned by Ruhrgas (Germany, 32 percent), Gazprom (Russia, 31 percent), Fortum (Finland, 10 percent), and smaller investors, and it has a long-term agreement with Gazprom for supply. Wind power is the only new renewable energy source commercially feasible in Estonia, but its use is still in its infancy.

ENVIRONMENT. A half century of incorporation into the closed economy of the Union of Soviet Socialist Republics (USSR) directed from the center in Moscow and aimed at building heavy **industry** and military might created an unbalanced economy in tiny Estonia with outdated machinery and technology and irrational use of natural resources. As a result, conflict arose between industry and preservation of the environment in several parts of Estonia. The impact of indiscriminate and uneconomic exploitation of natural resources began immediately when the USSR occupied Estonia and operated the military uranium refinery at **Sillmäe**, and it continued with the overexploitation of **oil shale** for underfiring massive electricity power stations and the uneconomic mining of **phosphate** for fertilizer used in far-off regions of the USSR. Because industrialization came to Estonia late, and because Estonian urban areas are small, Estonians have a close relationship with nature. The location and operation of industrial plants without any regard for environmental impact and the lack of controls over water and air pollution by chemical and mineral effluents and exhausts led to very high levels of pollution across the USSR, including Estonia. Decades of governmental disregard of the effects of pollution on the environment also produced a general lack of understanding of the consequences for animal and human health, with resulting high rates of illness and mortality. The massive monoculture of meat production **agriculture** in Estonia, and the carelessness of the Soviet military occupying large tracts of Estonia as bases, added considerably to chemical pollution of the soil and water table.

Nevertheless, when **perestroika and glasnost** allowed dissent in the late 1980s, the Estonian intelligentsia reacted strongly to the threat of potentially catastrophic pollution of the main groundwater aquifer posed by the proposal to build massive phosphate mines in **Northeast Estonia**, already the most polluted region of the country. The ensuing protest carried on largely through the media, known as the **Phosphate War**, was successfully won in 1987, and it provided much of the political mobilization of the Estonian people in the run-up to independence. Since the collapse of the Soviet economy, independent Estonia has conscientiously moved to restructure industry, agriculture, and human health to **European Union** (EU) standards. The national Environmental Strategy foresees a 30-year schedule to clean up the residue of the environmental pollution legacy of the Soviet period. Both the EU and the Nordic states have provided funding to assist Estonia in rectifying the most serious sources of pollution, such as cleaning up the Sillmäe nuclear and heavy metal pond, cleaning up the **Paldiski** naval nuclear reactors, and upgrading sewage systems. Still, even with EU financial assistance it will take until the end of 2013 to bring all of Estonia's drinking water systems up to EU standards, and 2015 for the oil shale burning **electricity** plants to become pollution-free, or be closed.

ERA OF SILENCE (Vaikiv Ajastu). The term was used to describe the years 1934–1940 by none other than **Kaarel Eenpalu**, a strong supporter of **Konstantin Päts**, *éminence grise* of the Era of Silence and prime minister in 1938–39. The period was ushered in by the **preemptive coup** of 1934, carried out by Päts to avert a feared takeover of the state apparatus by the League of **Veterans** of the **War of Independence**. Although historians have not uncovered any convincing evidence of the reality of such a threat, in the overheated atmosphere of 1934 in Europe, when Hitler had become a widely admired populist model for authoritarian nationalism, the credibility of the threat was accepted by a large majority of Estonian elites. Päts, using the authority of the newly adopted **Constitution of 1933**, proclaimed martial law on 12 March; appointed his trusted colleague **Johan Laidoner**, hero of the War of Independence but an opponent of the leadership of the League of Veterans, as commander in chief of the **armed forces**; shut down all veterans' organizations; arrested 400 of the organizations' members; and outlawed all organized political activity in the country. All members of the League of Veterans were also purged from local governments, the civil service, and the **Defense League**. These actions were immediately approved by the lame-duck parliament.

However, when Päts decreed postponement of the elections for both Riigivanem and **Riigikogu**, scheduled to be held in spring 1934 according to the new Constitution, opposition arose in a special session convened by the exiting parliament, since the Constitution did not allow postponements of elections by decree. His reaction was to permanently postpone the session and rule by decree until a new Constitution could be drawn up and adopted (*see* CONSTITUTION OF 1937). Thus, Päts's takeover of the government was not only a coup in fact, but also in law, since the whole process was illegal under the Constitution in effect in 1934.

The sobriquet "Era of Silence" well describes the silencing of all opposition to Päts's governing clique. However, it also reflects an apparent "national conspiracy" to go along with the suppression of civil and political rights in the interests of "order" after a decade of political turmoil. That his rule was not unduly harsh is demonstrated by nearly all of those jailed in 1934 being released by 1938, and by the fact that none of the former heads of state (Juan Kukk, **Ants Piip**, **Jaan Teemant**, and **Jaan Tõnisson**), who issued the Four State Elders' Memorandum in a Finnish newspaper in October 1936, calling on Päts to immediately end the curtailment of civil and political rights and to reinstitute democratic government, were ever harassed by the government. The fact that even when elections were held in 1938 under the new Constitution of 1937, the opposition only managed to elect 26 members to the government's 54, tends to support the view that that Era of Silence was acquiesced in by the vast majority of Estonians.

ERNESAKS, GUSTAV (1908–1993). Estonian conductor and composer, Ernesaks was born on 12 December 1908 at Perila in Peningi *vald.* After graduation in 1931 in music pedagogy and composition courses from Tallinn Conservatory, he taught in **Tallinn** schools in 1937–41. Thereafter he taught choir conducting at the Tallinn Conservatory for almost three decades (1944–72), where he was promoted to professor of music in 1945. Ernesaks formed the State Men's Choir in 1944 and acted as its conductor and musical director for the next five decades. During a prolific career spanning almost 70 years, he composed music for approximately 300 nationalistic choir songs and 20 solo songs and scores for five operas. During the Soviet period, he was honored by the Soviet state with several Lenin medals, named state laureate, and awarded other Estonian Soviet Socialist Republic (ESSR) state prizes and honors repeatedly from 1947 to 1978. Paradoxically, he composed both the ESSR state hymn (which Estonians ignored and never sang) and "Mu Isamaa on minu arm" ("My Fatherland Is My Refuge"), which quickly became the most-beloved "informal" national hymn sung repeatedly by 200,000–300,000 Estonians in defiance of Soviet power while standing at attention under the baton of Ernesaks at the conclusion of every **Song Festival** in Estonia for half a century. Despite the heavy load of Soviet approbation, Ernesaks was always regarded by Estonians as the quintessential patriot who kept the national flame of patriotism alive publicly even under the very noses of the Soviet occupants. Gustav Ernesaks died on 24 January 1993 in Tallinn, two years after having seen his beloved nation regain its independence.

***ESTONIA* DISASTER.** Shortly after 1:00 A.M. on 28 September 1994, the Tallinn-Stockholm ro-ro (drive-on) passenger-car ferry *MV Estonia* capsized and sank with the loss of 852 lives out of a total passenger and crew complement of 989. The ship, built for the Finnish-Swedish Baltic passenger traffic in 1980, entered the Estonian-Swedish passenger and truck-traffic service in 1992. It was on a routine overnight cruise to Stockholm in heavy seas averaging four meters in winds averaging 25 meters per second, when one or two very large waves hit it on the port bow at about 1:00 A.M. and tore open the upward-opening visor on the car deck, which allowed vast amounts of water to pour into it in a very short time. A severe starboard list developed quickly, aided by the winds on the port side as trucks and cars tore loose and shifted. At 1:15 A.M., the visor tore loose and fell into the sea. The ship quickly keeled over onto its starboard side and began to sink stern first; at 1:35 A.M., it was on its starboard side and disappeared under the waves at about 1:50 A.M. The keeling over to a list of 40–50 degrees, at which it is estimated evacuation from below open decks becomes impossible, took only about 10 minutes. It was so rapid that very few passengers were able to make their way to the open decks to life rafts.

An international Joint Accident Investigation Commission composed of Estonian, Finnish, and Swedish members issued its final report in December 1997. It found that the visor fastenings that had failed due to stress were the immediate cause of the accident. It did not inculpate the crew or safety inspections, the owners, the builders, or any individual with responsibility for the accident. However, it did recommend future design changes in ro-ro ship design.

ESTONIAN ACADEMY OF SCIENCES (Eesti Teaduste Akadeemia). The Estonian Academy of Sciences was originally established by presidential decree on 28 January 1938 as a personal academy honoring eminent Estonian scholars, in effect a copy of standard Western national academies of scholars. On 17 July 1940, a few weeks after it issued its first annual report, it was closed by the new Soviet order.

In 1945, the Council of Estonian National Commissars confirmed the list of 13 institutes that were to form the new Academy of Sciences of the Estonian SSR and appointed its organizing committee. The Council of Ministers of the Estonian Soviet Socialist Republic (ESSR), by a decree on 5 April 1946, formally established the new Academy, modeled on the All-Union Academy in Moscow and affiliated with it, as the highest state institution charged with academic research and its control as well as graduate teaching in the ESSR. The government also appointed the first 24 members of the Academy, 14 with the title of academician and 10 corresponding members. Subsequently, the allowable numbers in the two categories were increased to 22 academicians and 31 corresponding members. During the following 45 years, the number of institutes of the Academy increased to 15 divided into four divisions: three in the astronomy and physics division; two in informatics and engineering sciences; six in biology, geology, and chemistry; and four in humanities and social sciences (including the Institute of Philosophy, Sociology and Law, created in 1988). The total number of senior researchers employed in 1991 was 1,400, supported by a staff of 3,046 junior researchers, technicians, and others. Since the Academy not only had its own separate ESSR state budget line but received special project grants from Moscow as well, it also funded on a part-time basis most researchers at the universities. Moreover, it was in charge of all graduate work, while the universities taught undergraduates. Thus the Academy controlled science and research in Estonia, and the 52 academicians formed the center of control.

In 1988, the Academy's membership decided to revise its history, counted the date of its foundation as 1938 and renamed itself the Estonian Academy of Sciences.

After the restoration of independence, in an effort to reduce expenditures and reduce the inherited massive Soviet structure of the scientific establishment to one more appropriate to the scientific and financial capacity of a small state of 1.5 million, the Academy was reorganized as a personal academy, again honoring prominent scholars chosen by their peers, and all the institutes of the former state academy were hived off to the universities or became independent. The reorganization was finally completed when the act of a parliament governing it was promulgated on 29 April 1997.

But the legacy of the past lives on: the membership is still organized into the same four divisions: astronomy and physics has 15 members and three foreign members; biology, geology, and chemistry has 19 and four; informatics and engineering has 14 and three; and the humanities and social sciences 11 full and three corresponding foreign members. In 2000, 80 percent of the academicians had been appointed prior to the restoration of independence. The main change is that now there is only one category of national membership; the category of corresponding member is reserved for foreign members, all having been appointed since the reorganization. As in all Western academies, the membership is self-perpetuating and is strictly separated from government influence.

Today, the Academy still functions as the senior scholarly and scientific advisory organ of the state and acts as a national liaison with sister academies abroad. Since it no longer controls graduate degrees or institutes and has no money to disburse, its influence is limited to the sum of the stature of the individual members, as in the case of all Western academies.

ESTONIAN ALEKSANDER SCHOOL (Eesti Aleksandrikool). The attempt to found a higher secondary Estonian-language school (at the level of the county schools [*kreisikool*] that taught in Russian) was the first mass action of the Estonian farming communities in the 1860s. Initiated by farmers and schoolmasters in the parishes of Paistu and Tavastu and supported by **Johan Köler** and the **St. Petersburg Patriots**, a petition was submitted to the Estland provincial (*gubernya*) authorities in 1863 asking permission to organize the first Estonian language school, diplomatically named after the tsar. At the same time, a committee was formed to develop a curriculum. In 1869, permission was given to raise funding for the School, and in July 1870, the Central Committee of the Estonian Aleksander School was formed with **Jakob Hurt** as president. Supporting committees to collect money were formed across Estonia (in 1884, there were 146 such committees), and by 1888, 104,271 rubles had been collected—a considerable sum at the time.

But the unintended side effects of the fundraising action were perhaps even more important because the fundraising was accompanied by pan-Estonian agitation for education in the native Estonian language, an enhanced sense of national exclusiveness, and even demands for better teaching of Russian. The annual meetings of the Central Committee with the Supporting Committees (usually in **Tartu**) became well-reported public demonstrations of Estonian nationalism. The opposition of the Baltic landed nobility and much of the German-speaking **Lutheran** pastorate only increased the fervor of the movement.

Unfortunately, delays in actually founding the School led to rising conflicts, especially between the farming initiators, represented by the support committees, and the educated elites concentrated in the Central Committee. The main conflicts arose over whether to establish an agricultural school or an academic one, and over the composition of its board. In 1883, the annual meeting removed Hurt as president, but he refused to accept the decision and asked the authorities to close the support committees. The upshot was that in 1884 the provincial authorities in Livland closed both the support committees and the Central Committee as well, and they replaced it with a 25-member commission. In 1888, the fundraising action was liquidated and the moneys raised during the preceding 14 years were used to set up a Russian-language Estonian Aleksander School at the Kaarli Estate rear Põltsamaa, with an urban curriculum. In contrast to other county schools, it also taught the Estonian language. The school was closed by the authorities in 1906 since it was considered revolutionary because many of its teachers and pupils took part in the Revolution of 1905.

In 1914, the Estonian Aleksander Lower Agricultural School (Eesti Aleksandri Alampõllutöökool) was established at Käo Estate at the initiative of farmers' organizations and became the first institution to teach scientific farming. It was considered the successor to the Kaarli Estonian Aleksander School. It taught its three-year curriculum in Russian until 1917, with Estonian as an optional subject. In 1920, it was renamed the Estonian Aleksander Middle Agricultural School (Eesti Aleksandri Põllutöökeskool) and was transferred to Olustvere Estate in Põltsamaa vald, where it has continued operating under different names to date as an occupational middle school, at present as Põltsamaa Kodu ja Põllutöökool (Põltsamaa Home and Agricultural School).

ESTONIAN CANADIANS. The role that Estonians Abroad played in the life of Estonia during the half century of Soviet occupation is most clearly seen in the organization and activities of the Estonian community in Canada. As a microcosm of the Estonia of the 1930s, it was the most vibrant upholder of Estonian culture abroad and formed the model for all other Estonian communities abroad. However, its beginnings were not auspicious. Although some dozens of Estonian farmers emigrated to Canada around the turn of the 20th century, and seven farming settlements were founded in the Western provinces, the total number of Estonians in Canada did not exceed a few hundred at the end of World War I. During the interwar period, between 1922 and 1940, only 649 Estonians emigrated to Canada. It is estimated that there were about 2,000 Canadians of Estonian heritage before World War II.

Between 1947 and 1953, a wave of 13,037 Estonian immigrants to Canada created a distinct Estonian Canadian society with Toronto as their undisputed capital. Although sufficient numbers settled elsewhere in Canada to form congregations and associations, southern Ontario became their primary area of concentration, marked by the three children's summer and scout camp centers that have flourished there for five decades. Seventy percent of Estonians settled or resettled in southern Ontario, most in the metropolitan Toronto area. According to the Canadian censuses, the following numbers listed themselves as being of Estonian extraction: in 1961, 18,550; in 1971, 19,810; and in 1981, 15,915. The 1991 census showed 21,255 Canadians of Estonian extraction with 12,940 having only Estonian parents. By the 2001 census, these numbers had changed to 22,085 and 9,645 respectively.

The demographic configuration of the five-year postwar wave of political refugees consisted of a disproportionately large number of professionals, lawyers, military officers, and former politicians. Since they regarded themselves as temporary exiles, they set up organizations that would prepare them to return and rebuild their devastated homeland. Hence they established the elected and voluntarily financed Estonian Central Council in 1950 to lead and coordinate their political struggle for regaining independence. Its lobbying activities with the Canadian government proved very successful, especially since the fruitful cooperation developed with parallel organizations formed by Latvian and Lithuanian refugees led to the unique annual Baltic Evening held in the Parliament Buildings in Ottawa with participation of senators, members of parliament, and Cabinet members. And, although by the 1970s Estonians in Canada had become "Canadians" and considered it home, they nevertheless continued to behave as refugees and carried on the political struggle for independence of their homeland without any reduction in effort.

The refugees established approximately 200 copies of the social organizations that they had belonged to back home in order to propagate the culture that the communist occupiers were destroying in the homeland. Thus 13 **Lutheran,** two **Orthodox**, and five Evangelical congregations were formed, each with at least one choir and orchestra. The most important agencies to maintain Estonian culture and inculcate the values of patriotism among children and teens were the

Saturday primary and secondary schools and the Boy Scouts and Girl Guides teaching the Estonian language, history, and cultural values. Upon entering university, the freshman was usually recruited by an Estonian fraternity or sorority. Estonians in each Canadian municipality also organized annual **Independence** Day ceremonies, with the participation of local Estonian scouts, guides, choirs, and orchestras. The scout camp Kotkajärve (Eagle Lake) in Muskoka is not only a summer and winter scout retreat but also in 1967 became the site of the weeklong Metasülikool (Forest University) to bring together academics and young people from across Canada and the United States (and from Estonia since 1990) to foster the culture of Estonia and ensure that regaining and maintaining the independence of Estonia would be carried on by the children and grandchildren of the refugee generation.

In Toronto, the Estonians bought a derelict school building in the city center in 1950 and rebuilt it as Estonia House to serve as the nerve center of Estonians in Canada. It houses the Estonian Central Council, the Consulate of Estonia, the prosperous Estonian Credit Union, and the Saturday Estonian School, kindergarten, and Boy Scout and Girl Guides troops, and it provides the venue for most of the social, musical, and general cultural activities of the Toronto Estonian community. After 50 years of competition, the two community newspapers, *Meie Elu* (*Our Life*) and *Vaba Eestlane* (*Free Estonian*), were bought out by the Tartu College Foundation and a new weekly, *Eesti Elu* (*Estonian Life*), began publishing in 2002. To serve the increasing number of Estonian Canadians, whose Estonian is weak or nonexistent, it includes a 4–8-page section in English.

In 1969, Tartu College, an 18-story student residence on the edge of the campus of the University of Toronto, was built by the cooperative effort of the 600 alumni members of the 17 **student fraternities** to provide meeting rooms on the ground floor for the fraternities and earn income from the rented dorm rooms. The College funds the Tartu Institute, which runs lecture series on cultural issues; operates one of the two Estonian archives in Canada (the other is located in Estonia House and is run by the Estonian Federation in Canada); and supports a large library of Estonian books and a bibliography club that sends tens of thousands of donated books to libraries in Estonia. It also provided the funding for the **Chair of Estonian Studies** at the University of Toronto.

Political lobbying, educational, and cultural activities continue unabated in the 21st century and have been rejuvenated with the arrival of a couple of hundred immigrants from Estonia to Toronto and frequent visits in both directions. The Toronto community entered the 21st century vibrant and strong. Notably, it is the only community of Estonians abroad that has published one 500- and two 600-page cumulative folio volumes of its history: the first in 1975, the second in 1985, and the last in 1997, titled *Eestlased Kanadas* (*Estonians in Canada*) I, II, and III.

ESTONIAN CITIZENS' COMMITTEE (Eesti Kodanike Komitee). Two symbolically important events in the process of restoration of independence took place on **Independence** Day, 24 February 1989. At sunrise, the tricolor flag of the independent Estonian Republic was officially hoisted in the presence of the leaders of the Estonian Soviet Socialist Republic (ESSR), Head of State **Arnold Rüütel** and Prime Minister **Indrek Toome**, on the national flagstaff atop Pikk Hermann tower for the first time since the Soviet occupation in 1940. On the same day, the Heritage Society and the recently founded Estonian Christian Democratic League formed the Estonian Citizens' Committee at a meeting at Estonia Concert Hall with the objective of registering all who had been citizens of Estonia the day before the Soviet annexation in 1940 in order to call together a **Estonian Congress**. The action succeeded as Estonians formed local citizens committees for this purpose all over the country despite the hostility of the local communist authorities. By the end of the year, over 900,000 had registered themselves as citizens of the prewar Republic. The action was also strongly supported by **Estonians abroad**, so that when the Congress was actually elected and called together, it could claim that it represented all Estonian citizens of the de jure independent Republic of Estonia

ESTONIAN COMMITTEE (Eesti Komitee). *See* ESTONIAN CONGRESS.

ESTONIAN COMMUNIST PARTY (ECP) (Eesti Kommunistlik Partei, EKP). Marxism first arrived in Estonia at the **University in Tartu** in the 1880s when some students formed a study group. Revolutionary socialism began to spread among workers in **Narva** and **Tallinn** in the late 1890s under the leadership of activists from St. Petersburg. In 1901, the Leninist revolutionary newspaper *Iskra* (*The Spark*) was widely read among workers in Estonia when one of its enthusiastic supporters, Lenin's younger brother, Dmitri Ulyanov, studied medicine at Tartu. Lenin's close collaborator, Mihail Kalinin, worked as an agitator in Estonia in 1901–04, helped organize workers' committees in the growing industrial centers, and set up the Tallinn affiliate of the Russian Social Democratic Workers Party (RSDWP).

But soon, in 1905, Estonian social democracy split in two. Those who supported the building of the RSDWP into a federation of national parties formed the Estonian Social Democratic Workers Union (Eesti Sotsiaaldemokraatilik Tööliste Ühendus, ESDTÜ), whereas those who supported the idea of a centralized party in a centralized state remained with the RSDWP. Among the leaders of the latter were Aleksander Kesküla, Mihkel Martna, Hans Pöögelman, and **August Rei**. The party found most of its support among urban industrial workers. After the failed 1905 Revolution and the deadly work of the tsarist punishment units, membership dropped precipitously. Nevertheless, two years later, in February 1907 at the congress of the Estonian units of the RSDWP at Terijoki in Finland, the federalists joined again with the centralists and elected an executive committee. But, owing to the continued persecution by the tsarist police and widespread arrests of leading members, the revived party ceased activities within a few months for the next 10 years, as its remaining leaders withdrew from politics or fled abroad.

About the only socialist activity in the interim was the publication of the Bolshevik newspaper *Kiir* (*The Ray*) by **Jaan Anvelt** in Narva in 1912–14 and the carrying over to Estonia of the progressive deepening gulf between the **Bolshevik** (revolutionaries) and Menshevik (supporters of the parliamentary road to socialism) wings of the Social Democratic movement.

The February 1917 Revolution at one stroke transformed the Russian empire into a political arena where any and all political views could freely organize and compete. In Estonia there were now three leftist parties, the newest being the Socialist-Revolutionary Party (Sotsialistide-Revolutsionääride Partei) known as the *esseerid*, which demanded the replacement of the tsarist empire with a democratic republic and the division of landed estates among the peasants. Support for this party grew during World War I and was especially prominent among the non-Estonian peasant-stock soldiery and the Russian peasant-laborers imported to work the armaments factories. The intellectuals **Hans Kruus** and **Gustav Suits** were two prominent Estonian leaders of this party.

After the February Revolution, Bolsheviks made rapid inroads among the industrial workers, and the renamed RSDW(b)P ("b" for Bolshevik) became the largest party on Estonian territory, with **Jaan Anvelt**, **Viktor Kingissepp**, and Hans Pöölgelmann as leaders. The split with the Mensheviks became complete when the latter, spurning the unitary pan-Russianism of the Bolsheviks, formed their own party, the Estonian Social Democratic Union (Eesti Sotsialdemokraatlik Ühendus), with Mihkel Martna and August Rei as leaders.

On 29 November 1918, as the German occupation army retreated and the Red Army partially conquered Estonian territory, the Bolsheviks formed the Estonian Workers' Commune government. Six months later, on 5 June 1919, they were forced to liquidate it when the bourgeois Estonian Army drove the Red Army out of Estonia. Thereafter the Bolsheviks, now universally called communists, regrouped as an illegal organization in the independent Republic of Estonia. On 5 November 1920, the outlawed communist party held its first congress illegally in Tallinn; adopted its new wholly Estonian-language name, Eesti Kommunistlik Partei (EKP); and adopted a program to reestablish Soviet power in Estonia. It also elected Jaan Anvelt, Viktor Kingissepp, and Hans Pöögelmann, among others, to its Central Committee and became a section of the Moscow led Communist International (Comintern). Declared illegal, the ECP organized underground cells and in 1924 claimed 2,000 members, half of whom were industrial workers, one fourth farm workers, and one fourth poor peasants. In addition, it infiltrated the Estonian Working People's Party (Eestimaa Töörahva Partei), which it controlled. Thus, although its main leaders lived in exile in St. Petersburg or Moscow, a second echelon of "legal" leaders managed to elect members to the **Riigikogu** in the elections of 1920, 1923, 1926, 1929, and 1932.

However, the failure of the Comintern-inspired and Comintern-prepared Estonian communists' **attempted coup on 1 December 1924** put an end to the party as a political force in Estonia for 16 years. While its leaders fled to the Union of Soviet Socialist Republics (USSR) or were jailed, the remaining convinced communists went deep underground. Their estimated numbers (including those in jail) fluctuated between 70 and 200 during these years. According to the ECP's own records, there were only 150 party members in Estonia at the time of the Soviet occupation in July 1940.

Under the protection of the occupying Red Army and the direction of Andrei Zdanov, the member of the Politburo of the CP(b)SU (again, "b" for Bolshevik) Party sent to Estonia to reorganize it into the Estonian SSR, the ECP quickly revived, immediately added 1,300 new members, and restructured itself into the Estonian Communist (Bolshevik) Party to conform with the current practice in the USSR. On 12 September, its Central Committee was formed with Nikolai Karotamm, Johannes Lauristin, and **Johannes Vares** among the seven members. The party immediately set about turning bourgeois Estonia into a copy of the USSR: within a few months all large industries, all transportation companies, and all commerce were nationalized, and the Republic's political, judicial, and administrative structures were destroyed and new ones created in imitation of the Soviet models.

When Nazi Germany attacked the Soviet Union on 22 June 1941 and moved to occupy Estonia with its Army Group Nord in preparation for an attack on Leningrad, the EC(b)P set up an underground Party Center and the ESSR Volunteer Partisan Units Headquarters to organize guerilla warfare in German-occupied Estonia, before the Party leadership fled to the Soviet Union. Only 10 percent of the 2,084 party members and 1,667 candidates remained in Estonia, about half fell in battle, and 38 percent continued organizational work in the USSR. During the three ensuing years of exile, the Party hierarchy prepared 2,500 activists for Party, Komsomol, administrative, and propaganda work preparatory to freeing Estonia from the Germans. As the latter retreated on 10–11 September 1944, the Party Central Committee held its third plenary at Võru, where it elected Nikolai Karotamm as its first secretary. With the assistance of the CPSU and the occupying army, the ECP established total control over Estonia very quickly. Under his leadership, the Estonian Party carried out the total Sovietization of **agriculture** and transformed 92 percent of farms into collectives by 1950 (and 96.7 percent, by 1952, when only small outlying, unproductive "forest farms" of a few hectares were left in private hands)—in less than three years—as ordered by the 1947 decision of the CPSU Central Committee.

During the first five years after the Soviet reoccupation, Party membership grew from 2,409 in 1945 to 17,639 in 1950. However, since 57.2 percent of these were imported Russian workers, the Party was regarded by Estonians largely as foreign and as merely a wing of the Russian All-Union Communist Party. But although the Estonians in the leadership of the Estonian Party remained apart from the mass of the Estonian people, they nevertheless pursued moderate nationalist cultural policies and attempted to protect the small remnant of Estonian intelligentsia who had survived the war years and remained in Estonia. However, their masters in Moscow found these policies to be insufficiently communist and instituted a drastic reform of the hierarchy. Accordingly, the infamous VIII Plenary of the ECP in 1950 declared them guilty of "bourgeois nationalism," then removed Karotamm and virtually all the old pre-1940 cadre from Party positions. Hendrik Allik, Nigol Andresen, **Hans Kruus**, Lembit Lüüs, Aleksander Jõeäär, and Aleksander Aben were arrested and jailed, and August Hansen was later shot. They were replaced by **Johannes** (Ivan) **Käbin** as first secretary and other Russified Estonians in the Central Committee who had been nurtured by, and socialized to, the values of the All-Union (b) Communist Party.

After the death of Stalin and Nikita Khrushchev's denunciation of Stalin's personality cult at the XX Congress of the Communist Party of the Soviet Union (CPSU) in 1956, the chaotic years of "thaw," in which the Party attempted to reorganize and modernize agriculture and the administration of the state and the economy, allowed some freedom for local initiative. The Estonian party, now a carbon copy of the renamed CPSU and still under the strict oversight of the Moscow central, was able to take into account local needs and thus reorganize agriculture, increase consumer goods production, and build housing. Still, such pan-Soviet **industrial** policies such as those pertaining to the electricity and machine industries had to be given priority. The vast improvement of agricultural meant that the average annual production increased rapidly. Taking 1960–65 as the base, production increased by 20 percent in the next quinquennium; in 1970–75 it was 35 percent larger than the base, and in 1975–80, 52 percent larger than in 1960–65. Since these figures represent not value but actual gross tonnage, they are impressive indeed, and particularly so when compared to the Soviet average, where a food shortage persisted right until the collapse of the USSR. The resultant improvement in living conditions in the ESSR also improved the Party's image among the population.

However, after Leonid Brezhnev took over the Soviet leadership in 1964, pressures for **Russification** increased and eventually led to the downfall of Käbin, who, despite his Soviet-Russian upbringing, had slowly become Estonianized. Accused of supporting Estonian nationalism, like his predecessor, he was kicked upstairs and made the figurehead chairman of the ESSR Supreme Soviet in 1978 in a coup organized jointly with Moscow and engineered by its representative in the ECP Bureau. Since 1971, Moscow had placed a non-Estonian from elsewhere in the USSR as second secretary of the Bureau of the Central Committee of the ECP. The charge against Käbin of being guilty of Estonian nationalism was absurd, but nevertheless contained a grain of truth. The fact that he lasted 28 years as first secretary meant that he had to observe the dictates from Moscow. However, he had realized early on that he also needed the support of the local Estonians and consequently had become acclimatized to Estonian's local concerns about culture and **language** as well as local agricultural and industrial initiatives, such as developed during the Khruhschev thaw.

Käbin had quietly groomed **Vaino Väljas**, a graduate of history at Tartu University and a Bureau member since 1961 with a pro-Estonian reputation, as his eventual successor. In the event, **Karl Vaino**, born in 1923 in Russia of Estonian parents, educated there in technology, and totally Russified—even after 40 years, never learned to speak Estonian properly—was appointed his replacement. Vaino fitted in well with the prevailing Russification of the 1970s and early 1980s as introduced by Brezhnev. His closest comrades had always been the Russian directors of the centrally controlled industries in Estonia; he had no real Estonian friends. Nevertheless, he was not able to change the composition of the Bureau, which continued largely with the membership developed by Käbin.

During the 45 years of the Soviet period, two significant changes in the membership of ECP took palace. The first was that the party changed into a mass party. At the beginning of 1945, it consisted of a very small group of 2,409 convinced communists (of whom only 40 percent were ethnic Estonians), and the intake during the eight years was around a thousand new members per year to 22,320 (41.6 percent Estonians) in 1953. However, during the first years of the Khrushchev thaw in 1954–58, the intake doubled and during the second half, in 1959–64 the intake quadrupled to 4,000 a year; thereafter, recruitment stabilized at around 3,000 a year until 1986. Thus the ECP had 49,804 members in 1964 and 109,599 in 1986. Parallel with the growth in membership was the increase of ethnic Estonians in the Party to 51.7 percent in 1963. Thereafter, with some small blips, the Estonians' share remained around 50 percent. Although the ethnic composition of the Party was a deliberate policy, the Estonian Party members' proportion of the population remained at around 8 percent whereas the aliens proportion at 13 percent was noticeably higher.

Hence, the Party never achieved an Estonian identity and was regarded even by most of its careerist-oriented Estonian members as a branch of the occupying Soviet Union's state structure. Indeed, very few of those Estonians who joined the Party from the late 1950s onward identified ideologically with communism or regarded themselves as communists. They joined simply out of the reasoned conviction that independence was unlikely in the near future and one had to accommodate oneself to the prevailing demands of the occupying power. And it was a fact that all roads to economic and intellectual advancement required Communist Party membership everywhere in the Soviet Union. Even professorial appointments required Party membership or, at the very least, explicit Party approval.

The careerist orientation of ECP members meant that the repressions of Estonian culture and language under the Russophile Karl Vaino in the 1980s led to reactions (*see* DISSIDENTS) widely sympathized and supported by Party members. Indeed, leading Party members launched the anti-Moscow **Rahvarinne** mass protest movement, and it was the Party-controlled and Party-led Supreme Soviet of the ESSR that declared the sovereignty of the ESSR in 1988 and authorized free elections in 1989.

Of course, the Estonian Party needed the assistance of circumstance. Thus Mikhail Gorbachev played a key role when at the instigation of the Estonian ECP Bureau members (*see* INDREK

TOOME), he removed Karl Vaino for being a reactionary blocker of **perestroika** and replaced him with Vaino Väljas as first secretary in June 1988, who had been sidelined in 1978 and sent in 1980 to Venezuela and subsequently to Nicaragua as Soviet ambassador. Väljas, true to expectations, immediately decreed that the internal language of the ECP Central Committee and all its organs was henceforth Estonian. In any event, Väljas's appointment proved merely to confirm the Estonians' drive for self-rule. The ECP worked diligently for the next year and a half to restore independence for Estonia. Strangely, most of the nonethnic Estonian members of the ECP hierarchy went along with the process in 1988. After the negative reaction by Mikhail Gorbachev toward the **Declaration of Sovereignty** at the meeting of the Presidium of the Supreme Soviet of the USSR on 16 November 1988, however, the situation changed radically as the directors of the all-union factories in Tallinn organized their workers to agitate publicly against Estonian independence and formed the **Interfront**. The party soon split in two with the Moscow-oriented faction consisting virtually solely of Russians agitating against the Estonian traitors, the whole of the Estonian party hierarchy. Although the ECP continued in existence until the restoration of independence in 1991, and actually formally split in two at its XX Congress, on 25 March 1990 the Party decided to leave the USSR and declare itself an independent ECP. The radical pro-Moscow minority disagreed with the decision of the Congress and formed its own CPSU-associated faction.

Neither Party qua party, however, played any role in the politics of independence anymore. Large numbers of members had already begun to resign from the ECP in 1989, and by fall 1990 the ECP was but a shadow of itself. A large number of new noncommunist parties, most economically right wing and politically liberal or conservative, were formed during 1989–91 by different groups of former members of the ECP.

After the restoration of independence and its disbanding, the ECP disappeared completely from the consciousness of Estonians. Moreover, a decade later it was even difficult to find any Estonians who espoused any tenets of left-wing socialism. Unlike most postcommunist states, independent Estonia has no communist successor political party or even a radical left-wing party (*See* POLITICAL PARTIES).

ESTONIAN CONGRESS. The Estonian Congress was elected and met in 1990 to discuss questions of self-determination of Estonia. It was initiated at a meeting of the Eesti Rahvusliku Sõltumatuse Partei (ERSP, Estonian National Independence Party), Estonian Christian Federation (Eesti Kristlik Liit), and Society for the Protection of Estonian Cultural Heritage (Eesti Muinsuskaitse Selts, EMS) on 21–23 February 1989. On 11 November, the Estonian Republic's Citizens Preparatory Committee (Eesti Vabariigi Kodanike Peakommitee) was formed with **Tunne Kelam** as chair. In the Congress elections held from 24 February to 1 March 1990, 557,163 citizens participated, amounting to about 90 percent of those eligible. The Congress consisted of 464 delegates elected from the territory of Estonia, 35 living abroad, and 43 nonvoting delegates representing noncitizens who wished to apply for Estonian citizenship. The Congress delegates represented the whole spectrum of Estonian parties, movements, and associations: independents 109, **Rahvarinne** (Peoples' Front) 107, EMS 1,104, ERSP 70, and **Estonian Communist Party** (ECP) 39 seats. The Estonian Congress was the first time that a freely and popularly elected assembly representing the Estonian people had met since the Soviet occupation and annexation in 1940. The first session of the Congress met on 11–12 March 1990, and its 10th and final session met on 28 September 1992 when the results of elections to the new Parliament were proclaimed.

The Congress elected the Estonian Committee (Eesti Komitee) as its permanent organ with authority to act between sessions of the Congress. The first Committee elected on 12 March 1990 consisted of 78 members (71 citizens and seven noncitizens), and the second Committee was elected at the Congress's third session on 27 October 1990 and consisted of 55 members (50 citizens and five noncitizens). The first Executive Committee of the Committee was elected on 13 March 1990 and consisted of 11 members, and its second Executive was elected on 1 November 1990 and consisted of 12 members. Right-wing parties (ERSP, conservatives, and Christian Democrats) formed the vast majority of the membership of the latter.

The priorities of the Estonian Congress were to reestablish the Republic of Estonia on a constitutional basis and to maintain its legal continuity peacefully according to the norms of international law. Large numbers of restitutional resolutions were adopted, based on the concept of legal continuity of the Estonian Republic, the continuity of its citizenship, the territorial integrity of the state, the continuity of private property and the principle of its nonalienation, the principle of the continuing applicability of the 1922 **Peace Treaty of Tartu**, the illegality of the Soviet occupation and annexation and consequently its termination, the transfer of state authority to a constitutionally sanctioned representative body, and the indemnification of the damages caused by the Soviet occupation. The Congress declared itself competent to carry out the reestablishment of the Estonian Republic and indicated its readiness to take on the functions and powers of the state.

However, the Congress was unable to carry out these ambitious aspirations since it did not possess the necessary administrative structures. Instead it, and especially its Executive Committee, degenerated into a right-wing pressure group and acted as a popular rival to the left-center **Supreme Council**. At times of danger, such as the January 1991 disturbances in Tallinn and the **OMON** attacks in Vilnius and Riga, the Committee and Congress cooperated with the Supreme Council, but most of the time they were in opposition, not only to the latter but also to the politically centrist People's Front and the transitional government of **Edgar Savisaar**. Its economic program was weak and overly politicized; its geopolitical focus was exclusively on the West; its policies toward Moscow and Russia were narrow and inflexible; and its approach to the non-Estonian population, composed mainly of Russians, was harshly uncompromising. Its pretension to embody the ethical ethnicity of Estonia and Estonians led the Congress, and especially its Executive, to carry on an unremitting, furious propaganda war against the Supreme Council, the Peoples' Front, and the Savisaar government. This legacy persisted through the ensuing decade of independence in political partisanship as the former Estonian Congress activists saw themselves as morally superior Estonians. However, the overt right-wing partisanship of the Congress led to a rapid decline in popular esteem after its initial formation in early 1990. The only option it had was to face the inevitable and cooperate with the Supreme Council in forming the **Constitutional Assembly**.

ESTONIAN DEFENSE FORCES (EDF, Eesti Kaitsevägi). The **armed forces** of the independent Republic of Estonia were liquidated by the **Estonian Soviet Socialist Republic (ESSR)** puppet state soon after it was set up in 1940. During the long Soviet occupation after 1945, Estonian men were conscripted into the Soviet armed forces, where few chose to make a career as officers and very few rose to field rank.

On 3 September 1991, two weeks after the **Declaration of Independence**, the transition parliament passed an act to reestablish the Estonian Defense Forces and the transition government of **Edgar Savisaar** implemented it on 31 October 1991 by establishing the General Staff of the Estonian Defense Forces. The actual formation of the defense forces, however, proved to be much more difficult than 70 years earlier in the case of the **War of Independence** (*see also* ARMED FORCES). There were four reasons for this: first, the Soviet forces were held in low esteem by Estonians; second, Estonian former Soviet senior officers were not welcomed; third, the legacy of the Soviet forces' lack of discipline and morality created major ongoing problems in a small democratic force; and fourth, the foregoing problems were compounded by lack of funding, matériel, and clear political direction on the organization of the forces.

Initially, the formation of the forces was entrusted to former Soviet Colonel Ants Laaneots, who had been deputy commandant of the **Tartu** military district under General Dzjokar Dudaev (later president of Chechnya), and the newly formed Ministry of Defense under the politically inexperienced Minister Ülo Uluots (nephew of former prime minister and president ad interim **Jüri Uluots**). The independent-minded volunteer **Defense League**, composed of patriotic volunteers trained in the Soviet forces, and revived in early 1990 when Estonia was still part of the Soviet Union, regarded itself as the true Estonian defense force and refused to place itself under the command of the General Staff of the Defense Force. The League staged several attention-grabbing maneuvers in 1990, including an attempt to place border posts along Estonia's prewar frontier, now in Russia, which often drew criticism as being provocative.

Although in 1990 Estonia had been the first Soviet republic to defy the Soviet Army by offering alternative service to drafted Estonian youths, most Estonians simply avoided the draft. Consequently, after independence, when Estonia instituted its own compulsory military service, with a minimum term of one year beginning at age 18, young

Estonian men continued to spurn the call, and only one third of eligible draftees turned out for the spring 1993 conscription.

To remedy the situation in May 1993, President **Lennart Meri** appointed **Aleksander Einseln,** a retired U.S. Army colonel, as chief of the general staff of the defense forces, with Laaneots as his deputy. The appointment was only partly successful since Einseln soon became involved in conflict with his Soviet-trained colleagues. However, during his two-and-a-half year tenure, he was able to begin the organization of the forces into an effective modern defense force based on **North Atlantic Treaty Organization (NATO)** principles and matériel. He was also able to attract foreign assistance from the Nordic and NATO countries. The Finnish assistance in training a corps of noncommissioned officers, the backbone of all Western armies but entirely lacking in the Soviet Union, has been crucial in the development of the Estonian Defense Forces, as has the organization of the **Baltic Battalion (BALTBAT)** and the **Baltic Defence College**. Foreign armed forces also provided military education to Estonian junior officers in large numbers, with Finland taking an early lead. In 1996 a volunteer unit of retired staff rank officers was formed in the Finnish defense forces to coordinate assistance to build up the Estonian forces. Subsequently, senior Estonian officers were educated at the Finnish war college. Other countries also provide continuing training, including the United States, which in 1999–2000 educated **Johannes Kert**, then the chief of staff of the Estonian forces, at its National Defense College.

Estonia's security situation remained compromised until 1995, when the last Russian military left Estonian soil. Immediately after independence, Estonia began pressing the Soviet Union, and later Russia, for a speedy withdrawal of Soviet troops from its territory. Estonia insisted that the process be completed by the end of 1991. The Soviet government, citing a lack of available housing for its troops, said not before 1994. In January 1992, about 25,000 troops were left in Estonia, the smallest contingent in the Baltic States. Still, more than 80,000 hectares of land, including an inland artillery range, remained in the Russian military's hands. More than 150 battle tanks, 300 armored vehicles, and 163 battle aircraft also remained. The last troops did not leave until August 1994.

Disagreement over the pace of Russia's withdrawal from the Soviet naval enclave at **Paldiski**, only 35 kilometers west of **Tallinn**, added to the security dilemma. The Soviet navy had a submarine base there that included two nuclear submarine training reactors. Russian officials maintained that dismantling the reactor facility would take time; Estonia demanded faster action along with international supervision of the process. The last Russian warship, carrying 10 T-72 tanks, departed the base in August 1994. However, Russia retained control of the reactor facility in Paldiski until September 1995.

After 1995, once the land was cleared of Russian military, Western assistance increased quickly. Estonia was able to acquire matériel and munitions from Western nations and begin developing forces interoperable with the North Atlantic Treaty Organization (NATO). By 2000, the Estonian Defense Forces consisted of the Army, with five infantry battalions, an artillery group with field guns of Finnish make and trained by Finland, a peacekeeping unit (*see* BALTIC BATTALION), and a number of ancillary units, including a reconnaissance and intelligence unit; the coastal Navy with eight minesweeping ships acquired from Germany, Finland, and Denmark; and an elementary Air Force with some new helicopters, a few small former Soviet propeller aircraft, and a radar unit that enables Estonia to exercise minimal control over its airspace and cooperate and eventually integrate with NATO systems. A separate, Finnish-trained Coast Guard has adequate, mostly Finnish-donated patrol boats and new helicopters to maintain surveillance, monitor fishing, and carry on rescue operations in Estonian waters in peacetime.

In peacetime the primary function of the forces is to maintain preparedness, increase efficiency, provide support for NATO actions, and train a reserve of conscripts. The peacetime size of the forces consists of 6,000 men, of whom one third (24 percent officers and NCOs and 10 percent soldiers) form the professional cadre of the forces. Conscripts serving 8–11 months (55 percent) and the quartermaster corps (11 percent) complete the peacetime strength of the forces.

In 2000, to qualify for NATO membership, the government redefined the basic principles of Estonia's defense policy as deterrence, territorial defense, and the strengthening of security and stability in the region, leading to cooperation with and integration into the European and NATO institutions, and formulated them to accord with

NATO's Strategic Concept. Raising the share of defense expenditures to 2 percent of GNP by 2002 has been central to developing a viable defense position leading to NATO membership The five-year development plan (2000–2005) of the defense forces foresaw:

- An increase of the wartime manpower to 25,000–30,000
- The formation of three light infantry reserve brigades
- The further development of airspace surveillance capabilities
- The further development of mine warfare capabilities
- The development of rapid reaction capabilities
- The standardization of education
- The concentration of officer and NCO basic training in Estonia
- The development and reorganization of the current mobilization and readiness system
- The development of a Logistic Concept for the EDF

By the end of the period to improve the command and control structure of the defense forces, the General Staff of the Estonian Defense Forces (GSEDF) will be transformed into a joint staff responsible for the strategic planning and development, command, control and communication, and general personnel matters for the whole forces, and a subordinate Army Department will be established within the GSEDF.

ESTONIAN FOREIGN MINISTERS. *See* APPENDIXES.

ESTONIAN LANGUAGE. One of the Balto-Finnic subgroup of the Finno-Ugric language group, Estonian is spoken by approximately 1 million people, nearly all of whom live on the territory of the Republic of Estonia. Since the Estonian nation is small, and has been under the yoke of foreign overlords since the 13th century with the brief exception of the periods of independence between 1918 and 1940 and since 1991, its language has always played *the* key role in maintaining its existence as a separate nation. Thus language and nation are congruent concepts in the mind of every Estonian.

The only foreign language that is closely related to Estonian is Finnish, comparable to the relationship between German and Dutch or between Italian and Spanish. Hungarian, and a number of other Finno-Ugric languages still spoken by a score of ethnic groups on the territory of the Russian Federation (ranging in size from around

1 million Mari to a few hundred Vadjaks), are much more distant relatives, approximately as close as Polish is to Italian, in which cases only philologists can discern structural similarities.

Although before radio and television many dialects were spoken in the different counties in Estonia, the written language became standardized on the base of the North Estonian dialect during the last decades of the 19th century. A hundred years later only a few dialects remain in use by rural residents.

Estonian uses the Latin alphabet. Of its 32 letters, five occur only in foreign words. The 27 phonemes include nine vowels and 18 consonants. The letters of the Estonian alphabet are **a b c d e f g h i j k l m n o p q r s š z ž t u v w õ ä ö ü x y** (**š** and **ž** are used to indicate pronunciation in foreign words). Of these, **õ** is a recent addition, invented by **Otto Wilhelm Masing** in 1818. (For a description of pronunciation of letters not found in English, *see* READER'S NOTES.)

Because words in Estonian are 45 percent vowels and 55 percent consonants, the spoken language has a pleasant musical ring to it. The letters denoting Estonian sounds generally always have the same phonetic value, but there is a slight difference in pronunciation between long and short vowels. Double letters are used to indicate both long vowels and long consonants between vowels, but when a long consonant and another consonant appear between vowels single letters are used (for example *tk*, *ld*, and so on). Changing the duration of a sound alters the grammatical function of the word or changes its meaning altogether. Nouns are declined in 14 cases (one less than modern Finnish), and verbs are conjugated generally by adding endings to their roots. Some words in declension and in conjugation also change their root by replacing a vowel or a consonant, or by dropping it altogether. In addition, there are many prepositions but there are no articles in Estonian, nor any genders.

Most older loanwords originate in German or Old German (a total of more than 2,000 word roots), and around 350 have been borrowed from Russian. Many words related to the internationalization of life have entered the Estonian vocabulary as later loanwords, mainly from Latin, Greek, and English. Beginning with the age of information technology (IT) in the 1980s, despite the attempt to create new Estonian equivalents, mainly English words are entering the language and are Estonianized. Estonian is unique in that it can easily adopt foreign words because of its phonetic spelling merely by phonetizing their spelling and then using Estonian grammar to decline or conjugate them. Estonians are always creating or adapting new words, in some years perhaps a hundred new words or word forms, of which only a few enter common usage after some time. Hence, usage is the only determinant of the validity of a word in Estonian. This is also true of grammar and syntax. There is no equivalent of the Académie Française or the authority of the Bundestag in language in Estonia. The overnight transition from Estonianized Soviet Russian terminology and Russian language syntax to complete shunning of this terminology and a rapid reversal to the syntax standardized 50 years earlier, even in the daily press, demonstrates the flexibility of the Estonian language.

Although the first textbook written in Estonian appeared in 1637, it was not until 1869 that Ferdinand Johann Wiedemann published a comprehensive Estonian-German dictionary, followed by a grammar in 1875. Current written Estonian was modernized by **Johannes Aavik** during the 1910s and 1920s. His most important reform was the simplification of sentence structure, which allows for variation of mood and the use of the present tense when describing the past. He also made the coining of new words a respectable part of language development.

In the 1920s and 1930s, Johannes Voldemar Veski led the work of standardizing the Estonian scientific vocabulary, covering more than 100,000 terms. After World War II, Estonian linguists in exile carried on the effort: Andrus Saareste published an atlas of dialects and a conceptual dictionary; Julius Mägiste compiled an etymological dictionary; Valter Tauli wrote a scientific grammar, and Paul Saagpakk, professor at Yale, spent 40 years compiling an etymological Estonian-English dictionary, published by Yale University Press in 1980 and not surpassed to date.

In Estonia, during the Soviet occupation language studies were carried out at the **University of Tartu** and at the Institute of Linguistics of the **Academy of Sciences** in **Tallinn**, where all work of the compilation of dictionaries and grammar textbooks was concentrated. With the restitution of independence and the Academy being turned into a personal one, the Institute was transferred to the University of Tartu. The study of the Estonian language became a normal occupation at other universities as well.

Since it regained independence Estonian is again, as mandated by the **Constitution**, the sole official language of communication in all fields of activity in Estonia, including higher education, scientific research, business, and commerce. Russian is used mainly by Russian residents among themselves (as well as by Estonians in communicating with monolingual Russophones) whereas English has become the normal language of communication with foreigners. Because of Finnish television and the large numbers of Finnish tourists, Finnish is also spoken by many Estonians in Tallinn.

ESTONIAN LEARNED SOCIETY (Õpetatud Eesti Selts [ÕES], Gelehrte Estnische Gesellschaft). Estonian and Estophile **Baltic German** intellectuals under the leadership of **Friedrich Robert Faehlmannn**, Alexander Friedrich von Hueck, and Dietrich Heinrich Jürgenson formed the first scholarly organization, known universally in Estonia simply by its initials as ÕES, in **Tartu** in 1838 devoted to the study of the history and prehistory of Estonia; its **language**, **literature**, and folklore; and the country in general. It provided a major service in language analysis and in the development of scientific study of history, archeology, ethnography, numismatics, and **art** history in Estonia. The leadership of the society, which had been in the hands of Baltic Germans, was taken over by ethnic Estonian scholars only in the 1920s. Throughout its first period of activity, until 1950 when it was closed by the Soviet occupation, ÕES published 34 volumes of *Proceedings*, 72 yearbooks, as well as bibliographies. ÕES published the initial version of **Friedrich Reinhold Kreutzwald**'s **Kalevipoeg** in its *Proceedings* in 1857–61. Its collections of 25,000 books, 160,000 pages of manuscripts, and 60,000 eth nographic items were divided among various Estonian institutes. In 1988, ÕES was restored at the initiative of Herbert Ligi, professor of History at the **University of Tartu**. It has since resumed holding learned meetings and publishes a yearbook.

ESTONIAN LEGION. On 28 August 1942, the German Waffen-SS organized a formation for Estonian volunteers to fight the Soviet Union. The unit was established and trained at a military camp near Dębica in occupied Poland. By the end of January 1944, 11,000 Estonians had either joined the Estonian Legion voluntarily or been conscripted into it. The Legion consisted of the 33rd Training Battalion, the Narwa (Narva) Battalion, and the 3rd Estonian Brigade.

Since the Battalion Narwa was the first combat ready element of the Estonian Legion of the Waffen-SS, it was sent to join the 5th SS-Panzergrenadier Division Wiking in April 1943 as a replacement for the Finnish Volunteer Battalion of the Waffen-SS, which was being withdrawn to its homeland. It fought in Ukraine through 1943 and February 1944 but left for home in April and joined the battle against the Red Army in Estonia as part of the 20th Estonian Division.

The 3rd Estonian Volunteer Brigade, the second Estonian unit to become combat ready, fought from November 1943 to January 1944 on the Eastern front at Nevel, Ukraine. In January 1944, the 3rd Brigade was renamed the 20th Estonian Division and replaced the Estonian Legion which thus ceased to exist. In February the Division, together with its training reserve and support units, was brought to Estonia and fought a rearguard action against the advancing Red Army on the **Narva** and **Tartu** fronts as part of Army Group Nord as the Germans withdrew. At the end of September it retreated to Germany after suffering great battle losses, and it was re-formed in Breslau (now Wroclaw) between October 1944 and January 1945 when it fought in Silesia (eastern Poland) as part of Army Group Mitte to May, when it capitulated on the Czech northern border. Its reserve regiment surrendered on the border of Denmark in Schleswig-Holstein.

It should be pointed out that German law did not allow conscription of foreigners into its armed forces, but since the Waffen-SS was a "volunteer" army the restriction did not apply to it. Estonian youths were thus encouraged to "volunteer"; they saw this as a way to fight the hated Soviets and to gain experience for a future restored Estonian army. Few, if any, joined to fight for Hitler or Germany. Later, in February 1944, the German occupying forces imposed conscription. *See* JR200, OSTLAND.

ESTONIAN LENINIST COMMUNIST YOUTH LEAGUE. The Young Communists League of the Soviet Union is universally known as Komsomol. Its Estonian wing was named Estonian Leninist Communist Youth League (Eestimaa Leninlik Kommunistlik Noorsooühing, ELKNÜ), which operated under the direction of the **Estonian**

Communist Party to educate the youth of the country in communist ideology and to organize their social activities, including collective "voluntary" participation in such industrial activities as potato planting, harvesting, and constructing farm buildings.

ELKNÜ was first organized in **Tallinn** on 5 December 1920 as a section of the Communist Youth International under the name Pan-Estonia Young Proletarians League. By March 1921, it had 1,000 members but was forced underground when it was outlawed in April. In October 1921, the Central Committee of the ECP set up the ELKNÜ Temporary Central Bureau, which organized 35 underground communist youth collectives around the country. The first congress of the ELKNÜ took place at a farm on September 1922. By 1924, when the Komsomol took part in the **attempted communist coup,** it had 400 members. After the failure of the coup, the whole of ECP activity in Estonia was driven so far underground that its main task was to maintain contact among convinced communists; they had made no impact on political or social life in Estonia.

In July 1940, after the Soviet occupation, the ELKNÜ was reestablished as a legal organization that within the year recruited 10,000 members. After the German occupation in 1941, it was reformed in 1945 and held its second congress in May 1946. Its membership grew rapidly as units were formed at all schools and workplaces under the leadership of full-time professional Komsomol organizers. In 1946–47 9,800, in 1948–49 17,700 and in 1950–51 18,400 new members were recruited. ELKNÜ units took part in all pan-Soviet communist youth activities, such as brigades clearing virgin lands, building new settlements in Siberia and the Urals, and the formation of propagandistic elite pan-Soviet "building strike forces." The ideological work of the ELKNÜ was also all-encompassing, and ranged from organizing and leading the Pioneer (children's) organizations, organizing the patriotic travel movement "Know Your Country," establishing the Student Scientific Union, and organizing youth seminars, summer schools, and camps as well as publishing major newspapers, the Estonian language daily *Noorte Hääl* (*Voice of Youth*), the Russian language daily *Molodjozh Estonii* (*Estonian Youth*), the Estonian- and Russian-language weeklies *Säde* and *Iskra* (both meaning *Spark*), respectively, as well as the periodicals *Noorus* (*Youth*), *Pioneer*, and *Tähekene* (*Little Star*). On January 1986, the

ELKNÜ recorded its largest membership ever at 167,361. However, soon after the independence movement began in 1988, participation in Komsomol activities dropped rapidly and the organization disintegrated already in 1989 as young people joined the rush to support independence. Clearly, the ELKNÜ's past success was strictly based on its monopoly of youth activity and the control that it had over recommendations for jobs and postsecondary education in the closed party-state Soviet Estonia.

ESTONIAN PROVISIONAL GOVERNMENT. On 24 February 1918, the **Estonian Rescue (Salvation) Committee** appointed a provisional government to hold office pending the election of a **Constituent Assembly** to draft a **Constitution**. The main functions of the provisional government were to oppose the German military occupation, to organize Estonian **armed forces**, to lobby for diplomatic recognition abroad, and to organize elections to the Constituent Assembly at a propitious time. **Konstantin Päts** became prime minister and minister of trade and interior, **Jüri Vilms** was minister of justice, **Jaan Poska** was foreign minister, Juhan Kukk was minister of finance and state property, Jaan Raamot was minister of food and agriculture, **Andres Larka** was minister of war, Villem Maasik was minister of labor and welfare, Ferdinand Peterson was minister of roads, and Peeter Põld was minister of education. The cabinet was reorganized twice, first on 12 November because several ministers were abroad lobbying for recognition of the state and the retreat of German forces required an active government, and again on 27 November when it resigned to allow the first full meeting of the Estonian Provisional Diet, since it went underground in November 1917, a free hand in naming the government. After both reorganizations, Päts remained prime minister, but the political spectrum of the cabinet expanded to cover all points of view except that of the communists. After the Constituent Assembly met on 23 April 1919, the provisional government resigned on 9 May 1919 and was replaced by Estonia's first democratic cabinet responsible to the elected Constituent Assembly. *See also* DECLARATION OF INDEPENDENCE 1918; INDEPENDENCE 1917–1921; WAR OF INDEPENDENCE.

ESTONIAN RESCUE (SALVATION) COMMITTEE (Eestimaa Päästmise Komitee). Also known as Päästekomitee in Estonian history, this committee was appointed at a joint meeting of the Council of Elders and the Executive Committee of the **Eestimaa Kubermangu Ajutine Maanõukogu** (Provisional Diet of the Province of Estonia) on 19 February 1918. It was a three-man committee consisting of **Konstantin Päts**, **Jüri Vilms**, and Konstantin Konik, with all powers of the Provisional Diet. On 24 February 1918, the Päästekomitee issued the Estonian Manifesto of Independence and appointed the **Estonian Provisional Government** *See also* DECLARATION OF INDEPENDENCE 1918; INDEPENDENCE 1917–1921; WAR OF INDEPENDENCE.

ESTONIAN-RUSSIAN BORDER. *See* PEACE OF TARTU; PETSERIMAA.

ESTONIAN SOVIET SOCIALIST REPUBLIC (ESSR). The immediate origins of the ESSR are found in the the Secret Protocols of the 1939 **Molotov-Ribbentrop Pact** between the Soviet Union and Nazi Germany, which ceded the Baltic States to the Soviet Union. Accordingly, the following 17 June 1940, the Union of Soviet Socialist Republics (USSR) invaded and occupied Estonia and immediately began a brutal reign of terror. Within days Estonia found itself under military occupation, its armed forces were disarmed, and its government was replaced by one dictated by Andrei Zhdanov, the Politburo member designated by Joseph Stalin to act as political master of Estonia. Immediately the new puppet government of **Johannes Vares** called for elections in which only candidates approved by the **Communist Party of Estonia** were allowed to run. On 14–15 July, sham elections took place and on 21–23 the new parliament met; nationalized the banks, large industries, and all land; and passed a petition requesting the Supreme Soviet of the USSR to accept Estonia as member of the Union of Soviet Socialist Republics.

The independent Republic's political, judicial, and administrative structures were destroyed and replaced by Soviet models; all large industrial plants, transportation companies, as well as banking and commerce were nationalized. That the Soviet occupying forces were able to carry out such wholesale transformation in the short period between June 1940 and the German invasion on 22 June 1941 testifies to long and thorough preparation. Three years later when the

German Northern front collapsed, the Red Army reinvaded Estonia on 22 September 1944 and reinstituted the occupation that lasted for 47 years until 21 August 1991, when Estonia was able to declare itself a sovereign independent state once again. Prime Minister **Jüri Uluots** and some members of the government were able to flee to Sweden in 1944 and thus keep alive the de jure Republic, with the help of the **Stimson Doctrine**, under which the United States refused to accept the Soviet occupation of Estonia as legitimate. *See also* CONSTITUTION OF 1940 OF THE ESSR; CONSTITUTION OF 1978 OF THE ESSR; DECLARATION OF INDEPENDENCE IN 1991; DECLARATION OF SOVEREIGNTY; DEPORTATIONS; DISSIDENTS; ESTONIAN COMMUNIST PARTY; ESTONIAN LENINIST COMMUNIST YOUTH LEAGUE; ISEMAJANDAV EESTI (IME); KÄBIN; MOLOTOV-RIBBENTROPI PAKTI AVALIKUSTAMISE EESTI GRUPP (MRP-AEG); RUSSIFICATION; SAUL, BRUNO; SECOND NATIONAL AWAKENING; SUPREME SOVIET ELECTIONS OF THE ESSR IN 1990; SUPREME SOVIET OF THE ESTONIAN SOVIET SOCIALIST REPUBLIC; VAINO, KARL; VÄLJAS, VAINO.

ESTONIAN WORKERS' COMMUNE. During the **War of Independence**, a joint meeting of the Estonian sections of the Russian Communist (**Bolshevik**) Party and the Estonian Temporary Revolutionary Committee on 29 November 1918 in **Narva** set up the Estonian Workers' Commune as the government of the territory then occupied by the Red Army. The Commune was led by **Jaan Anvelt**, **Viktor Kingissepp**, and Hermann Pöögelmann—three extreme Bolshevik idealists who believed blindly in the victory of the international communist revolution. They instituted a dictatorial reign of terror on the territory, nationalized banks and industrial and commercial enterprises, closed churches, and proposed the transforming of landed estates into communes and *not* the redistribution of any land to the landless. The Workers' Commune controlled over half of Estonia's territory in January 1919 but lost it all when the Red Army was driven back in February. After retreating to Russia, it disbanded on 5 June 1919.

ESTONIANS ABROAD. Estonians abroad, known as *Väliseestlased* (literally, "foreign Estonians" or "external Estonians") and *Välis-*

Eesti ("Estonia Abroad"), are concepts that apply to the post–World War II Estonian diaspora in the West. Although many Estonians lived outside the homeland in earlier times (*see* EMIGRATION), there were no self-sufficient communities of Estonians abroad prior to World War II. The roughly 70,000 who fled the Soviet occupations to the West consisted largely of the intelligentsia who had most to fear from the new occupying communist regime, and coastal farmers and fishermen, who had the best opportunity to flee across the Baltic Sea. As a result, Estonians immediately on arrival in their refuges organized themselves into communities that reflected the Estonia that they had been forced to leave.

The first of the refuges for a large number was Sweden, where already during the War those who had fled in 1940 organized rescue activities for their politically vulnerable compatriots and lobbied the Swedish government on their behalf. The second refuge, Germany, was strictly temporary since it was a defeated and chaotic country where Estonians found themselves in displaced persons camps operated by the Western allies. Nevertheless, even in camp conditions Estonians organized themselves into a community and, together with Latvians and Lithuanians, set up and operated the **Baltic University** for four years, until the professors and students moved further West.

The Estonian postwar immigrants left Europe because they feared the Soviet Union and thus wanted to move as far away as possible to a safe refuge. The exodus from the initial lands of refuge, Sweden and the displaced persons camps in Germany, was caused by the repatriation of 167 Baltic officers who had served in the German armies to the Soviet Union from Sweden in 1945, and by the Swedish recognition of the incorporation of the Baltic states into the Soviet Union. Although only six of the returnees were Estonians, the sense of insecurity was very strong among all the Balts—and the United States and Canada were seen as preferred refuges. Ample evidence of the fear of the Soviet Union that pervaded Estonians in Sweden is provided by the 46 overcrowded "Viking" boats that left Sweden illegally between 1946 and 1949. These, manned by Estonians with a few Latvians, Lithuanians, and Ukrainians among them, sought refuge in the United States (17), Canada (10), South Africa (6), Argentina (5), England (3), and Brazil (1).

In three countries, Sweden, Canada, and the United States, where by the early 1950s 80 percent of the Estonian refugees found themselves, they formed three microcosms of the Estonia of the 1930s. Most Estonian émigrés expected to return to Estonia in a few years, since they believed that a new war would break out soon and the Soviet Union would be forced to leave the Baltic States by the victorious Western powers. Hence their political elites organized the new communities to reflect their refugee status in order to carry on the political struggle for the independence of their homeland.

Much smaller communities were formed in Australia (the largest in Sydney with others in Melbourne, Adelaide, and Perth) and in Great Britain (in Leicester, Bradford, in the Midlands, and in London). Eventually, re-emigration, mostly from Europe, led to small Estonian communities, still functioning in 2002, in Argentina (centered in Buenos Aires), Belgium, Brazil (São Paulo), France, Luxembourg, Netherlands, New Zealand, Norway (Oslo), South Africa (Johannesburg and Cape Town), Switzerland, and Germany. Even where there were only a few hundred Estonians, they still organized themselves as a refugee microcosm with an umbrella organization, Saturday schools, youth activities, and church congregations. And, wherever there are Estonians, they make a point of celebrating Independence Day together every 24 February. The description of organizational activities under **Estonian Canadians**, the most coherent group of Estonians abroad, applies in differing degrees to all Estonian communities abroad.

Naturally, the smaller scattered communities tended to decline in size and activity as their children grew up and melded with the local nation's society and economy. The most viable were those that had a large core group of refugee intelligentsia concentrated in a metropolitan area or within easy commuting distance. Thus, although the United States has the largest number of Estonians abroad, they are scattered across the continent in small groups in Albany, Buffalo, and Schenectady in New York State; Boston, Cleveland, Detroit, and in the environs of Minneapolis–St. Paul in Minnesota; Seattle in Washington State; and several places in Florida. The largest concentrations are found in the environs of New York City, with active organizations on Long Island, Lakewood, New Jersey, and in several towns in Connecticut; as well as in the Baltimore–Washington, D.C., and Los Angeles metropolitan areas. However, the Toronto Estonian community in Canada is the most vibrant of all Estonian communities abroad, with about 200 active organizations maintained by a hard core of 4,000, a number almost the same as in the 1950s, followed by the Estonian community in Stockholm, Sweden. Estonians are also organized in smaller numbers in Uppsala, just north of Stockholm, and in Lund and Gothenburg in southern Sweden.

The American, Canadian, and Swedish Estonian political lobbying organizations have operated on pan-national bases. The success of their efforts on behalf of regaining Estonia's independence was immeasurably increased by early cooperation with similar Latvian and Lithuanian political lobbying organizations. The Baltic Evening in the Parliament Buildings in Ottawa, preventing the U.S. government from recognizing the Soviet occupation of the Baltic States, and the lobbying by the **Baltic Appeal to the United Nations** (BATUN) in the United Nations prior to 1991 was possible only because of single-minded and consistent Baltic émigré cooperation. The cooperative political lobbying activities continue unabated into the new millennium and are aimed at facilitating membership in the **North American Treaty Organization** (NATO), as well as various political supports and economic assistance for the Baltic States.

In fact, apart from the political lobbying activities of the Estonian umbrella organizations abroad, there is little value in defining Estonians abroad by their non-Estonian citizenship (all rapidly acquired the citizenship of their lands of refuge in the 1950s) or country of domicile, since it is the common activities on a daily, weekly, and monthly basis that determine community. These obviously do not take place between scattered Estonian communities, apart from regional summer festivals, children's and scout camps, mutual choir visits, and sporadic contacts among different voluntary organizations, such as stamp collectors, fraternities, or rifle shooters.

EUROFACULTY. EuroFaculty was established by the Council of Baltic Sea States in 1993 at the initiative of Foreign Ministers Hans-Dietrich Genscher of Germany and Uffe Elleman Jensen of Denmark as a multistate institution to restructure the teaching and learning of law, economics, and public administration/political science at the **University of Tartu**, the University of Latvia in Riga, and Vilnius University, the classical national universities of Estonia, Latvia, and

Lithuania, respectively. Headquartered at Riga, the EuroFaculty operated centers at each of the three universities with cooperative programs in 10 faculties, institutes, and departments. The EuroFaculty was funded initially by the European Commission and the governments of Denmark, Finland, Germany, and Norway. Beginning in 1997 the governments of Estonia, Latvia, and Lithuania provided increasing financial support. Of the three centers, the transformation of teaching methodology and curriculum to Western international standards has proceeded most rapidly in public administration, political science, and economics at Tartu, with law lagging behind. Toivo Miljan, its founding director, was succeeded by the Norwegian economist Arild Saether in 1998, and by the Danish economist Gustav Kristensen in 2001.

EUROPEAN UNION (EU). Rejoining Europe had been an inseparable part of the demand for restoration of the independence of their country for Estonians throughout the long Soviet occupation, since Estonia had always been on the Western interface of the historic divide between East and West symbolized by the fortresses of **Narva** and Ivangorod facing each other across the River Narva since the 15th century. However, most Estonians were not interested in joining the European Union (or the European Community, as it was called until the Maastricht Treaty renamed it in 1993), which they considered as simply changing colonial rulers (i.e., the Soviet Union for the European Union).

Estonian cabinets, nevertheless, realized that Western financial help was crucial to the economic transformation to a capitalist economy, which they considered fundamental to successful political and social transformation. The **Isemajandav Eesti (IME)** program had been structured on the premises of minimalist government functions of ensuring the maximum conditions of freedom for entrepreneurial initiative to operate to allow wealth creation. Hence, the transition governments of **Edgar Savisaar** and **Tiit Vähi** faithfully initiated these policies, but it was not until the youthful first government of **Mart Laar** forced the pace of change between 1992 and 1994 that the Estonian transformation began to be taken seriously by the West.

What made the Laar initiatives possible was the European Union, which, under pressure from the government of Helmut Kohl as a result of the uniting of East Germany with West Germany, expanded the initial PHARE (Poland, Hungary, and Romania) program of transformation aid to include Poland, Czechoslovakia, Estonia, Latvia, and Lithuania in 1992. The formation of the **Council of Baltic Sea States (CBSS)** in 1992 helped educate Estonian governmental and parliamentary political consciousness on the necessity of compromise politics with the Europeans closest to them, and it taught them to negotiate for aid on compromise terms. Hence, aid started pouring in, as Estonian governments began to align Estonia's policies with the Europeans', in effect the EU's, since all CBSS members, except for Russia and Norway (which was negotiating membership at this time), were members of the EU. Moreover, the Commission of the EU also had a seat in the CBSS.

Eight developments gradually brought the EU into Estonian focus by the end of the Laar government, and vice versa. The Russian foot-dragging in withdrawing its military, its continuing complaints about Estonia's alleged mistreatment of the alien Russian population despite being proven groundless, and the reluctance of **North Atlantic Treaty Organization (NATO)** members to even consider Estonia's desire for membership in apparent deference to Russian opposition raised the expectation that membership in the EU would provide a soft security option by expanding the EU's economic sphere to Estonia. Hence, on 18 July 1994 the Free Trade Agreement with the EU was signed without any transition period, and on 24 November 1995 Estonia applied for EU membership. Three economic moves facilitated these developments and made them all but inevitable: the early introduction of the Estonian **kroon** in July 1992 and tying it in a **currency board** to the deutsche mark, the rapid rationalization of commercial **banking** in 1993, and the equally rapid beginning of an open international tendering process as the main vehicle of **privatization** of state enterprises. The final positive factors were the reorganization of the **court** system and judiciary during 1994, and the continuance by the second **Tiit Vähi** and **Mart Siimann** governments of the business- and investment-friendly policies established by the Laar government of a completely free trading nation, introduced tariffs, no restrictions on foreign ownership, and a flat-rate income tax. The growth and ensuing economic transformation brought Estonia into international focus and made it possible to consider it a serious partner.

It was the European Council of the EU that raised the possibility of membership in December 1993 when it established the Copenhagen Criteria for membership, which consisted of *political criteria* requiring stable institutions guaranteeing democracy, viable democratic institutions, the rule of law, human rights, and respect for minorities; *economic criteria* demanding a functioning market economy and the ability to withstand market competition in the EU; and the *ability to take on the duties of membership* and accept the objectives of the Treaty on European Union (the Maastricht Treaty), including political, economic, and monetary union as well as the ability to contribute to and support the Common Foreign and Security Policy. Moreover, any candidate for membership was required to adopt and implement the entire **Acquis Communitaire** upon accession. Two years later, in December 1995 at its Madrid meeting, the European Council asked the European Commission to prepare an opinion assessing the readiness of each of the applicant states to begin the process of membership negotiations. In June 1997, the Commission placed Estonia in the first group that it considered prepared to begin negotiations immediately, along with Poland, Slovenia, the Czech Republic, Hungary, and Cyprus. At its Luxembourg Meeting in December 1997, the European Council accepted the Commission's recommendations. Negotiations began between Estonia and the EU on 31 March 1998.

How did Estonia, only six years away from being an integral part of the Soviet Union and without even basic state structures such as a constitution, government, judicial system, central bank, its own currency, or a foreign and security policy or means to implement any of these, arrive among the first invitees, all of which had full state and governmental structures and their own **armed forces**, even though all except Cyprus had been dominated by the Soviet economy and polity? The answer may be found partly in the impressive policy thrust to "join the West" outlined above, but also in the serendipidous appointment of **Toomas Hendrik Ilves** as foreign minister engineered by President **Lennart Meri** in November 1996. It was Ilves, along with his predecessor in the portfolio, **Siim Kallas**, who brought Estonia to the attention of the EU, not least by incessantly lobbying each capital during the year preceding the Luxembourg invitation. Ilves exploited his knowledge of diplomacy gained as Estonia's first ambassador to Washington to the fullest in both propagandizing Estonia's rapid Westernization and in organizing the internal Estonian governmental EU responses.

However, it was only after Estonia was invited to begin negotiations that the internal structures were organized to provide both the necessary support for the negotiations and to channel the required implementation of the Acquis by the Estonian parliament. In this process, the Office of European Integration, established early in the spring of 1996 with two staff (expanded to 15 by 2001), by 1997 became the secretariat for the newly appointed minister of European affairs, the Ministerial Commission, and the Council of Senior Civil Servants on EU accession. The Ministry of Foreign Affairs was given the task of negotiating with the EU. In the structuring process as well as in the initial joint EU-Estonian review of the status of Estonian legislative conformance to the Acquis (completed in autumn 1999), the Finnish Ministry of Foreign Affairs provided invaluable assistance based on its own recent accession negotiations. The negotiating delegation formed on 3 February 1998 was headed by the foreign minister and consisted of 14 members of the main delegation and the heads of the 33 working groups who participated in negotiations in their specific areas of responsibility. All relevant ministries were represented at both levels.

The negotiations proper, on adoption of specific legislation in the Acquis Communitaire, moved rapidly with Estonia among the leading candidates in closing different chapters. The annual programs drafted since 1999 by the governments focused on Estonia completing its negotiations by 2002, with accession by 2003, while on 15 December 2001 at Laeken the European Council decided to conclude the negotiations by the end of 2002. On 12–13 December a year later, the European Council at Copenhagen extended formal invitations to the Czech Republic, Estonia, Hungary, Latvia, Lithuania, Poland, Slovakia, and Slovenia, as well as Cyprus and Malta, to join the EU on 1 May 2004.

Estonia found little difficulty in agreeing to adopt, legislate, and implement nearly all of the Acquis Communitaire, except for two items. First, Estonia and the EU agreed that it would take until 31 December 2013 to bring the drinking water in Estonia up to EU standards, and that 75 percent of the cost would be met by the EU; and second, Estonia negotiated a 10-year upgrading of its polluting shale oil underfired electricity plants since they provide the primary domestic energy source (and for employment reasons in **Northeast Estonia**), and the necessary parallel derogation in keeping the electricity market closed to EU-wide competition until 2012. All other concessions were minor, and many would be solved by accession. For example, in **agriculture** Estonia accepted the low 25 percent initial support of the full amount proposed for new members, but succeeded in its quest for higher production quotas to take advantage of future export potential based on the rapid increase in its agricultural productivity. Estonia agreed to give up its free trader status and institute EU-level duties on imports as a price of membership, but only on the date that accession becomes effective. Estonia also, unlike Poland, had no difficulty in accepting the delay in labor access to the EU posited by the current members to protect their labor markets, and since Estonia has no restrictions on foreign ownership of land it, unlike all the other East European candidates, did not even need to negotiate this issue.

The evident success of the negotiations reflected the rapid accommodation of lawmaking and implementation to EU standards, lauded by the European Commission in each of its annual reports. The reason for this is that the approach to the EU in Estonia was an elite process carried on by the bureaucracy and supported consistently by all parties in the **Riigikogu**. However, the population at large has always been skeptical toward the EU and lukewarm in its support. Studies show that Estonians' awareness of EU institutions is among the lowest among the candidate states, and support fluctuated around the 50 percent level even as the accession negotiations closed. One of the reasons was undoubtedly the overwhelming sense of insecurity among Estonians, demonstrated by the consistently higher level of support for NATO membership and the inverse relationship of support for the EU as the likelihood of NATO membership fluctuated. Another is that the average Estonian is immersed in the myriad problems of earning a living in a very competitive labor market and does not see how accession to the EU will affect him or her directly. Moreover, official information on the EU has only become widely available since 1998, when the first information distribution points were opened in the hinterland. Despite this, no organized opposition developed. A few academics spoke out intermittently and argued mainly for delay and specific derogations to guarantee that Estonia be able to maintain its liberal capitalist economy as well as its recently won independence of action.

Despite the lukewarm public support, which government programs of training central and local civil servants, commissioning research studies, and encouraging university programs on the EU, attempted to increase, no one expected the mandatory referendum on 14 September 2003, held to determine the Estonian public's acceptance of the invitation to join the EU and change the Constitution to allow for accession, to be lost. In the event, the fact that less than two thirds (64 percent) of electors bothered to vote and only two thirds cast affirmative ballots (66.8 to 33.2 percent), the lowest support among the Eastern European applicant countries, confirms the view that Estonians simply see EU membership as an inevitable evolution of moving back into Europe that may eventually bring benefits but is not a panacea that is expected to bring immediate changes to their well-being or their way of life.

– F –

FAEHLMANN, FRIEDRICH ROBERT (1798–1850). Estonian writer and medical doctor. Faehlmann was born on 31 December 1798 in Koeru *vald*, the son of an overseer of a **Baltic German** nobleman's estate. He was one of the first Estonians to be educated at **University of Tartu** where he obtained his doctorate in medicine in 1827 after 10 years of studies with a dissertation on inflammation of the heart, which, incidentally, laid the foundation for cardiology research at **Tartu** that continues to the present. While practicing medicine in Tartu from 1824 on, he also held the lectureship of **Estonian Language** at the University in 1842–50 and taught pharmacology in 1843–45. The founding of the **Estonian Learned Society** in 1838 was his idea and he served as its chair in 1843–50.

Faehlmann's importance in Estonian history is as the main precursor of the **National Awakening**. In his prolific writings and lectures, he condemned the Baltic overlords' cruelty to the Estonian peasantry while lauding the richness of the ancient culture and language of the Estonians. His publications of Estonian folktales in German as well as Estonian raised awareness of Estonian folklore abroad as well as at home. He also wrote on Estonian grammar, especially on the gradation of declinable words, the formation of comparative forms of words, as well as the derivation of words. But it is his collecting of folktales and their initial systematization, beginning in 1838, that provided the material for his friend and fellow doctor, **Friedrich Reinhold Kreutzwald**, after Faehlmann's early death at the age of 52 on 22 April 1850 in Tartu, to complete his work and publish the national epic poem ***Kalevipoeg***.

FASCISM. Although Soviet propaganda often referred to both the **Veterans** Movement and the regime of **Konstantin Päts** after the **preemptive coup** of 1934 as fascist, no evidence has been unearthed to date that either had any connections or even sympathies with either Mussolini or Hitler. Although there undoubtedly were individuals who sympathized with Hitler, especially among the **Baltic Germans**, there is no evidence of any organized fascist or Nazi movement in Estonia during independence. During the three-year German occupation from the fall of 1941 to the summer of 1944, the German Nazi Party attempted to form copies of its various branches in conquered Estonia, but with little success, because of the confusion of wartime occupation, the foreignness of the ideology, and the resentment of occupation. Even **Hjalmar Mäe**, who cooperated with the **German Occupation**, was rehabilitated by the Allies after the war. Similarly, the Estonian soldiers who fought in the Waffen-SS did so to fight for the freedom of Estonia and against the Soviet forces, and not for Germany or Hitler. *See also* ARMED FORCES, ESTONIAN LEGION.

FINLAND. The importance of Finland to Estonia from the mid-19th century onward cannot be overestimated, since the Finnish cousins have been acting as example, and provided guidance and strong support, to Estonian national aspirations unstintingly and consistently. The initial impact was the example of the Finnish epic *Kalevala*, the model for **Friedrich Reinhold Kreutzwald**'s ***Kalevipoeg***, which inspired the Estonian movement to collect folk verse (*see* JAKOB HURT *and* LITERATURE) and became the foundation of the Estonian **National Awakening**. At the turn of the 20th century, the University of Helsinki provided opportunities for Estonians to acquire doctorates in cultural studies. After the abortive 1905 Revolution, radicals sought by the tsarist police found refuge in Finland. In the **War of Independence**, Finnish volunteers were the first organized foreign contingent that arrived at a crucial time to stop the **Bolshevik** forces. In return, Estonian young men flocked to Finland in 1943–44 to assist the Finns to fight against Russia (*see* JR 200). But it was the moral support of ordinary Finns during the long Soviet occupation that gave the Estonians an advantage over all other conquered nations in the Union of Soviet Socialist Republics (USSR). That the support was partly conditioned by geography did not lessen the importance of it to Estonians. One of the most valuable and long-lasting supports was completely unintentional, namely Finnish **television**, which began broadcasting in 1956 and could be watched in the northern half of Estonia, with the result that large numbers of Estonians grew up speaking Finnish, possessed uncensored and unbiased information about the world, and were conversant with Western films and music. They also learned about modern commerce and competitive markets, for Finnish television was also commercial and partly dependent on advertising from its inception.

The reopening of the ferry service with Helsinki in 1980, when the Olympic regatta events were held in **Tallinn**, provided a major boon for Estonians in the form of a flood of 200,000 Finnish tourists a year who brought goods, literature, music cassettes, and videotapes to their friends. It was said in Tallinn that all that an Estonian needed was one Finnish friend to have access to the benefits of capitalism.

Beginning in 1989, Finnish business also made the first capitalist incursions into Estonia, initially by subcontracting textile processing, and subsequently by investing extensively in Estonian firms as well as subcontracting heavily. During the mid-1990s, Finnish law firms established in Tallinn began to dominate the international business dealings of foreign firms domiciled in Estonia as well as Estonian firms' foreign business, sending a clear signal for the need to rapidly upgrade legal education and the practice of law to the international level.

At the governmental level, Finland has been the strongest and most consistent foreign supporter of Estonia, and it has provided technical, financial, and political support unstintingly to Estonia from the beginning of renewed independence. Finnish assistance has also been given generously in developing the Estonian military and its foreign service.

Indeed, economically and politically, the two capitals, Helsinki and Tallinn, although separated by 75 kilometers of the Gulf of Finland, are in the process of forming the second Baltic conurbation, following the example of Copenhagen-Malmö at the southern end of the Baltic Sea.

FINNO-UGRIC PEOPLES. The Uralic family of **languages**, to which Estonian belongs, is divided into the Finno-Ugric and Samoyedic branches, and consists of over 30 languages spoken by approximately 23 million people. The Samoyedic branch with a total of about 30,000 speakers today is almost extinct, the largest remaining community being the Samoyeds in arctic Russia.

The Finno-Ugric branch consists of two major groups, the Finnic languages and the Ugric languages. The main language of the Ugric branch is Hungarian (or Magyar) with nearly 11 million speakers in Hungary and a further 3 million speakers in surrounding areas (for example, Slovakia, Romania, and Voyvodina in Serbia) as well as among emigrants in Western Europe and North America. Khanty (or Ostyak) has about 13,000 speakers, and Mansi (or Vogul) has around 3,000 speakers. Both of these languages are spoken east of the Urals, around the River Ob.

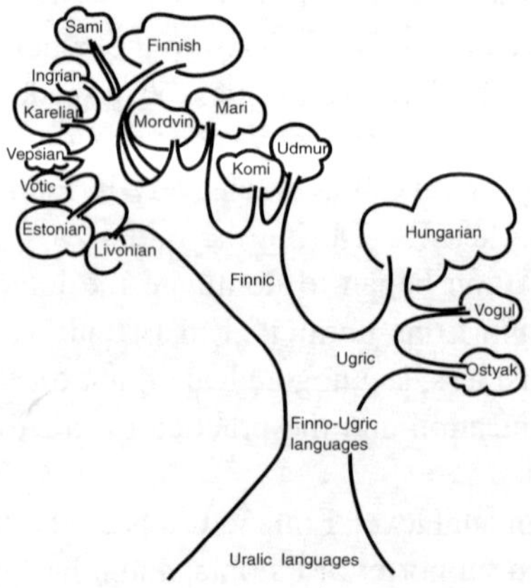

Adapted from http://www.ddg.com/LIS/InfoDesignF97/paivir/finnish/finnugr.html

Languages of the Finnic branch are spoken in the region between northern Norway and the White Sea: the whole of Finland, Estonia, and parts of Russia. The main language of the Finnic branch is Finnish, with over 5.5 million speakers in Finland, Sweden, Russia, and the United States. Estonian is spoken by over 1 million people, mainly in Estonia. Around 25,000 people speak Sami (formerly known as Lappish) in the north of Scandinavia. The remaining Finno-Ugric languages are spoken within Russia. Karelian, Vepsian, Ingrian, Livonian, and Votic are spoken in the Kola Peninsula in the north. Of these, Karelian is the most widespread with over 100,000 speakers. Vepsian has some 2,000 speakers. Ingrian, Livonian, and Votic all have very few speakers, and they may not survive for long.

Further in Russia, scattered around the central Volga region, are Mordvin (or Erza), Mari (or Cheremis), Udmurt (or Votyak), and Komi (or Zyryan). Mordvin is the most widely used, with 800,000 speakers. Mari is spoken by over 600,000, Udmurt by over 500,000, and Komi by approximately 250,000 people.

FLAG. *See* NATIONAL SYMBOLS.

FOUR-MAN PROPOSAL. *See* ISEMAJANDAV EESTI (IME).

– G –

GENOME PROJECT. In late 2000, **Riigikogu** authorized the Estonian Genome Foundation (EGF) to begin a pilot project that would eventually lead to compiling DNA profiles and health information of 75 percent of the 1.4 million Estonian population. This is only the second such project that aims to cover an entire country, Iceland with a population of 200,000 being the first. The Estonian project is more ambitious and is also different from the latter in that in Iceland, a private company has been given a license to run the country's health database for 12 years, whereas the Estonian EGF is nonprofit. Moreover, in Estonia the submission of data is voluntary, in contrast to Iceland where there is only a right to opt out. The initial result is that there is no opposition to the project in Estonia and a good deal of popular enthusiasm. It is expected that the project will generate sales of $100 million of anonymous data to drug firms, and public researchers will be given cost-free access. Individuals will also have access to their own files.

GEOSTRATEGIC POSITION AND DEFENSE STRATEGY. Located on the ice-free southern shores at the entry to the Gulf of Finland, Estonia's geographic position has been a prize for Russian rulers since Ivan the Terrible attempted to open a "Window to the West" via the Baltic States and initiated the **Livonian Wars**. **Peter the Great**, while building his "Western" capital at the iced-in bottom of the Gulf, and as part of his drive to move Russia into modern Europe, succeeded in conquering Estonia from Sweden, along with Latvia and Lithuania, in the **Great Northern War** at the end of the 17th century. Thus he moved the border of Russia to the shores of the Baltic Sea and opened up easy sea access to Western Europe. During the ensuing two centuries, St. Petersburg, behind the defensive cordon of the Baltic States and Finland, which the tsars acquired in 1808–09 from Sweden, grew into the prosperous European-oriented industrial showcase capital of a rural, backward Russian hinterland. **Tallinn**, Helsinki, and Riga were the gateways to the West and the Helsinki and **Tartu** universities the empire's elite educational institutions within the network of German universities.

Bases at Tallinn and Liepaja (Libau) in Latvia provided forward naval security to the empire, and toward the end of the 19th century Tallinn became an important armaments and industrial producer because of its ice-free port, its trading heritage since **Hanseatic League** days, and the educational strivings of the population (*see* EDUCATION).

World War I removed both the security cordon and the economic resources of the Baltics from Sovietized Russia. However, the new communist rulers understood well the value of the Baltic gateway, and planned a reconquest as soon as the Baltic States achieved independence (*see* ATTEMPTED COMMUNIST COUP OF 1924). The prelude to World War II provided the opportunity (*see* MOLOTOV-RIBBENTROP PACT) and the outcome of the war its implementation. Once again, the Baltic States provided a 200–400-kilometer-deep land security cordon; Liepaja, Tallinn, and **Paldiski** provided an ice-free forward naval bases; and Estonia and Latvia provided a well-educated labor force and modernizing industrial resources (*see* INDUSTRIALIZATION), as well as a highly developed and efficient source of agricultural products (*see* AGRICULTURE). The Soviet leaders quickly destroyed these states' governmental, administrative, and judicial structures and attempted unsuccessfully to destroy their **languages** and ethnic identities. They did everything in their power during the half century of occupation to totally integrate these states into the Soviet "Rodina" (the Russian concept of the nationless Soviet motherland) and state.

The collapse of the Soviet Union forced the empire run by the communist successors of the tsars reluctantly to cede control of the Baltics to their ethnic populations, who quickly threw off the legacy of communism and Russian orientations and language, and rapidly reclaimed their West European cultural orientation and transformed themselves into West European capitalist democratic states.

The very success of the Baltic States, and especially Estonia in the transformation process to democratic capitalism, which only six years after restored independence was invited to begin negotiating for membership in the European Union, was considered an insult by the still backward and mired-in-Soviet-heritage Russia. The insult was compounded when Russians, who still regarded Russia a great power, saw tiny Estonia being considered for membership in **North Atlantic Treaty Organization (NATO)** while transforming its military forces to NATO standards and interoperability.

But it is the loss of the security cordon that Russia felt most keenly. Its leaders began developing policies to regain at least security control of the Baltics even before they were forced to reluctantly, over almost four years, withdraw their forces from the restored state's territories. The defense policies of all Russian governments in the 1990s, and especially since the rise of President Vladimir Putin, have focused on regaining superpower status. The first demarche was the attempt to establish control over the disintegrating internal administrative system exemplified by the bloody war on Chechnya's aspirations for independence in 1994–96 and revived in 1999. The openly stated second phase was the expansion of the Russian sphere of influence, especially to the territory of the former Soviet Union, including the Baltic States, called "near abroad" by Russia.

Stated Russian defense doctrine sees three dangers: attempt to ignore Russia in solving international security problems denigrate Russia's role as a Great Power in what Russia sees as the "new multipolar world constellation"; expansion of military alliances and blocs reduce the security of Russia and its allies; and discrimination against Russian citizens abroad insult Russia's great power status. In peacetime, the primary role of defense policy is directed at supporting and defending Russian citizens living in foreign countries.

The Baltic States as a buffer is seen by Estonian analysts as being in the long-term Russian defense and foreign policy interests. Russians now refer to the historic western interface role of the Baltics as the "Baltic window to Europe" and hoped until 2002 that it would become a grey buffer zone against expansion of NATO and the European Union into Russia's self-defined sphere of influence—the near abroad. Such a buffer would also hinder the spreading of Western values into Russian culture. The ideal solution would be to reestablish the Russia's borders at the Baltic shores, which would prevent NATO using the Baltics as a bridgehead and at the same time reestablish Russian naval control over the Baltic Sea. The geostrategic position of St. Petersburg, Russia's second capital and its economic powerhouse, would also be secure. Added benefits would be the reacquisition of the developed modern Baltic economies and agriculture, as well as the ports of the Baltic States, crucial for western Russian access to trade.

Objectively viewed, little has changed in the geostrategic position of Estonia vis-à-vis Russia in four centuries except that attempts to establish control now depend on Estonian internal defense and foreign policies. Hence, the twin thrust to join the NATO military alliance as a full-fledged member and the European Union as a "soft" security option. Hence, also, the support by Estonia's Nordic and West European neighbors to build up its defense capability.

Given the unchanged geostrategic defense interest of Russia in the Baltic, combined with its stated defense doctrine, opportunities for reacquiring Estonia or any of the Baltic States could arise or be created by internal destabilizing crises, combined with weakness of defense forces. Prior to concrete membership in NATO, one early mooted possible scenario saw Russia taking on the role of a "peacemaker" to defend the interests of its citizens living in Estonia who as a fifth column would ask for assistance.

Three standard phases are used by foreign governments to escalate internal crises. First there is a campaign of discreditation, which actually has been going on unceasingly ever since the restoration of independence in Estonia and Latvia, over charges of "discrimination" against Russians. A land, air, and sea blockade follows. An initial attempt to do this was the doubling of tariffs on Estonian goods in 1996–2003 (although Russia stated that it would drop them at the beginning of 2002, they remained firmly in place). Disruption of energy and communication systems steps up the crisis. This is why Estonia quickly began building the oil terminals at Muuga (*see* TALLINN PORTS) already in 1992, diverted its oil dependence to Western oil companies, later set up oil reserves on standard NATO rules, attempted to sell half of its **electrical** power-generating capacity to an American firm, and is building a power cable to Finland to connect with the European electrical grid (*see* OIL SHALE). It also modernized its telecommunications systems initially by connecting directly with Finland and subsequently by placing its telecom shares on the London Stock Exchange and allowing multiple private international competing telecom services.

Membership in NATO and EU, starting in 2004, will not change the geostrategic location of Estonia, but the integration of Estonian defense structures and strategies with those of the North Atlantic partnership, together with its southern neighbors, will reduce the likelihood of any adventurism on the part of any future Russian government—provide Estonia keeps up its won commitment to collective defense. *See also* BALTIC BATTALION, BALTIC DEFENCE COLLEGE, BALTIC DEFENSE COOPERATION.

GERMAN OCCUPATION (1941–44). As part of the attack on Leningrad, German armed forces crossed the Estonian border on 5 July 1941 and reached **Tallinn** on 28 August. While Estonians welcomed the Germans as liberators from the Soviet oppression and expected the Republic to be restored, the Germans merely established what amounted to a puppet government and kept the reins to themselves as Estonia became a province in the new **Ostland** colony of the Third Reich. The economy was subjugated to serve the interests of the German army fighting the Soviets at the Leningrad front, nationalized property was not returned, and approximately 5,500 Estonians were executed in concentration camps as communist sympathizers. The period of the German occupation was a very trying one with brothers being forced to fight in both the Red Army and the Nazi war machine. Approximately 33,000 Estonians had been conscripted into the Soviet army and another 35,000 joined the retreating Soviet forces. The year of terror of the Soviet occupation of 1940–41 led young patriots to volunteer to German forces, but disillusion set in and enlistments dropped drastically as hundreds fled to volunteer to fight the Union of Soviet Socialist Republics (USSR) in Finnish forces (*see* ARMED FORCES, ESTONIAN LEGION, and JR 200).

When in February 1944 the Soviet Army again threatened Estonia, a general mobilization carried out by the German administration raised 40,000 to stop the Red Army at the Narva River. However, renewed attacks by the Soviet armies forced the Germans to retreat. In an attempt to reestablish the Republic during the interregnum **Jüri Uluots**, as acting president of the Eesti Vabariigi Rahvuskomitee (Republic of Estonia National Committee), appointed **Otto Tief** as acting prime minister on 18 September 1944. However, unlike 1918, no help came from the West, and the Soviet armies entered Tallinn on 22 September, thereby extinguishing four days of de jure independence for 47 years. Estonians regard the German occupation of 1941–44 as another bad interlude in the long Soviet rule from 1941 to 1991, differing from the two Soviet periods only in that there was a World War and hopes were very much alive that the end of the war would bring independence back again.

GERMANIZATION. Up to the late 19th century, the primary **language** of culture in Estonia was German as were the elites and the primary political and economic actors, the historic legacy of the conquest and settlement of these territories by the Teutonic **Crusading Orders** and their descendants. Hence, because the **Baltic Germans** dominated all economic, cultural, and social life, it was natural that local Estonians with ambition would attempt to rise into the *Herrenvolk* any way they could. Indeed, apart from schools teaching church cantors and local country schoolmasters, even the secondary educational institutions were German-language ones reserved for local upper-class offspring. Even the **University of Tartu**, when it was reestablished in 1802 as the university for Estland and Livland, was a purely German-language institution. Hence, it was normal for any Estonian or Latvian ambitious young man who aspired to rise socially and economically above the status of a peasant to adopt the culture of the Baltic German ruling class. It was not until the **National Awakening** of the 1860s that the **Estonian language** and culture began to attract attention as having intrinsic value among the aspiring classes—the result of concerted efforts by such literary figures as **Carl Robert Jakobson**, **Johann Voldemar Jannsen**, and **Lydia Koidula**.

As an educated middle class began to develop, naturally speaking German as well as Russian and Estonian, it consciously sought to develop an identity apart from the historically dominant German culture while copying much of it, but in Estonian. At the same time, as clumsy attempts to Russify the **Baltic Provinces** were made during the last two decades of the 19th century, some Germans began to propagate Germanization of the locals—something the elites had consciously avoided in the past when they treated the locals as *Undeutsch.* Among the local propagators of Germanization as an antidote to **Russification** in the 1890s Ado Grenzenstein proposed Germanization as the salvation of what he regarded as an unviable small nation in the vast sea of Russians. The German regime during the 1918 occupation attempted to reestablish German as the national language, but was ignored by the Estonians. During the **German occupation of 1941–44**, the policy of the occupiers was to denationalize Estonians and Latvians over a 20-year period and to turn them into Germans. As in the past, the Estonian population ignored the policy while speaking German with the Germans.

Of course there have always been Germanophiles among Estonians, who, however, have traditionally been pejoratively titled *kadakad* (junipers); they have had no impact on the population at large or on the national elites.

GLOBAL ESTO. In 1958, the first festival of Estonians in North America took place in Toronto involving 800 performers and 7,500 participants from the United States and Canada. The success of this led to a decision to hold a similar festival in New York City three years later in 1960 and a third one again in Toronto in 1964, followed by the fourth and last North American Estonian Festival at White

Plains, New York, in 1968. A week prior, the Estonian community in Sweden also organized a festival to commemorate the 50th anniversary of the **Declaration of Independence**. The success of these activities led to a decision to organize the first global Estonian Festival in Toronto in 1972. The festivals got their catchy new name from a Canadian TV documentary of the 1972 festival titled "ESTO." Thereafter, the world festivals were simply designated by sequential Roman numerals. Thus ESTO II took place in Baltimore in 1976, III in Stockholm in 1980, IV in Toronto 1984, V in Melbourne in 1988, VI in New York in 1992, and VII in Stockholm and **Tallinn** in 1996.

Although after the restoration of independence many questioned the need and function of continuing the ESTO tradition of **Estonians abroad** holding festivals, since the **Song Festivals** in Tallinn were now accessible to all Estonians wherever they found themselves in the world, it soon became evident that the ESTO tradition of bringing Estonians abroad together was too valuable to lose. Hence, ESTO VII in Stockholm was followed by ESTO 2000 (VIII) in Toronto and a decision to hold ESTO IX in Riga in 2004.

During the years of the Soviet occupation, the global Estonian cultural festivals brought together thousands of dancers and singers as well as theaters, orchestras, other musical groups, and exhibitions of paintings and crafts. At each festival, learned Estonian societies, fraternities, and cultural organizations from all Estonian communities abroad held global meetings. The highlights of each ESTO were the mammoth song-and-dance performances often combined with a sound and light show, with several thousand massed performers. Each ESTO also carried a political message that it demonstrated by a colorful march culminating at a rally, usually at a city hall square, where speeches and declarations reiterated the demand for Estonia's independence. Both the political message, spread by media around the world, and the cultural activities, to which home Estonians were always invited and which increasing numbers were able to attend in the 1980s, provided invaluable psychological support for the struggle against **Russification** and Sovietization of fellow Estonians in the occupied homeland.

GREAT NORTHERN WAR (1700–21). The succession of the 14-year-old Karl XII as king of Sweden on the death of Karl XI in 1697 provided Denmark with the opportunity to organize an anti-Swedish coalition with Poland and Russia to challenge its supremacy in the Baltic Sea basin. After two decades of continuous war, Russia supplanted Sweden as the regional great power. For Estonians and Latvians, this meant the beginning of two centuries of Russian domination as the provinces of Estland and Livland were incorporated into its empire by Tsar **Peter the Great**. For Estonians, the war meant the end of a peaceful century of growth and the introduction of more stringent control by the **Baltic German** barons who succeeded in having their privileges confirmed and strengthened by Peter the Great as the price of their support.

The three-year drought of 1694–97 immediately preceding the war, the greatest hunger ever faced by Estonians, brought with it large-scale death of both humans (70,000–75,000 or 20 percent of the population) and animals, and thus intensified the misery of the foraging armies when Karl XII landed at **Pärnu** in 1700 and marched via **Tallinn** to attack Peter successfully at **Narva**. However, Peter reorganized his army and soon turned the northern theater of the war into a rout for the Swedes. In 1702, he defeated the Swedish forces near **Tartu**, and the following year he conquered the Swedish fortifications on Lake Ladoga and founded St. Petersburg on the Neva River as a fortified base to defend the northern approaches against Sweden. In 1703, he also laid waste to large swathes of Estonia from Narva to Tallinn and from Tartu to Viljandi. The following year, he decisively defeated the Swedish forces at Narva.

The cost of the first four years of war to Estonians was enormous: foraging Swedish armies had to be supplied, and the Russians used scorched earth and terrorist tactics. After a five-year respite and the defeat of Karl XII at Poltava in 1709, the war again moved to the northern Baltics. In 1710, Riga capitulated to Russia, followed rapidly by garrisons at Kuressaare in Saaremaa, Pärnu, and Tallinn, where a capitulation treaty was signed on 29 September by the town burghers and the Estland nobility.

Since it was important to Tsar Peter to demonstrate to the West that he was a benign and enlightened ruler, all capitulation agreements were signed with the local Baltic barons and town burghers on a voluntary basis. As quid pro quo, he granted them all they asked for—retention not only of their privileges under Swedish rule but also the reinstatement of virtually complete self-rule (the so-called Baltic special order) of the Old Livonian Teutonic Order princedoms. The Baltic Provinces thus became insulated to a considerable degree from the pan-Russian policies of the imperial government.

But the indigenous population suffered. Drought in 1708 in northern Estland brought with it hunger and starvation. In 1710–11, plague killed off large numbers: in Tallinn two thirds of the population died, in southern Estonia about one third, and in northern Estonia over one third died. Although the war continued until the Treaty of Uusikapunki (Nystad, or Neustadt) in 1721, for Estonians and Latvian it ended in 1710. The aftereffects, however, lingered on—of the prewar population of 280,000 Estonians, only 120,000–140,000 were left in 1710. The countryside was devastated and marauded by displaced and hungry peasant guerrillas. Agriculture and economy revived very slowly; it took almost a hundred years for the population and the economy to reach its prewar level. At the same time, the socioeconomic lot of the peasants declined as the nobility reverted to treating the peasants as unprivileged serfs. It is no wonder that the **Swedish Era** has gone down in Estonian mythology as "the good old Swedish times."

– H –

HANSEATIC LEAGUE. This was a federation joining trading towns and cities under the leadership of Lübeck in the Low Countries to northern Germany and **Livonia**, as well as to the western Baltic Sea's prime trading cities of Stockholm and Visby in Gotland, from the end of the 13th to the end of the 16th century (formally 1669). As the most important trading system of the time, the League maintained offices in London, Norway, Denmark, and Novgorod. In Estonia, **Tallinn** and **Tartu** were important trading centers on the League's prime trade route linking its office in Novgorod to Lübeck, Hamburg, Brugge, and London. Pärnu and Viljandi served as secondary centers in this trade. Tallinn, jealous of **Narva**'s location nearer Novgorod, prevented it from achieving the status of a member town in the League. Staples such as furs, pitch, grain, linen, hemp, and lumber moved from the Russian interior west, and salt, herring, spices, as well as manufactures such as woolen cloth, metal goods, and jewelry, moved east. Hansa membership brought the Estonian towns into direct contact with the mainstream of the entrepôt trading and manufacturing cities of Europe. In Latvia, Riga was the main Hansa town connecting the Russian hinterland via the Daugava River to the system.

At its height in the 15th century, over a hundred towns and cities were members, and a total of 160 were members at one time or another. Beginning in 1356, representatives of member cities met regularly in council at annual Hansa Days. The Thirty Years' War disrupted trade, and its legacy made it impossible for the League to resume its activities. Moreover, the League had already begun to decline toward the end of the 16th century as England, Sweden, and Russia began to pursue mercantilist economic policies as opposed to the intra-League free trade approach.

After the restoration of independence to the Baltic States, a new Hansa League of former member cities has been established around the Baltic Sea, and annual Hansa Days are held in most, now as international festivals promoting trade and tourism.

HEADS OF ESTONIAN GOVERNMENT. *See* APPENDIXES.

HEADS OF STATE OF ESTONIA. Independent Estonia in line with the ultrademocratic sentiments of the first constitution created the position of Riigivanem (state elder) chosen by **Riigikogu** as head of state, who also served as head of government. Because the Riigivanem was head of government responsible politically and legally to the Riigikogu, his functions as prime minister were paramount and the head of state functions were strictly secondary and mainly ceremonial.

In the **Constitution of 1937**, the office of president was created to be elected by popular vote. **Konstantin Päts** was elected and served as the first president from 24 April 1938 until he was removed by the Soviet occupying powers on 23 Aug 1940.

The legal authority of the de jure Republic of Estonia was carried on by the prime ministers of the Estonian government in exile, exercising the authority of the president as mandated by the constitution of 1937 and the authority of President Päts, who transferred his powers to Prime Minister **Jüri Uluots** on the night prior to his arrest. Uluots, in exile, transferred these powers to **August Rei**, who similarly transferred them to his successor and so on until **Heinrich Mark** finally returned them to the constitutionally elected President **Lennart Meri** in 1992. Thus the continuity de jure of the Republic of Estonian was carried unbroken in exile. (*See* NONRECOGNITION OF SOVIET OCCUPATION).

Jüri Uluots	1944–45
August Rei	1945–63
Aleksander Warma	1963–71
Tönis Kint	1971–90
Heinrich Mark	1990–92

Lennart Meri was elected president on 5 October 1992 by popular vote as provided for by the **Constitution of 1992**, and he was reelected by the electoral college for a second and final term of five years in 1997, as provided by the Constitution of 1992.

Arnold Rüütel was elected by the electoral college and took office on 8 October 2001 as the third president of the Republic of Estonia.

Arnold Rüütel also served as chairman of the **Supreme Council of the Republic of Estonia** and thus as its head of state, starting 8 May 1990 when the Supreme Council renamed the then Estonian Soviet Socialist Republic (ESSR) the Republic of Estonia and declared a transition period to independence to end with the election of a Riigikogu under a new Constitution of the Republic. His interim mandate ended when President Meri took office on 8 October 1992.

HEALTH. Modern healthcare in Estonia traces its beginnings to the Faculty of Medicine at the University of Tartu, which by the third quarter of the 19th century had become a prominent center for medical research in the Russian empire, mainly because it was part of the German university system. Among its early graduates who worked to improve the health of the population were **Friedrich Robert Faehlmann** in **Tartu** and **Friedrich Reinhold Kreutzwald**, a country doctor in Võru for 44 years. Although the **Russification** of the University, which began in 1889, meant that many prominent German professors left, enough local talent remained for the reopened University to establish a nerve research clinic in 1921 and the Institute of Physiology, which attracted young Estonian researchers and taught doctors who provided services for the population at European standards in the 1930s.

The period from the first Soviet occupation in 1940 to the end of the 1950s was one of decline as the older remaining faculty retired and research was no longer funded. When the Union of Soviet Socialist Republics (USSR) again funded university research, the University of Tartu established a Central Medical Laboratory in 1961, under the aegis of which many researchers were able to study abroad. After the restoration of Independence, the Faculty of Medicine was restructured by the mid-1990s as a full-service medical research and teaching institution, and is the only medical school in Estonia. In 1999, a contemporary and efficient building for training and research, the Biomedicum, was built with a World Bank loan as part of the Estonian Health Project.

Despite progress in medical research, the health of the Estonian population in the Soviet period remained as poor as in the rest of USSR. This was the result of outdated medical practices, such as bed rest and long hospital stays; lack of modern medical technology; and the overuse of easily available and poor-quality pharmaceuticals, especially penicillin. Public health measures and education, apart from compulsory inoculations, were absent and, when combined with poor nutrition and cavalier attitudes toward workplace safety, led to health levels far below those of modern postindustrial societies.

Realizing the importance of a healthy population, Estonian governments began to restructure the inefficient, overspecialized, costly, and outdated health service infrastructure early in the 1990s by establishing a system of health insurance funds, paid for by special social taxes; reducing the number of hospital beds; and upgrading medical education. By the end of the 1990s, Estonia had pharmaceutical quality controls and occupational health, food, and veterinary safety systems in place. It had also moved away from palliative healthcare with its emphasis on medical specialists to preventive healthcare with the family physician as the primary caregiver. Drafted with the help of Sweden and using Sweden and Norway as benchmarks, the Estonian Hospital Master Plan 2015 was adopted in 2000. According to this plan, nearly all of the current 78 hospitals in Estonia, most small, nonacute-care, specialized tuberculosis, pediatric, psychiatric, oncology, or long-term geriatric hospitals, will be closed. The objective is to restructure the system to 13 acute-care hospitals in four catchment areas, with two regional major hospitals (the University Hospital in Tartu and one in Tallinn), the rest being closed or converted into local healthcare centers. Nonmedical geriatric care will be moved to an upgraded retirement nursing home system.

Although primary care physicians are already paid on a fee-for-service basis by the Central Health Insurance Fund, hospitals are still funded haphazardly from the Fund and municipalities and have no uniform operating rules. There is little evidence of outright fraud, but current financial audits in the healthcare field are inadequate. Naturally, since healthcare is a political matter and since reform will stretch over several elections and require erecting new contemporary buildings to replace the current outdated ones, the final result of restructuring will likely still leave Estonia with a system less efficient than those of the benchmark countries for some time. However, since costs will inexorably increase as medical technology develops, financial constraints will impose efficiencies, including drastic reductions both in length of hospital stays and in the number of specialized medical practitioners. Moreover, salaries of physicians and nurses in 2003 are so far below those in the benchmark countries that many are leaving Estonia to work in the Nordic countries.

Estonia's **population** is declining not only because of a low birth rate, but also because of low life expectancy. In 2000, it stood at 70 years at birth, and 15 years at age 65—far below the Nordic averages of close to 80 and 18, respectively. The reason is lifestyle. Estonians smoke and drink too much alcohol, both legacies of the Soviet period. As a result, Estonia has triple the rate of chronic liver diseases and twice the rates of cardiovascular diseases and lung cancers of Sweden. And although cigarette advertising has been regulated, alcohol controls are far below those instituted in 1640 by the Diet of Livland, which reduced the distillation of alcohol drastically.

HIRVEPARK. *See* MOLOTOV-RIBBENTROPI PAKTI AVALIKUSTAMISE EESTI GRUPP (MRP-AEG).

HOT SUMMER. *See* SECOND NATIONAL AWAKENING; SINGING REVOLUTION.

HUMAN RIGHTS. For eight centuries, the Estonians' collective rights to exist as an ethnic entity, as well as their individual human rights, have been routinely violated beginning with the **Crusaders**, continued by the **Baltic German** aristocratic rule, then two centuries of Russian imperial suzerainty, and finally the half century of Soviet occupation. Since the 13th century, Estonians have enjoyed only three decades of freedom—1918–40, and since 1991. It is thus understandable why they are extremely upset about the charges of human rights abuses that were levied against them by Russia repeatedly in the 1990s.

Even in its first **Constitution of 1920**, Estonia included and implemented the standard safeguards of civil and political rights then in vogue. The **era of silence** interfered with these rights in the name of national security, but much less than in other Central and Eastern European states in the 1930s. The **Constitution of 1992** includes all contemporary substantive and procedural human rights found in progressive Western constitutions. The innovative 1925 **Law on Cultural Autonomy**, providing protection of collective rights for citizens of non-Estonian ethnicities, was abrogated by the Soviet occupation but was revived by **Riigikogu** in 1993. Moreover, to reduce the tensions between the Estonian majority and the one-third Russian-speaking population imported during the Soviet occupation, the President's Round Table was established in 1993 to find practical solutions to problems of noncitizen **aliens**, and it is composed of representatives of all the major non-Estonian ethnic groups.

Beginning even before the regaining of independence, the Russian population in Estonia, agitated by elements in Moscow inimical to Estonian independence, began accusing Estonians of discrimination against Russians and abuse of their human rights. The **Citizenship Law** was criticized by the Russian Foreign Ministry and by some in the local Russian community as discriminatory. Some Western observers also urged that greater flexibility be shown, especially regarding **language** requirements for the elderly. However, numerous international fact-finding organizations, including the Finnish Helsinki Committee and the Organization for Security and Cooperation in Europe (OSCE), found that the Citizenship Law conformed to international standards. With respect to repeated Russian allegations of human rights violations among the alien population, both the OSCE mission in Estonia and the **OSCE High Commissioner on National Minorities**, as well as the commissioner on minorities of the **Council of Baltic Sea States (CBSS)** and the European Commission, have repeatedly declared that they could not find a pattern of human rights violations or abuses in Estonia.

However, certain current concerns of human rights, such as curbing violence against women, including the cavalier treatment of rape by both sexes; bringing ancient prisons up to date; and speeding up criminal trials requires both an infusion of money and time to be brought up to **European Union** standards. *See also* INTEGRATION; INTERFRONT; RUSSIANS IN ESTONIA; RUSSIFICATION.

HURT, JAKOB (1839–1907). Estonian poet, *literat,* and national activist. Hurt was born in Himmaste parish on 22 July 1839. Following theological studies at the **University of Tartu** (1859–63), he graduated with a *cand. theol.* degree and completed his Ph.D. at the University of Helsinki in 1886. After his first degree, he worked as a schoolmaster until 1872, since the German pastorate in Estonia refused to accept the nationalist Hurt as a colleague. Only after he became acknowledged as the leader of Estonian cultural nationalism was he elected pastor of the congregation at Otepää. But soon he ran into a serious conflict with his German colleagues and in 1880 decided to leave Estonia for the position as pastor of the St. John's Estonian congregation in St. Petersburg, which he served until 1901.

Hurt began the struggle for recognition of Estonian culture already as a student but rose to national notice only in 1869 when his address to the first national **Song Festival** at **Tartu** emphasized the need to develop a national ideology and the crucial role of **language** in the maintenance of the nation. His address formed the foundation for the **National Awakening** movement for the following decade. In 1870, he was elected president of the **Estonian Aleksander School** committee, then the premier attempt to introduce the **Estonian language** as a language of education. In 1871 Hurt became president of the Tartu Farmers' Society, and in 1872 president of the **Society of Estonian Literati**. Thus, within three years he was at the helm of the three primary nationalist organizations in Estonia. At the same time, he broadened his search into Estonian folklore and poetry and called for its collection across the country by amateurs, of whom 1,400 responded by sending in 261,589 units of poetry totaling 122,317 pages. Between 1888 and 1906, he published 156 analytical articles in the Estonian press on this material and thus spread the gospel of the value of the language as the carrier of a rich Estonian national culture. He died in St. Petersburg on 13 January 1907.

– I –

ILVES, TOOMAS HENDRIK (1953–). Estonian-American journalist, Estonian diplomat, politician, and long-serving foreign minister of Estonia. Ilves was born in Stockholm, Sweden, on 26 December 1953 to an Estonian family that had sought refuge from the Soviet occupation in 1944. After the family moved to the United States, Ilves completed secondary school and studied psychology at Columbia University, graduating in 1976. He received his M.A. in psychology from Pennsylvania University in 1978. His interest in language led him to teach English at the Englewood Educational Center at Englewood, New Jersey, in 1979–81, after which he moved to Vancouver, British Columbia, as director and arts administrator of the Vancouver Literary Centre in 1981–83 and then as lecturer of Estonian **literature** and linguistics at Simon Fraser University in Vancouver in 1983–84. In 1984, Radio Free Europe/Radio Liberty hired him as research analyst for Estonian broadcasts in Munich, West Germany. In 1988–93, he served as director of the Estonian broadcast service. Through his broadcasts, especially on literary topics and his own writings, he became well known to Estonians at home and abroad as an Estonian literary figure and nationalist activist.

Against this background, which included his intimate knowledge of Washington in his role as a manager of RFE/RL, President **Lennart Meri** asked him to give up his American citizenship and become ambassador of Estonia to the United States (and concurrently to Canada and Mexico). He served in this capacity from 1993 to 1996 and very quickly raised Estonia's visibility in governmental and political circles in Washington. When the second cabinet of Prime Minister **Tiit Vähi** fell apart with the resignation of Foreign Minister **Siim Kallas**, who was also leader of the coalition partner Reform

Party, President Meri again called on Ilves, this time to assume the post of foreign minister on a nonpartisan basis in the third coalition cabinet of Vähi. After a cabinet crisis when Vähi was replaced as prime minister by his party colleague **Mart Siimann** on 12 March 1997, Ilves remained as a nonpartisan foreign minister in the new cabinet.

However, by March 1999 Ilves had decided that if he wanted to continue in Estonian politics, he had to join a political party. Hence, he resigned from the cabinet and six months before the next elections formed a new party, the Peoples Party (Rahvaerakond), which amalgamated with the Moderates (Mõõdukad) shortly after the elections. During his six months out of politics, Ilves breathed new life into the Estonian North Atlantic Institute and used it as a platform to publicize his pro-**European Union (EU)** and **North Atlantic Treaty Organization (NATO)** foreign policy approaches. In the event, the electoral coalition of the Moderates (plus Peoples Party), Reform, and Pro Patria (Isamaa) together received a majority of the seats and Ilves was appointed foreign minister again in March 1999, and served until the resignation of the **Mart Laar** cabinet on 22 January 2002. In May 2001, Ilves was elected leader of the Moderate Party but resigned in October 2002 after his party was badly beaten in the local elections. He was the first Estonian party leader to resign on principle after electoral defeat. Although his party was reduced to a rump of 6 (from 17 in the 1999 election), he was personally reelected to Riigikogu in the general election on 3 March 2003, and was subsequently appointed as one of the Riigikogu's observers at the European Parliament pending Estonia's accession to the EU in 2004.

Ilves has, without a doubt in the minds of Estonians as well as his international colleagues and the foreign press, been one of the most effective foreign ministers of any country, and certainly of any Central and Eastern European country. It was largely due to his effective lobbying in the EU capitals that Estonia was accepted into the first round of candidates for membership of the EU, and it is largely due to his political acumen, foreign policy management, and knowledge of international processes that Estonia rose to general international acclaim as the leading transition country during his time in office. *See also* POLITICAL PARTIES.

IME PROJECT (Isemajandav Eesti, Economically Autonomous Estonia). The **Supreme Soviet of the ESSR** on 18 May 1989 adopted the IME Project program, organized on 1 April, and decided that Estonia would begin a transition to economic independence effective 1 January 1990. On 27 November 1989, the Supreme Soviet of the Union of Soviet Socialist Republics (USSR) acquiesced to this when it adopted a law on the economic autonomy of Estonia, Latvia, and Lithuania. The IME Project worked on a "conveyor belt" system to draft "100 laws to be adopted in 100 days." *See also* ISEMAJANDAV EESTI *and* PRIVATIZATION.

INDEPENDENCE (1917–21). The fall of the tsarist regime in February 1917 forced the issue of Estonia's political future. Vigorous lobbying by **Jaan Tõnisson** and the large Estonian population in Petrograd forced the Imperial Provisional Government to accept Estonia's territorial unification into one province, appoint **Jaan Poska** as governor of the Gubernya (Province) of Estland, and agree to the election of the Maapäev (**Eestimaa Kubermangu Ajutine Maanõukogu**) provincial assembly. Leftist parties, including the **Bolsheviks**, Social Democrats, and Social Revolutionaries, won significant support because of voting by the numerous imperial military personnel from outside Estonia serving in Estonia.

The Bolshevik takeover in Petrograd in November 1917 extended to Estonia as well, until Germany occupied Estonia in February 1918. Most of Estonia's noncommunist **political parties** realized they were caught between the two forces and agreed to begin an active search for outside support. Representatives were sent to the major European capitals to secure Western recognition of the **Declaration of Independence**. As the Bolsheviks retreated from **Tallinn** and just before the German occupation army entered the city, the Committee of Elders (the standing body) of the Maapäev declared the country independent on 24 February 1918, appointed the **Estonian Provisional Government**, and went underground. Although by May Great Britain and France accorded Estonia de facto recognition, the continuing German occupation meant that the provisional government was limited to helping **Johan Pitka** organize the **Kaitseliit** underground, negotiating in St. Petersburg, and continuing its lobbying abroad. The defeat of Germany in November 1918 and attack by the Red Army enabled the provisional government to organize an army to fight the **War of Independence** while simultaneously negotiating with Vladimir Lenin for armistice and peace. The prolongation of the War into the summer, and its widening to include the **Landeswehr War** against German mercenaries intent on creating puppet German states for the **Baltic German** barons, caused a shortage of manpower. Hence, the **Constituent Assembly**, elected during the wars on 5–7 April 1919, had to add to its duty of creating a **Constitution** the twin needs of finding manpower and financing for the armies. The solution to both, to strip the Baltic German nobility of their estates and promise land to every volunteer, arrived at on 10 October 1919 by the Land Reform Act, not only replenished the armies but also led to a major reorganization of Estonia after the wars into a petit bourgeois society with the consequent political struggles during the two decades of independence.

Although there was unity among the political parties in the Constituent Assembly on winning the wars and guaranteeing independence, there was major disagreement on the form of government. The Left wanted an ultrademocratic parliament without an independent executive and the Right a strong executive with a weak parliament. As the **Riigikogu Elections 1919–34** show, neither side won until the **preemptive coup of 1934** ushered in the **Era of Silence**. And the conflict between Left and Right over the form of state, a legacy of 1919, continues even in the 21st century, over establishing an executive presidency or at least one elected by popular mandate.

INDUSTRIALIZATION. For two centuries, from the incorporation of the Swedish Duchy of Estland into the Russian empire in 1710 to the formation of the Republic of Estonia in 1918, the Estonian economy was an integral part of the imperial Russian economy. Any surplus production of the nobles' manorial farms, as well of *Handtwerk* manufactures in the towns, was exported to St. Petersburg. As capitalist grain markets developed in Europe along with **agricultural** modernization during the 19th century, Estonian production was integrated into the imperial system. Large-scale industrial production of goods increased rapidly in the empire in the 1860s, including in Estonia, where the transition to factory-based production was completed during the third quarter of the century.

By the end of the 19th century, textiles formed the primary industrial sector, followed by the metals industry, which grew rapidly as industrial production became machinery-based and railroads were built. Increasing urbanization led to the establishment of the Kunda cement factory—a major industrial building materials producer in Estonia to the present. Wood processing, pulp, and paper industries developed rapidly. The textile and food processing industries dominated with 62 percent of industrial production at the turn of the century. Although **Narva** was the largest center of industry for a long time, around 1900 **Tallinn** passed it. In preparation for World War I, a number of large enterprises were established in Tallinn, including three large naval shipyards in 1912–13 alone. The value of industrial production in Estonia increased approximately 2.5 times between 1900 and 1913. Half of the factories were owned by Russian capital, and German, French, and English capitalists controlled a quarter. **Baltic Germans** were in third place, and Estonian entrepreneurs brought up the rear in fourth place. The rapid industrial growth was conditioned by Russian imperial interests: raw materials, machinery, and labor were imported, and most of the production was exported to the rest of the empire. Unfortunately, much of the armaments industries on Estonian soil were either evacuated or destroyed when the Russian armies retreated.

Hence, when the independent Republic was declared, it was faced with not only a communist Russia intent on reconquest but also with a partially destroyed industrial complex oriented to production for an extinct empire. All remaining large enterprises had to be closed and new, smaller ones formed better suited for a small country with limited local resources that also had to reorient its exports westward to Europe. By 1925–27 many smaller industries were operating successfully, and by 1938 the industrial structure of Estonia was in place and more-or-less level with Finland.

History was repeated when, after the Soviet takeover in 1940, Estonia's industries were nationalized and incorporated into the Soviet industrial complex. During the ensuing war, half of these industries were destroyed. After reimposing its occupation, in 1945 the Soviet Union began to expand existing industries and establish new ones as integral parts of its industrial complex. Stalin's policy of industrialization, based exclusively on building a heavy industry base, was applied to Estonia as well. Unfortunately, the policy became a mantra that outlived its creator, and despite Nikita Khrushchev's brief attempt in the early 1960s to introduce consumer industries, it remained the primary industrial policy of the Union of Soviet Socialist Republics (USSR) until its collapse.

Because of its manufacturing bias, a relatively well-educated labor force, a productive agricultural sector, forest resources, and its geographic location, Estonia, along with Latvia, was designated by the planners in Moscow for intensive industrial growth. That this required the importation of large numbers of workers also provided the political benefit that Estonia (and Latvia) could be more easily Sovietized and Russified (*see* RUSSIFICATION) and thus brought back into the Russian fold. Although exact statistics are not available, it has been estimated that Tallinn alone during the four decades of postwar Soviet occupation saw 7 million Soviet migrant workers trail through a city that grew from 145,000 in 1940 to 480,000 in 1989, half of them **aliens**. Several serendipitous factors speeded the forced pace of industrialization. Because **Tallinn port** was unscathed by the war, a large amount of the dismantled factories and machinery of German war reparations passed through it; but since the Russian railroad network was damaged and functioned badly, it was easier to simply leave the shipments in Estonia. These decisions were abetted by Estonian leaders who took advantage of the opportunity to rebuild the war-damaged industrial base. The maritime location with ice-free ports also encouraged the building up of a large merchant marine, shipyards and fishing and processing industries as integral parts of the Soviet industrial complex. Latvia, geographically similarly favored, was subject to similar development.

The **oil shale** deposits in **Northeast Estonia** provided the policy makers additional reasons for intensification of heavy resource industries, unavailable in Latvia, namely the decisions to supply Leningrad with electric power generated at two mammoth plants to be built at Narva, and manufactured gas produced at Kohtla-Järve. The apparent availability of uranium in the shale deposits encouraged Moscow to develop a rare metals refining industry. The mining, the power generation, and the rare metals refining required the importation of large numbers of workers with the result that urban areas of Northeast Estonia today are nearly exclusively Russian-speaking. Although the uranium discoveries proved in the longer run to be of too low grade to be effectively exploited, in 1945 when the USSR desperately needed to develop an atomic bomb, the decision was made to establish the **Sillamäe** refining complex, which processed imported uranium until the very end and left a huge **environmental** mess for the Western European taxpayer to clean up. The disregard of the environment by planners in Moscow led eventually to massively expand **phosphate mining** and to the ensuing **phosphate war**, which provided a major impetus to the mobilization of Estonians to fight for independence.

A serious unintended effect of Soviet industrialization policy was the bifurcation of the population along an ethnic class division. Since the heavy industries were almost exclusively manned by imported Russian-speaking workers, the hitherto strong Estonian working class disappeared as urban Estonians moved into the service sector. Two mutually excluding ethnic-linguistic-class communities quickly arose with few contacts across the divide. Somehow neither the planners nor the politicians in Moscow ever realized this negative impact of industrialization policy on the desired assimilation of Estonians with Soviet Russians.

The motivation for the restitution of Independence was expressed in the **Isemajandav Eesti** (IME, Economically Autonomous Estonia) proposal to establish an economically autonomous Estonia in 1987. The reaction to the inefficient massive heavy industry that produced ecological pollution of their native land but no well-being for Estonians, who instead saw an increasing decline in the Soviet standard of living, led to the desire to reorganize Estonian industry to provide economic benefits for Estonians. The **IME Project** produced the proposal adopted by the Supreme Soviet of the ESSR to pass 100 laws in 100 days in 1989 to restructure the politico-legal and socioeconomic systems to Western standards. Accordingly, policies were quickly developed to transform the Soviet Estonian industrial economy into an open competitive mixed capitalist economy in the shortest time possible. *See* ECONOMIC TRANSFORMATION.

INTEGRATION. Perhaps the most intractable problem with which Estonians had to grapple during the first decade of restored independence in the 1990s was the question of the alien, mostly ethnic

Russian, population who were brought into Estonia as labor during the Soviet occupation without consulting the Estonians. In the early years of the decade, there was a strong universal wish for all the aliens to leave in order that the monoethnic Estonia of the 1930s could be recreated. To encourage emigration back to Russia, an emigration assistance fund was established, and the granting of permanent residence status and naturalization were made difficult. Moreover, the Russian population, who during the Soviet period had been able to use the Russian language everywhere and thus had no reason to learn any Estonian, felt imposed on by the sudden demands of the Estonians to use only Estonian in all official and public dealings, and even in stores, offices, and workshops.

Although it had become evident already in the mid-1990s that very few of the Russian-speaking **aliens**, beyond the 70,000 who left between 1992 and 1995, would "go back to Russia" and that consequently an accommodation had to be reached with the remaining 400,000 who formed 35 percent of the country's population, it was not until membership in the **European Union** (EU) became a real possibility in the late 1990s that it became a political necessity to devise means to this end. Two other elements played a role in the development of the policy of integrating the Russian-speaking population into Estonia as a fully functioning part of the community. First, the research proving this necessity had already been done by sociological surveys beginning in the early 1990s, and second, both these surveys and official statistics showed that the whole **population** was rapidly aging and that nativity was dropping precipitously. In the decade from 1988 when 25,060 babies were born, to 2000 when 13,089 were born, nativity had dropped precipitously to half. The birth to death deficit since 1993 has stayed at 6,000–7,000, and will rise significantly in the next decade as the population ages. Political leaders began to understand that the economic consequences of an aging and declining population, with serious effects on social welfare funding and labor markets, beginning about 2010, required quick and resolute action.

Although sociological surveys had shown for a decade that the Russian and Estonian language communities, including the youth, lived isolated from one another, the diametrically opposite reactions of Russian and Estonian youths in March and April 1999 regarding

North Atlantic Treaty Organization (NATO) during the Kosovo air campaign shocked Estonians. Whereas Estonian youths were unanimous in supporting NATO, Russian youths expressed their opposition in raucous public demonstrations in front of the Russian embassy. The ensuing media discussion of the Russian community's isolation lasted two years and finally brought home the urgent need to solve the problem of the segregated non-Estonian-speaking foreign community. After lengthy analysis by a cabinet level committee, followed by debate and revision, **Riigikogu** adopted the program "Integration in Estonian Society 2000–2007" at the end of 2000.

Although the Russian language was their common language during the Soviet period, Russians and Estonians had became segregated into two linguistic-class communities from the beginning of Russian migration to Estonia (*see* INDUSTRIALIZATION). Until Estonia's independence became a reality, only a tiny fraction of Russian speakers bothered to learn Estonian. Yet Estonians were forced to learn Russian in order to communicate with most government offices, to communicate at work, and to shop. Hence, when Estonians again regained their independent state, which they unanimously viewed as the sole bulwark guaranteeing their linguistic and ethnic survival, they were adamant in recreating it as the monolingual, monoethnic state that it was before the Soviet occupation in 1940. The unreality of expectations of the aliens leaving only slowly penetrated Estonians' consciousness as Russians found life in Estonia far preferable to that in Russia. Even most of those who have opted for Russian citizenship seem to prefer to remain in Estonia.

The additional facts that Estonians, even after a decade of independence, could not get by without a knowledge of Russian in their second city, **Narva**, and that the Russians there continued to live in a Soviet time warp, finally produced polices to integrate the aliens into Estonia and make them loyal citizens of the Estonian state. Much of the Russians' isolation has been due to government policies based on the unrealistic expectations of emigration. Hence, for example, in a survey of the 175,000 Russian speakers who were still stateless in 2001, 60 percent said that one of the reasons they had not applied for naturalization was that they could not speak Estonian, but 50 percent said that it was matter of convenience—with an alien's passport, they could get Russian visas to Russia more easily than Estonian citizens! In 2000, Estonia and Russia ended this preferential treatment.

The integration program is based on the objectives of assisting Russian speakers to become loyal citizens while retaining an Estonian-Russian cultural identity. To this end, four subprograms were established. The basic one has the objective of making all Russian schools bilingual by 2007, when 60 percent of the teaching would be in Estonian, and all graduates could speak and write fluent Estonian. The problem lies in the difficulty of finding Estonian-language teachers, let alone teachers of other subjects, who would be willing to live and work in the current Soviet-mentality ghettoes of **Northeast Estonia**. To help solve the problem, Narva College was established as an affiliate of the **University of Tartu** to educate local Russian students as teachers able to teach in both Estonian and Russian. Similarly, Estonian Second Language teaching and learning programs were developed with the aim to eventually provide Estonian-language immersion programs for all Russian primary school children. The immersion project is based on 30 years of successful English Canadian programs of French immersion and is internationally funded. The first such classes were started in 2000 and will be added to progressively as new teachers are trained. In 1999 there were only 600 teachers of Estonian as a Second Language; in 2000 there were 700, but the backlog was 800.

The second subprogram provides support for Russians (and other ethnic minorities) to preserve their cultural distinctiveness by means of cultural societies of various kinds and Sunday language schools.

The third subprogram intends to encourage adult Estonian-language learning by providing both financial incentives by remission of half of the fees on successful completion of each segment, and dispensing with the language test on application for naturalization. The program is jointly funded by the Estonian taxpayer, the EU, and Western governments. The objective is to encourage adult, noncitizen Russian speakers to apply for naturalization and thus reduce the alien population as quickly as possible. Among the Russian-speaking youth, identification with Russia is already nonexistent, even in Narva, but surveys show that adults identify with an imaginary Russia rooted in the Soviet period of their youth. In 2000, naturalization was made easier for graduates of Russian secondary school who had passed the Estonian language courses, and in 2001 the mandatory test of knowledge of the Estonian **Constitution** was dispensed with for graduates who had passed the school Estonian civics course.

The fourth subprogram has the broad aim of developing good citizenship or civic values among non-Estonians, both naturalized citizens and those who are still aliens. It is multifaceted and includes increasing the number of professional Russian journalists trained in Estonia; to shift Russians media consumption from Russian **television** (currently the Russians' main source of information) to both Russian-language Estonian and Estonian-language television and **newspapers**; to develop Russian-language civic organizations, especially among youth; and to encourage interactivity between Estonian and Russian language media.

Although the program is perhaps overly ambitious about adults, seven years is a long time for children and youths. Thus, the goodwill, rooted in necessity, that appears to pervade the leadership of Estonian politicians, intellectuals, and businessmen is expected to significantly reduce Russian isolation in Northeast Estonia. *See also* ALIEN PASSPORTS; CITIZENSHIP; LANGUAGES; LANGUAGE LAW; RUSSIANS IN ESTONIA.

INTEGRATION IN ESTONIAN SOCIETY 2000–2007. *See* INTEGRATION.

INTERFRONT. On 19 June 1988, the Workers International Movement of the Estonian Soviet Socialist Republic (ESSR), known as Interrinne in Estonian and Interfront in English, was organized by Soviet centralist elements in Estonia as a direct challenge to the nationalist aspirations of the Estonians expressed by **Rahvarinne**. Although in retrospect Interfront proved unsuccessful in all its objectives, it nevertheless played a significant and disruptive role in opposing Estonian independence during its three years of existence until it was extinguished by the government of independent Estonia on 25 August 1991.

Shortly after its formation on 12 October 1988, its "general conception" demanded a two-chamber ESSR **Supreme Soviet**: a chamber of deputies and a nationalities chamber, in which Estonians and non-Estonians would be represented in equal numbers, with veto power for both groups. Moreover, Estonian and Russian were both to have status as official **languages** in a bilingual Estonia, and all people working or living in Estonia were to be granted citizenship. In November, an Interfront mass meeting in the city arena (Linnahall) condemned the new **Language Law** just passed by the ESSR Supreme Soviet, which established Estonian as the language of the country, and demanded the reorganization of the memberships of the **Estonian Communist Party (ECP)** and all ESSR government organs according to parity of nationality. In the same month, a congress established the United Council of Workers Collectives (Töökollektiivide Ühendnõukogu, TKNÜ), with 542 delegates representing 120,000 workers in 117 All-Union-controlled (that is, directly by Moscow ministries) enterprises. This demarche constituted a stepped-up challenge to Estonian independence, since it was led by politically well-connected large enterprise managers, such as its chairman, Vladimir Jarovoi, director of the mammoth military machine tool and metals enterprise Dvigatel in **Tallinn**. Thus, the factory directors in effect took over the leadership of Interfront and made it part of the workers' activities of their enterprises.

On 24 February 1989, as the ESSR government hoisted the blue-black-white tricolor from the national flagstaff atop Pikk Hermann for the first time since 1940, Interfront expressed nonconfidence in the government and began to organize strike committees in the All-Union enterprises. On 4 and 5 March, Interfront held its first congress with 742 delegates from 140 Union enterprises. Only 11 of the delegates were ethnic Estonians. The program adopted by the congress was diametrically opposed to that of Rahvarinne: it opposed the restoration of the bourgeois capitalist system, Estonian **citizenship**, **privatization** of means of production, a separate currency for Estonia, and the establishment of national **defense forces** units. A few weeks later, TKNÜ announced solidarity with Interfront. On 14 March, the two organizations held joint mass meetings in Tallinn, Kohtla-Järve, and **Tartu** with a focus of agitating against the national **flag** and the language law.

The close ties of Interfront with Moscow were openly demonstrated when the leaders of the two organizations met with the Politburo member Vadim A. Medvedev of the Communist Party of the Soviet Union (CPSU) in June. The following month, Interfront's Council of Strike Committees, together with TKNÜ, Soviet armed forces veterans' organizations, and serving soldiers' associations, organized a mass meeting on 21 July, the anniversary of the Soviet annexation of Estonia in 1940. Strikes at the end of the month were followed by a politically motivated general strike from 10 to 18 of August at all the All-Union factories following directives from Moscow. The categorical demand of the nearly exclusively non-Estonian strikers to the ESSR government to give up the policy of sovereignty was defied by the government. In November, Interfront and TKNÜ, together with the war veterans, held a mass meeting where they demanded the establishment of a separate Northeast Estonian Autonomous Soviet Socialist Republic with its own constitution and Supreme Soviet.

After this, Interfront began to agitate widely for the separation of Northeast Estonia and to viciously attack Rahvarinne. On 15 May 1990, a mass meeting at the Parliament Building on **Toompea** led to an attempt to physically remove the tricolor from the Parliament Building and replace it with the Soviet red flag. Strikes in Tallinn and Kohtla-Järve followed. The ESSR government denounced any attempt to divide Estonian territory.

The lack of success only led to increased attempts at organizing ever-widening opposition to the Estonian drive for independence. Accordingly, a congress of elected representatives at all state levels, from communes to the ESSR Supreme Soviet, together with representatives of enterprise works' collectives, consisting of Interfront members and sympathizers, met to form the Council of the National Economy (Rahvamajandusnõukogu) with the objective of carrying out President Mikhail Gorbachev's decrees and safeguard the constitution of the USSR. Interfront also set up television transmitters to broadcast its propaganda to **Northeast Estonia**. Toward the end of the year, mass meetings were organized to demand that the ESSR government sign Gorbachev's proposed new Federation Treaty, and the works' strike committees began to form workers' troop units. On 15 January 1991, a mass meeting on Toompea demanded that the ESSR Supreme Soviet meet their demands within 24 hours, which included the formation of a new government based on nationality quotas (at least half should be Russian), signing of the Federation Treaty, and giving up any thoughts of independence. The meeting also sent a request to Gorbachev to institute direct emergency presidential rule in Estonia. Meetings making similar demands took place at Kohtla-Järve.

On Bloody Sunday, 13 January, attacks by Soviet forces' **OMON** units in Vilnius cost 14 lives; on 17 January, 11 of the largest union enterprises in Tallinn went on strike; and on 18 January, the government built concrete block barricades around Toompea to protect Parliament from the strikers. The strikes spread to wholesale warehouses and to Tallinn airport. They ended on 30 January after negotiations between the government and directors of the striking All-Union enterprises. This strike proved to be the last hurrah of Interfront. It split shortly after its Second Congress on 2 February owing to charges of financial misconduct. Its falange held a rival Congress at Kohtla-Järve, but all signs pointed to the inevitability of the demise of Soviet-oriented action, as even the rapidly declining ECP (losing thousands of members each week) split into a national majority and a Soviet-oriented rump. On 25 August 1991, two days after the **Declaration of Independence** and the failure of the Moscow coup, the government of Estonia outlawed Interfront, the TKNÜ, and both wings of the ECP.

ISEMAJANDAV EESTI (IME, Economically Autonomous Estonia). The acronym IME means "miracle" in Estonian. The "Four-man Proposal" published in the **Tartu** newspaper *Edasi* on 26 September 1987 to establish Estonia as an economically autonomous republic, still within the Soviet Union, was originally written by a group of 12 members of the **Estonian Communist Party** (ECP) *nomenklatura*. However, only **Edgar Savisaar**, **Siim Kallas**, **Tiit Made**, and **Mikk Titma** found it possible to sign the proposal—the others feared major negative reactions from the Party. As it happened, three of the four were forced out of their jobs by the **Karl Vaino** regime. Only Tiit Made was able to continue working at the Institute of Qualification. On 16 November 1987, the Council of Ministers under **Bruno Saul** declared the IME proposal "noncompetent," but to no avail. The fuse of nationalism had been lit; within four years, Estonia regained its independence and the Soviet Union was no more.

The **IME Project** produced the proposal adopted by the **Supreme Soviet of the ESSR** to pass 100 laws in 100 days in 1989 to restructure the politico-legal and socioeconomic systems to Western standards. Accordingly, policies were quickly developed to transform the

Soviet Estonian industrial economy into an open competitive mixed capitalist economy in the shortest possible time.

– J –

JAAKSON, ERNST (1905–1998). "Grand old man" of the Estonian diplomatic corps. Jaakson was born in Riga on 11 June 1905 and began working for the Estonian Embassy in Riga in 1919 when still a student at the Riga German Gymnasium, where he served until 1926 while studying in the Faculty of Economics of the University of Latvia in 1925–26. After military service in the 10th Infantry Regiment from 1926 to 1928, he entered the foreign service of Estonia in 1928 and was appointed to the consulate in San Francisco in 1929. In 1932 he was transferred to the New York consulate, where he served first as consul and later consul-general until 1991. In 1934, he graduated from Columbia University with a B.A. in economics. In 1991 the restored independent Estonia appointed him ambassador to the United Nations and shortly thereafter ambassador to the United States, where he served until this retirement in 1993. Ernst Jaakson died in New York on 4 September 1998.

Jaakson performed the signal service to the Estonian Republic of maintaining the de jure continuity of the Republic and serving as the only Estonian diplomatic representative to the United States during the long Soviet occupation.

JAANIPÄEV (St. John's Day). The celebration of the summer solstice on 24 June since pagan times in northern Europe was Christianized by being named for the Apostle John in the Church calendar. The German Crusaders brought *Johannistag* to Estonians, who translated it as Jaanipäev. Despite the efforts of the Church, it has always been celebrated as the shortest night of the year (although the solar calendar has moved it to 22 June) over the centuries with bonfires, dancing, singing, drinking, and leaping over bonfires. It was the most important summer holiday in the Estonian peasants' cultural calendar since it signified the end of the spring season of sowing and partying by the village youth, and the beginning of the haying season. On the evening before St. John's Day, bonfires were lit and rooms in farmhouses were decorated with birch boughs. These customs are still followed across Estonia today. According to national mythology, money pits burn in the forest on this night and anyone who finds the flower of a fern, which purportedly blooms only on this night, is guaranteed great happiness and luck. During the period of Soviet occupation, Estonians made this night a celebration of nationalism, especially since from 1919 the St. John's bonfires have been called Victory fires in celebration of the victorious battle of Võnnu. *See* LANDESWEHR *and* VICTORY DAY.

JAKOBSON, CARL ROBERT (1841–1882). Estonian nationalist, social activist, writer, and teacher. Born on 26 July 1841 in Tartu as the son of Adam Jakobson (18 July 1817–18 December 1857), the local church choir director, parish schoolteacher, and clerk, Carl Robert received his elementary and secondary education from his father, studied at the Cimze seminary in Valga 1856–59, and succeeded his father as parish schoolmaster in 1859–61. After a conflict with the local pastor and the local noble, he moved to Jamburg in Russia where he worked as a schoolmaster. In 1865, he passed the examination as gymnasium teacher in German language and literature in St. Petersburg and taught inter alia at the tsarist court. In the same year he met **Johan Köler**, leader of the Estonian patriotic movement in the imperial capital, under whose influence the Germanized Jakobson converted to the Estonian cause. In his powerful and evocative prose in the newspaper *Eesti Postimees* (*Estonian Postman*), he quickly rose to prominence. In 1867 he issued the first part of *Kooli Lugemise Raamat* (*School Reader*), and in 1867 a geography text and atlas, both of which played a seminal part in **Estonian language** education. But he also laid the foundation of Estonian agricultural literature when he issued the first of his farmers handbooks, *Teadus ja Seadus Põllul* (*Knowledge and Rules in Agriculture*), in 1869. His prolific activity was catholic: in addition to newspaper articles on all kinds of subjects, he issued collections of music scores, wrote poetry, and in 1872 published the play *Artur ja Anna*, which became very popular.

Among Jakobson's greatest legacies to the Estonian people were his three patriotic lectures in Tartu in 1868–70 in which he criticized the **Baltic German** nobility for the seven centuries of serfdom that the Estonian nation had to endure and praised the ancient Estonian forebears for their struggle for freedom. Accordingly, he divided Estonian history into three periods: the era of enlightened self-government, followed by the darkness of Germanic serfdom, and the renaissance of the new era. The lectures were issued in book form in 1870 and have become the foundation of the Estonian self-conscious nationalist interpretation of their history as a people who have been hard-pressed by their neighbors and whose salvation and preservation as a nation lies in their own hands through a watchful eternal struggle against overwhelming foreign odds.

Throughout this time, Jakobson wrote polemic newspaper articles attacking the Baltic nobility and the church as its lackey in impoverishing the Estonian peasantry. This brought him into sharp conflict with **Johann Voldemar Jannsen**, whose poet daughter Lydia he gave the pseudonym **Koidula**, with the consequence that the pages of *Eesti Postimees* were closed to him. He then tried to establish a counter-newspaper but was denied permission form the imperial authorities. In 1872 Jakobson moved to Vändra as parish clerk and in 1974 he bought a farm in Kurgja, which he intended to make into a model farm using modern farming techniques. As a farmer, he became president of the Viljandi and Pärnu Farmers Associations and undertook a public educational program of speeches and writings to educate farmers in modernized farming. Under his leadership, they also became leading organs of the Estonians' national renaissance.

In 1878, Jakobson received permission to establish the newspaper *Sakala,* which from its first issue became the leading newspaper in the struggle for Estonians' national rights against the German barons. Despite his antichurch stance, which led to a split with his partner **Jakob Hurt**, and a yearlong suspension of the paper, by the 1880s *Sakala* had surpassed *Eesti Postimees* and had by far the largest circulation of any paper in Estonia. In 1881, Jakobson was the leading composer of what became known as the Major Memorandum (Suur Memorandum), which petitioned Tsar Alexander III to grant Estonia and Estonians more individual and national rights. This increased Jakobson's popularity and made him the undoubted leader of the Estonian national awakening at this time, but it also created even more conflict with the ruling Baltic-German nobility. His popularity was such that in 1882 he ousted the more moderate Hurt as president of the **Society of Estonian Literati** (Eesti Kirjameeste Selts), the premier collective of Estonian intelligentsia. Within a few months of reaching the pinnacle of leadership of Estonian nationalist aspirations, Jakobson died on 19 March 1882 at Kurgja, a few months before his 41st birthday, his ambitions for Estonia unfulfilled but well on their way.

JANNSEN, JOHANN VOLDEMAR (1819–1890). Estonian national-cultural activist, journalist, and writer. Born into a miller's family on 16 May 1819 in Vana-Vändra *vald*, his father died when he was only seven; hence, he was sent out to herd cattle to help earn his keep. Despite lack of material advantages, he completed the local parish and secondary schools and began work in 1838 as the organist of the local church and later as a church clerk and schoolmaster. In 1850, he moved to **Pärnu** and taught as the local secondary schoolmaster until 1863.

To make ends meet in 1843, after marriage, Jannsen began to write religious literature. The positive reception of his writings encouraged him to establish a newspaper. When permission was denied, he began publishing an annual *Sannumetoja* (*Courier*) in 1848 and issued seven volumes up to 1860. In 1856 he succeeded in receiving a license to publish the weekly *Perno Postimees* and edited it from 1857 to 1863, when he moved it to **Tartu** as the first Estonian professional journalist and edited the renamed *Eesti Postimees* until 1880. Among other innovations, he issued newspaper supplements on a regular basis, including *Eesti Põllumees* (*Estonian Farmer*), the first newspaper directed to the Estonian farmer in his own familiar language. Jannsen involved his whole family in the newspaper business, especially his daughter **Lydia Koidula** (real name, Lydia Emilie Florentine Jannsen), who received her early training in writing at the newpaper and later became Estonia's most famous female poet of all time.

Jannsen's home became a crossroads of patriotic agitation, providing a meeting place for the leading personalities of the Estonian national renaissance. In the 1860s, **Carl Robert Jakobson** was one of his intimates. In 1865, Jannsen, in pursuit of the **National Awakening**, initiated the song-and-drama organization Vanemuine, named after the Estonian god of music, and in 1867 led Vanemuine in innovating the first pan-Estonian song festival held in June 1869 with choirs and orchestras from all over Estonia and an audience of 12,000. The patriotic song that he wrote, "Mu isamaa, mu õnn ja rõõm" ("My Fatherland, My Happiness and Joy"), instantly became the popular national anthem, and was confirmed as such half a century later by the parliament of independent Estonia.

Jannsen, who had single-handedly created a popular consciousness of cultural exclusiveness and national cohesiveness among Estonians, surprisingly became cautious soon after the upswelling of popular nationalist sentiments that the song festival brought forth. Thus, although he continued to preach patriotism, his seeking accommodation with the Baltic German overlords led him into conflict with his close collaborators Jakobson and **Jakob Hurt**, both of whom he fired from his newspaper. By 1878, when Jakobson founded his competing and radical nationalist paper *Sakala*, the passive Jannsen had lost the support of the leading patriotic elites as well as popular readership. His last visible public act was the second pan-Estonian song festival, which he successfully organized in 1879. The next year a stroke left him incapacitated, and although he regained speech he was never able to work again. Ten years later, Jannsen died on 13 July 1890 in **Tartu**.

Jannsen's role in the Estonian National Awakening is seminal. Through his use of the vernacular **language**, he reached the kernel of the Estonian people—the increasingly independent farmers who bought their farms in a period when agricultural products were becoming a marketable commodity and farming was moving from sustenance to business (*see* AGRICULTURE). His newspapers propagated the national language, **education**, and modern farming methods as well as pride in national culture. He single-handedly created the popular support for the renaissance on which Hurt and Jakobson built.

JARVI, NEEME. *See* JÄRVI, NEEME.

JEWISH ESTONIANS. Although there are records of a few Jews in Estonia as early as the 14th century, permanent settlement dates only from the decree of Tsar Alexander II by which Jewish soldiers, tradesmen, artisans, and those with higher education were granted the right to settle beyond the Pale in the Russian empire. The first synagogues were formed in **Tallinn** in 1830 and **Tartu** in 1866, when 50 Jewish families settled there. These congregations built the only two temples in Estonia, both destroyed by fire in World War II. Small groups of Jewish tradesmen spread to Valga, **Pärnu**, and **Viljandi** where houses of prayer and cemeteries as well as schools to teach boys the Talmud were organized. Until World War I, all Jewish Estonian communities consisted of small tradesmen and artisans. The first Jewish Estonians who entered the **University of Tartu** at the turn of the century led the development of a Jewish Estonian intelligentsia beginning in the 1910s.

The tolerant attitude toward ethnic minorities of the newly independent Estonian republic, including the establishment of **Cultural Autonomy** in 1925, encouraged the flowering of Jewish cultural life. In 1919, the first Estonian Congress of Jewish Congregations led to the establishment of the Jewish Gymnasium in Tallinn and literary and sports associations in Tallinn, Viljandi, and **Narva** as well as an influx of students at the University of Tartu, where in 1934 100 Jewish Estonian students matriculated. In the same year, a chair of Judaica was established in the Faculty of Philosophy. In addition, in the 1930s two new Jewish schools, a secondary school in Tartu and an elementary one in Valga, opened.

These impressive activities were carried on by a minority that in 1925 numbered 3,045, barely making the cutoff limit of 3,000 needed to establish Cultural Autonomy. The elected Jewish Cultural Council operated the Jewish Cultural Autonomy and quickly attracted the attention of world Jewry for its management of Jewish cultural life in Estonia. These achievements are all the more impressive when it is realized that the census of 1934 counted only 4,381 Jewish Estonians.

The Jewish Estonian community was totally destroyed over the two years beginning in 1940 when the first Soviet occupation liquidated the cultural autonomies along with all of their institutions. After Nazi Germany drove out the Soviet army in 1941, those who had not been deported by the Soviets, or fled to Russia or the West, were murdered by the Nazis—variously estimated between 1,000 and 2,000 Jewish Estonians. The thriving community was utterly destroyed.

During the Soviet occupation after the war, some of the Jews who had fled to Russia returned but were unable to organize any semblance of Jewish cultural life or organizations as these were outlawed by the Soviet party state. Only a small congregation operated quietly in Tallinn. However, because of the relatively tolerant values of Estonians, many Jewish students and professors who could not gain admittance to the more anti-Semitic universities of Moscow, Leningrad, and Kiev made their way to Tartu (*see* JURI LOTMAN) and Tallinn and thereby enriched the academic level of Soviet Estonia. Some others migrated from other parts of the Soviet Union as well. However, although they were listed as "Jews" in their Soviet internal passports, few practiced either the religion or maintained any Jewish culture.

With the renewed independence of Estonia, the Jewish Cultural Society was established in 1988 and the Jewish Community as an umbrella organization was founded in 1992. Subsequently a synagogue was opened in Tallinn, but the fact that the Jewish Estonian community of approximately 1,000 is composed mostly of pensioners poses problems for its future viability as a community.

JR 200 (Finnish, Jalkaväenrykmentti 200). JR 200, or Infantry Regiment 200, in the Finnish Army was formed in 1944 from Estonian volunteers who had fled the forced mobilization into German forces during 1943 and early 1944. The unit fought in the Continuation War against the Red Army on the Karelian front. In August 1944, 1,800 of these accepted the amnesty negotiated by the Finnish government with the Germans and returned to help defend Estonia against the Soviet attack as the German troops retreated. A total of 3,273 Estonian volunteers served in the Finnish forces during the Winter War (1939–40) and the Continuation War (1941–44), most in JR 200. Of these, 126 were killed in battle and are buried in the War Heroes' graves section of the Hakaniemi Cemetery in Helsinki, 72 are missing in action, and 286 were wounded. *See also* ARMED FORCES.

JÄRVI, NEEME (1937–). Orchestra conductor. Born on 7 June 1937 in Tallinn, Järvi graduated from the conducting class at the Leningrad Conservatory of Music in 1960, was a conductor at the Estonian Radio and Television Symphony from 1960–63, was its conductor-in-chief from 1963 to 1979, founded the Tallinn Chamber Orchestra, and became conductor-in-chief of the Estonian Opera Orchestra. He came to international attention beyond the Soviet sphere and the Nordic countries initially in 1971 when he won the Sixth Conductors' Competition of the National Academy of St. Cecilia in Rome. Although he was lionized and honored with medals and titles in his homeland and in the Soviet Union, his dream to take his orchestra to the West and introduce Estonian composers to the world audience was thwarted by Soviet power. Hence, when the opportunity presented itself to emigrate to Israel in 1979, he took it and left his homeland. The next year, he moved to the United States, then he accepted the conductor's baton of the Gothenburg Symphony Orchestra in Sweden in 1982, as well as the Scottish National Orchestra, which he led from 1984 to 1988.

In 1990, while remaining with the Gothenburg Symphony, he also took on the conductor's baton of the Detroit Symphony. During the decades since he left his native land, Järvi has fulfilled his dream of introducing Estonian composers to the world, not only by including them in the repertoire of his orchestras but also by playing them in his demanding schedule of guest conducting and in his prolific recording program. Thus, among his 350 CDs of world composers, **Rudolf Tobias**, Heino Eller, **Arvo Pärt**, Eduard Tubin, and others have been represented. In addition to his musical leadership, which he used to build the Gothenburg Symphony into one of the stars of orchestral recording, he took the little-known Detroit Symphony to first rank and built a new $80 million home for it. Also, it is due solely to him that Estonian composers and Estonian music is known the world over for the first time in history.

His son older son, Paavo Järvi, is following in his father's footsteps as a recording conductor and guest conductor in demand the world over, and he was appointed music director of the Cincinnati Symphony Orchestra in 2001. His younger son, Kristjan Järvi, founded the avant-garde Asolute Ensemble in New York in 1993 and is following his older brother in making debuts as a guest conductor with orchestras around Europe. In 2000, he was also appointed conductor of the Umeå opera and symphony orchestras in northern Sweden. Neeme Järvi's daughter, Maarika, a well-known concert flutist, continues to appear regularly in her homeland, and has recorded concertos by Estonian composers, although she lives and works in France and Spain.

– K –

KABIN, JOHANNES. *See* KÄBIN, JOHANNES.

KAITSELIIT. *See* DEFENSE LEAGUE.

KALEVIPOEG. The Estonian national epic based on folklore, written originally by **Friedrich Reinhold Kreutzwald** in 1853 in 13,817 verses in the form of the old Estonian folk song, which he was not allowed to publish by the Russian Empire's censor. After thorough revision, it was published by the **Estonian Learned Society** in sections issued between 1857 and 1861 in the form of 19,087 verses. The final public version of 19,023 verses was published in Kuopio, Finland, in 1862.

The origins of the Kalevipoeg legend are found in ancient Estonian folklore. It records the battles and adventures of Kalev's son (Kalevipoeg), the mythical hero and ruler of ancient Estonians, and ends with his violent death and the country's conquest by foreign invaders. Initial written references were made to the folkloric legend in the 17th century and, although literary interest in it arose at the beginning of the 19th century, it was not until 1839 that **Friedrich Robert Faehlmann** presented the first collected synthesis of the folklore surrounding the legend. In the same year, influenced by the publication of the initial versions of the Finnish Kalevala epic in 1833–36 by Elias Lönnrot (final version published in 1849), **Baltic German** medical doctor and folklorist Georg Julius Schultz-Bertram proposed a schedule of writing the Estonian epic. However, it was not until the death of Faehlmann in 1850 that Kreutzwald began to work seriously on the project. Its impact on the development of the **Estonian language** and **literature** has been of seminal importance.

Although the work contains only about an eighth of the original verse from folklore, it is firmly anchored in the national folklore and provides a bridge with the mythical heroic past of the Estonian nation. Hence, it played a primary role in developing national consciousness in the period of the **National Awakening**, especially so since it systematized a folklore that was different yet in the same genre as that of the Finnish *Kalevala*. Its primary role in the development of the Estonian language lies in systematizing the unique verse form of Estonian folklore, the *regivärss*, that is, the Estonian form of runic verse—polyphonic prose or rhythmical prose employing the poetic devices of alliteration and assonance. The basic runic verse line is the trochaic tetrameter, with each line generally forming a conceptual whole. This runic-verse song-form is common to the majority of Balto-Finnic cultures and is presumed to date back to the first millennium B.C. Through translations using the Estonian folkloristic verse form into most of the languages of Europe, *Kalevipoeg* has served as a major literary ambassador for Estonia.

KALLAS, OSKAR PHILIPP (1868–1946). Estonian folklorist and diplomat. Born on 25 Oct 1868 in Kaarma parish, Kallas completed the **University of Tartu** in 1892, continued his studies at Helsinki in 1892–93, and earned his Ph.D. in 1901. In 1990 he married Aino Kallas, who became a well-known novelist in both Finnish and Estonian. Kallas worked as gymnasium teacher in **Narva** in 1893–95; in St. Petersburg in 1895–1903, where he also lectured at the University in 1901–03; and in **Tartu** in 1903–18, where he also served on the editorial board of *Postimees*. During the confusing period of 1918–20, he represented the Estonian government in Helsinki and became Estonia's first ambassador to Finland in 1920–22. Thereafter, he served as ambassador to London from 1922 until his retirement in 1934, and concurrently to The Hague from 1923. For the next 10 years he lived in active retirement in Tallinn, and he fled to Sweden in 1944 just before the second Soviet occupation.

Kallas's contributions to Estonian national development are myriad, though mostly hidden from public view, since as a born diplomat he had none of the self-promoting ethos of most of the other prominent figures of Estonian national development. Recent research, however, has discovered that he had a hand in many spheres. Among other achievements, he founded the Estonian National Museum in Tartu (the depository of all Estonian cultural artifacts); was the first Estonian to earn a doctorate in folklore, and as such laid the foundation of the scholarly study of Estonian folklore; and was the first professional Estonian diplomat as well as a businessman (as part owner of *Postimees*), journalist, teacher, and founder of the first Estonian girls' school. He was a close friend and adviser to **Jaan Tõnisson**, the politician and statesman, who, along with **Konstatin Päts**, dominated Estonian politics during the first four decades of the 20th century.

His role as Tõnisson's confidant apparently was responsible for Kallas's major disappointment in losing the lectureship of Estonian language and literature in 1909, when the council of professors of the University of Tartu appointed a less qualified but colorless "safe" candidate in opposition to the wishes of the Faculty of Philosophy. Kallas's dream of a professional academic career in the service of his nation thus lay in tatters. After all, he had given up his position as special lecturer in Finno-Ugric studies at St. Petersburg to return home. Although the University of Tartu granted him an honorary doctorate in 1929, he focused his academic energies for the rest of his life on the National Museum, which he served for a total of 56 years, until the Soviet occupation forced him to flee his homeland. Even as a working diplomat, he concentrated on introducing comparative Finno-Ugric approaches to the study of Estonian folklore and on building collections of Estonian folkloristic materials in the library of the Museum. Kallas died in Stockholm on 26 January 1946, two years after fleeing his homeland.

KALLAS, SIIM (1948–). Estonian politician, banker, and prime minister. Born on 1 October 1948 in **Tallinn**, Kallas graduated cum laude from the money and banking program in Economics at the **University of Tartu** in 1972; worked at the Ministry of Finance of the Estonian Soviet Socialist Republic (ESSR) in 1975–79, as director of the Savings Banks in 1979–86, and then as deputy editor of *Rahva Hääl*, the newspaper of the **Estonian Communist Party (ECP)** and the government of the ESSR, in 1986–89. In 1989, during the struggle for independence, he was appointed chairman of the Association of Labor Unions of the ESSR, where he served until appointed the second president of the newly formed **Bank of Estonia**. On 5 March 1995, Kallas was elected to **Riigikogu** VII as leader of the Reform Party and served as foreign minister in the first **Mart Laar** coalition cabinet in 1995–96. Thereafter, he remained opposition leader of the

Reform Party in Parliament until the formation of the three-party coalition government after the Riigikogu IX election on 7 March 1999, when he became finance minister in the second Laar cabinet. After the collapse of this cabinet in December 2001, engineered by **Edgar Savisaar** and himself, on 22 January 2002 Kallas became prime minister of a minority coalition government of the Reform and Center parties and served until 10 April 2003. After the general election of 3 March 2003, although Kallas's party, which came third, entered into a coalition with Res Publica and the Coalition parties, Kallas himself stayed outside the cabinet but remained leader of the Reform Party.

Kallas rose to prominence as one of the signatories to the Four-man Proposal on **Isemajandav Eesti (IME)**, published on 26 September 1987 in the Tartu newspaper *Edasi.* His public visibility continued as he was elected to the People's Congress of the Union of Soviet Socialist Republics (USSR) and to the ESSR Supreme Soviet in 1989–91. As a member of the ECP from 1972 to 1990, he was one of the prominent young Estonians who pursued an independent political future for Estonia consistently from the mid-1980s, joined **Rahvarinne**, served on its central council, and was one of the founding members of the Vaba Eesti (Free Estonia) political movement out of which in 1994 he helped form the Reform Party and was elected its leader. He and Reform represent the classical liberal capitalist approach in Estonian politics. His coalition with Savisaar's Center Party, which represents a welfarist center approach to governing, was a triumph of pragmatic politics over ideology and an indication of the developing flexibility of the Estonian political class. Kallas's cabinet was regarded by observers as one of the most effective in Estonia, and Kallas received high praise as prime minister from his European colleagues. *See also* POLTICAL PARTIES.

KELAM, TUNNE (1936–). Estonian politician and writer. Born on 10 July 1936 in Taheva *vald*, Kelam graduated in history from the **University of Tartu** in 1959 and then worked for the State Historical Archives in **Tartu** until 1964 while continuing graduate studies in the history of art. For the next 10 years, 1965–75, he worked for the *Estonian Encyclopedia* as an editor. His anti-Soviet proclivity was noted already in 1957 when, still a student, he began to lecture on international politics in the academic voluntary society Teadus (Science). From 1959 to 1965, he also commented on foreign affairs for the Tartu newspaper *Edasi*. In the 1970s, he became an active opponent of the Soviet regime when he joined the nationalist-democratic underground movement.

In 1972, Kelam drafted a memorandum to the United Nations on behalf of the Estonian Democratic Movement and the Estonian people, which outlined a program for ending the Soviet occupation and reestablishing the independent Republic of Estonia. The KGB marked him and forced him to resign from the *Encyclopedia* in 1975, when he found work in the Kreutzwald State Central Library but was again forced to leave in 1980 for a job as a night worker in a chicken production unit at a **sovokhoz**, where he stayed until 1988, when **perestroika** allowed him to join the newly established journal *Akademia* as its **Tallinn** representative. Throughout, he continued his illegal activities of spreading uncensored information, developed contacts with Western democratic organizations, and organized nationalist oriented groups.

In 1988, Kelam was among the leading founders of the Eesti Rahvuslik Sõltumatuse Partei (ERSP, Estonian National Independence Party) and in 1989 of the Estonian Citizens' Committee movement, and he became the chair of its Executive Committee. In 1990 he was elected to the **Estonian Congress** and became chair of the **Estonian Committee**. In 1991, he was elected to the **Constitutional Assembly** and has been elected to all four parliaments of independent Estonia since 1992, first as member of the ERSP and, after its demise in 1995, as member of the Pro Patria Party. Kelam also served as one of the two deputy speakers of the **Riigikogu** from 1992 to 2003. In 1996 and 2001, he ran unsuccessfully for president of Estonia. Kelam has been active in international parliamentary affairs and, as chair of Riigikogu's European Affairs Committee, has participated actively in Estonian-European Parliamentary, European Council, and Inter-parliamentary Union activities, facilitated by his knowledge of English, Finnish, Russian, German, French, Polish, Italian, and Hindi. During the Soviet period, he also translated widely from these languages.

KERES, PAUL (1916–1975). Estonian chess master. Born on 7 January 1916 in **Narva**, Keres studied mathematics at Tartu in 1938–41 but did not complete his degree; his life revolved around chess. Already at the tender age of 13, he beat all adults at a local tournament in Narva. After achieving the title of Estonian chess master in 1935, he rose to international attention in the same year when he became European champion in postal chess and won the 1936 international tournament at Bad Nauheim. By 1938, he was classed among the eight chess masters competing for the world championship, but he never made it—thrice he was runner-up, and he became known as the perpetual No. 2. Keres's contributions to international chess, however, are considerable: in addition to participating in numerous chess teams (four times with the Estonian team between 1935 and 1939, which he led to a bronze medal at Buenos Aires in 1939), he also achieved gold medals on seven occasions as a member of the Soviet team between 1952 and 1964. The greatest international accolade, however, was the offer of election to the presidency of FIDE as a result of his reputation for integrity as well as his mastery of the theory of the game. Unfortunately, he had to turn the offer down since, as a Soviet citizen, he would not have been able to make any decisions independently of Moscow. As he put it, "The only thing I can do without Moscow is write my books on chess." His legacy, apart from the memory of gentlemanly and scrupulous attention to the rules of the game, consist of a large theoretical literature available to any chess enthusiast.

For Estonians, in the 1930s along with the wrestler **Kristjan Palusalu**, Keres represented international visibility of achievement as he was the most celebrated Estonian in the world at the time. During the Soviet occupation, Keres became a symbol of the survival of integrity in the face of the totalitarian repression of morality and pressure to conform to the dictates of the communist ideological teleology. The system used his mastery of chess, allowed him to travel widely (he died on 5 June 1975 in Helsinki en route home from a chess tournament in Canada), and even honored him with the usual medals, but it never made him into a subject of the Party state ideology. The Estonian population turned out in the tens of thousands to pay their respects at his funeral and honor him as much as the symbol of national integrity as national chess master.

KERT, JOHANNES (1959–). Estonian general. Kert was born in Petseri on 3 December 1959 in Petseri and graduated from the Faculty of Physical Education at the **University of Tartu** in 1981 as a wrestling coach. During his university career, he also received officer training in the motorized infantry and was commissioned lieutenant. In 1981–83, during his compulsory military service, he took battalion command courses at the Soviet Army's Higher Armored Command College at Kharkhov and was then sent to serve in the tank battalion of the motorized infantry regiment in Kaliningrad. After military service, he worked as a youth leader in **Tartu** for the next six years. In 1990, Kert resumed his military career as the first instructor of the **Defense League**'s Kalev Malev and was elected later that year as its commander. In 1991, he was appointed by the newly instituted Estonian Defense Headquarters as head of the Defense League's Operations Group, and was sent to organize and head the first noncommissioned officers' school at Võru. In 1992, he began organizing the independent Kuperjanov infantry commando battalion and became its commander. At the end of the year he was appointed commander of the Defense League and organized a group of disparate and often undisciplined unit of volunteers into a structured, operating organization under the control of the **Estonian Defense Forces** (EDF) command.

In 1996, after the resignation of General **Aleksander Einseln,** President **Lennart Meri** appointed him commander of the Estonian Defense Forces. He was promoted to captain in 1992, major in 1993, lieutenant colonel in 1994, colonel in 1996, major general in 1997, and lieutenant general in 1998. In 1998–99 he completed the Finnish National Defense College's general staff course, and in 1999–2000 he took the staff course at the U.S. Army War College in Carlisle, Pennsylvania. Shortly before graduation and while still in the United States, President Meri proposed to Kert that he resign as commander of the EDF and take up the new, shortly to be established, Land Forces Command. On his refusal, Meri dismissed him and assigned him to the Reserve. The matter became a political cause célèbre amid charges that the president had acted unconstitutionally, since it is the president's prerogative to recommend but Parliament's right to appoint, as well as remove, the commander of the EDF. After both Kert and Meri appeared before the **Riigikogu**, Kert's dismissal was approved by a single vote (by a member who later claimed that he had mistakenly pressed the "Yes" voting button on his desk, in the belief that he was voting in support of Kert). Despite several weeks of public controversy, the only plausible reason advanced for the president's action was that **Jüri Luik**, the minister of defense, a protégé of Meri's, wanted a more politically flexible commander of EDF. The choice was Rear Admiral Tarmo Kõuts, hitherto head of the Border Guard, who had demonstrated administrative efficiency as well as leadership and political acumen in inveigling appropriations to build up effective border controls both on land and at sea.

Eventually, Kõuts talked Kert into accepting the new subordinate position and on 19 December 2000 appointed him commander of land forces.

KINGISSEPP, VIKTOR (1888–1922). Estonian revolutionary communist leader. Born in Kaarma-Suure *vald* in Saaremaa on 24 March 1888, Kingissepp, an ideological **Bolshevik**, was one of the founders of the **Estonian Communist Party** (ECP). He received his secondary education at the Kuresaare Middle School and studied in the history, language, and law faculties at St. Petersburg University off and on from 1906 to 1917. He picked up his socialist ideology already in secondary school, joined the Estonian section of the Russian Social Democratic Workers' Party in St. Petersburg, and participated in its illegal underground activities in Estonia, St. Petersburg, and Moscow as a political propagandist and journalist. As deputy chair of the Estonian Revolutionary War Committee during the Bolshevik coup in October 1917, he led the formation of the Estonian Red Army, and served on the Executive Committee of the Estonian Soviets. In 1918, he was elected to the All-Russia Executive Committee of the Russian Soviets.

During the Estonian **War of Independence**, while serving on the Estonian Central Committee of the Russian Communist Party and simultaneously as commissar of internal affairs of the Estonian Workers' Commune, Kingissepp is reputed to have fought fanatically against the Estonian Republic. When the ECP was formed in 1920, he was elected to both its Central Committee and its Central Bureau. In the independent Republic, he formed an underground organization with the objective of overthrowing the regime and incorporating Estonia into the Soviet Union. On 3 May 1922, he was shot as a traitor by a field war court. In the Estonian Soviet Socialist Republic

(ESSR), he was regarded as a hero, and Kuressaare was renamed in his honor (a decision reversed by the reinstated Republic in 1992), and a new town in the Leningrad Oblast in Russia was also named for him, where his name has survived the collapse of the Union of Soviet Socialist Republics (USSR).

KOIDULA, LYDIA (Lydia Emilie Florentine Jannsen) (1843–1886). Koidula was born on 24 December 1843 in Vana-Vändra *vald* when her father **Johann Voldemar Jannsen** was still an unknown parish clerk and country schoolmaster, which later fortuitously provided her with the source for her evocative poetry of country life. After being educated by her father and the family's subsequent move to **Pärnu** in 1850, she completed the German Girls' School there in 1861, where she experimented with poetry initially in German. In 1862, she graduated with the certificate of the **University of Tartu** as a home schoolmaster—the highest educational qualification achievable by women at the time. When her father moved to **Tartu** in 1863 to edit *Eesti Postimees*, she became his right hand and soon took charge of the literature section, for which she also wrote stories and poetry. In 1867 when **Carl Robert Jakobson** included her poetry (and "gave" her her pseudonym) in his school text on literature, she became known widely across Estonia. In the same year her second collection of poetry, *Emajõe ööbik* (*The Nightingale of the Mother River*—the river running through Tartu, which is mythologized by Estonian intelligentsia as the cradle of Estonians), especially with her evocative patriotic and rural idyllic poems, including "Mu isamaa on minu arm" ("My Fatherland Is My Happiness"), "Sind surmani" ("Even unto My Death"), and "Ema süda" ("A Mothers' Heart"), spread her fame even more broadly. As her father's close collaborator, she naturally assisted in the creation of the first pan-Estonian Song Festival in 1869 and in the work of the Vanemuine theater. In 1870, the performance of her play *Saaremaa Onupoeg* (*The Nephew from Saaremaa*) on the fifth anniversary of the Vanemuine company is taken as the beginning of Estonian theater. In her position at the epicenter of the Estonian **National Awakening**, she came to know all its leading figures; maintained frequent contact and a large correspondence (much of which has been published) with them, including **Friedrich Reinhold Kreutzwald**, the creator of **Kalevipoeg**; and picked up and distilled wisdom from them.

Koidula also traveled and came to know European nationalist romantic movements firsthand, initially with her father with whom she visited Finland in 1879 and later with her husband, the Latvian naval doctor Eduard Michelson, whom she married in Tartu in 1873 and with whom she spent 1876–78 in Germany and Austria, where he pursued postgraduate medical studies. Although she was forced to make her home at the imperial naval base of Kronstadt outside St. Petersburg from 1873 onward, she never accommodated to it and was always homesick for Tartu, which she visited often, maintaining her connections and writing for her father's newspaper. While dying of breast cancer, she issued her last collection of poetry, patriotic to the very end, *Enne surma—Eestimaale* (*My Last Testament—to Estonia*). During a writing career of 25 years, Lydia Koidula produced over 300 poems, 86 short stories, seven evaluative articles, and four plays, all of which are still in print. Her complete archive survived and is deposited in the Museum of Literature. In 1946, 60 years after her death on 11 August 1886, her remains were brought from Kronstadt and reinterred at the national cemetery in **Tallinn**. Since her poetry first spread through the schools in the 1860s, all Estonians have read her poems and found in them their own expression of patriot love for the nation and its land.

KOLER, JOHANN. *See* KÖLER, JOHANN.

KOLKHOZ (Estonian, Kolhoos; Russian, Kolkoz, contraction of *kollektivnoje hozjaistvo*, collective enterprise, collective farm). Kolkhozes were the main agricultural production units in the Soviet Union; they have continued as such through the decade after the collapse of the Union of Soviet Socialist Republics (USSR) in most successor states in the Commonwealth of Independent States (CIS), including Russia. In Estonia, the kolkhozes were privatized beginning in 1990 and the land was returned to the original owners or their successors by the mid-1990s. *See also* AGRICULTURE; SOVKHOZ.

KOMSOMOL. *See* ESTONIAN LENINIST COMMUNIST YOUTH LEAGUE.

KOPP, JOHAN. *See* KÕPP, JOHAN.

KREUTZWALD, FRIEDRICH REINHOLD (1803–1882). Estonian writer and medical doctor. Born on 26 December 1803 at Jõepere manor in Kadrina parish into a serf's family that was freed only in 1815, Kreutzwald obtained an education thanks to his father's drive (representative of the desire for education of the newly freed Estonian peasantry) and the support of friendly members of the **Baltic German** nobility. On finishing the **Tallinn** county school in 1820, he worked as an elementary school teacher and gained admission to the medical faculty at the **University of Tartu** in 1826. After graduating in 1833, he served as city doctor in Võru for 44 years, until 1877. Like his friend and medical colleague, **Friedrich Robert Faehlmann**, he lived a dual life—on the one hand he worked hard as a medical practitioner providing services to a population still at the edge of subsistence, and on the other, his love of his fatherland led him to write and publish stories in Estonian. The latter earned him the popular title "Nightingale of Võru." Kreutzwald's concern about the low level of health of the Estonian peasant in 1854 led to the publication of the first popular medical handbook written by an Estonian, which remained in circulation for decades.

Through his prolific writings, Kreutzwald laid the foundations of the **National Awakening**. But, although he took over his friend Faehlmann's collection of Estonian folk verse and completed it by writing it up as **Kalevipoeg**, which immediately became *the* national epic of Estonia, and although he corresponded extensively with all of them, he was never at the center of the movement. Still, he was the first Estonian to be honored abroad for his literary contributions: in 1855 he was elected corresponding member of the Finnish Literary Society, and in 1871 corresponding member of the Hungarian Academy of Sciences. Kreutzwald died on 25 August 1882 in Tartu.

In Estonia, Kreutzwald's role in the formation of national consciousness and his influence on the seminal figures of the Estonian renaissance was widely acclaimed only in the 20th century. Statues of him were erected in five cities between 1926 and 1958 (three during the Soviet occupation!), and a memorial museum was opened in Võru in 1941. Between 1953 and 1979, five volumes of his collected works and six volumes of his correspondence were published. However, in literary history both in Estonia and abroad, his claim to greatness is forever the national epic Kalevipoeg.

KROON (EEK). The kroon as national currency of Estonia was originally adopted in 1928, to replace the mark (introduced in 1919 to replace the Russian ruble), which had lost its value as a result of political meddling and had become a political liability. The new kroon, divided into 100 senti, was handled better by the semi-independent central bank and maintained its credibility throughout the 1930s, until the Soviet occupation abolished it in 1940. In 1928, its value was set at 0.4072 grams of gold or 1 Swedish krona; and after the general demonetizing of gold in 1935, its value was reset at 1 £ = 19.20 kroons

The kroon was reinstituted as the national currency of Estonia on 20 June 1992. Its value was pegged by an act of parliament to the deutsche mark at the rate of 8 kroons to 1 deutsche mark (1 DM = 8 EEK). Six hundred million kroons were issued (in both cash and deposits converted from rubles) equivalent to $US50 million dollars (USD). The kroon at issue was backed by assets totaling $US120 million, mostly in monetary gold. An act of **Riigikogu** also established a **currency board** system whereby the issuance of kroons was tied to foreign exchange at full and free convertibility. The value of the kroon can thus only be changed by an act of parliament—a difficult process in the Estonian Parliament, in which no party has ever enjoyed a majority and the cabinet is always made up of at least three minority parties. With the disappearance of the DM on 1 January 2001, the value of the Estonian kroon automatically changed to the DM's equivalent in euros (1 euro = 15.64664 EEK). *See also* BANK OF ESTONIA; CURRENCY BOARD.

KROSS, JAAN (1920–). Estonian writer. Born in **Tallinn** on 19 February 1920, Kross obtained a law degree from the **University of Tartu** in 1944 and taught there until 1946. He was then deported to the Union of Soviet Socialist Republics (USSR) as part of a hunt for "nationalist" scapegoats and spent the next eight years in the Komi Autonomous Republic and Kransnojarsk Oblast. He returned home in 1954 but was not "rehabilitated" until 1960 when he was allowed to join the Writers Union of the Estonian Soviet Socialist Republic

(ESSR), of which he became secretary in 1976–81 and later deputy chair and chair. Between 1958 and 1971, Kross published five collections of poetry and one long satirical poem, "Tuule Juku" ("Weathervane"). Colleagues and critics lauded him for introducing a thought-provoking style and creative freshness to Estonian poetry in the early 1960s, a time of transition from the Khrushchevian "thaw" to the Brezhnevite stagnation. Since the 1970s Kross has been writing historical novels, novellas, and stories that deal with the problems of accommodation in the lives of both real and imagined historical Estonian figures who manage to rise from subject status under historical overlords. The Estonian public regarded Kross's historical writing as satire of the then current subjugation of Estonians to the Soviet yoke, permitted by the authorities only because of the overlay of historical antifeudalism in the novels, and they consistently bought out all editions of his books. Kross, although repeatedly queried about it, has never acknowledged the apparent autobiographical aspects in his writings. Once during the paroxysms at the end of the Soviet party-state in 1989–90, his overt nationalism, although camouflaged by history and an elegant writing style, led to an attempt by Moscow to censor him. The attempt was unsuccessful because of the cohesiveness of the Estonian writers who refused to support the accusations of antistate writing against him. In the 1980s and 1990s, Kross was repeatedly proposed for the Nobel Prize in Literature but just as repeatedly lost out. One likely explanation is that of his score of books, only *Rock from the Sky* (1984), *The Czar's Madman* (1993), *Professor Marten's Departure* (1994), and *The Conspiracy and Other Stories* (1995) are available in English, although most are available in Finnish, and many in German and French.

KRUUS, HANS (1891–1976). Estonian historian and politician, and the most curious combination of political revolutionary and solid, staid academic in modern Estonia. Kruus was born on 22 October 1891 in **Tartu** into an industrial worker's family who in 1900 moved to a farm that his father had bought. While studying at the Tartu Teachers College in 1907–11, he began to write for newspapers, which he continued after graduation and daytime work as a teacher until 1914 when he entered the history faculty at the **University of Tartu**. In 1916, his studies were interrupted by mobilization and a year's training at an officer's school at Odessa, after which he was posted to the First Estonian Regiment, where he also became politically active. Accordingly, in May 1917 Kruus was elected to the **Maapäev** and in June to the Estonian Soldiers' Supreme Soviet. In September, along with Villem Ernits, Joahnnes Semper, **Gustav Suits**, and others, he formed the Estonian Socialist-Revolutionary Party (Eesti Sotsialistide-revolutsionääride Partei, universally known as *esseerid*) and was elected its leader. In contrast to the **Bolsheviks**, this party focused on nationalism and the gaining of independence. In January 1918, Kruus presented the party's memorandum defending Estonian independence to Joseph Stalin, then commissar of national questions in the Russian Revolutionary government. In 1919, he was elected to the **Constituent Assembly** on his party's list. After independence, the party renamed itself the Independent Socialist Workers Party with Kruus as chair of its central committee.

In 1920, Kruus was elected to the first **Riigikogu** on his party's list. In the summer, he visited Moscow and petitioned the Comintern to accept his party as a member, but without success. He resigned from both his party and parliament in 1922, gave up politics, and focused on academic work. In 1923, he completed his first degree and continued graduate studies at Tartu, completed his doctorate in history in 1931, and was appointed professor extraordinary of history. In 1934, he was elected professor of Nordic history and was concurrently appointed prorector in 1934–37. As a result of a conflict with President **Konstantin Päts**, he was proscribed from teaching at Tartu during 1939–40. He actively supported the Soviet occupation in 1940, was deputy prime minister in **Johannes Vares**'s cabinet, and was a member of the new Estonian Soviet Socialist Republic's (ESSR) parliament. In August 1940, he joined the **Estonian Communist Party (ECP)**, and in September he was appointed rector of the University of Tartu.

During the **German occupation** in 1941–44, Kruus fled to Russia, where he worked on historical research. With the return of the Soviet occupation in 1944, he returned as rector of the university and professor of history until 1948. Concurrently, in 1944–50 he served as ESSR foreign minister, as president of the ESSR Academy of Sciences 1946–50, and as a member of the ESSR Supreme Soviet 1947–50. After the infamous VIII Plenary of the Central Committee of the

ECP in 1950, he was removed from all his positions, accused of the crime of bourgeois nationalism, and imprisoned for four years during the inquiry into the accusations. On being freed in 1954, he worked in Moscow in the History Institute at the USSR Academy of Sciences, returned to Estonia in 1958, and worked as senior historian in the History Institute of the **Estonian Academy of Sciences** until his death on 30 June 1976 in **Tallinn**.

Despite his variegated political career, Kruus is honored among Estonian historians as one of the founders of the professional scholarly study of history in Estonia. During the two decades of independence, he produced scores of articles and monographs that covered diverse periods of Estonian history. Among the most important are: *Linn ja Küla Eestis* (*City and Village in Estonia,* 1920); *Eesti Ajaloo Lugemik* (*Reader in Estonian History*) I and II (1924–29); *Vene-Liivi sõda 1558–1561* (*The Russo-Liv War 1558–1561*, 1924); and ***Eesti Aleksanderikool*** (*The Estonian Alexander School*, 1939). His work in the Soviet period work is prolific as well, with his research of the role of the home in Estonian culture especially valued. He devoted the last two decades of his life to this research as head of the Academy of Sciences Home Research Commission 1958–76, under whose aegis he edited the *Kodu-uurija Käsiraamat* (*Home Researcher's Handbook*) in 1966, and numerous papers and articles dealing with home and family in the various regions of Estonia.

During the 1920s and 1930s, his contributions to intellectual inquiry in Estonia extended to editorial membership in 1924–40, and editor in 1932–36, of the *Ajaloo Ajakiri* (*Historical Journal*), the premier Estonian scholarly history periodical; executive membership of the Eesti Kirjanduse Selts (Estonian Literary Society) in 1927–40; deputy chairmanship of the Academic Historical Society in 1928–40; membership of the editorial board of *Eesti Kirjandus* (*Estonian Literature*) in 1929–40; membership of board of the Estonian Cultural Archives; and membership of the executive of the 1905 Society in 1929–40. His contributions to academic history were formally recognized by his colleagues when the University granted him an honorary doctorate in 1938.

KÕPP, JOHAN (1874–1970). Estonian theologian, historian, and educator. Kõpp was born at Holdre on 9 November 1874. While studying at the faculty of theology at the **University of Tartu**, which he completed in 1906, he also worked in the editorial office of the newspaper *Postimees* and was active in the **Eesti Üliõpilaste Selts** (EÜS), the most nationalist of the Estonian fraternities, and served as its president on three occasions. In 1906, he was one of the 24 in Tartu who signed the telegram published in St. Petersburg newspapers protesting the savagery of the tsar's punitive squads, which killed over 300 and executed 652 after court-martials in the three Baltic provinces for their part in the 1905 Revolution. In 1907–09, while completing his pastoral internship, he also taught at the gymnasium in **Pärnu**. From 1909 to 1919, as the first native Estonian pastor in the Laius parish, Kõpp became *the* standard-bearer of the nationalist aspirations of his flock, was elected to represent them in the Tartu County Council in 1917 and at the National Congress in **Tallinn**, and in 1919 was elected by the Christian Peoples' Party to the **Constituent Assembly**.

In 1917, Kõpp also began his career at the University as docent in theology. With the reopening of the University of Tartu as the national university in 1919, he became both dean and professor of theology, serving in the latter capacity until 1944 with a break in 1940–41 during the first Soviet occupation. From 1923 to 1928, he also served as prorector of the University and as rector from 1928 to 1937. In 1939 he was elected archbishop of the Estonian **Lutheran** Church and served as such until 1964, both in Estonia until 1944, and thereafter as archbishop of the legally recognized Estonian Lutheran Church in exile, resident in Sweden. He died at Stockholm on 21 October 1970.

At **Tartu**, Kõpp is remembered as a strong supporter of the University as an autonomous academic as well as national cultural institution, despite its role as the sole university in Estonia and funded by state taxes. In internal university dealings, he had a reputation of strict neutrality tempered by balanced thoughtful conclusions and solutions to problems. As an academic, he instituted the discipline of the study of theology as a national cultural phenomenon, and studied both methodology and theory of theology. During his time at Tartu, Kõpp participated actively in all the learned societies as well as the nationalist ones, and wrote copiously on current events in the press. Among the most valued of his many books by posterity are his *Lai-*

use kihelkonna ajalugu (*History of Laius Parish,* 1937), reputedly the most thorough analysis of any parish in Estonia, as well as his *Kirik ja rahvas* (*Church and Nation,* 1959), a frequently cited historical treatment of spiritual development of the Estonian nation during the 17th century.

KÄBIN, JOHANNES (IVAN) (1905–1999). Estonian communist politician. Although born in Estonia in Kalevi *vald* on 26 September 1905, Käbin grew up in Russia, joined the Communist Party of the Soviet Union (CPSU) in 1927, and attended the Red Professors' Institute in Moscow in 1936–38. Thereafter, his life was devoted to service to the Party. He returned to Estonia with the occupation forces and served in 1940–41, and in 1943–44 while the **Estonian Communist Party** (ECP) was in exile in the Union of Soviet Socialist Republics (USSR), as director of the press section of the Central Committee of the ECP. Thereafter, in 1944–47 he was deputy director of the propaganda and agitation section, in 1947–48 he was director of the ECP Institute of History, and he was elected first secretary of the Central Committee of the ECP in the infamous VIII Plenary of the CC of the ECP in 1948, in which capacity he served for 28 years until 1978. In 1978–83 he was chairman of the Presidium of the Supreme Soviet of the Estonian Soviet Socialist Republic (ESSR) and deputy chairman of the Presidium of the Supreme Soviet of the USSR. He was also elected to the USSR Supreme Soviet in 1950–84 and to the ESSR Supreme Soviet in 1951–1985, the Central Committee of the CPSU in 1952–78, the Central Committee of the ECP in 1948–86, and the bureau of the CC of the ECP in 1948–83.

Thus, for almost three decades Käbin exercised as total control over the ESSR as any trustee of the Moscow Politburo possibly could. According to both those who worked closely with him as well as the Estonian population at large, and despite his ideological commitment to communism to his dying day, he provided as good a government to Estonia as possible under the yoke of the USSR. He was a very private man who eschewed the vanity and showy lifestyle usual among high communist functionaries. He apparently not only "saved" Estonian **agriculture** from the excesses of Nikita Khruschev's enthusiasm for maize production, for which the climate and soil of Estonia are unsuitable, but also from much interference from

Moscow in Estonia. He maintained a middle course by skillfully and effectively tacking between the various political demands of his Muscovite masters. As a result, Estonian agricultural production increased rapidly to become the showpiece of the USSR and Estonians had better material conditions and also somewhat more freedom to express themselves than people in other parts of the Soviet Union. His successor, **Karl Vaino**, first secretary from 1978 until Mikhail Gorbachev removed him in 1988, was a completely Russified Estonian whose command of the Estonian language was almost nonexistent, and who in vivid contrast to Käbin pursued a deliberate policy of **Russification** and uniformization with the rest of the Soviet Union. After the restoration of independence, Käbin remained in Estonia, while Vaino moved to Moscow. Käbin died in his modest apartment in Tallinn on 26 October 1999.

KÖLER, JOHANN (1826–1899). Estonian painter, a founder of Estonian national painting, and a leader of the National Awakening. Köler, born on 18 March 1826 in Suure Jaani parish, received his early education in Viljandi, and studied to become a painter at Cēsis in Latvia. In 1846, he moved to St. Petersburg and studied painting at the Imperial Academy of Art in 1848–55, where he received the small gold medal for his diploma painting. In 1857, Köler made a painting and study tour through Germany, Holland, and Belgium. In 1858 in Paris he painted the altar painting for the Cēsis (Võnnu) Church, exhibited a variation of this painting while in Rome in 1858, and in 1861 was granted the title academician by the Imperial Academy of Art on the strength of the painting. In Italy, Köler painted landscapes, action scenes, and portraits, while moving from a rigid classical to a freer romantic coloring and style. He also developed into a superb aquarellist and became a member of the Royal Belgian Aquarellists Association in 1874.

From 1862 on, Köler taught at the St. Petersburg Art Development School, in 1869–70 also at the Imperial Academy of Art, as well as teaching art to the tsar's family. In 1867, he was granted the title of professor and became a sought-after St. Petersburg society portraitist. During the 1870s, he painted romantic landscapes in the Crimea. Köler participated widely in exhibitions in Russia and abroad, including individual exhibitions in Vienna in 1889 and Riga in 1892. After his death on 22 April 1899 in St. Petersburg, a commemorative exhibition was held in 1900. In Estonia, his paintings became popular only after his death. His fresco *Come to Me* in St. Charles Church in Tallinn is the first monumental painting in Estonia. Aside from being a painter, in 1863–64 he joined the leading Estonian intellectual elites and began to participate actively in the nationalist movement. Focusing particularly on the peasants' struggle for land, he argued against the power of the nobility and their special rights in the Baltic Provinces. As the founder of the **St. Petersburg Patriots** in 1863–64, because he had entré to the elites of the empire, he was able to perform signal service to the cause of Estonian nationalism.

– L –

LAAR, MART (1960–). Estonian politician and historian, twice prime minister. Born on 22 April 1960 in Viljandi, Laar studied history at the **University of Tartu** in 1978–83 and completed a *mag. phil.* degree in 1994. In 1983–85 he worked as a history teacher at a **Tallinn** secondary school, and in 1987–90 as director of the division of preservation cultural artifacts at the Ministry of Culture of the Estonian Soviet Socialist Republic (ESSR). Laar's political career began in 1990 when he was elected to the **Supreme Council of the ESSR**, and simultaneously to the competing **Estonian Committee**. In 1991–92 he served on the **Constitutional Assembly**, and in 1992 he was elected to the reinstituted **Riigikogu** on the Pro Patria Party list, and became prime minister of a coalition cabinet, which he led until 1994. During his two-year tenure, his right-of-center government established Estonia's road to democratic capitalism by radical policies of **privatization**, currency, and **banking** reform as well as an open approach to foreign investment. In addition to his own youth—he was only 32 when he became prime minister—the youthfulness of his cabinet, averaging under 40, with Foreign Minister **Jüri Luik** merely 26—and the radicalism associated with youth, as well as their command of the English language, brought Estonia sharply to the attention of the West. After the collapse of his coalition, Laar continued as leader of the Pro Patria party in parliament and was reelected in 1995 as a leader of the opposition. In the Riigikogu election of 1999, he was again reelected and formed a new coalition cabinet consisting of Pro Patria, the Moderates, and the Reform Party, which lasted for almost three years until internal strains broke it up in January 2002. After he led his party to defeat in the local elections of October 2002, Laar became the second Estonian party leader to resign on principle (the first was Toomas Ilves). Half a year later, in the Riigikogu election of 2 March 2003, Pro Patria received only seven seats, having lost 11, although Laar was reelected himself.

From his student days, Laar has been a social activist: in 1978–83 he was one of the founders of the nationalist semi-underground association Noor Tartu (Young Tartu), and has been a member of the cultural-nationalist Estonian Heritage Society, the Union of Learned Students (Üliöpilaste Teaduslik Ühing), the PEN Club, the fraternity **Eesti Üliõpilaste Selts** (EÜS), and the Jaan Tõnisson Institute, among others. As a historian, Laar has published primarily on contemporary history as well as books popularizing the Estonian national heritage in Estonian, Finnish, and English. His English-language *War in the Woods*, published in 1993, deals with the resistance movement during the second Soviet occupation after World War II (*see* BRETHREN OF THE FOREST), and his German-language *Das estnische Wirtschaftswunder* (2001) is a largely biographical description of the transition period and his initiative-laden first government. *See also* POLITICAL PARTIES; ECONOMIC TRANSFORMATION; COURTS.

LAIDONER, JOHAN (1884–1953). General Johan Laidoner is the best known Estonian soldier-statesman of independent Estonia, because of his services in the **War of Independence**, and for his role in the successful **preemptive coup of 1934**. Born on 12 February 1884 in Viiratsi *vald*, Laidoner graduated from the Vilnius Military Academy in 1905, and from the General Staff War Academy in St. Petersburg in 1912. He fought in World War I in the Imperial Russian army on the western front from 1915 to 1917, and from December 1917 to February 1918 was commander of the Estonian Division in the imperial army. After the **Declaration of Independence**, he organized the Estonian armed forces, and sought assistance from abroad for his units. He was appointed commander in chief of the Estonian forces on 23 December 1918 and successfully directed the War of

Independence, first against the Red armies on the eastern front, and then defeated the Stahldivision of General Rüdiger von der Goltz at Võnnu (Cēsis, Wenden) and drove it out of Estonia in the summer of 1919 when the latter led the Baltische **Landeswehr**. This army had been organized by the German government in the aftermath of the confusion of the Brest-Litovsk treaty to create Balticum, an independent German puppet state to consist of the former Russian Provinces of Kurland, Livland, and Estland. On 21 March 1920, he was promoted to lieutenant general and retired. As a civilian, he was elected to the first three parliaments (1921–29) for the Agrarian Party and served as chair of the foreign affairs, budget, finance, and defense committees.

Laidoner was recalled to active service as commander in chief on 1 December 1924 to put down the **attempted communist coup** led by **Viktor Kingissepp**, then he retired again in January 1925 after successfully clearing the land of the insurrectionists. In 1925, he was appointed by the League of Nations to chair the commission to determine the borders of Iraq. He returned to active politics and national defense when he helped organize the preemptive coup of 12 March 1934, which put **Konstantin Päts** into power, who appointed him again as commander in chief until his deportation by the Soviets in 1941.

In 1937, he served in the Constituent Assembly (Rahvuskogu) elected to draft a new **constitution**, and in his capacity as commander in chief he was an ex officio member of the new upper house, the State Council (Riiginõukogu), from 1938 to 1940. Throughout the 1930s, he actively sought to develop cooperation with Latvia, Finland, and Poland in foreign and defense policies. On 17 June 1941 in Narva, he was forced to sign agreement to the ultimatum by which Soviet forces peacefully invaded Estonia with 90,000 troops under the pretext that Estonia had not been able to provide security to the Union of Soviet Socialist Republics as agreed in the 1939 **Soviet Estonian Mutual Assistance Treaty** of 1939. A month later, on 19 July 1940 he was deported by the Soviet occupying regime to Pensa, but not arrested until 1941, after which he made a circuit of several concentration camps and died in one on 13 March 1953.

LAIKMAA, ANTS (until 1935, Hans Laipman) (1886–1942). Estonian painter. Laikmaa was born on 5 May 1866 in Vigala *vald* and studied painting at the Art Academy in Düsseldorf in 1891–93 and in 1896–97. He then worked as a painter in Tallinn and Haapsalu between 1899 and 1907, and opened the first painting studio in Estonia in Tallinn in 1903, where he taught on and off until 1932. Laikmaa traveled widely in Europe, especially in Belgium, Holland, France, Germany, Austria, and Finland during the first decade of the new century. He came under the influence of impressionism and painted a large number of interpretive pastel portraits of well-known Estonians and peasant models during this period. Laikmaa helped organize the first general art exhibition in Estonia in Tartu in 1906 and founded the Estonian Art Society in Tallinn in 1907. In 1907–09 Laikmaa painted mostly in Finland, traveling through the art centers in Western Europe in 1909–13 while making the isle of Capri and Tunisia his home during 1910–12. During this period his painting, especially of landscapes, was influenced by European postimpressionism and became more expressionist, his handling of color more contrast seeking, and his forms more stylized. On his return to Tallinn in 1913, he taught and painted at his studio at the Estonian National Museum, and at the Estonian Art Society, and he painted his first Estonian landscapes focusing on the noteworthy peculiarities of the western coast and the islands. He also began to paint flowers, especially chrysanthemums, during the 1920s, while his style moved toward realism. In 1932, Laikmaa closed his Tallinn studio, moved to his farm in Tacbla *vald* in Kadarpik parish, and designed a new house with the help of his architect friends, where he painted and wrote his memoirs until his death on 19 September 1942.

Laikmaa's influence, through his painting, teaching, critical writings, as well as organizational genius, determined the development of painting in Estonia in the early decades of the 20th century. In addition, his outgoing personality and his romantic involvements, not least with **Marie Under**, the poetess, endowed him with popular star quality as well. His image of a romantic artist hero has been propagated for three generations by Endel Nirk's biographical novel, *Kaanekukk* (*Cock of the Walk*), which depicts Laikmaa's life.

LAKE PEIPUS (Peipsi Järv; Russian, Chudskoye Ozero). The lake forms most of the Estonian-Russian border and stretches for 143 kilometers from north to south. Its total area (3,600 square kilometers/

1,390 square miles), is actually divided into three: the Big Lake (Suurjärv, 2,555 square kilometers) proper in the north and Lake Pihkva (Russian, Pskov Ozero; 708 square kilometers) in the south, separated by the small and narrow Lake Lämmijärv (Russian, Typloe Ozero; 232 square kilometers). The surface of the lake is divided almost evenly between Estonia and Russia. Over 30 small rivers and creeks flow into the lake; it empties into the Narva River, which flows north into the Gulf of Finland at the city of Narva. The lake is very shallow, averaging eight meters with 15.3 meters at its deepest. The bottom is mostly gray mud with sand in the southern part; as a result, it is rich in fish and is used for commercial fishing by both Estonians and Russians. The lake has about 60 small islands, with two of the larger and inhabited ones in Russia and the third, Piirisaar, in Estonia. Because of its shallowness, the lake is frozen for three to five months most winters.

The Lake was the site of the "Battle on the Ice" made famous by the 1938 classic epic film *Aleksander Nevsky* by Sergey Eisentstein with musical score by Sergey Prokofiev, which he also turned into a highly acclaimed cantata for choir and orchestra. In 1239, the Livonian Knights began a military campaign in northwestern Russia to expand their territory and convert the Russians to the western Catholic church, but in 1242 Alexander Nevsky led his Russians to a heroic victory over the Christianizing Germans on frozen Lake Peipus. He thus put an end to Germanic attempts to conquer Russia and fixed the border between Eastern and Western culture that has lasted to the present.

LANDESWEHR. This was a military force formed in Riga in December 1918 by **Baltic Germans** for the purpose of gaining control over Estonian and Latvian territory after the conclusion of the 1918 peace treaty between Germany and Russia in order to colonize them with Germans, thus setting up new German states. Their forces were sufficiently strong on Latvian territory that they were able to depose the Latvian government of Karlis Ulmanis on 16 April 1919 and form a pro-German government under Andrievs Niedra. Thereafter, on 22 May the Landeswehr, together with the Stahldivision of General Rüdiger von der Goltz, composed of battle-hardened veterans of the German Army who had volunteered to fight for a Baltic Germany, advanced on Estonia in the Võnnu-Valga salient in the rear of the Estonian southern flank. After a series of battles over Võnnu from 6 to 9 June, at the instigation of Allied representatives a short-lived armistice was signed. After both sides had reinforced their positions on 19 June, the combined German forces attacked the 100-kilometer Estonian lines, defended by 5,000 men (including 1,400 Latvians), with 189 machine guns, 28 field guns, and two armored trains under the command of Major General Ernst Põdder. The enemy forces consisted of 5,300 men, 310 machine guns, 50 field guns, 12 mortars, one armored train, and some airplanes, under the command of General von der Goltz.

After two days of attack and counterattack in which the Estonian armored trains played a significant role, the Estonian forces routed and put the enemy to flight on 23 June, and followed up by pursuing them to the outskirts of, and were poised to take, Riga. However, allied military representatives demanded an armistice, which allowed the Landeswehr forces to escape to Jelgava, from where they dispersed. The brilliant victory, commemorated by bonfires on **Victory Day** on 23 June, put an end to the Baltic and homeland Germans' ambitions to recover their rule over the Baltics. *See also* WAR OF INDEPENDENCE.

LANDTAG. *See* DIET.

LANGUAGE LAW. On 18 January 1989, the **Supreme Soviet** of the Estonian Soviet Socialist Republic (ESSR) adopted the Language Law, which declared **Estonian** as the sole official language and relegated Russian to the category of "other" **languages**. At the time, it was a courageous move since Russian was not only the state language of the whole Union of Soviet Socialist Republics (USSR) but also the language used habitually in the ESSR Supreme Soviet since many of the deputies did not speak Estonian. Moreover, Russian was the exclusive language of the many local councils and governments, especially in **Northeast Estonia**. The new law specified the use of Estonian in all public and private institutions, including **courts**, schools, and organizations. A transition period of four years was specified during which Estonian was to be progressively introduced as the primary language of use in the country. On 23 November 1990, the transition government appointed the Official Language Office with the mandate to implement the transition to Estonian.

Even though Estonian typographic hardware and software did not become universally available for some years, Estonian speakers began to use their language immediately in all public and private contexts. However, it was not until the latter half of the 1990s that the mass of Russian speakers accepted the reality that Estonia was officially a monolingual country and that anyone who wished to live there and participate in its sociocultural, economic, and political affairs had to be able to understand and speak Estonian adequately. The recalcitrance of an Estophobe segment of the Russian population, located primarily in **Narva**, was agitated by pan-Slavic elements in Moscow, such as Duma Deputy Speaker and Russian ultranationalist leader Vladimir Zhirinovsky, to accept Estonia neither as a monolingual ethnic state nor indeed as an independent state. The Russian Duma's and government's continuing complaints were primarily responsible for bringing the **Estonian language** issue into the international arena. Hence, the involvement of Organization of Security and Cooperation in Europe (OSCE) Commissioner **Max Van der Stoel**; Ole Espersen, Commissioner on Democratic Institutions and Human Rights, Including the Rights of Persons Belonging to Minorities, of the **Council of Baltic Sea States**; the Council of Europe; and the United Nations Human Rights Commission. Although the latter two consistently reported that the Russian complaints of human rights discrimination against Russian speakers were groundless, the former two, especially Van der Stoel, worked tirelessly to assist the Estonian government and **Riigikogu** to revise the language and citizenship legislation to conform to West European norms.

By 1995, due to increasing experience with language issues as well as advice from abroad, a new revised and more precise Language Act was enacted. In 1999, after Estonia had been invited to join the first wave of applicants for European Union (EU) membership, the Act was revised to reflect both the Estonian desire to maintain a monolingual Estonian ethnic state yet met the minimum basic language requirements of the EU for movement of persons, goods, and services. Both the Russian community and the OSCE commissioner were actively involved, the former vocally, the latter quietly as advisors to both the parliamentary committee dealing with language questions and the government.

The Act specifies three levels of proficiency in the Estonian language required for various public and private uses in article 5, paragraph 5:

> 1) basic level—limited oral and elementary written proficiency in Estonian. The person can manage in familiar language situations, understands clear speech on everyday topics, understands the general meaning of uncomplicated texts and can complete simple standard documents and write short texts for general use;
>
> 2) intermediate level—oral and limited written proficiency in Estonian. The person can manage in various language situations, understands speech at normal speed, understands the contents of texts on everyday topics without difficulty and can write texts relating to his or her area of activity;
>
> 3) advanced level—oral and written proficiency in Estonian. The person can express himself or herself freely irrespective of the language situation, understands speech at high speed, understands the contents of more complicated texts without difficulty and can write texts which are different in style and function.

The usage requirement in private business was solved by article 5, paragraph 3:

> In order to comply with requirements for the work environment and consumer protection and in the interests of the protection of the environment, health and security, employees of companies, non-profit associations and foundations, and sole proprietors shall, upon offering goods or services and forwarding information, use Estonian at the level which is necessary to perform their employment duties.

In article 10, the Act also continues the right to use Russian in local governments:

> Where the majority of permanent residents are non-Estonian speakers, the language of the national minority constituting the majority of the permanent residents of the local government may be used alongside Estonian as the internal working language of the local government on the proposal of the corresponding local government council and by a decision of the Government of the Republic.

Different aspects of the Language Law are implemented by various Acts. One that raised a great deal of attention in Estonia and abroad was the removal of the Estonian language requirement for candidacy to the Riigikogu and local governments, by an amendment to the Elections Act on 21 November 2001, to bring Estonian law into conformity with the **Acquis Communitaire** of the European Union.

However, parliament simultaneously passed an amendment to its Rules making Estonian its language of business. The former change, however, was enough for the Council of the OCSE to decide that its work in Estonia had been completed and to close its mission.

LANGUAGES. Although Estonians have occupied the same territory for at least a thousand years, the dominant language for centuries was German, the language of the land-owning, **Baltic German**, aristocratic successors of the Christianizing **Crusading Orders**. Estonian was a little-regarded language spoken by the peasants, who were generally called *Undeutsch* by the overlords. Estonian was also split into many local dialects and, although the first textbook in the Estonian language was published in 1637, the first grammar did not appear until 1875 at the time of the **National Awakening**. The prime developers of the language were **Johannes Aavik** and Johannes Voldemar Veski as late as the first half of the 19th century. **Education** in local dialects at the local village church schools by cantor-schoolmasters was begun during the **Swedish Era** (*see* LITERACY) using mainly catechism and the Bible, but teaching in all secondary schools was conducted in German until the period of **Russification** at the end of the 19th century, when attempts were made to force Russian on all schools, which did not succeed at village level owing to the poor Russian skills of the schoolmasters. The six-decade-long public campaign to open the first purely Estonian-language secondary school, the **Estonian Aleksander School**, did not succeed until after **Independence**. Estonian was taught at some secondary schools, especially at **Treffner Gymnasium**, the only secondary school with a majority of Estonian students before Independence, but Russian was the required teaching language. **The University of Tartu** taught in German from its reopening in 1802 to the Russification in the 1890s, when Russian was decreed the main language in lectures. Even after Independence, it took the University a decade to gradually shift to Estonian as the teaching language as Estonian-speaking staff were hired.

The centuries-long official negation of the Estonian language did not weaken it but had the unintended consequence of strengthening Estonian national consciousness and led to Estonians learning German and Russian, which provided access to both West European and

Russian culture. The long stubborn struggle for recognition of a collective ethnic status, and the struggle to turn their language into a modern cultural language (*see* LITERATURE; MASING, OTTO W.; YOUNG ESTONIA) means that Estonians equate their language and culture with their nation. When the language weakens or disappears, the Estonian nation weakens or disappears. In the minds of Estonians, their independent state was formed as the "Estonian nation-state" to safeguard the Estonian nation and its language—the carrier of Estonian culture. The focus during the two decades of Independence between the world wars was on strengthening the culture of the nation. Hence, the strong antagonism to the Soviet occupation and the forced use of Russian as the main language of official communication (*see* DISSIDENTS; RAHVARINNE). The antipathy toward the Russian language was reinforced by the importation of a large number of Russian-speaking laborers during the half century of Soviet occupation without consulting the Estonians, which reduced the ethnic Estonian share of the **population** from 90 percent to 62 percent by 1989. Worse, the Russian speakers did not bother, nor did they have any incentives, to learn Estonian, whereas Estonians had to learn Russian. Hence, it is understandable that on reacquiring their independent state, Estonians wanted to reestablish their lost monoethnic, monolingual, Estonian-speaking state. Although the former objective has proven to be impossible to carry out, Estonians have consistently pursued the objective of restoring Estonia as an Estonian-speaking state. Hence the **Language Law**, which makes Estonian the sole official language, and the **Integration** program to convert monolingual Russian speakers to bilingual Estonian speakers. Although this creates difficulties for older Russian speakers who cannot acquire Estonian **citizenship** without adequate language skills, they are nevertheless able to get along almost anywhere in Estonia since most adult Estonians speak adequate Russian, whereas it is still impossible for Estonians to be served in Estonian in **Northeast** Estonia, where only 3 percent of the population is Estonian speaking.

Still, at the beginning of the 21st century, despite lingering antagonism, the Russian language is guaranteed a future as a cultural language in Estonia since Russian primary schools are able to teach in Russian and Russian secondary schools are scheduled to eventually move to a 40:60 ratio of Russian and Estonian as teaching languages. The main problem for the next decade is training enough teachers able and willing to teach in Estonian Russian schools because few native Estonian teachers are interested in teaching in such schools and because most ethnic Russians who train as Estonian-language teachers are offered much better-paying jobs by business firms. In the meantime both Estonians and Russophones are learning English, and conversations between Estonian and Russian youths are often carried on in English.

LARKA, ANDRES (1879–1943). Estonian soldier and politician. Born on 5 March 1879 at Pilistvere in Kabala *vald*, Larka fought in the Russo-Japanese war as an officer and graduated from the army command college at St. Petersburg in 1912. He then fought in World War I and rose to the rank of major general in 1918. In the same year he was appointed minister of war in the Estonian Provisional Government and led the newly organized Estonian **armed forces** as chief of staff during the battles of the **War of Independence** in November–December 1918. Larka served as assistant to the minister of war from 1919 to 1925. After retirement, he was elected in 1930 as chair of the League of Veterans of the War of Independence (*see* VETERANS) and as their candidate for Riigivanem in 1934. After **Konstantin Päts**'s coup on 12 Mar 1934, he was jailed twice (1934–35 and 1935–37) for alleged conspiracy to overthrow the government against which Päts carried out his **preemptive coup**. There is no real evidence that any overthrow was planned (*see* SIRK). In fact, during the collection of signatures for nomination for head of state, on 1–5 March 1934, Larka's supporters gathered 52,346 to the combined total of 29,975 by his three opponents (**Johan Laidoner**, Päts, and **August Rei**). He was clearly a victim of the general hysterical fear among the mainstream politicians of a fascist-type democratic victory by the disaffected Veterans. During the **Era of Silence**, which lasted until just before World War II, all criticism of the Päts government was forbidden under the guise of national security. After the Soviet occupation of Estonia in 1940, Larka was arrested again and died in prison on 8 January 1943 at Malmõz in Kirov Oblast.

LAURISTIN, MARJU (1940–). Estonian politician, sociologist, and journalism professor. Born on 7 April 1940 in **Tallinn**, Lauristin studied journalism part time at the **University of Tartu** while working for Estonian Radio in 1962–66. Subsequently she studied sociology at Tartu in 1967–70 and served as head of the Sociology Laboratory at the University from 1970 to 1972, when she moved to the Journalism Department, with which she is still associated. In 1983, she was promoted to docent and served as the head of the department from 1987 to 1992. In 1995, she was elected professor of social policy in the new Faculty of Social Sciences and served as interim dean of the faculty in 1995–96. Although a member of the **Estonian Communist Party** (ECP) from 1968 to 1990, she began her political career as one of the signatories of the **Letter of the Forty** in 1980, and subsequently participated in the academic opposition wing in the ECP. In 1988, she became one of the founders of the **Rahvarinne** along with **Edgar Savisaar**; and was elected to the Union of Soviet Socialist Republic's (USSR) Peoples' Congress and the Estonian Soviet Socialist Republic's (ESSR) Supreme Soviet in 1989. In 1990, she was elected one of the associate speakers of the **Supreme Council of Estonia**. Lauristin was a prominent member of the **Constituent Assembly** and member of the first **Estonian Committee**. She was elected to the VIII (1995–99) and IX (1999–2003) parliaments and served as minister of social services in **Mart Laar**'s cabinet in 1992–94. In 1990, she founded the Estonian Social Democratic Independence Party and became the leader of the Estonian Social Democratic Party when the former amalgamated with it. Subsequently, she served as the leader of the Moderate Party, and strongly influenced its ideological development, which the various social democratic parties had coalesced into initially as an electoral alliance. While working as full-time professor of social policy at the University of Tartu in 1995–2003, she was elected to both the VIII and IX parliaments and participated actively in the affairs of the Moderates and in the **Riigikogu**. In the 2003 election, Lauristin lost out by a few votes as a result of the swing against her party. She is an active researcher and writer and publishes in foreign languages as well as in Estonian. Her best known work in English, *Return to the Western World*, published in 1997, is cowritten and edited with Peter Vihalemm et al. and deals with the postcommunist Estonian transition.

Marju Lauristin, one of the most widely respected of Estonian leaders of the independence movement, was born to an ideological communist family. Her father was Johannes Lauristin (29 October 1899–28 July 1941) who served as the first secretary of the ECP in the annexed ESSR in 1940 but was killed during the evacuation to the Soviet Union a year later. Her mother, Olga Lauristin (born 28 April 1903, she celebrated her 100th birthday in 2003), a prominent and active ideological Communist Party member, was jailed in the aftermath of the **attempted communist coup in 1924**, and served as a minister in the ESSR government and member of several ESSR and USSR Supreme Soviets.

LEGAL SYSTEM. The legal system of Estonia in the 21st century is an amalgam of foreign systems imposed by past conquerors mixed with increasing adoption of laws drawn from the **Acquis Communitaire** of the **European Union** (EU) in order to meet entry requirements, and influences of Anglo-American common law, especially in transborder commercial and business transactions, as well as environmental protection. The impact of the foreign legal sources is uneven and has not been systematized by Estonian lawmakers, scholars, jurists, or lawyers.

The reason is found in the political history of Estonia, which shows at least seven centuries of foreign rule by German Christianizing crusaders, who settled as colonists and developed a feudal **Baltic German** legal system, which operated until the end of the 19th century. But it, too, was interrupted and changed by Danish, Swedish, and Polish overlords in different parts of the Estonian homeland. Beginning in 1710 in **Tallinn** and 1720 in the rest of Estonia, the Russian legal system increasingly imposed itself on the Baltic German one, until it supplanted most of the latter at the end of the 19th century. Unfortunately, the Baltic German legal system was developed in the interests of a colonial overlord and had little impact, apart from public order and criminal law, on the indigenous, mostly peasant population. Nevertheless, a comprehensive, if characteristically feudalistic, uniquely "Baltic" legal system operated in the Baltic Provinces of imperial Russia in the first half of the 19th century.

The Russian tsars were slow to impose their legal system on the Baltic nobility, which enjoyed a privileged position in the empire as a result of **Peter the Great** making a deal that allowed them to keep their privileges, known as the **Special Baltic Order**, in return for loyalty to the imperial crown, which the Baltic nobility kept unswervingly. Hence, legal reforms emanating from St. Petersburg were slow to penetrate the Baltic Provinces. However, during the 19th century modernization of the imperial legal system became a necessity, driven by the increasing exposure of Russia to world markets as a result of the industrialization, urbanization, and transportation revolutions in Western Europe. In the Baltic, St. Petersburg made another deal with the ruling nobility to apply the modernized imperial general penal code in the Baltic Provinces in return for a promise that the remaining existing law in force in these provinces would be recorded in five volumes of a planned Baltic Provinces legal code. But only three volumes were completed when the tsar in 1864 signed into law the Baltic private law volume and also signed a resolution that the last two, the civil and criminal proceedings volumes, would not be proceeded with and that the general court system and procedures of the empire would be implemented in the Baltic provinces only sometime in the future (*see* COURTS).

The hybrid system that developed in the Baltic Provinces during the half century before the collapse of the empire was inherited by independent Estonia. During the two decades of independence, Estonia began to rapidly develop a legal system appropriate to a modern, democratic, urbanizing, and industrializing European state. The most urgent reforms concerned public law to implement state sovereignty. Although planning proceeded on a comprehensive 15-volume code of laws, and as new laws were passed owing to necessity, a new hybrid system developed. New Acts of the Estonian Parliament and the laws of the Russian empire, including the remnants of the Special Baltic Order, valid on Estonian territory on 27 October 1917 (the date chosen being prior to the Russian Revolution), were incorporated into the legal system of the Republic, pending review and modernization. The political and economic problems of the 1930s ending in the occupation of Estonia by the Soviet Union in 1940, annexation and incorporation into the Soviet empire followed by the Nazi German occupation 1941–44, and the subsequent renewal of occupation by the Soviet Union for the next 47 years meant that the hybrid legal system in force in 1940 continued as the de jure law of the Republic of Estonia, whereas the Soviet Union's laws and those passed by the Supreme Soviet of the Estonian Soviet Socialist Republic (ESSR) were the de facto laws on the territory of Estonia.

Prior to the restoration of independence, instead of a ***restitutio ad integrum*** of the laws of the Republic of Estonia recognized de jure by the leading Western states throughout the Soviet occupation, the democratically elected transition parliament (*see* SUPREME COUNCIL), though still under ESSR electoral law, for reasons of pragmatic politics decided to follow the analogous decision of 1918: "All normative acts currently in force on the territory of Estonian shall remain in force" (16 May 1990).

Further confusion was added when, instead of restoring the **1937 Constitution**, a new **Constitution** was passed by referendum in 1992. The government elected under the provisions of the new Constitution decided in 1993 not to proceed from existing laws in reforming the legal system, but to draw on foreign examples, principally Austria and Germany, in developing a new legal order. However, in reality examples have been drawn from many counties—the bankruptcy act, for example, is mainly based on France; the income tax act on Portugal; environmental law has American overtones; and so on. Owing to inexperience and pragmatic electoral politics as well as partisanship, the **Riigikogu** has proceeded very unevenly with legal reform. Some laws have been amended virtually every year, for example laws covering real property, restitution, compensation, and the rights of rival claimants (owners versus occupiers) to property. Rivalry among legal experts also plays a part. In the case of the penal code, two plans competed during most of the 1990s until an amalgam of the existing code and the French and the German codes was completed in 1999.

Since 1997, when Estonia was selected for fast-track membership in the European Union, EU examples (especially Finnish ones) are taken as models and often simply passed into law. Moreover, the government in January 2000 undertook to pass all the laws required for Estonia to meet the Acquis Communitaire by the end of 2001, a practical impossibility. In the case of Finland, 30,000 laws had to be reviewed and accommodated to the EU demands when it joined in 1993. But Finland was a full partner in the European Free Trade Area (EFTA) and deeply involved in international trade for decades, fully integrated into the Western trading system. Its legal system was also fully developed. Since the 16th century, it had developed as a uniform system based on the Swedish one, and has developed in harmony with the other Nordic countries since 1953.

In contrast, the Estonian legal system has the advantage in that, since it is in fact not a uniform system but merely a collection of laws, it can develop rapidly as a truly "European" one within the EU as its internal economic and social arrangements become increasingly conditioned by Brussels.

LEMBITU (?–1217). Ancient military leader and folk hero of Estonia during the Estonians' fight for freedom in the Christianizing crusade of 1208–27. Knowledge of Lembitu is almost exclusively derived from the Chronicle of Henrik of Livonia (*see* CHRONICLES), a lay priest of Latvian extraction in the service of Bishop Albert of Riga. Lembitu, a leader of the Sakala tribe in southern Estonia, participated in the retributory attack in 1211 on the Christianized German stronghold on the banks of the River Jumere near the present-day city of Valmiera in Latvia and defeated the forces of the Brethren of the Sword (*see* CRUSADING ORDERS) and the bishop of Riga. In 1217, when the German forces had been driven from Estonia, Lembitu organized a campaign to drive them out of **Livonia** as well. In the subsequent battle on St. Matthew's Day (21 September) against German and Christianized Latvian and Livonian elite units, Lembitu fell, apparently slain by the Latvian leader Veko. Lembitu has throughout the past 800 years been a symbol of the heroic Estonian struggle for freedom against superior foreign forces.

LETTER OF THE FORTY. *See* DISSIDENTS.

LIPPMAA, ENDEL (1930–). Estonian physicist, chemist, and politician. Lippmaa was born on 15 September 1930 in Tartu, graduated from the Tallinn Polytechnical Institute in 1953, received his doctorate in theoretical physics in 1971, was awarded an honorary doctorate by Jyväskylä University in 1972, and was elected to the Estonian Academy in 1975 and the Finnish Academy in 1990. In 1961–80, he served as director of the physics laboratory of the Institute of Cybernetics of the Estonian Soviet Socialist Republic's (ESSR) **Academy**

of Sciences, and became director of the Biochemical Physics Institute in 1980. As an internationally recognized scientist, Lippmaa has researched magnetic resonance, high-temperature reactions, catalysis, and biophysics. He rose to political prominence first in 1987 when he organized opposition to opening new environmentally damaging **phosphate mines** (*see* PHOSPHATE WAR) in **Northeast Estonia**. Lippmaa was elected to the Peoples' Congress of the Union of Soviet Socialist Republics (USSR) in 1989, participated in the Estonian Commission on the **Molotov-Ribbentrop Pact** where he helped publicize the illegality of the pact, was elected to the **Estonian Congress**, and was a member of its first executive committee. He served as minister without portfolio responsible for relations with the East during 1990–01 in the transition cabinet of **Edgar Savisaar**. During the preindependence period, Lippmaa was politically very active and used his international connections and visibility in the interests of independence for Estonia. In 1989, he popularized the term ***restitutio in integrum*** as a political objective of independence. After leaving the transition cabinet, he withdrew from active politics and returned to rebuild and consolidate his Institute in the changed conditions of independent Estonia.

LITERACY. Estonians trace the beginnings of widespread knowledge of reading to the end of the 17th century when authorities of the **Swedish era** established the public primary school system, which Estonians refer to as Rahvakool (literally, people's school, meaning the ethnic Estonian peasantry's school). Bengt Gottfried Forselius played a seminal role in this when he operated the first seminary for village schoolmasters for four years and graduated 160 teachers from 1684–88. By the end of the century, thousands of peasants could read and literacy became sought after. Contemporary Lutheran pastors, themselves Germans, **Baltic Germans**, or Swedes, remarked on the Estonians' enthusiasm to learn to read. In 1739, the Lutheran Consistory of the Province of Lettland demanded that all children between seven and 12 attend school or learn to read at home. Thus, schooling had been compulsory for Estonians for over two and a half centuries. Although it is estimated that 10 percent of the peasantry could read at the beginning the 18th century, when it ended 60 percent of adults knew how to read. The desire to learn to read was supported by the appearance of books in Estonia: the New Testament in the North Estonian dialect in 1715, the first Estonian-language calendar in 1720, and the **Bible** in Estonian in 1739. The Imperial Russian census of 1897 found that 91.2 percent of the population could read and that 77.7 percent could write. By 1934, full literacy had risen to 96.1 percent in Estonia, and by 1970 to 100 percent, as reported by the census of the Union of Soviet Socialist Republics (USSR) of that year. *See also* EDUCATION; LUTHERANISM.

LITERATURE. Estonian literature can be grouped into 11 categories, as follows.

The Folklore Period. Long before the coming of Christianity and the written word, literature in Estonia consisted of folklore, which, however, developed artistically only in the three centuries after the Crusades (from about 1300 to 1600) at about the same time as in Western Europe. Although much was in the form of recited verse, there were also proverbs, mythical stories, and songs for occasions such as courtship, weddings, births, funerals, haying, Midsummer (Jaanipäev), St. Martin's Day (Mardipäev), St. Catherine's Day (Kadripäaev), Halloween, and so on. Folklore created in the 18th and 19th centuries was heavily influenced by German ballads and poetry. Despite a few sporadic publications (one as early as 1695), the systematic recording of Estonian folklore did not begin until just before the **National Awakening**, inspired in part by the writings of the German nationalist Johann Gottfried von Herder (who, incidentally, began his writing career in Riga, where he served as a cleric from 1764 to 1770). The initial collecting of folkloric verse was carried on by German Estophiles. It was not until **Friedrich Robert Faehlmann** (1798–1850) and **Friedrich Reinhold Kreutzwald** (1803–82) that native Estonians became involved. The publication of **Kalevipoeg** provided a powerful stimulus to preserving the rapidly disappearing oral heritage. **Jakob Hurt**'s (1839–1907) public appeal in 1883 brought in 45,000 folksongs and 10,000 fables. In 1875, 1886, 1904, and 1904–07, Hurt issued the first monumental collections of Estonian folksongs. **Oskar Kallas** (1868–1946), the first Estonian holder of a doctorate in folklore, helped found the Estonian National Museum in 1908. In 1927, the Estonian Folklore Archives were founded in **Tartu**, and are now housed in the Estonian Literary Museum there.

Religious Literature (1550–1750). The second historical strand in the formation of **Estonian language** literature consisted of the professional handbooks written in Estonian by the **Lutheran** clerics for their brethren who needed to preach in the native language after the Reformation. These writings, between 1550 and 1750, laid the foundation of the written language. Toward the end of the 17th century, reading knowledge had spread sufficiently for catechisms and songbooks to be published in Estonian. In the decades after the **Great Northern War**, didactic storybooks appeared, along with a grammar. The publication in 1739 of the **Bible** in the North Estonian dialect established the latter as the dominant written form of the language. However, the first almanac for the peasantry was written in the South Estonian dialect in 1739; the first almanac in North Estonian was not published until 1799. The almanac tradition, containing short stories as well as practical farming and household advice, survived until Independence. The second half of the 19th century saw reading spreading to all parts of the country, so that by 1898, 97 percent of the population was literate.

Estophile Enlightenment (1750–1840). Educated German immigrants and local **Baltic German** nobles' sons educated at German universities introduced Enlightenment ideas of rational thinking to Estonia, which propagated freedom of thinking and brotherhood and equality. Soon, the French Revolution provided a powerful motive for the enlightened local upper class to create literature for the peasantry for their edification, entertainment, and **education**. The freeing of the peasantry from serfdom on the nobles' estates in 1816 and 1819 by Tsar **Aleksander I** abetted the movement. The Estophile period formed the transition from religious literature to belles-lettres and newspapers written in Estonian for the mass public. **Otto Wilhelm Masing** (1763–1832), of mixed heritage, was the first Estophile with complete command of the Estonian language. His conviction that the language of the peasants is capable of expressing complex thoughts was viewed with derision among the Baltic German elites. It was also very likely the reason why he lost the competition for the lectureship in Estonian at the newly reopened **University of Tartu**. In addition to writing prolifically and providing official translations of laws, he published the first Estonian-language newspaper, *Marawhva Näddala-Leht* (*Country People's Weekly Paper*), which contained both local and foreign news as well as short stories and poems. His work was carried on by Heinrich Rosenplänter (1782–1846), who demanded that all clerics, estate owners, and bureaucrats speak correct Estonian. Courageously he expressed the hope that eventually native Estonians would rise to leading positions in Estonia, and thereby preserve the Estonian language and culture. The first Estonian-language theater performance took place in Pärnu in 1824. Toward the end of the Estophile period, native Estonian authors issued original novels, stories, and poems, in addition to translations and adaptations from German. **Kristjan Jaak Peterson** (1801–22) was the most original of the highbrow native poets of the time.

Romantic Pre-awakening Period (1840–60). Although conflicts arose between the native peasantry and the ruling elites subsequent to the imperial crackdown after the Decembrists' uprising and the ascension to the throne of Tsar Nikolai I, the freeing of the peasantry by Aleksander I resulted in the spread of schooling, the rise of a middle class with secondary education, and a small professional class. One of the latter, Eduard Ahrens (1803–63), published an Estonian grammar in 1843–53 that established a new systematic written form of the hitherto mainly oral language. When **Kreutzwald** popularized it in his writings it became the standard form, and is used today. In 1838, under the leadership of Faehlmann, the **Estonian Learned Society** (known for decades under its German name, Gelehrte Estnische Gesellschaft) was founded and became the focal point for Estonian literary efforts. After his early death in 1850, Kreutzwald, known as "the Nightingale of Vöru" because of his prolific lyrical writings, composed the national epic **Kalvipoeg**, based on the folk verse collected by Faehlmann, in addition to handbooks on health (he was a practicing country doctor) and other diverse writings. During this period, **Johann Voldemar Jannsen** (1819–90) became the first professional newspaper editor-publisher, and after starting two newspapers he ended by founding *Eesti Postimees* in Tartu in 1864, today the largest newspaper in Estonia under the shortened title *Postimees*.

National Romanticism of the National Awakening (1860–90). The imperial defeat in the Crimean War and the death of Tsar Nikolai I in 1855 led his successor, Aleksander II, to institute reforms with far-reaching consequences in the Baltic provinces. The replacing of corvée labor with money rent, local government reform, a new **education** law, and the opening up of travel, together with general economic growth in Europe and the Russian empire, led to prosperity and the movement to purchase freeholds in the 1860s. Leading freeholders and schoolmasters, along with a few town professionals, formed a self-conscious cultural nationalist pan-Estonia movement, later referred to as the **National Awakening**. The great figures of the period were all writers, such as the politically opposed newspapermen **Jakob Hurt** and **Carl Robert Jakobson** (1841–82), and the poet and editor **Lydia Koidula** (1843–86, daughter of J. V. Jannsen). Their objective was to forge a cultural Estonian nation out of the parochially separated counties and villages of Estonian peasantry, by instilling pride in the common past and in the language. The **Song Festival** of 1869 founded a tradition that time has only strengthened. For almost a century and half, it has regularly brought together Estonians from across the country (and abroad) to massive celebrations in song and music of the sense of belonging to a unique nation. The literature of the National Awakening is unabashedly patriotic and romanticizes the virtues of the homeland with its fields, forests, sea, and nature in general as uniquely "Estonian." A hundred years later, Lydia Koidula's odes to Estonia comforted Estonians' hearts through the long years of the Soviet night:

> My fatherland, my deepest love
> I'll never thee forsake,
> And should I die a thousand deaths,
> That penalty I'll take,
> Let jealous strangers do their part,
> They'll never tear thee from my heart
> My fatherland!

The explosive flowering of Estonian language literature of all kinds imbued the value of the Estonian language so strongly in the whole native population that when the **Russification** wave of the late 1880s and the 1890s hit Estonia (along with the other peripheries of the empire), its main impact was to reinforce Estonian nationalist aspirations along with the value of their language.

Critical Realism (1890–1905). The 15 years around the turn of the century saw the stabilization of Estonian society, along with an unprecedented increase in freehold farmers and urban working, middle, and professional classes who spoke Estonian as a matter of course. However, along with wealth and educational and functional differentiation, social cleavages created conflicts among the hitherto largely cohesive rural Estonian-speaking population. Socialism arrived and created dissention over inequities. In Tartu, **Jaan Tõnisson** (1868–1941; died in Soviet gulag) and **Villem Reiman** (1861–1917), publishing *Postimees*, pursued an idealistic but politically cautious radical nationalism combined with an economic conservatism that emphasized self-sufficient entrepreneurship. In Tallinn, a rapidly growing industrial port city, **Konstantin Päts** (1871–1956), editing *Teataja*, demanded social and political rights for Estonians who still suffered the twin imperial and Baltic baronial yokes. **Eduard Vilde** (1865–1933), who debuted in 1882 as a 17-year-old with a criminal novelette, quickly became Estonia's realist writer par excellence, and published 15 books by the time he reached 27. His painstakingly researched novels reflected the recent historical downtrodden position of the Estonian peasant classes and the contemporary working-class milieu, not only in Estonia but abroad, in Denmark for example, as well. The work of Vilde and his contemporaries, Juhan Liiv (1864–1913), Ernst Särgava (1868–1958), Anna Haava (1864–1957), and others, was in tune with the similar German, Russian, Scandinavian, French, and Hungarian literature read by educated Estonians (who as a matter of course spoke German, Russian, and Finnish, and many spoke French and English as well). By the turn of the century, translations (e.g., two separate editions of Tolstoy's *War and Peace* were published in the 1890s) had made the leading contemporary foreign works available to all Estonians, who had already become the most voracious readers in Europe.

The Young Estonia Movement and the New Romanticism (1905–40). The abortive revolution of 1905 opened the twin floodgates of the Estonians' grievances toward the **Baltic German** ruling class and their desire for self-government. Estonians took control of the **Tallinn** City Council from the Germans in the first decade and built new imposing theater buildings with voluntary contributions (Vanemuine in **Tartu** in 1906, Endla in **Pärnu** in 1912, and Estonia in Tallinn in 1913), established the Estonian Literary Society (as a successor to the **Society of Estonian Literati** closed by **Russification** in the 1890s) in 1907, and opened the Estonian National Museum in 1908. **Gustav Suits** (1883–1956) formed the literary movement **Young Estonia** in imitation of similarly named movements across Europe with the call: "More culture, more European culture! Let us be Estonians but become Europeans!" The objective was to professionalize Estonian culture, to move it from the inward-looking romanticization of the peasant past and the struggles against the ruling class to one that would be outward-looking at the level of West European aesthetics. He was joined by **Friedebert Tuglas** (1886–1971), Juhan Aavik (1884–1982), Vello (Grünthal) Ridala (1885–1942), and Bernhard Linde (1886–1954). By Independence, the group had taken Estonian writing into the mainstream of Western literature. Literary criticism was one of the primary methods in this endeavor, and Tuglas and Suits were its preeminent masters. Through the short Independence of only 20 years, these writers as well as their predecessors, all born in the latter part of the 19th century, and their successor generation, carried on the modernist realist-psychological European styles of the time in the Estonian setting.

The writers **A. H. Tammsaare** (1878–1940), **Oskar Luts** (1887–1953), August Gailit (1891–1960), Peet Vallak (1893–1959), August Jakobson (1904–63), August Mälk (1900–87), and August Sang (1914–69); the playwright Hugo Raudsepp (1883–1952); and the poets Marie Under (1883–1980), Henrik Visnapuu (1890–1951), Betti Alver (1906–89), **Johannes** (Barbarus) **Vares** (1890–1946), Johannes Semper (1892–1970), Juhan Sütiste (1899–1945), Artur Adson (1889–1977), Kersti Merilaas (1913–86), and a dozen others continued as the literary lions of Estonia until the foreign occupations of World War II. Young Estonia also established a press and published most of the belles-lettres of the period—1,400 books with a combined circulation of 2 million copies between 1918 and 1940.

Soviet Estonian Literature (1940–90). To eradicate capitalism and independent thinking, the Soviet Union nationalized all publishing houses and newspapers within weeks of occupying Estonia in 1940. Socialist realism became the only style of writing allowed. The main impact of the three years of German occupation, which followed in 1941, was the exiling to the Soviet rear of those writers who had supported the Soviet order. The reoccupation in 1944 led to a deepening of the demand for Party-prescribed proletarian literature and the expulsion from the Writers Union in 1948 of leading prewar writers who had remained in Estonia, thus making it impossible for them to publish their works (*see* ESTONIAN COMMUNIST PARTY). Two well-known writers were arrested and died in prison: Hugo Raudsepp (1883–1952) and Heiti Talvik (1904–1945).

The 1940s and the 1950s added little of merit to Estonian literature, although Juhan Smuul (1922–1971) did lighten up stringent socialist realism in 1955 with his *Kirjad Sõgedate Külast* (*Letters from the Village of the Benighted*), containing descriptions of the daily life of his native primitive "collective farm" on Muhu island, which he subsequently turned into a historical museum village. Aadu Hint (1910–89), a professional writer already in the 1930s, published the first volume of his four-part proletarian epic of life on the island of Saaremaa, *Tuuline Rand* (*The Windswept Shore*, 1951–66), which begins with the Revolution of 1905. Rudolf Sirge (1904–70), a professed socialist already when he published his fist novel in 1927, wrote *Maa ja Rahvas* (*The Land and the People*) in 1955, the first Soviet era novel that slipped the bonds of history and dealt with more contemporary and touchy issues, in this case the year 1940–41 culminating in the **deportations** of the summer of 1941.

The Khrushchev thaw opened a new chapter in the literature of occupied Estonia in the late 1950s, when the proscribed writers were rehabilitated (among them Semper, Tuglas, Sang, and Alver) and the works of other writers of "bourgeois" Estonia were reprinted. Poetry reemerged first with nine new collections published in 1958, among them **Jaan Kross**'s first work, *Söerikastaja* (*The Coal Concentrator*). The mid-1960s saw the arrival of six new poets—**Paul-Eerik Rummo** (b. 1942), Jaan Kaplinski (b. 1941), Viivi Luik (b. 1946), Mats Traat (b. 1936), **Hando Runnel** (b. 1938), and Enn Vetemaa (b. 1936), as well as the reemergence of Betti Alver, August Sang, and Kersti Merilaas of the prewar generation. Simultaneously, the short story made its debut in Soviet Estonia with Mati Unt (b. 1944), Arvo (Vallikivi) Valton (b. 1935), and Enn Vetemaa (b. 1936) publishing their first collections in which they broke many of the puritanical taboos and strictures of conformism to "correct" thinking and behavior.

They were soon joined by Aimée Beekman (b. 1933), who became a productive novelist; Ellen Niit (b. 1928 and married to Jaan Kross), poet and prolific children's writer; and **Lennart Meri** (b. 1929), an essayist (and president of Estonia, 1992–2001) who combined history and documentary realism in his travelogues and essays (and subsequently turned some into internationally awarded films). In the 1970s and the 1980s, Jaan Kross became the best-known Estonian writer internationally through translations of his evocative historical novels, such as the four-part *Kolme katku vahel* (*Between Three Plagues,* 1970–80), which to Estonians seemed to suggest a veiled historical allegory of contemporary Estonia, as did his 1978 *Tsaari Hull* (*The Emperor's Madman*).

In addition to fanning the flames of national culture through their poetry and novels, the generation of writers who arose after 1960 played a central role in the process of restoring Independence for Estonia in the late 1990s (*see* SECOND NATIONAL AWAKENING), and many entered elective politics in 1989–89, among them Kross, Valton, Meri, and Kaplinski.

Restored Independence: The 1990s. The restoration of Independence brought with it an avalanche of publication of novels, essays, historical and other studies, and autobiographies that had been gathering dust as manuscripts, some because either they or their authors had been refused or were deemed unacceptable, and some because the authors had simply written for their desk drawers. Although some had literary merit, many were published simply as a reaction to the lifting of censorship. The decade of restored Independence has seen the reissuing of a very large number of the Estonian archive of novels and poetry as well as a continuing flood of translations of English-language bestsellers, detective novels, and potboilers.

Since the disappearance of state support for writers, the reprinting of Estonian classics, the appearance of foreign translations, and the reduction in reading, the professional writer has had to earn a living from other employment. As the older generation's output declined, it was added to in the 1980s by that of Toomas Vint (b. 1944), Mari Saat (b. 1947), Teet Kallas (b. 1943), Jaak Jõerüüt (b. 1947), Mihkel Mutt (b. 1953), and a dozen others, who continue sporadically to issue new works in the mainstream of contemporary Western literary styles.

At the Turn of the 21st Century. At the end of the 1990s and the beginning of the 21st century, a few new writers, all born in the 1970s and 1980s, appeared. The new generation, who were teenagers in the last confusing decade of the Soviet era, then grew to adulthood in independent Estonia, has no personal experience of repression and occupation, is free of recent historical-cultural complexes, and is able to experiment with different genres as any writers in the Western world. Mehis Heinsaar (b. 1973) published two collections of short stories; Jan Kraus (b. 1974), a collection of short stories and a novel; Urmas Vadi (b. 1977), a collection of short stories and a play as well as several plays for children; Berk Vaher (b. 1976), two collections of short stories; Mihkel Samarüütel (b. 1976), a book of short stories; and Matt Barker (b. 1980), a medical student, a collection of short stories and a novel. Although magazine articles by these writers appeared in the second half of the 1990s, they came to the attention of the literary critics and the reading public at the turn of the century as their books were published between 1999 and 2002. Their writings are characterized by imagination, a sense of the absurd, playfulness, and diversity of style—which short stories easily allow.

Estonian Writers Abroad (1940–2000). The three occupations of the World War II period led to an exodus of writers who fled either the Soviet occupation or the German one, or were deported to Siberia. The Soviet reoccupation of 1944 led to a final departure, which meant that over half, including all the prominent writers, disappeared from the homeland. Among those who fled west were Gustav Suits, Marie Under, Aino Kallas (1878–1956), August Gailit, August Mälk, Henrik Visnapuu (1890–1951), Ants Oras (1900–82), Karl Ristikivi (1912–77), Bernard Kangro (1910–94), and Artur Adson (1889–1971). All had left "temporarily," as had nearly all the refugees who fled west, since all were convinced that the Soviet occupation was not only morally reprehensible but also illegal under international law, and consequently the Western Allies would quickly drive out the Soviets once the Nazis were defeated. They continued their writing activities in the expectation of an early return home. Their productivity in the 1950s far exceeded that of their compatriots at home, although the refugee community did not exceed 100,000 in total. As the 1950s waned and the hope of an early return disappeared, the exile writers took on a self-imposed duty to keep Estonian "bourgeois" literature alive and well outside the occupied homeland.

Among writers who reached their artistic prominence abroad were Karl Ristikivi with his historical novels, the poet Kangro who published more than 10 novels abroad, Kalju Lepik (1920–99), Pedro (Peeter) Krusten (1897–1987), Gert Helbemäe (1913–74), Raimond Kolk (1924–92), Arvo Mägi (b. 1913), and Ain Kalmus (b. 1906). A new generation of Estonian writers abroad arose with the poets Ivar Grüunthal (1924–96), cofounder of *Mana*, the Estonian literary journal abroad; Arno Vihalemm (1911–90); Ilmar Laaban (1924–2001); Aleksis Rannit (1914–85); Ivar Ivask (1927–92), editor of the international literary journal *Books Abroad* (later *World Literature)*, who did more than anyone during the 20th century to introduce Estonian writers to the world audience; Harri Asi (b. 1922); Hannes Oja (b. 1919); and the prose writers Ilmar Talve (b. 1990), Aino Thoen (b. 1913), Ilmar Jaks (b. 1923), Helga Nõu (b. 1934), and Enn Nõu (b. 1933).

Hellar Grabbi (b. 1929) edited *Mana* for 30 years, maintained the writing of Estonian literary criticism at the international level, and introduced Estonian writers in Soviet Estonia to his audience abroad. The interaction provided by this journal, more than anything else, maintained an artistic connection between the two camps of writers and their readers forced to live apart by political reality.

LIVONIA. This is the English form of the German Livland, the Estonian Liivimaa, and the Latvian Livonija. Livland was the name of the late medieval state that the German crusaders (*see* CRUSADING ORDERS) established on the territory of present-day Latvia and Estonia. This state is also known as Old Livonia to distinguish it from the later Province of Livonia. The crusaders first conquered and Christianized the coastal areas around the south shore of the Gulf of Riga settled by **Livs**, before moving inland and conquering the Latvians (Latgals) who lived in the present-day Latvian province of Vidzeme. In 1210–20 Latgale and southern Estonia were conquered, followed by northern Estonia in 1227. Between 1347 and 1561, Livonia consisted of the whole area controlled by the Livonian Order: the Bishopric of Riga, including **Tartu**; the Saare bishopric; and the confederation of the Kurland (Courland, Kurzeme) bishopric—in other words, the whole of Estonia and the present-day provinces of Vidzeme, Kurzeme, and Zemgale in Latvia. After 1560, when Estonia was conquered by Sweden, and after the Polish-Swedish war of 1600–29, when Kurzeme and Zemgale were lost to Poland, the Province of Livonia was created out of the rump—the southern half of Estonia, including Tartu, and the present-day province of Vidzeme in Latvia. The remaining territory of present-day Estonia became the Province of Estland. As a result of the **Great Northern War** (1700–20), the Province of Livonia was ceded by Sweden, along with the Province of Estland, to Russia, where both remained until 1918. In 1917, Pärnu, Saare, Viljandi, and Võru counties were transferred from the Province of Livland to the Province of Estland for ethnic and historical reasons. Thus, for the first time in history, the ethnically Estonian territories were united under one administrative authority, one year before gaining sovereign independence. The original home territory of the Livs remained as part of the modern-day Latvia.

LIVONIAN ORDER. *See* CRUSADING ORDERS.

LIVONIAN WARS (1558–83). The middle of the 16th century saw a power struggle in the eastern Baltic Sea littoral among Poland-Lithuania, Denmark, Sweden, and Russia. The political conflicts among the Livonian states (later known as Old Livonia) and their inability to cooperate made them tempting targets for all, but especially Russia, which needed an outlet to the Baltic Sea. Russia had already attacked Livonia in 1476, 1501, and 1502 and annexed part of eastern Livonia. In 1557, the peace treaty lapsed and Ivan the Terrible launched a quarter-century-long war of conquest with an attack on the Bishopric of Tartu in January 1558, defeated it within six months, and deported its German burghers to Russia. When, in the following years, the Livonian Order demonstrated its weakness by losing battles, the various vassals of Old Livonia transferred suzerainty over their territories to the competitors of Russia. The Bishop of Saare, who controlled the islands of Saaremaa and Hiuumaa plus as much territory on the mainland of western Estonia, sold his bishopric to the Danish king. The vassal knights controlling **Tallinn**, Harju-Viru in northern Estonia and Järvamaa in central Estonia, transferred their fealty to Sweden. Finally, the Livonian Order, together with the bishop of Riga, placed their territories under the protection of the newly formed union of Poland-Lithuania. Thirty years of intermittent warfare thus finally led to peace treaties whereby Russia withdrew, keeping only a small slice in the east of present-day Latvia and Lithuania and left the field to be divided between the new Baltic powers of Poland-Lithuania and Sweden. Old Livonia disappeared with the Estonian settlement area split under the rule of Denmark (the islands of Saaremaa and Hiiumaa), Sweden (the northern half of the Estonian territory, known as the Province of Estland), and Poland (southern Estonia and the rest of Old Livonia).

LIVS. The Livs were an ethnic group that, from the sixth century A.D., inhabited the southern shore of the Gulf of Riga. Around 1000 A.D., their settlements expanded north from present-day Riga along a 60–100-kilometer band on the eastern shore of the Gulf to the Estonian settlement areas. Ethnolinguistically, the Livs are part of the Finno-Ugric group and speak a language distantly related to Estonian. Over the centuries, after their subjugation by the German **Crusading Orders** as the first of the peoples in the area to be Christianized, they slowly assimilated into the dominant Latvian ethnic population with the result that by the beginning of the 19th century, there were only 2,000 people who could speak the Liv language left on the southern shore of the Gulf. By 1990, only 35 could still speak the language; a decade later, there were still fewer native speakers, but the numbers who understand the language and can speak it avocationally had grown. Since restoration of independence in Latvia, three Liv societies have been founded, a Liv cultural museum was opened in the village of Staicele in northwestern Latvia, and Liv cultural days and a Liv choir have been organized. The Latvian government has supported these activities. The **University of Tartu** also teaches the language as an academic subject and assists in maintaining the Liv cultural museum. Today, Livs are an anthropological, historical, and academic curiosity and not a viable ethnic group. The most visible contribution of the Livs is the historical provision of their name to the **Livonian Order**, its medieval Old Livonian state, and the Russian Province of Livland.

LOCAL GOVERNMENT. Historical name, *vald.* Although local self-government structures operated in prehistoric ancient Estonia (*see* COURTS), the Christianizing conquest by the **Baltic Germans** quickly reduced them to merely formal and empty shells, and eventually removed them altogether. It was not until 1866, well after the Russian imperial power abolished serfdom in the Province of Estland in 1816 and in Livland in 1819, that the Balti Vallaseadus (Baltic Commune Law) reinstituted local government by Estonians and Latvians. The *vald* (equivalent to the Scandinavian commune or the North American township) became the lowest administrative regional organ, in which the peasant landlords, noble estates' tenant farmers, landless farm workers, and estate workers were provided with representation according to status in *vald* councils, and *vald* administrators became civil servants. Approximately 1,000 *vallad* (Estonian, plural of *vald*) were created usually by grouping the villages around estate lands. Between 1891 and 1893, the combining of small *vallad* resulted in a reduction of their number to 400. By decree on 12 June 1917, the *vald* councils became democratically elected and were authorized to administer estate lands. From 1920 to 1934, the local governmental system consisted of the same number of communes, market towns, and towns—387, 19, and 13, respectively—that existed in 1899. But by 1933, amalgamation had reduced the *vallad* to 369. In 1934–39, a further amalgamation was carried out to reduce the number of economically weaker *vallad*, leaving only 265 in 1939.

Counties in History. The second level of self-government, the counties (*maakond* in Estonian, *Kreis* in German), arose in ancient Estonia as cooperating administrative units with common military commands in wartime. At the beginning of the 13th century, there were eight large and five smaller counties. After the conquest, the counties were replaced by bishoprics and Teutonic Order statelets. The historic county names of Sakala, Ugandi, Revelia, and Rotalia disappeared forever along with the counties (and were recalled only as names of **Student Fraternities** at the beginning of the 20th century). After 1580, the Swedish conquerors reorganized the disintegrated system of Old **Livonia** into counties based on the Swedish system and created Harju, Järva, Lääne, and Viru counties in northern Estonia and Tartu and Pärnu counties in southern Estonia, as well as Saaremaa as a separate county in 1645. As in the case of the Teutonic statelets, these counties were administrative structures controlled by the local Baltic barons, augmented by newly created Swedish nobles—they were not organs of self-government of the Estonian peasantry. The Russian imperial period saw the continuation of the county system of administration by the Baltic nobility, with periodic creation and restructuring of some counties. Viljandi and Võru, for example, became net additions. In 1917, all received elected self-governing councils. From 1918 to 1934, democratically elected councils with appointed executives responsible to the elected councils governed the counties. During 1934–38, after the **preemptive coup**, the councils were dismissed and the minister of the interior appointed interim county governments. From 1938 to 1940, elected councils again appointed county executive committees that, however, were now headed by county governors appointed by the president of the Republic. During the 1930s serious planning and discussion took place on reducing the number of local governmental units to an economically viable number, and in the early 1940s a reform would certainly have been carried out but for the intervention of the Soviet occupation.

Soviet Period. During the occupations, both the Soviets and the Germans maintained the administrative structure of the independent republic of 11 counties with 33 towns and 248 communes until 1944. However, soon after the reoccupation, the Soviets soon began a series of apparently haphazard reforms with the intent of eventual conformity with the Soviet system. The first move in 1945 created the village soviet (*külanõukogu*) as the primary unit and in 1950, as the rural **collectivization** was about to be completed, the whole of the old administrative structure was destroyed and replaced by 39 rural regions (*maarajoon*) to which 28 towns, 21 market towns, and 636 village soviets were subordinated. After further reforms, including extensive amalgamation of village soviets as the collective farms of which they basically consisted were amalgamated, and various reorganizations of the regions by the early 1960s local administration in the ESSR remained stable. At the end of the Soviet period, Estonia was divided into 15 regions, with 189 village soviets, 24 market towns, and 33 towns.

Since 1989. Since the original objective of the restoration of independence was to restore the prewar republic, one of the first actions of the nationalist leadership of the **Estonian Supreme Soviet** already in 1989 was to restore the grassroots level of government. Under a law passed on 10 November 1989, local matters were to be decided by local governments, with communes, market towns, and towns as the primary level of government and the counties as the secondary level. The implementation of reform began with the regions being renamed counties and the villages communes (renamed *vald* in Estonian); the towns and market towns became independent. A two-level system of local government was established when on 1 January 1990 *vallad* (plural of *vald*), market towns, and towns formed the primary level of elected councils, and the counties with their old prewar names formed the second, also with elected councils and executives. Thus between 1990 and 1993, Estonia was divided into 198 rural *vallad*, 11 market towns, and 46 towns within 15 counties. In 1993 the market town designation was abolished, as were the elected county councils. The practical difference between *vald* and town was also removed. Thus Estonia was left with a single-tier elected system of local government consisting of 247 municipalities (*vallad*) and a supervening level of 15 county administrations, modeled on the Finnish system and akin to the French prefecture, appointed by the minister of the interior. The local municipal councils organized "voluntary" county associations to discuss common local problems, and even delegated duties to these voluntary bodies.

However, by 2000 the very large variation in population and local taxing powers of the municipalities led the government to propose a drastic rationalization of the system: amalgamation and reduction of the counties to nine and the municipalities to a maximum of 107. The government hoped thereby to create viable communes, to reduce unnecessary duplication, and to save a large amount of tax funds. It was hoped to have the new system in place in time for the local elections scheduled for 2002. In the event, the interests of local councilors in keeping their jobs intervened and only a few municipalities voluntarily joined together; thus forcible amalgamation was put off yet again. The period of the mandate was also to be lengthened from the historic three years to four (the latter was passed by the VIII **Riigikogu** as one of its last acts in February 2003). Strong opposition by local government politicians, led to a consequent inability by the second **Mart Laar** three-party coalition government to act decisively in 2000–01 and the breakup of the coalition at the end of 2001, and to yet another shelving of the reforms to reduce the number of local governments. The **Siim Kallas** government right after its appointment devised a system of financial incentives for the amalgamation of the *vallad* and predicted that eventually the smaller uneconomic *vallad* would inevitably be amalgamated, either voluntarily or forcibly, as the **European Union** (EU) rules of financing came into effect in Estonia. During 2001, EU officials had also criticized the financial and administrative inefficiency of the large number of communes in Estonia.

It should be noted that the electoral rules originally established for local government councils in the restored Republic are still in force: in addition to citizens, **aliens** legally resident in the municipality for at least three years may vote in local elections, but only citizens may contest council seats.

LOTMAN, JURI (YURI) (1922–1993). Internationally acclaimed founder of the **Tartu** school of cultural semiotics. Lotman, a Russian, was born on 22 February 1922 in Petrograd, as St. Petersburg was then called. After service in World War II, he completed his degree in literature at the University of Leningrad in 1950 and moved to Tartu to teach at the Teachers College since he was unable to find an academic appointment in Russia owing to his Jewish heritage, despite being a member of the Communist Party of the Soviet Union (CPSU) since 1943. In the more liberal and tolerant Estonian Soviet Socialist Republic (ESSR), he was able to pursue his research into the sources and impact of culture relatively freely, apart from some routine harassment at the hands of the KGB who interviewed him intermittently after he achieved international acclaim for his work in cultural semiotics. He transferred to the **University of Tartu** in 1954 and served as chair of the Department of Russian Literature from 1960–76, was granted a Ph.D. in 1962, and was promoted to professor in 1963.

Although the external world recognized Lotman's achievements early on, as shown by his election as vice president of the International Association of Semiotics already in 1967 (in which capacity he served to the end of his life), to the British Academy in 1981, and to the Norwegian Academy of Sciences in 1986, it was not until 1987 that the ESSR honored him with its Order of Scholarly Merit. Subsequently he was elected to the Estonian Academy of Sciences in 1990, only three years before his death at Tartu on 28 October 1993. Lotman leaves a large legacy of writings from his lifelong study of the development of 18th- and 19th-century Russian literature, and the resultant works in the study of semiotics. He was the primary developer of the foundations of structural semiotics in the study of semiotics. Since a group of Moscow colleagues participated regularly at the summer seminars that he organized at the University of Tartu's sports camp at Kääriku, the Tartu school of semiotics is known in Russia as the Moscow-Tartu school of semiotics.

Although Lotman only wrote in Russian, his work has become internationally known, with the Russian editions of his writings found in university libraries across the world. The best known of his works in foreign languages are *Aufsätze zur Theorie und Methodologie der Literatur und Kultur* (Kroneberg: Scriptor, 1974); *Kunst als Sprache: Untersuchungen zum Zeichencharakter von Literatur und Kunst* (Leipzig: Reclam, 1981); *The Semiotics of Russian Culture* (Ann Arbor: University of Michigan, 1984); and *Universe of the Mind: A Semiotic Theory of Culture* (Bloomington: Indiana University Press, 1990).

LUIK, JÜRI (1966–). Estonian politician and diplomat. Born on 16 August 1966 in **Tallinn**, Luik graduated from the journalism program at the **University of Tartu** in 1989, and then worked for two years as an editor of the popular magazine *Vikerkaar* while participating actively in the politics of independence together with a group of his former fellow student activists, with whom he had organized such nationalist actions as the Second Student Forum on Higher Education in **Tartu** in 1998. In 1989–91, he served also as the Anglo-American expert for **Lennart Meri** at the Estonian Institute, which the latter had just established. In 1991–92, he was appointed director of the Political Department by Foreign Minister Lennart Meri, and recruited to the Pro Patria Party, organized by Meri's protégés. In 1992, Luik was elected to the newly reinstituted **Riigikogu** and appointed by Prime Minister **Mart Laar** as minister without portfolio. In 1993–94, he served as leader of the delegation negotiating with Russia, after which Laar appointed him minister of defense. From January to April 1995, Luik served as foreign minister, at 28 the youngest foreign minister in Estonian history. After the defeat of his party at the polls, he spent the year 1995–96 as a researcher with the Carnegie Endowment in the United States. In 1996, he was appointed ambassador to the **North Atlantic Treaty Organization** (NATO) and the Benelux in Brussels. With the return to power of Pro Patria in March 1999, he was recalled and appointed minister of defense, at 33 the youngest such minister in Europe, serving until the collapsed Laar coalition was replaced in January 2002. Subsequently, on 26 November 2002, Luik was named as head of the Estonian Delegation negotiating membership in NATO.

LURICH, GEORG (1876–1920). Estonian wrestler and weightlifter. Born 22 April 1876 at Väike-Maarja, Lurich turned professional early in life and fought matches in Russia and Western Europe for 25 years (1895–1920) as a world champion in classical wrestling. In 1913–17, he also fought freestyle in the United States. He won records in weightlifting as well as one-arm wrestling and even in bodybuilding contests. He owed his championship status to his mastery of technique and his speedy use of it. As a result, he fought and beat most world champions during his heyday. For Estonian youth and men, Lurich was a lifelong model to be emulated. He used his hero status in Estonia to encourage bodybuilding, temperance, and a healthful lifestyle and propagated this in articles and appearances. His reputation has survived for almost a century after his death from an acute typhus infection on 22 January 1920 at Armavir in the Caucasus. Since 1956, an annual Lurich wrestling meet has been organized in **Tallinn**, and his name again spread around the international wrestling world at the beginning of the 21st century.

LUTHERANISM. *See* RELIGION.

LUTS, OSKAR (1887–1953). Estonia's most popular writer of the 20th century. Luts was born on 7 January 1887 in Kaarepere *vald*, and he attended local schools and the **Tartu** Realgümnasium. After secondary school, he became an apprentice pharmacist in 1903 and worked in Tartu, **Narva**, **Tallinn**, and St. Petersburg until 1911, when he entered the Department of Pharmacology at the University of Tartu graduating in 1914. He served in World War I as a pharmacist, but changed occupations and worked in the university library in 1919–20, changing again in 1922, when he sold books for two years. From 1922 on, he earned his living as a professional writer.

However, despite a prolific output of scores of books and short stories as well as articles and plays, Luts never reached the heights of his early adventure novel *Kevade* (*Spring*) I–II published in 1912–13, which he later turned into a series of the life experiences of the farm-boy Toots, with *Suvi* (*Summer*) I–II, published in 1918–19; *Tootsi pulmad* (*Toots' Wedding*) (1921); *Argipäev* (*Weekday*) (1924); and *Sügis* (*Autumn*) I (1938) and II issued posthumously in 1988, 35 years after his death on 23 March 1953 in Tartu. These books have been so popular that each succeeding generation of Estonians has made Toots its own folk hero. Toots and his friends appeal to the Estonian psyche since they reflect both the dream of a golden, simple past and the kaleidoscope of personalities that Estonians recognize among their friends. Consequently, these books have never gone out of print. Luts's *Collected Works* were issued in 27 volumes in 1937–40, and reissued in 11 volumes during the Soviet era between 1952 and 1967.

– M –

MAAPÄEV (German, Landtag; Russian, Zemstvo; English, Diet). The aristocratic and estate owners' Diets of the Provinces of Estland and Lettland were disbanded on Independence in 1920 by Estonia and Latvia. On 30 March 1917, the Russian Provisional Government transferred the Estonian settlement area of northern Lettland to the Province of Estland, thus joining Estonians for the first time into a single administrative territorial unit, and decreed the establishment of a temporary Zemstvo for the newly consolidated Province (Gubernya in Russian) of Estonia, to be elected by universal indirect suffrage. The new provincial assembly was known colloquially as the Maapäev. Of its 62 members, those representing rural communes were elected by two-tier elections in May–June while the town representatives were chosen after municipal elections in July–August 1917. On 15 November, just before it was dissolved by the Bolshevik Estonian Military Revolutionary Committee, which had taken over power in the Gubernya of Estonia after the October Revolution in St. Petersburg, the Maapäev declared itself the sole sovereign power in Estonia until a **Constituent Assembly** could be democratically elected. It transferred its powers to its Committee of Elders and Executive Committee and went underground. On 24 February 1918, in the power vacuum between the retreat of the **Bolsheviks** from **Tallinn** and the arrival of German troops from the west, the Committee of Elders declared Estonia an independent Republic and appointed a provisional government headed by **Konstantin Päts**. *See also* DECLARATION OF INDEPENDENCE.

MADE, TIIT (1940–). Estonian economist, journalist, and politician. Born on 13 March 1940 in **Tallinn**, Made graduated in 1965 in economics from Tallinn Polytechnical Institute (TPI, now Tallinn Technical University). He taught at TPI while continuing graduate studies at Moscow State University, from which he received his *cand. econ.* degree in 1971. Made served as consular attaché at the Soviet embassy in Stockholm in 1974–77, and he worked as director of the Information Institute of the Estonian Soviet Socialist Republic's (ESSR) State Planning Committee in 1979–84. Thereafter, he taught as senior lecturer at the Institute of Qualification, and as lecturer at the Teachers Continuing Education Institute until 1989. Simultaneously, he worked as a freelance commentator on economic and foreign affairs for Estonian Radio and Television. His political career began in 1987 when he cosigned the Four-man Declaration on **Isemajandav Eesti** (IME), which was published in the **Tartu** newspaper *Edasi* (now again with its original name *Postimees*) on 27 September. Subsequently, he became one of the founders of the Estonian Green Movement in 1988, and of the Eesti Ettevõtjate Erakond (Estonian Entrepreneurs Party) in 1990, serving as its chair until 1991. He was elected president of the Federation of Estonian Cooperatives and Private Entrepreneurs in 1989 and served until 1994 in this capacity. Having joined the **Estonian Communist Party** in 1971, he left it in 1989. In 1989, he was elected to the Supreme Soviet in Moscow where he served on the Foreign Affairs Committee, until he resigned in 1991 to participate directly in Estonian electoral politics, being elected to the Estonian **Supreme Council** (Soviet) in 1990 and to **Riigikogu** VII in 1992 and VIII in 1995. After being defeated in the 1999 elections, Made returned to teaching and journalism.

MARK, HEINRICH (1911–). Estonian lawyer and exile politician. Born on 1 October 1911 in Karaski village in Kõlleste *vald*, Mark graduated in law from the **University of Tartu** in 1938, while working as a primary school teacher from 1933 to 1938. He practiced law in Tartu in 1939–40 and in **Tallinn** in 1943, but was forced to teach school again during the Soviet occupation in 1940–41, as well as in 1941–42 during the German occupation. Mark fled to Finland in 1943 and to Sweden the following year. For the next four decades, he was a leading force in the Estonian exile community in Sweden, serving as a leader of the Estonian Committee in Stockholm from 1945 to 1981, and as secretary-general of the Estonian National Council in Sweden from 1951 to 1979. In 1953, he was appointed state secretary in the Estonian Government in exile and served until 1971 when he was named acting **prime minister**. In 1990, he became acting **president** of the de jure Republic of Estonia. In 1992, Mark transferred the legal powers of the Republic to President **Lennart Meri**, after the latter's election on the basis of the new **Constitution of 1992** approved by referendum, having thus provided the legal continuity of the Republic established in 1918.

MASING, OTTO WILHELM (1763–1832). The first Estonian writer and theologian of the Enlightenment. Born on 8 November 1763 at Lohusuu to an Estonian parish clerk father and a mother of aristocratic Swedish origin, young Masing received the education of a gifted Baltic noble. After studies at the Narva City School and Torgau Gymnasium in Germany, he entered the University of Halle, at the time a prominent center of rationalist Enlightenment learning in Germany, where he studied theology in 1783–86. He returned home and for two years tutored a noble family and did the Grand Tour of Europe with one of his pupils. In 1788 when, at the age of 25, he became pastor of the Lüganus parish, he began a career of enlightening his flock by sermons and writings. In 1795, he published his first major work, the first school reader in Estonian. After moving to the richer neighboring parish of Viru-Nigula, he married a **Tartu** burgher's daughter, who died in 1809, whereupon the 55-year-old country pastor married a 26-year-old marquise who was born in Naples but had grown up in St. Petersburg. Prior to his marriage in 1815, Masing had moved to the parish of Ärksi, which had the twin advantages of closeness to Tartu, and a larger, wealthier parish estate. Here his influence grew rapidly, and his Enlightenment colleagues named him to the post of assessor of the Province of Livland in 1818. In 1821, Masing was appointed bishop of Tartu. Thus he rose to a central position in the religious life of the Baltic Provinces.

The Ärksi period turned out to be the most productive in Masing's life and coincided with the emancipation from serfdom of the peasantry. In 1819 he, as the recognized expert in the **Estonian language**, was asked to provide the official translation of the Law on the Peasantry, which was published in 1820. For a number of years thereafter, Masing translated laws and decrees of the provincial administration. In 1821, he began publishing the *Marahwa Näddala-Leht* (*Country People's Weekly*) and managed to keep it going for four years, until 1825, despite the opposition of the **Baltic German** nobility and the poverty of his readers. This was the first newspaper in the Estonian language and was dedicated to inform and educate the peasantry. Masing also wrote and published calendars, books, and booklets for the edification of the peasants, as well as school texts on arithmetic, Bible stories, and school readers. His contributions to the written language are equally notable: he invented the letter "õ" (pronounced as the vowel in the English *no* or *known*) and used it for the first time in print in 1818. Through his writings, he strengthened the North Estonian dialect as the written language in southern Estonia, which until 1918 was part of the Province of Livland. Masing died on 15 March 1832 at Ärksi without realizing either of his final dreams, a teachers' college for parish schoolmasters and a definitive Estonian language dictionary. The disappearance of the manuscript of his dictionary—the result of 40 years of labor—is a major loss to Estonian culture.

MASING, UKU (1909–1985). Estonian writer, poet, theologian, and philologist. Masing was born as Hugo Albert on 11 August 1909 in Lipa village in Raikküla *vald.* In 1937, he changed his name to Uku Masing. He graduated with a master's degree in theology from the **University of Tartu** in 1930, continued studies at Berlin and Tübingen in 1930–33, and received his doctorate in theology from Tartu in 1948. Masing taught in the theology faculty at the University of Tartu from 1933 to 1940 and, after the Soviet occupation closed the faculty, at the Institute of Theology of the Estonian Evangelical **Lutheran** Church from 1949 to 1963. His catholic writings cover New

Testament studies as well as Finno-Ugric peoples' belief systems, folk poetry, and linguistics. He also translated Asian, ancient Greek, and Latin literature as well as the **Bible**. He is best known to Estonians for his expressive yet intellectually complex poetry, most of it published abroad during the Soviet period but widely circulated in Estonia. After his death on 25 April 1985, and with the arrival of **perestroika and glasnost**, one original volume of poetry and one novel were published in Estonia in 1988 and 1989. Since independence, all of his poetic works have been reissued.

MERI, LENNART-GEORG (1929–). Writer, filmmaker, diplomat, and politician; president of Estonia, 1992–2001. Meri was born on 29 March 1929 in **Tallinn** to the family of a prominent Estonian diplomat, Georg Meri. He received his primary education in Berlin and Paris, where his farther was stationed; and he received his secondary education in Jansk, Russia, where his family was exiled until 1946 after **deportation** in 1941, and in Tallinn after the family was allowed to return to Estonia. As a result, he is fluent in German, English, Russian, and French as well as in Finnish. After receiving his degree in history from the **University of Tartu** in 1953, he worked in 1953–55 as a writer for Vanemuine Theater in Tartu, in 1955–61 as editor of broadcast plays at Estonian Radio, and thereafter as an independent writer, playwright, and film director.

From 1985 to 1987, Meri was secretary for foreign relations for the Estonian Writers Union; in 1988 he founded the Estonian Institute, which he headed until 1990, when he was appointed foreign minister and served in the **Edgar Savisaar** and **Tiit Vähi** transition governments. In spring 1992, he was appointed ambassador to Finland but was elected in September by popular vote as the first post-Soviet president of independent Estonia. In 1996, he was reelected president by the Electoral College for a second and constitutionally final five-year term.

Meri has published seven novels, several collections of speeches, essays, and documents, as well as Estonian translations of German, French, English, and Russian authors such as Erich Maria Remarque, Jean Bruller Vercors, Graham Greene, and Alexander Solzhenytzin. Between 1970 and 1997, he also produced and directed five full-length films depicting the Finno-Ugric peoples and cultures. As a result, Meri became well-known in Finland long before Estonia regained independence: among other honors, he was elected corresponding member of the Finnish Writers Union in 1977 and honorary member in 1982. In 1977, his film *Linnutee tuuled* (*Winds of the Flyway*) won the silver medal at the New York Film Festival. After being elected president, Meri took on the role of *Landesvater* (father of the nation) and lifted the spirits of the Estonian people through well-crafted speeches. He focused the attention of European politicians and publics on Estonia as a progressive state-society worthy of early membership in the **European Union** in equally well-crafted speeches in English, French, German, and Finnish. As an intellectual-writer-politician, he is often compared to Vaclav Havel of the Czech Republic.

Shortly after his retirement from the office of president, Meri was elected to the Humanities and Social Sciences division of the **Estonian Academy of Sciences**, and in February 2002 was appointed by the **Siim Kallas** government as its delegate to the Constitutional Convention of the 15 members and 13 applicant countries, convened to reorganize the institutions of the European Union in order to accommodate its expansion. Just as he created the role of the modern president as *Landesvater* in Estonia, Meri is creating the role of the former president as a national mediator and international ambassador of Estonia.

MOLOTOV-RIBBENTROP PACT (MRP). On 23 August 1939, Vyacheslav Molotov and Joachim Ribbentrop, foreign ministers of the Soviet Union and Nazi Germany, respectively, signed a nonaggression treaty in which the two countries agreed not to attack each other, either independently or in conjunction with other powers, or to support any third power that might attack the other party to the pact.

However, it was the Secret Protocols to the pact that turned out to be the real reason for the pact, and by which the whole of Eastern Europe was divided into German and Soviet spheres of influence with half of Poland roughly east of the Vistula in the Soviet sphere along with Estonia, Latvia, Lithuania, and Finland. Moreover, Bessarabia was to be separated from Romania. Three secret supplementary protocols made specific demarcations. The first two, signed on 28 September 1939, specified the new borders of Lithuania between the two signatories, demarcated the new Polish-German border, and assigned Bessarabia to the Soviet sphere. In the third Secret Protocol, signed as late as 10 January 1941, Germany renounced its claims to parts of Lithuania (formerly in East Prussia) in return for Soviet payment of a sum agreed upon by the two countries.

The first fruits of the protocols became evident within a few weeks as Germany and the Soviet Union both attacked Poland and divided it up between themselves.

Shortly thereafter, in November 1939 the Red Army attacked Finland, overran the Baltic States under the pretext of needing to secure their defensive perimeter by placing bases in the three between October 1939 and July 1941 (*see* SOVIET-ESTONIAN MUTUAL ASSISTANCE TREATY), and annexed the three states in July–August 1940.

Although the Molotov-Ribbentrop Pact was discarded when Germany attacked the Union of Soviet Socialist Republics (USSR) on 22 June 1941, the borders that the Soviet Union established at the conclusion of World War II were essentially those agreed in the Pact. After the defeat of Nazi Germany, the USSR had claimed the victor's right to conquered territory—territory that it had acquired as a direct result of the political division with Nazi Germany in the Secret Protocols.

Until 1989, although the Secret Protocols became known soon after the war, the Soviet Union refused to acknowledge their existence, primarily because Balts vociferously argued the illegality of continued occupation based on agreement with Nazi Germany. In 1988, Estonians organized the **Molotov-Ribbentropi Pakti Avalikustamise Eesti Grupp** (MRP-AEG) mass movement, which demanded the publication and acknowledgement of the Secret Protocols by Moscow. Although most prominent members of the **Estonian Communist Party** (ECP) signed declarations to this effect and although the protest caught the imagination of the population, leading to the **Baltic Chain** on the 60th anniversary of the MRP in 1989, the Soviet Union never acknowledged the existence of the protocols. Its successor state, Russia, has never acknowledged or apologized for the illegality of the 50 years of occupation resulting from the Secret Protocols.

MOLOTOV-RIBBENTROPI PAKTI AVALIKUSTAMISE EESTI GRUPP (MRP-AEG). The Estonian Group for Making the Molotov-Ribbentrop Pact Public announced on 15 August 1987 that it had been formed by a group of concerned people to publicize the Secret Protocols of the **Molotov-Ribbentrop Pact**. The group's chair was the former political prisoner Tiit Madisson, who was also president of the Pärnu Heritage Society. Other freed prisoners of conscience, including **Lagle Parek**, Heiki Ahonen, Arvo Pesti, Klaju Mätik, and Erik Udam, were the activists behind the initiative. In its announcement, the MRP-AEG called for a mass meeting on 23 August, the anniversary of the signing of the pact. In the event, the meeting took place at Hirvepark (Deer Park) on the southern slope of Toompea, just below the Parliament building, and the medieval Pikk Hermann tower, the site of the national flagstaff.

The Hirvepark meeting was the first planned overtly political challenge to Soviet authority and took advantage of General Secretary Mikhail Gorbachev's atmosphere of **perestroika and glasnost**, promising renewal and tolerance. The inspiration for the demonstration and the demand for public acknowledgement by Moscow of the secret protocols were the actions of émigré Estonians, Latvians, and Lithuanians in the United States, Canada, and Western Europe who had marked 23 August for a decade with black armbands in an effort to bring the illegality of the Soviet occupation of their homelands to the attention of the world's public and politicians. The Hirvepark demonstration resounded in the Western media thanks to the émigré contacts who had organized a letter from the American senators to Gorbachev and the Baltic Soviet Socialist Republics' leaders to allow the Hirvepark meeting to proceed undisturbed. As a result, the demonstration was allowed to take place. Unlike previous attempts at bringing attention to the illegality of the Soviet occupation, no one was imprisoned or even harassed for speaking out at Hirvepark, as in the case of the signers of the **Letter of the Forty**. That it was not suppressed and that the Soviet Estonian press and broadcast media reported it created a sense of political breakthrough among the Estonian people, who breathlessly sensed the possibility of actual change in the system that hitherto had rigidly controlled any deviation from the Communist Party line and not allowed any organizing not directed by the Party.

MUUGA. A new port was built by the Soviet Union between 1982 and 1986 at the town of Muuga, 13 kilometers east of **Tallinn**, primarily for grain imports by deep-sea freighters. On regaining independence, Estonia immediately expanded the port by building several oil terminals as well as additional loading and terminal warehouse facilities. In 1992, Muuga port became part of the Tallinn Ports complex, which includes the Old Port in the city center and the Paldiski South Port, a deep-sea harbor 40 kilometers west of Tallinn on the **Paldiski** peninsula, served by a rail connection built for heavy military traffic by the Soviet military. Tallinn Ports, because of their efficiency and relatively low costs, have become so successful as a transit operation for Russian raw oil exports and for industrial goods imports for the St. Petersburg market that the Russian government is building several ports close to St. Petersburg to draw off this transit trade.

The petroleum shipping ports at Primorsk and Ust-Luga became operational at the end of 2001, and Vysots is expected to come on stream at the end of 2003. However, given that all three are iced in part of the year and are almost 400 kilometers from the open sea at the bottom of the Gulf of Finland—whereas the Tallinn ports are the only ice-free ones in the Gulf, their trade is growing at a brisk rate, and they are constantly increasing their efficiency—the competition is not expected to reduce the transhipment through Estonia.

Historically, the first references to port facilities in Tallinn are found in reports by traders from Gotland in 1230. In 1370, the first protective stone breakwater was built, and it was renovated in the 17th century. In 1714, in the midst of the **Great Northern War** with Sweden, Tsar **Peter the Great** began expanding the harbor to accommodate his naval vessels as a defensive outpost for his new capital of St. Petersburg. From 1860, when the harbor facilities were placed under the control of the city government, Tallinn grew rapidly as a commercial port. In 1903, a separate Tallinn Ports Authority was established and operated until it was taken over by the Soviet government in 1941. It was revived in 1992 and privatized in 1996.

– N –

NARVA. Located on waterfalls near the mouth of the Narva River, which connects the Gulf of Finland with Lake Peipsi (Peipus), the town of Narva grew as a trading post on the Varangian trade route to Greece during Viking times from the 6th to the 9th centuries A.D. In 1345, when it had become an important trading center on the Scandinavia-Novgorod trade route, King Valdemar VI Atterdag of Denmark granted it a charter with town privileges. During the ensuing centuries, Narva gradually supplanted Novgorod as the intermediary of European-Russian trade as the northeasternmost member of the **Hanseatic League**. Its greatest flowering as a trading center took place in **Swedish times** during the 17th century before the founding of St. Petersburg, which grew into Russia's premier westernmost metropolis in the 18th century.

As the Narva River has divided the Russian and Orthodox East from the ethnic Estonian and Roman Catholic (later Protestant) West since time immemorial, so the town of Narva became a military outpost at this interface. The fortified castle of Narva, begun in the 13th century by Danes and finished in the 15th century by the Teutonic Order, has faced the Russian castle of Ivangorod across the river ever since. At the end of the 14th century, a surrounding town wall fortified with towers was built. During the next two centuries, the medieval towers were reconstructed into artillery towers able to withstand the newly developed cannon and constructed to cover firing angles along the whole fortification. In the 17th century, the Swedish overlords constructed bastions of Italian and German types, and in the 1680s, they built a grandiose new defensive line with French-type bastions around the castle. The victory over the larger forcers of Tsar **Peter the Great** in the first battle of Narva in 1700 made the reputation of the young Swedish King Charles XII as an astute military commander. However, in the second battle in 1704, Peter regained Narva and the Russian empire subsequently controlled it until its demise in the Russian Revolution.

The remarkable defensive ensembles of both Narva and Ivangorod castles have survived and, in facing each other across the river, continue to symbolize the dividing line between East and West today. Unfortunately, the old walled medieval city of Narva, built with the wealth of trade over centuries and containing irreplaceable architectural gems, including the unique Narva baroque style, was totally destroyed by Soviet bombardment and deliberate destruction by retreating German troops between March and July 1944.

The **industrialization** of the second half of 19th century brought the Kreenholm Manufacture to Narva. Utilizing the cheap energy of the waterfalls, it became one of the largest textile mills in Europe at the time. At the World Exhibition in Paris in 1900, it even won the Grand Prix for its textiles. And although the mill is again producing textiles for export today, it is the partially surviving architectural ensemble of the Kreenholm industrial complex that is of historical interest. The architects, schooled in St. Petersburg, built an industrial-residential complex that incorporated the prevailing late 19th-century sociological and philosophical ideas about industrial cities of the future.

The present-day Narva is an industrial town marked by the legacy of the Soviet Union: in addition to the historic textile manufacturing, a furniture factory and two huge power stations fueled by locally mined shale oil were built, producing energy not only for Estonia but also with half exported to Latvia and to St. Petersburg. Although one of these has been mothballed since the economic transformation after the collapse of the Soviet Union, the imported labor that these massive undertakings required has left Narva with the second-largest urban population in Estonia. Moreover, of the 80,000 inhabitants in 2000, only 3 percent were ethnic Estonian. To house this population, most of whom were imported in the 1950s and 1960s, huge soulless Soviet industrial housing subdivisions were built, and continue to mark the city as a leftover of the recent past.

To counteract this vista, the city rebuilt and renovated small parts of its past during the 1990s and proudly displays them as its symbols: the town hall, a few old houses, the belt of the Narva bastions, and the Orthodox Cathedral of the Resurrection of Christ.

NATIONAL ANTHEM. *See* NATIONAL SYMBOLS.

NATIONAL AWAKENING (Rahvuslik ärkamine). Estonians call the period roughly between 1860 and 1885 the National Awakening, since the quarter century saw systematic agitation by activists to raise Estonians to a consciousness of their unique national culture. The period was dominated by romantic notions of culture and ethnicity and was rooted in organizing the rural farmers and tenants to participate in choirs and orchestras all over the countryside. Although the leaders, such as **Carl Robert Jakobson**, **Johann Voldemar Jannsen**, and **Lydia Koidula**, were well educated and well aware of the mainstream of contemporary European thought and literature, the foot soldiers in the field awakening the population were mainly the local schoolmasters and **Lutheran** pastors. There was widespread encouragement of literacy by means of **newspapers** and almanacs containing both practical modern farming advice and short stories and poetry. Music was encouraged by means of choirs, orchestras, and **Song Festivals**. These endeavors, together with the preservation of local heritage by means of amateur archaeology, led to the awakening of the mass of the Estonian people, who at the time were overwhelmingly rural—peasant farmers, tenants, and landless farm laborers—to their ethnic Estonian-language national culture. Up to this time, the **Baltic German** nobility, owners of most of the land, looked down at them as *Undeutsch*, spoke German or pidgin Estonian to them, and generally treated them with contempt as uncivilized peons. The National Awakening instilled pride in the Estonian nation and in the Estonian language, encouraged farmers to teach their sons to read, and made education the norm for social and economic advancement.

NATIONAL SYMBOLS. The following three national symbols have been especially significant to Estonia.

Flag. The national flag of Estonia is rectangular in shape and divided into three horizontal bands of equal size. The upper band is blue, the middle one is black, and the lowest band is white. The proportions of the flag are 11:7, and its normal size is 165 x 105 centimeters. The blue-black-white flag was first consecrated at Otepää on 4 June 1884, as the flag of the **Eesti Üliõpilaste Sel**, the Estonian University Students Association (universally known by the acronym EÜS). Subsequently, it became a hallowed national symbol as the students led the process of nation building.

The provisional government of Estonia on the 21 November 1918 proclaimed the blue-black-white flag the state flag. After the annexation of Estonia by the Soviet Union in June 1940, the flag was banned.

During the **singing revolution** in 1987–88, the flag (referred to by Estonians simply as the *sini-must-valge lipp* or blue-black-white tricolor flag) was openly flaunted as the symbol of independence. On the 24 February 1989, the then still Estonian Soviet Socialist Republic's government flew the blue-black-white national flag of Estonia from the national flagstaff atop the Pikk Hermann tower as the national flag of Estonia once again.

Coat of Arms of Estonia. The Estonian coat of arms shows three blue lions passant gardant (facing and pacing on guard) on a golden shield framed on each side by gilded oak leaf branches with the stems of the branches crossing at the base of the shield. The design of the shield originates in the XII century, when Danish King Valdemar II presented the City of **Tallinn** (then Reval) with a coat of arms similar to that of the state of Denmark, showing three lions. The motif was transposed to the coat of arms of the Province of Estonia proclaimed by Tsarina Catherine II on 4 October 1788.

The **Riigikogu** of the Republic of Estonia adopted the state coat of arms on 19 June 1925. After the forcible annexation of Estonia by the Soviet Union in 1940, the coat of arms was outlawed, along with all symbols of independent Estonia. The use of the historic coat of arms as the state coat of arms of the Republic of Estonia was readopted on 7 August 1990.

National Anthem. The national anthem "Mu isamaa, mu õnn ja room" ("My Native Land, My Joy and Delight") is a choral melody, originally arranged in 1843 by Fredrik Pacius, a Finnish composer of German origin. In Estonia, Johann Voldemar Jannsen's lyrics were set to this melody and sung at the first Estonian **Song Festival** in 1869. It gained in popularity during the growing national movement. In Finland, it first became popular only as a students' song, but soon also became more widely accepted. When both Estonia and Finland became independent after World War I, this identical melody with different words was recognized as the national anthem by both nations. Estonia adopted it officially in 1920, after the **War of Independence**. During the decades of the Soviet occupation of Estonia, the melody was strictly forbidden and people were sent to Siberia for singing it. However, even during the worst years, the familiar tune could be heard over Finnish **radio**, every day at the beginning and end of the program. Thus, the melody could never be forgotten. With the restoration of Estonian independence, the national anthem has, of course, been restored, too.

NEWSPAPERS AND PERIODICALS. The first newspaper published in Estonia was the German-language *Revalsche Post-Zeitung*, which lasted from 1689 to 1710. The first Estonian-language regularly issued publication was the weekly *Lyhike öppetus*, of which 41 issues appeared in 1766–67, published at Põltsamaa. The *Tartomaa Näddala-Leht*, which appeared in 1806, is regarded as the first proper Estonian-language newspaper. And the 19th-century tradition of the Estonian press as a tool of national awakening, with a cultural-educational orientation, including modernization of agricultural techniques, was created by **Otto Wilhelm Maasing**'s *Marahwa Näddala-Leht* (1821–23). The first illustrated periodical was **Friedrich Reinhold Kreutzwald**'s *Maailm ja monda mis seal sees leida on*, which appeared in five issues from 1848 to 1849. In the second half of the century, the press in Estonia became politicized as a nationalist cultural opinion maker and became a tool in the **National Awakening**.

The first regularly published and "permanent" newspaper in Estonia was *Perno Postimees*, edited by **Johann Vilhelm Jannsen** in 1857–63, who moved it to Tartu in 1863 and renamed it *Tartu Postimees* and edited it until 1905. This newspaper is still published today under the title *Postimees. Sakala*, founded in 1878 and published by **Carl Robert Jakobson**, was the first overtly partisan political newspaper in Estonia. During the last two decades of the century, the number of journalists and newspapers increased rapidly. At the beginning of the 20th century, Social Democratic and worker's newspapers and periodicals began to appear. The right-wing political newspaper *Päevaleht* appeared in 1905 and continued until it was closed by the Soviet occupation in 1940. In 1923, the literary and cultural journal *Looming* was founded.

During the two decades of independence, all the larger newspapers in Estonia became associated with political parties, with the result that after the **preemptive coup of 1934** some were closed and others continued under politically emasculated reorganized nonpartisan publishing houses. The newspaper *Uus Eesti* became the voice of the government and the Isamaaliit party. The **Silent Era** is marked by a radical reduction of the press—although the number of newspapers had risen to 121 in 1933, by 1940 it had declined to only 47. Of these, *Vaba Maa* and *Päeveleht* had circulations up to 50,000. However, the periodicals press, less concerned with partisan politics and more focused on literary, cultural, scientific, and associational interests and activities continued apace at over 200 titles.

During the first period of Soviet occupation in 1940–41, seven national newspapers were published and new periodicals such as *Viisnurk*, *Nõukogude Kultuur*, *Pioneer*, and *Kehakultuur* appeared. *Looming* was the only major periodical that continued publication, but with Communist Party–friendly articles in the content.

After the resumption of the Soviet occupation after the war, the main national newspapers and periodicals of the first Soviet period resumed publication with *Rahva Hääl*, *Noorte Hääl*, *Edasi* (printed on the presses and premises of *Postimees* in Tartu), and *Maaleht* among the main ones. In addition, all kinds of collectives began to publish their own newspapers and information periodicals, such as student organizations, collective farm associations, and industrial organizations. 1953 saw the largest numbers of newspaper titles in Soviet Estonia when 123 were published. Subsequently, with **radio** and **television** becoming prime entertainment and information media, *Eesti Radio* and *Television*, the two weekly program guides, became the most popular regularly circulating publications. With the drastic increase in the Russian-speaking population (from under 3 percent in 1944 to 38.5 percent in 1989), the Russian-language press increased apace. In 1985, there were 103 regularly published periodicals in Estonia with total circulation of 31.2 million copies; of these, Estonian-language titles numbered 70 with a circulation of 24.4 million copies, the remainder being Russian-language; and 49 newspapers had a combined circulation of 272 million copies, of which the 35 Estonian-language papers accounted for 222 million.

In the run-up to regaining independence, interest in the press increased rapidly. Large numbers of new newspapers and journals began publishing, and although many disappeared just as quickly, by 1990 165 newspapers with a total circulation of 380.5 million copies were published. In the same year, 434 journals appeared with a combined circulation of 26.2 million copies, significantly below the 1995 figure. Clearly, many startups had limited appeal. In 1995, the year when the initial enthusiasm of the freedom to start a newspaper, and to publish and read whatever one wished, had waned, partly also the result of the commercial realities of steeply rising publishing costs in a market economy, Estonian-language papers numbered 110 and

Russian titles 36. During the following five years to 2000, a consolidation of titles reduced Estonian ones to 82 and Russian ones to 27. Total circulation had declined drastically by 1995 to an average of 9,544 copies per issue and then declined slowly further to 8,737 copies per issue in 2000. In contrast, periodical titles had increased to 501 by 1995 and their circulation had increased to 20.2 million copies per year (or 3,793 per issue). Of the total, Estonian-language publications numbered 426 and Russian ones 75. The share in total circulation of the Estonian language periodicals was 77 percent. By 2000, the number of periodical titles had increased to 956 (Estonian titles, 778), but their total circulation had declined slightly to 19.8 million copies (Estonian copies, 18.4) per annum. Although Russian titles increased to 18 percent, their share of total circulation had decreased to 8 percent.

During the second half of the 1990s, a consolidation of the main dailies in the country took place, with Swedish, Norwegian, and Finnish investors taking large shares in the remaining ones. By the beginning of the 21st-century *Postimees*, restituted to the **Tõnisson** family, had sold a large share to Norwegian investors, moved physically to Tallinn, and become *the* national quality newspaper, with a circulation of 61,000 copies per issue in 2002. Its circulation was exceeded only by *SL Õhtuleht*, an evening tabloid, at 66,000 copies. Its only remaining competitor, *Eesti Päevaleht*, sold 35,000 copies and *Äripäev*, the Estonian business daily version of the Swedish Bonniers publishing stable, sold 31,000 copies daily. Two provincial dailies, *Pärnu Postimees* with 15,000 copies and *Sakala* with 10,800 copies, were the only other papers with circulations over 8,000. Their closest competitors were the weekly *Eesti Ekspress*, with 45,600, and *Maaleht* (the national farmers' weekly) with 42,600 copies per issue. Among Russian-language papers, the dailies *Molodezh Estonii* and *Estonija* reached circulations of 8,000 and 6,500, respectively, and the Russian weeklies *Den za Dnem* and *Molodezh Estonii Subota* sold 12,900 and 10,500 copies, respectively.

All of the main newspapers and many of the local ones have online editions, as do over 100 periodicals.

NONRECOGNITION OF SOVIET OCCUPATION. Of the 37 states that never recognized the occupation of Estonia, Latvia, and

Lithuania by the Soviet Union in June 1940, the United States' position was crucial. On 23 July 1940, Secretary of State Sumner Welles instituted the American policy of nonrecognition of the Soviet occupation by declaring that the United States would continue to recognize these three countries individually. The policy of nonrecognition was an extension of the Stimson Doctrine of 1932, under which the United States had refused to recognize the Japanese, German, and Italian occupations during the 1930s.

The nonrecognition policy, which Washington maintained through the 51 years of occupation, permitted the Estonian, Latvian, and Lithuanian de jure governments' diplomatic and consular representatives to continue their activities in the United States and to represent their governments to the U.S. government as fully accredited diplomatic representatives. The United States facilitated the continuation of these diplomatic activities by allowing drawings on blocked Baltic States' deposits at Fort Knox for use not only in the United States but also by the Baltic States' diplomatic representatives in all countries where they were recognized.

U.S. presidents and members of Congress periodically reiterated the American commitment to Baltic freedom in their addresses and declarations. President Dwight D. Eisenhower reaffirmed the right of the Baltic States to independence in his address to a joint session of Congress on 6 January 1957. After the signing of the Helsinki Final Act in July 1975, the House of Representatives passed a resolution declaring that the Final Act would not affect the continuity of U.S. recognition of the sovereign and independent Baltic States. On 26 July 1983, on the occasion of the 61st anniversary of the de jure recognition of the three Baltic countries by the United States in 1922, President Ronald Reagan reaffirmed the recognition of the independence of Estonia, Latvia, and Lithuania. Ambassador Jeane J. Kirkpatrick also read this declaration to the United Nations.

Throughout the 51 years of Soviet occupation, all American official publications and maps that in any way touched the Baltic States included a statement of U.S. nonrecognition of the Soviet occupation. This unwavering American support for Baltic independence provided not only enormous moral support to all Balts in their struggle for restoration of independence, but was also a constant reminder that did not allow less idealistic or more pragmatic nonrecognizing states to let lapse their polices of nonrecognition. It also acted as a constant reminder to the Soviet hierarchy of the illegality of their control over the Baltic States.

NOOR EESTI. *See* YOUNG ESTONIA.

NORTH ATLANTIC TREATY ORGANIZATION (NATO). Membership in NATO has been seen by Estonians as *the only real* guarantee for the long-run security, defense, and continued independence of Estonia from the beginning of the restoration of independence in 1992. This view was not unique to Estonians, but was shared by all former East European satellites and by Latvia and Lithuania. Thus, all began lobbying to join soon after the unification of Germany in 1992. By 1997, the pressure exerted by Polish, Hungarian, Czech, as well as German lobbies had convinced the United States to offer them membership in 1997, effective in 1999. However, European and American sensitivity to Russian antagonism of membership of former Warsaw Pact members joining NATO meant that troops from Western NATO counties will not be permanently stationed in these new member states.

Instead of membership, the United States offered the Baltic States a political Charter of Partnership in January 1998, which declared American support of Baltic aspirations to become integrated with European and transatlantic institutions such as the **European Union**, Organization of Security and Cooperation in Europe (OSCE), the World Trade Organization, and NATO. It reiterated the general statement of the NATO Madrid Summit of 1997 and reaffirmed U.S. policy that NATO's partners can become members "as each aspirant proves itself able and willing to assume the responsibilities and obligations of membership, and as NATO determines that the inclusion of these nations would serve European stability and the strategic interests of the Alliance."

Subsequently, Estonia sharply stepped up its lobbying by joining with the other membership hopefuls (Albania, Bulgaria, Latvia, Lithuania, Macedonia, Romania, Slovakia, and Slovenia) in joint declarations, by receiving strong support for membership from the Nordic countries (especially neutral Finland and Sweden), and by radically increasing the defense budget from under 1 percent of GDP in 1999 to 2 percent in 2002. In its Annual National Program for 2000, Estonia outlined a drastic and rapid upgrading of its armed forces to a wartime size of 25,000–30,000 troops and developing a high level of NATO interoperability by 2005.

Three factors inhibited Estonia's and the other two Baltic States' membership ambitions throughout the 1990s. First, all lacked armed forces, since they had been integral parts of the Soviet Union; second, the former Soviet (now Russian) forces did not evacuate their manpower and installations until 1994, unwillingly and after long negotiations; and third, various Russian high officials and the Duma continued their vocal opposition to Baltic NATO membership, which they considered "provocative." The Russian opposition was mainly a reflection of the loss of status and a realization that Moscow had been relegated to a position of inferiority. This opposition continued to play a significant role in some European NATO members' reluctance to support rapid Baltic membership. In the summer of 2000, for example, the German deputy minister of defense went so far as to publicly state that the Baltic States' membership depended on Russian approval. Although he was forced to recant after strong negative reaction by the Balts' Western supporters, it was clear that some Europeans states considered Russian sensitivity more important than Baltic fears for their security.

The controversy also highlighted the Balts' argument that only when they are actually members within the NATO collective security alliance would they find security from any possible future Russian designs on them. Membership would also insulate them from both the Russians' hectoring and the Western allies' political sensitivities to Russia. Moreover, only membership in NATO will erase the bitter memory of 1940 when internal hope of the Western allies' support proved to be ephemeral self-delusion. Hence, Estonian leaders continued to lobby for support, in European capitals, but especially in Washington, together with Latvia, Lithuania, and increasingly all the other applicants. Although the election of George W. Bush as president in 2000 raised the Balts' hopes of an invitation at the Prague NATO meeting in fall 2002, it was the serendipitous aftermath of the tragedy of September 11, 2001, that brought about the certainty of an invitation for membership. Three specific developments were the quick and unreserved support for the United States in the fight against terrorism by the Balts, the equally rapid and astute reaction by President Vladimir Putin in placing Russia firmly in the American-led antiterrorist camp, and the consequent reward of the creation of the 21-member Russia-NATO Council (replacing the five-year-old Russia-NATO Permanent Joint Committee of NATO plus Russia) on 1 June 2002. Within the month, Putin made it clear that Russia no longer objected to the inclusion of the Baltic States in NATO.

Given the new level of cooperation between NATO and Russia, enhanced by making Russia a full member of the Group of Eight announced at the Kananaskis Summit in Canada on 28–29 June 2002, and the provision of $20 billion to safeguard and destroy Russia's decrepit nuclear stocks, NATO can no longer be regarded as a Cold War military bulwark against Russia/Soviet Union. But whatever its future role, membership in it will help to normalize relations with Russia, just as in the case of Poland, and as it already has—in June 2002, Russia also moved on the border issue and made promising noises on removing the double duties that it had imposed on Estonian imports. As expected, the NATO annual meeting at Prague on 21–22 November decided to extend an invitation for membership to Estonia, Latvia, and Lithuania effective 2004. For Estonians, the long road to full membership in NATO thus entered its final stretch in achieving military security *and* a formal acknowledgement by the Great Powers of its irrevocable right to independent statehood. *See also* BALTIC BATTALION; BALTIC DEFENCE COLLEGE; BALTIC DEFENSE COOPERATION; GEOSTRATEGIC POSITION AND DEFENSE STRATEGY.

NORTHEAST ESTONIA (Kirde Eesti). The northeastern part of Estonia, comprising the County of Ida-Virumaa (East Virumaa), includes the city of **Narva** and the towns of **Sillamäe** and Kohtla-Järve, and is the center of Estonia's **oil shale** mining and the industries based on it—the electrical power stations near Narva and the oil shale processing chemical plants at Kiviõli and Kohtla-Järve. The region became progressively synonymous with **Russification** in Estonian minds after the Soviet reoccupation in 1945 as Moscow intensified the exploitation of the oil-bearing shale deposits and imported increasing numbers of unskilled and semiskilled Russian-speaking labor to man these industries. In the 1970s, Estonians' awareness of the **environmental** damage caused in the ecologically sensitive region, which contains Estonia's prime aquifer, by insensitive far-off Moscow ministries that controlled the exploitation, led to resistance to industrial expansion in the area. In the 1980s, the threat of massive phosphate mining led to public protests, which mobilized Estonians to the drive for independence.

The ecological damage of Soviet exploitation is being repaired slowly over the next decades as the mining industry is restructured on international lines of profitability and environmental sustainability. The legacy of the imported Russian-speaking population is a more difficult and politically sensitive problem—internally and internationally. Whereas in 1939 the Russian-speaking population of the whole of Estonia numbered 80,000, in 2000 it numbers around half a million or 33 percent, down about 100,000 from its height in 1989 when it formed 39 percent of the total population. Almost half of this population is found in the four urban areas of Ida Virumaa, with most of the rest in **Tallinn**. They also form 80 percent of the population of the county. These towns are totally Russian speaking. Ethnic Estonians, who live in the countryside, form only 3 percent of the urban population in Northeast Estonia. At the time of the collapse of the Soviet Union and the restoration of independence, these Russians overwhelmingly opposed it and for a time even proposed secession from Estonia.

During the second half of the 1990s, economic growth fostered by foreign investment in Narva, emigration of rabid Russophiles, and accommodative polices of the national government, culminating in the 2000 **Integration** project, have reduced the tensions in the region and are rapidly moving Russian speakers to teach their children Estonian. The stark contrast between orderly and prosperous Estonia and the chaotic economy and political atmosphere across the border in Russia is also building loyalty to the Estonian state among Russian speakers. Moreover, the Estonians are also becoming accommodative. No longer does a reference to Kirde Eesti call forth outbursts of anti-Russian sentiments among average Estonians in the rest of the country, as was the case in the early 1990s. *See also* INDUSTRIALIZATION; RUSSIANS IN ESTONIA.

NUCLEAR WASTE. *See* PALDISKI *and* SILLAMÄE.

– O –

Note to Reader: In Estonian alphabetization, the letter Ö follows the letter W, and Ö entries in this dictionary are listed according to this convention.

OIL SHALE EXPLOITATION. Although "burning rock" was reported in northern Estonia as long ago as 1725, and the first scientific paper on it was published in 1791 by academician J. Georgi of St. Petersburg, it was not until the coal shortage of 1916 during World War I that oil shale was exploited as emergency fuel for heating plants, locomotives, and cement and lime furnaces in the imperial capital of St. Petersburg. In 1918, 17,000 tons were mined for this purpose. The new government of independent Estonia decided to establish a shale oil industry and formed the State Oil Shale Industry to operate mines, an oil extracting plant, and a downstream chemical plant in parallel with other private firms owned by Estonian, German, English, and Swedish capital. By 1939, Estonia was energy self-sufficient and even exported oil products and gasoline, which formed fully 8 percent of Estonia's exports.

After World War II, the industry added gas to its product line, but this was replaced by natural gas in the 1970s as the Russian gas net was extended to Estonia. From the 1950s, however, owing to Stalin's electrification drive, oil shale was mainly used for underfiring the electrical power plants, with a small share used as feedstock for the Kohtla-Järve and Kiviõli chemical plants and for firing the aggregate in the Kunda cement plant. In 1974, mining output was increased when the new 1,400-megawatt Baltic Thermal Power Station was brought on stream. Mining oil shale for underfiring was increased yet again in 1973 when a second large plant, the Estonian Thermal Power Station with a 1,600-megawatt capacity, began operations. Less than half the output of these generating plants was used by Estonia; the rest was intended for Leningrad and Latvia. Thus, when the Sosnovoi Bor Nuclear Power Station began operations in the Leningrad Oblast in 1981, demand for oil shale in Estonia dropped and mining decreased from just over 30 million tons in 1980 to 21 million tons in 1990. With the subsequent collapse of the Union of Soviet Socialist Republics (USSR) and its power-hungry industries, the demand for oil shale declined to just 12 million tons in 1995.

The share of oil shale in the production of electricity in Estonia was around 90 percent in 2000. Of the oil shale mined, 74 percent was used for electrical underfiring, 10 percent was for underfiring district heating and hot water systems, 13 percent was converted into oil, and 1 percent was used for chemical feedstock. Future projections indicate little change apart from some fluctuations in the demand for electricity.

The latter may increase, however, if Eesti Energia (the owner of the two old generating stations now combined and renamed Narva Electric Plants) is successfully modernized. After several years of negotiations in 2000, it looked like Eesti Energia, with the American energy firm NRG as its 49 percent partner, would have sufficient international investment to modernize the old, inefficient plants into environmentally friendly ones meeting the emission standards agreed to with Finland and subsequently with the **European Union** as part of the **Acquis Communitaire**. However, widespread partisan and public opposition, and a demand for state guarantees by NRG bank lenders (specifically forbidden by legislation), led to Estonia annulling the sale in 2002. It is expected that the state firm will be able to modernize its boilers with EU funding assistance and Estonian private funding. Increased production would then mainly depend on sales to the Baltic electricity net (mainly to Latvia), as well as to the St. Petersburg industrial area. A transmission cable under the Gulf of Finland is being planned to link Estonia to the Nordic electricity net, both as a balance to the Russian net, and for commercial reasons since Finnish consumption is increasing at a rate that has already led to Finland's decision to eventually build a fifth nuclear power station.

Since the restoration of independence, the oil shale utilization has been rationalized to serve Estonian national interests, including the preservation of the **environment**, as well as meeting national energy needs and developing industry. At the beginning of the 21st century, Estonia has three oil shale–utilizing firms: the partially privatized Eesti Energia electric power company, the private Viru Chemical Group shale oil cracking plant and its chemical downstream plants (low-viscosity oils, oil pitch, phenols), and the private Kunda-Nordic Cement cement-producing company. *See also* OIL SHALE RESOURCES.

OIL SHALE RESOURCES. Two types of oil shale are found in Estonia: the Middle Ordovician Kukersite and Lower Ordovician Dictyonema shale. The Kukersite deposits, which extend into Russia west of St. Petersburg, are the only deposits so far mined. The Dictyonema shale deposits are much larger and cover an area of around 11,000 square kilometers in the northern and northwestern parts of Estonia in seams varying in thickness from one to eight meters at a depth of 10–90 meters. However, the energy content of this shale is very low and thus uneconomic at current world energy prices.

The Kukersite shale is the principal mineral resource of Estonia and is found in two main deposits. The Estonia deposit is located in the northeast close to the Gulf of Finland and stretches in a triangle from west of Rakvere to the Russian border at **Narva** and south to Lake Peipus. The productive seam varies in thickness from about three meters in the northern part of the deposit to between 1.4 and 2.0 meters in the southern and western parts at depths ranging from close to the surface to deeper than 70 meters. Most of the unexploited reserves are found at depths below 40 meters, which makes opencast mining uneconomical, and requires underground mines at added costs of exploitation. In 2000, three opencast and six underground mines were in operation.

The Tapa Kukersite deposit, located southwest of the Estonia deposit, has a maximum seam thickness of 2.0–2.3 meters at depths ranging from 60 to 170 meters below the surface. This deposit is not being mined at this time. The Estonia and Tapa deposits cover an area of about 5,000 square kilometers.

Extensive analyses of the oil shale deposits conducted since the restoration of independence have established economically mineable resources at 10 billion tons, with a minimum energy content of 1450 kilocalories/kilograms of shale and a minimum seam thickness of 0.5 meters under an overburden of 10 meters, or thickness of 1.4 meters under an overburden of over 10 meters. At foreseeable rates of mining, mostly for underfiring the Narva electric power stations at full capacity, these reserves are expected to last for 30 years. At present, Dictyonema shale deposits are not carried on the books as part of the mineral or energy resource balance of Estonia.

OJULAND, KRISTIINA (1966–). Estonian diplomat and politician. Born on 17 December 1966, in Kohtla-Järve, Ojuland graduated from the Faculty of Law at the **University of Tartu** in 1990 and immediately joined the newly organized Ministry of Justice, where she drafted legislation while simultaneously attending the Estonian School of Diplomacy, which the then Foreign Minister **Lennart Meri** had established in 1990. On completing it, she joined the Political Department of the Ministry of Foreign Affairs and represented Estonia at the Council of Europe. From 1994 to 1996, Ojuland served as managing director of the Estonian Broadcasting Association and entered **Riigikogu**, since she had been elected in the 1992 **Riigikogu elections** as an alternate member on the Pro Patria Party list. In 1995, she was elected to Parliament on the Reform Party ticket and was also elected to the Tallinn City Council in 1996, then reelected in 2000 (until 2003, it was possible to serve in the Riigikogu and simultaneously as an elected municipal councilor). From 1997 to 2001, Ojuland was also director of the Euro-Integration program at the private Concordia International University in Tallinn. From 1999 to 2002, she represented the Estonian Parliament at the Parliamentary Assembly of the Council of Europe, and was elected president of the Liberal, Democratic and Reformers Parties Group, while also serving as vice president of the Parliamentary Assembly of the Council of Europe from 1996 to 2002. Ojuland was thus not only seasoned in parliamentary and municipal politics but was also very well versed in European affairs when Prime Minister **Siim Kallas** chose her as Estonia's first female foreign minister in January 2002. After a successful year, during which Estonia was invited to join both the **European Union** (EU) and the **North Atlantic Treaty Organization** (NATO), when she again won election to the Riigikogu in March 2003, Ojuland was reappointed to her portfolio by Prime Minister **Juhan Parts** in his new coalition cabinet.

At the end of 2002, she was listed as one of the 100 under-40 Global Leaders for Tomorrow 2003 nominated by the World Economic Forum/Davos and published by *Newsweek.*

OLD BELIEVERS. *See* RELIGION.

OLD LIVONIA. *See* LIVONIA.

OMON (Otriad Militsii Osobennogo Naznechenii). The Special Task Militia Unit of the Ministry of the Interior of the Union of Soviet

Socialist Republics (USSR) is referred to by the acronym OMON in Russian as well as English and is also known as the Black Berets. On Sunday, 20 January 1991, a detachment of OMON attacked the Latvian Ministry of Internal Affairs building in Riga, which had been under the control of pro-independence forces since the election in 1990, and killed five people, including a student and two filmmakers. This attack took place a week after Soviet army tanks attacked the Vilnius **television and radio** tower early in the morning of Sunday, 13 January 1991 (subsequently known as Bloody Sunday), claiming that they were being fired on by Lithuanians who had occupied the tower and were broadcasting anti-Soviet messages. Fourteen people (13 Lithuanian civilians and one Russian soldier) were killed and more than 140 were injured. News films of the assault, broadcast throughout the world, contradicted Soviet media claims that the army was reacting to shots from the television tower. As a result, barricades were built around the Lithuanian, Latvian, and Estonian parliament buildings, and were not dismantled until the following year after independence had been achieved and the USSR had collapsed totally. OMON operated in Lithuania until the **abortive Moscow coup of 1991** and led to a number of Lithuanian deaths. Of the three Baltic States, only Estonia escaped any attacks by Soviet military forces and did not suffer any deaths in the struggle for independence.

OPIK, ERNEST JULIUS. *See* ÖPIK *preceding* YOUNG ESTONIA.

ORDERS OF MERIT OF THE REPUBLIC OF ESTONIA. The Republic of Estonia has established six Orders of Merit, five during its first period of independence and one since the restoration of independence:

The Cross of Liberty was instituted in 1919 to recognize services in the Estonian **War of Independence**; it has not been awarded since 1925. The Cross of Liberty is a military award for extraordinary military service in the event of war in defense of the freedom of Estonia.

The Order of the National Coat of Arms was instituted in 1936 in commemoration of the Proclamation of Independence on 24 February 1918. It is the highest decoration for services rendered to the state and is awarded in six classes, normally to public servants and politicians.

The Order of the White Star was instituted in 1936 to commemorate the Estonian nation's struggle for freedom and is awarded to Estonians in recognition of public service, and to foreigners for services to the Estonian State. The order comprises seven classes.

The Order of the Cross of the Eagle was instituted by the **Defense League** in 1928 on the 10th anniversary of Estonian independence. It is awarded in recognition of military service in national defense in eight classes, normally to serving military personnel.

The Order of the Estonian Red Cross was instituted by the Estonian Red Cross Society in 1920 and is awarded in recognition of humanitarian services to the Estonian nation and for saving lives. The order comprises six classes.

The Order of the Cross of St. Mary's Land was established in 1995 and is awarded to foreigners, such as heads of state, prime ministers and ambassadors, who have rendered special services to the Republic of Estonia. The order consists of six classes. St. Mary's Land (Maarjamaa) has been the poetic synonym for Estonia since 1215.

The Orders are awarded by the president of the Republic on the recommendations of an advisory Committee on Decorations.

ORGANIZATION OF SECURITY AND COOPERATION IN EUROPE'S (OSCE) HIGH COMMISSIONER ON NATIONAL MINORITIES. In 1992, the Conference on Security and Cooperation in Europe (institutionalized as the Organization for Security and Cooperation in Europe on 1 January 1995) established the post of high commissioner on national minorities to identify and seek early resolution of ethnic tensions that might endanger peace, stability, and friendly relations among the states members of the OSCE. The high commissioner was to be "an instrument of conflict prevention at the earliest possible stage." Operating independently, he conducts onsite missions and engages in preventive low-visibility diplomacy at the earliest stages of tension, seeking to promote dialogue and build confidence and cooperation between parties at risk of conflict.

On 15 December 1992, Max van der Stoel was appointed high

commissioner; his term was extended three times until Rolf Ekéus took over on 1 July 2001. Van der Stoel was a former member of the Dutch Parliament and the Consultative Assembly of the Council of Europe, foreign minister of the Netherlands (1973–77 and 1981–82), and Dutch ambassador to the United Nations (1983–86). He also served as special rapporteur of the United Nations Commission on Human Rights from 1991 to 1999.

Van der Stoel's low-key engagement in influencing Estonia's governments and parliaments from 1993 to 2000 was the crucial catalyst in Estonia's slow but progressive acceptance of the need to accommodate the civil rights needs of the non-Estonian ethnic alien population brought into Estonia during the Soviet period (*see* ALIEN PASSPORTS; ALIENS; RUSSIANS IN ESTONIA; RUSSIFICATION). Although various forces in Moscow (including the government, Duma, and several political parties) repeatedly charged Estonia with persecution and discrimination against the non-Estonian population, van der Stoel never found any basis for these accusations. Nor did he find any incidents of interethnic violence. From the beginning, he received assurances from the Estonian government that it intended to respect fully its OSCE commitments, including to the minorities. Moreover, all the different Estonian governments worked with van der Stoel to make certain that Estonia would meet all international criteria respecting **human rights**, citizenship, and **language** matters (*see* INTEGRATION).

In order to fulfill his mandate to prevent future conflicts and to assist Estonia to meet its obligations, the commissioner proposed a list of recommendations in 1993. These included the rapid reduction of stateless persons permanently residing in Estonia by granting citizenship to children of stateless persons born in Estonia and the equitable application of Estonian-language requirements for naturalization. Most important, any discrimination on the grounds of nationality or ethnicity should be avoided. The use of the **Estonian language** in private business and organizational affairs should not be made mandatory. Efforts to teach Estonian to non-Estonians should be enhanced and the media, especially television, should be used to inform them of the legislation and practical questions relating to naturalization and language matters. For too long, many Estonians (including many politicians) felt that these recommendations constituted an unwarranted intrusion into Estonia's internal affairs and represented a misunderstanding of Estonians' legitimate objective of safeguarding their ethnicity and language within their own nation-state. Nevertheless, partly as a result of the patient low-key advice of Commissioner van der Stoel, the Estonian governments and parliaments implemented most variations of the recommendations quickly by 1996, the final ones on citizenship of stateless children in 1998, and a revised **Language Law** in 2000. To most Estonians, there seemed little reason to maintain an OSCE mission in Tallinn already in 1996. In fact, the mission encouraged Russians to cooperate with Estonians in **Northeast Estonia**, where the mass of Russians lives. In December 2001, the Council of the OSCE concluded that its mission in Estonia was completed and closed its office there.

The one recommendation made by van der Stoel that the Estonian government did not agree to was the establishment of a national commissioner on ethnic and language questions, Instead, President **Lennart Meri** in 1993 set up the President's Roundtable on Ethnic Minorities, which has functioned successfully as an informal contact point between the Estonian government and the Russian minority.

ORTHODOX CHURCH. *See* RELIGION.

OSTLAND. In 1941, Nazi Germany established the Reichskommissariat Ostland with headquarters in Riga to administer the conquered territories of Estonia, Latvia, Lithuania, Byelorussia, and eastern Poland. Each became a Generalbezirk (main district), named after the respective country, except for the last, which was named Generalbezirk Weissruthenien. Each was administered by a Generalkommissar (commissioner-general), the Estonian one by Karl Sigismund Litzmann. Since the colonial department in Berlin under Minister Alfred Rosenberg (born in **Tallinn** in 1893) looked on the Estonians favorably as Finno-Ugrians and thus as "Aryans," and since the Generalkommissars had great latitude amidst the chaotic Nazi German administrations (only the formal structures drawn on paper were well organized, but the actual operations were not), Litzmann authorized a Landeseigene Verwaltung, or local national administration, to assist him.

The Estonian Omavalitsus, as it was called in Estonian, was

headed by **Hjalmar Mäe**. However, it soon became evident to Estonians that this "national" civilian administration was merely an attempt by Litzmann to provide a sense of local autonomy and thereby to inveigle Estonian cooperation. Since all power was distributed among the competing German Reichskommisariat hierarchy, the security service (Sicherheitsdienst, SD), the German railroads administration, the Army, and the Schutzstaffel (SS), the Omavalitsus was left only the role to attempt to ameliorate the foreign colonizer's oppression as best it could. Disillusioned, Estonians found that Germany was no more interested in restoring Estonian statehood than the Soviets had been. In fact, the Germans did not denationalize anything and simply carried on with the structures that the retreating Soviets had left behind. It should also be noted that Estonia was burdened as well with a German military administration governing the Leningrad-Narva front, which required logistics support from the Generalbezirk Estland. The dual control lasted from the initial **German occupation** in July 1941 to the retreat of the German armies in September 1944.

– P –

PAINTING. The earliest paintings in Estonia date from the 13th century and consist of religious panels and frescoes in the Valjala, Karja, Muhu, Kaarma, and Ridala churches. The Renaissance period began in Estonia in the 16th century with Michel Sittow (1469–1525) as the most important painter of allegorical and moralizing scenes and altar compositions as well as some portraits. The latter became popular in the Baroque period in the 17th century in addition to the usual Biblical themes and figural compositions. The Baroque period also saw the use of ceiling murals and ornamentally painted beams. Although the earlier artists were mostly homegrown Baltic Germans, most of the artists in the 18th and 19th centuries were of German extraction. In the latter century, the period of classicism in Estonia, Dutch painters were also attracted to Estonia. Landscapes, including of Estonia, and sources drawn from ethnography, antiquity, and more recent history as well as still life studies became popular additions to portraiture at this time. Techniques of painting became more varied as watercolors, glass painting, and silhouette cutouts were added to fresco and oil painting. A rich variety of views of **Tallinn**, especially panoramas, date from this period.

It was only in the second half of the 19th century that the first native Estonian artists came on the scene, but they lived and worked mostly abroad, where they had also studied. The best known are **Johan Köler**, Karl Ludwig Maibach (1833–1889), Paul Raud (1865–1943) and his brother **Kristjan Raud**, **Andres Laikmaa**, Tõnis Grenzstein (1863–1916), and Alfred Hirv (1880–1918). With democratization, industrialization, urbanization, and the growth of wealth during the early decades of the 20th century, artists' societies were formed, art exhibits were organized, and art institutions were founded in Tallinn and **Tartu**. The four decades up to 1940 were marked by flux, as genres and styles changed with great rapidity: expressionism, cubism, impressionism, fauvism, and so on, formed and reformed and melded one into the other. During the foreign occupations of World War II, many artists fled to the West, including **Eduard Wiiralt**, Estonia's most famous graphic artist of the 20th century.

During the ensuing half century of Soviet occupation, Estonian artists found that by using the socialist realism approach they could relatively freely develop nationalist-cultural themes in their paintings. Artistic expression in the occupation began with thematic motifs of war and reconstruction, but moved rapidly toward relative freedom in the Khrushchev thaw of 1958–64 as styles, techniques, and subjects became varied. By the 1980s, indigenous Estonian painting was following the international color and form movement and had added a satiric allegorical approach to life in the Soviet world. The notable painters during the Soviet period were Richard Sangrits (b. 1910), Evald Okas (b. 1915), Lüüdia Vallimäe-Mark (b. 1925), Aili Vint (b. 1941), Jüri Arrak (b. 1936), Tiit Pääsuke (b. 1941), and Enn Põldroos (b. 1933). Most of these painters were also active in the first decade after the restoration of Independence in the 1990s, but the enthusiasm with which the public followed their earlier work disappeared, with a resultant quiescence in Estonian painting, not least because of competing attractions, easy access to foreign art, and the loss of the need for artistic release of the frustrations of grayness of life under socialism.

PALDISKI. Located on the Pakri peninsula 47 kilometers west of **Tallinn**, Paldiski was a closed military town during the Soviet occupation. The peninsula contained the Paldiski Soviet Naval base with two nuclear reactors (commissioned in 1968 and 1982) and formed the main training base for the Soviet Baltic Fleet's nuclear submarine crews. After the restoration of independence, lengthy negotiations with the Russian state led to eventual withdrawal of Russian forces, and an international effort with Swedish, Finnish, and American financial and physical assistance, as well as Russian personnel, to remove and decontaminate the nuclear sites. By 30 September 1995, the work was completed and the base was demilitarized.

Paldiski contains two ice-free deep-water harbors and is connected to Tallinn and **Narva** with a railroad bed capable of carrying heavy cargo traffic. Hence, there are plans to develop it as a major port. By 2000, some passenger ferry services to Sweden and Germany and regular cargo shipping used the renewed port.

PALUSALU, KRISTJAN (until 1935, Kristjan Trossmann) (1908–1987). Estonian wrestler and national hero. A physically strong boy born on 10 March 1908 on a farm in Salulepi *vald*, Palusalu discovered classical wrestling only in 1930, during the last few months of his military service when he was already 22. Nevertheless, he began to win national matches in the heavyweight class by the following year. In 1933, he came in fourth at the European Master's tournament in Helsinki, but in 1936, when his mastery of technique had caught up to his strength, he won gold medals in both free and classical wrestling at the Berlin Olympics. The fact that Palusalu beat the German favorite with Hitler in attendance (who left his seat without a word) was sweet revenge to Estonian national pride for the centuries of **Baltic German** domination and provided a vicarious sense of national accomplishment. The gift of a 45-hectare farm, the Estonian government's recognition of his accomplishment, perfectly reflected the popular respect—for physical strength and farming—of a society with peasant roots. Although Palusalu won the European Master's title in Greco-Roman wrestling in 1937 in addition to a total of 12 Estonian titles, his Olympic achievement has always remained his crowning glory in the Estonian national consciousness. In 1941, he was mobilized by the Red Army, but deserted across the battle front to the Finnish side in the same year, returned to Estonia after the retreat of the Soviets, and was imprisoned for a short time after the Soviet reoccupation. Because of this, and his position as a national hero, he was never again allowed to participate officially in the sport. He ended his career as a volunteer trainer while working as a construction worker. A year after his death on 17 July 1987 in **Tallinn**, the annual Palusalu International Wrestling Competitions were instituted to commemorate his achievements.

PAREK, LAGLE (1940–). Estonian freedom fighter and politician. Born on 17 April 1941 in **Pärnu**, Parek was deported with her family to Siberia in 1949, returned to Estonia in 1954, and completed the **Tallinn** Construction Technical School in 1960. Subsequently she worked at various rural construction projects as well as for the State Heritage Monuments Planning Institute, and was jailed in 1983–87 for her anti-Soviet activities. After her release, she worked actively for Estonian independence as a founding member of the **Moltov-Ribbentropi Pakti Avalikustamise Eesti Grupp** (MRP-AEG) (The Estonian Group for Making the **Molotov-Ribbentrop Pact** Public), and as an organizer of the commemoration of the date of the MRP in Hirvepark in 1987, the first of the major events of the Singing Revolution. In the same year, she cofounded the Eesti Rahvusliku Sõltumatuse Partei (ERSP, the Estonian National Independence Party), and became its chair in 1988–93. Parek served as a member of the **Estonian Committee** in 1990–92, was the candidate of the ERSP in the presidential election of 1992, and served as minister of the interior in the **Mart Laar**'s first cabinet in 1992–94. Since 1997, she has worked for a nonprofit organization.

PARLIAMENT. *See* RIIGIKOGU.

PARLIAMENTARY ELECTIONS. *See* RIIGIKOGU ELECTIONS.

PARNU. *See* PÄRNU.

PART, ARVO, *See* PÄRT.

PARTS, JUHAN (1966–). Lawyer, politician, and prime minister. Parts was born on 27 August 1966 in Tallinn, graduated as lawyer from the **University of Tartu** in 1991, and immediately entered the newly reestablished Ministry of Justice's department of economic law. A year later he was appointed assistant secretary general responsible for legislative drafting until 1995, when he became the head of the Ministry as its secretary general. In 1998, the **Riigikogu** appointed him to the position of auditor general. In both functions he participated in the restructuring of the court system and the reintroduction of private law in Estonia. On 24 August 2002, Parts was elected leader of Res Publica, a party founded the previous year at the initiative of **Rein Taagepera** to counter the apparent self-servingness of the existing political parties. The party received broad public support at the municipal elections in October 2002 and achieved 28 seats in the Riigikogu in the elections of 2 March 2003, which enabled Parts to become prime minister at the age of 36 and form a broad-based tripartite coalition government with the Reform and Coalition parties. At 36 Parts became the youngest prime minister in Europe; in Estonian history, only **Mart Laar**, at 32, was younger when he became prime minister in 1993.

PATS, KONSTANTIN. *See* PÄTS, KONSTANTIN.

PEACE OF TARTU (Tartu Rahu). Although the **War of Independence** with Soviet Russia was won by the Estonian side already in August 1919 and peace negotiations began that September on the initiative of Vladimir Ilyich Lenin, the Entente powers forced Estonia to suspend the negotiations during the unsuccessful Russian Whites' offensive led by General Nikolai Judenich in October. The peace negotiations, led on the Estonian side by veteran diplomat **Jaan Poska**, were not resumed until 5 December. Even then, the Soviet side mounted several unsuccessful attacks on the **Narva** front in an attempt to influence the negotiations. An armistice was agreed on 3 January 1920, and the peace treaty was signed on 2 February in **Tartu**. In the treaty, Soviet Russia recognized Estonia as a sovereign state and renounced all claims to Estonian territory in perpetuity. The Soviets also agreed to pay 15 million gold rubles (weighing 11.6 metric tons) in partial compensation for factories evacuated during the war, confiscated funds, and so on; authorized Estonia to build a railroad to Moscow; and provided Estonia with preferred access to cutting 10,000 square kilometers of forests in Russia. The land border was fixed at the armistice line—an even 10 kilometers east of Narva in the north and on the eastern border of Setumaa (County of **Setu**) in the southeast (renamed **Petserimaa**), areas that had been historically part of Russia, but had been settled partly by Estonians. The Peace Treaty, the first signed by Soviet Russia largely due to the negotiating skills of Poska, was followed by similar peace treaties with Lithuania in July, Latvia in August, and Finland in October. The Peace of Tartu quickly led to international recognition of Estonia as a sovereign state and to membership in the League of Nations on 21 September 1921.

After the restoration of independence in 1991, the Soviet Union and, in 1992, Russia, its successor state, refused to recognize the Peace of Tartu. Under the dubious international legal doctrine of *rebus sic stantibus*, it claimed that the treaty had lapsed since it was concluded with Soviet Russia, which had ceased to exist when the Union of Soviet Socialist Republics (USSR) was formed, as had the prewar Republic of Estonia when it became part of the USSR in 1940. Consequently, the Russians argued, the current Republic was a successor state to the USSR, created only in 1991 and thus obliged to accept the borders that the latter had legislated.

Estonia resisted the Russian arguments for several years, partly to buttress its claim that it was *not* a successor state to the USSR but had been illegally militarily occupied, but mainly to regain the territories lost east of the Narva River, including Setu County, which had been transferred back to Russia during the Nikita Khrushchev era. After Russia unilaterally began marking the border in 1994, and Estonia discovered that Western states were not interested in supporting its border claims, Estonian negotiators gradually gave up insisting on the legality of the Tartu peace treaty. Agreement was reached on a new border draft treaty in 1996. However, although Estonia quickly ratified it, Russia had not ratified it even after Estonia's pro-EU referendum decision on 14 September 2003, apparently because it had hoped to delay Estonia's entry into the **European Union** (EU) and the **North Atlantic Treaty Organization** (NATO), both of which had insisted on Estonia settling its border with Russia. Inexplicably, Russian recalcitrance to ratify continued after Estonia was invited to join both NATO and the EU in late 2002. This recalcitrance continued even after Estonia's membership had been confirmed by both organizations and the Russian foreign minister had congratulated Estonia on its acceptance by NATO and on Estonia's decisive pro-EU referendum result!

PEIPSI JÄRV. *See* LAKE PEIPUS.

PEOPLE'S FRONT. *See* RAHVARINNE.

PERESTROIKA AND GLASNOST. The long 18-year reign of Leonid Brezhnev as general secretary of the Communist Party of the Soviet Union (CPSU) was marked during the late 1970s and early 1980s by a gradual slide in living standards, the rapid spread of corruption and cronyism within the Soviet bureaucracy, and generally dispiritedness of life. This was the result of the policy of building a formidable military-industrial structure with large armed forces and massive armaments at the expense of consumer goods. Advancing senility in the mediocre and cronyist Politburo exacerbated the malaise. When Brezhnev died in office just before his 76th birthday, his successor, Yuri Andropov, who was 68 and had been head of the KGB for 15 years, was probably the only senior Party official who realized the seriousness of the decline of the socioeconomic fabric of the Soviet Union. He might have staved off the collapse of the system for some time if he had lived, although his initial prescription of reinstilling the ethic of discipline and hard work by reducing the role of alcohol was clearly misdirected and insufficient. In any event, he died only 15 months into his term, after spending the last six months ill and out of the public eye. He was replaced by Konstantin Chernenko, a 73-year-old crony of Brezhenev's on the Politburo, who immediately began reappointing the officials whom Andropov had replaced with younger and less corrupt ones. When Chernenko died a year later, in February 1985, the disillusion with the corruption of the CPSU hierarchy had irreparably weakened its legitimacy to control the creaking economic, social, and political system.

When Mikhail Gorbachev, at 54 the youngest general secretary since Joseph Stalin at age 43, took over the reins of power in 1985 he did not understand the deep crisis of the Soviet Union in all its facets. He thought that the system itself was sound and needed only restructuring to allow growth to accelerate. Accordingly, he launched the policy of "perestroika," or renewal, defined by the CPSU Plenum of January 1987, as

> the decisive defeat of the processes of stagnation . . . the final goal . . . a profound renewal of all aspects of the nation's life, imparting to socialism the most contemporary of social organizations, and the most complete disclosure [development] of the human character of our society in all its decisive aspects—economic, social-political, moral.

Unfortunately, perestroika remained an ephemeral declaratory policy without concrete direction, and became a hodgepodge of discrete attempts to get the economy moving, such as uncoordinated and clumsy attempts toward freeing the economy from the restraints of central control by dozens of ministries in Moscow and in the republics, mainly by allowing some degree for freedom of enterprise by permitting state firms to form new subsidiaries and by freeing some prices.

Gorbachev soon ran into the opposition of vested interests and devised the policy of "glasnost," or openness, to encourage the uncovering of corruption and stagnant thinking. Glasnost allowed the media freedom to expose corruption and point fingers at reactionary party leaders with impunity.

In Estonia, the speech by Gorbachev to the 27th Party Congress in 1986, which emphasized the role of the local soviets "to serve as one of the most effective means of mobilizing the masses for the effort to accelerate the country's social-economic development," served as the clarion call to autonomy. Hence, the Four-man Declaration on **Isemajanadav Eesti (IME)** in October 1987. After the failure of the EKP chief, Karl Vaino, to stop the **Estonian Communist Party** (ECP) hierarchy's massive move to take advantage of the freedoms promised by perestroika and glasnost to move toward autonomy and independence, Estonians began to devise policies and to implement them without recourse to Moscow. Estonians interpreted the two policies liberally, yet attempted to show in the years 1988 and 1989 that they were fully within the spirit of the confused declaratory policies. But by 1990, the Estonian press and leaders following the policy of glasnost had earned the trust of the masses and had totally destroyed any remaining legitimacy of Muscovite rule over Estonia.

PETER THE GREAT (1672–1725). Russian tsar. Born on 30 May 1672 in Moscow, Peter became tsar of Russia in 1682 jointly with his brother Ivan and became sole tsar in 1696 on the death of his brother. He died on 28 January 1728 in his new capital city of St. Petersburg. History regards Peter as the first great modernizer and Europeanizer of Russia. He brought the best European engineers, shipbuilders, architects, craftsmen, and merchants to Russia and sent hundreds of Russians to Western Europe to be educated and learn arts and crafts. Peter considered access to the Baltic Sea through Finland and the Baltic duchies the "Window to the West" as his primary move in modernizing Russia, and he built the new capital named eponymously St. Petersburg at the head of the Gulf of Finland. He began the **Great Northern War** with Sweden in 1700 and by 1721 had conquered the Baltic duchies and incorporated them as the Baltic Provinces (Gubernya) in his empire. Sweden ceded these territories and part of Karelia and Ingermanland in the Treaty of Nystad (German, Neustadt; Finnish, Uusikaupunki). In 1703, Peter began building his new capital in the conquered territory of Ingermanland and moved his government there in 1710.

Peter granted the **Baltic German** aristocracy greater autonomy of government over the new provinces than they had enjoyed under Swedish suzerainty; Swedish reforms were abrogated and all lands were returned to their original owners. These concessions became known as the **Special Baltic Order** and lasted in modified form until 1917. The old **Hanseatic** cities were also granted broad autonomy. These acts ensured the loyalty of the Baltic German nobility to the Russian empire for two centuries. The Kadriorg (German, Katarinenthal) Palace and the surrounding Kadriorg Park in **Tallinn** were designed by the Italian architect Niccolo Michetti and built under Peter's personal supervision as a summer house for his consort Katarina. Later, the Palace, since 1946 restored as an art museum, was used as the Province of Estland Governor's palace, and as the Estonian Presidential Palace from 1928 to 1940. Even before the interior had been completed, Peter died from a chill and was buried in the Cathedral of the St. Peter and St. Paul Fortress in St. Petersburg.

PETERSON, KRISTIAN JAAK (born Christian Jacob Petersohn) (1801–1822). Estonian writer. Born on 14 March 1801 in Riga to an

Estonian church verger, Peterson lived his entire short 21-year life in the Latvian city, where he also died on 4 August 1822, apart from 18 months (1819–20) studying at the **University in Tartu**. His writings inspired both **Friedrich Robert Faehlmann** and **Friedrich Reinhold Kreutzwald** to study Estonian ancient folk religion. Although he wrote poetry from an early age and published a number of articles in German about the **Estonian language**, he became a national cultural icon only in the 20th century, after 1901 when 21 of his extant Estonian-language and three of his German-language manuscripts were found in the archives of the **Estonian Learned Society**. He is credited as the first Estonian writer to have confidence in the Estonian language as a literary language, and not merely as a vernacular language of peasants. The curious facts that his mother was Latvian and that he lived in Latvia all his life add dramatic piquancy to his championing of the Estonian language.

PETERSOO, UDO (1934–). Estonian **Lutheran** clergyman and archbishop of the Estonian Lutheran Church in exile. Born on 8 May 1934 in **Tallinn**, Petersoo fled from Estonia to Sweden in 1944 and then emigrated to Canada with his parents in 1951. He graduated from Waterloo Lutheran University (renamed Wilfrid Laurier University in 1973), in Ontario, Canada, and from Waterloo Lutheran Seminary (also in Ontario, Canada) in 1974, and he was ordained in the Lutheran Church in 1975. Petersoo served as pastor of the Estonian St. Peter's Lutheran Congregation in Toronto, moved subsequently to St. Andrew's Estonian Congregation in Toronto, and was elected assessor and bishop of the Canadian diocese of the Estonian Evangelical Lutheran Church. In 1990, he was elected archbishop of the Church in exile. Petersoo has actively participated in most of the principal social activities of the Estonian community in Canada, and has served as chair of both the Estonian National Central Council in Canada and the Estonian National World Congress. Although the Lutheran Church in Estonia and the Church in exile have remained separate, Petersoo and the archbishop in Estonia have cooperated and extensively coordinated the work of the two churches, most recently through the development of a modern hymnal. *See also* ESTONIAN CANADIANS.

PETSERIMAA (also Petserimaakond). The County of Petseri was created by the **Peace of Tartu** in 1920, when Russia ceded the border Setumaa settled by an Estonian ethnic group, speaking the **Setu** dialect, most of which had been under Russian imperial rule since the Duchy of Pskov (Estonian, Pihkva) lost its independence to the tsars in the 16th century. The county was located at the extreme southeast corner of Estonia bordering on Russia and Latvia along the southwest shore of **Lake Peipus** (Peipsi Järv). As late as 1934, only 22 percent of Petserimaa's population was Setu, and 65 percent were ethnic Russians. Since that time, statistical data on the actual number of Setus has not been available. In 1945, seven of the 11 parishes of Petserimaa were allocated to the Pskov Oblast in the Russian Federated Soviet Socialist Republic, along with a small adjoining slice of Latvia; four parishes were incorporated into Võru County in the Estonian Soviet Socialist Republic (ESSR). After regaining independence in 1991, Estonia demanded the return of the lost territory along with territory also annexed to Russia east of the Narva River north of Lake Peipus according to the Peace of Tartu. Russia, however, refused to recognize the Peace of Tartu as still in force. Estonia eventually gave up the lost territory and agreed to recognize the existing border. Since Estonia recognizes as **citizens** all who were citizens prior to the Soviet occupation of 1941, not only Setus but also ethnic Russians living in the Russian part of the former Petseri county are able to claim Estonian citizenship. Special simplified border crossing arrangements have been negotiated between Russia and Estonia for such people living in both countries.

PHOSPHATE MINING. The mining and processing of phosphate rock into phosphate powder began in Estonia in 1922 and was subsequently upgraded to produce mixed superphosphate fertilizers. After World War II, the nationalized combined mining and chemical operation was expanded at Maardu, on the seashore 40 kilometers east of **Tallinn**. In 1965, the underground mine was replaced by an opencast mine. Since phosphate fertilizers are mainly useful for acid soils and since Estonian soils are heavily limed, very little of the product of the Maardu plant was used in Estonia. After the restoration of independence, the plant quickly declined and was closed after bankruptcy. Today there is a privately owned freeport named Kristiine Center on the site.

After the war, large deposits of phosphate rock covering over 200 square kilometers were discovered in **Northeast Estonia** at Rakvere, 100 kilometers east of Tallinn and halfway to **Narva**. Exploration and outlining of these during the 1970s and 1980s provided evidence that they were among the largest in the Soviet Union. However, there were two problems that needed to be solved before they could be exploited. The first was the overlay of intermixed Dichtyonema Argillite, which covers the northern third of Estonia from the island of Hiiumaa running east inland for 100 kilometers and then on an irregular northerly concave line to the head of **Lake Peipus** south of Narva. Dichtyonema shale veins are found in varying thickness at varying depths below the surface and contain a variety of organic and heavy metal minerals in a matrix that tends to self-ignite on contact with oxygen. To prevent pollution by burning toxic minerals, the dichtyonema shale must be isolated quickly and carefully buried in oxygen-deprived sites. Even so, mine tailings will inevitably contain some self-igniting Argillite, which will burn underground for years, as was the case with the much smaller Maardu mine and its dumps. The second problem to be solved was the prevention of pollution and depletion of the main Estonian aquifer of Pandivere, which underlies the main phosphate deposits, since the mines need to be pumped constantly to keep them dry.

Although technical solutions have been found to these problems, the local farming population in the prospective mining areas, environmentalists, intellectuals, and the nation's political leaders continue to refuse to accept the viability of the technical data. Their opposition in the 1980s was based on four arguments: first, given the existing experience of any massive Moscow-run mining and industrial operation (the proposal was for mining 18 million tons of ore a year), maximum air and ground pollution and depletion of the national aquifer would be inevitable and severely affect the ecology of over a quarter of the territory of Estonia; second, the phosphate mined and processed in Estonia would be exploited not in the interests of Estonia but for use in other parts of the Soviet Union, where most of it would be wastefully utilized as well; third, Northeast Estonia would become a wasteland of mines and dumps, unusable for agriculture; and finally, the necessary importation of 40,000 to 45,000 Russian-speaking unskilled labor needed for the mines and the processing plants would totally Russify the county of Virumaa, effectively removing Estonians from their historic northeastern settlement area. In addition, there was the argument that the ore was really not of sufficiently high quality for economic exploitation at existing world market prices.

An evaluation by staff of the Mining Department of Tallinn Technical University in 1997 concluded that world prices would have to increase at least to $250 from the current $80–100 a ton to make it economically exploitable—a rise unlikely to occur for a century. Indeed, the latter factor, combined with ecological pollution, has meant that independent Estonia is not carrying any phosphate deposits on its mineral resource balance. Important additional current realities are the international demands to limit emission of pollutants both into the Gulf of Finland and into the air, and the **European Union** directives controlling pollutants, which Estonia exceeded in 2000 in all sectors, even with the drastically reduced heavy industry and **oil shale** mining after the collapse of the Soviet economic structures. *See also* ENVIRONMENT.

PHOSPHATE WAR. Most Estonians regard the Phosphate War (Fosforiidisöda) during two fateful years from 25 February 1987 to 6 December 1988 as the catalyst that led to the destabilization of the Soviet Union and its rapid dissolution. The "war" was fought over opening new phosphate mines in **Northeast Estonia** and was the first sustained open popular expression of dissent in the Soviet Union ever. The public struggle against opening new phosphate mines succeeded because the intelligentsia and most of the **Estonian Communist Party** (ECP) leadership were against the further destruction of the fragile ecology of their Estonian homeland by the insensitive remote hand of Moscow. Moscow's Sovietizing drive of the past two decades had created a fear among Estonians that their very existence as a nation was at stake. Now the dangerous massive mining for a chemical of minimal utility threatened to turn a large part of their country into a moonscape as had been done by Moscow mining ministries in other parts of the Soviet Union with large mineral deposits. Moreover, in Estonia the new phosphate mines were to be opened in the one region, the Pandivere highlands, which contained the main aquifers of Estonia and from which the majority of its rivers rise.

Although the struggle against large-scale phosphate mining in Estonia had been carried on since the 1970s behind closed doors among chemists, mining engineers, and environmentalists, among them **Endel Lippmaa**, the public had been largely fed misinformation to keep them docile.

The decision to go ahead with mining the phosphate in Estonia was precipitated by the decline in the prison population of the gulags in the 1970s, which had been the mainstay of the mining of phosphate in the frozen Russian north. The required voluntary labor that gold and nickel mines in Siberia used was too expensive for the low-value mining of phosphate. Hence, the All-Union Ministry of Fertilizer Industries eagerly seized the opportunity provided by the Estonian deposits. Voluntary labor, even at low rates, would be easy to entice to Estonia, since it had a reputation of being "Western" and had a high standard of living.

The catalyst that mobilized the Estonian people to a massive protest was the statement by the deputy minister of the All-Union Ministry of Fertilizer Industries on a widely watched environmental **television** program that a decision had already been made to begin large-scale phosphate mining next year in northern Estonia, which contradicted the public position of the ECP leadership that the decision was to be made by the Estonians in the future and only after the ecological dangers had been adequately addressed. Clumsy attempts simultaneously to deny that the decision had already been made to which they had acquiesced and to justify it publicly showed the ineptness of the senior ECP leadership around **Karl Vaino**, and their lack of contact with the Estonian people. The seizing of the issue by the intelligentsia and **kolkhoz**, town, and regional party leaders as well as the press generated a popular resistance, supported by respected Estonian-minded party leaders, and awakened hopes in Estonians' hearts that they would finally be able to stop Moscow from destroying the land of their forefathers.

But the unintended consequence of the process of stopping the expansion of mining was even more important than the outcome, since it demonstrated the power of collective action against the hated foreign colonizer and showed that the Estonian people could act together in defense of their homeland. It also showed the inability of Moscow to act in the periphery of the empire in the age of **pere-**

stroika and glasnost. As the protest action continued through the summer, leadership of the republic slipped away from the ECP led by Karl Vaino to media-wise younger intellectuals and Estonian-minded party members, who used the openness and "democracy" of Mikhail Gorbachev's policy of perestroika and glasnost to pursue the self-determination promised by the "sovereignty" clause in each Soviet republic's constitution. Courage and universal support by the intelligentsia, including university and secondary school students, and by pro-Estonia and anti-Vaino senior party hierarchy led directly to the **Isemajanadav Eesti** (IME) action, followed by the "hot summer" of the **Singing Revolution** in 1988, and the creation of **Rahvarinne** in 1989. *See also* PHOSPHATE MINING.

PIKK HERMANN. Toompea castle, on the site of the ancient Estonian settlement of Lindanisa in **Tallinn**, was originally built by the Schwertbrüder **Crusading Order** in 1227–29. In 1360–79, the southern wall was built up to 9.5 meters (28 feet) and a tower was added on the southeastern corner; in beginning of the 16th century, it was extended to its current height of 50 meters and other towers of 40–50 meters were also built in corners of the castle walls. Since the castle was built on a hill (Toompea) 20 meters high, it presented an imposing fortification seen from a distance by anyone approaching Tallinn from land or sea until the 17th century. The medieval castle was later replaced by a governor's palace, which was rebuilt in the 1920s into a neoclassical **Parliament** Building, incorporating basically only the foundations and parts of the original walls. Today only the tallest tower, Pikk Hermann ("tall Herman"), survives the medieval building.

The flagstaff atop Pikk Hermann has borne the symbol of the masters of the castle and of the rulers of the Province of Estland for centuries. Since 1918, Pikk Hermann and the flag at the top of the national flagstaff has symbolized independence (*see* NATIONAL SYMBOLS). Thus, one of the first acts of the Soviet Union was to replace the Estonian flag with the red flag of the **Estonian Soviet Socialist Republic** (ESSR) in 1940. The Estonian flag was again hoisted to its rightful place atop Pikk Hermann at sunrise on 24 February 1989 to the strains of the long-forbidden national anthem in an emotional ceremony attended by the government and 100,000 Estonians fully two years before Estonia regained its independence in 1991. Today strict protocol controls the flag—it may only be flown form sunrise to sunset, except for **Jaanipäev** at midsummer, when it flies symbolically around the clock for 24 hours.

PITKA, JOHAN (1972–1944). Seaman, shipping company owner, founder of the Estonian navy and **Defense League**, politician, and hero of the **War of Independence**. Pitka, born on 19 February 1872 in Võhmuta *vald*, as a youth studied at the Käsmu, Kuressaare, and Paldiski marine colleges during winters while sailing the Baltic and the North seas in the summers. He sailed the oceans of the world from 1889 to 1907 in various capacities on merchant marine ships of different nationalities, after 1895 as captain. In 1904, he moved to England, where he first sailed out of Hull as a captain of sailing ships, and then set up a shipping agency in Liverpool. In 1911, he moved to **Tallinn** and founded the successful shipping firm Joh. Pitka and Ko.

After the February Revolution in 1917, he was a whirlwind of activity in organizing national military forces. He was not only a member of the Estonian Soldiers Supreme Council but also personally financed the newspaper *Eesti Sõjamees* (*Estonian Soldier*), financed local county recruitment offices, and often paid for the arms and supplies for the newly formed units as well. He also organized the volunteer Omakaitse (Home Guard). After the October Revolution the **Bolsheviks** ordered his arrest, but he evaded them and continued his organizing work underground. His Omakaitse forces provided the first reliable support for the **Estonian Provisional Government** when it declared independence on 24 February 1918. During the German occupation, he continued organizing the national **armed forces** underground. The Eesti Kaitse Liit (later **Kaitseliit**), the result of his secret activities, became operational on 11 November 1918. In the ensuing War of Independence, Pitka exceeded his previous efforts in organizing the building of armored cars and armored trains, initially at his own shipyards at his own cost; he formed the Estonian navy; organized volunteer attack units, directed the Kaitseliit, reorganized retreating units, defused the workers' opposition in the Tallinn shipyards, and fought at the front against the Red Army. He personally directed the crucial naval operations in the battle for **Narva** and Ingermanland, the bombardment of the German defenses of Riga, and the laying of minefields in the Gulf of Finland. The stress was so great that at the end of the war, with his health ruined, although he was promoted to rear admiral and granted honors by Estonia and Latvia, as well as a knighthood by Great Britain (along with **Konstantin Päts** and **Johan Laidoner**, his close colleagues, the only Estonians so honored), he was forced to retire from active service to his country.

But his energy soon returned when he saw war profiteers and others who had not sacrificed their fortune, nor risked their lives, taking prominent parts in running the country. Pitka formed his own party with the stated objective of counteracting corruption and self-serving politicians. Unfortunately, although his party won four seats, his plain talk and injudicious attacks left him outside parliament in 1923. Embittered, he left the country and emigrated with his family to British Columbia, where he attempted to establish a settlement. In 1930, after six years of fruitless hard work, he abandoned Canada and returned home, where he was rewarded with a state pension for his wartime services and was made president of the Central Board of the Estonian Consumers Federation.

But the siren call of politics enticed Pitka to once again try his luck. This time he joined the **Veterans** of the War of Independence, but characteristically organized his own Brothers of Battle Club, which demonstratively marched out of the Third Congress of the Estonian Veterans of the War of Independence over a conflict of principles. Despite this, he continued his work as director of the Submarine Force Foundation and was even elected in December 1936 to the Rahvuskogu (Constituent Assembly) established to work out the new **Constitution of 1937**. At the same time, he worked his farm and wrote assiduously, including four volumes of memoirs in 1938–39, in addition to his 1921 memoirs of World War I and the War of Independence.

In 1940, Pitka fled to Finland and joined the Erna group and later attempted to enlist in the **JR 200** Regiment of Estonian volunteers being formed by the Finnish army, but was rejected because of age—he was over 70. In April 1944, he returned to Estonia and urged cooperation with the Germans to prevent a second Soviet occupation. With the deterioration of the German front, he organized the "Admiral Pitka" unit of about 200 volunteers and fought a retreating battle with the invading Soviet army in western Estonia. Pitka was apparently killed toward the end of September 1944 somewhere in Läänemaa during the confusion of the retreat.

In the 1990s, Pitka's memoirs, *Meresõit Leaga* (*Sea Voyage with Leah*), were reissued, including the stirring tale of his years as master of a barquentine at the end of the 19th century. An authentic hero of the 20th century is being rediscovered, at least in Estonia, since so far his books are available in Estonian only. In 2002, a bust of Pitka was unveiled near the headquarters of the Kaitseliit at the base of Toompea in Tallinn to commemorate his fundamental role in the War of Independence and in the founding of the Kaitseliit.

PODDER, ERNST. *See* PÕDDER, ERNST.

POLITICAL PARTIES. Because of the half century of Soviet occupation when the political, social, and economic structures of Estonia were destroyed, the history of political parties in Estonia consists of two separate periods: 1905 to 1940 and 1988 to the present.

The first Estonian parties grew out of Russian social democracy at the dawn of the 20th century as illegal underground groups. The Estonian Social Democratic Workers' Union (ESDWU) (Eesti Sotsiaaldemokraatlik Tööliste Ühisus, ESDTÜ) was the first to be formalized as an Estonia-oriented political party in 1905, whereas those oriented toward imperial centralism set up an Estonian affiliate of the Russian Social Democratic Workers Party (*see* ESTONIAN COMMUNIST PARTY). In the same year, the Estonian Progressive Party was formed as a right-wing party in imitation of the Russian Cadet Party.

However, it was not until the revolutionary year, 1917, that party formation took off in Estonia. In that year, four groupings were formed—the standard three on the left, in the center, and on the right, plus ethnic minority parties. The left consisted of the Bolsheviks, who in 1920 formed the Estonian Communist Party, which was outlawed as a party after the **attempted coup of 1924** but whose members were allowed to continue successful electoral activities under the guise of various small left-wing parties; and the successor parties to the ESDWU, which split, reorganized, joined with other left-wing parties, and finally re-formed as the Estonian Socialist Workers'

Party (Eesti Töörahva Partei) in 1926. The center consisted of the Labor Party (Tööerakond), which split into two with the former landless peasants who had been given land in 1919, forming the Homesteaders' Party (Asunikud) in 1923; and the Radical Democrats (Radikaal-demokraatilik Erakond), with whom the Democratic Party (Demokraatlik Erakond) amalgamated in 1919. The right grew mainly out of the Progressive Party (Eduerakond), which in 1917 split into the Democratic Party just referred to, and the Farmers' Union (Maarahva Liit). In 1919, the Christian Nationalist Party (Kristlik Rahva Erakond) was also formed on the right. The ethnic minorities parties (one German party and several Russian parties) never played any significant part in Estonian politics—their combined representation in the **Riigikogu** I–IV ranged from five to eight mandates. Other ethnic parties (two Jewish ones and a Swedish one) never elected members to parliament and disappeared after a single electoral outing. In addition to the parties mentioned between 1919 and 1932, almost 30 other parties were formed, mostly in pursuit of single interests. Of these, the National Liberal Party, the Renters, and the **Veterans** received mandates (four, one, and one, respectively) only in the election of 1923, and the Landlord's Party received one mandate in 1920, two in 1923 and 1926, and three in 1929.

In 1932, a major realignment took place, which briefly consolidated the fractious partisan landscape. Although each of the three sectors on the Left-Right continuum received about one third of the seats in the first four parliaments, there was considerable reformation of parties. In contrast, Riigikogu V elections gave the new United Agrarian Party (Põllumeeste Kogud), a coalition of all right-wing parties, 40 percent of the seats while the new National Center Party (Rahvuslik Keskerakond), an amalgam of center parties, was reduced to 23 percent and the left to 27 percent (Estonian Socialist Workers' Party with 22 percent and communists with 5 percent).

Unfortunately the Depression, which hit Estonia hard, compounded both constitutional weakness, which prevented decisive action by the government and exacerbated the conflict between Left and Right. Between 1919 and 1933 there were 21 cabinets, four in 1932 alone; half were led by the right-wing Agrarians and half by center parties. The Social Democrats, although the largest party in parliament prior to 1932, led only one cabinet. Amidst the constitutional crisis of 1932–33, the sudden surge of popularity of the ultraright Veterans movement and their unexpected decision to run for the presidency led to the **preemptive coup** by Riigivanem **Konstantin Päts** in 1934, and the subsequent suspension of political parties during the **Era of Silence**. In the elections of 1938 under the new **Constitution of 1937**, the Päts government excluded all formal party candidates except for the officially sanctioned Fatherland League, based primarily on Päts's own United Agrarian Party.

The foreign occupations by the Soviet Union in 1940, Germany in 1941–44, and the Soviet Union again from 1944 to 1988 prevented any partisan political activity apart from that within the revived ECP.

As a result of **perestroika and glasnost**, the political landscape in Soviet Estonia had changed so drastically by 1988 that both mass political movements and nascent parties began to be formed. Among the latter, the Estonian National Independence Party (Eesti Rahvusliku Sõltumatuse Partei, ERSP) was organized already in January. By summer 1988 a rejuvenated new Estonian independence-oriented reform leadership had taken over the ECP, **Rahvarinne** (Peoples' Front) had been formed and a number of pro-Soviet anti-Independence as well as Estonian nationalist movements had been organized and were engaged in mass politics. Two years later, in February 1990, 31 political parties and groupings participated in the elections to the **Estonian Congress**. The rapid politicization of the Estonian population was caused by the explosive demand for independence and for the self-expression and national participation so long forbidden by the Muscovite overlord. The opposition to the Estonians' aspirations, formed by all of Moscow's central institutions and by Russian migrants who organized into the **Interfront** in Estonia, simply encouraged greater participation by the Estonians. A mad surge of **electoral democracy** was unleashed in Estonia by Mikhail Gorbachev's calling for the election of an expanded People's Congress of the Soviet Union with considerable freedom from the Communist Party tutelage to propose candidates.

In the elections on 28 March 1989, of the 26 elected by Estonians, only six had been nominated by the ECP (all were reform communists) and all the others represented newly organized political movements (People's Front won 16 seats, the green movement three, and the anti-independence Interfront three).

These elections were followed by four more before independence was regained, and another four in quick succession between June 1992 and October 1993. The electoralism itself generated widespread party formation. This time, however, in contrast to the first period, 70–80 years earlier, all the parties that were formed in time to participate in the elections to Riigikogu VII on 20 September 1992 were center and right in orientation. The Communist Party disappeared altogether and did not leave any successor parties. Although party names changed, and amalgamations and new parties have been formed for each of the four elections since renewed independence, the new party system was established in the Riigikogu VII election.

The most remarkable aspect of it is that all elected parties since 1992 have been ideologically center-right, whatever designation they may give themselves from time to time for public relations purposes, the only exception being the Russian ethnic parties, which are Social-Democratic in orientation, and which did not elect a single member in 2003 because of their inability to cooperate and because of the attractiveness of Estonian parties, especially the Center Party, to their electors. The second characteristic of the party system is a latent rural-urban conflict, which is reflected in the continued existence of a separate agrarian party even after most rural people joined the Coalition Party. The third and most visible characteristic of the party system is the government-opposition chasm. This developed early and is based in the conflict of personalities.

The first government formed after the elections of 1992 consisted of Pro Patria, the Estonian National Independence Party, and the Moderates (Mõõdukad), a coalition of three newly organized nominally Social Democratic parties, and it set up a clear "ins-and-outs" conflict partly based on a claimed purity from Soviet-era contamination by the youthful cabinet. Prime Minister **Mart Laar** was 32, Minister without Portfolio **Jüri Luik** was 26 (and later became foreign minister at 28), and few were over 40, in contrast to the Coalition and Center parties' members who had been instrumental in the independence movement inside the Estonian Communist Party as well as members of the transition government. The conflict carried on through the 1995 elections when the center-right Pro Patria–led coalition lost to the former opposition, the center-left and center-right Coalition-led coalition government with the Center Party, and later with the newly formed right-of-center Reform Party. In 1999, after the electorate had again grown weary of the squabbling in the government, a new wall-to-wall center-left, center-right, Pro Patria–led coalition cabinet with the Moderates and Reform Party was formed and the personality conflict continued between it and the Center and Coalition parties, now in opposition. After close to three years, the coalition broke down at the end of 2001 and a new minority cabinet was formed between the Reform Party and the Center Party, hitherto the main opposition party in January 2002. Shortly thereafter, the small United Russian Peoples' Party with five members decided to amalgamate with Reform, thus guaranteeing the coalition a majority in parliament. This is a clear example of pragmatism and the continuation of the "ins-and-outs" of ministerial party politics.

As support for Pro Patria and the Moderates collapsed and the new right-of-center Res Publica was formed and "won" the 2003 elections (although the Center Party also received the same number of mandates—28), the old conflict continued: a coalition of Res Publica, Reform, and Coalition parties refused any cooperation with the Center Party and relegated it to opposition.

To the outside observer, the policies of all the governments since the transition cabinet in 1990 appear to follow the same trend of emphasis on national wealth creation with the government's role limited to creating favorable conditions for growth, but with minor differences in policies over rates of growth and expenditures on social services. Naturally, given the poverty and tiny population base of under 1.4 million, with a budget of only US$2 billion in 2000, even small differences in expenditures lead to large political battles in parliament between government and opposition, but die as soon as a vote is taken and a decision is made. All cabinets have also followed nearly identical policies of accession to both the **European Union** (EU) and **North Atlantic Treaty Organization** (NATO), consistently supported by all parties in the Riigikogu.

POPULATION. Until 1782, the population figures for Estonia were based on estimates, ranging between 150,000 and 180,000 in 1200, about 250,000 in 1550, down to 120,000 in 1640 due to war and plagues, up to between 350,000 and 400,000 in 1696, and down to between 150,000 and 170,000 in 1712 due to war, starvation, and plague.

Between 1782 and 1858, seven population counts took place, the first of which found a population of 485,000 on the territory of present-day Estonia. In 1863, the Estland and Livland *gubernyas* organized statistical committees and proceeded to carry out censuses according to principles laid down at international conferences on statistics, first in towns in Livland on 3 March 1863, and then in **Tallinn** in Estland on 16 November 1871. On 29 December 1881, the first comprehensive censuses of the whole populations of Estland (excluding the town of **Narva** and **Petserimaa**) and Livland were carried out, followed by the first census of the whole of the Russian Empire on 28 January 1897. Independent Estonia carried out only two censuses, in 1922 and 1934, and the German occupation forces in 1944 conducted a population registration with seven questions. After the war, the Soviet Union carried out censuses on 15 January 1959, 15 January 1970, 17 January 1979, and 12 January 1989. The first census of the re-independent Estonian Republic took place in May 2000. (See table 1 for Estonian population figures.)

The Estonian Statistical Office and other government agencies also keep population registers, which provide basic breakdowns of urban-rural, male-female, ethnic origin, and citizen-noncitizen data. Unfor-

Table 1 Population, 1881–2000

Year	*Total Population (thousands)*	*Ethnic Estonians (% of total in brackets)*	*Urban Population (% in brackets)*
1881	881	792 (89.9%)	
1897	958	868 (90.6%)	190 (19.2%)
1922	1,107	970 (87.6%)	277 (24.0%)
1934	1,126	993 (88.2%)	323 (28.7%)
1944	850	827 (97.3%)	
1950	1,097		
1959	1,197	893 (74.6%)	676 (56.4%)
1970	1,356	925 (68.2%)	881 (65.9%)
1979	1,466	948 (64.7%)	1,022 (69.7%)
1989	1,566	963 (61.5%)	1,127 (71.6%)
2000	1,370	930 (67.9%)	923 (67.4%)

Note: Based on census data, which is not strictly comparable, since different measures were used. The 1944 figure is based on a German occupation questionnaire, which, because of wartime confusion, refugee movements, conscription, and deliberate avoidance of official notice, is not very accurate. The 1950 figure is an estimate.

tunately, long-term official data are not available on the breakdown of the ethnic division of the population between urban and rural areas (see table 2). However, it is estimated that the rural dwellers are nearly all ethnic Estonians, and that the remnants of the indigenous Russian Estonian farmer-fishermen on the western shore of **Lake Peipus** form nearly the whole of the non-Estonian rural population.

The above tables reflect four temporal trends of the Estonian population: a steady growth up to World War II due to births exceeding deaths and a steady increase in life expectancy; a drastic decline during the war due to emigration, war deaths, and **deportations**; a rapid growth due to immigration of labor from the Soviet Union from 1945 to 1989; and a rapid decline thereafter, owing to **emigration** of 100,000 mainly to Russia, and decline in births while death rates have increased. Since 1939, the ethnic composition of the country has changed twice. First, the **Baltic Germans** left under Hitler's program of *Umsiedlung*, or resettlement, to populate conquered western Poland, encouraged by the Soviet occupation of 1940, followed by

Table 2 Population, 1986–2002 (average for year)

Year	*Total Population (thousands)*
1986	1,540
1987	1,552
1988	1,561
1989	1,568
1990	1,569
1991	1,561
1992	1,533
1993	1,494
1994	1,462
1995	1,436
1996	1,415
1997	1,399
1998	1,386
1999	1,375
2000	1,369
2001	1,364
2002	1,361

Note: Data for 1989–2002 recalculated by Estonian Statistical Bureau on the base of the 2000 census.

the persecution and exit under both the first Soviet occupation and the German one, with the result that the population of Estonia by 1944 was almost purely ethnically Estonian. Second, after the Soviets reoccupied Estonia at the end of the war, a massive 40-year influx of Russian-speaking, mostly ethnic Russian labor, changed the composition drastically by 1989 to almost 40 percent non-Estonian, which declined slightly during the ensuing decade of independence to only one-third nonethnic Estonian. In no other society in the world has such a drastic ethnic restructuring taken place in less than 50 years. Only Latvia approaches such cataclysmic ethnic reversals, but Latvia began with a much larger foreign ethnic share.

The decline in Estonia's population actually began already in the 1930s as live births declined, but was masked by the continuing influx of young labor during the Soviet occupation. The end of both immigration and emigration since the collapse of the Soviet Union has meant that the secular trend of deaths outstripping births takes place in parallel among both ethnic and nonethnic Estonians. The trend is exacerbated by two legacies of the recent past—an abortion rate twice the live birth rate, and a very high death rate among men due to alcoholism. Both reflect the continuing focus on curative rather than preventive public health programs, resulting in low levels of **health** among the whole population. The general effect is a negative growth in population, combined with aging, which by 2020 is expected to lead to a major decline in the labor force with a consequent need to reorganize the economy to accommodate a smaller labor force and an increasingly larger group of pensioners with increasing health and social service demands.

POSKA, JAAN (1866–1920). Estonian statesman and lawyer. Poska was born on 24 January 1866 in Laiuse *vald*, the fifth of 12 children of a Russian Orthodox parish clerk/schoolmaster. He received his early and secondary education at the Church's school and seminary in Riga and then entered the medical faculty at the **University of Tartu** but soon transferred to law, which he completed in 1890. Poska was the first lawyer of Estonian extraction admitted to the bar in **Tallinn**, where he worked assiduously to further Estonians' interests against the ruling **Baltic German** nobility; was elected to the city council in 1904; and served as mayor from 1913 to 1917. In this position, he reformed the city's finances, medical services, and social assistance and set up innovative schools such as the School of Commerce for Women and the School for Artisans.

After the February Revolution in 1917, the imperial Russian Provisional Government named him commissar (temporary governor) of the expanded Gubernya (Province) of Estland, which it created by uniting the Estonian-speaking northern part of the Gubernya of Livland with the historic Gubernya of Estland as a result of the intense lobbying by the Estonians in St. Petersburg. In the fall of 1917, he was elected to the Russian Constituent Assembly, and although deposed as governor by the short-lived Estonian **Bolshevik** government of **Viktor Kingissepp** in October, Poska continued to work for Estonia's independence. He is reputed to have declared when he heard of the October Revolution in St. Petersburg: "Now we have no alternative but to declare Estonia independent." Thus this self-made member of the Baltic elite, fully at home in imperial St. Petersburg circles, became a revolutionary nationalist activist. In January 1918 he, along with **Jüri Vilms** and Julius Seljamaa, visited the ambassadors of Great Britain, France, and the United States in St. Petersburg to lobby for foreign recognition of Estonia's ambitions for independence. After the **Declaration of Independence** and the establishment of the provisional government of Estonia in February 1918, Poska became Estonia's first foreign minister. Against major odds during the German military occupation from March to November 1918, he diligently pursued recognition by the Allies of Estonia as an independent state. During this time, he worked especially closely with the Finnish government (itself under siege by the Bolsheviks) and became convinced that the only way to break the stranglehold of the Baltic German nobility in Estonia was to confiscate their landholdings and distribute them among Estonian peasants—a process that was carried out between 1921 and 1924. During the **War of Independence**, he continued to serve as foreign minister and was reappointed as such in the first regular Cabinet of the new Republic. Thus, it fell to him through the stormiest period of the formation of the Estonian state to negotiate not only financial, munitions, and volunteer manpower support from foreign powers during the war but also recognition of the new state at the Peace conference in Paris from reluctant Allies more concerned with continuing the war to defeat the Bolsheviks.

Poska's lasting greatness in Estonian history is that he negotiated a most advantageous peace treaty with Vladimir Lenin's new Bolshevik Russian state. The **Peace of Tartu**, signed on 2 February 1920, provided the financial foundation for Estonia and expanded Estonian territory to its largest ever size. In the treaty, Russia recognized Estonia as an independent state, gave up forever any claims on Estonian territory (which was expanded for strategic defense purposes to include sections never before part of historic Estonia), transferred 11.6 metric tons of gold (worth 15 million gold rubles) from its state hoard, returned all goods removed from Estonian territory during the Revolution and its aftermath, and gave Estonia claim on felling a vast tract of forest in Siberia as compensation; this treaty was never honored by Russia. After this triumph, Poska participated in the **Constituent Convention** and as an experienced lawyer helped draft the new **Constitution**. Shortly after, and before seeing his memoirs of the Versailles peace conference published, he died suddenly on 7 March 1920 in Tallinn at the early age of 54. The record shows that 20,000 Estonians mourned him at his funeral.

PREEMPTIVE COUP OF 1934. *See* ERA OF SILENCE *and* VETERANS.

PREHISTORIC PERIOD. *See* ARCHAEOLOGY; ARCHITECHTURE.

PRIBALTIKA. *See* BALTIC PROVINCES.

PRIVATIZATION. In the late 1980s, Estonians believed that the basic means of transforming Sovietized Estonia into a democratic society required the rapid denationalization of the centralized command economy. In 1988–89, the creation of private ownership of the means of production as the primary form of the economy was also seen as the basic way to differentiate Estonia from the Soviet Union and thereby to weaken the control of the latter over it. But it was the hidden political agenda behind the relatively modestly stated objectives of the **Isemajandav Eesti** (IME) project that caught the imagination of the Estonian elites and population. IME thus became the universally perceived fundamental vehicle for political independence. However, the economic aspects were not abandoned: an independent Estonia was to be a capitalist Estonia where Estonians were private owners with the state as their servant, and not vice versa.

Hence, privatization in Estonia had a drastically different meaning from that in capitalist Western societies such as Great Britain and Sweden, which were also going through a major wave of privatization in the 1980s. In these, it was mostly the large public infrastructural industries with their bloated staffs and inefficient and costly operations that were sold to commercial owners to get them off the taxpayers' backs and force them to operate on competitive economic grounds. In contrast, in Estonia, and in all the other socialist states of Eastern Europe, the objective was to create a capitalist society.

In Estonia, this clear objective was complicated until 1992 by the lack of complete control over the state's levers. Until after the **abortive Moscow coup** in August 1991, as far as the world was concerned, Estonia was "legally," although only de facto, part of the Soviet Union and therefore under the control of Moscow (*see* NON-RECOGNITION OF SOVIET OCCUPATION). This meant, among other factors, that only the housing stock, the collectivized farms, and a very limited number of industrial sectors that the latter recognized as being under the control of the constituent republics could be turned over to private owners. A second main problem, not solved until June 1992, was the lack of Estonia's own currency operated by its own central bank (*see* BANK OF ESTONIA), with the consequence that both internal financing and international borrowing capacities were lacking. Moreover, there was also the problem of a widespread idealized and politically inspired expectation that in independent Estonia, all Estonians would become "owners" in compensation for the years of captivity under Soviet occupation. This quickly ran into the opposite demand that the restitution of the independent Estonian Republic of 1940, which all Estonians (including the members of the Supreme Soviet of the Estonian Soviet Socialist Republic, ESSR) recognized, also required the restitution of the illegally confiscated property to their rightful owners or legal heirs.

Thus, privatization in Estonia was not only intimately tied to the resuscitation and development of private property after a half century of dormancy, but was regarded initially as *the* primary means of reestablishing private property.

The process of creating private property began when the **Supreme Soviet of the ESSR** on 18 May 1989 adopted the **IME Project** program (which had been organized on 1 April) and decided that Estonia would begin a transition to economic independence effective 1 January 1990. On 27 November 1989, the USSR Supreme Soviet acquiesced to this when it adopted a law on the economic autonomy of Estonia, Latvia, and Lithuania. The IME Project worked on a "conveyor belt" system to draft "100 laws to be adopted in 100 days." The first new autonomy laws to be passed by the Supreme Soviet of the ESSR were the first Property Act and the Joint Stock Companies Act, both effective 1 January 1990. The latter allowed real companies to be formed for the first time in place of the shadow "cooperatives" and small subsidiaries that Mikhail Gorbachev had permitted earlier. After the elections to the XII Supreme Soviet of the ESSR on 18 March 1990, won by the newly formed democratic parties supporting political independence for Estonia, the legislature changed the name of the state to the Republic of Estonia, its own name (in the interim prior to a new **Constitution** and new elections) to Supreme Council to distinguish itself from the Soviet Union, and appointed the creator of the IME Project, **Edgar Savisaar**, as prime minister of the transition to independence, which would end when elections took place for the reinstituted **Riigikogu** under a new Constitution. All this took place in a carefully calculated defiant interpretation of the Soviet authorization of "economic autonomy" and the interpretation of the meaning of "sovereignty" in the ESSR constitution.

An avalanche of economic reform acts from the IME project was passed, not in 100 days but during 1990–91, which set the foundations of democratic capitalist society and economy. The crucial one allowing private ownership was "The act on the principles of ownership reform" (Omandireformi aluste seadus), adopted on 13 June 1991. The fact that it has been amended frequently since, sometimes several times in one year, underscores the difficulty of moving a society from state to private ownership.

The actual process of privatizing began initially in 1990 with local governments allowing service industry personnel (e.g., hairdressers, photographers, and shoe repairers) to buy their service units and rent the premises. Privatizing the housing stock, collective farms, land, and industrial enterprises required first the establishment of the State

Property Office (Riigivaraamet) in 1990, which initially needed to make an inventory, and was then given the authority to begin privatizing housing and smaller enterprises. The process, however, quickly ran into conflicting interests among the population and the many **political parties** representing them. In 1990–91, the main conflict was over the rights of the prewar owners, whose houses and farm property had been forcibly confiscated by the Soviet state, and the "new owners" who lived in these houses or had acquired them in good faith during the Soviet period. Since it was obvious to nearly everyone that the legal continuity of the Estonian republic also meant the legal continuity of ownership of property, these properties had to be returned. But politically, restitution could not be allowed to create new inequities to the new owners, who formed the vast majority of owners.

At the same time, the voucher privatization craze, pioneered by the Czechs, swept Eastern Europe and the former Soviet Union. By this scheme, everybody was to be entitled issuance of a number of vouchers (State Obligation Certificates) of a nominal value based on the number of years he or she had had to live under the socialist yoke, plus the number of years he or she had been employed, as well as various miscellaneous entitlements (e.g., for repression or years in Siberia). The main problem was what to use these vouchers for. In Estonia, it was decided that they could be used to purchase the state apartments that people currently lived in, with any remainder of the state-fixed price to be paid in cash. Eventually, a final deadline of 1996 was set for this opportunity.

All prewar real property, including housing, was divided into two classes: returnable and compensationable. The former would be returned, with existing tenants ("new owners") being given several years to find new housing, as well as preference on empty state apartments, while the former legal owners were set a deadline to make their claims, adjudicable by the courts. Real property ruled by the state (national and municipal governments) to be in the national or cultural interests would not be returned but would be compensated by vouchers. Any disputes would be settled by the **courts**; many cases are still ongoing a decade after independence. Real property owned by prewar joint stock companies would not be returned, but shareholders would have the right of first refusal to purchase the property and any factory or business located on it.

In enterprise privatization, the main conflict was between the existing management, who pushed for distribution of shares among their workers, and the IME Project economists, who saw the need to sell to the highest bidder in order to bring in new management and new investments to transform the dying Soviet factories still producing goods that no longer had markets. The first approach, used by every former socialist state either in full or partially—most disastrously in Russia—inevitably resulted in management buying up the workers' shares and becoming robber-baron capitalists without a new infusion of expertise or funds. In Estonia, quick action by Olari Taal (about to be named minister of economics) and Prime Minister **Tiit Vähi** in 1992, to bring in advice from the German Treuhand and subsequently to either sell at local auction for cash or to advertise internationally for tenders and sell after negotiation to a strategic investor, was adopted as the primary method of privatizing industry. The demand for people's participation, which had not completely disappeared, was met by allowing limited percentages of some auctioned firms' shares to be sold for vouchers.

Unlike Treuhand, which was given all East German industry to bring up to saleable standards (using West German tax funds) and then to sell to the highest bidder, the Estonian Privatization Agency (Eesti Erastamisagentuur), set up in 1993, was given only the function of finding suitable strategic investors to whom to sell, and to complete the process of selling and financing the sale. After all, Estonia was poor and did not have any taxpayers' money to invest. In the event, the need to sell to viable owners to bring in foreign investments to revive and restart the dying firms in the new Europe-oriented economy proved successful. None of the firms thus sold has gone bankrupt, although several have been closed by new owners in efforts at consolidation.

But Estonia went further. After completing the sale of all industrial plants to private owners, in 1998 it embarked on selling its infrastructure as well. In the process, the airline, the shipping line, bus firms, harbors, railroads, and city water and sewage systems have been sold, many to foreign bidders. By 2001, Estonia had become the most capitalist, free-enterprise state in the world, surpassing even Hong Kong. *See also* ECONOMIC TRANSFORMATION.

PROVINCE OF ESTLAND. The Province of Estland, consisting of the northern half of present-day Estonia, existed from 1584 to 1917, first as a province under Swedish suzerainty and from 1710 as part of Imperial Russia. From 12 April 1917, when the Russian Provisional Government transferred the northern Estonian-speaking area of the Province of Livland to it, until the Declaration of Independence on 24 February 1918, the province contained the whole of the historic settlement area of Estonians.

PROVISIONAL DIET OF THE PROVINCE OF ESTLAND. *See* EESTIMAA KUBERMANGU AJUTINE MAANÕUKOGU.

PROVISIONAL GOVERNMENT. *See* DECLARATION OF INDEPENDENCE 1918.

PÕDDER, ERNST (1879–1932). Estonian soldier, victor of the Battle of Võnnu, and hero of the **War of Independence.** Põdder was born on 10 February 1879 in Aleksander *vald* in Võru county, graduated from the Military College in Vilnius in 1900, and fought in the Russo-Japanese War of 1904–05, where he rose to the rank of lieutenant. Thereafter he continued to serve in the Russian imperial army in the Far East until 1914. At the beginning of World War I, he was promoted to colonel and given command of a regiment. On 22 July 1917, he joined the Estonian national units, then still part of the imperial army (*see* ARMED FORCES), and took command of the First Regiment and subsequently the Third Regiment. During the German occupation of 1918, he was one of the main organizers of the **Defense League**, along with **Johan Pitka**.

Promoted to major-general at the beginning of the **War of Independence**, Põdder served first as head of internal security and then, after being given command of the Third Division, destroyed the German **Landeswehr** and the Stahl Division under von der Goltz at the battle of Võnnu (Latvian, Cēsis; German, Wenden) on 19–23 June 1919. He signaled the victory by ordering Estonians to light victory bonfires on hills. Subsequently, 23 June was declared **Victory Day** in Estonia, and the bonfires lit in the evening preceding St. John's Day (**Jaanipäev**) are known as Victory fires. After the war, Põdder commanded the First and Third Divisions in succession and participated in the suppression of the **attempted communist coup of 1924**. In 1926, he was named as a permanent member of the Estonian War Council, and he was honored as their sole honorary member by the **Veterans** of the War of Independence. Põdder continued until his death on 24 June 1932 in **Tallinn** as an active member of the Council of Elders of the Defense League. General Põdder was awarded the highest level of the Cross of Liberty for his services in the War of Independence (*see* ORDERS OF MERIT OF THE REPUBLIC OF ESTONIA).

PÄRNU (German, Pernau). The fourth largest city in Estonia with a population of 45,700 in 2000. Pärnu's recorded history reaches back to a 1242 reference to its port. In 1251, the city was founded by the Saare-Lääne bishopric for the first time on the right bank of the river Pärnu as a church center with a cathedral. After being sacked and burned by pagan Estonians, the **Teutonic Order** reestablished the city on the left bank in 1265, where the city center has remained. The city's first period of growth took place from 1318 to the end of the 15th century when, as a member of the **Hanseatic League**, it served as a transshipment point on the river trade route to Novgorod. With the decline of the League, it gradually became a county administrative center for its hinterland and during the Swedish period its transit role was replaced by an export trade of timber, flax, and other such staples. For a short two decades, the city also hosted the university as the Academia Gustaviana was moved to it from **Tartu** in 1699 at the beginning of the **Great Northern War**. During the ensuing Russian imperial times, the city continued in its main role as a port. In 1838, however, with the rebuilding of a tavern on the seashore into a bathing house, Pärnu embarked on its career as a *Kurort* or summer bathing resort. In 1888, the city instituted a program of building parks and pleasant walks along the seashore combined with special-purpose restorative baths of seawater and mineral mud brought in from Haapsalu. In 1906, the Pernauer Yacht Club laid the foundations to the city's reputation as a sailing center.

During the Soviet occupation, the city developed as a favorite summer resort for professionals from Leningrad and a year-round health and convalescence center with half a dozen such institutions. After the restoration of independence, the health resorts were privatized and became resort hotels with year-round visitors from Finland as well as from Estonia. In addition, the city organizes festivals of different kinds during the summer months, which bring large numbers of visitors to its growing restaurants, clubs, and theaters. The city has also taken advantage of its port facilities and has become a transshipment, warehousing, and trading center for the region. In the late 1990s, the city became once again a university town as the **University of Tartu** opened the affiliate Pärnu College. Today Pärnu remains the premier beach resort in Estonia. Located at the river mouth at the bottom of the sheltered waters of the deep half-moon-shaped Gulf of Pärnu on the west coast opposite the island of Saaremaa, the city's wide sand beaches are equally accessible to visitors from Tallinn, only 140 kilometers north, and Riga, 189 kilometers south on the Tallinn-Riga highway.

PÄRT, ARVO (1935–). Estonian composer. Pärt was born on 11 September 1935 at Paide. While studying composition at **Tallinn** Conservatory beginning in 1958, Pärt worked at Estonian **Radio** as a recording engineer until 1967. During his studies, he composed music and won recognition in Eastern Europe, and he took first place in the Soviet All-Union Young Composers' Competition for his early popular work, "Meie aed" ("Our Garden," 1959), a cantata for children's choir and orchestra, and for the oratorio "Maailma samm" ("The World's Stride," 1960). He experimented with the 12-tone system first developed in the early 1900s by Arnold Schoenberg, in the striking composition "Nekrolog" (1960), the first 12-tone piece written in Estonia. Soon after graduation in 1963 he composed "Symphony No. 1" (1964) and "Symphony No. 2" (1966); the latter includes quotations from the music of other composers. He also used this collage technique in "Credo" (1968), a work for piano, mixed chorus, and orchestra. Banned in the Soviet Union because of its religious text, "Credo" also signaled the end of Pärt's experimentation with the 12-tone system. At the beginning of the 1970s, after a period of withdrawal and study of medieval music, he wrote a few transitional compositions in the spirit of early European polyphony, the "Third Symphony" of 1971 being an example: "a joyous piece of music" but not yet "the end of my despair and search."

Shortly after, Pärt again turned to self-imposed silence, during which he delved back through the medievalism of his "Third Symphony" and to the very dawn of musical invention. After a radical transformation, he reemerged in 1976 with a unique technique to which he has remained loyal and which he calls *tintinnabuli* (from the Latin, "little bells"). As he puts it:

> I have discovered that it is enough when a single note is beautifully played. This one note, or a silent beat, or a moment of silence, comforts me. I work with very few elements—with one voice, two voices. I build with primitive materials—with the triad, with one specific tonality. The three notes of a triad are like bells and that is why I call it tintinnabulation.

The principle of tintinnabulation is composing two simultaneous voices as one line—one voice moving stepwise from and to a central pitch, first up then down, and the other sounding the notes of the triad. He first displayed it in the short piano piece "Für Alina."

Having found his new métier, Pärt produced prolifically with three of the 1977 pieces ("Fratres," "Cantus in Memoriam Benjamin Britten," and "Tabula Rasa"), still among his most highly regarded compositions. As his music began to be performed in the West, while he continued to struggle against Soviet officialdom, his frustration ultimately forced him to emigrate in 1980 to Vienna, where he took Austrian citizenship. Subsequently he moved to West Berlin, where he still lives.

Since leaving Estonia, Pärt has concentrated on composing music based on religious texts. Large-scale works include "St. John's Passion" (1982), "Te Deum" (1984–86), and "Litany" (1994). Choral works, such as "Magnificat" (1989) and "The Beatitudes" (1990), have proved popular with choirs around the world. He is also writing a growing number of works for strings and chamber ensembles, including numerous versions of "Fratres," "Cantus in Memoriam Benjamin Britten," (1977/1980), "Festina Lente" (1988), and "Siloun's Song" (1991). His works have been recorded by ECM Records. **Neeme Järvi**, his Estonian compatriot who conducted the premiere of "Credo" in Tallinn in 1968, has introduced Pärt's compositions to American and European audiences through performances and recordings. Pärt has been widely acclaimed and honored abroad since the 1990s and is acknowledged by the music world as one of the great composers of the late 20th century.

PÄTS, KONSTANTIN (1874–1956). Undoubtedly the most prominent Estonian statesman and politician of the interwar years, not least because of the **preemptive coup** Päts carried out with the assistance of General **Johan Laidoner** in 1934 to prevent a feared fascist coup. Subsequently, he became the first Estonian head of state to carry the title president.

Päts was born on 23 February 1874 on a farm in Tahkuranna *vald* and graduated in 1898 from the **University of Tartu** with a law degree. From 1901 to 1905, he published the nationalist newspaper *Teataja* and became deputy mayor of **Tallinn** in 1905. In the aftermath of the abortive Revolution of 1905, when an imperial punishment detachment secretly sentenced him to death in 1906, he fled to Switzerland, then moved to Finland, returned to Estonia in 1909, and was imprisoned in St. Petersburg in 1910–11. On his release he edited the newspaper *Tallinna Teataja* until 1917 when, as chair of the Estonian Soldiers' Supreme Council, he helped establish the Estonian **armed forces**. In the same year, he led the Estonian Interim Government (Eesti Maavalitsus), served on the Estonian Diet (**Maapäev**), and spent one month in jail after the **Bolshevik** Revolution of October 1917. In 1918, Päts led the **Estonian Rescue (Salvation) Committee** (Estimaa Päästmise Komitee), and after the **Declaration of Independence** in 1918 he served as prime minister, minister of war, minister of the interior, and minister of trade and industry in the **Estonian Provisional Government** (Eesti Ajutine Valitsus). From June to November 1918, he was imprisoned by the German occupation forces.

During the politically chaotic first decade of independence, Päts served as **Head of State** (Riigivanem or "State Elder") on five separate occasions (January 1921–March 1922, August 1922–March 1924, February 1931–February 1932, November 1932–May 1933, and October 1933–January 1934). After the preemptive coup of 1934, he dismissed parliament and ruled as prime minister exercising the authority of Riigivanem until 1937, and as Riigihoidja (regent), in the interim between the proclamation of the new **Constitution of 1937** and his election as Estonia's first president in 1938.

Päts was also elected to the **Constituent Assembly** (Asutav Kogu) in 1919 and was elected to all prewar **Riigikogu** (I through VI). In 1935, he became one of the founders of the Fatherland Union Party

(Isamaaliit), which had supported the coup of the previous year and became the only legally allowed party in Estonia. On 23 July 1940, the Soviet occupation authorities arrested and deported Päts with his family to Russia, where he died in prison at Burashevo in Kalinin oblast on 18 January 1956. His remains were brought to Estonia in 1990 and reburied at the national Forest Cemetery (Metsalkalmistu) in Tallinn.

During the first four decades of the 20th century, Päts and **Jaan Tõnisson** were the most visible political figures in Estonia. But although the latter was an idealist, Päts was primarily a pragmatic realist who believed that the natural order was one of balance and harmony. His overwhelming objective, which he began pursuing already as editor of *Teataja* immediately after military service, was self-government for the Estonians. Accordingly, he became above all the prime state builder of Estonia, building it institution by institution. He was able to do this because he was a natural politician who understood that all politics is the "art of the possible," which he combined with superb organizing abilities. His first success came quickly when he succeeded in displacing the **Baltic German** majority with Estonians on the Tallinn City Council in the election of 1904. The next objective, achieving autonomous government for a united Province of Estonia, took longer and because of the Bolshevik Revolution and World War I, led to a major change in approach, the establishment of an independent state—a pragmatic accommodation to changed circumstances that was easy for the realist Päts. Indeed, Päts played the most important role of any Estonian politician in the revolutionary period leading up to **Independence** as prime minister and minister of defense in the Salvation Committee and the provisional government. With the help of Johan Pitka and Laidoner, he built the armed forces of Estonia and won the **War of Independence**. As well, during the War of Independence, Päts agitated and had the Constituent Assembly pass the Land Reform law that expropriated the aristocratic estates and divided them among the landless. The allocation of small landholdings to all war veterans made the wartime conscription a success and ensured a personal interest among the soldiers in victory. Later, Päts's partisan political support was located mainly among the small farmers.

Although Päts participated in the heady confusion of building the new state as prime minister longer than any other leader before the preemptive coup, the results were mixed owing in no small measure to the ultrademocratic parliamentary system that the political Left had forced through in the Constituent Assembly. In 1933, the international economic effects of the Depression on Estonia added to the political instability that the **Constitution of 1920** had fostered in the petit bourgeois society that it had created, and this led to popular demands for Constitutional change. The **Constitution of 1933**, however, had swung too far in the direction of pure presidentialism and when the **Veterans** of the War of Independence appeared poised to win the presidential election and lead Estonia down the path of authoritarian nationalism, Päts moved quickly in using the new constitutional powers to preempt them. Ruling with constitutionally sanctioned emergency powers, Päts brought economic and political stability to the nation—at the expense of liberal democracy. However, his rule was not particularly authoritarian in practice, even during the first three years, after which he called together a partly elected, partly appointed representative council to draft a new Constitution, based on his long-held belief that representation in parliament ought to reflect not only the ideological and class party interests but also the corporate functional occupational interests. The latter, he believed, would ameliorate the ideological and class conflicts and better allow pragmatic conciliation and compromise. His proposal to include this in the 1920 Constitution had failed, but using contemporary examples from Germany and France he was able to have **Jüri Uluots** construct the new presidential-parliamentary system on this basis. **Riigikogu elections** were carried out in 1938, but World War II, the Soviet invasion, and the **German occupation** intervened before the new system could be tested with free and reorganized **political parties**. Päts also worked diligently to restructure **local government** to contemporary standards, but ran out of time.

That he allowed his government to give in to Soviet demands without the Estonian army firing a single shot may be explained by his pragmatic approach to the realities of conflict resolution. The symbolic defiance against vastly superior armed forces (*see* SOVIET-ESTONIAN MUTUAL ASSISTANCE TREATY) would not have changed the outcome, but many Estonians would have been killed. Moreover, Päts along with most Estonians apparently was convinced that the coming war between Germany and the USSR would break out within a couple of months and in consequence Estonia would again become free.

– R –

RADIO AND TELEVISION. Radio broadcasting began in Estonia on 18 December 1926 when the private company Radio-Ringhääling began operating, with stations in **Tallinn**, **Tartu**, and later Türi. Felix Mohr, an able newsreader as well as producer and director, introduced radio plays and so-called radio evenings in 1928. In 1934, the government of President **Konstantin Päts** reorganized radio broadcasting into the state monopoly Riigi Ringhääling, which in 1939 broadcast nine hours daily to an audience of 100,000.

Although broadcasting became a tool of the party-state during the Soviet occupation, toward the middle of the period in the daily 35-hour schedule of three radio stations (the basic Raadio I, the music and information Vikerraadio, and Raadio III, a stereo program) a number of programs were ideology-free and became very popular. Among these were the musical programs "Good Morning Farmers" and "Family and Home." Among information broadcasts, the news programs were followed by most of the population as were lectures and discussions of literature, plays, comedy programs, and round-table discussions about political and economic matters. In 1969, the information, culture, and music program "Midnight Hour" was one of the first of the relatively ideology-free programs that became popular and thus increased demand for more. In 1970, the Estonian radio was the first in the Soviet Union to begin broadcasting commercial advertising announcements paid by diverse Soviet state firms; and in 1971 it began broadcasting in stereo.

In 1989, at the end of the Soviet period, Estonian Radio reorganized its programming toward the **Isemajandav Eesti** (IME) project, and it played a significant role in informing the population about political, national-cultural, and economic activities and policy proposals. It also took on the function of mobilizing the population to support its leaders during the Singing Revolution in 1989 and the transition period of 1990–92.

In 1990, the Estonian Soviet Socialist Republic's (ESSR) State Television and Radio Committee was disbanded and Eesti Ringhääling was established as a state board directly responsible to Parliament. Two separate operating state firms, Eesti Raadio and Eesti Television, were formed responsible to the state holding company Eesti Ringhääling. In 1991, both state radio and TV lost their monopoly status as private local radio and TV stations were authorized. Although both state firms are subsidized by the state, they also compete for advertising with private stations.

By the end of the 1990s, large numbers of commercial radio firms had been established, all with limited transmitting power. Thus in 2000, there were a total of 25 broadcast stations with 93 transmitters, including those owned by the state firm, and two religious nonprofit ones. Radio broadcast hours increased rapidly from 65,000 in 1993 to over 214,000 in 1997, with the share of entertainment rising from 50 percent to over 70 percent. Own production dropped slightly, from 94 percent to 80 percent. The share of Estonian-language broadcast hours remained stable at over 80 percent, whereas the Russian-language share rose steadily from 6 to 16 percent, squeezing out other foreign languages completely by the end of the 1990s.

Television broadcasting in Estonia began in July 1955 and quickly expanded to include central Soviet television as well as Leningrad stations, which covered the country. Tallinn residents, however, were able to watch Finnish television stations from 1956, which operated on a commercial basis, broadcast in both Finnish and Swedish, and used subtitles on foreign films. Tallinners not only watched Western newscasts and learned Finnish and English, but, uniquely in the Soviet Union, developed an awareness and understanding of capitalism. Thus, when independence was regained, Estonia moved quickly and issued the first private television broadcasting license in 1992. The next year, when transmission of television broadcasts from Moscow and St. Petersburg were stopped, saw an explosion of television stations to eight, with one going out of business the next year but two new ones appearing for a total of nine in 1995. Subsequently, the reality of a small market of only 1.4 million and the widespread penetration of cable TV reduced the number to five in 2000. By 2002, there were only two private television companies (including TV3, owned by the Nordic MTG broadcast company) and the state ETV, plus one local channel in Tartu. Only ETV covered the whole country, whereas the private broadcasters left some sparsely populated areas uncovered. In addition, all cities and towns were covered by one of seven cable companies, which carried over 60 Finnish, Russian, British, German, and other foreign, including digital, channels.

The broadcast scene in Estonia at the beginning of the 21st century has become fully integrated into the European commercial broadcast system, and includes foreign investors in both radio and television.

RAHVARINNE (People's Front). The concept of the people's front was originally proposed by Secretary General Georgi Dimitrov at the VII Congress of the Comintern in 1935 as a method of fighting fascism. It was first used in Spain in the following year, when the Frente Popular was elected to power. In 1936–37, the short-lived French socialist government of Léon Blum was based on the Front Populaire, a coalition of socialists, radical socialists, and communists. In most East European states under Soviet occupation after World War II, the communists organized popular fronts as a means of seizing power.

Thus it was ironic that the Estonian Rahvarinne was set up in 1988 by leading **Estonian Communist Party** (ECP) members **Edgar Savisaar** and **Marju Lauristin** to deliberately crush communism in Estonia. When the Estonian Peoples' Front to Support Perestroika (its original full name) became the model for similar popular fronts to counteract the Communist Party of the Soviet Union (CPSU) and the local communist parties in the other Baltic Soviet Socialist Republics, Ukraine, Moldavia (now Molodva), Byelorussia (now Belarus), and other countries, revenge was complete.

The Rahvarinne, or RR as it was invariably called in print, was the culmination of almost two years of uncoordinated popular protest actions against Soviet power in Estonia, beginning with the widespread voicing of opposition in 1986–87 to the opening of new and expanded open-pit **phosphate mines** in **Northeast Estonia**, which would add measurably to the pollution of almost 20 percent of the territory of the country. At the same time, the media (still under the control of the ECP) were also rapidly opening their pages and opinion programs to the one-sided antistatist debate that went into high gear after the **Four-man Proposal** on **Isemajandav Eesti** (IME) in the newspaper *Edasi* on 29 September 1987. The Hirvepark meeting on 23 August 1987 was the start of public mass street demonstrations, and the congress of the Creative Associations (artists, writers, and musicians) on 1–2 February 1988 made it clear to all that the Estonian elites were unanimous in supporting an anti-Soviet action to free Estonia from its yoke.

Thus, two weeks later after a regular evening **television** discussion program, *Mõtleme Veel* (*Let's Continue Rethinking*), Savisaar and Lauristin proposed the establishment of the RR. It quickly caught the imagination of the people and led to the Estimaa Laul (The Estonian Song, implying that the Estonians were now singing their own tune) **song festival**/rally at the Song Festival Grounds in **Tallinn** with 300,000 participants including **Vaino Väljas**, the new first secretary of the ECP, the major public declaration of yearning for independence of the Estonian people. A year later, on 23 August 1989, on the 50th anniversary of the **Molotov-Ribbentrop Pact**, the **Baltic Chain** of 2 million Estonians, Latvians, and Lithuanians holding hands from Tallinn to Vilnius was a demonstration to the world of the solidarity of the Baltic peoples' determination to be free. Although RR continued to operate until 1993, its influence declined rapidly after more outspoken activists in the Heritage Society and the newly formed radical independence political party, the Eesti Rahvusliku Sõltumatuse Partei (ERSP) (*see* POLITICAL PARTIES), dominated the independence dialogue in 1990. Although the RR fielded candidates in the 1992 presidential and parliamentary elections, it soon split up into several political parties and decided to disband at its closing congress on 13 November 1993. Its role in the two crucial years, 1988 and 1989, in providing leadership and inspiration to the mass of the Estonian people and focusing on their aspirations, was crucial in the struggle for independence.

RAUD, KRISTJAN (1865–1943). Estonian painter and renowned cultural figure. Raud was born on 22 October 1865 in Viru-Jaagupi *vald* to a freehold farmer. Kristjan and his twin brother, Paul (who died on 22 Nov 1930 in **Tallinn**), were only able to study art because of prominent patrons. Paul was financed by Baroness Natalie von Uexküll, a member of one of the oldest noble families in the Baltic. Kristjan's studies were financed by the tsar's family, arranged by the society painter **Johann Köler**. Although Paul devoted his life to painting and became a well-known painter, Kristjan entered the pantheon of Estonian culture only partly for his art, but mostly because of his leadership in the preservation and development of Estonia's cultural heritage. He studied at the Art Academy in St. Petersburg from 1892 to 1897 and continued his studies at Düsseldorf in 1897–98, and at Munich in 1898–1903. He returned to Estonia and opened an atelier in **Tartu** in 1904, where he worked until 1914 when he moved to Tallinn.

As a cultural activist during his Tartu years, Kristjan Raud joined **Young Estonia**, the Estonian Farmers Society, and the Estonian Art Society, and was one of the driving forces in establishing the Estonian National Museum (Eesti Rahva Muuseum). His services in preserving folk art are significant: in 1909–13, he led the collection of cultural artifacts for the Museum, and he organized a national collection in 1920. In 1918, Raud founded the Museum's Tallinn branch and organized and became leader of the Estonian Museum Society. During the 1920s he also taught at various schools, including the State Artisan School.

Most of Raud's artworks are pencil and charcoal drawings, although he also painted in oils, tempera, gouache, and watercolors. The primary theme in his work revolves around the Estonian people and their fate and heritage. As an artist, he is best known for the depiction of the mythological hero, **Kalevipoeg**, whom he depicted in a series of drawings in 1913–17, especially those published in 1935 in the 100th anniversary issue of **Friedrich Reinhold Kreutzwald**'s epic work, and a series of subsequent paintings of the mythical hero. Raud continued to paint at the studio in his house in Tallinn until his death on 19 May 1943. Most of his best work is located in the Tartu and Tallinn Art Museums. His house in Tallinn has also been turned into a memorial museum, and a statue was erected in his memory in Tallinn in 1969.

REBANE, ALFONS (1908–1976). Estonian soldier and the premier Estonian hero of World War II. Born on 24 June 1908 in Valga, Rebane studied at the **University of Tartu**, graduated from the Estonian War College in 1929, and then served in various capacities in the Estonian armed forces. When the Estonian Army was taken over by the Soviet Union after it annexed Estonia in 1940, he was appointed to command the reconnaissance battalion of the new Red Army 22 (Estonian) Territorial Corps. Soon, however, he was relieved of his command and discharged from the Army, apparently because the new masters did not consider him trustworthy. With the outbreak of German-Soviet hostilities, he sought out companions to form units to fight to free Estonia from foreign domination, and he organized the guerilla Viru Malev that operated in northeastern Estonia, destroying Soviet Army communications and attacking smaller units and local communist administrative offices. Shortly after the arrival of the German occupation, Rebane was appointed early in 1942 to organize the volunteer Security Company 181, later renamed the 15th Company of the 4th (East) Battalion, in the German Army. He fought valiantly with his company against the Red Army on the German front east of the Estonian border in the battles of spring 1942.

When Estonian relations with the Germans worsened in the fall of 1942 and the number of volunteers declined, the six Estonian battalions were consolidated into three and Rebane was appointed commander of the 1st East (Estonian) Battalion. In March 1944, his unit was brought back from the Russian front, reorganized, and incorporated into the 20th (Estonian) Division of the Waffen-SS as the 2nd Battalion of the 47th Regiment. Rebane refused initially to join the Waffen-SS but was soon forced to change his German Wehrmacht major's insignia for those of a Sturmbannführer of the Waffen-SS. In command of his men, once again he fought against the Red Army on the eastern front of Estonia from **Narva** to **Tartu**. At the battle for Tartu, he was promoted to command of the 46th Regiment and fought a rear-guard action as the Germans retreated across Estonia and Latvia during the summer and fall of 1944, at the end of which his unit was shipped to Germany. Rebane's realistic evaluation of the military-political situation at this time was that any attempt at guerrilla warfare on Estonian territory against the Red Army would be pointless, and that the only service he could perform would be to continue to fight against the Russians on the Polish front. Accordingly, he distinguished himself and was awarded oak leaves to his Iron Cross and promoted to Standartenführer (colonel). Rebane is the only Estonian soldier to have been honored with the Iron Cross with oak leaves.

At the end of the war, most Estonian forces were on the Czechoslovak front and thus became prisoners of the Soviet Army. Rebane, however, made his way with a small unit into the British Occupation Zone in defeated Germany and surrendered there. After a short period of imprisonment, he was appointed as the Estonian expert at the Intelligence School in London, and helped to fight the KGB in its attempts to infiltrate the West. After retirement, he spent the last 20 years of his life in Germany, where he was active in both Estonian émigré and German organizations. He died on 8 March 1976 at Augsburg, Germany. In 1999, Rebane was reburied at the national cemetery in Tallinn in a state funeral, despite strong political criticism by Moscow. Colonel Rebane is held in high esteem by Estonians everywhere as a war hero who fought valiantly for Estonia's freedom against its historical enemy. *See also* ARMED FORCES; BRETHREN OF THE FOREST; ESTONIAN LEGION; GERMAN OCCUPATION; JR 200; OSTLAND.

REFUGEES. *See* DEPORTATIONS; EMIGRATION; ESTONIAN CANADIANS; ESTONIANS ABROAD.

REI, AUGUST (1886–1963). Estonian statesman and lawyer. Rei was a central figure in the struggle for independence of the Estonian people for over 60 years. From the time of the abortive Revolution of 1905 in the Russian empire, through independence and its loss in World War I, to the struggle to maintain the Republic de jure, and in the consciousness of the West in the postwar period, he was at the center of the action. No other Estonian statesman approaches his six-decade record of service during this fateful period of Estonian history.

Rei was born on 22 March 1886 in Pilistvere parish and began to serve the Estonian cause already as a young student at **Tartu** Gymnasium from 1896 to 1903, where he cofounded a student nationalist group. His activism led to his expulsion and a forced transfer to Novgorod to complete his secondary education, which he did in 1904, whereupon he entered law studies at St. Petersburg. When the Revolution of 1905 closed the University, he returned to Estonia and became one of the leaders of the Social Democratic movement. His flair for writing made him the principal author of the movement's flyers and other propaganda. With the crushing of the Revolution, he was charged and imprisoned but was released after five months owing to lack of evidence. He continued underground as editor of the outlawed newspaper *Sotsiaaldemokraat*. In 1907–11, while completing his studies in law, he took an active part in the Estonian student movement's political work in St. Petersburg.

After voluntary military service in the imperial army with discharge as lieutenant in the reserves, Rei practiced law briefly in Viljandi and served in the artillery in St. Petersburg during World War I. In 1917, he was elected deputy chair of the Supreme Committee by the First Congress of Estonian Soldiers, with the duty of organizing the Estonian national armed forces (*see also* PITKA, JOHAN; PÄTS, KONSTANTIN), while he also helped found the Estonian Social Democratic Workers' Party (ESDWP). After the German collapse, he was appointed minister of labor and welfare in the provisional government, but was forced to resign as a result of an article critical of the conduct of the Finnish civil war, since the Estonians were seeking assistance from the Finnish government. Perhaps because he had become leader of the right wing of the ESDWP, he was sufficiently acceptable to the bourgeois parties to be elected chair of the generally left-leaning **Constituent Assembly** on 23 April 1919. Consequently, for the next year and a half he carried the authority of the nascent Estonian state, until the **Constitution** was adopted, when Prime Minister Ants Piip became Riigivanem on 20 December 1920.

During the 1920s, Rei served repeatedly as chair of his party's executive committees as well as editor of its newspaper. He was elected to all six interwar **Riigikogu**. In 1928–29, he formed a coalition cabinet consisting of his Social Democrats, the Union of Settlers, State Tenants and Small Farmers, and the Christian Nationalist Party and served as Riigivanem for seven months until the ensuing general elections. In 1932–33, he served as foreign minister in the Päts's IV government, while continuing as chair of the **Tallinn** City Council. At the beginning of 1934, he attempted to form a new cabinet but was upstaged by the **preemptive coup** carried out by Päts and Johan Laidoner. However, since he was among the right-wing socialists who supported this action, he was rewarded by Päts in 1936 with the position of deputy foreign minister, and in 1937 was sent to Moscow as ambassador. As such, he was a member of the delegation forced to sign the Bases Agreement with the Union of Soviet Socialist Republics (USSR) in September 1939. He was in Tallinn during the fateful days of June 1940 since Päts intended to name him prime minister, but was overruled by Commissar Andrei Zdanov, backed by the Soviet Army. In September 1944, he served as foreign minister in the short-lived **Otto Tief** cabinet on Estonian soil between the retreating German and the advancing Soviet armies. Fleeing to Sweden, he joined Prime Minister **Jüri Uluots** in his exile government. On the latter's death, Rei became prime minister in exile, exercising the authority of the president from 1945 to his own death on 29 March 1963 in Stockholm.

In Estonia, Rei's activities and interests extended far beyond politics: he continued his legal practice and maintained a reputation as a highly competent lawyer, and he was a long-serving president of the Alliance Française, deputy chair of the Estonian Foreign Relations Association, as well as an active member of workers' theater, sports, and social clubs. In exile he worked tirelessly, often in cooperation with Latvian and Lithuanian colleagues, to regain independence for his homeland, by publicizing the illegality of the Soviet occupation and annexation in writings, appeals, and conferences. He also worked diligently to maintain the focus of his exiled compatriots and served as chair of the Estonian National Foundation in 1946–49 and as chair of the Estonian National Council in 1947–63. Rei's remarkable vitality enabled him to begin writing his memoirs in his mid-seventies, but fate intervened and he died after completing only the first volume.

REIMAN, VILLEM (1861–1917). Clergyman, historian, social activist, and one of the founders of Estonian cultural self-consciousness. Born into a deeply religious and ascetic tenant-farm family on 9 March 1861 in Suure-Kõpu *vald*, Reiman received a top-notch classical secondary education at **Pärnu** Gymnasium, which he attended from 1872 to 1877. In 1882, he entered the theology faculty at the **University of Tartu** and became member of the **Society of Estonian Literati**. In 1883, along with eight friends, he founded **Eesti Üliõpilaste Selts (EÜS)**, and in 1884 participated at Otepää in the dedication ceremony of its blue-black-white national flag (*see* NATIONAL SYMBOLS), subsequently adopted as the Estonian national flag. He served as president of EÜS in 1886 and maintained a close connection with this nationalist student fraternal organization throughout his life. Reiman began his lifelong writing career at university when his first anti-**Russification** articles appeared in Karl August Herrmann's *Postimees* in 1886, in which called on Estonians to develop a national high culture as the only guarantee of national survival. After graduating with a *cand. phil.* in 1887, Reiman served his mandatory pastoral candidacy year at **Jakob Hurt**'s congregation in St. Petersburg, where he deepened his interest in national cultural history. In 1890, he was confirmed pastor of the Kolga-Jaani parish, despite the opposition of the local **Baltic German** nobility. He married Paula Norman in the following year, and subsequently they formed one of the first educated Estonian families where the home language was Estonian.

From 1890, Reiman began his long association with the temperance movement, became its soul as well as temporal leader, and spoke out in sermons, writings, and speeches against alcohol and for a sound, healthful, and ascetic lifestyle. His continued public speeches against Russification, in defense of the **Lutheran** faith, and against the Russian empire's Orthodox Church brought him into frequent conflict with the state authorities. In 1891–94, he was placed under police surveillance and for 10 months under house arrest. In 1893, the year when over a hundred pastors were charged with antistate activity, he was defrocked by the Riga district court and sentenced to 10 months in jail, but received an amnesty.

During the 1905 Revolution, he actively condemned violence but defended those condemned to death by the punishment squads sent out by the imperial government in St. Petersburg. In the same year, he became one of the founders of the Estonian National Progressive Party as well as its ideologue. One of his demands was the replacement of the Baltic German control over the Lutheran Church by a national church controlled by leaders freely elected by the congregations.

In 1896, Reiman had led the group that helped **Jaan Tõnisson** to purchase *Postimees* from Herrmann. He was able to provide the largest contribution owing to having charge of one of the largest (1,600 hectares) and wealthiest parish estates in Estonia. His support extended to assisting in editing the paper, and in 1897–1901 he wrote a large number of cultural-historical articles for it. His literary output included editing the first five issues of the EÜS album (I–V, 1888–1902), an annual calendar (1896–1907), a compendium on Estonian culture in five volumes (1911–15), and the annual of the Estonian Education Societies (1909–10).

In addition to his writing activity, Reiman's social organizational activism in the opening decades of the 20th century was dedicated to building up institutions of Estonian culture. In 1907, with Tõnisson, he established the Estonian Literary Society, a revival of the moribund Society of Estonian Literati as a broader manifestation of the aspirations of the national culture, and served as its chair from 1907 to 1914. He participated in the establishment of the Estonian National Museum in 1909, founded the Viljandi Education Society in 1908, and served as its chair until 1913, helping it establish a middle school for girls in Viljandi in that year. He died suddenly at the early age of 56 on 25 May 1917 at Kolga-Jaani.

In Estonian history, Reiman is known as one of the great and moderate leaders of the later period of the **National Awakening** prior to **independence** who formed the direction of development of the high nationalist culture of Estonia. His life was characterized by idealism, ethnocentrism, pietism, and ascetism. He opposed violence and exalted morality, probity, responsibility, law and order, and ethical motivation in one's actions. He was convinced that with "God's help," Estonia would inevitably achieve independence.

RELIGION. Christianity most likely was introduced to Estonians from the east as the Kievan Rus proselytized Russians on the borderlands around 1054, the year of the Great Schism. Western attempts to convert the Estonians began in the following century when Fulco was named apostle to the Estonians and in 1165 became bishop of the Estonians. By the middle of the 13th century, bloody **Crusades** led by Germans and Danes had Christianized first Latvia and then Estonia by the sword. The process involved combining the spiritual with military force when Albert Buxhoevden, bishop of Riga, in 1202 founded the Fratres Militiae Christi, popularly known as the Brethren of the Sword (Schwertbrüder), which later folded into the Teutonic Order (Deutsche Orden) (*see* **CRUSADING ORDERS**). Monks and nuns from newly founded monasteries followed, with Dominicans and Cistercians especially eager to convert the heathen. In the western parts of Estonia, the Catholic Church ruled supreme, and in the eastern borderlands controlled by Russian princelings, the Orthodox rite of the rulers held sway.

Beginning in 1523, the Lutheran Reformation quickly spread across Catholic Estonia as the **Baltic German** landlords converted and placed Lutheran pastors in the village churches. In the 17th century, Sweden conquered Estonia and enforced the Lutheran liturgy, held vernacular services, and encouraged Bible reading by parishioners. The Catholic Church became virtually extinct in Estonia.

Until the middle of the 19th century, membership in the Russian Orthodox Church in the Estonian settlement areas of the Gubernyas (Provinces) of Estland and Livland was limited to Russians in the towns and the **Setus** in the Gubernya of Pskov. Owing largely to mostly unfilled expectations of land grants and other preferential advantages from the tsar (who was head of the church), a segment of the Estonian peasantry converted to Orthodoxy. Thus, by **Independence**, the Orthodox Church had about 200,000 members in Estonia, although the majority of the population belonged to the Lutheran Church. The religious revivals that swept across Europe in the late 19th and early 20th centuries also rapidly reached Estonia. With complete religious freedom during the two decades of independence, the denominations founded by Evangelical movements flourished.

Since Estonians had not been particularly religious in modern times, the suppression of religion during the Soviet occupation succeeded in removing religion from the lives of the vast majority of people, except for small cores of older believers. However, as the Soviet yoke lifted, organized religion revived as most church buildings in the villages and countryside were rebuilt during the 1990s, often with foreign assistance, and the functions of baptism, confirmation, marriage, and burial were again carried out by a newly trained ministry. Although the **Constitution of 1992** guarantees absolute religious freedom in contemporary Estonia, the state still plays a role in registering churches as well as other voluntary organizations, and still has ownership or guardianship of some church buildings, a legacy of the Soviet period. The religious denominations of historical and modern Estonia are summarized below.

Lutheran Church. Lutheranism was introduced into the Baltic when the Diet of Volmar in 1544 recognized the principle of freedom of faith. After 1555, when the Livonian Order signed the Treaty of Augsburg, the principle of *cuius regio eius regio* ("the ruler determines the religion of the ruled") converted practically all churches in Estonia to Lutheranism, as the **Baltic German** nobility controlled appointments of pastors to all parish churches. With the arrival of the Swedish conquest at the end of the century, a systematic organization of church life began with the establishment of a consistory in **Tallinn** and the development of strict church discipline. The Swedish Law on Churches of 1686 came into force in Estonia in 1694. When Estonia passed under the suzerainty of Russia after the Peace of Nystad (German, Neustadt; Finnish, Uusikaupunki), the tsar granted the aristocracy the right to appoint clergy. A century later, in 1832, this right was removed by Tsar Nikolai I in a new church law. After independence in 1919, a national nonstate Lutheran church was established. In this respect, the Estonian Church differs from those of the Nordic countries, where the Lutheran Church remains the state church and performs such basic state functions as registering births, deaths, and marriages. As all religion was repressed during the Soviet period, the Estonian Evangelical Lutheran Church also came under the control of the state authorities but continued in operation with a small number of clerics and congregations. The Estonian Evangelical Lutheran Church in Exile was organized by Archbishop Johan Kõpp under the authority granted to him in 1943 by the home church and operates with 67 congregations in Australia, Canada, Sweden, as well as several other European and Latin American states. The Estonian and the Exile churches recognize each other but continue to operate separately with two archbishops. The home church has 165 congregations divided into 12 bishoprics and claimed 176,000 members in 2000.

Roman Catholic Church. Catholicism reemerged in the 18th century with the first post-Reformation congregation building its church in 1844 in **Tallinn**, but with most of the members being foreigners. After independence, the Catholic Church of Estonia was separated from the Bishopric of Riga, and in 1936 the German Jesuit Eduard Profittlich became the first bishop of the Estonian church. During the Soviet occupation, the church was again united with the Riga Bishopric. In 1992, Rome sent Archbishop Justo Mullor Carcia to act as bishop of the restored Bishopric of Estonia. In 1934, the Roman Church had 2,327 Estonian members and a like number of Polish guest workers who attended mass; the number of Catholics in independent Estonia at the beginning of the 21st century is around 3,000. The Church also has one restored monastic order of monks and two of nuns.

The Orthodox Church. A report exists of an Orthodox congregation in Estonia in 1030, but records of the Orthodox Church before the 18th century are scarce and uneven since the ruling aristocracy supported competing churches and either ignored or repressed the Orthodox faith. In the 18th century, Orthodoxy in Estonia came under the Pskov Diocese, but when the Riga Diocese was established in 1850 Estonian congregations were brought under its control. Until 1917 none of the bishops were Estonian, but in that year Platon (Paul Kulbusch) was ordained bishop of Riga and vicar of **Tallinn**. In 1919, he was murdered as a public enemy by the **Bolsheviks**. In the same year, the Church's first Estonian plenary decided to declare its autonomy within the Eastern Church. A year later Tihon, the patriarch of the Russian Orthodox Church, recognized the independence of the Estonian Apostolic Orthodox Church (EAOC). The Church elected Archbishop Aleksander and ordained him for life as its head. In 1923, the Estonian Church at its own request was canonically subordinated to the Patriarchate of Constantinople, thus severing any residual connection with the Russian Patriarchate. By 1938, the EAOC had three elected bishops, 55 high priests, 95 priests, and 30 deacons, for a total of 183 clerics; it had a monastery in Petseri, two convents in Estonia proper, a priory in Tallinn, a seminary in Petseri, and a chair of orthodoxy in the Faculty of Theology at the **University of Tartu**.

In 1944, with the second Soviet occupation imminent, the head of the Church, Metropolitan (Archbishop) Aleksander, along with 22 clergymen and thousands of believers, fled for the West and continued to operate in exile as the legal Estonian Apostolic Orthodox Church under the authority of the 1935 Synod rules. In March 1944, the Patriarchate of Moscow dismissed the remaining members of the synod of the EAOC and established a new Diocesan Council under the control of the Moscow Patriarchate, with a bishop who did not speak Estonian as its head.

In 1993, under the authority of the Law on Churches and Congregations, the EAOC reregistered in Estonia and thus was able to claim the return of its church buildings and other properties confiscated by the Soviet state on 16 June 1940. Also in 1993 Alexius II, the patriarch of Moscow and all the Russias (and, incidentally, an ethnic Estonian), issued a *tomos* (church decree) that the Estonian Orthodox Church, formerly the Diocese of Estonia, would remain subordinate to the Patriarchate of Moscow. In 1995 he elevated its head, Bishop Kornelius, to archbishop of Estonia. In 1996, the patriarch of Constantinople renewed the *tomos* granting the EAOC its status as in 1923, and named the archbishop of Karelia and All Finland as his *Locum Tenens* (vicar) on all matters concerning the EAOC.

Sixty Orthodox congregations have decided to join the EAOC, and 30 others have expressed a wish to remain affiliated with the Moscow Patriarchate. The 60/30 division, which also reflects the division of the 60,000 Orthodox Christians in Estonia, splits the Church along language lines. It involves legal disputes over property as well as the struggle between the Patriarchates of Moscow and Constantinople over control of Estonian Orthodoxy. Despite legal action up to the Supreme Court of Estonia, the Church headed by the Moscow faction has not been granted the right to use the name EAOC or title to any property, nor have any of its congregations been registered. In January 1999, at a meeting with the Estonian prime minister, the Moscow patriarch expressed a willingness to settle the dispute with the registered EAOC in order to receive legal recognition for its separate church and the property used by its congregations.

However, the dispute now revolved around the name that the Russian-controlled Church would use in Estonia. The Moscow Patriarchate insisted on a name that the Estonian government considered misleading since it suggested that the Russian controlled Church is an independent Estonian one. In 2001, after the Russian Patriarchate brought a suit of discrimination against the Estonian government, the matter of name was settled by negotiation as the Estonian Orthodox Church of the Moscow Patriarchate because the **Constitution** guarantees the right of any religious group to be registered. Hence, Estonia now has two legally recognized Orthodox Churches, thus reflecting its position as the historic borderland between Eastern and Western Christianity more clearly than at any time in its history.

Old Believers. During the reign of **Peter the Great**, church reform in Russia alienated a number of faithful who refused to accede to the modernization of the liturgy. The recalcitrants were placed under interdict by the Church, which was headed formally by the tsar; persecuted; and forced to the borderlands of the empire, such as to Estonia. Known as Old Believers, a large number settled along the western shores of **Lake Peipus** in villages of peasant farmers and fishermen. Although they were forbidden to build churches, they formed congregations and actively practiced their faith. During the 1920s and 1930s, they were able to operate freely as were all other religious denominations, and they survived the religious persecution of the Soviet occupation by following their successful practice in the empire of not attracting attention to themselves and not proselytizing. Today, there are 11 Old Believer congregations in Estonia with about 10,000 members, still in the same villages along Lake Peipus, still speaking Russian, and still following their old rites. In 1994, they formed the Union of Old Believer Congregations and joined the World Council of Old Believers.

Jewish Estonians. *See* JEWISH ESTONIANS.

Other Denominations in Estonia. The first Baptist congregations were formed in 1884 by Swedish and German missionaries. By 1900, their numbers were large enough to form the Estonian Baptist Union. At the beginning of the century, both the Pentecostal movement and the Free Evangelical movement also arrived in Estonia. During the 1930s, many of these congregations joined the Baptist Union. In 1945, the Soviet occupying authorities amalgamated all three and other Evangelical Free congregations into the Union of Evangelical Christians and Baptists of the Soviet Union. But even before the restoration of independence, the small confessional congregations began to separate with the assistance of their exile co-confessionals. Thus, in 1989 the independent Estonian Evangelical Christians and Baptists Union was formed, consisting of Baptist congregations, and it grew rapidly to 89 congregations and 6,500 members. The first Estonian Christian Pentecostal Church was formed in 1991 and by 2000 had grown to 38 congregations and 2,500 members. The first Estonian Methodist Church was founded in 1910 in Saaremaa and soon spread to the mainland, but it never acquired many adherents. It was revived in the 1990s with the help of the North European Central Conference of the United Methodist Church and reestablished 24 congregations with 1,900 members. The Seventh Day Adventist

Church was initiated by German missionaries from St. Petersburg in 1897 and by the end of the 1930s had grown to 38 congregations with 2,000 members. The church remained active in small congregations meeting at homes during the Soviet regime and was thus able to maintain a stable membership. In 2002, it consisted of 18 congregations with 2,000 members.

RESTITUTIO IN INTEGRUM. The Latin phrase, taken from ancient Roman law, is used principally today in copyright and trademark law, and it means restoration in whole to a state prior to a breach of copyright. In 1989 **Endel Lippmaa**, then prominently involved in the politics of independence, used the phrase as a legal justification to restore Estonia's sovereignty in toto as it existed prior to the Soviet takeover based on the illegal secret protocol of the **Molotov-Ribbentrop Pact**. The phrase became popular among Estonians and was incorporated in the declaration of transition to independence by the last **Supreme Soviet** of the Estonian Soviet Socialist Republic (ESSR) on 30 March 1990. Subsequently, the phrase was used to demand total restoration of property confiscated or transferred by, or under, both the German and Soviet regimes, and it created a rift between the former real property owners and their heirs and those who occupied the property. After long confusion, however, the principle of sanctity of property ownership was adhered to, except for property declared to be of national value or importance, for which compensation was paid. *See also* PRIVATIZATION.

RIIGIKOGU. Literally State Assembly, the Riigikogu is the unicameral parliament of Estonia. According to the **Constitution of 1920**, which established it, the Riigikogu consisted of 100 members elected for a term of three years by universal suffrage. Five parliaments, titled Riigikogu I to V, were elected between November 1920 and May 1932. Elections were fixed for the first Sunday in May of the third year of the parliament (*see* RIIGIKOGU ELECTIONS 1920–1932).

In 1933, after years of squabbling between those who supported an assembly-centered government where the executive power was severely restricted by the legislature and a presidential-parliamentary system where the executive president would have separate constitutionally sanctioned powers, a draft constitution leaning toward the latter was approved in a referendum and entered into force as the **Constitution of 1933**. On 12 March 1934, Riigivanem **Konstantin Päts** used the power of ruling by decree authorized by the new Constitution to avert a rumored coup and declared a state of emergency, instituted martial law, adjourned the Riigikogu, and thus ushered in the **Era of Silence**. After a brief session, he again adjourned Riigikogu V on 2 October 1934 and never recalled it. On 5 March 1935, all activities of political parties were prohibited.

On 18 February 1937, a partly elected, partly appointed National Assembly was convened to draft a new presidential-parliamentary Constitution, which was adopted by a referendum on July 28 of the same year (*see* CONSTITUTION OF 1937). The new Riigikogu consisted of two chambers: the Riigivolikogu (Chamber of Deputies), an 80-member body elected on a majority basis by universal suffrage; and the 40-member Riiginõukogu (State Council), appointed by the president. The VI Riigikogu took office in February 1938 after elections to the Riigivolikogu (*see* RIIGIKOGU ELECTIONS 1938).

Within two years, on 17 June 1940, before the new Constitution and parliament could begin to repair the damage of the constitutional crisis of the preceding decade, Estonia was occupied by the Soviet Union. A year later it was occupied by Germany, and in 1944 again by the Soviet Union. During the brief interregnum between the German withdrawal and the second Soviet occupation in September 1944, a nonpartisan government was formed on the basis of the Constitution of 1937. Within days, its members were either imprisoned by Soviet forces or fled to the West, where they maintained the de jure government in exile of the Republic of Estonia until the restitution of independence.

The new Soviet occupation lasted for 47 years, during which elections to the Estonian Supreme Soviet, a standardized Soviet style legislature, were regularly held under the aegis of the **Estonian Communist Party** (ECP), which was the sole political party allowed by the Soviet constitutions of the Estonian Soviet Socialist Republic (ESSR) (*see* CONSTITUTION OF 1940 OF THE ESSR; CONSTITUTION OF 1978 OF THE ESSR).

In the middle of the **Second National Awakening**, elections in March 1990 to the **Supreme Soviet** (*see* SUPREME SOVIET ELECTIONS) took place on a largely democratic basis and led to the new body preparing the restitution of independence for Estonia.

Since the restitution of Independence, three parliaments have been elected on the principles of the Constitution of 1920 as reiterated in the **Constitution of 1992**. To reduce electoral instability, the mandate was increased to four years and the membership was increased by one to the odd number 101. The 1992 Elections Act fixes the date of the elections as the first Sunday in March in the fourth year of the parliament. To maintain constitutional continuity, the parliaments have been titled Riigikogu VII to X (*see* RIIGIKOGU ELECTIONS 1992–2003).

RIIGIKOGU ELECTIONS 1920–1932. During the liberal democratic regime of the Estonian Republic's first period of independence lasting from 1920 to 1933, five general elections took place. The 100 seats were filled by proportional representation in which each citizen over 21 (who had held Estonian citizenship for at least one year) cast a single vote in a secret ballot for a party list in multimember electoral districts. The Riigikogu (literally, State Assembly) was elected for a three-year term, and each parliament was numbered using Roman numerals beginning with I (see table 3).

RIIGIKOGU ELECTIONS 1938. On 24–25 February 1938, elections were held to the Chamber of Deputies (Riigivolikogu) of the two-chamber Riigikogu. In the first elections after the adoption of the Constitution of 1937 by referendum, only one party and individuals running without party affiliation were allowed to campaign for office. Despite these restrictions, the official government party, the Popular Front for the Implementation of the Constitution, won only 47 percent of the votes cast to 53 percent for the independent candidates. The Popular Front, nevertheless, won an overwhelming majority of the 80 seats, since the elections were conducted on a first-past-the-post basis rather than the traditional proportional system hitherto used in Estonia. Moreover, in eight constituencies there was no voting since the only candidate represented the Popular Front. In addition, 10 members who had campaigned as individuals joined the 54 official party members elected or acclaimed after the elections, and thus raised the government bloc to 64 seats. The opposition consisted of the eight-member Democratic Faction (comprising the Center and Settlers parties' members and two **Veterans**), and the six-member

Table 3 Riigikogu Elections, 1920–1932

	Number of Seats in Riigikogu				
Party	*I 1920*	*II 1923*	*III 1926*	*IV 1929*	*V 1932*
Left					
Communists	5	10	6	6	5
Independent Socialists	11	5	—	—	—
Social Democrats	18	15	—	—	—
Social Workers Party	—	—	24	25	22
Center					
Labor Party	22	12	13	10	—
National Party	10	8	8	9	—
Homesteaders	—	4	14	14	—
National Center	—	—	—	—	23
Other parties	—	6	—	—	—
Right					
Christian National Party	7	8	5	4	—
Farmers Party	21	23	23	24	—
United Agrarian Party	—	—	—	—	42
Landlords Party	1	2	2	3	—
National minorities' parties	5	7	5	5	8
Totals	100	100	100	100	100

Working People's Unity Faction (consisting of communists and left-wing socialists).

RIIGIKOGU ELECTIONS 1992–2003. Restored Estonia's political parties are all rooted in the struggle for independence between 1988 and 1991. In consequence, the current party system is very different from the prewar one. Whereas the latter was based on left-right ideological and class conflicts, the current one does not have any left-wing political parties, apart perhaps from the mildly Social-Democratic Russian coalition party, which, however, plays no significant role in national politics. All the other parties, however they may title and describe themselves for electoral purposes, are really center-right parties pursuing indistinguishable entrepreneurial policies. Even the rural-based Coalition and the Country People's parties pursue free trade. As a result, Estonia is the only country in the world with no tariff protection, even for **agriculture**. All parties supported rapid **privatization** (completed by 1998, except for a few utilities), have provided solid support for quick accession to both the **European Union (EU)** and the **North Atlantic Treaty Organization (NATO)**, and have pursued stable, conservative economic policies consistently lauded by the International Monetary Fund (IMF), with the result that from 1992 through 2002 Estonia had the highest per capita foreign investment of any transitional country. See table 4 for a breakdown of party representation from 1992 to 2003.

In the Estonian context, center-left signifies primarily that they are committed slightly more to governmental social activism than the center-right parties, which lean more toward fiscal conservatism and the creation of wealth. The Moderates and Center Party are the only center-left parties, the others are center-right, and, apart from the splinter parties on the right that were elected in the first or the second elections, the Reform Party is the most right-wing of the center-right parties. The Independent Royalists were a unique party composed of

Table 4 Party Representation, 1992–2003

Parties	*Riigikogu VII* *20 Sept. 1992*	*Riigikogu VIII* *5 March* *1995*	*Riigikogu IX* *7 March 1999*	*Riigikogu X* *2 March 2003*
Moderates	12	6	17	6
Center Party	15	16	28	28
Coalition Party	17	41	7	13
Country People's Party			7 (with Coalition Party)	
Pro Patria	29	8	18	7
Estonian National Independence Party	10			
Res Publica				28
Reform Party		19	18	19
Better Estonia/ Estonian Citizen	8			
Entrepreneurs' Party	1			
Right Wingers' Party		5		
Independent Royalists	8			
Greens	1			
Estonian United People's Party (ethnic Russians)			6 (coalition of two parties)	6
Total	101	101	101	101

successful Soviet-era comedians whose function was to act as court jesters of the first resurrected parliament, after which they disappeared. That Estonians actually elected eight members of the Independent Royalists, a clearly marginal and not politically serious party that had a tongue-in-cheek platform of creating a new "independent" kingdom of Estonia, is testimony to the exuberance of a newly freed democracy but was mainly a reflection of the star quality of comedians in Soviet Estonia, who built a strong following by their carefully constructed, irreverent anticommunist political satire.

A realignment took place among the right-of-center parties when Res Publica was founded in 2002, then won large numbers of seats in the municipal elections that fall and 28 seats in the Riigikogu in 2003, at the expense of Pro Patria and the Moderates, owing to widespread disillusion with the second Laar government among these parties' supporters.

Note also that some of the "parties" are either formal or informal electoral coalitions, notably the Coalition and Russian parties. Each election has also seen a number of minor parties unsuccessfully seek representation in parliament. *See also* ELECTORAL SYSTEM.

ROMAN CATHOLIC CHURCH. *See* RELIGION.

RUMMO, PAUL-EERIK (1941–). Estonian poet, dramatist, writer, and politician. Rummo, born on 19 January 1941 in **Tallinn**, graduated from the **Estonian language** and **literature** course at the **University of Tartu** in 1965 and thereafter worked as a writer at the Vanemuine Theater in **Tartu** and for the Drama Theater in Tallinn for the next 13 years, from 1976 to 1989. In 1987–89, he was secretary of the Estonian Writers Union and an active participant in the independence movement, led in the beginning by the writers and other creative artists. Thus he took part in the **Estonian Congress**, as well as the Estonian Committees' Constitutional Assembly, where he served as a committee chair in 1992. His partisan political life began in 1989 when he formed and led the Estonian Liberal Democratic Party until 1994, when it amalgamated with the Reform Party. After serving as consultant on cultural affairs in the State Chancellery during the transition government in 1990–92, he was elected to **Riigikogu** VII in 1992 and served as minister of culture and education in the **Mart Laar** coalition cabinet of 1992–94. In 1995 and 1999, he was reelected to parliament on the Reform Party list, but lost his seat in the 2003 elections. His parliamentary work has focused on cultural affairs and European matters.

During the Soviet period of the 1960s and 1970s, Rummo the poet provided important national-cultural nourishment to the Estonian people by his poetry. In the 1960s, his large output of lively and happy verses cast rays of sunlight on socialist reality; but in the 1970s his emphasis on the dreary reality and his political outspokenness brought censorship to his works, which nevertheless circulated in *samizdat* (literally self-publication in Russian, this terms refers to manuscripts typed in multiple copies, retyped, and circulated illegally by readers underground) became well known, and influenced the path of Estonian poetry. The proscribed works were subsequently published in collections during the **perestroika** of 1985 to 1989. In addition, his avant-garde play, *Cinderella Game*, which premiered in 1969, provided a watershed in the development of the Estonian theater. During his long career as a theater writer and critic, he produced a large number of plays and film scenarios. Along with his parliamentary career, Rummo continued to write critical literary essays as well as to translate poetry from English, Italian, Finnish, and Russian.

RUNNEL, HANDO (1938–). Estonian writer and poet. Runnel was born on 24 November 1938 in Võhmuta *vald.* After agricultural studies at the Estonian Agricultural Academy (now Agricultural University) in 1957–62, he turned to **literature** and obtained employment with the literary periodical *Looming*, for which he worked from 1967 to 1971. Almost two decades later (1989–91), he again worked as an editor for a literary journal, this time for the newly founded *Akademia.* Since 1992, he has lectured in arts and humanities at the **University of Tartu** and worked as an editor while continuing his creative literary activities.

Runnel's primary commitment, however, has always been to writing. In the 1960s and 1970s, he became a much-loved poet and published five collections in 1965, 1967, 1970, 1972, and 1976. His poetry in the 1960s reflected the age-old yearning of Estonians—a peasant people tenants in their own land under the yoke of foreign overlords—for the ownership of their own idyllic land. Because he was a *kolkhoznik*, so certified by his Soviet agronomist's diploma, the communist authorities at first did not understand his nationalist appeal to the hearts of Estonians. However, as he progressively became bolder in his irony of the Soviet demagoguery of democracy and rewriting of history, some of his poetry was censored in the 1970s, and was not published until 1988 and 1992. But Runnel's appeal to the Estonians increased, particularly when his poetry began to reflect the vulgarism of the prosaic life of Soviet Estonia. By 1982, his poetic collection contained hymns to individualism and the Estonian fatherland. Thus, his published poetry during the 1970s and 1980s formed a public protest against the party-state, and he became lionized as a fearless patriot by the Estonians to whose souls he provided solace and whom he encouraged to solidarity with the nation and its historic culture. Runnel was the conscience of Estonians. In addition to poetry, Runnel has published collections of essays and a number of children's books as well as numerous articles.

RUSSIANS IN ESTONIA. The history of Russian settlement on Estonian territory reaches back at least a thousand years and is composed of two sources—religion and trade. In 1030, Yaroslav the Wise founded the town of Jurjev (Yurijev) on the ancient Estonian stronghold of Tarbatu (Tartu). However, in 1061 the Estonians conquered the town. During Yaroslav's reign, the first Russian churches were founded, although Estonia was not Christianized until the 13th century by German, Danish, and Swedish crusaders. Later, the Western Russian trading towns of Novgorod and Pskov (Estonian, Pihkva) became members of the **Hanseatic League** along with **Tallinn** and **Tartu**, thus leading to close commercial ties and the settlement of Russian traders in the Estonian towns. In some farming villages along the ethnic border area as well as in the town of **Narva**, some mixing of populations took place. However, after the Christianizing of Estonia, the ethnic border also became a religious dividing line between the Eastern and the Western Churches, and, after the Reformation, between the Orthodox and the Lutheran faiths (*see* RELIGION). Despite records of some purely Russian villages along the western shore of **Lake Peipus** (Peipsi), the Russian population on Estonian territory is estimated at under 1 percent as late as the end of the 18th century, despite the establishment of Russian suzerainty over the Baltic Provinces in the Treaty of Nystad.

Russian immigration began in earnest at the end of the 1830s when Old Believers (the followers of the Russian Orthodox Church who resisted church reforms) began to move to eastern Estonia and Latvia, and established new congregations. The Baltic Provinces offered a more tolerant atmosphere at this time owing both to the influence of the Enlightenment on the Baltic aristocratic rulers and the dominance of **Lutheranism**. Later in the 19th century, the construction of railroads increased both commerce and movement of people, with the result that the census of 1867 recorded 8,500 Russians in Estonia; the census of 1881 recorded 16,000. The latter figure, nevertheless, still formed only 2 percent of the total population of Estonia.

The first major increase of Russians in Estonia occurred with the redrawing of the border in the **Peace of Tartu** in 1920, in which Estonia regained the town of **Narva** (part of Novgorod province since 1720 but where the Estonians were in the majority) and gained the right bank of the Narva River and the historically ethnically mixed **Petserimaa** (Pechora) county in the southeast. Thus, in 1922 Estonia had a Russian population of 92,000, or 8.2 percent of the total. This ethnic Russian share in the Estonian population was considered indigenous by Estonians and remained constant until the massive migration of labor orchestrated by the Soviet Union took place beginning during World War II. Although the aftermath of the Bolshevik Revolution had seen an influx of political refugees into Estonia and even some political anti-Soviet activities by them in the 1920s, many moved on to France and other Western countries. Thus the number who integrated into the Estonian Russian community was small.

The Soviet occupation and annexation of 1940–41, the German occupation of 1941–44, and the Soviet reoccupation of 1944 cost the indigenous Russian Estonians dearly as all leading figures were murdered or deported along with their ethnic Estonian counterparts, while Russian political émigrés in Estonia fled to the West. By the end of the war, the local Russian Estonians were headless and overwhelmed by the influx of Soviet Russians. Young people moved from the Estonian Russian villages to the towns, and many integrated into the ethnic Estonian population. Moreover, the county of Petseri and the right bank of the Narva River were reincorporated into Russia proper. Both the rural Russian Estonian settlements and most of the Russian Estonians' identity thus disappeared very quickly. Only the small number of fishing-peasant farming villages of Old Believers along Lake Peipus maintained their community.

The labor migration policy of the Soviet occupation during the half century from 1940 to 1990 increased the share of the Russian-speaking population to 40 percent. The majority of these had no ethnic consciousness or attachment to any "homeland" or loyalty to any territorial home area and considered themselves as part of the new Soviet man, with the whole Soviet Union as its homeland—a concept known in Russian as *Rodina.* Nearly the whole of this 600,000-strong population consisted of unskilled industrial working classes, which meant that during the 50-year period of the Soviet occupation, there was little Russian cultural life in Estonia. In fact, the Russian theater performances in Tallinn usually had more ethnic Estonians in the audience, and most of the Russians attending the universities in Tartu and Tallinn came from elsewhere in the Soviet Union. On the restitution of independence, most Estonians wanted to get rid of the Russophone migrants but only about 70,000 left. This led to almost a decade-long debate among Estonians on the "aliens problem," which is not completely settled yet at the beginning of the 21st century, although it is no longer a major political issue. *See also* ALIEN PASSPORTS; ALIENS; INTEGRATION; NARVA; NORTHEAST ESTONIA; RUSSIFICATION.

RUSSIFICATION. The term "Russification" as used in Estonia describes the attempt to force the use of the Russian language on Estonians in the last two decades of the 19th century and in the 1970s. The imperial policy of Russification was introduced by the nationalist government of Alexander III, after the assassination of the liberal Tsar Aleksander II on 13 March 1881, and lasted into the first decade of the 20th century. The policy was applied in the non-Russian western periphery, from Finland in the north to Poland in the south, to bring them into conformity with the rest of the Russian empire. Although Russian nationalist and pan-Slavist sentiments had circulated widely in St. Petersburg from the 1860s on demanding an end to the **Baltic Germans**' semiautonomous status in the **Baltic Provinces**, it was not until 1887 that systematic Russification began. The first law applied to all the peripheries of the empire and replaced the old self-perpetuating city councils with elected ones based on tax rolls and the appointment of mayors directly by the Ministry of the Interior. In 1888–89, the policing and judicial functions were taken over by St. Petersburg and Russian was mandated as the language of all public administration, and of instruction in all schools, including at the **University of Tartu**, which was renamed Imperial Jurjev University and brought under direct control of the imperial Ministry of Education, as were all lower schools.

Although the intent of these policies was to break both the privileges of the Baltic nobility (*see* SPECIAL BALTIC ORDER) and thus the separatist status of the Baltic provinces (and the similar privileges of the Polish nobility in the Polish-Lithuanian periphery and the Swedish upper class in Finland), its clumsy universal application gradually turned the anti-Germanic Estonians and Latvians inward toward their own **languages** and national cultural values in disregard of the imperial edicts. Moreover, the Estonians and Latvians noticed that the hand of the distant monolingual Russian foreign overlord was even harsher than that of the known Baltic German nobles. The Russification of **education** at the lower levels failed largely since most teachers had poor Russian language skills, and instead emphasized the value and beauty of the national language. At the higher levels, Russification produced an Estonian elite who spoke fluent Russian in addition to Estonian, German, and Finnish (and often French and English as well). Forcing the **Estonian Aleksander School**, funded by a widely supported 20-year public subscription campaign as the ideal Estonian-language school, to open instead as a Russian-language school in 1888 was probably the one act of the imperial government that turned Estonians inward and westward more than any other.

Thus, the unintended effect of Russification was to support **national awakening** instead. The resultant increased political activity of Estonians and Latvians (it should be noted that Estonia was divided until 1917 into the two Provinces of Estland and Livland, the latter shared with Latvians) led to electoral successes at municipal levels. In the 1904 local elections, Estonians gained control of the City Council of Tallinn for the first time, enabling **Konstantin Päts** and **Jaan Poska**, among others, to develop political skills and public support.

Although many Estonians would characterize the whole of the Soviet occupation as the second period of Russification, it is more correctly a period of Sovietization, a largely successful reorganization of the Estonian governmental, administrative, judicial, political, economic, and social structures as integral parts of the Soviet Union. For most of the half century of occupation, there was little pressure to reorient the language and ethnic culture of the people. However, the large-scale importation of non-Estonian Russian-speaking labor (*see* POPULATION) throughout the period and the three waves of **deportations** may be seen as a deliberate attempt to reduce the ethnic nation to impotence, that is, national genocide.

The infamous VIII Plenary of the Central Committee of the **Estonian Communist Party** (ECP) in 1950 saw the Estonian national-oriented ECP hierarchy replaced by returning Russified Estonians, many of whom could not even speak the local language. As a result, large numbers of the surviving elite were removed and repressed in the arts, sciences, and literature (including communist sympathizers) and replaced with Russians or Russified imports. Harsh Moscow-centered party and administrative rules were instituted. Still, the policy of Russification proper was ushered in gradually only with the 1961 Communist Party of the Soviet Union (CPSU) party program and the new Soviet constitutions of 1977. At the anniversary ceremonies commemorating the founding of the Union of Soviet Socialist Republics (USSR) in 1972, General Secretary Leonid Brezhnev announced the beginning of a new historical period, the building of a Soviet people with a new internationalist culture. The objective was to assimilate all the peoples of the Soviet Union into a homogeneous Russian-speaking mass—to create the so-called New Soviet Man or *Homo sovieticus*.

However, its implementation in Estonia began in earnest only in 1978 with the appointment of **Karl Vaino** as first secretary of the ECP. The legal basis for this was the secret decree of the USSR Council of Ministers of 12 October 1978: "On measures for implementing the further development of the learning and teaching of Russian in the federated republics." This decree enabled the ECP Central Committee to pass an ambitious 19-point plan to radically increase the use of Russian at the expense of the Estonian language. Although the writing of theses and dissertations in Russian only had been made obligatory earlier, even in Estonian philology, now an attempt was made to impose Russian as the universal language in Estonia. Among other measures, Russian suddenly became the language of instruction in kindergarten; the share of Russian was increased by a third in school curricula at the expense of other subjects; the teaching of Russian was favored in various ways, including establishing a new faculty to raise the qualifications of Russian-language teachers at the Pedagogical University; a new methodological journal of teaching Russian was founded in Estonia; and Russian-language teachers were given a 15 percent salary premium. At the same time, translation into Estonian of foreign language literature that had already appeared in Russian became difficult, local Russian authors were given preference in publishing, and Russian operas, plays, and films were performed or shown only in Russian. Moreover, Estonian became increasingly difficult to use in the capital city as monolingual Russian speakers were imported for jobs in the commercial, transport, media, communications, and banking sectors.

Although the immediate impact of these measures was unpleasant, their consequence was the strengthening of Estonian cultural consciousness and deepening of the commitment to linguistic and ethnic exclusiveness. The first public reaction was the Baltic Appeal of 23 August 1979, signed by 45 Estonian, Latvian, and Lithuanian citizens and addressed to the governments of the USSR, West Germany, and East Germany, the governments that had signed the Atlantic Charter in 1941, and to Kurt Waldheim, secretary-general of the United Nations (*see* DISSIDENTS). This was followed the next year by student demonstrations in Tallinn and the **Letter of the Forty** on 28 October 1980, shortly after the Olympic regatta had concluded in Tallinn. The speaking out on national consciousness and the expression of outrage at the pollution (*see* PHOSPHATE WAR) of the cherished Estonian national landscape was encouraged by General Secretary Gorbachev's policies of **perestroika and glasnost**, which were ushered in shortly thereafter and led to a melding of the xenophobic anti-Russian anti-Russification (Estonians did not distinguish between them) mentality and the inward-looking nationalism encouraged by its repression. In the event, this policy of Russification produced a stronger reaction than the earlier one in the 19th century and underlay the explosive developments that led to the restoration of independence. It also left a residue of animosity toward **Russians**, which a decade of independence has not completely removed (*see* INTEGRATION).

RUSSOW (RÜSSOW), BALTHASAR (c. 1536–1600). Medieval Estonian chronicler. Born around 1536 in **Tallinn**, the son of country teamster Simon Rissa, Russow was educated at the Tallinn City School, caught the attention of the pastor of St. Olaus's (Oleviste) Church, and was sent to Stettin, Wittenberg, and Bremen to study classical languages and theology. In 1563, he was ordained in Tallinn and became assistant pastor of the Estonian congregation at Holy Ghost (Pühavaimu) Church, and in 1567 its pastor, where he remained until his death on 24 November 1600. Russow's social career was even more remarkable. A landless peasant's son, he first married a German parish clerk's daughter; upon her death, he married the daughter of the bishop of Estonia; and on her death, he married the widowed daughter of one of the Great Guild's leading members, and thus entered the highest social circle of the **Hanseatic** town of Tallinn.

His great historical achievement is the Low German language *Chronica der Prouintz Lyffland* (*Chronicle of the Province of Livland*), first published in Rostock in 1578, which was immediately sold out, reprinted a second time in the same year, and reissued in a second updated edition in 1584. The *Chronicle* describes the history of Old Livland (*see* LIVONIA) from the 12th century to 1583. Its most valuable contribution to history is its detailed description of the social and economic conditions prior to the Liv War. Although the *Chronicle* immediately became a classic work in Low German, it also earned Russow the undying enmity of the **Baltic German** nobility who never forgave him for his less-than-gentle description of their rule. Russow's chronicle has been cited more by succeeding historians than any other Baltic chronicle except for Hendrik's *Chronicle* (*see also* CHRONICLES). The latest Estonian edition of Russow's *Chronicle* was published in 1993.

RÜÜTEL, ARNOLD (1928–). Agronomist, Estonian statesman, and third president of Estonia. Born on 10 May 1928 in Laimjala parish in Saaremaa, he graduated from the Estonian Agricultural Academy in **Tartu** in 1964 while working full time at the Estonian Institute of Animal Husbandry. He was director of the Tartu Model State Farm in 1963–69, and rector of the Agricultural Academy in 1969–77. Having joined the **Estonian Communist Party** (ECP) in 1964, Rüütel served as its secretary of agriculture in 1977–79, and after serving as first deputy to the chairman of the Estonian Soviet Socialist Republic's (ESSR) Council of Ministers in 1979–83 he rose to the chair of the Presidium of **Supreme Soviet of the ESSR** (in effect, president of the ESSR) and held that position until 8 May 1990. On March 1990, that body had declared Soviet authority on Estonian territory null and void and instituted a period of transition to independence to end with the formation of constitutionally constituted state organs of the Republic of Estonia. On 8 May, the ESSR Supreme Soviet declared the name ESSR null and void, reestablished the name of the country as the Republic of Estonia, reinstituted national regalia, and changed its English name to the Supreme Council of the Republic of Estonia. It elected Rüütel as its chair (effectively president of the Republic, since the structures of the **ESSR Constitution** continued in effect), in which capacity he served until the election of President **Lennart Meri** under the new constitution in 1992.

In addition to his political career, Rüütel continued his academic research and a connection with the Agricultural Academy. In 1991, he defended his doctoral thesis. In the same year, Bentley College in the United States granted him an honorary doctorate for his political work. In Estonia his old school, now renamed the Agricultural University, honored him by naming him professor emeritus and by granting an honorary doctorate.

Despite his long career in the ECP, as member from 1964 to 1989, in the Central Committee from 1971 to 1989, and in the Bureau (Estonian Politburo) from 1977 to 1989, Rüütel was never an ideological communist but a pragmatist who always served the interests of Estonia. In the confusing and difficult 1988–92 period, he worked diligently with progressive forces for Estonia's independence and stood up to the pressure exerted by Mikhail Gorbachev and the Communist Party of the Soviet Union (CPSU) central organs on him and on the Estonian government. In 1989–92 he, together with Prime Minister **Edgar Savisaar**, made the decisive moves in the Supreme Soviet and in the Supreme Council, as well as in negotiations with Moscow and in the public eye in Estonia. The result was that the fatherly looking and loquacious Rüütel had become the most popular politician in Estonia at the end of the Soviet period. In the 1992 presidential election, he won 41.8 percent of the popular vote, short of the 50.1 percent requirement, but lost to Lennart Meri, who had received only 29.5 percent, when the election, by the rules of the new Constitution of 1991 (only the first post-independence president was to be elected by popular vote), moved to the newly elected **Riigikogu**, which preferred a literary figure without a communist party past (*see* ELECTION OF PRESIDENT).

Rüütel, always highly regarded by the rural population, formed the center-right Rural Party, reorganized it in 1999 together with other rural parties into the Estonian People's Union, and served as its chairman from 1994 to 2001. As its leader Rüütel was elected to Riigikogu VIII in 1995 and IX in 1999 with large majorities; in 1995–97, he served as speaker of the Riigikogu and sat on its committees dealing with agriculture and ecology, the latter one of his special interests.

In October 2000, when parliament could not agree on a successor to retiring President Meri, and the election moved to the presidential electoral college, composed of members of parliament and representatives of all the municipal councils, Rüütel won in the second round of voting against younger, more intellectually accomplished rivals owing to his continuing popularity among the country folk. As a testimony to his pragmatic ability to create consensus, within months of his election his support ratings among all classes rivaled those of Meri's at his height. Owing to his grandfatherly mien and his agricultural roots, Rüütel has maintained his popularity among common people, and has received acceptance among the intelligentsia, who accord him the respect due to a head of state and who no longer compare him to Meri. Since his election, Rüütel has worked consistently as the Great Conciliator attempting to heal the apparent rift between the "winners and losers," the educated younger urban elites and the older, rural population. Indeed, his election as president was widely regarded as the revenge of the "losers," whose interests the **Mart Laar** cabinet had consistently disregarded, and which led directly to the formation of Res Publica and the consequent decline of Pro Patria and the Moderates parties in 2002–03 (*see* POLITICAL PARTIES).

– S –

SAUL, BRUNO (1932–). Long-serving party politician in the Estonian Soviet Socialist Republic (ESSR). Born on 8 January 1932 in **Narva**, Saul graduated in 1956 as an engineer from the (ESSR) Leningrad Electrotechnical Communications Institute, and subsequently earned an *econ. cand.* degree in 1977. In 1973, he graduated from the Higher Party School of the Central Committee of the Communist Party of the Soviet Union (CPSU). He then worked as an engineer and head of the ESSR Radio Center in 1961–64 and as chief engineer in the ESSR Ministry of Communications in 1964–66. From 1969 to 1975, Saul served as minister of communications, from 1975 to 1983 as first deputy of the ESSR Council of Ministers, and as prime minister from 1984 to 1988. Saul was a member of the **Estonian Communist Party** (ECP) from 1960 until 1990, when he resigned his membership. From 1984 to 1990, he also served as a member of the Supreme Soviet of the Union of Soviet Socialist Republics (USSR) and from 1975 to 1990 as a member of the ESSR Supreme Soviet.

On 7 December 1988, he was dismissed by the ECP Central Committee's XII Plenary as Chairman of the Council of Ministers (prime minister) because of popular pressure successfully exerted for the first time in Soviet Estonia, resulting from the Four-man Proposal on **Isemajandav Eesti** (IME) of September 1987 to establish Estonia as an independent economically autonomous republic within the Soviet Union. On 16 November 1987, the Saul Council of Ministers declared the IME proposal unacceptable ("noncompetent") and chastised the authors. Popular sentiment, however, boiled over since other leading party members supported IME. In June 1988, the Hot Summer of the **Singing Revolution** had forced Mikhail Gorbachev to remove First Secretary **Karl Vaino**. The rest of the recalcitrant old-line party leadership, tainted with reactionarism, was removed along with Saul at the XII Plenary, after **Vaino Väljas** had been made party leader.

SAVISAAR, EDGAR (1950–). Estonian politician, prime minister, and mayor of Tallinn. Savisaar was born on 31 May 1950 in Harku. After graduating in history from the **University of Tartu** in 1973, he earned a *cand. phil.* degree in 1981 and worked as planning commission chair of Mere borough in Tallinn in 1980–85, then as division manager in the Estonian Soviet Socialist Republic's (ESSR) Planning Committee in 1985–88. After being forced to leave because of his espousal of economic independence for Estonia—he was one of the four signatories of the **Isemajandav Eesti** (IME) proposal—he joined the newly formed semiprivate consulting firm Mainor, which had been formed as a result of Mikhail Gorbachev's **perestroika and glasnost**, where he worked on the **IME project** in 1988–89. After **Vaino Väljas** replaced **Karl Vaino** as leader of the **Estonian Communist Party** (ECP), Savisaar was appointed minister of economics and head of the Planning Committee in the **Indrek Toome** government in 1989–90 and became prime minister of the transition government of 1990–92, until he was forced to resign in favor of **Tiit Vähi** on 29 January 1992. Subsequently, he has been elected to all four **Riigikogu** of independent Estonia, each time with the largest individual vote of any member. He served as deputy speaker of parliament in 1992–95, and as minister of the interior in the Vähi government in 1995. However, Savisaar was forced to resign both from the government and as leader of the Center Party, which he had founded, as a result of the so-called taping scandal (he had surreptitiously taped negotiations with other parties preceding the formation of the Vähi coalition cabinet) in October 1995. Although his party was the second largest in parliament, all five of its ministers were also forced to resign and Vähi formed a new coalition, this time with the Reform Party, on 6 November 1995. He was condemned by President **Lennart Meri** and shunned by all parties, and although a small group left the party, he was returned with an overwhelming vote as leader of the Center Party at its congress only six months later in May 1996. Subsequently, he was elected as chair of the Tallinn City Council in 1996 and served until 1999, in addition to his mandate as a member of parliament. In 1999, his party narrowly lost the majority in the city council elections, and the tripartite national government coalition of Pro Patria, Moderates, and Reform managed to stitch together a majority of one or two with the help of some Russian council members. However, in 2001 he formed a coalition with the Reform Party and was elected mayor of Tallinn. Although he resigned from the Riigikogu, Savisaar maintained his position as leader of the Center Party, was reelected to it with a resounding majority in April 2002, and as his party's leader he continued to play a major role in the policy making in the **Siim Kallas** Reform Party–Center Party coalition. In the municipal elections on 20 October 2002, the Center Party won an absolute majority in Tallinn but continued its coalition with Reform. In the Riigikogu elections of 2 March 2003, Savisaar again received the largest number of votes by far, but resigned his seat while continuing as mayor of Tallinn and as leader of the national Center Party. Savisaar's services in achieving the restoration of independence for Estonia are unsurpassed: he was the moving force behind the IME project and its popularization in the media, as well as the creator of **Rahvarinne**. He coordinated the work of the government and parliament during the transition period, and led Estonia to independence as prime minister.

It is no exaggeration to argue that the direction of all the Estonian governments' policies since 1990 have been based on Savisaar's vision of an economically prosperous independent state (although this is disputed by his detractors). It is also not surprising that Savisaar has found it difficult to maintain popularity. His forceful, even overbearing, personality and rapidly calculating analytical mind alienate him from many, since he lacks the schmoozing, back-slapping style of the natural politician. The conflict with rivals is exaggerated by Estonia's endemically fractious multiparty system with a maximum of 200 professional politicians in a tiny national elite of 2,000.

The endemic partisan conflict began when rivalry for position in new **Riigikogu elections** in 1992 among putative leaders broke up the Rahvarinne, of which Savisaar was the undisputed leader. The recriminatory attacks on each other were especially sharp against Savisaar, disparaging his autocratic style; his logical, apparently insensitive mind; and the large support he enjoyed (which continues to the present) among the Russian-speaking population. Savisaar, nevertheless, continues to win large personal majorities in Riigikogu elections. He led his party to the largest plurality in parliament in the 1999 elections, and in 2003 his party won more votes than any other but received the same number of seats as the new Res Publica Party, which formed the government together with the Reform and Coalition Parties, leaving Center in opposition. Although in 2001–02 Savisaar was able to organize cooperation with the right-wing Reform Party, the Pro Patria and Moderate Parties still loathed him so much that even in opposition (and reduced to rump size in the 2003 election), they found it hard to cooperate with the Center Party. Among the public, however, Savisaar maintains his popularity, as demonstrated yet again in December 2002 when he was voted the most influential politician of the year, ahead of both President **Arnold Rüütel** and Prime Minister **Siim Kallas**. *See also* POLITICAL PARTIES.

SCULPTURE. The earliest sculptures in Estonia date from the 13th century. Most prevalent are sculptural decorations on church and town buildings. Notable among these are the sculptures of Saaremaa's Karja Church, the terracotta figures in St. John's Church in **Tartu**, and the portal sculpture of the Dominican Monastery in **Tallinn**. Some mausoleum and sarcophagus bas reliefs of this period have also survived. The most notable secular sculptures are represented by the wooden figures in Tallinn Town Hall. Early period sculpture is mostly Gothic in style.

The Renaissance style is found in the cenotaphs in St. Mary's Chapel in St. Olaus Church in Tallinn and the burial monuments in the Tallinn Cathedral. The Baroque style of the 17th century is found in stone portals, window columns, and sarcophaguses, mainly in Tallinn. Wooden carvings of the period are found in the altars, pulpits, pews, epitaphs, and heraldic shields in churches. Until the end of the 19th century, the sculptors were mainly artists from Germany and Holland.

The fist native Estonian sculptors were August Ludwig Weitzenberg (1837–1921) and Amandus Heinrich Adamson (1855–1929) whose monuments, respectively depicting the mythological Linda (mother of **Kalevipoeg** and the modern form of the ancient name of Tallinn, Lindanise; thus the female symbol of Tallinn) on Harju Hill beside Parliament, and the Russalka memorial in Kadriorg Park, remain important Tallinn sights over a century later. Beginning in the 1920s, Estonian sculptors turned to portraiture in addition to decorative carvings and cemetery memorial monuments. The best known are Jaan Koort (1883–1935), Ferdi Sannamees (1895–1963), Herman Halliste (1900–1973), Enn Roos (1908–1990), August Vomm (1906–1976), and Anton Starkopf (1889–1966). During the post–World War II period, the initial focus of socialist realist sculpture honoring heroic workers gave way in the 1960s to portraiture, figural compositions, and freeform sculpture using different media, including wood, bronze casting, welded iron, and fiberglass. The leading sculptors of this period were Matti Varik (b. 1939), Riho Kuld (b. 1936), Erika Haggi (b. 1922), Mare Mikof (b. 1941), Jaan Vares (b. 1927) Arseni Mölder (b. 1910), and Olav Männi (1925–1989). No notable new sculptors have arisen since.

SECOND NATIONAL AWAKENING. Forty-five years had elapsed since Estonia had lost its independence to the Soviet occupying forces in 1940, when General Secretary Mikhail Gorbachev announced a policy of liberalization and renewal of Soviet society and economy at the April 1985 plenary of the Communist Party of the Soviet Union (CPSU) (*see* PERESTROIKA AND GLASNOST). To prevent a revolutionary explosion from below, the decision had been forced on Gorbachev by the obvious economic decline, thoroughgoing corruption, and bureaucratic gridlock of the Soviet Union.

The Estonian elites quickly recognized this as an opportunity for national renewal and began to rebuild the national memory of Estonian culture, which the Soviet party-state had openly and systematically been destroying since the infamous VIII Congress of the **Estonian Communist Party** (ECP) in 1948. Initial steps were the same as in the first **National Awakening** over a hundred years earlier, namely insertion of the songs of that period in concerts, and essays and descriptions of the roles of such great nationalist notables as **Jakob Hurt** and **Villem Reiman** in the press. In the fall of 1986, the heritage movement became active in towns and villages across the country, and in 1986–87 the antiphosphate mining campaign (*see* PHOSPHATE WAR) took off, activated by the mining bureaucracy in Moscow, which planned to set up a major phosphate mine in Toolse. The danger of environmental catastrophe was publicized by the journalist Juhan Aare in a large number of articles in the popular press and on **television**. A protest wave swept across Estonia: petitions were signed against the mines and students and intellectuals held meetings where they expressed lack of confidence in the Estonian Soviet Socialist Republic's (ESSR) government. The **Tartu** newspaper *Edasi* (*Forward*) and the monthly *Vikerkaar* (*Rainbow*) incited an ideological battle over **environmental** pollution and the danger of a bilingual Estonia.

Since the **Russification** of Estonia had long been a serious cause of concern for the Estonian elites, the mining proposal, which would have required yet another massive influx of migrant labor from the far reaches of the Soviet Union, provided a fortuitous convergence of two popular protest items. On 23 August 1987, a mass rally was held at **Hirvepark**, just below the Parliament building on **Toompea**, which demanded publicizing the secret protocols to the **Molotov-Ribbentrop Pact** of 1939, which had relegated the Baltic States to the Soviet Union. Although the repressive backward regime of **Karl Vaino** forced the Hirvepark organizer Tiit Madisson to leave Estonia and although the regime began to spy on and harass the heritage movement, this rally proved to be the turning point. After this, the public of Estonia could no longer be restrained in expressing their national aspirations for first cultural, and then political, independence.

On 27 September 1987, *Edasi* published the Four-man Manifesto proposing an economically autonomous Estonia—**Isemajandav Eesti** (IME). The acronym IME, which also means "miracle" in Estonian, within months became a code word for regaining the sovereign independent Estonian state and a powerful, emotive focus for all nationalist forces and aspirations. Thus, within a few months of the call for IME, networks of organizations appeared across Estonia oriented toward renewal of all facets of the nation. After almost five decades of repression under the yoke of the Soviet party state, societal voluntary organizations burst forth like flowers in spring right after the Party newspaper *Edasi* dared to call for the miracle of independence. The first and most encompassing of these was the Heritage Societies network (Muinsuskaitse Selts), which held its national founding congress in December 1987. On 24 February (Independence Day) 1988, a mass meeting of 10,000 took place at the **Tammsaare** monument in central **Tallinn**.

At the beginning of April 1988, the most important signal to date of the Estonians' determination to escape the Soviet Union was given by the Creative Associations (comprising writers, painters, and musicians—in short, the elite that had been coopted and carefully nurtured by Moscow to produce propaganda for its policies) in a congress where they unanimously demanded the implementation of IME, the prioritizing of national consciousness as state policy in Estonia, the deepening of openness (Gorbachev's glasnost), the public acknowledgement by Moscow of the illegality of the mass **deportations**, the stopping of immigration, and the decentralization of cultural life. The congress also expressed dissatisfaction with First Secretary **Karl Vaino** and Chairman of the Council of Ministers **Bruno Saul**. On 13 April 1988, during a live broadcast of a televised discussion, **Edgar Savisaar** proposed the formation of the People's Front (**Rahvarinne**). An initiative group was formed on the spot. On 14 April 1988 during the heritage days in Tartu, the national blue-black-white tricolor flag (*see* NATIONAL SYMBOLS) was flown in public for the first time since it had been declared an illegal bourgeois symbol in 1940.

During May and June, the hitherto unimaginable mass activity of the entire population continued: the Estonian Green Movement was formed, support groups for the People's Front were organized across the country, the First Youth Forum united all the newly formed independent youth organizations, and pickets began to demand the freeing of **dissidents**. In June, the "night song festivals" began with up to 100,000 people gathering in parks and squares in Tallinn to sing patriotic songs during the long white evenings. These impromptu "song festivals" gave the name "**Singing Revolution**" to the Estonian struggle for freedom and led Estonians to claim that they sang themselves to freedom.

Criticism of the party-state became more open and sharper and was now directed at specific individuals. The crisis in the ECP became deeper as the nationalist members of its Central Committee openly joined and led the demonstrations. The People's Front seized the initiative and called the masses to a meeting at the Song Festival Grounds in Tallinn to support and send off the delegates to the Moscow Party Congress. Such a demonstration of expected popular anti-Party sentiments, however, threatened such extreme destabilization of Party control that the Moscow Party central reacted quickly to remove the focus of popular antagonism. Accordingly, Karl Vaino was replaced by the Estonian nationalist communist **Vaino Väljas** as ECP first secretary. Although this last-minute move was successful in removing the threat of massive public demonstrations against the Party, it backfired in that the meeting, held on schedule on 17 June, now turned into a massive nationalist celebration of victory over the

Party by 150,000 jubilant Estonians who greeted Vaino Väljas as one of their own.

Then followed a rapid updating of national historical memory as information relating to the **Molotov-Ribbentrop Pact** was publicized by the ESSR government, as hitherto closed library holdings and archives were opened, as monuments to the **War of Independence** were rebuilt and rededicated, as political prisoners were freed, as the former "bourgeois" names of streets were resurrected, and so on. During the summer of 1988, Estonia was clearly the leader of perestroika and of popular movements in the Soviet Union. Latvia and Lithuania quickly followed in Estonia's wake, with Ukraine and other regions following later. The 11th of September 1988 saw the culmination of the Singing Revolution as the People's Front organized the festival "Estonian Song" with 300,000 participants. At this rally, the demands for independence from the Soviet Union and the restoration of the Republic of Estonia were voiced openly as self-evident.

However, during July and August those opposed to Estonian independence also organized themselves. The International Movement or **Interfront** was formed by the managers of the Soviet federal enterprises who organized their non-Estonian migrant workers to demonstrate in favor of keeping Estonia as part of the Soviet Union, and to oppose the proposed **language law** making Estonian the official language as well as the proposed restoration of Estonian citizenship on the basis of the prewar bourgeois laws.

At the beginning of October 1988, the Rahvarinne was formally established as a legal organization, nascent political parties began to form, the language law was debated in the **Supreme Soviet of the ESSR**, and the latter adopted a **declaration of sovereignty** of Estonia and a consequent amendment of the ESSR **Constitution** in November. The year 1988 was the seminal year in the restoration of Estonia's independence, which awakened the collective consciousness of the nation to the realization that its long-subdued desire to be a free and independent nation once again was a realistic goal.

SERFDOM. The indigenous populations of the territories of Estonia and Latvia, conquered by the German Christianizing **Crusading Orders** in the beginning of the 13th century, were progressively enslaved by the their new masters by the 14th century as the arable land was divided into estates granted to the crusading knights. Already during the 13th century, the reigning princes granted their vassal estate owners policing authority over their tenants, to which in the next century they added judicial authority and forced peasants who moved away from an estate to pay a fine to the noble landlord. In the first half of the 15th century fleeing tenants were forcibly returned to their estates, and in the second half the landowners began to buy and sell peasants. By the 16th century, virtually all peasants were tied to estates. The following two centuries saw the yoke of serfdom increase as the sale of landless peasants became common.

Toward the end of the 18th century, the Enlightenment influenced some nobles, who realized the economic ineffectiveness of serfdom, to experiment with corvée labor rents. Tsarina **Catherine the Great**, influenced by the Enlightenment, began with such reforms in 1765, which eventually led Alexander I to enact Emancipation laws in the Provinces of Estland and Livland in 1816 and 1819, respectively. The peasant was legally freed from ties to the estate, but all the land still belonged to the noble estate owners. It took another half century before peasants could dream of purchasing land, and a century before the nobles' estates were confiscated and the land distributed to the indigenous populations by the newly independent Republics of Estonia and Latvia in 1920.

SETUS (Estonian, Setud). The Setus are a minuscule Estonian ethnographic group located in the extreme southeast corner of Estonia, as well as in the adjacent villages of the Pskov Oblast in Russia. Because their sparsely settled territory was acquired by Russia in the 16th century, not only the Setu Estonian dialect but also their architecture, religion, folk costumes, and way of life have been influenced by Russian traditions, unlike the rest of Estonia, which lived under **Baltic German** suzerainty for eight centuries. From 1920 to 1945, Setumaa was the Estonian county of **Petserimaa**, when the Union of Soviet Socialist Republics (USSR) annexed seven of its 11 parishes to Pskov Oblast, and transferred the remaining four to the Estonian County of Võru. The Setus are the only remaining group in Estonia with a distinct ethnic subculture and dialect. As such, the dialect is taught in the schools in the Setu settlements, along with its close cousin, the Võru dialect, in some Võru schools. Today several thousand speak the dialects among themselves in Setu areas in Russia and in the countryside in Võru County, along with speaking "proper" Estonian in their contact with other Estonians.

SILLAMÄE. This is a town of 20,000, built on terraces at the mouth of the valley of the Sõtke River as it cuts its way through the 56-meter coastal cliffs on the Gulf of Finland 25 kilometers west of **Narva** and 180 kilometers east of **Tallinn** on the St. Petersburg coastal highway just north of the forested scenic Blue Hills highlands (Sinimäed) rising to 85 meters, was known as a pleasant seaside resort town until the end of World War II. The only industry was a small **oil shale** processing plant built in 1928, which has since closed.

In 1946, the town became a secure military town as the Soviet Union established its first uranium enrichment plant there. Initially local uranium ore was used, but it was replaced in 1954 with much higher grade ore imported from East Germany and Hungary since the uranium content at 0.03 percent in the local Dichtymous Argillite shale proved to be too low for efficient or economic enrichment. Between 1946 and 1990, 100,022 tons of enriched uranium dioxide was produced at Sillamäe, which made it the third largest producer in the Soviet bloc.

In 1970, the processing of rare metals and rare earths was added to the Sillamäe complex, with Lopartite from the Kola Peninsula used as raw material. In 1990, even before the restoration of independence, uranium enrichment processing was stopped and, after perfunctory radioactive decontamination and evacuation by the Soviet military, the town was opened to civilians shortly after the restoration of independence. The production complex was fully privatized in 1997 and the reorganized firm Silmet continues the processing of rare metals and rare earths from imported rare earth concentrates from Russia. It is the largest processor of these in Europe and is an alternative western source of supply to the Chinese suppliers. Its products, nearly all exported, are cerium, neodymium, lanthanum, samarium, europium, gadolinium, and so on; rare metals such as tantalum and niobium; and their compounds.

Sillamäe's main claim to the world's attention, however, is sinister. It contains a 12-million-ton makeshift radioactive lake-sized tailings pond, located only 30 meters from the edge on top of the coastal cliffs, into which all the tailings during the whole period of uranium dioxide production were dumped. Nitrates have been seeping through the mud and rock containment walls into the sea, as have small quantities of radioactive particles of uranium, thorium, barium, strontium, and arsenic. The site emanates radon gas and radioactive dust.

The danger of collapse of the 25-meter containment embankment, built haphazardly over 40 years and filled with gravel, pit sand, and ashes from the depository as well as with solid tailings, led to an urgent need to safeguard the deposit and make it harmless. International action was required since Estonia had neither the expertise nor the required money. Moreover, the tailings pond is judged to be the fourth most environmentally dangerous of 7,000 uranium production facilities in the world. Hence, the international Sillamäe Radioactive Tailings Pond Remediation Project was set up, and was cofinanced by the **European Union** (EU), Denmark, Finland, Norway, Sweden, the Nordic Investment Bank, the Nordic Environmental Finance Corporation, and the Estonian state, to begin making the pond less hazardous. In 1999, remediation work began to fortify the 40-hectare lake with concrete walls, construct a breakwater to prevent waves from undermining the cliffs, and eventually seal the entire site in a virtual sarcophagus. The massive project, the first site of the 29 radioactive Soviet relics in Eastern Europe to be safetied, is proceeding apace and is expected to be completed on schedule in 2006. Parallel with the uranium lake project, Silmet, with American assistance, is developing an environmentally safe waste management system for its ongoing operations. *See also* ENVIRONMENT.

SINGING REVOLUTION. During the white nights of June and July 1988, nightly gatherings of Estonians on the streets and squares of **Tallinn** to sing patriotic folksongs generated a historically never-seen nationalistic fervor among the Estonian population and infused them with a belief in the inevitability of regaining independence. These impromptu gatherings became known as the "Singing Revolution" and created the myth that Estonians sang themselves to freedom. The singing and the numerous political meetings have also become known as the "Hot Summer." *See also* SECOND NATIONAL AWAKENING.

SIRK, ARTUR (1900–1937). Estonian soldier and politician. Sirk was born on 25 September 1900 in Lehiste *vald.* After graduation from military college in 1919, he served as a junior officer in the **Tallinn** Student's Battalion in the **War of Independence**, was decorated with the Cross of Freedom for valor, and retired from the army in 1921. Thereafter, Sirk studied agriculture in 1921–22, and then law in 1922–26, while again serving in the army from 1923–26. From 1930, he practiced law in Tallinn and became chair of the Estonian League of **Veterans** of the War of Independence. As its leader, he was accused after the **preemptive coup** by President **Konstantin Päts**'s government of complicity in plotting a coup, and he was imprisoned pending an investigation. He escaped and fled to Finland, where he reportedly actually began plotting a coup. To escape the Päts government, he moved on to England and then to Luxembourg, where he died on 2 August 1937 at Echternach in unknown circumstances.

Although the authoritarian government's propaganda during the **Era of Silence** that followed Päts's coup in 1934, and that lasted almost until World War II, did not allow the publication of any other interpretation than the official one that the Veterans were fascist-leaning and were conspiring to overthrow the legal government and establish fascist rule, subsequent research, including 1990s analyses of documentation, shows that the Veterans and their leaders were operating legally and would likely have won the largest plurality, even a majority, at the polls in 1934. There is no evidence of any plotting of coups, nor of any connection to Nazism or Fascism.

SOCIETY OF ESTONIAN LITERATI (Eesti Kirjameeste Selts, EKS). Active in **Tartu** from 1872 to 1892, the Society of Estonian Literati was the first association of writers in Estonia and worked diligently to support the publishing of **Estonian language** books, the collection of Estonian cultural artifacts, and the development of science and scholarship in Estonia. Meetings of the EKS were generally considered events of cultural importance. Under the leadership of **Jakob Hurt** during its first half, from 1872 to 1881, it represented a moderate approach. However, when it came under the influence of the more radical nationalists **Carl Robert Jakobson, Hugo Treffner**, and **Johann Köler**, the conflicts between the two groups generated quarrels of such proportions that the Society ended in 1893.

In 1907, the society was resurrected under the name Eesti Kirjanduse Selts (EKS, Estonian Society of Literature) by the intellectuals grouped around the newspaper *Postimees* to carry on the work of its predecessor to propagate and popularize the language and culture of Estonia. It published an annual (1909–40) and the journal *Eesti Kirjandus* (*Estonian Literature*) from 1909 to 1940, and founded its own publishing house to enable it to publish classics of Estonian and international belles-lettres using state subventions in the 1920s and 1930s. It also published a three-volume Estonian language dictionary; English-, Russian-, and Swedish-Estonian dictionaries; schoolbooks; and series on science, world literature, and biographies of notables. The Society was closed by the Soviet occupiers in 1940.

SONG FESTIVALS. Although Estonians have been spontaneously breaking into song at festivities and when they are happy or sad since time immemorial, it was the **Lutheran** Church that introduced choral music to them in its village schools. By the end of the 17th century, at least five choral music books for schools had been published. Influenced by **Baltic Germans**, who had imported the custom of village song and orchestra societies from Germany, multivoice choral singing spread across Estonia and Latvia at the beginning of the 1830s. The first pan-Estonian Song Festival was organized by **Johann Voldemar Jannsen** and took place in 1869 in **Tartu** with 51 choirs and 845 singers from across Estonia and the participation of a public of 15,000 over two days. This, the first National Song Festival, also marked the beginning of the **National Awakening**. By the end of the century, five more Song Festivals had been held with a steady increase in participating choirs to 410 with 5,681 singers in 1896. During the first two revolutionary decades of the 20th century, only the 1910 Song Festival took place, but it too showed increased participation, to 527 choirs and 10,100 singers.

After **Independence**, the first Song Festival in 1923 established a five-year interval for future festivals, held in 1928, 1933, and 1938. After the interruption of the World War II years, the first Song Festival during the Soviet occupation was held in 1947 on the anniversary of the Russian Revolution, with a decreed Soviet orientation praising communist achievements, and with a reduced share for Estonian national-cultural and folkloric songs. The public numeration of the

Song Festivals (XII) was also forbidden in order to formally demonstrate a break with the "bourgeois nationalist" Estonian past culture. From 1950, the five-year cycle was again observed (except for the XVIIth in 1969 that commemorated the 100th anniversary) and allowed as a result of Nikita Khruhschev's thaw, which relaxed strict centralized ideological control over the constituent republics of the USSR. However, the ascension of the reactionary **Karl Vaino** to the leadership of the **Estonian Communist Party** (ECP) in 1978 led to an emphasis on Sovietization and **Russification** as promoted by General Secretary Leonid Brezhnev. Thus, the 1980 and 1985 Song Festivals were again marked by communist ideology and the demand to carry portraits of Party leaders in the traditional procession.

Official repression of their **language** and culture had been familiar to Estonians from the earliest days of the Song Festivals. Not only did it take two years to get permission to stage the first national festival from the government of the Gubernya of Lettland controlled by **Baltic German** nobles, but subsequent ones were also marked by the need to pay obeisance to the Russian Imperial crown during the first period of Russification. However, all attempts at foreign control had the opposite impact—a strengthening of nationalist consciousness as the Song Festival became the premier folk festival and a prime symbol of Estonian nationalist solidarity. Thus, during the Soviet occupation, as important as the formal massed choirs averaging 25,000 singing was the audience of 100,000–250,000 (300,000 in 1999) singing patriotic songs after the conclusion of the official program. Even in 1947 when **Lydia Koidula**'s poem "Mu isamaa on minu arm" ("My Fatherland Is My Refuge"), arranged as a choral song by conductor **Gustav Ernesaks**, was removed from the program, the massed choirs nevertheless sang it. At the conclusion of all subsequent Song Festivals, the public sang it spontaneously, standing at attention, as a substitute for the forbidden national anthem.

The tactic of Jannsen and **Jakob Hurt**, the main speaker at the first Song Festival, to use the combination of performance and participation as a social mobilizer to create a sense of a cultural Estonian nation among the still disparate peasants who continued to refer to themselves as *maarahvas* (country folk or people) or *talurahavas* (peasants or people of the farm), succeeded in initiating the National Awakening. A hundred years later, it proved to be an important element in sustaining the national community when the Soviet empire tried to negate the very existence of the Estonian nation. The myth that Estonians sang themselves free, which circulated widely after the **Singing Revolution** of the hot summer of 1988 when thousands gathered to sing patriotic songs in Tallinn nightly during the long white nights of June and July, was actually born in the first Song Festival in 1869, and played as important a role among **Estonians abroad** as at home.

After the restoration of independence, the XXII Song Festival in 1994 returned to the five-year cycle on the base of 1869, with succeeding ones in 1999 and 2004. *See also* GLOBAL ESTO.

SOVIET-ESTONIAN MUTUAL ASSISTANCE TREATY. Shortly after the August conclusion of the **Molotov-Ribbentrop Pact**, the Union of Soviet Socialist Republics (USSR) demanded without warning on 24 September 1939 that Estonia join a 10-year mutual assistance pact under which the USSR would be granted army, navy, and air bases in Estonia for the duration of the war. Isolated behind the **Baltic Sea**, which was dominated by German and Soviet navies, and without any hope of Western assistance, neutral Estonia with a peacetime army of 16,000 was forced to acquiesce to Soviet demands after only four days of intensive negotiations. The treaty, allowing the stationing of 25,000 Soviet military with equipment in Estonia, was signed on 28 September. Similar treaties were immediately forced on Latvia and Lithuania. Three weeks later, on 18 October, 25,000 Soviet troops crossed the Estonian border and took up the ceded bases. When Finland refused to conclude a similar pact, the USSR bombed Finland on 30 November 1939 using Estonian airfields in cavalier defiance of the Bases Agreement (as Estonians refer to the pact), which naturally led to tensions with Estonia, although the troops were carefully isolated on bases out of contact with the Estonian public. At the conclusion of the Finnish Winter War (13 March 1940), valiant Finland was forced to cede the province of Karelia, cede 12 percent of its territory (which Russia has not returned), and lease the Hanko peninsula to the USSR for military bases, which the USSR did not give up until 1956 (*see also* PETSERIMAA).

Coinciding with the rapid advance of German forces in France, the Soviet Union decided to implement the secret clauses of the

Molotov-Ribbentrop Pact, and simultaneously prepare for a possible German attack, by occupying Lithuania on 15 June 1940, followed by Latvia and Estonia on 17 June. In the case of Estonia, the USSR accused Estonia on 16 June of collaborating with Lithuania and Latvia in a military alliance directed against it and demanded free passage for troops to garrison the most important centers of Estonia. In addition, the ultimatum, to be answered in eight and a half hours, demanded that Estonia replace the current government with one capable of carrying out the "honest execution" of the Mutual Assistance Treaty!

On the morning of 17 June, Commander in Chief General **Johan Laidoner**, on instructions from President **Konstantin Päts**, signed the order allowing the passage of 90,000 Soviet soldiers into Estonia. Within days, Estonia found itself under military occupation, its armed forces were disarmed, and its government was replaced by one dictated by Andrei Zhdanov, the Politburo member designated by Joseph Stalin to act as political master of Estonia. Immediately the new puppet government of **Johannes Vares** called for elections in which only candidates approved by the **Estonian Communist Party** were allowed to run. On 14–15 July elections took place, and on 21–23 the new parliament met; nationalized the banks, large industries, and all land; and passed a petition requesting the Supreme Soviet of the USSR to accept Estonia as a member of the Soviet Socialist Republic. The process was similar in the other Baltic States. On 20 June in Latvia, a new government handpicked by Moscow was announced, then called for sudden rigged elections. On 21 July, the new parliament asked for Latvia to be incorporated into the Soviet Union. On the same day, after similarly rigged elections, the new Lithuanian parliament made a similar request. Both were accepted by the Supreme Soviet, and both countries were incorporated into the Soviet Union on 3 August 1940; three days later, on 6 August, Estonia was accepted as the 15th Soviet Republic. Prior to that, on 19 July General Laidoner, and on 30 July President Päts, were deported to Soviet concentration camps as "enemies of the people." Both died in the camps.

SOVKHOZ (Estonian, Sovhoos). State farm in the Soviet Union. In contrast to the **kolkhozes**, the sovkhozes were created by the Ministry of Agriculture on uncultivated land, often of marginal agricultural value in Estonia, and peasants were brought in from surrounding villages to operate them. There were few sovkhozes in Soviet Estonia. *See also* AGRICULTURE.

SPECIAL BALTIC ORDER. The historic privileges of the **Baltic German** nobility of the princedoms of the Old Livonian Teutonic Order, including the lawmaking and implementing authority, which had developed over the centuries in Estland, Lettland, and Kurland, were confirmed by Tsar **Peter the Great** in return for transferring their allegiance from the Swedish king during the second half of the **Great Northern War** between 1710 and 1720. These became known as the Special Baltic Order since the Baltic Provinces were the only parts of imperial Russia able to operate as virtually independent self-governing territories, much as before the conquest, with privileges and laws outside the control of the government in St. Petersburg. *See also* BALTIC GERMANS; COURTS; LEGAL SYSTEM.

ST. GEORGE'S NIGHT REBELLION or UPRISING 1343–1345 (Jüriöö Mäss or Ülestõus). The last attempt by the Estonians to rid themselves of the feudal German and Danish crusaders originated from the worsening economic conditions of the peasantry caused by increased demands of the colonizing overlords. The uprising began in the Danish fiefdom of Harju county in northern Estonia on St. George's Night (23 April 1343), when a force of 10,000 peasants conquered the fortified monastery at Padise in a surprise attack, burned churches and mansions, and surrounded the fortified town of **Tallinn**. The rebellion quickly spread to Läänemaa and the island county of Saaremaa, lasted two years, and led to the killing of almost all Germans in the countryside. It took the Livonian Order (*see* CRUSADING ORDERS) two years of bloody warfare to finally crush the rebellion and required assistance from its mother Teutonic Order. As a result of the uprising, Danish King Valdemar IV sold the Harju and Viru counties to the Teutonic Order in 1346, which in turn sold them to the Livonian Order in 1347, thus making all Estonian territories German fiefdoms. The failure of the uprising and its severe crushing led to a loss of confidence among the Estonians, and a final loss of independence with no serious revolts for three centuries, until 1560.

For modern Estonians, the Jüriöö Ülestõus signifies the indomitable spirit of rebellious independence of the Estonian nation.

ST. PETERSBURG PATRIOTS (Peteburi patrioodid). This is the name given to the group of Estonian intelligentsia living in St. Petersburg between the end of the 1850s and the beginning of the 1870s, under the leadership of **Johann Köler** from 1862, and consisting of the pedagogue F. Dankman, the first Estonian agronomist Jakob Johnson, the civil servant A. Jüriev, the tsar's personal physician Philipp Karell, the artist Niklaus Friedrich Russow, and **Carl Robert Jakobson**, who assisted Estonian peasants to write and present petitions to the imperial authorities; prepared for the establishment of the **Estonian Aleksander School**; made preparations for establishing a democratic Estonian newspaper, *Perno Postimees* (originally intended to be published in St. Petersburg); and played the main role in forming the democratic bourgeois direction of the **National Awakening**.

STIMSON DOCTRINE OF 1932. *See* NONRECOGNITION OF SOVIET OCCUPATION.

STRANDMAN, OTTO (1875–1941). Estonian politician. The son of a schoolmaster and parish clerk born on 30 November 1875 in Undla *vald*, Strandman received his early education from his father and his secondary education in several different Rakvere, **Tartu**, and St Petersburg schools. After passing his matriculation exam in 1896, he worked for three years in the office of the State Bank in **Tallinn** and then studied law at Tartu and St. Petersburg, graduating from the latter in 1903. He set up a practice in Tallinn, defended the working man against abuse of power by estate owners and civil servants, and participated actively in the social life of the city with the result that he was elected to the city council in 1904. During the 1905 Revolution, he gathered around himself radical-minded younger members of the Tallinn intelligentsia and Social Democrats who found both **Jaan Tõnisson** and **Konstantin Päts** too moderate. His reward was a brief exile in Switzerland until 1909, when he returned to Tallinn to continue his legal practice.

In 1905, Strandman began to pursue autonomy for Estonia in the

Russian empire when he participated in the Autonomists' congress in St. Petersburg, worked on the projected law during his Swiss exile, and formed an autonomists' club at the beginning of World War I. After the February Revolution in 1917, he joined the group drafting the law on autonomy and helped push it though the imperial government. He was elected to the Estonian Provincial Assembly (**Maapäev**) and became its deputy speaker. He actually chaired the historic meeting on 15 November 1917 when the Maapäev declared itself the sovereign political authority in Estonia. Simultaneously, he continued his job as procurator in the Tallinn State Court, belonged to the city council, and led the Estonian Federation that united the various Estonian voluntary organizations. He became a trusted member of the Radical Socialist Party (later renamed the Workers Party) and, after **Jüri Vilms**'s death, its leader.

Strandman served as minister of justice in the first **Estonian Provisional Government** formed in February 1918, then became minister of agriculture in the second government formed that fall. He supported radical land reform, took control of abandoned estates, and began to distribute the estate lands to tenants and the landless. When the Left won a majority in the elections to the **Constituent Assembly**, he was asked to form the first constitutional government of Estonia, which he did on 8 May 1919, and which during its six months in office succeeded in solving many problems caused by the confusion of the war. Subsequently, Strandman was elected to all four **Riigikogu** before the **preemptive coup** and served on many committees in each. In 1921, he was elected speaker of parliament, served as foreign minister in Ants Piip's cabinet in 1920, and served as foreign and finance minister in Friedrich Akel's cabinet in 1924.

As finance minister, Strandman quickly established the framework of a reorganized economy, suitable for a small independent state. From 1927 he was sent to Warsaw as ambassador, but then was recalled in 1929 and asked to form a cabinet. This time, despite the onset of the global Depression, Strandman, owing to his ability to solve economic problems and create consensus, was able to keep his coalition cabinet going for a full 19 months—a record not surpassed until 1990. When his cabinet fell, he managed to have himself sent to Paris as an ambassador, where he remained for eight years. His deep democratic beliefs were demonstrated when in 1936, despite his official position, he supported publicly the Four State Elders' Memorandum critical of President Konstantin Päts's authoritarian rule.

World War II ended Strandman's political career. He returned from Paris in the fall of 1939 and lived quietly at his farm in his home in Kadrina *vald* through the early months of the Soviet occupation. On 16 February 1941, however, Strandman committed suicide rather than face imprisonment and **deportation** when the NKVD asked him to show up for an interview.

STUDENT FRATERNITIES. Soon after its reopening in 1802, students at the **University of Tartu** formed student fraternities in imitation of the *Studentenverbindungen* at German universities, with the one difference that here they called themselves *Corporationes* (*Korporatsioonid*) and that they formed themselves according to the geographic origin of their members. The first one, Corporation Curonia, was formed in 1808 by students from the Province of Kurland (Kurzeme). Students originating from the Province of Estland formed Corp! Estonia in 1821, and those from Livland formed Corp! Livonia in 1822. Despite their Baltic names, these were German fraternities and consisted of **Baltic Germans** since almost no locals attended university at this time. They copied the chivalrous rules of behavior of the *Studentenverbindungen*, including the wearing of caps and sashes bearing their colors, hierarchies based on seniority, solving quarrels by courts of honor and duels, and so on. During 1830–63 and the period of **Russification** from 1889 to 1905, the authorities forbade the public display of identifying color regalia by fraternity members.

The first ethnic Estonian student fraternity, **Eesti Üliõpilaste Selts**, known universally by its initials EÜS, was formed in 1870 as a self-consciously patriotic Estonian organization whose members were uniformly Estonian *talupojad* (singular *talupoeg*, literally farmer's son, the Estonian's term of perverse pride in their common peasant origins), and not the Germanized students who joined the German-language Baltic German fraternities.

Subsequently, as fear of German dominance dissipated with the growth of an Estonian ethnic national elite, new fraternities were formed, in frank imitation of the Baltic German ones. Thus Estonian students at the Riga Polytechnic formed Corp! Vironia in 1900 (this was moved to **Tartu** in 1920), while at Tartu they formed Fraternitas Estica in 1907, Sakala in 1909, Ugala in 1913, and Fraternitas Liviensis in 1918, naming themselves after provinces of ancient Estonia. The only other fraternity formed before independence was Korp! Rotalia, which was organized at St. Petersburg in 1913 by dissidents from a locally organized EÜS. Before settling in Tartu in 1919, this fraternity moved to Warsaw and Berlin as its members sought graduate degrees and recruited new members from among Estonians studying at these foreign universities. The patriotic fervor of the fraternities was demonstrated by most of them joining the army *in corpore* to fight in the **War of Independence**.

After independence, four more fraternities were formed at Tartu: Leola in 1920, Revelia in 1920, Tehnola in 1921, and Fraternitas Tartuensis in 1929. The fraternities formed a federation, Eesti Korporatsioonide Liit (EKL), in 1915 to look after their common interests. In keeping with its self-designated status as a nonelitist organization and a noncorporation, EÜS has never joined EKL. Women students formed their sororities in the first few years of the University of Tartu's reopening as the national university: Filiae Patriae in 1920, and Indla, Lembela, and Amicitia in 1924.

When the Soviet occupation in 1940 disbanded all the fraternities—a ban continued by the Nazi occupation—existing fraternity members continued to meet in private based on the bonds of friendship forged during student years, but new members could not be recruited. However, chapters of the fraternities, including EÜS, were formed abroad wherever Estonian émigré communities were found and thus became global organizations, each with its own worldwide organization and a local federation (EKL) in each major center of the Estonian Diaspora. Despite half a century of foreign residence, these organizations inculcated national values of patriotism in their young student recruits and thus helped maintain viable Estonian-speaking ethnic communities in Sweden, the United States, Canada, and Australia for 50 years and contributed significantly to the struggle for the restoration of independence.

With the surge of nationalism in 1988, the foreign branches of the fraternities joined with the remnants of the aged members in Estonia and reestablished the original chapters in Tartu and **Tallinn** by 1989. Subsequently, they played a key funding role in the recovery and rebuilding of the original chapter houses in Tartu and Tallinn. The fraternities are flourishing and rapidly reacquiring their prewar role as clubs instilling patriotic values in the Estonian intelligentsia. Two new fraternities have also formed since the renewal of independence: Ave in 1987 and Arminia Dorpatensis in 1994.

SUITS, GUSTAV (1883–1956). Estonian writer and renowned professor of **literature**. Suits was born 30 November 1883 in the village of Võnnu, and after attending local schools he entered the **University of Tartu** in 1904 but in the following year transferred to the University of Helsinki, where he completed his *cand. phil.* in European literature and Finnish language, literature, and folklore in 1911. Subsequently, he worked at the University's library for the next two years, taught Swedish and Finnish in the Russian Gymnasium in Helsinki in 1913–17, and went to Paris in 1914 on a fellowship but had to curtail it at the outbreak of World War I.

During 1917–19, the decisive years for Estonian independence, Suits participated actively in politics: he joined the newly founded Estonian Socialist-Revolutionary Party, led its activities in Helsinki, was elected to its central committee, and in 1918 managed the office of the Estonian Foreign Delegation in Stockholm. In 1917, he was among the first to raise the idea of an independent Estonia as opposed to the prevailing sentiment for autonomy within the Russian empire. He also propagated the idea of a federated state of Estonia-Finland.

With the reopening of the University of Tartu as the national university on 1 December 1919, Suits was sent back to Helsinki on a fellowship to prepare himself for a teaching position. He began teaching at Tartu in 1921 as a lecturer, was promoted to professor extraordinary in 1924, and served as professor of literature from 1931 to 1944. During the two decades of independence, Suits established a wide circle of academic contacts on his many research trips to the Nordic countries, Germany, Holland, and the Soviet Union. He was honored with memberships in the Finnish Literature Society in 1931 and the French Académie Septentrionale in 1936, as well as the Estonian Academy in 1938. In 1944, Suits fled to Sweden via Finland and obtained a Nobel Institute fellowship, which enabled him to continue his academic life of research, lecturing, and conference travel until his death at the age of 73 on 23 May 1956 in Stockholm.

Suits's contributions to the development of Estonian literature and high culture had already begun at the turn of the century when he edited the student literary compilations *Kiired* (*Rays,* vols. I–II, 1901–03); became an outspoken leader of the Noor Eesti (**Young Estonia**) movement and edited its albums (vols. I–V, 1905–15), as well as its journal, *Noor Eesti*, in 1910–11. His 1905 call: "More culture! More European culture! Let us be Estonians, but let us also become Europeans!" became the mantra of the intelligentsia of the developing nation-state and was as powerful an energizer of Estonian youth then as at the turn of the millennium a hundred years later. It was Suits and Noor Eesti who "professionalized" Estonian culture by demonstrating that Estonians were capable of doing it themselves without the intermediation of Germans or Russians. Ever since, the self-conscious sense of inferiority exhibited by all peripheral peasant peoples has been absent among Estonians, who instead revel in the self-ascribed superiority of a separate unique culture by participating in the amorphous general "European" culture.

As a naturally left-leaning intellectual but also a humanist and creative writer, Suits attempted from his earliest writings during the 1905 Revolution to bridge the socialist-liberal gap, and to temper both the demand for justice and the demand for individual rights by espousing moderation and compromise. This, naturally, bought him into conflict with both the Marxists, who he saw as nihilists, and the nationalists, whom he accused of clericalist narrow-mindedness.

As an academic, Suits's service to the development of Estonian professional study of literature and its history is seminal. Together with **Friedebert Tuglas**, he is regarded as one of the fathers of professional criticism of literature and the theater. His primary fields of study throughout his life were the history of Estonian literature and poetry and comparative West European and Russian literature. He wrote copiously on all these themes, with the main works being a history of Estonian literature published in 1932, and another history of Estonian literature published in Stockholm in 1953. Despite his activism and academic commitment, his favorite preoccupation was poetry, of which he published collections beginning in 1905 and ending with different collected works published in 1963, and posthumously as late as 1992.

SUPREME COUNCIL OF THE REPUBLIC OF ESTONIA. *See* SUPREME SOVIET OF THE ESSR.

SUPREME COURT (Estonian, Riigikohus, literally "state court"). Because Estonia has been under the suzerainty of foreigners for nearly all of its recorded history, its legal systems and **courts** have been conditioned by foreign authorities. Moreover, at times various parts of the territory of Estonia have been under the control of different sovereigns. Hence, the history of law and the courts in Estonia is heterogeneous. Nevertheless, because the German crusaders settled permanently in the territories of the Estonians and the Latvians, German law as it developed in Germany provided the main influence on the development of the **legal systems** of Estonia and Latvia. In the 17th century, when Estonia came under the control of the Swedish king the first "supreme court," the Tartu Õuekohus (Swedish, Hovrätt), was established as the Crown Appeals Court in Livland in 1630; it survived until the end of the 19th century. In 1720, when Sweden lost the **Great Northern War** and Estonia was ceded to Russia, for political purposes the old Baltic Germanic legal system was reinstituted with a vengeance and became known as the **Special Baltic Order**. Only in the 19th century was the Russian legal order gradually and partly extended to Estonia and Latvia.

After the **Declaration of Independence in 1918**, the **provisional government** of Estonia issued a decree establishing provisional courts, and this was subsequently regularized by the **Constituent Assembly** on 21 October 1919 when it adopted the Law on the Supreme Court. The new Supreme Court of Estonia held its first session on 14 January 1920 in **Tartu**, where it remained until 1936, when the authoritarian government of President **Konstantin Päts** moved it to the political capital of **Tallinn**. In 1940, the Union of Soviet Socialist Republics (USSR) liquidated the Supreme Court as well as the existing legal system immediately on illegally annexing the country, and it imported Soviet copies. Less than a year later, these were in turn supplanted by the Nazi German legal system and courts, and when they were driven out in late 1944, the USSR reimposed the Soviet legal order. This time it lasted until 1991. During this period, the Supreme Court of the Estonian Soviet Socialist Republic (ESSR) adjudicated all Soviet law on Estonian territory, although in certain circumstances it was possible to appeal to the Supreme Court of the USSR in Moscow.

On 27 May 1993, the Supreme Court of the Republic of Estonia, refounded on the authority of the new **Constitution of 1992**, held its first session. The Supreme Court was again placed in the university city of Tartu, almost 200 kilometers south of Tallinn, to symbolize the separation and independence of the court system from the political authority of the state and government.

The Supreme Court consists of 17 justices, appointed for life. The chief justice is appointed by the Riigikogu on nomination by the president of the Republic; the puisne justices are appointed by parliament on nomination by the chief justice. Although the Supreme Court may sit en banc, it does so normally only for internal administrative matters. In one of its first plenary sessions, it organized itself into three chambers: the criminal, civil, and administrative law chambers. A fourth, the constitutional review chamber, consisting of the chief justice and four other justices (members of the three classical chambers), is elected for five-year terms by plenary sitting of the Court, and has the authority to provide judicial opinions on bills referred to it by the president prior to signing, as well as the usual judicial review functions of any constitutional review court. The uniting of the final appeals constitutional review functions distinguishes the Estonian Supreme Court from other European highest courts where there are separate causation and constitutional courts, and moves it toward the common law model as it operates in the United States and the British Commonwealth.

The rotating-membership appeals selection committee, of three members with one replaced every three months, determines whether to grant leave for appeals in criminal, civil, and administrative law cases. Appeals on constitutional matters are determined solely by the constitutional review chamber. Normally, each classical chamber sits in three-member panels, but it may sit in any numbers, including full chamber, and may coopt members of other chambers if additional expertise is needed. A plenary sitting of the Court is competent to act when at least 11 members are present.

SUPREME SOVIET ELECTIONS OF THE ESSR IN 1990. Elections to the **Supreme Soviet** of the Estonian Soviet Socialist Republic (ESSR) were carried out on a pro forma basis with nominees approved by the **Estonian Communist Party** (ECP) as the only candidates in the elections. The number of candidates was equal to the seats to be filled.

The first and only multiparty, free, and open election to the Supreme Soviet of the ESSR took place on 23 March 1990. Nine political movements, parties, associations, workers' collectives, and local meetings of citizens nominated 462 candidates for the 101 seats (plus four elected by the military in the ESSR). With the participation of 78 percent of the electorate, 14 Communist Party functionaries; 12 leaders of municipal councils; 11 directors of enterprises and banks; 15 state farm (**kolkhoz** and **sovkhoz**) leaders; 13 higher educational and research institute, school, and medical organization leaders; 27 academics, teachers, journalists, and doctors; two workers; four military officers; and seven representing other occupations were elected. According to political commentators, one third represented the left and one third the right, with the remaining third being neutral. Although the majority supported regaining an independent Estonian Republic, most of the elected Russians opposed independence. Throughout its life, the different factions in the last Supreme Soviet were constantly changing members and reforming. Nevertheless, this was the body that adopted a series of important acts leading to the restitution of the Estonian Republic that, together with the resolutions of the **Estonian Congress**, laid the foundations for legal authority of the reestablished independent Republic of Estonia.

SUPREME SOVIET OF THE ESTONIAN SOVIET SOCIALIST REPUBLIC (ESSR) (Eesti Nõukogude Sotsialistliku Vabariigi Ülemnõukogu, normally rendered as ENSV Ülemnõukogu). The unicameral legislative assembly of the ESSR, established by the **Constitution of 1940**, was modeled on the All-Union Supreme Soviet in Moscow. It consisted of 101 deputies elected for four-year terms (changed to five-year terms in the **Constitution of 1978**) from multimember districts on the basis of one member per 10,000 citizens of the Union of Soviet Socialist Republics (USSR) resident in the ESSR, nominated by any registered organization and vetted by the **Estonian Communist Party** (ECP). Only as many candidates were approved for election by the electoral commissions consisting of Party members as there were seats to be elected; very few non-party members were allowed to contest elections. Soviet military personnel stationed in Estonia also had designated seats. The Supreme Soviet usually met only twice a year to approve legislation passed between its meetings by its legislative-executive committee, the Presidium, of which the chairman acted as **head of state**, whereas the Council of Ministers functioned as its administrative implementing body. The legislation was based on central directives from the Communist Party of the Soviet Union (CPSU), which developed policies for the All-Union Supreme Soviet in Moscow, and then passed them on to the component republics' Communist Parties. Ministries in Moscow also dictated implementation policies to ensure harmonized legislation in the USSR. Component republics were allowed some variations on matters of strictly local concern but within All-Union policy frameworks.

The last election of the Supreme Soviet of the ESSR was carried out on a free, multiparty basis on 10 March 1990, except for the representatives of the military who were elected (as in the past) by soldiers at the direction of their Communist Party political officers and consisted of 101 deputies plus four deputies elected by Soviet Army units stationed in the ESSR (*See* SUPREME SOVIET ELECTIONS OF THE ESSR IN 1990). On 30 March, the ESSR Supreme Soviet declared the annexation of Estonia to the Soviet Union null and void from inception and instituted a period of transition to Independence, to be declared completed on the adoption of a new **Constitution** of the independent Republic of Estonia. On 8 May, the Supreme Soviet readopted the Republic of Estonia as the official name of the country and changed its own name to the Eesti Vabariigi Ülemnõukogu, officially translated in English as the Supreme Council of the Republic of Estonia.

SWEDISH ERA. Estonians still fondly recall the memory of the 17th century, when they and most Latvians lived under the suzerainty of the Swedish kingdom, as the "good old Swedish times." Although the indigenous peasantry in Livland and Estland remained tied to the land under the yoke of the foreign **Baltic German** and newly imported Swedish nobles, the Swedish kings, accustomed to a free peasantry back home, sought to ameliorate the lot of the Baltic **serfs**

by introducing compulsory elementary **education** and translating the **Bible** into the local languages. In 1630, Governor Johan Skytte opened a gymnasium in **Tartu**, another in **Tallinn** in 1631, and the **University of Tartu** in 1632, although these were restricted to the nobles and burghers. In 1684, a teachers' seminary was opened near Tartu to educate indigenous schoolmasters for the new elementary schools, which produced 160 teachers during its four-year existence. The first printing press was established in Tartu in 1632 and soon books were printed in Tallinn, **Narva**, and **Pärnu**. The first **Estonian-language** grammar was published in 1637, and at least 45 Estonian-language books were printed between 1631 and 1710. Estonians' typically reserved attitude toward the church also improved somewhat as a result of the founding of elementary schools attached to local parish churches and the publication of religious literature in their native language. Moreover, the Swedish period saw a radical improvement in the education of the clergy—by the end of the period, most were university educated and a large number spoke Estonian.

However, the peasantry remained wedded to old customs and beliefs, among them worship of their forefathers and the observation of a mixed pagan and Roman Catholic cultural calendar. The **Lutheran** pastorate abhorred such beliefs and customs and instituted witch-hunts. This led to 175 people accused of witchcraft between 1600 and 1709, of whom 53, or 30 percent, were burned to death on pyres. Nevertheless, the spread of literacy began slowly to displace the old pagan beliefs and customs (*see* RELIGION).

Reorganization of the judicial system was the most radical reform carried out during the Swedish era. The lowest **courts**, the *vakukohus* (by now effectively estate courts dominated by the local noble), remained, but appeals could be made to regional castle courts (*lossikohus*) and finally to the Crown Court (Õuekohus) in Stockholm. In 1630, a Crown Appeals Court was also established in Tartu (Tartu Õuekohus). For the first time the peasant, although tied to the land, could demand justice beyond his local village and estate.

The Swedish era also saw the introduction of large manual labor-based industries, such as brickyards, glassworks, sawmills, spinning and knitting shops, and paper manufactures. Narva rose to preeminence as a trade center with Russia, Tartu declined, and Tallinn maintained its trading status. The main exports to the West consisted of grain, linen, pitch, spars and masts for ships, sawn lumber, and animal skins. Imports consisted of salt, metal manufactures, luxury goods, alcohol, spices, paper, tobacco, and fruits. Trade continued to be dominated by the Baltic German burghers.

The Swedish conquest of the provinces of Estland and Livland came about as a result of the disintegration of the balanced relations among the Teutonic Order princedoms of Old **Livonia** in the competition for influence in the area among Sweden, Denmark, Russia, and Poland. Their eagerness for control was fueled by trade—whoever controlled Livland controlled the lucrative Western trade with Russia. In the event, Sweden was able to expand its authority because of civil war in Russia in the early 17th century and the Thirty Years' War in Germany, which vitiated German and Polish power.

The Swedish era in Livland and Estland coincided with the Swedish Great Power period, gained at the cost of constant war with its neighbors, against the Catholic princes in Germany and Poland and against Russia. In contrast, after the initial conquest Livland and Estland enjoyed a century of peace under the benevolent rule of the Swedish kings. In retrospect, for Estonians and Latvians, the Swedish era has taken on a rosier hue than sanctioned by objective reality because the century was bracketed by war, pestilence, and starvation at both ends. *See also* SWEDISH ESTONIANS.

SWEDISH ESTONIANS. The ethnic Swedish population on the islands and the coastal area of northwest Estonia arrived between the 13th and 14th centuries and is most likely connected with the similar but much larger settlement of the western and southern coasts of Finland at the same time. Records indicate that the earliest colonized areas belonged to the Church; thus the settlements appear to be part of the northern Christianizing crusades. Ironically, in contrast to the ethnic Estonian population, which to this day looks back on the golden **Swedish era** as the "good old Swedish times," the Swedish population lost the privileges of protection of Swedish law under which they enjoyed personal freedom and limited financial responsibility, in contrast to the Estonian peasants who were attached to the soil. With Swedish control established over the new Duchy of Estland in 1584 during the **Livonian Wars**, the Church lands were secularized and given as fiefs to the nobility, and peasants' land was included in the new manorial estates. The feudal aristocracy did not recognize the special legal status of the Swedish settlements and treated them as they did the Estonian **serfs**.

With the coming of independence in 1918, the economic condition of the Swedish Estonians, who were for the most part small farmers and fishermen, remained behind that of the average Estonian peasant, in that they remained as subsistence farmers and fishermen largely because of their psychological and geographical remoteness from the mainstream of the new class of independent Estonian farmers (*see* AGRICULTURE). Moreover, they did not have a middle- or upper-class leadership as did the **Baltic Germans** and **Jewish Estonians**. Their one Estonian national political leader, a government minister, soon lost his position owing to partisan maneuvering in the complexities of the multiparty system, and the Swedes were left with a national secretary in the Ministry of Education. Partly for similar reasons, the Swedish population did not take advantage of the **Cultural Autonomy**; but since they did live in their historic settlements they had their own village councils that, however, had to make do with inadequate local tax income. Nor did the Swedish State pay any attention to their kinfolk in Estonia. Most Swedish tourists preferred to regard their visit to what Estonians called *Noarootsi* (knife Sweden, a reference to the tenuous hold of the Swedish Estonian fishermen-farmers on the narrow coastal strip and the agriculturally poor tiny coastal islands) as a visit to a living museum of the past.

The first Soviet occupation forced many Swedish Estonians from their homes on the islands that were taken over by the Soviet military; and many were also conscripted into the Soviet army along with other Estonian men, and later into the German ones. With the collapse of the German front imminent in the summer of 1944, the Swedish government organized a repatriation of the remaining Swedish Estonian population. Altogether, 7,000 Swedish Estonians left the country during the war years. Since their total population had been 7,641 in the 1934 census, this represented the disappearance of the Swedish ethnic heritage from Estonia. The 1989 Soviet Estonian census confirmed this: only 297 people listed themselves as having Swedish ethnicity. Less than 100 still spoke their distinct Swedish dialect in the mid-1990s.

The Swedish Estonians who fled to Sweden have melded into the general population, and none have returned to the totally devastated lands that they once occupied, today mostly returned to forest. The only reminder of 700 years of their history is their umbrella voluntary association Svenska Odlingens Vänner and their publication *Kustbon* in Stockholm.

– T –

TAAGEPERA, REIN (1932–). Estonian and American political scientist and political activist. Born on 28 February 1933 in **Tartu**, Taagepera as a youth fled with his parents via Germany to Morocco and then to Canada. After completing his first degree in engineering physics at the University of Toronto in 1959, he studied nuclear physics and received his M.A. in 1961 at Toronto, then continued Ph.D. studies in solid state physics at the University of Delaware, which he completed in 1965. While working as a research physicist in 1964–70, he began studying international relations at the University of Delaware, and earned his M.A. in the field in 1969. In 1970, Taagepera was hired by the newly organized behaviorist-oriented School of Social Sciences at the University of California, Irvine, to teach political science; was promoted to professor in 1978; and took early retirement in 1994 to devote his time to the **University of Tartu**. In 1989, he had already began working with the newly elected rector, Jüri Kärner, to establish a School of Social Sciences at Tartu modeled on his California institute. Thus, when the new school opened in 1992 he served as its first dean, while arranging leaves from California until 1994, when he relinquished the deanship and accepted the appointment as Tartu's first professor of political science in the School's Department of Political Science, serving until mandatory retirement in 1998.

It is solely due to Taagepera's efforts that Tartu, alone among post-Soviet universities, developed a modern political science department with rigorous western social sciences curricular standards graduating students on a level comparable to Nordic universities within eight years of the collapse of the Soviet power in Estonia. He began by rigorously training a group of local former lecturers of Marxism and history willing to subject themselves to retraining, and followed by insisting on student-entry standards of a very high order, including knowledge of English, since most political science literature is available mainly in that language.

However, Taagepera's services to rebuilding Estonia are not limited to academic pursuits since the late 1980s but date from his student days, when he worked diligently to maintain Estonian culture alive among the émigré Estonian students in Canada and the United States. From 1967 to 1975 he issued a bimonthly newsletter, *Baltic Events*, which provided timely information in English on events in the Baltic republics to a wide audience, and he wrote widely in academic journals on Estonian and Baltic issues. He became so well known for his propagation of independence for Estonia that the Soviet Union refused to let him or any members of his family into Estonia for 17 years. During the independence movement beginning in 1988, he was frequently an outspoken visitor to Estonia. He served as the secretary of the Estonian Heritage Society Abroad in 1988–90, and was a member of **Estonian Committee** II, and of the **Constitutional Assembly** in 1991–92. In 1990, he was awarded the Tuglas prize for his *Livland, Lieveland* collection of novellas. Thus, he was sufficiently well known to be asked to run for the presidency in the 1992 election. Since he hesitated and thus entered the contest late, he received only 23.4 percent to **Lennart Meri**'s 29.5 percent and **Arnold Rüütel**'s 41.8 percent of the popular vote. According to law, the runoff was decided by the **Riigikogu** between the two top candidates, with Lennart Meri being chosen president (*see* ELECTION OF THE PRESIDENT). In 2001, Taagepera, disappointed with the apparent self-interest politics of the established parliamentary parties, helped organize a new party, Res Publica, and served as its interim leader until its founding congress in late summer 2002, in ample time for the Riigikogu elections in March 2003, which the Party "won" with sufficient seats to enable **Juhan Parts**, the new leader, to form a coalition cabinet (*see* POLITICAL PARTIES).

Internationally, Taagepera is known for developing the Laakso-Taagepera formula for determining effective electoral systems in multiparty systems. His major work, written together with his doctoral student at California, Matthew Soberg Shugart, *Seats and Votes, the Effects and Determinants of Electoral systems* (Yale University Press, 1989), is regarded as the definitive study of electoral systems.

TALLINN. After Reykjavik, Oslo, Stockholm, and Helsinki, Tallinn is the fifth most northerly capital city in the world, only 82 kilometers from Helsinki, 280 kilometers from Riga, 315 kilometers from St. Petersburg, and 380 kilometers from Stockholm. Hence it has access to over 11 million people within a radius of 400 kilometers and 80 million within a radius of 860 kilometers—the distance to both Copenhagen and Moscow, respectively. Its location in a sheltered bay on the ice-free northwest corner of Estonia at the mouth of the Gulf of Finland has made it a natural trading harbor on east-west trading routes between Scandinavia, the Russian hinterland, and the Black Sea ever since Viking times. Estonian tribes named Revelians, Harians, and Vironians built a fortified settlement on the limestone Toompea Hill rising 47 meters above the harbor. In ancient times, the fort and the settlement were variously called Lindnäs by Scandinavians, Lindanise by Estonians, and Kolovan or Lednets by Russians. In 1219, Danish King Valdemar II conquered northern Estonia and built a stone fortress on the hill, as well as the Dome Church, which was completed during the next century and a half of Danish control. The fort, along with the town, gradually became known as Taani linna (Danish fort) to Estonians, and was subsequently shortened to Tallinn. Similarly, the Dome Church gave its name to the hill, contracted to Toompea ("domehead," or height).

In 1248, the burgeoning trading town was granted a town charter by Lübeck, and in 1285 it became a member of the **Hanseatic League**. The German colonizers of the rest of Estonia and the mostly German traders in the city, as well as the Danes, called the city Reval or Revel (a name used by foreigners, especially Germans, right up to the end of the 20th century) after the ancient tribe that had settled the county around Tallinn.

As a result of the **St. George's Night Uprising**, Danish King Valdemar IV sold Tallinn and northern Estonia to the Teutonic Order in 1346, which in turn sold them to the **Livonian Order** in 1347. During the two centuries of the latter's suzerainty until 1561, a strong medieval stone wall with 66 defensive towers was built around the settlement below the hill, known as the Lower Town. The Vanalinn (Old Town) on Toompea Hill was completed with palaces for the landed Baltic German nobility and wealthy burghers. Although both the town on the hill and the lower town have been modernized with renovations and additions over the centuries, the Old Town, as both parts are known today, survives as the only original medieval walled city in northern Europe. Since its founding, the only destruction that Old Tallinn has been subjected to are six great fires, from the first in 1288 to the firebombing in 1944, which, however, did not destroy any buildings on the hill. The Old Town was renovated for the 1980 Olympics when the sailing regattas were held in Tallinn. Since the restoration of Estonia's independence, it has been undergoing major restoration and renovation. As a result, it has become a major north European tourist magnet.

Despite being handed from the Danes to the Livonian Order, to **Swedish** control in 1561, and finally to the Russian empire in 1710, when it capitulated to Tsar **Peter the Great** a decade before the end of the **Great Northern War**, Tallinn managed to keep an independent town government throughout and even had privileges added with each change of suzerain. Thus the Tallinn town government continued speaking German and operated under its own rules for almost two centuries until the population growth brought about by **industrialization** and imperial policies of **Russification** in 1877 ended the Lübeck charter and replaced it with Russian administrative law.

The Russian imperial period also left a valuable architectural legacy in Tallinn: the Kadriorg Park and its palace (*see* ARCHITECTURE); the government buildings on Toompea, including the parliament building; plus several churches, theaters, and a number of bank and school buildings.

The growth of modern Tallinn began in 1857 when a rail line was built to connect it with **Narva** and St. Petersburg. As a result of its ice-free port, Tallinn became a major industrial center and one of the most important ports in the European part of the Russian empire. The population multiplied sixfold in 50 years and reached 160,000 in 1917 as rural workers flocked to the factories and as industrial workers were sent to Tallinn from Russia. When, immediately before World War I, Tallinn became an imperial naval base, in addition to large shipyards established in the west end in Kopli armaments factories were also built. After Tallinn became the capital of Estonia in 1918, its character shifted from an emphasis on industry and shipping to a political, administrative, judicial, and cultural center, competing in the latter category with **Tartu**, the intellectual hearth to Estonia.

During World War II, Tallinn suffered only one bombing during the night of 9–10 March 1944 when 600 died and 20,000 became homeless. The damage to the city caused by mobilization into the armies of the two occupiers, and the **deportations**, **emigration**, and occupations, meant that the city was largely shorn of its leading citizens. During the half century of Soviet occupation, in addition to reviving as the capital of Estonia, it was also developed as the major Estonian industrial center with most of the labor imported from the Soviet hinterland. According to some estimates, Tallinn became a railroad station with an estimated 7 million migrant laborers passing through during the four decades since the war. As a result, Tallinn in 1991 had a bifurcated population with the normal, social class–structured Estonian half alienated from the alien, monolingual, Russian-speaking, and largely working-class half.

With the restoration of independence, the city revived quickly as it reestablished contact with the Western world, especially with Finland and Sweden, and turned its back on Russia except for the transit trade through its ports (*see* MUUGA). The heart of the city was rapidly reoriented into a commercial and financial center with new department stores, shopping malls, high-rise glass towers, and business and tourist hotels. The ferry, fixed-wing air, and helicopter connections with Helsinki and Stockholm brought over 7 million visitors to Tallinn in 2000.

Tallinn's population declined to 410,000 as 70,000 **aliens** (about half from Tallinn, comprising 28 percent of its population) left Estonia soon after independence. The ethnic composition of Tallinn today is half ethnic Estonian, 40 percent Russian, and 10 percent other nationalities. Although the ethnic and social class structure of Tallinn has not changed much in a decade of independence, the relationships are very different as the aliens are learning Estonian, applying for citizenship, and being integrated into Estonian society (*see* INTEGRATION).

The city fathers have drawn up major redevelopment plans to make it a modern livable city with good roads, other amenities, and low-rise housing, including single-family dwellings to replace the Soviet era high-rise blocks. The legend of the Old Man of Ülemiste tells that he is prepared to drown the city with the waters of the lake overlooking the city if it is ever completed. Hence Tallinn is constantly constructing new buildings to ensure that the city will never be completed. The building boom unleashed by restored independence should keep the city safe from the threat of the Old Man of Lake Ülemiste for decades to come.

TALLINN PORTS. *See* MUUGA.

TAMMSAARE, A. H. (Anton Hansen) (1878–1940). Estonian writer. Tammsaare was born on 30 January 1878 in Albu *vald.* After studies at Väike-Maarja parish school and at Treffner Gymnasium in 1898–1903, Tammsaare worked in the editorial section of the newspaper *Teataja* in 1903–05 and then studied law at **Tartu** in 1907–11, but owing to tuberculosis had to leave a few months before graduating. From 1911 to 1919, he lived with his brother in a forest ranger's farm, except for the year 1912–13, which he spent in the mountains of the Caucasus curing his disease. This proved to be his only trip outside Estonia. In 1919, he moved to **Tallinn**, married, and earned a good living as a professional writer until he died of a heart attack at his desk on 1 March 1940.

Tammsaare's work is marked by erudition learned from catholic yet systematic reading in several languages. Although he had been writing since gymnasium days, it was only during his law studies that he made the decision to become a professional writer. He prepared for this by studying natural science, philosophy, psychology, sociology, and law, since he viewed the writer's function as being a thermometer of society. As such, a writer must be in touch with all that moves and concerns society. That, to Tammsaare, required immersion in such secularizing tendencies of European culture and society as reflected in these disciplines. Tammsaare was also unique in that he was one of the few members of the Estonian intelligentsia born at the end of the last century who was indifferent to religious spirituality, but sought salvation from the sufferings of contemporary European civilization in culture.

Tammsaare produced a very large oeuvre that, despite his own wide knowledge of languages, remains accessible only to readers of Estonian. His works consisted of complex analytical novels, popular articles, and essays on the search for truth and justice. Indeed, his major work is the pentalogy *Tõde ja Õigus* (*Truth and Justice*) published over the period 1926 to 1933. Its first volume has been reissued 11 times, the others 7 times. The 1964–69 reissue amounted to 50,000 copies of each volume—an impressive number for an Estonian-speaking population of 900,000. It is regarded by many as a five-course university education for the Estonian people in psychology, culture, and philosophy. It also made his reputation as the greatest Estonian writer of all time. In 1952–68, his works were published in 13 volumes and in 1978–93 his collected works were published in 18 volumes. Although the continuing importance of *Tõde ja Õigus* in Estonian culture may be compared to that of Shakespeare in English culture, the outside world has no access to it basically because of the difficulty of effectively translating the country dialect used as well as the uniquely parochial setting of the stories in late 19th–early 20th century transition of peasant to petty bourgeois Estonian culture. Estonians mythically relate to this transition as if to their individual pasts. Only a few of Tammsaare's other works have been published in Russian, and one each in Latvian, English, and French, largely because of the intervention of the war and his death at its beginning. *See also* LITERATURE.

TARAND, ANDRES (1940–). Estonian politician and environmentalist. Tarand was born on 10 January 1940 in **Tallinn**, where he also received his primary and secondary education. After graduating in meteorology from the **University of Tartu** in 1963, he did his compulsory service in the Soviet army. Tarand then entered graduate studies at the Tallinn Botanical Gardens in 1965–68, and received his *cand. geog*. from the University of Tartu in 1973. In the meantime he participated in the Soviet Antarctic Expedition of 1968–70, and joined the staff of Tallinn Botanical Gardens on his return in 1970, where he worked in various capacities until he became its director in 1988–90.

In the mid-1980s, he became involved with the nationalist environmental movement that attempted to stop the unchecked exploitative open-pit mining of **phosphate** and **oil shale** in **Northeast Estonia**. This naturally led him into active politics as a leader, not only because of his environmental expertise but also mainly because of his accommodating personality and his persuasive abilities. He participated in the Green and **Rahvarinne** movements in 1998–90, served on the **Estonian Committee**, and was elected to the **Estonian Congress** and to the **Constituent Assembly**. He was also elected to the **Supreme Council** in the first free elections in Soviet Estonia in 1990, and subsequently has been elected to the **Riigikogu** in the general elections of 1992, 1996, 1999, and 2003. He joined the Mõõdukad (Moderate) Party and in 1996 became its chair. Tarand served as minister of the environment in the first **Mart Laar** cabinet 1992–94 and as compromise prime minister for five months in 1994–95 leading the so-called Christmas Peace Cabinet when Prime Minister Laar was forced to resign. Since 1999, Tarand's main function has been to chair his party, both in and out of parliament; to be a possible presidential candidate of his party; and to be a political commentator trusted by many Estonians as a balanced elder statesman. *See also* ENVIRONMENT.

TARTO, ENN (1938–). Estonian freedom fighter and politician. Tarto was born on 25 September 1938 in **Tartu**. After completing secondary school in Russia in 1958 where the family had been **deported** during the war, he studied Estonian language and literature at the University of Tartu in 1969–72. In 1956–60, 1966–67, and 1983–88, he served time in gulag concentration camps for anti-Soviet propaganda and agitation. After his return to Estonia in 1988, he became actively engaged in the politics of Estonian independence and was elected to and participated in all the extraparliamentary representative organizations during 1989–91, including the Executive Committee of the Citizens of the Republic of Estonia**, Estonian Committees** I and II, as well as the Constitutional Assembly. After independence, he was elected to the **Riigikogu** in 1992, 1995, and 1999, but lost his seat in 2003 when his party, the Moderates, won only 6 seats, down from 11 in the previous Riigikogu.

TARTU (German, Dorpat). Estonia's second city and the intellectual and cultural hearth of Estonia. Tartu also has the distinction of being the oldest historical reference in Estonia, found in an ancient Russian chronicle that describes the raid of the Kievan prince Yaroslav the Wise on Tartu in 1030, building his own fort and naming it Jurjev. Since the Brethren of the Sword in 1224 during the Christianizing Crusades captured Tartu, it has been the seat of a bishopric, and for two centuries the capital of the Tartu Episcopal statelet in the Livonian League. Since Tartu was also on a trade route to Novgorod, it became a member of the **Hanseatic League** in 1280. Its prominence as a religious, administrative, and trade center brought the Lutheran Reformation to it already in 1525 and led to the violent stripping of churches by townsmen. A quarter century later at the beginning of the **Livonian Wars**, Tartu was attacked by Tsar Ivan the Terrible in 1558, but it took three quarters of a century of warfare and several changes of suzerain before Sweden conquered Tartu in 1625, then established the first printing house in Estonia in 1631; the university, Academia Gustaviana, in 1632; as well as Forselius Seminary, the first teachers' college in Estonia, which operated in 1784–88 (*see* EDUCATION). But soon a century of disasters struck—Tsar **Peter the Great** conquered Tartu in 1704; great fires raged in 1708, 1763, and 1775; and the population dropped to 3,421 by 1789 after having reached 6,000 two centuries earlier

The reopening of the **University of Tartu** in 1802 saw the beginning of the golden age of Tartu. By 1854, the population grew to 13,000; Tartu became the intellectual and cultural capital of Estonia as the University attracted bright minds; the first **song festival** in Estonia was held there in 1869; the fist national theater opened in 1870; and the **Society of Estonian Literati** was founded in 1872. By 1900, Tartu's population had reached 40,000 and it had developed into not only an academic, cultural, and administrative center but also had become the manufacturing center of southern Estonia as well. The severing of southern Estonia from the Province of Livland in 1917, the uniting of Estonia, the signing of the **Peace of Tartu** with the Soviets in 1920, and the reopening of the University as the national university ushered in the modern era of intellectual and cultural renaissance of Tartu. After a population decline during World War II, by 1950 it had grown to 55,000 and to 100,000 by 1977, its size today. The University and the Agricultural Academy (now the Agricultural University) allowed Tartu to remain largely ethnically Estonian and provided the intellectual ferment necessary to maintain national cultural values. Significantly, it was the Tartu Communist Party newspaper *Edasi*, which published the Four-man Proposal on **Isemajandav Eesti** (IME). In 1993, after a hiatus of half a century, the reestablished independent **Supreme Court** was again placed in Tartu, symbolically a 200-kilometer distance from the seat of the government in Tallinn.

At the beginning of the third millennium, Tartu is a modern university, administrative, commercial, and manufacturing center with a vibrant musical and theater scene. It began to rebuild its town center during the mid-1990s and to restore its historical artifacts, the ruins of the medieval Episcopal cathedral on Toomemaägi (Dome Hill), the many statues of national heroes destroyed by the Soviet occupation, and the war-damaged 19th-century St. John's Church, as well as upgrading its many museums and providing new facilities for its citizens, such as modernized roads, hospitals, and a water park.

TEEMANT, JAAN (1872–1942?). Estonian politician, statesman, and lawyer. Born on 24 September 1872 in Vigala *vald*, Teemant completed **Treffner Gümnasium** in 1893, and studied law at St. Petersburg. After graduation in 1903, he practiced law in **Tallinn**. His advocacy of the rights of tenant farmers against the **Baltic German** baronial estate owners and his public criticism of the nobility and the anachronistic land law of the **Special Baltic Order** brought him immediately into the limelight, and facilitated his election to the Tallinn city council in 1904.

In the revolutionary year of 1905, Teemant demanded a judicial inquiry into the police breaking up the May Day demonstration in Tallinn, organized a petition to the imperial government, negotiated with the barons on a proposed revised land law, and drafted a law on autonomy for the Estonian province in a commission established for this purpose. As a result of this radical activism, he was elected chair of the All-Estonian Congress called by the moderate **Jaan Tõnisson** on 27–29 November in **Tartu**. The meeting soon split. Tõnisson and the moderates left the hall for a second venue, leaving Teemant in charge of the radical majority, which adopted such revolutionary resolutions as the calling of a constituent congress, self-government, nationalization of land and the means of production, and arming the population. Even though Teemant did not support all these resolutions, he was nevertheless elected to a five-man executive committee to implement them. When a war emergency was declared, he fled to Switzerland just before being condemned to death in absentia. In exile, he continued his political activity and even drafted a law on autonomy for Estonia. In 1908, with the rescinding of the emergency he returned to Estonia and, although the death sentence had been annulled, he was nevertheless sentenced to prison for two years plus two years of exile in the northern Russian province of Archangelsk for his anti-imperial politics.

On his return, Teemant worked at his legal practice in Tallinn until the outbreak of the February Revolution in 1917, when he was elected to the **Maapäev** (Provincial Assembly) and served as its chair from July to October. In the spring of 1919, he was elected to the **Constituent Assembly** on the ticket of the Agrarian League, but was soon named procurator-general of the new Republic in which function he had to fight the agitation and subversive activities of the **Bolsheviks**. At the end of the **War of Independence**, he resigned from politics and returned to the practice of law. However, a scant four years later he answered the siren call of politics again and was elected to **Riigikogu** II and all subsequent parliaments (III, IV, and V) until the **Era of Silence**. Between 1925 and 1927, he formed three successive coalition cabinets as Riigivanem (state elder, functioning as both head of government and state). In February 1932, he formed his fourth cabinet, which lasted for five months during the deepest economic crisis of the Depression in Estonia. Despite having to pass drastic measures, his personal popularity remained high.

As a convinced democrat, Teemant warned the new powerbrokers at the last session of Riigikogu V in 1934 of the illegality of their action, opposed them, and defended those charged with anti-Estonian activities by the new government in court. In October 1936, along with three other former heads of government and state (Juhan Kukk, **Ants Piip**, and Jaan Tõnisson), he issued the "Four State Elders' Memorandum" calling on **Konstantin Päts** to immediately end the curtailment of civil and political rights and to restore democratic government. The memorandum, published in a Finnish newspaper because of the censorship of anything critical of the government at home, but immediately known by everyone in Estonia, demonstrated publicly for the first time the extent of elite opposition to Päts's authoritarianism. During the remaining years of independence, Teemant continued his legal practice in Tallinn and was named by Päts as the Estonian member of the joint Estonian-German commission dealing with the repatriation of **Baltic Germans** to the Third Reich. Immediately on the Soviet occupation, on 23 July 1940, Teemant was arrested and on 21 February 1941 was sentenced to 10 years of imprisonment by a Soviet war tribunal for repressing the working class, and for supporting war criminals and the landed gentry! No reliable information is available as to his fate after this date, except that he was **deported** to serve his imprisonment somewhere in the Soviet Union and is believed to have died in 1942.

TELEVISION. *See* RADIO AND TELEVISION.

TEUTONIC ORDER. *See* CRUSADING ORDERS.

TIEF, OTTO (1889–1976). Estonian statesman and lawyer. Tief was born in the village of Uusküla in Rapla *vald* on 14 August 1889. After graduating from local schools, he studied law at St. Petersburg form 1910 to 1916 where, among other activities, he became a co-founder of the fraternity Rotalia (*see* STUDENT FRATERNITIES). In 1918, he became a member of the Estonian Soldiers Central Committee and served as deputy battalion commander of the Kalev Malev in the **War of Independence**. Tief graduated from the **University of Tartu** in law in 1921 and served as minister of health and welfare in 1926–27, then as minister of justice in 1928. Thereafter, he carried on a private legal practice while also serving as legal counsel to the Estonian Land Bank. He was elected to **Riigikogu** III and V in 1926 and 1932. In 1944, he joined the Eesti Vabariigi Rahvuskomitee (Republic of Estonia National Committee) and served as prime minister and minister of the interior in the government named by **Jüri Uluots** on 18 September 1944. During the few days of interregnum between the German armies' retreat and the Soviet reoccupation, Tief's cabinet proclaimed a declaration regaining independence and attempted to organize a defense of **Tallinn** against the advancing Soviet army. On 10 October 1944, Tief was imprisoned and in 1945 the Soviet Union's Supreme Court sentenced him to 10 years in prison, which he served in Siberia and Kazakhstan. On release he returned to Estonia for two years, 1956–58, but left for Ukraine in fear of a new repression. After 1965 he lived in Ainazi, Latvia, just outside the Estonian border. On his death on 5 March 1976 in Ahja, Estonia, the Soviet authorities, still intent on repression, would not allow him to be buried in the national cemetery in Tallinn. However, in independent Estonia, he was reburied there among other national heroes in 1993.

TIGER LEAP (Tiigrihüpe). Initiated by **Jaak Aaviksoo**, the Estonian national information technology (IT) program was launched on 21 February 1996 by President **Lennart Meri** with the goals of modernizing the Estonian **educational** system, creating conditions for the formation of an open learning environment, and adapting the nation to the demands of an information society. The immediate objective was to put a computer in every classroom in every school in Estonia, and to rapidly introduce information and communications technology (ICT) in the public and private sectors. By 2000, four short years later, ICT access had moved Estonia into the front ranks of Internet use in Europe.

The Tiger Leap Foundation, with Jaak Aaviksoo as the chair, was created in February 1997 as a nonprofit body consisting of the Ministry of Education and 37 computer companies and private individuals to organize the execution and financing of the program. Initially, to the general public, Tiger Leap became associated with the slogan "one computer for every 20 pupils." The Foundation rapidly evolved a three-level strategy with the national level developing the target program; the county level coordinating the supply of computers and skills; and at local levels, each school implementing the ICT program of learning and utilization of IT resources.

The educational part of the program provided training for teachers, computers, and software; assisted in setting up **Estonian language** educational databases for schools; and encouraged pupils to set up chat rooms and online newspapers.

The Tiger Leap program caught the imagination of the Estonian population and became the motor of virtualization of the Estonian economy and the public sectors. In consequence, already at the end of 1999 almost all government forms were accessible to the public on the Internet, and the administrative reform of 2000 began with making all internal documents available online to eliminate paper jams. All ministries, including the prime minister's office, sent Christmas cards in 1999 online only. To encourage Estonians to use IT outside work and education, the foundation has provided a large number of public-access Internet sites around the countryside. By 2000, Cabinet meetings used only documentation read on computer screens, and traveling ministers participated in cabinet meetings by laptop Internet connection. In 2002, the **Tallinn** City Council inaugurated its own advanced Tiger Leap to increase the number of computers in the schools from the current one per 42 pupils to one for every 10 by 2005; and in June, a program funded by banks and telecom firms was inaugurated to teach computer and Internet access skills to 100,000 computer-illiterate adults in Estonia.

TITMA, MIKK (1939–). Estonian sociologist. Born on 2 November 1939 in **Tallinn**, Titma studied law at the **University of Tartu**, graduated in 1963, studied sociology, and earned a *cand. soc.* degree in 1968 and his doctorate in 1975 from the Sociology Institute of Academy of Sciences of the Union of Soviet Socialist Republics (USSR) in Moscow. In 1968–74, he taught at the **University of Tartu**, and in 1975–88 headed the sociology section in the Institute of History of the Academy of Sciences of the Estonian Soviet Socialist Republic (ESSR). In 1988–90, he served as director of the newly founded Institute of Philosophy, Sociology and Law of the Academy. In 1989–90, he served also as third (ideological) secretary of the Central Committee of the **Estonian Communist Party** (ECP) and was a member of the **Supreme Soviet of the ESSR** in 1990–91. In 1991, Titma left Estonia for the United States and worked until 1999 as a researcher in sociology at Stanford University, when he was elected professor of sociology at the University of Tartu. Although Titma's academic output is considerable in Estonian, Russian, and English, with over 160 publications, and he is internationally well known as an expert on intergenerational sociological studies, his claim to fame among Estonians is his role as coauthor and signer of the Four-man Proposal on **Isemajandav Eesti** (IME) published in the **Tartu** newspaper *Edasi* on 26 September 1987. His primary research and publications are on social cleavage, generational studies, and the comparative study of societies in transition.

TOBIAS, RUDOLF (1873–1918). Estonian organist, composer, and the "father" of Estonian classical music. Born on 29 May 1873 in Käina, Tobias graduated in 1897 from studying the organ and Nikolai Rimsky-Korsakov's composition classes at St. Petersburg Conservatory. From 1898 to 1904, he was choir leader and organist at the Estonian St. John's Church in St. Petersburg, then moved thereafter to **Tartu** where he taught music, conducted, gave piano recitals, and wrote articles on musical events in the press. In 1908, he moved abroad and lived in Paris, Leipzig, and Berlin, where he taught theory at the Berlin Music Academy and gave concerts of his own compositions from 1912 to his death on 29 October 1918.

Tobias is regarded as the father of Estonian classical music: he composed many firsts in Estonian music—a symphonic work, the prologue *Julius Cesar*, 1896; the cantata *Johannes of Damascus*, 1897; the piano concerto *Concertstück*, 1897; a sonata for piano in 1897; a string quartet in 1899; the oratory *Salvation of Jonah*, in 1909; and a programmed instrumental work, the *Burlesque of Walpurgis*, 1910, among others. He wrote ballads and choir, piano, organ, and orchestral music, some with national-cultural themes. His compositions are powerfully monumental and are characterized by the use of counterpoint technique. His compositions have been extensively played in Estonia and are thus familiar to and beloved by Estonians. More recently, during the last quarter century, **Neeme Järvi** has frequently included Tobias in his conducting repertoire, has recorded all of his music, and has thus brought Tobias to attention of the international music world.

Tobias also left a family of musicians. His daughter, Silvia (1908–1985), a harpsichordist, played in the Estonia Theater orchestra in 1935–70 and moved to New York in 1972, where Tobias's younger daughter, Helen Tobias-Duesberg (born in New York in 1919), an organist and composer, had lived since 1949. Helen studied composition in Tallinn and New York, and taught at the Manhattan Music School from 1951 until retirement. She also composed melodramas; ballads for symphony orchestras; a requiem for soprano, choir, and orchestra; as well as chamber and song music, much of it since the 1970s.

TOOME, INDREK (1943–). Estonian politician. Born on 19 September 1943 in **Tallinn**, Toome graduated from Tallinn Polytechnical Institute (now Tallinn Technical University) in 1968 as an electronics engineer. He then made a career in the **Estonian Communist Party** (ECP) until 1990, when he resigned from the Party. From 1968 to 1970, he served as a leader of the youth wing of the Estonian **Komsomol** and then as its first secretary until 1978 when he was appointed first secretary of the Tartu City Committee of the ECP. In

1984, he became deputy to the chair (prime minister) of the Council of Ministers of the Estonian Soviet Socialist Republic (ESSR) and served from January to November 1988 as third (ideological) secretary of the Central Committee of the ECP, and as prime minister of the ESSR from 1988 to 1990. Toome became one of the leaders of the reform wing of the ECP during **perestroika and glasnost** and in June 1988 took the lead, together with Enn-Arno Sillari, first secretary of the ECP's Tallinn committee, and Karl Kortelainen, the KGB head in Estonia, in asking Mikhail Gorbachev, general secretary of the Communist Party of the Soviet Union (CPSU) to replace the reactionary antiperestroika and **Russifying** ECP First Secretary **Karl Vaino** with the moderate Estonian nationalist **Vaino Väljas**. Väljas's accession to the ECP's leading position marked the public acceptance of the ECP of the **Singing Revolution**. Toome's government resigned on 30 March 1990 when the ESSR **Supreme Soviet** declared the beginning of the transition to independence, and handed over the reins of government to Prime Minister **Edgar Savisaar**.

Toome served as a member of the ESSR Supreme Soviet from 1972 to 1990, and as a member of the renamed transition **Supreme Council of the Republic of Estonia** elected democratically on 18 March 1990, until its dissolution in 1992. Toome then withdrew from politics and has devoted himself to private business. His reputation suffered as both the **Mart Laar** and **Tiit Vähi** cabinets in 1993–94 pursued him in the **courts** for corruption for illegally obtaining an Estonian passport for an **alien**. He was convicted and paid a fine.

TOOMPEA. Although Toompea is the name of the hill on which Old Tallinn was built (hence the Old City on the hill is known as Toompea), the term is also used to refer to Toompea Castle or Palace on Toompea where **Riigikogu** is located. Since the prime minister's office and the State Chancery (Riigikantselei or Cabinet Office/Executive Office) were also located in one wing of the Parliament Building until 2000, and are now in the Stenbock Building only 150 meters away on the hill, both Parliament and government (Valitsus) are often referred to as "Toompea." *See also* TALLINN.

TRADE. *See* AGRICULTURE; ECONOMIC TRANSFORMATION; INDUSTRIALIZATION.

TREFFNER, HUGO HERMANN FÜRCHTEGOTT (1845–1912). Estonian nationalist, national-language school activist, and educator. Born on 17 July 1845 in Kanepi *vald*, Treffner passed the home (private) schoolmaster's exams at the **University of Tartu** in 1865 and taught in various places, including Poland, thereafter. Subsequently he completed studies at the Faculty of Theology at **Tartu** in 1880 and in 1883 succeeded in opening Treffner Gümnasium, a private school for boys, which he directed to the end of his life. Beginning in 1886 he also taught religion at the Russian-language St. Mary's School in Tartu, which he also did in 1899 at the Pushkin Gymnasium for Girls. In the 1870s he joined in the nationalist renaissance movement of **Carl Robert Jakobson**. As part of his contribution to the movement, Treffner became a founder and leader of both the **Eesti Üliõpilaste Selts** (EÜS) and the **Society of Estonian Literati**. He was a member of the central committee of the **Estonian Aleksander School** and the 1879 **Song Festival** committee. Treffner owned and edited *Postimees* in 1887–88, but sold it in 1888. He also edited the periodical *Oma Maa* (*Own Land*) from 1886 to 1891. He was one of the most colorful personalities in Tartu in his time and was the model for Maurus, the hero of the epic novel *Tõde ja Õigus* (*Truth and Justice*) written by his former pupil, **A. H. Tammsaare**. Treffner died on 13 March 1912 in Tartu, full of honors but short of seeing Estonian as the teaching **language** of his school.

His nephew, Konstantin Edmund Treffner (born 13 October 1885 in Koorküla, died 9 December 1978 at Loksa) followed in his uncle's footsteps after finishing Treffner Gümnasium, initially working as a private teacher and then, after graduating in mathematics from Tartu, taking over in 1917 as director of the school and running it until dismissed by the Soviet occupation authorities in 1940. K. E. Treffner also served as minister of education in 1919–20. In 1917, he was elected to represent the Estonian Teachers' Central Federation at the pan-empire teachers congress, where he defended Estonian as a language of instruction.

Treffner Gümnasium started as a German-language school, switched to Russian in 1889 as a result of the **Russification** thrust of the empire, and finally became an Estonian-language school in 1918. During Hugo Treffner's lifetime, it was the only secondary school with a basically Estonian student body. As such, it played a central role in the formation of an educated Estonian elite. After the founder's death, the school was financed by a supporters' organization, which in 1935 was turned into a foundation. During the Soviet occupation the school's name was changed variously to Tartu IVth Secondary School, Tartu 1st Secondary School, and A. H. Tammsaare Secondary School, until 1990, when it regained its original name.

TREFFNER GÜMNASIUM. *See* TREFFNER.

TUGLAS, FRIEDEBERT (until 1923, Friedebert Mihkelson) (1886–1971). Estonian writer, literary critic, and translator. Because of his central role in leading the development of the citification and modernization of Estonian culture, he was known in the prewar decades as the "Pope of Estonian literature." And, although he never studied at university, in 1946 he was inducted into the **Estonian Academy of Sciences**. Tuglas was born on 2 March 1886 in Ahja and began publishing in 1901 while still a student at **Treffner Gümnasium**, from which he graduated in 1905. He quickly became a leader of the **Noor Eesti** movement and participated in the 1905 revolution, for which he was imprisoned at the end of 1905 for four months by the provincial government, after which he fled the country and traveled around Europe as a political émigré, living primarily in Finland but also for short periods in Paris, St. Petersburg, Germany, Belgium, Switzerland, Italy, and North Africa. He returned to **Tartu** in 1917 and moved to **Tallinn** in 1944.

During his years in Tartu, in other words during the entire span of the first Republic, the literary and cultural life of Estonia revolved around him. He participated in the founding of the periodical *Siuru*, edited it, and founded and edited three more literary periodicals—*Odamees*, *Ilo*, and *Tarpita*. Between 1923 and 1939, he was elected chair of the Estonian Writers Union five times while also serving as chair of the Estonian Literary Society in 1929–40. In 1923, he founded *Looming*, which quickly became the premier cultural periodical of Estonia, and served as its first editor until 1926. In addition, he found time to participate actively on the local cultural and literary scene and sat on the boards and participated in numerous Estonian and foreign associations and organizations, including the Tartu theater Vanemuine, the art academy Pallas, the Finnish Writers Union, and the London PEN Club, among others. During the first Soviet occupation in 1940–41, he again edited *Looming* and belonged to the executive of the Estonian Soviet Socialist Republic's (ESSR) Writers Union. In 1946, he was honored with the title People's Writer by the ESSR government. However, at the end of the decade as a result of Stalin's Sovietizing of cultural policy, he was thrown out of the Writers Union and his works were proscribed. In 1955, after a change in Soviet cultural policy, he was rehabilitated and allowed to resume his position as the literary icon of Estonians. After his death on 15 April 1971, his colleagues turned his house into a shrine-museum.

Tuglas's literary output is prodigious and encompasses hundreds of short stories and literary critiques, and scores of novels. He experimented with different literary styles of belles-lettres, and used romanticism, elegiac symbolism, impressionism, realism, and psychological interpretation. Early in his career, in 1909 and 1912, he wrote two books on method and style in literature, which proved to be decisive in their influence on Estonian writers. Two decades later his eight-volume critical analysis (*Kriitika*, vols. I–VIII, 1935–36) established a solid critical foundational review of Estonian literature to date, and provided the major influence on the direction and development of Estonian writing. His catholic grasp of the human condition extended to writing travelogues on Spain (1918) and North Africa (3 vols., 1928–30), which established the norm for Estonian cultural-literary travel writing. That he could also write for the popular reader is shown by his humor-laden "A Norwegian Chronicle," published anonymously in 1939. Moreover, Tuglas was a prolific translator who introduced Estonians to Finnish and Russian writers of note.

His literary output has been issued in collected editions several times: three volumes of short stories in 1939–40, eight volumes of *Works* in 1957–62, two volumes of collected short stories in 1971, a final memoir in 1973, and seven volumes of collected works in 1986–96. Although some of his output has been translated into Finnish, Latvian, Hungarian, German, and Russian, very little is available in English. Thus, Tuglas remains primarily an Estonian literary giant available only to Estonian readers.

TÕNISSON, JAAN (1868–1941?). Estonian statesman, politician, and lawyer. Born into a well-off farm family on 22 December 1868 in

Viljandi *vald*, Tõnisson devoted his life to building a cultured Estonian nation-state on principles of liberal democracy. Hence, after graduating from the **University of Tartu** with a law degree in 1882, he joined the editorial board of *Postimees.* After a two-year stint in 1894–96 in Russia as an apprentice judge and court investigator, he returned to **Tartu**, bought *Postimees* together with **Oskar Kallas** and Karl Koppel and the help of **Villem Reiman**, and became its editor. This single act, more than any other, marked the change of generations in the leadership of the Estonian nationalist movement. It also marked the beginning of the "renaissance" of Tartu, as it again became the center of agitation for cultural nationalism. In 1898, Tõnisson joined the Tartu Estonian Farmers Society and immediately began a campaign of educating farmers to modernize and intensify farming practices by means of courses and annual exhibitions, which soon became manifestations of national cultural aspirations. The first and second pan-Estonian agricultural congresses organized by him in 1899 and 1905 brought together and built solidarity among Estonian farmers; Tõnisson was also instrumental in founding the agricultural cooperative movement in Estonia. In 1907, he joined Villem Reiman in establishing the Estonian Literary Society, a revival of the moribund **Society of Estonian Literati**, as a broader manifestation of the aspirations of the national culture.

Tõnisson's liberal democratic ideology, to which he remained true to the end of his life, led him to oppose not only the ongoing **Russification** of the late 19th century and the **Baltic German** reactionaries but also Estonian radical democrats and socialist revolutionaries. Thus, he came into early conflict with **Konstantin Päts**, and remained in lifelong opposition as the quintessential liberal-democrat to the pragmatic social-democratic authoritarian Päts. Although Tõnisson condemned the 1905 Revolution, he was caught up in it. In November 1905 he founded the Estonian National-minded Party and early in 1906 worked diligently to stop the murderous actions of the punishment squads sent out by St. Petersburg to bring the revolutionaries to rough field "justice." Thus, although he was elected from the Province of Livland to represent the Autonomists at the first imperial Duma in 1906, he was nevertheless removed as editor of his paper for a period and even sentenced to prison for three months in 1908 for his part in the January 1906 protest of the Tartu intelligentsia against the punishment squads.

Between the revolutions of 1905 and 1917, Tõnisson was not only the most respected but also arguably the most influential political leader of Estonia. However, his role declined in the confusion of the revolutionary period during World War I as his moderate liberal-democratic views were spurned by the politicians leading the radicalized demands of the urban working classes, who had grown to large numbers during the **industrializing** boom of the prewar decade. Still, he soldiered on as the conscience and leader of liberal democracy. To accommodate to the times, his party was refounded several times, but throughout with Tõnisson as leader: in 1917–19 as the Estonian Democratic Party, 1919–32 as the Estonian People's Party, and in 1932–35 as the National Party. One of his strongest holds on public opinion was his newspaper, which he edited up to 1935, when Päts removed him as editor.

Tõnisson's role as a liberal-democratic nationalist found expression in his participation at the center of Estonian politics: in the All-Estonian Congress (which he convened in 1917), in the **Constituent Assembly** in 1919, and all **Riigikogu** from 1920–34 and 1938–40. He served on the Estonian Foreign Delegation in 1917–18, as minister without portfolio in 1918–19, as prime minister in 1919–20, as speaker of the parliament in 1923–25 and 1932–33, as **Riigivanem** in 1927–28 and 1933, and as foreign minister in 1930–32 in Päts's and **Jaan Teemant**'s cabinets. He fell out completely with Päts after the **preemptive coup**, and was removed from politics and silenced in 1935. He found employment as professor of cooperatives at the University of Tartu in 1935–39. Despite the proscription on his writing and speaking, he nevertheless garnered the largest number of votes in the 1938 Riigivolikogu election. But as chair of only the Defense Committee in parliament, he had no influence on the development of foreign relations leading up to the Soviet occupation. After his arrest on 12 December 1940, Tõnisson was interrogated in Tallinn until April 1941 by the NKVD. Although there is no reliable information on his subsequent fate, it is surmised that he was murdered by the NKVD in July 1941.

– U –

ULUOTS, JÜRI (1890–1945). Last prime minister of independent Estonia from 12 October 1939 to 16 June 1940, when he resigned as a result of the Soviet ultimatum and occupation of Estonia. On his authority as acting president under the **Constitution of 1938** in the absence of deported elected President **Konstantin Päts,** Uluots appointed **Otto Tief** as prime minister and asked him to form a government on 18 September 1944 in the brief interregnum between the German retreat and the Soviet reoccupation of Estonia. Uluots's action served to establish the continuity of the Republic and led to the recognition by 37 Western states of the Republic of Estonia as a de jure state throughout the Soviet occupation. Uluots fled to Sweden when the Soviet Union reoccupied Estonia, established a new government in exile on the base of the members of the Tief government who had escaped, and died in exile in Stockholm a few months later, on 9 January 1945.

Uluots was born on 13 January 1890 and graduated in 1915 from the law faculty at the University of St. Petersburg, where he continued graduate studies in Roman and private law. In 1919, he was elected to the Estonian **Constituent Council** and to the first, second, and third **Riigikogu** in the 1920s. In 1920, he began to teach Roman law at the **University of Tartu**, was appointed professor in 1925, and served as dean of the faculty of law twice (1924–31 and 1942–44) as well as prorector from 1931–34. He was intimately involved with the university and continued to teach there even while prime minister. Uluots was one of the primary founders of the discipline of legal studies in Estonia and formed much of Estonian private law. He was a member of the partly appointed, partly elected National Assembly (Rahvuskogu) to draft the new **Constitution of 1938**, and was one of its main authors. In 1938, he was elected to the new Riigikogu and served as speaker of its newly created lower chamber, the Riigivolikogu, until he became prime minister on 12 April 1939, serving until forced to resign by the Soviet occupation on 21 June 1940. He was also one of the main organizers with **Konstantin Päts** and **Johan Laidoner** of the authoritarian regime of the **Era of Silence**.

UNDER, MARIE (1883–1980). Estonian poet. After studies at the **Tallinn** German Girls School 1891–1900, Under, born on 27 March 1883 in Tallinn, worked at the Tallinn newspaper *Teataja* in 1901–02 and on marrying in 1902 moved to Moscow. After the birth of two children, the family moved to Tallinn, where Under worked as a professional writer. After some time, irreconcilable differences led to divorce from her husband in 1917. She married the writer Artur Adson (1877–1970) in 1924 and stayed with him until his death.

Under showed an aptitude for poetry already at a very young age; read widely in German, French, and Russian; and was especially enamored of Johann Wolfgang von Goethe, Friedrich Schiller, Friedrich Nietzsche, and Henrik Ibsen. Her development as a poet was influenced by **Eduard Vilde**, who encouraged the 17-year-old to switch from German to writing her poetry in Estonian. He arranged for her to join **Konstantin Päts**'s newspaper *Teataja* in 1901, which at the time was one of the contact points of the political and cultural elite in Estonia. Her home in Tallinn became a literary salon during the prewar years and her visibility as a poet rose when she became chair of the writers cooperative Siuru. *Sonetid* (*Sonnets*), her first collection of poetry, was published in 1917 and made her an instant celebrity. Two additional collections followed the next year and confirmed her status as a poetic star.

Under's romantic-erotic poems were like a thunderbolt that shocked and then liberated Estonians from the straitlacedness of the prevailing faux-religious public morality in the midst of the morbid uncertainties of World War I. She was read and discussed by everyone, because everyone found an echo of him or herself in her poems.

In her mature years during the 1920s and early 1930s, her prolific production of 10 collections confirmed Under as the most important Estonian national poet of all time. Her poems, now shorn of overt eroticism, nevertheless still exuded sensuality and expressed a self-confident national-cultural consciousness. In the eyes of her contemporaries, she was the incarnation of the spirit of Estonian national culture, whose poems became the measure of both past and future Estonian poetry.

In her long exile in Sweden, from 1944 to her death almost four decades later, her poems again reflected the sentiments in the hearts of her fellow Estonians, both at home and abroad, as she expressed the pain of loss of home. Now, her poetry also became a political statement of the stubbornness and unbending will of Estonians to regain their independent nation-state. Her poetry remains popular in Estonia and during her lifetime was translated into 20 languages. Under died on 25 September 1980 in Stockholm at the age of 97, honored by many countries.

UNITED STATES BALTIC CHARTER. On 16 January 1998 in Washington, D.C., the presidents of the United States of America and of the Republics of Estonia, Latvia, and Lithuania signed the Charter of Partnership between these four countries. The objective of this diplomatic demarche was to assuage Baltic security fears of being left out of the **North Atlantic Treaty Organization** (NATO) on the pragmatic grounds of leading European states' desire to accommodate Russian concerns about NATO encroachment on its self-declared security sphere along its borders. In the charter, the United States declared its support for Baltic aspirations to integrate fully into the European and Atlantic economic and security institutions. An annual meeting reviews progress in these endeavors. The charter was also accompanied by separate funding assistance arrangements to bring the Baltic States' military preparedness up to NATO standards and interoperability.

UNITED STATES' NONRECOGNITION OF SOVIET OCCUPATION. *See* NONRECOGNITION OF SOVIET OCCUPATION.

UNIVERSITY OF TARTU. The university was established as a four-department Latin academy in 1632 during the reign of Gustavus II Adolphus as the second university in the Swedish empire modeled on the first, the University of Uppsala. The operations of the University during the **Swedish era** were frequently interrupted by war, and after the transfer of Estonia to the Russian empire in 1721, the University was closed. It was reopened in 1802 as the sole German-language university in the Russian empire. As such, it became a natural part of the German-speaking universities of Europe where it was normal for students and professors to "wander" among the universities. Hence it also occupied the unique position of intermediary between Russia and Europe, and attracted and developed such world-renowned scholars of the 19th century as Karl Ernst von Baer, the founder of embryology; Wilhelm Friedrich Ostwald, the founder of physical chemistry; as well as the physicists H. F. E. Lenz and Moritz Hermann Jacobi, among others, to teach, study, and carry on research at Tartu. The idyll ended when, in the last decade of the 19th century, the policy of **Russification** swept across the empire and forced Tartu to teach in Russian, thus taking it out of the system of German universities, and consequently removing it from the West European cultural realm.

After 30 years, the renaissance of the University of Tartu as a European university took place concurrently with the establishment of the Republic of Estonia. On 1 December 1919, it reopened as Estonia's national university, with teaching to be carried on in Estonian, German, and Russian. During the first two decades of the Estonian Republic, the University began to regain its position among its West European cohorts and established a solid research base in the work of neurologist Ludvig Puusepp, geobotanist Teodor Lippmaa (**Endel Lippmaa**'s father), archaeologist Harri Moora, chemist Paul Kogerman, zoologist Johannes Piiper, and astronomer **Ernest Öpik**.

During the half century of Soviet occupation, the University of Tartu, although under the constraints of communist state authority, managed to maintain its position as the hearth of Estonian culture and the intellectual home of its intelligentsia, with most of its teaching in Estonian in all faculties (with some parallel courses in Russian). Although it attracted liberal-minded Russian colleagues, especially from Leningrad and Moscow, and maintained a reputation as one of the best universities in the Soviet Union, the only area where it had a world reputation was in semiotics, thanks to **Juri Lotman**, a Russian Jew who had sought refuge in liberal-minded Tartu from the reactionary and anti-Semitic atmosphere of Leningrad. Finno-Ugric studies was also relatively unscathed and even flourished under the direction of Paul Ariste, who was able to maintain contacts with both Finnish and Hungarian colleagues and had easy access to the large numbers of Finno-Ugric ethnic groups in the Soviet Union. Nevertheless, research in all fields suffered, but especially in the sciences, because of lack of routine competitive contact with western universities and colleagues, as well as the dearth of up-to-date library collections. In the so-called national disciplines, such as Estonian history, **language** and **literature**, archaeology, and linguistics, the lack of competitive contact led to the propagation of the archaic methodologies of the 1930s well into the 1980s. The politically sensitive disciplines of economics, law, sociology, and psychology were badly distorted by mandatory Marxist-Leninist ideological underpinnings directed by the party-state. Despite a large degree of collusion among faculty members to evade abject subservience to

Party dictates, the very length of 45 years of Marxist teachings meant that by the 1980s all of the professoriate was exclusively Soviet-trained.

At the coming of **perestroika and glasnost**, the staff and students at Tartu quickly moved to rebuild. With the death of the incumbent Party hard-line rector, Arnold Koop, the new rector, biologist Jüri Kärner, was elected in 1988 (and served until 1993) by open balloting of students and faculty. He quickly established contact with the émigré intelligentsia abroad and instituted a modernization process. The initial contacts established by the hard science faculties with Western universities during the 1980s were rapidly expanded to enable students and staff to study at and visit European and North American universities, updated computers and printing equipment were provided by a consortium of the **Estonian Canadians** in Toronto, and a social sciences faculty was established by 1992 with **Rein Taagepera,** a political scientist from the University of California, Irvine, as the first dean. The transformation of the social sciences was further assisted by the **EuroFaculty**, instituted in 1993, and strongly supported by the Rectorate. These policies were followed by the next two rectors, psychologist Peter Tulviste and physicist **Jaak Aaviksoo**, who both launched extensive renewal processes by upgrading faculty qualifications (one method was to appoint professors on a competitive basis for only five-year terms), and reducing redundant and overaged staff (the Soviet universities were overstaffed with individuals with questionable qualifications doing "research"). In addition, the University restructured its curriculum to a largely Anglo-Saxon format with an initial baccalaureate degree followed by a master's and a doctorate. The Soviet-era habilitation degree was removed.

By the end of the 1990s, the University was refurbishing its buildings and adding new ones of international standards, and the teaching was rapidly moving to international levels as older staff were gradually replaced by Western-trained younger people and as the University actively sought to employ foreigners. Although the primary language of teaching remained Estonian, the University sought to become trilingual with English and Russian as the other two languages of instruction. Unfortunately, the use of Russian declined rapidly as ethnic Russian students preferred to become fully competent in Estonian and few came from the east. Instead, the combination of low fees, proximity, and rapid Westernization, attracted large numbers of Finnish students to Tartu, adding immeasurably to the Westernization of the processes of learning and teaching because, as fee payers, the Finnish students demanded that professors give lectures and tests at the international standard. Thus, by the new millennium, the University of Tartu was well along the road of regaining its former position as a leading European institution of higher learning and research.

– V –

VAINO, KARL (1923–). Leading reactionary Estonian communist politician. Vaino was born in Tomsk in the Russian Federated Soviet Socialist Republic (RFSSR) on 28 May 1923 to Estonian parents who had remained in Russia after the **War of Independence**. He graduated from the Tomsk Institute of Electromechanical Transportation Engineering in 1947 and joined the Communist Party of the Soviet Union (CPSU) in the same year. In the following year, Vaino was sent to Estonia as a functionary of the **Estonian Communist Party** (ECP). A decade later, he attended the Higher Party School of the Central Committee (CC) of the CPSU, which he completed in 1957, and a brief three years later was appointed a secretary of the CC of the ECP. In 1978, at the direction of the Moscow CPSU central and against the wishes of the then first Secretary, **Johannes Käbin,** who had been grooming **Vaino Väljas** as his successor, Karl Vaino was promoted to first secretary.

Vaino's tenure as leader of the ESSR was marked by a period of **Russification** and Sovietization in Estonia ushered in by Leonid Brezhnev to counter the liberalization of Nikita Khrushchev's thaw. Vaino never learned to speak Estonian properly and was regarded by Estonians as Moscow's "man in Estonia." In 1981, he was honored by being appointed a member of the CC of the CPSU, where he served until 1989. As a result of his reactionary policies, his reformist Estonian nationalist ECP colleagues (*see* INDREK TOOME), pressured by a popular reaction massively expressed by the **People's Front** (Rahvarinne), persuaded General Secretary Mikhail Gorbachev to replace him with Vaino Väljas as First Secretary of the ECP on 16 June 1988 during the "hot summer" of the **Singing Revolution**. He left Estonia immediately to live in Moscow.

VAN DER STOEL, MAX. *See* ORGANIZATION OF SECURITY AND COOPERATION IN EUROPE'S (OSCE) HIGH COMMISSIONER ON NATIONAL MINORITIES.

VARES, JOHANNES (Barbarus) (1890–1946). Estonian poet, public figure, politician, and member of the **Estonian Communist Party** (ECP). Born on 12 January 1890 in Heimtal parish, Vares graduated in medicine from Kiev University in 1917, fought in the **War of Independence**, and was awarded a high decoration by the new republic. During the two decades from 1920 to 1939, Vares carried on a practice as a physician in **Pärnu** but moved to **Tallinn** in 1939. In June 1940, the occupying Soviet power made the well-known and respected left-wing humanist and antifascist Vares prime minister. From August 1940 to his death, he served as the head of state of the Estonian Soviet Socialist Republic (ESSR), formally chair of the Presidium of the ESSR Supreme Soviet. On 6 August 1940, he led the delegation that petitioned the Union of Soviet Socialist Republics (USSR) to accept Estonia as a member SSR, an action that forever tainted him as a traitor among Estonians. The cause of his death in on 29 November 1946 in Tallinn is still unclear—he either committed suicide or was murdered on the orders of his superiors in the Party.

As a writer, he debuted in 1910 and published his first collections of poetry, *Fata-Morgana*, in 1918 and *Inimene ja Sfinks* (*Man and Sphinx*) in 1919. These were followed at regular intervals by 10 more collections of poetry until 1939. His works reflected a sensitive humanist awareness of social conflicts and stresses. He also wrote novellas, literary criticism, and travelogues. However, both his poetry and his other writings of 1940–44 were characterized by political polemics.

VEKSA. The acronym stands for Väliseestlastega Sidemete Arendamise Komitee, translated as the Committee for Developing Contacts with Estonians Abroad. It was created in 1960 and was run jointly by the **Estonian Communist Party** and the KGB to influence the very cohesive and culturally strong Estonian communities of refugees abroad in two ways: ideally to convince them that the Soviet order in Estonia was beneficial to Estonian culture and national interests, or at the very least to show them that it was possible to develop cooperation with Estonians in the Estonian Soviet Socialist Republic (ESSR). The hidden agenda was to split these communities and thereby weaken their successful anticommunist struggle and propaganda function in the West. Initially in the 1960s, this policy had some success since older **Estonians abroad** condemned any contacts with Estonians at home as tantamount to legitimizing the communist regime. However, by the 1970s the growing contacts, especially among younger Estonians abroad with Estonia, rapidly spread information at home about Western democracy and the flourishing Estonian culture and communities abroad, and led to the opposite result. The contacts, including the travels of selected cultural figures to Estonian communities abroad, who were required to report in detail on all their contacts with foreign Estonians, supported the growing disenchantment with the regime and encouraged the developing dissident movement. Despite its lack of success, VEKSA continued operating on its original strategy and even increased its propaganda-oriented contacts into the late 1980s.

VETERANS (Eesti Vabadussõjalaste Liit, League of Veterans of the War of Independence; colloquially called Vapsid). The veterans of the Estonian **War of Independence** (1918–19) originally formed pressure groups to insure that the promises made by the government to provide them with land and other perks would be honored. However, when the worldwide Depression hit Estonian exports hard and combined with the prolonged constitutional crisis of 1932–34, the Veterans' local organizations, composed of men who regarded themselves as true patriots, formed a new national central league led by heroes of the War of Independence. The constitutional crisis was ushered in by political parties in parliament creating an impasse of ungovernability: four cabinets in 1992 alone, and an average life of 9.5 months for governments since 1921. Those on the center and the right of the political spectrum laid the blame for the governing crisis on the lack of a strong executive presidency in the **Constitution** engineered by the left-wing majority in the **Constituent Assembly** in 1919–20.

In this atmosphere of political confusion, the Veterans League provided a clear objective of pursuing the objective of the integral Estonian nation-state and safeguarding it against all predators, internal as well as external, and of uniting the nation into one organic whole in the interests of all its citizens. That the Veterans' message reflected the nation's mood is shown by the results of the third constitutional referendum in 14 months, in which their proposed constitution won by a landslide of 72.2 percent of the votes cast on 14–16 October 1933. Whether the Veterans League, which immediately decided to turn itself into a **political party** and to contest the subsequent elections for the new **Riigikogu** and the presidency, would have behaved any differently from existing parties was never demonstrated since the acting (under the new Constitution) Riigivanem **Konstantin Päts** carried out a **preemptive coup** on 12 March 1934, just before the scheduled elections, to prevent the Veterans from gaining power. The subsequent outlawing of all party activity ushered in the **Era of Silence**.

There has been much debate as to whether the Veterans were a fascist organization. Although condemned as such by President Päts and his many supporters as well as by the political left (communists and socialists), well-corroborated historical evidence shows that they had no contact with Italian fascism or the Nazi Party of Germany at all. Nor did their newspaper, *Võitleja*, extol either foreign ideology or movements. Their primary foreign examples and contacts were the contemporary Veterans' organizations and the anti-Marxist Lapua movement in Finland, which mobilized public opinion and practically dictated the agenda for the Finnish government from 1930 to 1932. *See also* ARTUR SIRK.

VICTORY DAY (Võidupüha). On June 23 1919, the Estonian forces defeated the German **Landeswehr** at the Battle of Võnnu (Latvian, Cēsis; German, Wenden) in Latvia, and thus put an end to any threat of Germans reasserting suzerainty over Estonia or Latvia. This great military victory on the eve of Midsummer has been celebrated ever since as a holiday and is marked by bonfires. *See also* JAANIPÄEV.

VILDE (WILDE), EDUARD (1865–1933). Estonian journalist, writer, playwright, and literary critic. Born to a servant family at the

Puldivere baronial estate on 4 March 1865, Vilde grew up at another estate where his father worked as a warehouse keeper and his mother as a housekeeper. Despite his humble origins, Vilde acquired his elementary and secondary education in German-language schools in **Tallinn**. His childhood may also be regarded as quintessentially representative of the **National Awakening** among the peasantry, who respected **education** and did everything in their power to educate their children. Vilde himself read widely, followed most of the Estonian **newspapers**, and began to write adventure stories already in secondary school. This led to his being hired as writer by the newspaper *Virulane* in 1883, a year after he left school, which he left in 1887 to work for *Postimees* for a year, after which he moved on to the German-language *Zeitung für Stadt und Land* in Riga for a year in 1889.

In 1890–92, Vilde worked as a freelance journalist in Berlin, where he came under the influence of German socialism and acquired a social-democratic political outlook. He returned to the *Postimees* in 1893–96, lived in Moscow in 1896–97, edited *Virmaline* in Narva in 1897–98, then moved to Tallinn where he worked for *Eesti Postimees* in 1898–1901 and for *Teataja* in 1901–04, and then moved to Tartu to work for *Uudised* in 1904–05.

In the fall of 1904, he visited the Estonian settlements in the Crimea, became involved with the Revolution at home in 1905, and was forced to flee into exile for the following 12 years. During this period he moved around a lot, to Switzerland, Finland (where he edited the periodical *Kaak* in 1906), Germany, Austria, the United States (1911), and Denmark. On his return home in 1917, he was appointed artistic director and playwright by the Estonia Theater in Tallinn and worked there for two years, until the government appointed him ambassador to Copenhagen and Berlin in 1919–20. He remained in Berlin until 1923, working as a freelance journalist and writer, and thereafter continued as a professional writer in Tallinn until his death on 26 December 1933. He was the first cultural figure to be buried at the Forest Cemetery in Tallinn, the Estonian pantheon.

Vilde's journalistic career was but a minor aspect of his contribution to Estonian culture. His career as a novelist began with adventure and humor stories in the 1880s, and came into full flower in the 1890s when he began to strive for realism in depicting the life conditions of

Estonians. His 1896 novel, *Külmale maale* (*To the Cold Land*), is regarded as the seminal work in critical realism in Estonian **literature**. He continued to produce novels on a regular basis, using as his settings such diverse places and conditions as textile workers in **Narva** (*Iron Hands*, 1898), the mid-19th-century peasant movement in Estonia in a trilogy published between 1902 and 1908, the life of the Danish proletariat (*Salvation,* 1909), as well as a series of plays between 1912 and 1922. The best known of his works, and one still in regular repertoire, is his 1913 *Pisuhänd*, about an Estonian mythological goblin bringing fortune. Later in Tallinn, he edited his oeuvre and published it in a 33-volume collected *Works* between 1923 and 1935. Many of his writings were reissued in a 14-volume *Works* series in 1951–61. Vilde's popularity has been memorialized in monuments raised in three cities in his honor in the 1950s and 1960s, and in a memorial museum in Tallinn.

VILJANDI (German, Fellin). In prehistoric times, a fortified commercial and communications center was established on the hills overlooking Lake Viljandi in southcentral Estonia in the middle of the ancient county of Sakala. After conquest by the **Teutonic Order**, it was rebuilt as a military fort in 1224 and the surrounding civilian settlement of Viljandi was given a town charter by Riga in 1283. The town's prosperity as a trading center was enhanced by its membership in the **Hanseatic League**. In 1783 to 1796, it served as the county seat of Viljandi county and was again designated as such in 1888. With the coming of the railroad in 1897, it maintained its role as a regional commercial center and added a modest industrial base, mainly in woodworking. At various times during the 20th century, diverse vocational training was provided in Viljandi, including nursing, teacher training, business, and tailoring. In 1991, the Viljandi Occupational Arts School, originally founded in **Tallinn** in 1952 and transferred to Viljandi in 1960, was raised to degree-giving status and renamed Viljandi Kultuurikolledz (Viljandi Arts College). With a staff of 56, it offers diploma and degree courses in music, dance, theater, librarianship, and the teaching of national handicrafts. Despite the implicit emphasis on culture, Viljandi's architectural heritage is limited to the ruins of the medieval fort and some late 18th-century buildings, but most are 19th- and early 20th-century constructions.

After steady growth from a base of 13,000 in 1913, since 1970 the town's population has stabilized at slightly over 20,000 inhabitants.

VILMS, JÜRI (1889–1918). Estonian politician, lawyer, and journalist Vilms was born on 13 March 1889 in Arkama village in Kabala *vald* in Viljandi county. After graduation from the faculty of law at the **University of Tartu** in 1911, he practiced law in **Tallinn**. In 1917, while working as political editor of the newspaper *Eesti Päevaleht*, he became involved in politics, assisted in the formation of Estonian military units, and founded the Estonian Radical Socialist Party (later the Eesti Tööerakond, or Estonian Workers Party). He was elected to the **Maapäev** and became a member of the **Estonian Rescue (Salvation) Committee** and subsequently minister of justice and deputy prime minister in the first **Estonian Provisional Government**. On his way across the frozen Gulf of Finland to Finland from German-occupied northern Estonia to seek military and financial assistance during the **War of Independence**, he was caught by German soldiers on 24 March 1918 and executed in Helsinki a week after reaching age 29.

VÕNNU. *See* LANDESWEHR; VICTORY DAY.

VÄHI, TIIT (1947–). Estonian politician and industrialist. Born on 10 January 1947 at Kaagvere, Vähi graduated from Tallinn Polytechnical Institute (now Tallinn Technical University) in mechanical engineering in 1970, began working for the Valga Transport Depot in 1972, and was appointed its manager in 1976. He served as minister of transport in the last government of the Estonian Soviet Socialist Republic (ESSR) in 1989–90 and as minister of transport and Communications in **Edgar Savisaar**'s transition government in 1990–92. Vähi became prime minister after Savisaar resigned in January 1992 and served for eight months until the ensuing general elections in October. In opposition during the next parliamentary mandate, Vähi was elected chair of the Tallinn City Council and chair of the Federation of Estonian Cities from 1993 to 1995. After the elections in March 1995, Vähi formed his second coalition government consisting of the Coalition Party together with the Rural Party and the Center Party and served as prime minister from April 1995 to March 1997, when he was forced to resign in favor of his party comrade Mart Simann. In 1991, he was one of the founders of the Coalition Party and served as its chairman until 1997. He did not stand for the **Riigikogu** at the 1999 elections, returned to private business, and has since managed the rare metals enterprise Silmet at **Sillamäe**. *See also* POLITICAL PARTIES.

VÄLJAS, VAINO (1931–). Estonian politician and diplomat. Väljas was born on 28 March 1931 in Emmaste *vald*, graduated in 1955 from the Faculty of History at the **University of Tartu**, and received his *cand. hist.* degree in 1973. He rose steadily in the ranks of the **Estonian Communist Party** (ECP), beginning with the post of secretary of the University **Komsomol** as a student in 1951–52 and ending as the first secretary of the ECP in 1988–92. As a result of hardliners' intrigues, although clear heir-apparent to the retiring First Secretary Johannes Käbin, he was passed over in 1980 and was sent to Venezuela as Soviet ambassador instead, where he served until 1988, and concurrently to Nicaragua in 1986–88. In the spring of 1988, General Secretary Mikhail Gorbachev recalled him to replace the incumbent, **Karl Vaino**, his erstwhile reactionary rival, whose resistance to **perestroika and glasnost** was creating problems in Estonia. Väljas, a pragmatic nationalist career communist, led the reform of the ECP and participated actively, if cautiously, in the movement toward independence for Estonia. Väljas, a member of the Communist Party of the Soviet Union (CPSU) from 1952 to 1990, was elected democratically to the transitional Estonian Supreme Council in 1990–92. After the ECP split in 1990, he led its nationalist Estonian wing, which renamed itself the Estonian Democratic Workers Party after independence in 1991, but resigned as its leader in 1992 and retired from politics. This party and the ECP have died out totally and have no successor parties, or even factions, in Estonia.

– W –

WAR OF INDEPENDENCE. The War of Freedom (Vabadussõda), as it is known in Estonian, was a 15-month war (1918–20) against both the Russian **Bolsheviks** and **Baltic-German** and German forces (*see*

LANDESWEHR). The fight for independence, which cost the lives of 3,600 Estonians and left 14,000 wounded, was concluded in the **Peace of Tartu** with Russia in 2 February 1920. In the treaty, Moscow relinquished all claims to Estonia in perpetuity.

With the capitulation of imperial Germany, the **Estonian Provisional Government** (Eesti Ajutine Valitsus) took over governmental powers in **Tallinn** with the support of the **Defense League** organized by **Johan Pitka**. On 16 November, on the strength of voluntary mobilization it began to organize the Estonian army, initially consisting of one division, with **Konstantin Päts** as minister of war, Major General **Andres Larka** as chief of staff, and Major General Aleksander Tönisson in command of the division.

The war began when the Red Army attacked **Narva** on 22 November but was driven back by retreating German forces. A week later, on 28 November, the Red Army's Seventh Army attacked Narva again with 7,000 infantry, 22 field guns, an armored train, 111 machine guns, two armored cares, two airplanes, and the cruiser *Oleg* supported by two destroyers. South of **Lake Peipus** (Peipsi Järv), around Petseri (Russian, Pechory), the Bolshevik army had deployed the Second Novgorod Division with 7,000 infantry, 12 field guns, 50 machine guns, two armored trains, and three armored cars. At this time, the Estonians had only 2,000 men in the army-in-formation armed with light weapons, and 14,500 men in the Defense League who were similarly armed. Thus only 1,100 men with 13 machine guns could be deployed on the Narva front and about 200 on the Petseri front. By the evening of the 28th, the Russians had landed 750 men behind the Estonian lines and were about to surround the Estonians. General Tõnisson decided to retreat and let the Russians take Narva. The Bolshevik army was able to enter Valga (18 December), Tartu (22 December), and Tapa (24 December) virtually unopposed. By the New Year, the Red Army controlled nearly all of Estonia along a line running from just east of Tallinn, southeast just west of Tartu, and then southwest to Heinaste (Ainazi), the present coastal border point with Latvia. On the conquered territory, the Bolsheviks formed a puppet government, the Estonian Workers Commune (Eesti Töörahva Kommuun), with **Jaan Anvelt** as their leader.

In the meantime, Colonel **Johan Laidoner**, who had been appointed commander in chief of the Estonian **armed forces** on 23 December, succeeded within a few days in recruiting 600 officers and 11,000 soldiers to the new army, which by New Year had a strength of 13,000. He reorganized the forces by setting up the Second Division in southern Estonia under the command of Colonel Viktor Puskar, as well as a number of independent battalion-sized commando-type units composed of volunteers, such as the Kuperjanov Battalion, the Partisan Battalion, and the Kalev Malev. The government also succeeded in its quest for foreign assistance from Finland and Great Britain: on 5 December Finland delivered 5,000 rifles and 20 field guns together with ammunition, and on 12 December a British naval fleet squadron, commanded by Rear Admiral Sir Edward Alexander Sinclair, arrived off Tallinn. On 31 December, the British fleet delivered 6,500 rifles, 200 machine guns, and two field guns. The Royal Navy also captured two Russian destroyers and donated them to Estonia. During January 1919, two Finnish volunteer units with a combined strength of 3,500 men arrived in Estonia.

The strengthened Estonian forces succeeded in stopping the Red Army in decisive battles along the entire front on 2–5 January 1919 and began their counter-offensive on 7 January on the Viru, or northern, front. Three armored trains built in Tallinn, under the command of Captain Anton Irv, played a significant role in the ensuing campaign. On 9 January Tapa was retaken, followed on 14 January by Tartu. A combined assault of the main Viru front by the army and a commando unit landed in the rear drove the Bolshevik army out of Narva on 18 January. Thereupon, the northern front stabilized along the Narva River and the war moved to the southern front, where a drawn-out battle began over the important rail junction at Valga. On 30 January, Lieutenant Julius Kuperjanov's partisans, together with the Finnish volunteer regiment, Sons of the North, succeed in defeating the enemy in violent battle over Paju Mansion, the last Red Army stronghold before Valga. By 4 February Valga, Võru, and Petseri were in Estonian hands. All of Estonia having been freed, the battlefront now followed the border of the historic Estonian ethnic settlement. On the first Independence Day, 24 February 1919, the Estonian forces at the front consisted of 19,000 men, 70 field guns, and 230 machine guns.

The Red Army concentrated 80,000 men, with 200 field guns and 1,100 machine guns and supported by five armored trains, 14 armored cars, and 14 airplanes, in attacking Estonian forces at the beginning of March. The Estonian lines held and concentrated their counter-offensive in three theaters—Narva-Petrograd (St. Petersburg) in the north, Pihkva (Pskov)-Petseri in the southeast, and northern Latvia in the south. The commander in chief formed a new division, the Third, with Major General **Ernst Põdder** in command to fight the southern front.

The objective of the three-front offensive was to carry the war into enemy territory and prevent it from encroaching on Estonian territory. To this end, the government formed three foreign units on Estonian territory—the Ingermanland Regiment (300 men), the (White or anticommunist) Russian Northern Corps (2,750 men), and the North-Latvian Brigade (1,500 men). Simultaneously, Estonian recruitment continued apace. Thus, by the beginning of May, the Estonian forces numbered 74,000 men. By this time, the Finnish volunteers had done their valuable duty to fight for Estonia and had left for home, but new volunteer companies had arrived from Denmark and Sweden.

On 12 May, Estonia attacked in the north and pierced the peripheral defensive fortifications of the Kronstadt naval base off Petrograd (St. Petersburg) the next day; on 16 May the successful offensive on the southern front began. Pihkva (Pskov) fell to the Estonians on 25 May, and on 5 June the Estonians entered Jekabpils (Jakobstadt) in Latvia, where they made contact with Polish forces on the southern bank of the Daugava (German, Düna; Russian, Dvina) River. At this time, the Estonian armed forces reached their all-time high of 86,000 men in the regular army and 32,000 in the first (fighting) ranks of the Defense League. Their armaments consisted of an armored train division with 10 trains, 300 artillery pieces, 2,000 machine guns, six armored cars, and 28 airplanes. The naval arm, under the command of Rear Admiral Pitka, consisted of 24 attack vessels and 11 support ships at sea and five attack and eight support vessels on Lake Peipsi.

A new war, the **Landeswehr** war, broke out on the southern front in Latvia on 5 June 1919, which the Estonians won, forcing the Germans to withdraw. Because of the weakness of Latvian forces, the Estonian Third Division remained in northern Latvia until late fall 1919 to defend it against Russia. In consequence, the Russian Red Army did not again attack in the south and the front remained quiet.

Warfare on the northern and eastern fronts continued into late fall, in rapidly changing circumstances. Initially, as a result of military defeats, Vladimir Lenin's Bolshevik Russian government gave up on conquering Estonia; disbanded the Estonian Workers' Commune, whose government had been in exile in Russia since early January; and proposed negotiations for a peace treaty on 31 July 1919. The first phase of negotiations was held in Pihkva in September. By November, the White Russians' Southwest Army suffered defeat at the hands of the Reds and collapsed. Estonia refused to let its remnants retreat to Estonia to regroup, and it disarmed and interned them.

At the same time, the Red Army concentrated six divisions totaling 125,000 men on the Narva front and attacked the 40,000-man Estonian forces consisting of two divisions, the First and the Third, which had been hastily redeployed from Latvia. In armaments, the two armies were more evenly balanced; the Russians and Estonians had six armored trains to four, 205 field guns to 160, and 826 machine guns to 667, respectively. The Red Army lost 35,000 dead and wounded in two months of attacks on well-fortified Estonian defensive positions and finally collapsed. (It should be noted that all the forces and armament figures cited are based on pre–World War II sources, and have not yet been authenticated by more recent historically objective research and analyses.) As a result, the peace negotiations resumed at Tartu on 5 December 1919, and were concluded successfully at 10:30 on 3 January 1920 when hostilities ended. The **Peace of Tartu** was signed on 2 February 1920.

WIIRALT, EDUARD (also Viiralt) (1898–1954). Estonian graphic artist. Probably the best-known and most popular artist in Estonia, his works have received broad exposure and are widely owned by private individuals. Born on 20 March 1898 on the Kalitino estate near St. Petersburg to an Estonian family, Wiiralt studied at the Tallinn School of Artisans during 1915–18, participated in the **War of Independence**, and continued studies at the newly founded Pallas Art Academy in **Tartu** in 1919–24, taking a year's sojourn at the Dresden Art Academy in 1922–23. Although his formal studies were more in sculpture than graphics, the Dresden period influenced him especially to experiment with the then prevailing expressionism in Germany, and particularly in portrayal of the city's nightlife and the exotic animals in the zoo. After completing Pallas, he taught graphic art there for a year but did not take to teaching. Thus when he obtained a scholarship to Paris, he left with alacrity in 1925 and remained there until the outbreak of World War II.

Wiiralt's first Paris period may be divided into two artistic parts. Until 1933 he lived the typical bohemian life of an artist, marked with drinking bouts and poverty alternating with ascetic concentration on work—it was a period of learning and maturing and international recognition in group exhibitions, as well as individual exhibitions, in Europe and America. From 1933, after a serious liver ailment and a long convalescence, his work was marked by harmony and naturalness, and gone were the extremes of the past. His first exhibit in Estonia took place in 1936 and his second only posthumously in 1957. His 1938–39 trip to Morocco was especially productive. After returning to Estonia in 1939, he found it too narrow for his talent and at the first opportunity in 1944 he left and reached Paris in 1946 after a circuitous route via Germany, Denmark, and Sweden. The second Paris period was very productive and raised his reputation in France to a new high, but it was brought to a premature end by cancer of the liver, which was discovered in 1953. He died on 8 January 1954 and was buried at Père Lachaise cemetery among other artistic luminaries.

As a human being, Wiiralt was a sympathetic, balanced, and humble man. He spoke Estonian, Russian, German, and French freely and read Spanish and English. He always lived a simple life, even after World War II when his reputation brought him wealth. His art, on the other hand, was thematically variegated, yet executed with precision, using every imaginable graphic technique and material available. It included abstract compositions, portraits, animals, landscapes, and compositions of natural phenomena, but it focused primarily on the human form. His popularity in Estonia was much enhanced by his international reputation, and to the present Estonians regard him as the master graphic artist of the 20th century. *See also* ART.

– Ö –

ÖPIK, ERNEST JULIUS (1893–1985). Estonian astronomer and founder of astronomy as an academic discipline in Estonia; best known for his studies of meteors and meteorites. Öpik was born on 23 October 1893 at Kunda and received his degree in astronomy from Moscow University in 1916, where he continued research until 1920. He joined the staff of the Tashkent Observatory for a year when he returned to Estonia to work at the Astronomical Observatory in **Tartu**, where he remained until 1944. Öpik received his *dr. plil. nat.* from the **University of Tartu** in 1923. Many of his major contributions to astronomy were made in Tartu and include inter alia the elucidation of the theory of the entry of high-speed bodies into the atmosphere, the result of a cooperative venture with Harvard colleagues, where he was a visiting professor in 1930–34. At this time, he also advanced research methodology by developing the double-count method of tallying meteors, where two observers work simultaneously at different locations. Consequently, he was able to correctly predict the frequencies of craters on Mars years before the NASA *Mariner* probe proved him right. He also contributed to cometary studies and in 1932, together with his Dutch colleague Jan Hendrick Oort, proposed that a reservoir of comets (the Öpik-Oort cloud) orbits the Sun and provides the source of those few comets that assume orbits sufficiently eccentric to bring them close enough to the Sun to be visible.

In 1922, Öpik proved that the source of stellar energy was nuclear and heavily dependent on temperature. At this time, he also made an estimate of the distance of the Andromeda Nebula that remained valid for half a century. In the 1930s and 1950s, he estimated the age of the universe from meteorites and from galactic and extragalactic statistics. In 1944, with the return of Soviet occupation, Öpik fled to Germany and taught in 1945–47 at the **Baltic University** at Pinneberg. In 1948, he moved to Great Britain, where he joined the staff of the Armagh Observatory in Northern Ireland. From 1956 until his death on 10 September 1985 at Armagh, he also held a position on the faculty of the University of Maryland at College Park, and divided his time equally between Armagh and Maryland.

In addition to numerous honorary doctorates, memberships in scientific organizations, and gold medals from many countries, Öpik is memorialized in our constellation: planet No. 2009, orbiting between Mars and Jupiter, is named after him. Öpik is without a doubt the greatest and internationally most known and honored Estonian natural scientist of the 20th century.

– Y –

YOUNG ESTONIA (Noor Eesti). This was a movement of national-cultural renewal that was propagated by literary and artistic figures with the object of developing a national professional culture as an integral part of the wider West European culture. The movement arose out of student groups meeting underground in **Tartu** in 1903–04. Although its visibility was highest in the decade leading up to World War I, when it declined rapidly, its influence on Estonian culture was both profound and lasting. Its leading activist-writers, **Gustav Suits**, **Friedebert Tuglas**, **Johannes Aavik**, Villem Grünthal (pseudonym Ridala), Bernhard Linde, and P. Ruubel, all prolific writers, caught the imagination of Estonians in the crisis year 1905 with their revolutionary refocusing of Estonian culture from its parochial inward-lookingness of the past to a wider outward-lookingness toward Western Europe.

Their call for "more European culture" was central to their endeavor of bringing the aesthetics of the Western cultural Romantic revival into the mainstream of Estonia. By becoming more European, Estonian culture would withstand the politico-cultural onslaught of Russia and carve out its rightful niche as an integral part of European culture. Among the specific intellectual aims were to develop a synthesis of Europe and Estonia, socialism and individual liberty, self-conscious creativity and a deepening national collectivism, realism and romanticism, as well as aesthetics and science. To counteract the strong German and Russian intellectual heritage of 19th-century Scandinavia, France, and Italy became the new sources for examples of cultural renewal. Finland, where many of the activists had studied and lived for long periods, was looked to as the principal partner and facilitator of change. This brought with it a reevaluation of the work of past literary figures such as **Kristjan Jaak Peterson** and **Friedrich Reinhold Kreutzwald**, critical attention to style and form in **literature**, and a linguistic modernization of the **Estonian language**. Prose reached contemporary international standards in short-story writing, poetry, and literary criticism. The use of symbolism was valued as a means of aesthetic expression, and sociology, psychology, and biology became additional sources for belles-lettres.

The principles and values of the movement strongly influenced the plastic **arts** (such as painting and book design) as well as critique in the performing arts. The group organized four art exhibits (1910–11, 1913, and 1914) with the participation of **Kristjan Raud** among others.

Noor Eesti established its own publishing house and issued five collections (1905, 1907, 1909, 1912, and 1919); published two periodicals, *Noor Eesti* (1910–11) and *Vaba Sõna* (1914–16); and published novels and other writings by its members. The publishing house survived the organization and continued publishing works by the members of the defunct organization until its closing by the Soviets in 1940. It was the largest publisher of original works in Estonia, issuing 1,400 books with a combined circulation of 2 million copies between 1918 and 1940.

Appendix A
Heads of Estonian Government

1.	24.02.1918–26.11.1918	9 months	Konstantin Päts, PM* and Minister of Interior
2.	26.11.1918–09.05.1919	5.5 months	Konstantin Päts, PM and Minister of Interior
3.	09.05.1919–18.11.1919	6+ months	Otto Strandman, PM and Minister of War
4.	18.11.1919–28.07.1920	8+ months	Jaan Tõnisson, PM
5.	28.07.1920–30.07.1920	3 days	Ado Birk, PM
6.	30.07.1920–26.10.1920	3 months	Jaan Tõnisson, PM
7.	26.10.1920–25.01.1921	3 months	Ants Piip, PM and Minister of War; Riigivanem** from 20 December
8.	25.01.1921–21.11.1922	1 year, 10 months	Konstantin Päts, Riigivanem
9.	21.11.1922–02.08.1923	8 months	Juhan Kukk, Riigivanem
10.	02.08.1923–26.03.1924	8 months	Konstantin Päts, Riigivanem
11.	26.03.1924–16.12.1924	8.5 months	Friedrich Akel, Riigivanem
12.	16.12.1924–15.12.1925	1 year	Jüri Jaakson, Riigivanem
13.	15.12.1925–23.07.1926	7 months	Jaan Teemant, Riigivanem
14.	23.07.1926–04.03.1927	7.5 months	Jaan Teemant, Riigivanem
15.	04.03.1927–09.12.1927	9 months	Jaan Teemant, Riigivanem
16.	09.12.1927–04.12.1928	1 year	Jaan Tõnisson, Riigivanem
17.	04.12.1928–09.07.1929	7 months	August Rei, Riigivanem
18.	09.07.1929–12.02.1931	1 year, 7 months	Otto Strandman, Riigivanem
19.	12.02.1931–19.02.1932	1 year	Konstantin Päts, Riigivanem
20.	19.02.1932–19.07.1932	5 months	Jaan Teemant, Riigivanem
21.	19.07.1932–01.11.1932	3 months	Karl-August Einbund (after 1935, Kaarel Eenpalu), Riigivanem
22.	01.11.1932–18.05.1933	5.5 months	Konstantin Päts, Riigivanem
23.	18.05.1933–21.10.1933	5 months	Jaan Tõnisson, Riigivanem
24.	21.10.1933–09.05.1938	4 years, 7 months	Konstantin Päts, Riigivanem, State Regent from September 1937, President from 24 April 1938

25.	09.05.1938–12.10.1939	1 year, 5 months	Kaarel Eenpalu, PM
26.	12.10.1939–21.06.1940	8 months	Jüri Uluots, PM
27.	09.1944	5 days	Otto Tief, Acting PM and Minister of Interior
28.	08.05.1990–29.01.1992	1 year, 8.5 months	Edgar Savisaar, PM
29.	30.01.1992–21.10.1992	8 months	Tiit Vähi, PM
30.	21.10.1992–08.11.1994	2 years, 0.5 months	Mart Laar, PM
31.	08.11.1994–17.04.1995	5 months	Andres Tarand, PM
32.	17.04.1995–06.11.1995	8 months	Tiit Vähi, PM
33.	06.11.1995–12.1996	1 year, 1 month	Tiit Vähi, PM
34.	12.1996–17.03.1997	4 months	Tiit Vähi, PM
35.	17.03.1997–25.03.1999	2 years, 1 week	Mart Siimann, PM
36.	25.03.1999–28.01.2002	2 years, 10 months	Mart Laar, PM
37.	28.01. 2002–10.04.2003	1 year, 5 weeks	Siim Kallas, PM
38.	10.04.2003–		Juhan Parts, PM

* Prime Minister

* * Riigivanem, literally state elder. Under the 1920 Constitution, the head of the cabinet was also the head of state.

See also **HEADS OF STATE OF ESTONIA**.

Appendix B
Estonian Foreign Ministers

1919	Jaan Poska
1919	Ants Piip
1919–1920	Ado Birk
1920	Kaarel Robert Pusta
1920–1921	Otto Strandman
1921–1922	Ants Piip
1922–1923	Aleksander Hellat
1923–1924	Friedrich Akel
1924	Otto Strandman
1924–1925	Kaarel Robert Pusta
1925–1926	Ants Piip
1926–1927	Friedrich Akel
1927	Aleksander Hellat
1927–1928	Hans Rebane
1928–1931	Jaan Lattik
1931–1932	Jaan Tõnisson
1932	Mihkel Pung
1932–1933	August Rei
1933	Ants Piip
1933–1936	Julius Seljamaa
1936–1938	Friedrich Akel
1938–1939	Karl Selter
1939–1940	Ants Piip
April 1990–March 1992	Lennart Meri
April–Oct. 1992	Jaan Manitski
Oct. 1992–Jan. 1994	Trivimi Velliste

Jan. 1994–April 1995	Jüri Luik
April–Nov. 1995	Riivo Sinijärv
Nov. 1995–Nov. 1996	Siim Kallas
Nov. 1996–Oct. 1998	Toomas Hendrik Ilves
Oct. 1998–March 1999	Raul Mälk
Oct. 1999–Feb. 2002	Toomas Hendrik Ilves
Feb. 2002–	Kristiina Ojuland

Appendix C

Estonian Participation in Free and Mostly Free Elections, 1989–2003

Date	*Election*	*Eligibility*	*Turnout Percentage*	*Candidates and Parties/Groupings*	*Mandates*
26.03.1989	USSR Congress of People's Deputies	Permanent residents + Soviet military	87.1	107 candidates + 12 appointed; 3 major tendencies	32 (Upper House) + 4 (Lower House) elected; 12 appointed
10.12.1989	Local Councils of People's Deputies of the Estonian SSR	Permanent residents + Soviet military	72.0	9,192	4,256
24.2–1.03. 1990	Estonian Congress	Pre-1940 citizens and their descendants	70.0	1,200 candidates; 4 major tendencies	499 + 43 advisory representatives
8.03.1990	Supreme Soviet of the Estonian SSR	Permanent residents + Soviet military	78.4	392 candidates; 3 major tendencies	101 + 4 (military)
3.03.1991	Referendum on Independence	Permanent residents	82.9	—	—
28.06.1992	Referendum Adopting the Constitution	Estonian citizens	66.8	—	—
20.09.1992	Riigikogu	Estonian citizens	67.8	628 candidates; 17 parties/ coalitions, 25 independents	101
20.09.1992	President of Estonia	Estonian citizens	68.0	4 candidates; 4 groupings	1
17.10.1993	Local Government Councils	Permanent residents	52.6	8,948 candidates; 12 parties, 51 associations, 781 candidate lists, 811 independents	3,513
5.03.1995	Riigikogu	Estonian citizens	68.9	1,256 candidates; 7 coalitions, 9 parties, 13 independents	101

Date	Election	Eligibility	Turnout Percentage	Candidates and Parties/Groupings	Mandates
August–September 1996	President of Estonia	2/3 majority required in Riigikogu; if none, run-off election by electoral body		2 candidates in 3 rounds in Riigikogu, 5 candidates in 2 rounds in electoral college	1
20.10.1996	Local Government Councils	Permanent residents	52.5	11,128 candidates; 19 parties (120 party lists, 99 coalitions), 554 local candidate lists, 409 independents	3,453
7.03.1999	Riigikogu	Estonian citizens	57.4	1,884 candidates; 12 party lists, 19 independents	101
17.10.1999	Local Government Councils	Permanent residents	49.8	12,801 candidates; 4 parties (180 party lists, 18 coalitions), 570 local candidate lists, 159 independents	3,355
Aug–Sept. 2001	President of Estonia	2/3 majority required in Riigikogu; if none, run-off election by electoral college	367 members of electoral college	3 candidates in 3 rounds in Riigikogu; 4 candidates in two rounds in electoral college	1
20.10.2002	Local Government Councils	Permanent residents	52.5	15,203 candidates; 13 parties (874 party lists); 121 individual candidates	3,291
2.03.2003	Riigikogu	Estonian citizens	58.2	963 candidates; 11 party lists; 16 independents	101
14.09.2003	Referendum on accession to EU	Estonian citizens	64.0	—	66.83 percent for; 33.17 percent against

Source: Table adapted from *Estonian Human Development Report 2000*, table 1.2; 2002 and 2003 elections and referendum data compiled from Estonian Electoral Committee database at www.vvk.ee.

See also ELECTORAL DEMOCRACY.

Glossary

Bolshevik—The Russian term for "majority." The Russian Democratic Workers' Party split in 1903 into a majority (Bolsheviks) who propagated violent revolution and a minority (Mensheviks) who supported a parliamentary road to socialism. Hence, "Bolshevik" became synonymous with "communist."

Bureau (*Büroo* in Estonian)—The equivalent in the Central Committee of the Estonian Communist Party of the Politburo of the Central Committee of the Communist Party of the Soviet Union.

Estland—The German (and also Swedish) term for Estonia; it is Igaunija in Latvian. Estland is used to describe both the principality of Estland under the Teutonic Order and Swedish rule and the Imperial Russian province of Estland, consisting of the northern half of Estonia in Imperial Russia to 1917, when the Estonian-speaking northern half of the province of Livland was transferred to the province of Estland, which declared independence in 1918 as the Republic of Estonia.

gubernya—Province in imperial Russia.

kihelkond—Originally church parish, later civil parish in the province of Estland; abolished in independent Estonia.

***kolhoos* (*kolkhoz* in Russian)**—A contraction of *kollektivnoje hozjaistvo* (collective farm), the main agricultural unit in the Soviet Union.

Kurland—The German term for Courland; it is Kurzeme in Latvian and Kuramaa in Estonian. The imperial Russian province of Kurland today forms the Latvian province of Kurzeme.

Lettland—The German (and also Swedish) term for Latvia; it is Latvija in Latvian and Läti in Estonian.

Livland—The German term for Livonia; it is Liivimaa in Estonian. The Imperial Russian province of Livland consisted of the present-day Latvian provinces of Vidzeme and Zemgale (i.e., the central northern and southern half of Latvia) and the southern half of present-day Estonia.

maa—Land. County when used as suffix, for example Harjumaa; also used as suffix to denote the large islands of Saaremaa and Hiumaa.

maakond—County.

malev—Army of one or several counties in ancient Estonia. A county or city military unit in the Kaiseliit in modern Estonia, equivalent to a regiment.

***nomenkatuur* (*nomenklatura* in Russian)**—In the Soviet Union, all organs of the Communist Party, from the local *rayon* committee up to the Central Committee of the Communist Party of the Soviet Union, had secret lists of persons who were acceptable for appointments to public and economic positions. Thus the *nomenklatura* formed a network of those trusted by the Party.

oblast—Administrative territorial subdivision, a province or component state in the Russian Federated Soviet Socialist Republic, and in independent Russia since 1992.

Põhiseadus—Constitution.

Rahvuskogu—National Assembly established to draft the new Constitution of 1937

Riigihoidja—Regent, in the interim between the proclamation of the new constitution of 1937 and his election as Estonia's first president in 1938.

Riiginõukogu—State council. The 40-member upper house of the Riigikogu, appointed by the president, under the Constitution of 1937.

Riigivanem—State elder. The prime minister, who also functioned as head of state under the Constitution of 1920.

Riigivolikogu—Chamber of Deputies. The 80-member elected lower house of the Riigikogu under the Constitution of 1937.

***sovhoos* (*sovkhoz* in Russian)**—State farm established by the Soviet state, usually on marginal agricultural land, and operated similar to the *kolhoos.*

Toompea—Since both Parliament and the Cabinet Office are located on Toompea Hill in the Old City in Tallinn, "Toompea" is commonly used to refer to all three, depending on the context.

Umsiedlung—Hitler's program of resettlement of the Baltic Germans to populate conquered western Poland.

vald—Commune, township.

Valitsus—Government, Cabinet.

Bibliography

This bibliography consists of English, German, Finnish, and Swedish writings, with a few French- and Italian-language items. The four main languages reflect the historical context of foreign languages' contiguity in Estonian history. Until World War II, German was the main foreign language for international publication in Estonia; its preeminence was based on the role of the Baltic Germans in Estonia from the Conquest in 1227 to Independence, and the continuing connections of Estonian academics with German colleagues in the 1920s and 1930s. During the Soviet occupation after World War II, German held its own as a foreign language of publication because of the membership of the German Democratic Republic in the Soviet bloc. Thus, although Estonians published in Estonian and Russian (which, incidentally, never became a language of academic publishing during the imperial period from 1700 to 1918), they also continued to do so in German, although at a reduced rate. Estonian academic writers who had fled abroad also continued to publish in German.

During the Soviet period, Baltic German historians who had resettled in Germany in World War II delved into their history and published extensively. Historical, political, and cultural analyses by Swedes, Finns, and Estonians abroad were also published during the postwar decades. English was the language of publication mainly of the new generation of Estonian academics born in North America. Very few works written by Estonians in the homeland during the Soviet period appeared in English—many were propagandistic or limited to politically acceptable topics, as is evident in the bibliography. However, with the restoration of independence, Estonians at home, after unleashing a flood of books in Estonian, turned to English as the primary foreign language of publication, both of translation and of original work. At the same time, foreign academics also became interested in Estonia and the Baltic States and have published mostly in English.

Nevertheless, the bibliography shows that coverage of topics in foreign languages is very uneven. Cultural subjects, such as music and theater, are represented by only a few works, whereas recent political and economic analyses abound. Non-Estonian speakers also find that they have little access to the rich Estonian-language literature since very little has been translated into English, German, or French.

The bibliography does not include any works in Estonian since those who read the language can find materials easily via the Internet at the Library of Congress, the library of the University of Helsinki, and the various Estonian libraries.

Older reference works in Estonian, such as encyclopedias, are scarce. Before World War II, only the one-volume *Väike Entsüklopedia* (1,679 pp.) was published in 1937. During the Soviet period, the politically slanted eight-volume *Eesti Nõukogude Entsüklopeedia* (known familiarly as *ENE*) appeared between 1968 and 1976, with an addendum volume in 1978. In 1985, a new edition began appearing, but only four volumes were published by 1989; then, in 1990 with volume 5, the term *Nõukogude* (Soviet) was dropped and it became *Eesti Entsüklopeedia* (known as *EE*). Volumes 6 to 9 were published between 1992 and 1998, with an addendum in 1999; and volume 11, covering 20th-century Estonian state, culture, science, and education, appeared in 2002. A completely new and up-to-date short encyclopedia, *Väike Entsüklopeedia* (1,455 pp.), appeared in 2002 and was joined by the first volume of the 20th-century chronology on Estonia, *Eesti XX sajandi kroonika I osa, 1900–1940* (528 pp.).

In the meantime, several specialized lexical works were published: *Eesti Kunsti ja Arhitektuuri Biograafiline Leksikon* (614 pp.) on arts and architecture in 1996, *Eesti Kooli Bibliograafiline Leksikon* (304 pp.) on education in 1998, *Eesti Rahvaste Raamat* (598 pp.) on ethnic minorities in Estonia in 1998, *Eesti Teatri Biograafiline Leksikon* (814 pp.) on Estonian theater in 2000, the revised *Eesti Rahvakultuuri Leksikon* (413 pp.) on national culture in 2000, *Eesti Elulood* (670 pp.) on prominent Estonians (including Estonians abroad) as volume 14 of the *Encyclopedia* in 2000, volume 1 of *Eesti Teaduse Biograafiline Leksikon A-Ki* (704 pp.) on scholars and scholarship in 2002, and a popular second edition of *Eesti Spordi Biograafiline Leksikon* (800 pp.) on Estonian sports in 2002.

This bibliography has been organized in two parts: the first dealing with history in a chronological order by periods, with the earlier comprising centuries and the more recent comprising decades; and a topical part consisting of matters of either past or current interest, some topics covering centuries, such as Tallinn and the Baltic Germans, and others limited to decades, such as education and science.

Since Estonia regained its independence just as the Internet became universally available, Estonians were able to take advantage of it from the very beginning. Thus, the Estonian government developed an encompassing online information network that covers every detail of politics, public administration, and judicial activity, most of it available in English. Universities as well as cities, financial institutions, and businesses compete in providing online information. Moreover, four newspapers, *Eesti Ekspress*, *Eesti Päevaleht*, *Postimees*, and *Äripäev*, have online accessible archives, but only in Estonian, going back to late 1995 or early 1996.

CONTENTS

I. HISTORY

1. General Histories of Estonia and the Baltic States

Chambon, Henry de. *La république d'Estonie*. Paris: Editions de la Revue Parlementaire, 1936.

Helk, Vello. *Estlands historie: kort fortalt*. Odense, Denmark: Odense universitets forlag, 1993.

Hiden, John, and Patrick Salmon. *The Baltic Nations and Europe: Estonia, Latvia and Lithuania in the Twentieth Century*, rev. ed. Reading, Mass.: Addison-Wesley, 1995.

Jackson, J. Hampden. *Estonia*, 2nd ed. London: George Allen & Unwin, 1948.

Kahk, J., and E. Tarvel. *An Economic History of the Baltic Countries*. Stockholm: n.p., 1997.

Kiaupa, Z., A. Mäesalu, A. Pajur, and G. Straube. *The History of the Baltic Countries*. Tallinn, Estonia: Avita, 1999.

Nodel, Emanuel. *Estonia: Nation on the Anvil*. New York: Bookman Associates, 1963.

Ojamaa, M. *Viron historia*. Helsinki, Finland: W. Söderström, 1944.

Page, Stanley W. *The Formation of the Baltic States; A Study of the Effects of Great Power Politics Upon the Emergence of Lithuania, Latvia, and Estonia*. New York: H. Fertig, 1970.

Pekomäe, Vello. *Estland genom tiderna*. Stockholm: Välis-Eesti & EMP, 1986.

Pick, Frederick Walter. *The Baltic Nations: Estonia, Latvia and Lithuania*. London, Boreas, 1945.

Plakans, Andrejs. *The Latvians: A Short History*. Stanford, Calif.: Hoover Institution, 1995.

Plasseraud, Yves, with Francis Moulonguet. *Pays baltes*. Paris: Autrement, 1991.

Raun, Toivo U. *Estonia and the Estonians*, 2nd ed. Stanford, Calif.: Hoover Institution Press, 2001.

Ruggiero, Adriane. *The Baltic Countries—Estonia, Latvia, and Lithuania*. Parsippany, N.J.: Dillon Press, 1998.

Scheffel, Friedrich Alexis. *Kriegsfahrt in die baltischen Lände*. Ansbach: C. Brügel & Sohn, 1929.

Smith, Graham, ed. *The Baltic States: The National Self-Determination of Estonia, Latvia, and Lithuania.* London: Macmillan, 1994.

Uustalu, Evald. *The History of the Estonian People.* London: Boreas, 1952.

Vuorela, Toivo. *The Finno-Ugric Peoples.* Indiana University Publications, Uralic and Altaic series, no. 39. The Hague: Mouton, 1964.

Walter, Eginhard. *Estland, Lettland, Litauen; das Gesicht der baltischen Staaten.* Berlin: Steiniger-Verlage, Verlagsabteilung Reimar Hobbing, 1939.

Wittram, Reinhard. *Geschichte der Ostseelände Livland, Kurland, 1180–1918.* Munich: R. Oldenbourg, 1945.

Ylikangas, Heikki, Petri Karonen, and Martti Lehti. *Five Centuries of Violence in Finland and the Baltic Area.* Columbus: Ohio State University Press, 2000.

Ziedonis, Arvids, Jr., Rein Taagerpara, and Mardi Valgemäe, eds. *Problems of Mininations: Baltic Perspectives.* San Jose, Calif.: Association for the Advancement of Baltic Studies, 1973.

Ziedonis, Arvids, Jr., William L. Winter, and Mardi Valgemäe, eds. *Baltic History.* Columbus, Ohio: Association for the Advancement of Baltic Studies, 1974.

2. Conquest to 1700: Crusades, Danish, and Swedish Periods

Arens, Ilmar. *Das Wackenrecht und die rechtliche Schichtung der bäuerlichen Bevölkerung im estnischen Kreise Wiek am Anfang des 16. Jahrhunderts.* Heidelberg, Germany: 1946.

Blum, Jerome. "The Rise of Serfdom in Eastern Europe." *American Historical Review* 62 (1957): 807–36.

Brundage, James A., trans. and ed. *The Chronicle of Henry of Livonia.* Madison: University of Wisconsin Press, 1961.

Bunge, Friedrich Georg von. *Das Herzogthum Estland unter den Königen von Dänemark.* Hannover-Döhren, Germany: H. v. Hirschheydt, 1973.

Christiansen, Eric. *The Northern Crusades.* London; New York: Penguin, 1997.

———. *The Northern Crusades: The Baltic and Catholic Frontier, 1100–1525.* Minneapolis: University of Minnesota Press, 1980.

Federley, Berndt. *Konung, ståthållare och korporationer; studier i Estlands förvaltning 1581–1600.* Helsinki, Finland: Societas Scientiarum Fennica, 1962.

Helk, Vello. *Die Stadtschule in Arensburg auf Ösel in dänischer und schwedischer Zeit (1559–1710).* Lüneburg, Germany: Nordostdeutsches Kulturwerk, 1989.

Johansen, Paul. *Die Estlandiste des Liber Census Daniae.* Copenhagen: H. Hagerup, 1933.

Loit, Aleksander. *Kampen om feodalräntan: reduktionen och domänpolitiken i Estland 1655–1710.* Studia Historica Upsaliensia 71. Stockholm: Almqvist & Wiksell, 1975.

Loit, Aleksander, Evalds Mugurevics, and Andris Caune, eds. *Die Kontakte zwischen Ostbaltikum und Skandinavien im frühen Mittelalter.* International conference, 23–25 October 1990. Studia Baltica Stockholmiensia 9. Stockholm: Almqvist & Wiksell International, 1992

Loit, Aleksander, and Helmut Piirimäe. *Die Schwedischen Ostseeprovinzen Estland und Livland im 16.–18. Jahrhundert.* Studia Baltica Stockholmiensia 11. Stockholm: Almqvist & Wiksell, 1993.

Nordling, Carl O. *Gåtorna kring Birger jarl, Ösel och Borgå: omvärdering av historiska teorier rörande svensk östpolitik och finsk och estnisk kolonisation under tidig medeltid.* Lidingö, Sweden: Faktainformation, 1976.

Saks, Edgar V. *Commentaries on the Liber Census Daniae: Studies in Mediaeval European History.* Montreal: RKT, 1974.

———. *The Estonian Vikings.* Cardiff, Wales: Boreas, 1985.

Seraphim, Ernst. *Geschichte Liv-, Est- und Kurlands von der "Aufsegelung" des Landes bis zur Einverleibung in das russische Reich.* Reval (Tallinn), Estonia: F. Kluge: 1895–96.

Seresse, Volker. *Des Königs "arme weit abgelegenne Vntterthane [Untterthanen]": Oesel unter dänischer Herrschaft 1559/84–1613.* Frankfurt, Germany: P. Lang, 1996.

Soom, Arnold. *Der baltische Getreidehandel im 17. Jahrhundert.* Stockholm: Kungl. Vitterhets-, historie- och antikvitetsakademiens handlingar, 1961.

———. *Handel Revals im siebzehnten Jahrhundert.* Wiesbaden, Germany: O. Harrassowitz, 1969.

———. *Politik Schwedens bezüglich des russischen Transithandels über die estnischen Städte in den Jahren 1636–1656.* Tartu, Estonia: Õpetatud Eesti Selts, 1940.

Tarvel, Enn. *Der Haken: die Grundlagen der Landnutzung und der Besteuerung in Estland im 13.–19. Jahrhundert.* Tallinn, Estonia: Perioodika, 1983.

Thomson, Harry. *Schweden und seine Provinzen Estland und Livland in ihrem gegenseitigen Verhältnis 1561–1710: Materialien u. Betrachtungen.* Schliersee: H. Thomson, 1975.

Urban, William L. *The Baltic Crusade.* Dekalb: Northern Illinois University Press, 1975.

———. *The Livonian Crusade.* Washington, D.C.: University Press of America, 1981.

3. In the Russian Empire: 1700 to 1914

Arbusow, Leonid. *Grundriss der Geschichte Liv-, Est- und Kurlands.* Hannover-Döhren, Germany: H. v. Hirschheydt, 1967.

Ehstländische Bauer-Verordnunge. St. Petersburg, Russia: n.p., 1816.

Erdmann, Karl Eduard. *System des Privatrechts der Ostseeprovinzen Liv-, Est- und Curland.* Riga, Latvia: N. Kymmel, 1889–94.

Kahk, Juhan. *Die Krise der feudalen Landwirtschaft in Estland (Das Zweite Viertel des 19. Jahrhunderts).* Tallinn, Estonia: Eesti Raamat, 1969.

———. *Peasant and Lord in the Process of Transition from Feudalism to Capitalism in the Baltics: An Attempt of Interdisciplinary History.* Tallinn, Estonia: Eesti Raamat, 1982.

Karjahärm, Toomas. "Das estnisch-deutsche Verhältnis und die Russiche Revolution von 1905." *Nordost Archiv* 4, no. 2 (1995): 431–51.

———. "The Political Organization of Estonian Society and the Political Parties in Estonia in the Years 1900–1914." In *The Baltic Countries 1900–1914*, edited by Aleksander Loit, 131–45. Studia Baltica Stockholmiensia 5. Stockholm: Almqvist & Wiksell, 1990.

Kirby, David. *The Baltic World 1772–1993: Europe's Northern Periphery in an Age of Change.* London: Longman, 1995.

Land-Rolle des Herzogthums Ehstland nach der Revision von 1765, oder, Verzeichniss der zu dem Herzogthume Ehstland gehörigen Güter, deren Grösse, nebst den Namen der Familien, welche dieselben im Besitze haben. Reval (Tallinn), Estonia: Verlegts Johann Jacob Illig, Buchh, 1766.

Liv-, est- und curlaendisches Privatrecht. Zusammengestellt auf Befehl des Herrn und Kaisers Alexander II. St. Petersburg, Russia: Buchdr. der Zweiten Abtheilung Seiner Kaiserlichen Majestät eigener Kanzlei, 1864.

Loit, Aleksander, ed. *National Movements in the Baltic Countries During the 19th Century.* Studia Baltica Stockholmiensia 2. Stockholm: Almqvist & Wiksell, 1985.

———, ed. *The Baltic Countries 1900–1914.* Studia Baltica Stockholmiensia 5. Stockholm: Almqvist & Wiksell, 1990.

Raun, Toivo U. "The Development of Estonian Literacy in the 18th and 19th Centuries." *Journal of Baltic Studies* 10 (1979): 115–26.

———. "The Estonians." In *Russification in the Baltic Provinces and Finland, 1855–1914,* edited by Edward Thaden, 287–354. Princeton, N.J.: Princeton University Press, 1981.

———. "Estonian Social and Political Thought, 1905–February 1917." In *Die baltischen Provinzen Russlands zwischen den Revolutionen von 1905 und 1917*, edited by Andrew Ezergailis and Gert von Pistohlkors. Quellen und Studien zur Baltischen Geschichte 4. Cologne, Germany: Bohlau, 1982.

———. "Language Development and Policy in Estonia." In *Sociolinguistic Perspectives on Soviet National Languages: Their Past, Present and Future*, edited by Isabelle T. Kreindler. Berlin: Mouton de Gruyter, 1985.

———. "The Revolution of 1905 in the Baltic Provinces and Finland." *Slavic Review* 43 (1984): 453–67.

Rechtskraft und Rechtsbruch der liv- und estländischen Privilegien, rev. ed. Berlin: Duncker & Humblot, 1999.

Richter, Christoph Melchior Alexander von. *Geschichte der dem russischen Kaiserthumeinverleibten deutschen Ostseeprovinzen bis zur Zeit ihrer Vereinigung mit demselber.* Hannover-Döhren, Germany: H. v. Hirschheydt, 1972.

Schmidt, Oswald. *Rechtsgeschichte Liv-, Est- und Curlands*. Hannover-Döhren, Germany: H. v. Hirschheydt, 1968.

Thaden, Edward, ed. *Russification in the Baltic Provinces and Finland, 1855–1914*. Princeton, N.J.: Princeton University Press, 1981.

Wrangell, Otto Fabian von. *Landrath Wrangell's Chronik von Ehstland nebst angehängten Ehstländischen Capitulations-Punkten und Nystädter Friedensschluss*. Hannover-Döhren, Germany: H. v. Hirschheydt, 1969.

Zelnik, Reginald E. *Law and Disorder on the Narova River: The Kreenholm Strike of 1872*. Berkeley: University of California Press, 1995.

4. World War I and the War of Independence

Arens, Olavi. "Soviets in Estonia, 1917/1918." In *Die Baltischen Provinzen Russlands zwischen den Revolutionen von 1905 und 1917*, edited by Andrew Ezergailis and Gert Von Pistohlkors. Cologne, Germany: Böhlau, 1982.

Aun, Karl. "The 1917 Revolutions and the Idea of the State in Estonia." In *Die Baltischen Provinzen Russlands zwischen den Revolutionen von 1905 und 1917*, edited by Andrew Ezergailis and Gert Von Pistohlkors. Cologne, Germany: Böhlau, 1982.

Estonian War of Independence, 1918–1920. New York: Eesti Vabadusvõitlejate Liit, n.d.

Hehn, Jürgen von, Hans von Rimscha, and Hellmuth Weiss. *Von den baltischen Provinzen zu den Baltischen Staaten: Beitr. z. Entstehungsgeschichte d. Republiken Estland u. Lettland*. Marburg (Lahn), Germany: J.-G.-Herder-Inst., 1971–1977.

Helanen, Vilho. *Suomalaiset Viron Vapaussodassa*. Helsinki, Finland: Kustannusosakeyhtiö Kirja, 1921.

Hovi, Olavi. *Suomalaiset heimosoturit Viron vapaussodassa ja Itä-Karjalan heimosodissa vuosina 1918–1922*. Turku, Finland: 1971.

Jaanson, Kaido. *Soldiers of Fortune: Swedish and Danish Volunteers in the Estonian Civil War, 1918–1920*. Tallinn, Estonia: Perioodika, 1988.

Martna, M. *Estland, die Esten und die estnische frage*. Olten, Switzerland: W. Trösch, 1919.

———. *L'Estonia; gli Estoni e la questione estone*. Rome: A. Signorelli, 1919.

———. *L'Esthonie; les Esthoniens et la question Esthonienne (préface de C. R. Pusta)*. Paris: A. Colin, 1920.

Niinistö, Jussi, and Jukka I. Mattila. *Pohjan Pojat: kuvahistoria suomalaisen vapaaehtoisrykmentin vaiheista Viron vapaussodassa 1919*. Helsinki, Finland: Lak-Kustannus, 1999.

Paris. Peace conference, 1919. Estonia. *Mémoire sur l'indépendance de l'Esthonie présenté à la Conférence de la paix par la délégation esthonienne*. Paris: Imp. de la Bourse de Commerce, 1919.

Schücking, Lothar Engelbert Levin. *Ein Jahr auf Oesel, Beiträge zum System Ludendorff*. Berlin-Steglitz: F. Würtz, 1920.

Wheeler-Bennett, John. *Brest-Litovsk: The Forgotten Peace, March 1918.* London: Macmillan, 1956. (Originally published in 1938.)

5. Independent Estonia: 1920–1940

Angelus, Oskar. *Die Kulturautonomie in Estland Estnischen Zentralkomitee für Westdeutschland.* Detmold: Buchdruckwerkstätte Tölle, 1951.

Aun, Karl. *Der völkerrechtliche Schutz nationaler Minderheiten in Estland von 1917 bis 1940.* Hamburg, Germany: Hansischer Gildenverlag J. Heitmann, 1951.

Bank of Estonia. *Estonian Economic Year-book.* Tallinn, Estonia: Eesti-Pank, 1934–1938.

Fromme, Ernest. *The Republic of Esthonia and Private Property.* Berlin: Baltischer Verlag u. Ostbuchhandlung, 1922.

Gerber, Hans. *Kulturautonomie als Eigenart minderheitenrechtlicher Ordnung und ihre Verwirklichung nach der estnischen Verfassung.* Berlin: G. Stilke, 1926.

Grundmann, Karl-Heinz. *Deutschtumspolitik zur Zeit der Weimarer Republik: e. Studie am Beispiel d. dt.-balt. Minderheit in Estland u. Lettland.* Hannover-Döhren, Germany: H. v. Hirschheydt, 1977.

Hiden, John, and Aleksander Loit, eds. *The Baltic in International Relations between the Two World Wars.* Studia Baltica Stockholmiensia 3. Stockholm: University of Stockholm, 1988.

———. *Contact or Isolation? Soviet-Western Relations in the Interwar Period.* Studia Baltica Stockholmiensia 8. Stockholm: Almqvist & Wiksell, 1991.

Horm, Arvo. *Estland fritt och ockuperat: en studie över landets sociala förhållanden under självständighetstiden och under rysk och tysk ockupation.* Stockholm: Tidens förlag, 1944.

Hovi, Kalervo. *Estland in den Anfängen seiner Selbständigkeit: die Tagebuchaufzeichnungen des dänischen Generalkonsuls in Reval Jens Christian Johansen 13. 12. 1918–29. 5. 1919.* Turku, Finland: Institut für Geschichte, Allgemeine Geschichte, Universität Turku, 1976.

Isberg, Alvin. *Med demokratin som insats: politiskt-konstitutionellt maktspel i 1930-talets Estland (mit einer Zusammenfassung in deutscher Sprache).* Stockholm: Center for Baltic Studies, University of Stockholm, 1988.

Kasekamp, Andres. "The Estonian Veterans' League: A Fascist Movement?" *Journal of Baltic Studies* 24 (1993): 263–68.

———. "The Nature of Authoritarianism in Interwar Estonia." *International Politics* 33 (1996): 57–65.

———. *The Radical Right in Interwar Estonia.* New York: St. Martin's Press, 2000.

Katz, Zev, ed. *Handbook of Major Soviet Nationalities.* New York: The Free Press, 1975.

Klesment, Johannes. "Reform of the Estonian Constitution." *Revue Baltique* 1 (1940): 54–67.

Köll, Anu-Mai. *Peasants on the World Market: Agricultural Experience of Independent Estonia 1919–1939.* Studia Baltica Stockholmiensia 14. Stockholm: Almqvist & Wiksell, 1994.

Köll, Anu-Mai, and Jaak Valge, eds. *Economic Nationalism and Industrial Growth: State and Industry in Estonia 1934–1939.* Studia Baltica Stockholmiensia 19. Stockholm: Almqvist & Wiksell, 1998.

Kuuli, Olaf. *Six Years of Fascist Dictatorship in Estonia.* Tallinn, Estonia: Perioodika, 1975.

Lipping, Imre. "December 1, 1924: The Communist Coup in Estonia." *Yearbook of the Estonian Learned Society in America* 5 (1968–1975): 43–46.

Maddison, Eugen. *Die nationalen Minderheiten Estlands und ihre Rechte.* Tallinn, Estonia: Tallinna Eesti Kirjastusühisuse Trükikoda, 1926.

Meder, Walter. *Das Dekretrecht des Staatspräsidenten in Estland.* Tartu, Estonia: J. G. Krüger, 1936.

Mothander, Carl. *Baroner, bönder och bolsjeviker i Estland.* Helsinki, Finland: Lars Hökerbergs Bokförlag, 1943.

Parming, Tönu. *The Collapse of Liberal Democracy and the Rise of Authoritarianism in Estonia.* Beverly Hills, Calif.: Sage Publications, 1975.

Pullerits, Albert, ed. *Estonia: Population, Cultural and Economic Life.* Tallinn, Estonia: State Central Bureau of Statistics, 1935, 1937.

Rauch, Georg von. *The Baltic States: The Years of Independence: Estonia, Latvia, Lithuania, 1917–1940.* London: C. Hurst, 1974; New York: St. Martin's Press, 1995.

Sahlström, André. *Under blåsvarta färger: den estniska konstitutionella krisens verkningar i de finsk-estniska relationerna åren 1934–1938.* Helsinki, Finland: Suomalaisen Kirjallisuuden Seura, 2000.

Schmidt, Erik. *Optical Illusions: The Life Story of Bernhard Schmidt, the Great Stellar Optician of the Twentieth Century.* Tallinn, Estonia: Estonian Academy Publishers, 1995.

Stryk-Helmet, Erik von. *Die Verfassungen von Finnland, Estland, Lettland und Litauen in rechtsvergleichender Darstellung.* Cologne, Germany: Druck von E. Pilgram, 1928.

Sunila, August. *The Armed Uprising of the Estonian Proletariat on December 1, 1924.* Tallinn, Estonia: Kodumaa, 1974.

Uibopuu, Henn-Jüri. "The Constitutional Development of the Estonian Republic." *Journal of Baltic Studies* 4 (1973): 11–35.

Vardys, Stanley V. "Democracy in the Baltic States, 1918–1934: The Stage and the Actors." *Journal of Baltic Studies* 10 (1979): 321–35.

Vardys, V. Stanley, and Romuald J. Misiunas, eds. *The Baltic States in Peace and War, 1917–1945.* University Park: Pennsylvania State University Press, 1978.

Vesterinen, Emil. *Agricultural Conditions in Esthonia: A Short Survey.* Helsinki, Finland: Tietosanakirja-osakeyhtiö, 1922.

Zetterberg, Seppo. *Suomi ja Viro 1917–1919: poliittiset suhteetsyksystä 1917 reunavaltiopolitiikan alkuun.* Helsinki, Finland: Suomen Historiallinen Seura, 1977.

6. World War II: The Soviet and German Occupations

Cube, Hans Eberhard von. *Überleben war alles: Aufzeichnungen eines baltischen Umsiedlers von 1939 bis 1946.* Lüneburg, Germany: Nordostdeutsches Kulturwerk, 1986.

Generalkommissar in Reval, 1941–1944. *Statistische Berichte für den Generalbezirk Estland.* Reval (Tallinn), Estonia: Generalkommissar in Reval, n.d.

Gurin-Loov, Eugenia. *Eesti juutide katastroof 1941 = Holocaust of Estonian Jews 1941.* Tallinn, Estonia: Eesti Juudi Kogukond, 1994.

Hiden, John, and Thomas Lane, eds. *The Baltic States and the Outbreak of the Second World War.* Cambridge: Cambridge University Press, 1992.

Hippius, Rudolf. *Die Umsiedlergruppe aus Estland.* Posen: 1940.

Hough, William. "The Annexation of the Baltic States and its Effect on the Development of Law Prohibiting Forcible Seizure of Territory." *The New York Law School Journal of International and Comparative Law* 6, no. 2 (1985).

Isberg, Alvin. *Zu den Bedingungen des Befreiers: Kollaboration und Freiheitsstreben in dem von Deutschland besetzten Estland 1941 bis 1944.* Stockholm: Almqvist & Wiksell, 1992.

Jackson, J. Hampden. *Estonia: With a Postscript on the Years 1940–1947.* Westport, Conn.: Greenwood Press, 1979.

Jurs, August. *Estonian Freedom Fighters in World War Two.* Hamilton, Ont., Canada: Vôitleja Relief Foundation, n.d.

Littlejohn, David. *Foreign Legions of the Third Reich.* San Jose, Calif.: R. J. Bender, 1979–1987.

Loeber, Dietrich André, ed. *Diktierte Option: die Umsiedlung der Deutsch-Balten aus Estland und Lettland 1939–1941.* Neumünster, Germany: K. Wachholtz, 1972.

Lükens, Markus. *Die Uhr aus der Seife: Bericht über eine Flucht.* Düsseldorf, Germany: Erb, 1985.

Nielsen-Stokkeby, Bernd. *Baltische Erinnerungen: Estland, Lettland, Litauen zwischen Unterdrückung und Freiheit.* Bergisch Gladbach, Germany: Gustav Lübbe Verlag, 1990

Nørgaard, Erik. *Mændene fra Estland: dokumentation af hidtil hemmeligholdt materiale om baggrunden for det politiske mord i Kongelunden fastelavnsmandag 1936 og den kommunistiske magtovertagelse af Estland i 1940.* Copenhagen: Holkenfeldts, 1990.

Oras, Ants. *Baltic Eclipse.* London: V. Gollancz, 1948.

Panksejev, A. *The Estonian People in the Great Patriotic War.* Tallinn, Estonia: Perioodika, 1980.

Raud, Villem. *Developments in Estonia, 1939–1941.* Tallinn, Estonia: Perioodika, 1987.

Rei, August. *Balticum och Sovjetunionens säkerhet.* Uppsala, Sweden: Baltiska kommittén, Almquist & Wiksell, 1944.

———. *Have the Baltic Countries Voluntarily Renounced Their Freedom? An Exposé Based on Authentic Documentary Evidence.* New York: n.p., 1944.

———. *Have the Small Nations a Right to Freedom and Independence?* London: Boreas, 1946.

———, ed. *Nazi-Soviet Conspiracy and the Baltic States: Diplomatic Documents and Other Evidence.* London: Boreas, 1948.

Sanden, Einar. *An Estonian Saga.* Cardiff, Wales: Boreas, 1996.

Shtromas, Alexander. "Soviet Occupation of the Baltic States and their Incorporation into the USSR: Political and Legal Aspect." *East European Quarterly* 19 (1985): 289–304.

Siniveli (pseudonym). *Viro taistelee vapaudestaan: vuosi 1944 tuntemattoman todistajan silmin Siniveli.* Helsinki, Finland: Alea-kirja, 1991.

Tomson, Edgar. "The Annexation of the Baltic States." In *The Anatomy of Communist Takeovers,* edited by Thomas T. Hammond, 214–28. New Haven, Conn.: Yale University Press, 1975.

Trapans, Andris. *Soviet Military Power in the Baltic Area.* Stockholm: Latvian National Foundation, 1986.

United States Congress. House Select Committee on Communist Aggression. *Report of the Select Committee to Investigate Communist Aggression against Poland, Hungary, Czechoslovakia, Bulgaria, Rumania, Lithuania, Latvia, Estonia, East Germany, Russia, and the Non-Russian Nations of the U. S. S. R.* Second Interim Report to the Select Committee on Communist Aggression, House of Representatives, Eighty-third Congress, second session, under authority of H. Res. 346 and H. Res.438. Washington, D.C.: GPO, 1954.

Uustalu, Evald. "The National Committee of the Estonian Republic." *Journal of Baltic Studies* 7 (1976): 209–19.

———. *For Freedom Only: The Story of Estonian Volunteers in the Finnish Wars of 1940–1944.* Toronto: Northern Publications, 1977.

We Demand Freedom for Estonia; Memoranda Presented to the Delegations at the Paris Conference, 1946. London: Boreas, 1947.

Weiss, Gottfried. *Abschied von Estland und deutsche Schicksalsjahre: Erinnerungen und Zeitbilder von 1914–1933 erzählt von einem Sonntagskind.* Melle: E. Knoth, 1990.

Weiss-Wendt, Anton. "The Soviet Occupation of Estonia in 1940–41 and the Jews." *Holocaust and Genocide Studies* (1977): 207–22.

Wieselgren, Per. *Från hammaren till hakkorset; Estland, 1939–1941.* Stockholm: Idé och Form Förlag, 1942.

7. Estonia in the Soviet Union: Views from Inside and Outside

Eliaser, Elga. *Estonia Past and Present.* Stockholm: Estonian Information Center, 1959.

Estonian Democratic Movement and the Estonian National Front. *Two Memoranda to UNO from Estonia.* Stockholm: Estonian Information Center, 1974.

Holzapfel, Gerhard. *Die Landwirtschaft der Estnischen SSR.* Berlin: Urania, Sektion Agrarwissenschaften, 1967.

Jänes, Harri. *Health Care in the Estonian SSR.* Tallinn, Estonia: Perioodika, 1980.

Kaelas, Aleksander. *Das sowjetisch besetzte Estland.* Stockholm: Eesti Rahvusfond, 1958.

Kahk, Juhan, and Karl Siilivask. *History of the Estonian SSR.* Tallinn, Estonia: Perioodika, 1985.

Kareda, Endel. *Techinque of Economic Sovietisation.* East and West 3. London: Boreas, 1947.

———. *Estonia in the Soviet Grip: Life and Conditions under Soviet Occupation 1947–49*. East and West 5. London: Boreas, 1949.

Karklins, Rasma. *Ethnic Relations in the USSR: The Perspective from Below.* Boston: Allen and Unwin, 1986.

Klesment, Johannes. "The Forms of Baltic Resistance to the Communists." *The Baltic Review* 8 (1956): 24–42.

Küng, Andres. *Estland zum Beispiel: nationale Minderheit u. Supermacht.* Stuttgart, Germany: Seewald, 1973.

———. *A Dream of Freedom: Four Decades of National Survival versus Russian Imperialism in Estonia, Latvia, and Lithuania, 1940–1980.* Cardiff, Wales: Boreas, 1980.

Kurman, George. "Literary Censorship in General and in Soviet Estonia." *Journal of Baltic Studies* 8 (1977): 3–15.

Laar, Mart. *War in the Woods: Estonia's Struggle for Survival, 1944–1956.* Washington, D.C.: Compass, 1992.

Laigna, Karl, ed. *A Thousand and One Facts about Soviet Estonia: General Data, Nature, and Population; History and Social Organization; Economy; Education, Science, and Culture.* Tallinn, Estonia: Perioodika, 1984

Lauk, Epp. "Practice of Soviet Censorship in the Press: the Case of Estonia." *Nordicom Information* 21, no. 3 (1999): 27–40.

Loeber, Dietrich A., V. Stanley Vardys, and Laurence P. A. Kitching, eds. *Regional Identity under Soviet Rule: The Case of the Baltic States.* Hackettstown, N.J.: Association for the Advancement of Baltic Studies, 1990.

Maley, William. *The Politics of Baltic Nationalism.* Canberra, Australia: Research School of Pacific Studies, 1990.

Misiunas, Romualdas, and Rein Taagepera. "The Baltic States: Years of Dependence, 1980–1986." *Journal of Baltic Studies* 20 (1989): 65–88.

———. *The Baltic States: Years of Dependence 1940–1980*, 2nd rev. ed. London: Hurst and University of California Press, 1993.

Naan, Gustav, ed. *Soviet Estonia: Land, People, Culture.* Tallinn, Estonia: Valgus Publishers, 1980.

Olevsoo, G. *Soviet Estonia.* Tallinn, Estonia: Eesti Raamat, 1970.

Paalberg, H., and E. Vint. *The Estonian SSR Economy: Industry and Agriculture.* Tallinn, Estonia: Eesti Raamat, 1973.

Parming, Tõnu. *The Collapse of Liberal Democracy and the Rise of Authoritarianism in Estonia.* London: Sage, 1975.

———. "The Electoral Achievements of the Communist Party in Estonia, 1920–1940." *Slavic Review* 42 (1983): 426–47.

———. "The Jewish Community and Inter-Ethnic Relations in Estonia, 1918–1940." *Journal of Baltic Studies* 10 (1979): 241–62.

———. "Long Term Trends in Family Structure in a Soviet Republic." *Sociology and Social Research* 63 (1979): 443–66.

———. "The Pattern of Participation of the Estonian Communist Party in National Politics, 1918–1940." *Slavonic and East European Review* 59 (1981): 397–412.

———. "Population Changes in Estonia, 1935–1970." *Population Studies* 26 (1972): 53–78.

Parming, Tõnu, and Elmar Järvesoo, eds. *A Case Study of a Soviet Republic: The Estonian SSR.* Boulder, Colo.: Westview Press, 1978.

Purre, Arnold. *Soviet Farming Failure Hits Estonia.* Stockholm: Estonian Information Center, 1964.

Roos, Aarand. *Estonia: A Nation Unconquered.* Baltimore, Md.: Estonian World Council, 1985.

Saar, Asmu, ed. *A Thousand and One Facts about Soviet Estonia.* Tallinn, Estonia: Perioodika, 1989.

Soviet Estonia. Tallinn, Estonia: n.p., 1967.

Sinilind, Sirje. *Viro ja Venäjä havaintoja Neuvostoliiton kansallisuuspolitiikasta Virossa 1940–1984.* Helsinki, Finland: Alea-Kirja, 1985.

Taagepera, Rein. "Citizens' Peace Movement in the Soviet Baltic Republics." *Journal of Peace Research* 23 (1986): 183–192.

———. *Softening without Liberalization in the Soviet Union: The Case of Jüri Kukk.* Lanham, Md.: University Press of America, 1984.

———. "Soviet Documentation on the Estonian Pro-Independence Guerilla Movement, 1945–1952." *Journal of Baltic Studies* 10 (1979): 91–106.

Toome, Indrek. *The Youth of Soviet Estonia: Organization and Activities.* Tallinn, Estonia: Perioodika, 1980.

Uibopuu, HennJüri, and Andrejs Urdze. *Die Aufarbeitung der kommunistischen Vergangenheit in Estland und Lettland.* Cologne, Germany: Bundesinstitut für Ostwissenschaftliche und Internationale Studien, 1997.

Vanatoa, Endel. *Estonian SSR: A Reference Book.* Tallinn, Estonia: Perioodika, 1985, 1987.

Vardys, Stanley V. "Human Rights Issues in Estonia, Latvia, and Lithuania." *Journal of Baltic Studies* 12 (1981): 275–98.

———. "Modernization and Baltic Nationalism." *Problems of Communism* 24, no. 5 (1975): 32–48.

———. "The Role of Baltic Peoples in Soviet Society." In *The Influence of East*

Europe and the Soviet West on the USSR, edited by Roman Szporluk, 147–49. New York: Praeger, 1976.

Vihalemm, Peeter, and Marju Lauristin. "Political Control and Ideological Canonisation: the Estonian Press during the Soviet Period." In *Vom Instrument der Partei zur "vierten Gewalt,"* edited by E. Mühle. Marburg, Germany: Herder-Institut, 1997.

We Demand Freedom for Estonia. Memoranda Presented to the Delegations at the Paris Conference, 1946. London: Boreas, 1947.

8. Transition and Independence on the Way to the European Union (EU): 1988–2002

Cullen, Robert. *Twilight of Empire: Inside the Crumbling Soviet Bloc.* New York: Atlantic Monthly Press, 1991.

Dalhoff-Nielsen, Peter. *Baltisk oprbrud: Estland, Letland och Litauens forvandling efter glasnost.* Copenhagen: Vindrose, 1990.

Drechsler, Wolfang. "Estonia in Transition." World Affairs 157, no. 3 (winter 1995): 111–17.

Lauristin, Marju, et al., eds. *Return to the Western World: Cultural and Political Perspectives on the Estonian Post-Communist Transition.* Tartu, Estonia: Tartu University Press, 1997.

Lieven, Anatol. *The Baltic Revolution: Latvia, Lithuania, Estonia, and the Path to Independence.* New Haven, Conn.: Yale University Press, 1993.

Nørgaard, Ole, et al. *The Baltic States after Independence*, 2nd ed. Cheltenham, UK: Edward Elgar, 1999.

8.1. Economy

Aho, Simo, et al. *Making the Way into the Market Economy: Transformation in Estonia with a Focus on Food and Light Industries.* Helsinki, Finland: Ministry of Labor, 1996.

Andersen, Erik André. *An Ethnic Perspective on Economic Reform: The Case of Estonia.* Aldershot, UK: Ashgate, 1999.

The Baltic States. London: Economist Intelligence Unit, 1990.

Bank of Estonia. *Inflation and Monetary Policy in Estonia.* Tallinn, Estonia: Eesti Pank, 1997.

———. *Monetary Developments & Policy Survey.* Tallinn, Estonia: Eesti Pank, 1998.

———. *Rahareform Eestis 1992a. = The Monetary Reform in Estonia, 1992.* Tallinn, Estonia: Eesti Pank, 1992.

Borrmann, Christine, Peter Plötz, and Andreas Polkowski. *Wirtschaftslage und Reformprozesse in Mittel- und Osteuropa: Estland, Lettland, Litauen.* Hamburg, Germany: HWWA—Institut für Wirtschaftsforschung—Hamburg, 1999.

Cavalcanti, Carlos Brandão, and Daniel Oks. *Estonia, the Challenge of Financial Integration.* Washington, D.C.: World Bank, Europe and Central Asia [Region], Poverty Reduction and Economic Management Sector Unit, 1998.

Doukas, John, Victor Murinde, and Clas Wihlborg, eds. *Financial Sector Reform and Privatization in Transition Economies.* Amsterdam: Elsevier, 1998.

Eamets, Raul, ed. *Estonian Labour Market and Labour Market Policy.* Viljandi: Ministry of Social Affairs of Estonia, 1999.

Eamets, Raul, Kaia Philips, and Tiina Annus. *Background Study on Employment and Labour Market in Estonia.* Tartu, Estonia: Faculty of Economics, University of Tartu, 2000.

Ennuste, Ülo, and Lisa Wilder, eds. *Harmonisation with the Western Economics: Estonian Economic Developments and Related Conceptual and Methodological Frameworks.* Tallinn, Estonia: Estonian Institute of Economics at Tallinn Technical University, 1999.

Fritsche, Ulrich, Peter Plötz, and Andreas Polkowski. *Wirtschaftslage und Reformprozesse in Mittel- und Osteuropa: Estland, Lettland, Litauen.* Hamburg, Germany: HWWA—Institut für Wirtschaftsforschung—Hamburg, 1997.

Hansson, Ardo H. *Transforming an Economy while Building a Nation: The Case of Estonia.* Helsinki, Finland: United Nations University, World Institute for Development Economics Research, 1993.

———. *Macroeconomic Stabilization in the Baltic States.* Stockholm: Stockholm Institute of East European Economies, Stockholm School of Economics, 1995.

Hood, Neil, Robert Kilis, and Jan-Erik Vahlne, eds. *Transition in the Baltic States: Micro-Level Studies.* New York: St. Martins's Press, 1997.

Kaasik, Tõnis, ed. *Ida-Virumaa: Man, Economy, Nature: A Survey of the Problems Facing Ida-Virumaa in the Context of Sustainable Development.* Tallinn, Estonia: Commission on Sustainable Development of Ida-Virumaa and Stockholm Environment Institute, 1995.

Laar, Mart. *Das estnische Wirtschaftswunder.* Bonn, Germany: Konrad Adenauer Stiftung, 2002.

Lösch, Dieter, Peter Plötz, and Andreas Polkowski. *Wirtschaftslage und Reformprozesse in Estland, Lettland und Litauen im Herbst 2000.* Hamburg, Germany: Hamburgisches Welt-Wirtschafts-Archiv, 2000.

Lugus, Olev, and George A. Hachey, Jr. *Transforming the Estonian Economy.* Tallinn, Estonia: International Center for Economic Growth, 1995.

Miljan, Toivo. "The Proposal to Establish Economic Autonomy in Estonia." *Journal of Baltic Studies* 20 (1989): 149–64.

Noorkõiv, Rivo, et al. *How Estonia's Economic Transition Affected Employment and Wages, 1989–95.* Washington, D.C.: World Bank, African Human Development Department, 1997.

Orazem, Peter F., and Milan Vodopivec. *Male-Female Differences in Labor Market Outcomes during the Early Transition to Market: The Case of Estonia and Slovenia.* Washington, D.C.: World Bank, 1999.

Ratas, Rein. *Main Outlines of Sustainable Development in Estonia.* Tallinn, Estonia: Ministry of the Environment, 1997.

Reedik, Vello, and Tiit Kaps. *Impact Study, 1992–1997 Estonia.* Tallinn, Estonia: n.p., 1998.

Schumacher, Torsten. *Transformation und wirtschaftliche Selbstverwaltung—das Beispiel Estland.* Frankfurt, Germany: P. Lang, 1997.

Shen, Raphael. *Restructuring the Baltic Economies: Disengaging Fifty Years of Integration with the USSR.* Westport, Conn.: Praeger, 1994.

Siwiânska, Joanna. *The External Public Debt of Baltic and Selected CIS Countries in Years 1992–1997: Estonia, Latvia, Lithuania, Kazakhstan, Kyrgyz Republic, Moldoa, Russian Federation and Ukraine.* Warsaw, Poland: Center for Social and Economic Research, 1999.

Terk, Erik. *Privatisation in Estonia: Ideas, Process, Results.* Tallinn, Estonia: Estonian Institute for Futures Studies, 2000.

Tiusanen, Tauno, and Jari Jumpponen. *The Baltic States in the 21st Century: Western Investors in Estonia, Latvia, and Lithuania.* Lappeenranta, Finland: Lappeenranta University of Technology, 2000.

Tiusanen, Tauno, and Kirsti Talvitie. *The Baltic States in the 1990's: Western Companies in Estonia, Latvia and Lithuania.* Porvoo, Finland: Werner Söderström Osakeyhtiö, 1998.

Venesaar, Urve, and George A. Hachey, eds. *Economic and Social Changes in the Baltic States in 1992–1994.* Tallinn, Estonia: Institute of Economics, 1995.

8.2 Polity

Arter, David. *Parties and Democracy in the Post-Soviet Republics: The Case of Estonia.* Brookfield, Vt.: Dartmouth, 1996.

Berg, E., and S. Oras. "Writing Post-Soviet Estonia on to the World Map." *Political Geography* 19, no. 5 (2000): 601–25.

Berg-Schlosser, Dirk, and Raivo Vetik, eds. *Perspectives on Democratic Consolidation in Central and Eastern Europe.* Boulder, Colo.: East European Monographs, 2001.

Drechsler, Wolfgang, and Taavi Annus. "Die Verfassungsentwicklung in Estland von 1992 bis 2001." In *Jahrbuch des öffentlichen Rechts der Gegenwart,* vol. 50, 473–92. Tübingen, Germany: Mohr Siebeck, 2002.

Eesti Kongress. *Eesti Kongress = The Congress of Estonia = Kongress ç Estonii.* Tallinn, Estonia: The Congress of Estonia, 1991.

Gerner, Kristian, and Stefan Hedlund. *The Baltic States and the End of the Soviet Empire.* London: Routledge, 1993.

Grofman, Bernard, Evald Mikkel, and Rein Taagepera. "Electoral Systems Change in Estonia, 1989–1993." *Journal of Baltic Studies* 30, no. 3 (1999): 227–49.

———. "Fission and Fusion of Parties in Estonia, 1987–1999." *Journal of Baltic Studies* 31 (2000): 329–57.

Kionka, Riina. "Economic Woes and Political Disputes." *Report on the USSR* 3, no. 1 (1991): 45–47.

———. "The Estonian Citizens' Committees: An Opposition Movement of a Different Complexion." *Report on the USSR* 2, no. 12 (1990).

Lauk, E. "Who Are We? Restoring the Language, Cultural Memory and Identity of Estonia." In *Communication and Reconciliation: Challenges Facing the 21st Century,* edited by P. Lee, 46–60. London: World Association for Christian Communication, 2001.

Lukkari, Matti. *Viron itsenäistyminen: kerran me voitamme kuitenkin.* Helsinki, Finland: Otava, 1995.

Klöcker, Georg, ed. *Ten Years after the Baltic States Re-entered the International Stage.* Baden-Baden, Germany: Nomos, 2001.

Made, Tiit. *Mu isamaa: Viron toivo ja pelko.* Helsinki, Finland: Kirjayhtymä, 1988

McHale, Vincent E. "The Party System of the Baltic States: a Comparative European Perspective." *Journal of Baltic Studies* 17 (1986): 295–312.

Mikkel, Evald. "The Opinion Proximity of Russians and Estonians in Estonia during the Early 1990s." *Journal of Baltic Studies* 30, no. 2 (1999): 162–79.

Miljan, Toivo. "Democratization in Estonia." *Lituanus: Lithuanian Quarterly Journal of Arts and Sciences* 37, no. 2 (summer 1991).

Misiunas, Romualdas, and Rein Taagepera. "The National Renaissance of 1988." *Baltic Forum* 5, no. 2 (1988): 1–21.

Oplatka, Andreas. *Lennart Meri: ein Leben für Estland.* Zürich, Switzerland: Verlag Neue Zürcher Zeitung, 1999.

Ostrow, Joel M. *Comparing Post-Soviet Legislatures: A Theory of Institutional Design and Political Conflict.* Columbus: Ohio State University Press, 2000.

Pettai, Vello. "The Baltic States: Straddling the Post-Communist Divide." In *Democracy in the New Europe: The Politics of Post-Communism*, edited by Julie Smith and Elizabeth Teague. London: Greycoat Press, 1999.

———. "Estonia and Latvia: International Influences on Citizenship and Minority Integration." In *International Influences on Democratic Transition in Central and Eastern Europe*, edited by Alex Pravda and Jan Zielonka. Oxford: Oxford University Press, 2001.

———. "Estonia: Positive and Negative Engineering." In *Institutional Engineering in Eastern Europe*, edited by Alex Pravda and Jan Zielonka. Oxford: Oxford University Press, 2001.

———. "Estonia: The Right's Return." In *1999 Annual Survey of Central and Eastern Europe*, edited by Peter Rutland. Prague, Czech Republic: OMRI/East-West Institute, Internet Publication, 2000.

Pettai, Vello, and Marcus Kreuzer. "Institutions and Party Development in the Baltic States." In *Party Development and Democratic Change in Post-Communist Europe*, edited by Paul G. Lewis. London: Frank Cass, 2001.

———. "Party Politics in the Baltic States: Social Bases and Institutional Context." *East European Politics and Societies* 13, no. 1 (spring 1999): 150–91.

The Popular Front of Estonia: Charter, General Congress of the Popular Front of Estonia on October 2, 1988. Tallinn, Estonia: Perioodika, 1989.

Raun, Toivo U. "Democratization and Political Development in Estonia, 1987–1996." In *The Consolidation of Democracy in East Central Europe*, edited by Karen Dawisha and Bruce Parrott. Cambridge: Cambridge University Press, 1997.

Smith, Graham, ed. *The Baltic States: The National Self-determination of Estonia, Latvia, and Lithuania.* New York: St. Martin's Press, 1994.

Steen, Anton. *Between Past and Future: Elites, Democracy and the State in Post-communist Countries: A Comparison of Estonia, Latvia, and Lithuania.* Aldershot, UK: Ashgate, 1997.

———. "Confidence in Institutions in Post-Communist Societies: The Case of the Baltic States." *Scandinavian Political Studies* 19, no. 3 (1996): 205–25.

Taagepera, Rein. *Estonia: Return to Independence.* Boulder, Colo.: Westview Press, 1993.

———. "Estonia's Road to Independence." *Problems of Communism* 38, no. 6 (1989).

U.S. Commission on Security and Cooperation in Europe. *Human Rights and Democratization in Estonia.* Washington, D.C.: Author, 1993.

———. *Renewal and Challenge: The Baltic States, 1988–1989*. Washington, D.C.: GPO, 1990.

8.3. *Society*

Berg, E., and S. Oras. "Writing Post-Soviet Estonia on to the World Map." *Political Geography,*" no. 5 (2000): 601–25.

Estonian Human Development Report. Annual (1995–). Published by UNDP until 2000; by Institute of International and Social Studies, Tallinn Pedagogical University, since 2001.

Estonian Medical Statistics Bureau, Latvian Medical Statistics Bureau, Lithuanian Health Information Center. *Health in the Baltic Countries.* Tallinn, Estonia: Estonian Medical Statistics Bureau, 1993.

Hanhinen, Sari. *Social Problems in Transition: Perceptions of Influential Groups in Estonia, Russia, and Finland.* Helsinki, Finland: Aleksanteri Institute, 2001.

Joonsaar, Anne, et al. *Estonian Women in a Changing Society.* Tallinn, Estonia: National Report of Estonia, 1995.

Kaaına, Marina, et al. *Public Health in Estonia.* Tartu, Estonia: Elmatar, 1998.

Kirch, Marika, and David D. Laitin, eds. *Changing Identities in Estonia: Sociological Facts and Commentaries.* Tallinn, Estonia: Estonian Academy of Sciences, 1994

Lauristin, Marju. "Estonia Is Looking for Its Own Welfare Model." In *Social Protection of the Next Generation in Europe*, edited by D. Pieters. The Hague: Kluwer Law International, 1998.

———. "The Social Development of Estonia." In *Ten Years after the Baltic States Re-entered the International Stage*, edited by G. Klöcker, 127–34. Baden-Baden, Germany: Nomos, 2001.

———. "Transformations of Public Sphere and Changing Role of the Media in Post-Communist Society." In *Building an Open Society and Perspectives of Sociology in East-Central Europe*, precongress volumes of the 14th World Congress of Sociology, edited by P. Sztompka. Montreal: International Sociological Association, 1998.

Löfgren, Joan, and Graeme P. Herd. *Estonia and the EU: Integration and Societal Security in the Baltic Context.* Tampere, Finland: Tampere Peace Research Institute, 2000.

Narusk, Anu, ed. *Every-day Life and Radical Social Changes in Estonia: A Sociological-empirical Overview of Changes in Estonians' Life Values, Attitudes, Living Conditions, and Behaviour during the Transition from Soviet to Post-Soviet.* Tallinn, Estonia: Eesti Teaduste Akadeemia Kirjastus, 1995.

Narusk, Anu, and Leeni Hansson. *Estonian Families in the 1990s: Winners and Losers.* Tallinn, Estonia: Estonian Academy Publishers, 1999.

Pettai, Vello, with Aksel Kirch, Marika Kirch, and Tarmo Tuisk. "Changing Ethnic and National Identities in Estonia." In *States of Mind: American and Post-Soviet Perspectives on Contemporary Issues in Psychology*, edited by Diane F. Halpern and Alexander E. Voiskounsky. Oxford: Oxford University Press, 1997.

Raska, E., and J. Saar, eds. *Crime and Criminology at the End of the Century.* Ninth Baltic Criminological Seminar, May 22–25, 1996. Tallinn, Estonia: Estonian National Defense and Public Service Academy, 1997.

Raun, Toivo U. "Perestroika and Baltic Historiography." *Journal of Soviet Nationalities* 2, no. 2 (1991): 52–62.

Reinikainen, Jouni. *Right against Right: Membership and Justice in Post-Soviet Estonia.* Stockholm: University of Stockholm, Department of Political Science, 1999.

Runnel, P. "The Tiger Leap Project and the Toilet Wall: Development of the Internet and IT Consciousness in Estonia." *Nord Nytt* 82, special issue: "Computers and Culture" (2001): 51–65.

Saar, Andrus. "What Did the Plebiscite and Referendum in Estonia Reveal about the Statehood of Estonia and the Soviet Union?" *The Monthly Survey of Estonian and Soviet Politics* (March 1991): 12–16.

8.4. Public Administration

Kungla. Tarvo. "Die estnischen Kommunen und ihre Finanzen." In *Die selbstverwaltete Gemeinde. Beiträge zu ihrer Vergangenheit, Gegenwart und Zukunft in Estland, Deutschland und Europa*, edited by Wolfgang Drechsler, 111–22. Berlin: Duncker & Humbolt, 1999.

OECD (SIGMA) and European Union. *State Administrations in Central and East-*

ern European Countries Applying for Accession to the European Union. OECD (SIGMA) and European Union, 1999.

Randma, Tina. "Pitfalls of Foreign Aid: Lessons from Estonia." (World Bank) *Transition Newsletter* 13, no. 2 (March–April 2002): 28–30.

———. "Public Administration Education: Estonia." In *Building Higher Education Programmes in Public Administration in CEE Countries*, edited by Tony Verheijen and Juraj Nemec. Bratislava: NISPAcee/EPAN, 2000.

———. "Public Administration Education: Estonia." In *Civil Service Careers in Small and Large States: The Cases of Estonia and the United Kingdom*, Administrative Organisation, Tasks of the State, and the Civil Service series, vol. 47, edited by Tony Verheijen and Tiina Randma. Baden-Baden, Germany: Nomos, 2001.

———. "A Small Civil Service in Transition: The Case of Estonia." *Public Administration and Development* 21 (2001): 41–51.

Randma-Liiv, Tina. "Small States and Bureaucracy: Challenges for Public Administration." *Trames* 6 (56/51), no. 4 (2002): 374–89.

8.5. Media

Høyer, Svennik, Epp Lauk, and Peter Viahlemm. *Towards a Civil Society: The Baltic Medias's Long Road to Freedom.* Tartu, Estonia: Nota Baltica Ltd., 1993.

Lauk, E. "Trends in the Development of the Estonian Media Market in the 1990s." *Media Development*, no.3 (1999): 27–32.

Lauristin, Marju, and Peeter Vihalemm. "Current Media Politics in Estonia." In *The Role of Media in a Changing Society*, edited by Svennik Høyer, Bjarne Skov, and Line Sandsmark. Papers from the Baltic-Norwegian Conference October 1991. Oslo, Norway: Oslo University Press, 1992.

———. "Politiske forandringen og massemedier i Estland." In *Pressens Årbog 1990.* Copenhagen: Fredriksstad, 1991.

NORDICOM. *Nordic Baltic Media Statistics 1998: Denmark, Finland, Iceland, Norway, Sweden, Estonia, Latvia, Lithuania.* Gothenburg, Sweden: NORDICOM, 1999.

Vihalemm, Peeter. "Development of Media Research in Estonia." *Nordicom Information* 23, no. 2 (2001): 63–76.

———, ed. *The Baltic Media in Transition.* Tartu, Estonia: University Press, 2002.

9. The European Union and the North Atlantic Treaty Organization (NATO)

Arnswald, Sven, and Marcus Wenig, eds. *German and American Policies Towards the Baltic States: The Perspectives of EU and NATO Enlargement.* Baden-Baden, Germany: Nomos, 2000.

Bungs, Dzintra. *The Baltic States: Problems and Prospects of Membership in the European Union.* Baden-Baden, Germany: Nomos, 1998.

European Parliament. *The Social Dimension of Enlargement: Social Law and Policy in the Czech Republic, Estonia, Hungary, Poland, and Slovenia.* Luxembourg: European Parliament, 1998.

Henderson, Karen, ed. *Back to Europe: Central and Eastern Europe and the European Union.* London: UCL Press, 1999.

Hubel, Helmut, ed. *EU Enlargement and Beyond: The Baltic States and Russia.* Berlin: Berlin Verlag Arno Spitz, 2002.

Jopp, Mathias, and Sven Arnswald, eds. *The European Union and the Baltic States: Visions, Interests and Strategies for the Baltic Sea Region.* Helsinki, Finland: Ulkopoliittinen Instituutti, 1998.

Liuhto, Kari, ed. *The Baltic States and the European Union Integration.* Turku, Finland: Turku School of Economics and Business Administration, Business Research and Development Center and Institute for East-West Trade, 1997.

Malfiet, Katlijn, and Wim Keygnaert. *The Baltic States in an Enlarging European Union: Towards a Partnership between Small States.* Leuven, Belgium: Institute for European Policy, Katholieke Universiteit Leuven, 1999.

Nunberg, Barbara. *Ready for Europe: Public Administration Reform and European Accession in Central and Eastern Europe.* Washington, D.C.: World Bank, 2000.

Raik, Kristi. *Towards Substantive Democracy? The Role of the European Union in the Democratisation of Estonia and the Other Eastern Member Candidates.* Tampere, Finland: Tampere Peace Research Institute, University of Tampere, 1998.

Schürmann, Bernd. *Die Gestaltung der Beziehungen zwischen Estland und der Europäischen Union.* Berlin: Berliner Interuniversitäre Arbeitsgruppe "Baltische Staaten," 1996.

II. GENERAL: DESCRIPTIONS, TRAVEL, AND HANDBOOKS

The Baltic States: A Reference Book. Tallinn, Estonia: Estonian Encyclopaedia Publishers, 1991; Riga, Latvia: Latvian Encyclopaedia Publishers, 1991; Vilnius, Lithuania: Lithuanian Publishers, 1991.

Champonnois, Suzanne, and François de Labriolle. *L'Estonie des Estes aux Estoniens.* Paris: Karthala, 1997.

Davies, Ellen Chivers. *A Wayfarer in Estonia, Latvia and Lithuania.* New York: R. M. McBride, 1937.

Joint Accident Investigation Commission of Estonia, Finland, and Sweden. *Final Report on the Capsizing on 28 September 1994 in the Baltic Sea of the Ro-ro Passenger Vessel MV Estonia.* Helsinki, Finland: Joint Accident Investigation Commission of Estonia, Finland, and Sweden, 1997.

Peil, Tiina. *Islescapes: Estonian Small Islands and Islanders through Three Centuries.* Stockholm: Almqvist & Wiksell International, 1999.

Peterson, Olaf. *Die Universitätsstadt Dorpat (Tartu).* Marburg an der Lahn, Germany: Johann-Gottfried-Herder-Institut, 1982.

Ransome, Arthur. *"Racundra's" First Cruise (Sailing along the Western Coast of Estonia).* London: George Allen & Unwin, 1923; New York: B. W. Huebsch, 1923.

Rei, August. *The Drama of the Baltic Peoples.* Stockholm: Vaba Eesti, 1972.

Rigby, Elisabeth. *Letters from the Shores of the Baltic.* London: John Murrat, 1849.

Rutter, Owen. *The New Baltic States and Their Future: An Account of Lithuania, Latvia and Estonia.* Boston: Houghton Mifflin Company, 1926.

Seth, Ronald. *Estonian Journey: Travels in the Baltic.* New York: R. M. McBride, 1939.

Stavenhagen, Wilhelm Siegfried. *Album ehstlaendischer Ansichten.* Gelting: Artus-Verlag, 1966.

Taska, Artur. *Die Grenzen des Küstenmeeres Estlands.* Lund, Sweden: n.p., 1974.

Varnusz, Egon. *Paul Keres' Best Games*, translated by Andras Barabas, edited by Frank Boyd. Oxford: Pergamon, 1990.

Walter, Gert. *Estland.* Berlin: Verlag der Nation, 1968.

Washburne, Marion Foster. *A Search for a Happy Country.* Washington, D.C.: National Home Library Foundation, 1940.

Wistinghausen, Kurt von. *Estland, ferne Welt: ein Jugendweg.* Stuttgart, Germany: Verlag Urachhaus, 1969.

III. TOPICAL STUDIES

1. Agriculture

Agricultural Policy and Rural Development in the Baltic States. International Conference Research Papers, February 15, 2000, Vilnius. Vilnius, Lithuania: LIAE, 2000.

Bogdanov, Georgiæi. *Agrarian Reform in Esthonia: A Means of Suppressing the Racial Minority.* Berlin: Baltischer Verlag u. Ostbuchhandlung, 1922.

Fock, Achim. *Estonia into the EU: Quantitative Analysis of the Agricultural and Food Sector.* Kiel, Germany: Vauk, 2000.

Järvesoo, Elmar. "Early Agricultural Education at Tartu University." *Journal of Baltic Studies* 11 (1980): 341–55.

Lomp, Kalju. *Vinni, Model State Farm.* Tallinn, Estonia: Perioodika, 1980.

Luiga, Georg Eduard. *Die Agrarreform in Eesti.* Helsinki, Finland: Mercators tryckeri, 1920.

———. *Die neue Agrarverfassung in Eesti, ihre geschitlichen Ursachen und sozialpolitischen Auswirkungen.* Tartu, Estonia: Buchdr. des Postimees, 1924.

Luiga, Georg Eduard, and A. Warep. *Die neue Landordnung*. Tartu, Estonia: Buchdr. des Postimees, 1924.

Maiste, Juhan. *Eestimaa mõisad = Manorial Architecture in Estonia*. Tallinn, Estonia: Kunst, 1996.

Minstry of Agriculture, Estonia. *Agricutlture and Rural Development: Overview 1999*. Tallinn, Estonia: 2000.

Organization for Economic Cooperation and Development. *Review of Agricultural Policies: Estonia*. Paris: Organization for Economic Cooperation and Development, 1996.

Pajo, M., M. Tamm, and R. Teinberg. *The Restructuring of Estonian Agriculture*. Talinn: Estonian Ministry of Agriculture, 1994; Ames: Midwest Agribusiness Trade and Information Center, Center for Agricultural and Rural Development, Iowa State University, 1994.

Royal, Roland. *Das estnische Bauerngehöft*. Mainz, Germany: 1951.

Sepp, Kalev. *The Methodology and Applications of Agricultural Landscape Monitoring in Estonia*. Tartu, Estonia: Tartu University Press, 1999.

Stryck, Gustav von. *Das Agrargesetz in Livland, Lettland und Estland*. Tartu, Estonia: J. G. Krüger, 1922.

Taagepera, Rein. "Soviet Collectivization of Estonian Agriculture: The Deportation Phase." *Soviet Studies* 32 (1980): 379–97.

———. "Soviet Collectivization of Estonian Agriculture: The Taxation Phase." *Journal of Baltic Studies* 10 (1979): 263–82.

Tõnurist, Edgar. *Agriculture in Soviet Estonia*. Tallinn, Estonia: Perioodika, 1978.

Weller, Arthur. *The Agrarian Reform in Esthonia from the Legal Point of View*. Berlin: Edition Baltischer Verlag u. Ostbuchhandlung, 1922.

2. Baltic Germans

Angermann, Norbert, et al. *Wolter von Plettenberg: der grösste Ordensmeister Livlands*. Lüneburg, Germany: Verlag Nordostdeutsches Kulturwerk, 1985.

Dehio, Walter. *Erhard Dehio: Lebensbild eines baltischen Hanseaten 1855–1940*. Heilbronn, Germany: E. Salzer, 1970.

Dellingshausen, Eduard, Freiherr von. *Im Dienste der Heimat!* (in Estonian, *Kodumaa teenistuses: Eestimaa Rüütelkonna peamehe mälestused*). Tallinn, Estonia: Olion, 1994.

Garleff, Michael. *Deutschbaltische Politik zwischen den Weltkriegen: die parlamentarische Tätigkeit der deutschbaltischen Parteien in Lettland und Estland*. Bonn-Bad Godesberg, Germany: Verlag Wissenschaftliches Archiv, 1976.

Gernet, Axel von. *Forschungen zur Geschichte des baltischen Adels*. Hannover-Döhren, Germany: Verlag H. v. Hirschheydt, 1978.

Jahrbuch des baltischen Deutschtums. Lüneburg, Germany: Schriftenvertrieb der Carl-Schirren-Gesellschaft, 1927.

Jahrbuch des baltischen Deutschtums in Lettland und Estland. Riga, Latvia: Jonck & Poliewsky, 1928–1931.

Kühn, Lenore. *Erinnerungen an livländisches Landleben: Herausgegeben und mit einer Einleitung versehen von Detlef Kühn.* Lüneburg, Germany: Verlag Nordostdeutsches Kulturwerk, 1983.

Lundin, Leonard C. "The Road from Tsar to Kaiser: Changing Loyalties of the Baltic Germans, 1905–1914." *Journal of Central European Affairs* 10 (1950): 222–55.

Piirimäe, Helmut, and Claus Sommerhage. *Geschichte der Deutschen in Dorpat.* Tartu, Estonia: Universität Tartu, Lehrstuhl für deutsche Philologie, 1998.

Rechtskraft und Rechtsbruch der liv- und estländischen Privilegien. Leipzig, Germany: Duncker & Humbolt, 1887.

Ritscher, Alfred. *Vom Tode Wolters von Plettenberg bis zum Untergang des Deutschen Ordens in Livland (1535–1561).* Bonn, Germany: Kulturstiftung der Dt. Vertriebenen, 2001.

Schilling, Erich Baron. *Die Rittergüter im Kreise Jerwen seit der Schwedenzeit: ein Beitrag zur Güter- und Familiengeschichte Estlands.* Hannover, Germany: H. v. Hirschheydt, 1970.

Schlau, Wilfried, et al. *Die Deutschbalten.* Munich: Langen Müller, 1995.

Seesemann, Heinrich. *Dorothea (Doris) von Ungern-Sternberg, 1787–1828 [i.e. 1829]: e. Lebensbild, nach Briefen u. anderen.* Hannover-Döhren, Germany: H. v. Hirschheydt, 1979.

Seraphim, Ernst. *Aus Livlands Vorzeit, deutsche Ritter und Kaufleute als Kulturbringer im Baltenland.* Leipzig, Germany: Koehler & Amelang, 1925.

Wedel, Hasso von. *Die estländische Ritterschaft und ihre Institutionen, vornehmlich zwischen 1710 und 1783.* Berlin: Ost-Europa-Verlag, 1935.

Weiss, Gottfried. *Abschied von Estland und deutsche Schicksalsjahre: Erinnerungen und Zeitbilder von 1914–1933 erzählt von einem Sonntagskind.* Melle: E. Knoth, 1990.

Wistinghausen, Henning von. *Aus meiner näheren Umwelt: eine estländische Kindheit vor 100 Jahren = Pilte minu lähemast ümbrusest: üks lapsepõlv Eestimaal saja aasta eest.* Tallinn, Estonia: Avita, 1995.

———. *Quellen zur Geschichte der Rittergüter Estlands im 18. und 19. Jahrhundert: (1772–1889).* Hannover-Döhren, Germany: H. v. Hirschheydt, 1975.

———. *Versunkene Welten: Erinnerungen einer estländischen Dame / Theophile von Bodisco.* Weissenhorn: A. H. Konrad, 1997.

———. *Zwischen Reval und St. Petersburg: Erinnerungen von Estländern aus zwei Jahrhunderten: im Auftrag der Estländischen Ritterschaft.* Weissenhorn: A. H. Konrad, 1993.

3. Culture

3.1. Archaeology

Nerman, Birger. *Die Verbindungen zwischen Skandinavien und dem Ostbaltikum in der jüngeren Eisenzeit.* Stockholm: Akademiens förlag, 1929.

Selirand, Jüri. *Jatkuvuus Viron muinaistieteen vakiintumisessa.* Oulu, Finland: Oulun Yliopisto, 1990.

———. *Viron Rautakausi: Viron nuoremman rautakauden aineiston pohjalta.* Rovaniemi, Finland: Pohjois-Suomen Historiallinen Yhdistys, 1989.

Selirand, Jüri, and E. Tõnisson. *Through Past Millennia: Archaeological Discoveries in Estonia.* Tallinn, Estonia: Perioodika, 1984.

3.2. Architecture

Hein, Ants. *Palmse = Palms: ein Herrenhof in Estland.* Tallinn, Estonia: Kirjastus Hattorpe and Eesti Entsüklopeediakirjastus, 1996.

———. *Viljandimaa mõisad = The Manor Houses of Viljandi County, Estonia.* Viljandi, Estonia: Hattorpe, 1999.

Mäeväli, Sulev. *Historical and Architectural Monuments in Tallinn.* Tallinn, Estonia: Perioodika, 1981.

Maiste, Juhan. *The House of the Brotherhood of Blackheads.* Tallinn, Estonia: Kunst, 1995.

Mazing, Viktor Viktorovich. *Ancient Mires as Nature Monuments.* Tallinn, Estonia: Estonian Encyclopaedia Publishers, 1997.

Ränk, Gustav. *Die älteren baltischen Herrenhöfe in Estland: Eine bauhistorische Studie.* Uppsala, Sweden: Lundquistska Bokhandel, 1971.

Soom, Arnold. *Der Herrenhof in Estland im 17. Jahrhundert.* Lund, Sweden: Estonian Learned Society in Sweden, 1954.

Thomson, Erik. *Korps, ein Herrenhof in Estland im Wandel der Zeiten.* Lüneburg, Germany: Nordostdeutsches Kulturwerk, 1986.

Thomson, Erik, and Georg Baron von Manteuffel-Szoege. *Schlösser und Herrensitze im Baltikum; nach alten Stichen.* Frankfurt, Germany: W. Weidlich, 1959.

Thomson, Erik, and Hildegard Thomson. *Dome, Kirchen und Klöster im Baltikum.* Frankfurt, Germany: W. Weidlich, 1962.

Tuulse, Armin. *Die Burgen in Estland und Lettland.* Tartu, Estonia: Dorpater Estnischer Verlag, 1942.

———. *Gotland och Estlands medeltida byggnadsskulptur.* Lund, Sweden: n.p., 1945.

———. *Monument och Konstverk som förstörts i Estland 1941–1944.* Stockholm: Estonian Learned Society in Sweden, 1948.

3.3. Art

Antik, Richard, et al. *Estonian Art in Exile 1980 = Eesti kunst eksiilis 1980.* Stockholm: Estonian World Festival 1980 in Sweden, 1980.

Baigell, Renee, and Matthew Baigell. *Peeling Potatoes, Painting Pictures: Women Artists in Post-Soviet Russia, Estonia, and Latvia: The First Decade.* New Brunswick, N.J.: Jane Voorhees Zimmerli Art Museum and Rutgers University Press, 2001.

Feinstein, Stephen C. "The Avant-Garde in Soviet Estonia." In *New Art from the Soviet Union*, edited by Norton Dodge and Alison Holt. Washington, D.C.: Acropolis Books, 1977.

Kodres, Krista, Juhan Maiste, and Vappu Vabar, eds. *Sten Karling and Baltic Art History = Sten Karling und Kunstgeschichte im Ostseeraum.* Tallinn, Estonia: Estonian Academy of Arts, 1999.

3.4. Folklore and Folk Culture

Aarne, Antti. *Estnische Märchen- und Sagenvarianten Verzeichnis der zu den Hurt'schen Handschriftsammlungen gehörenden Aufzeichnungen.* Hamina: Suomalaisen Tiedeakatemian kustantama, 1918.

Baruch, Jacques. *Légendes d'Estonie.* Brussels: Thanh-Long, 1975.

Kallas, Oskar Philipp. *Die Wiederholungslieder der estnischen Volkspoesie.* Helsinki, Finland: Druckerei der Finnischen Litteraturgesellschaft, 1901.

Korb, Anu, Janika Oras, and Ülo Tedre. *Estonian Folklore Archives.* Tartu, Estonia: Estonian Folklore Archives, 1995.

Loorits, Oskar. *Grundzüge des estnischen Volksglaubens*, 3 vols. Lund, Germany: C. Bloms boktr., 1949–1957.

Manninen, Ilmari. *Die Sachkultur Estlands.* Tartu, Estonia: Õpetatud Eesti Selts, n.d. (1930s).

Moora, H., and Ants Viires. *Abriss der estnischen Volkskunde.* Tallinn, Estonia: Estnischer Staatsverlag, 1964.

Peterson, Aleksei. *Zur finnougrischen Volkskunde.* Tallinn, Estonia: Valgus, 1985.

Ränk, Gustav. *Vanha Viro, kansa ja kulttuuri.* Helsinki, Finland: Suomalaisen Kirjallisuuden Seura, 1955.

Tedre, Ülo. *Estonian Customs and Traditions.* Tallinn, Estonia: Perioodika, 1995.

———. *From Ancient Estonian Customs to Modern Rites.* Tallinn, Estonia: Perioodika, 1985.

Värv, Ellen. *Estonian Folk Costumes.* Tallinn, Estonia: Estonian Institute, 1998.

Viires, Ants. *Über die Herkunft und Verbeitung des Krummholzes im Pferdegeschirr.* Debrecen, Hungary: n.p., 1971.

———. *Woodworking in Estonia.* Jerusalem: Israel Program for Scientific Translations, 1969.

———, ed. *Finno-Ugric Studies in Archaeology, Anthropology and Ethnography.* Estonian Papers presented at the Sixth International Finno-Ugric Congress, Syktyvkar, 24–30 July 1985. Tallinn, Estonia: Estonian Academy of Sciences, Institute of History, 1990.

3.5. Music

Allpere, Anne. *Cantometrics—Applied on Estonian Runo Songs.* Tallinn, Estonia: Eesti NSV Teaduste Akadeemia, 1988.

———. *Estonian Cantometric Attempt.* Tallinn, Estonia: Eesti NSV Teaduste Akadeemia, 1989.

———. *Estonian Cantometric Attempt II: The Sacred and the Profane, Can It Be Heard?* Tallinn, Estonia: Eesti NSV Teaduste Akadeemia, 1989.

Anderson, Walter. *Studien zur Wortsilbenstatistik der älteren estnischen Volkslieder.* Tartu, Estonia: Tartu University Press, 1935.

Olt, Harry. *Estonian Music.* Tallinn, Estonia: Perioodika, 1980.

Tennar, Fred. *Aspects in the Development of Estonian National Music.* Silver Spring, Md.: Shazco, 1998.

Topman, Monika. *An Outline of Estonian Music.* Tallinn, Estonia: Perioodika, 1978.

3.6. Theater

Rähesoo, Jaak. *Estonian Theater.* Tallinn, Estonia: Estonian Theater Union, 1999.

Rosen, Elisabet, Baronesse. *Rückblicke auf die Pflege der Schauspielkunst in Reval; Festschrift zur Eröffnung des neuen Theaters in Reval im September 1910.* Hannover-Döhren, Germany: H. v. Hirschheydt, 1972.

4. Education

Blosfeld, Paul Ferdinand Hermann. *Geschichte des deutschen Schulwesens in Estland, 1919–1935.* Tallinn, Estonia: F. Wassermann, 1935.

Inno, Karl. *Tartu University in Estonia during the Swedish Rule (1632–1710).* Stockholm: Vaba Eesti, 1972.

Peck, Bryan T., and Annabelle Mays. *Challenge and Change in Education: The Experience of the Baltic States in the 1990s.* Huntington, N.Y.: Nova Science Publishers, 2000.

Peremees, H. *Higher Education in the Estonian SSR.* Tallinn, Estonia: Perioodika, 1980.

Rajangu, Väino. *Das Bildungswesen in Estland: Grundlagen, Tendenzen, Probleme.* Cologne, Germany: Böhlau Verlag, 1993.

Rajangu, Väino, and Mai Meriste. *Educational Institutions for Ethnic Minorities in Estonia.* Tallinn, Estonia: Center for Educational Research at Tallinn Technical University, 1996.

———. *Estonian Schools Abroad and Educational Institutions for Ethnic Minorities in Estonia.* Tallinn, Estonia: Center for Educational Research at Tallinn Technical University, 1996.

Reinhop, H. *Education in Soviet Estonia.* Tallinn, Estonia: Eesti Raamat, 1967.

Teacher Training in the Baltic States: Nordic Plan of Action. Copenhagen: Nordic Council of Ministers, 1995.

Virkus, Rein. *Education in the Estonian SSR.* Tallinn, Estonia: Perioodika, 1975.

5. Ethnic Minorities

Aklaev, Airat. *From Confrontation to Integration: The Evolution of Ethnopolitics in the Baltic States.* Frankfurt, Germany: Peace Research Institute, 2001.

Andersen, Erik André. *An Ethnic Perspective on Economic Reform: The Case of Estonia.* Aldershot, UK: Ashgate, 1999.

———. *Privatiseringens konsekvenser for den russiske befolkning i Estland perioden 1987–1995.* Frederiksberg: Samfundslitteratur, 1998.

Berg, Eiki. "Ethnic Mobilization in Flux: Revisiting Peripherality and Minority Discontent in Estonia." *Space & Polity* 5, no. 1 (2001): 5–26.

———. "Minority Conflicts in Eastern Europe." In *Politics and Identities in Transformation: Europe and Israel*, edited by Shlomo Avineri and Werner Weidenfeld. Bonn, Germany: Europa Union Verlag, 2001.

Birckenbach, Hanne-Margret. *Preventing Diplomacy through Fact-finding: How International Organisations Review the Conflict over Citizenship in Estonia and Latvia.* New Brunswick, N.J.: Transaction Publishers, 1997.

Katus, Kalev, Allan Puur, and Luule Sakkeus. "The Demographic Characteristics of National Minorities in Estonia." In *The Demographic Characteristics of National Minorities in Certain European States*, vol. 2, Population Studies 21. Strasbourg, France: Council of Europe, 2000.

Kionka, Riina. "A Russian Speaks Frankly about Non-Estonians." *Report on the USSR* 2, no. 39 (1990): 22–24.

Kirch, Aksel, ed. *The Integration of Non-Estonians into Estonian Society: History, Problems, and Trends.* Tallinn, Estonia: Estonian Academy Publishers, 1997.

Laitin, David. *Identity in Formation: The Russian-Speaking Populations in the Near Abroad.* Ithaca, N.Y.: Cornell University Press, 1998.

Lauristin, Marju, and Mati Heidmets, eds. *The Challenge of the Russian Minority.* Tartu, Estonia: Tartu University Press, 2002.

Pettai, Vello. "Estonia's Controversial Language Policies." *Transition* 2, no. 24 (November 1996): 20–22.

———. "Shifting Relations, Shifting Identities: The Russian Minority in Estonia after Independence." *Nationalities Papers* 23, no. 2 (June 1995).

Raun, Toivo U. "Ethnic Relations and Conflict in the Baltic States." In *Ethnic Nationalism and Regional Conflict: The Former Soviet Union and Yugoslavia*, edited by W. Raymond Duncan and G. Paul Holman. Boulder, Colo.: Westview, 1994.

Rose, Richard, and William Maley. "Nationalities in the Baltic States: A Survey Study." *Studies in Public Policy* 222 (1994): 39–41.

Semjonov, Aleksei, ed. *Ethnic Minorities in Estonia: Domestic Laws and International Instruments.* Legal Information Center for Human Rights and the Presidential Round Table on National Minorities International Seminar, Tallinn, Estonia, 25–26 April 1997.

Shafir, Gershon. *Immigrants and Nationalists: Ethnic Conflict and Accommodation in Catalonia, The Basque Country, Latvia, and Estonia.* Albany: State University of New York, 1995.

Taagepera, Rein. "Ethnic Relations in Estonia 1991." *Journal of Baltic Studies* 23 (1992): 121–32.

———. *The Fenno-Ugric Republics and the Russian State.* London: Hurst, 1999.

Trifunovska, Snezana, ed. *Minorities in Europe: Croatia, Estonia, and Slovakia.* The Hague: Kluwer Law International, 1999.

Verschik, Anna. *Estonian Yiddish and Its Contacts with Coterritorial Languages = Eesti jidiš ja selle kontaktid Eestis kõneldavate keeltega.* Tartu, Estonia: Tartu University Press, 2000.

Vetik, Raivo. "Ethnic Conflict and Accommodation in Post-Communist Estonia." *Journal of Peace Research* 30, no. 3 (August 1993): 271–80.

———. *Inter-ethnic Relations in Estonia, 1988–1998.* Acta Universitatis Tamperensis. Tampere, Finland: Tampere University Press, 1999.

———. "Russians in Estonia: New Development Trends." In *Changing Identities in Estonia. Sociological Facts and Commentaries,* edited by Marika Kirch and David D. Laitin. Tallinn, Estonia: Estonian Academy of Sciences, 1994.

Vihalemm, Triin. "The Estonian Language Competence: Performance and Beliefs about Its Acquisition among the Russian-Speaking Habitants of Estonia 1989–1997." *International Journal of Sociology of Language* 139 (1999): 69–85.

———. Formation of Collective Identity among Russophone Population of Estonia. Tartu, Estonia: Dissertationes de mediis et communicationibus Universitatis Tartuensis, 1999.

———. "Group Identity Formation Processes among Russian-Speaking Settlers of Estonia: A Linguistic Perspective." *Journal of Baltic Studies* 30, no. 1 (1999): 18–39.

6. Estonians Abroad

Aun, Karl. *The Political Refugees: A History of the Estonians in Canada.* Toronto: McClelland and Stewart, 1985.

Birskys, Betty, et al. *The Baltic Peoples in Australia: Lithuanians, Latvians, Estonians.* Melbourne, Australia: AE Press, 1986.

Pennar, Jaan, with Tõnu Parming and P. Peter Rebane. *The Estonians in America, 1627–1975: A Chronology & Fact Book.* Dobbs Ferry, N.Y.: Oceana Publications, 1975.

7. Foreign Relations: 1918–2002

Arumäe, Heino. *At the Crossroads: The Foreign Policy of the Republic of Estonia in 1933–1939.* Tallinn, Estonia: Perioodika, 1983.

The Baltic States 1940–1972; Documentary Background and Survey of Develop-

ments, Presented to the European Security and Cooperation Conference. Stockholm: Baltic Committee in Scandinavia, 1972.

The Baltic States: Survey of the International Relations of Estonia, Latvia and Lithuania. Stockholm: n.p., 1968.

Clemens, Walter C., Jr. *Baltic Independence and Russian Empire.* New York: St. Martin's Press, 1991.

———. *The Baltic Transformed: Complexity Theory and European Security.* Lanham, Md.: Rowman & Littlefield, 2001.

Crowe, David M. *The Baltic States & Great Powers: Foreign Relations, 1938–1940.* Boulder, Colo.: Westview, 1993.

Hansen, Birthe, and Bertel Heurlin. *The Baltic States in World Politics.* New York: St. Martin's Press, 1998.

Hiden, John. *The Baltic States and Weimar Ostpolitik.* Cambridge: Cambridge University Press, 1987.

Hiden, John, and Aleksander Loit, eds. *The Baltic in International Relations between the Two World Wars.* Studia Baltica Stockholmiensia 3. Stockholm: Almqvist & Wiksell International, 1988.

Hinkkanen-Lievonen, Merja-Liisa. *British Trade and Enterprise in the Baltic States, 1919–1925.* Studia Historica 14. Helsinki, Finland: Suomen Historiallinen Seura, 1984.

Mattisen, Edgar. *Searching for a Dignified Compromise: The Estonian-Russian Border, 1,000 years.* Tallinn, Estonia: ILO, 1996.

Newman, Edward William Polson. *Britain and the Baltic.* London: Methuen, 1930.

Nokkala, Arto. *Sotilaspolitiikan haasteita Pohjois-Euroopassa.* Tampere, Finland: Center for Peace Research, University of Tampere, 1998.

Page, Stanley W. *The Formation of the Baltic States: A Study of the Effects of Great Power Politics upon the Emergence of Lithuania, Latvia, and Estonia.* New York: H. Fertig, 1970.

Petersen, Nikolaj, ed. *The Baltic States in International Politics.* Copenhagen: Jurist- og økonomforbundets forlag, 1993.

Royal Institute of International Affairs. *The Baltic States: A Survey of the Political and Economic Structure and the Foreign Relations of Estonia, Latvia, and Lithuania.* Westport, Conn.: Greenwood Press, 1970.

Talvar, H. *The Foreign Policy of Estonia, 1918–1921.* Tallinn, Estonia: Perioodika, 1978.

———. *The Foreign Policy of Estonia, 1920–1939.* Tallinn, Estonia: Perioodika, 1982.

Vares, Peter, ed. *Estonia and the European Union: In Search of Security.* Tallinn, Estonia: EuroUniversity, 1999.

Vendt, Alfred. *Estnische Handelspolitik.* Emsdetten, Germany: Verlags-anstalt H. & J. Lechte, 1938.

Vihalemm, Peeter. "Baltic Space: Estonia and its Neighbours." *Journal of Baltic Studies* 30, no. 3 (1999): 250–69.

Volmars, Janis. *Zollunion Lettland-Estland als historisches, theroetisches und ökonomisch-konstruktives Problem.* Riga, Latvia: A. G. Valters und Rapa, 1934.

8. The Estonian Language

Bjarnson, Donald Einer. *Teaching Estonian to Americans: A Comparison of Two Methods.* Ph.D. diss., Indiana University, 1982.

Gutslaff, Johann. *Observationes grammaticae circa linguam Esthonicam = Grammatilisi vaatlusi Eesti keelest.* Translated into Estonian and edited by Marju Lepajõe. Tartu, Estonia: Tartu Ülikooli Kirjastus, 1998.

Gutsleff, E. *Anweisung zur ehstnischen Sprache grammatica Vocabularium, Proverbia, Aenigmata, Colloquia E. Gutsleff* [von Ant, Thor Helle]. Halle: n.p., 1732.

Hasselblatt, Cornelius. *Lehrbuch des Estnischen.* Wiesbaden, Germany: Harrassowitz, 1995.

Hinderling, Robert. *Die deutsch-estnischen Lehnwortbeziehungen im Rahmen einer europäischen Lehnwortgeographie.* Wiesbaden, Germany: Harrassowitz, 1981.

Kurman, George. *The Development of Written Estonian.* Indiana University Publications; Uralic and Altaic Series 90. The Hague: Mouton, 1968.

Mägiste, Julius. *Estnisches etymologisches Wörterbuch.* Helsinki, Finland: Finnisch-Ugrische Gesellschaft, 1982.

———. *Vanhan kirjaviron kysymyksiä; tutkielmia viron kirjakielen varhaisvaiheista 1200-luvulta 1500-luvun lopulle.* Helsinki, Finland: Suomalaisen Kirjallisuuden Seura, 1970.

Moseley, Chris. *Colloquial Estonian.* London: Routledge, 1994.

Mürk, Harry William. *A Handbook of Estonian: Nouns, Adjectives and Verbs.* Bloomington: Indiana University, Research Institute for Inner Asian Studies, 1997.

Nemvalts, Peep. *Case Marking of Subject Phrases in Modern Standard Estonian.* Stockholm: Almqvist & Wiksell, 1996.

Õim, Haldur, ed. *Estonian in the Changing World.* Tartu, Estonia: University of Tartu, Department of General Linguistics, 1996.

Oinas, Felix J. *Estonian General Reader.* Bloomington: Indiana University Press, 1972.

———. *Basic Course in Estonian.* Bloomington: Indiana University Press, 1975, 1993.

Raag, Raimo. *Från allmogemål till nationalspråk: språkvård och språk politik i Estland från 1857 till 1999.* Uppsala, Sweden: Acta Universitatis Upsaliensis, 1999.

———. *Lexical Characteristics in Swedish Estonian.* Uppsala, Sweden: Academia Upsaliensis, 1982; Stockholm: Almquist & Wiksell, 1982.

Raag, Virve. *The Effects of Planned Change on Estonian Morphology.* Uppsala, Sweden: Uppsala University Library, 1998.

Raun, Alo, and Andrus Saareste. *Introduction to Estonian Linguistics.* Wiesbaden, Germany: O. Harrassowitz, 1965.

Saari, Henn. *Ein Weg zur Wortgrammatik, am Beispiel des Estnischen.* Tallinn, Estonia: Eesti Keele ja Kirjanduse Instituut, 1997.

Sivers, Fanny de. *Analyse grammaticale de l'estonien parlé.* Clermont-Ferrand, France: G. de Bussac, 1969.

Söderman, Tiina. *Lexical Characteristics of the Estonian North Eastern Coast Dialect.* Uppsala, Sweden: AUU, 1996.

Tauli, Valter. *Standard Estonian Grammar.* Stockholm: Almqvist & Wiksell, 1973, 1983.

Tiivel, Irene. *English and Estonian: Some Idiomatic Differences.* Tartu, Estonia: Ilmamaa, 1998.

Tuldava, Juhan. *Estonian Textbook: Grammar, Exercises, Conversation.* Bloomington: Indiana University, Research Institute for Inner Asian Studies, 1994.

Virtaranta, Pertti, and Seppo Suhonen. *Viron kirjakieli = Estonian, the Literary Language.* Helsinki, Finland: Suomalaisen Kirjallisuuden Seura, 1985.

Weiss, Andreas von. *Hauptprobleme der Zweisprachigkeit: eine Untersuchung auf Grund deutsche estnischen Materials.* Heidelberg, Germany: C. Winter, 1959.

9. Literature

9.1. Literature in Translation

Airik-Priuhka, Silvia, ed. *Våra sånger fick vi med oss: lyrik av 12 estniska skaldinnor i urval och översättning.* Stockholm: Välis-Eesti & Emp, 1983.

Eelmäe, August. *The Sailors' Guardian: A Selection of Estonian Short Stories.* Tallinn, Estonia: Perioodika, 1984.

Eerme, Karl, ed. *Estonian Poetry.* Translated by E. Howard Harris. London: Estonian National Fund in Great Britain, 1950.

Kääri, K., and H. Peep. *A Glimpse into Soviet Estonian Literature.* Tallinn, Estonia: Eesti Raamat, 1965.

Kallas, Aino Krohn. *The White Ship: Estonian Tales.* Freeport, N.Y.: Books for Libraries Press, 1971.

Kreutzwald, Fr. R. *Kalevipoeg: An Ancient Estonian Tale.* Moorestown, N.J.: Symposia Press, 1982.

Kross, Jaan. *The Conspiracy & Other Stories.* London: Harvill Press, 1995.

———. *The Czar's Madman: A Novel.* New York: Pantheon Books, 1993.

———. *Die Frauen von Wesenberg, oder, Der Aufstand der Burger: Roman.* Munich: Carl Hanser Verlag, 1997.

———. *Professor Martens' Departure.* New York: New Press, 1994.

Kurrik, Juhan. *Ilomaile: Anthology of Estonian Folk Songs with Translations and Commentary.* Scarborough, Ont., Canada: Maarjamaa, 1985.

Maas, Selve, comp. *The Moon Painters, and Other Estonian Folk Tales.* New York: Viking Press, 1971.

Maas, Selve, and Peggy Hoffmann. *The Sea Wedding and Other Stories from Estonia.* Minneapolis, Minn.: Dillon Press, 1978.

Matthews, William Kleesmann. *Anthology of Modern Estonian Poetry.* Westport, Conn.: Greenwood Press, 1977.

Moroz, Elvina. *The Love that Was: Stories of Estonian Writers.* Moscow: Progress, 1982.

Mutt, Eugenie. *Fairy Tales from Baltic Shores; Folk-lore Stories from Estonia.* Philadelphia: The Penn Publishing Company, 1930.

Oras, Ants. *Acht estnische Dichter; ausgewählt und übertragen von Ants Oras.* Stockholm: Verlag Vaba Eesti, 1964.

P.E.N. Club, Estonia. *Anthologie des conteurs estoniens.* Paris: Editions du Sagittaire, 1937.

The Play: Short Stories by Young Estonian Authors. Tallinn, Estonia: Perioodika, 1984.

Pranspill, Andres, ed. and trans. *Estonian Anthology; Intimate Stories of Life, Love, Labor, and War of the Estonian People.* Milford, Conn.: n.p., 1956.

Pruul, Kajar, and Darlene Reddaway, eds. *Estonian Short Stories.* Evanston, Ill.: Northwestern University Press, 1996.

Puhvel, Heino, ed. *Estonian Short Stories (Eduard Vilde et al.).* Tallinn, Estonia: Perioodika, 1981.

Puhvel, Madli. *Symbol of Dawn: The Life and Times of the 19th-century Estonian Poet Lydia Koidula.* Tartu, Estonia: Tartu University Press, 1995.

Sørensen, Egon. *Djævelens ansigt: roman fra Estland.* Hornslet: Limosa, 1991.

Straumanis. Alfred, ed. *Confrontations with Tyranny: Six Baltic Plays with Introductory Essays.* Prospect Heights, Ill.: Waveland Press, 1977.

Talvet, Jüri, ed. *The Piper: A Selection of Estonian Fairy Tales.* Tallinn, Estonia: Perioodika, 1987.

Tuglas, Elo. *Elon kirja: Elo Tuglaksen päiväkirjamerkintöjä vuosilta 1952–1958.* Helsinki, Finland: Suomalaisen Kirjallisuuden Seura, 1990.

Unt, Mati. *Hyvää iltaa, rakkaat vainajat näytelmä.* Oulu, Finland: Pohjoinen, 1986.

———. *Kuunpimennys.* Helsinki, Finland: Gummerus, 1985.

———. *Murha hotellissa.* Helsinki, Finland: Taifuuni, 1993.

———. *Selections.* Tallinn, Estonia: Eesti Raamat, 1985.

Viirlaid, Arved. *Graves without Crosses.* Toronto: Clarke Irwin, 1972.

Withers, Carl. *Painting the Moon: A Folktale from Estonia.* New York: E. P. Dutton, 1970.

9.2. Literature: Bibliography and History

Aav, Yrjö. *Estonian Periodicals and Books in Finnish Libraries.* Zug, Switzerland: Switzerland Inter Documentation Company, 1970.

Harris, E. Howard. *Estonian Literature in Exile.* London: Boreas, 1949.

———. *Literature in Estonia.* London: Boreas, 1947.

Hasselblatt, Cornelius, und Volker Pirsich. *Estnische Literatur in deutscher Sprache, 1802–1985: Bibliographie der Primär- und Sekundärliteratur.* Hamburg: H. Buske, 1988.

Judas, Elizabeth. *Russian Influences on Estonian Literature; A Study of Jakob Tamm and Anton H. Tammsaare.* Los Angeles: Wetzel, 1941.

Kabur, V., ed. *Eesti kirjandus võõrkeeltes, 1978–1984 = Estonskaia literatura na inostrannykh iazykakh, 1978–1984: bibliograficheskii ukazatel' = Estonian Literature in Foreign Languages, 1978–1984: A Bibliography.* Tallinn, Estonia: Fr. R. Kreutzwaldi nim, Eesti NSV Riiklik Raamatukogu, 1985.

Kruus, Oskar, ed. *Eesti kirjarahva leksikon = Estnisches Schriftstellerlexikon.* Tallinn, Estonia: Eesti Raamat, 1995.

Kõressaar, Viktor, and Aleksis Rannit, eds. *Estonian Poetry and Language: Studies in Honor of Ants Oras.* Stockholm: Kirjastus Vaba Eesti for Estonian Learned Society in America, 1965.

Kuldsepp, T. *Viron kirjallisuus Suomessa.* Helsinki, Finland: Suomalaisen Kirjallisuuden Seura, 1977.

Mägi, Arvo. *Estonian Literature.* Stockholm: Baltic Humanitarian Organization, 1968.

Mallene, Endel. *Estonian Literature in the Early 1970s: Authors, Books, and Trends of Development.* Tallinn, Estonia: Eesti Raamat, 1978.

Mauer, Mare, ed. *Eesti kirjandus võõrkeeltes: bibliograafianimestik = Estonian Literature in Foreign Languages: a Bibliography = Estonskaia literatura na inostrannykh iazykakh: bibliograficheskii ukazatel.* Tallinn, Estonia: Fr. R. Kreutzwaldi nim. Eesti NSV Riiklik Raamatukogu, 1978.

Nirk, Endel. *Estonian Literature: Historical Survey with Bibliographical Appendix*, 2nd ed. Tallinn, Estonia: Perioodika, 1987.

———. *Viron kirjallisuus.* Helsinki, Finland: Suomalaisen Kirjallisuuden Seura, 1986.

9.3. Children's Literature

Maran, Iko. *A Long Day.* Tallinn, Estonia: Perioodika, 1983.

McBride, Gisela, comp. *Tales from Estonia.* Trexlertown, Pa.: G. McBride, 1982.

9.4. Literary Criticism

Devoto, Giacomo. *Storia delle letterature baltiche.* Milan: Nuova academia, 1957.

Doderer, Heimito von. *Von Figur zu Figur: Briefe an Ivar Ivask über Literatur und Kritik.* Munich: Beck, 1996.

Epner, Luule, and Pekka Lilja, eds. *Taasleitud aeg: Eesti ja soome kirjanduse muutumine 1950–1960 aastatel = Kadonneen ajan arvoitus viron ja Suomen kirjal-*

lisuuden muuttuminen 1950- ja -1960- luvulla. Tartu, Estonia: Tartu ülikooli, 2000.

Hasselblatt, Cornelius. *Die estnische Literatur und ihre Rezeption in Deutschland.* Lüneburg, Germany: Institut Nordostdeutsches Kulturwerk, 1994.

Jänes, Henno H. *Geschichte der estnischen Literatur.* Stockholm: Almqvist & Wiksell, 1965.

Kallas, Aino Krohn. *Nuori Viro: Muotokuvia ja suuntaviivoja.* Helsinki, Finland: Otava, 1918.

Kirby, William Forsell, comp. *The Hero of Esthonia, and Other Studies in the Romantic Literature of that Country* (from Esthonian and German Sources). London: John C. Nimmo, 1905.

Kurman, George. *Literatures in Contact: Finland and Estonia.* New York, Estonian Learned Society in America, 1972.

Lapin, Leonhard. *Pimeydestä valoon: Viron taiteen avant-garde neuvostomiehityksen aikana.* Helsinki, Finland: Kustannusosakeyhtiö, 1996.

Loorits, Oskar. *Estnische Volksdichtung und Mythologie.* Tartu, Estonia: Akadeemiline Kooperatiiv, 1932.

Mägi, Arvo. *Viron kirjallisuuden historia.* Helsinki, Finland: Suomalaisen Kirjallisuuden Seura, 1965.

Rubulis, Aleksis. *Baltic Literature: A Survey of Finnish, Estonian, Latvian, and Lithuanian Literatures.* Notre Dame, Ind.: University of Notre Dame Press, 1970.

Salokannel, Juhani. *Sielunsilta: Suomen ja Viron kirjallisia suhteita.* Helsinki, Finland: Suomalaisen Kirjallisuuden Seura, 1998.

Suits, Gustav. "Die estnische Literatur." In *Die osteuropäischen Literaturen und die slawischen Sprachen*, edited by A. Bezzenberger and A. Brückner. Berlin: B. G. Teubner, 1908.

Thomson, Erik. *Estnische Literatur: ihre europäische Verflechtung in Geschichte und Gegenwart.* Lüneburg, Germany: Nordostdeutsches Kulturwerk, 1973.

Wagner, Kerttu. *Die historischen Romane von Jaan Kross: am Beispiel einer Untersuchung der deutschen und englischen Übersetzungen von Professor Martensi ärasõit.* Frankfurt, Germany: P. Lang, 2001.

10. Nature and Natural Resources

Estonian Riigikogu. *National Environmental Strategy Approved by Parliament 12 March 1997.* Tallinn, Estonia: Estonian Environment Information Center, 1997.

Karoles, K. ed. *Estonian Forests.* Tallinn, Estonia: Estonian Forest Dept., 1995.

Markus, Eduard. *Der Brennschieferbau Estlands: eine geographische Analyse.* Tartu, Estonia: K. Mattiesens Buchdr, 1938.

Masing, Matti. *Taxonomy and Status of Wild Mammals in Estonia, 1945–1994.* Tartu, Estonia: Sicista, 1999.

Peterson, Kaja. *Nature Conservation in Estonia: General Data and Protected Areas.* Tallinn, Estonia: Huma, 1994.

Raukas, Anto, and Aada Teedumäe, eds. *Geology and Mineral Resources of Estonia.* Tallinn, Estonia: Estonian Academy Publishers, 1997.

Roose, Antti. *Estonia Built on Oil Shale.* Rakvere, Estonia: Virumaa Foundation, 1991.

Tenno, Koidu, and Veena Räägel. *Estonian Oil-shale: Resources, Mining, Power Engineering, Oil-shale Chemistry.* Tallinn, Estonia: Informare Ltd., 1991.

Thomson, Erik. *Die Grossschmetterlinge Estlands.* Stollhamm: Rauschenbusch, 1967.

11. Religion

Amburger, Erik. *Die Pastoren des Konsistorialbezirks Estland, 1885–1919.* Cologne, Germany: Böhlau, 1988.

Estonian Evangelical Lutheran Church in Exile. *Church in Bondage.* Stockholm: Estonian Evangelical Lutheran Church, 1980.

Helk, Vello. *Die Jesuiten in Dorpat 1583–1625: ein Vorposten der Gegenreformation in Nordosteuropa.* Odense, Denmark: Odense University Press, 1977.

Hollberg, Wilhelm. *Das russische Altgläubigentum: seine Entstehung und Entwicklung.* Tartu, Estonia: Tartu Ülikooli Kirjastus, 1994; Cologne, Germany: Mare Balticum, 1994.

Isberg, Alvin. *Kyrkoförvaltningsproblem i Estland 1561–1700.* Uppsala, Sweden: Universitetet, 1970; Stockholm: Almqvist & Wiksell, 1970.

———. *Svensk mission och kyrklig verksamhet i Estland 1873–1943 = Schwedische Mission und kirchliche Tätigkeit in Estland 1873–1943.* Uppsala, Sweden: Uppsala universitet, Teologiska institutionen, 1978.

Karjahärm, Toomas. "Konfessionen und Nationalismus in Estland zu Beginn des 20. Jahrhunderts." *Nordost Archiv* 7, no. 2 (1998), 543–53.

Kimbrough, S. T., Jr., ed. *Methodism in Russia and the Baltic States: History and Renewal.* Nashville, Tenn.: Abingdon Press, 1995.

Paucker, Eduard Peter Heinrich. *Ehstlands Kirchen und Prediger seit 1848.* Hannover-Döhren, Germany: H. v. Hirschheydt, 1968.

Paulson, Ivar. *The Old Estonian Folk Religion.* Indiana University Publications. Uralic and Altaic Series, no. 108. The Hague: Mouton, 1971.

Philipp, Guntram. *Die Wirksamkeit der Herrnhuter Brüdergemeine unter den Esten und Letten zur Zeit der Bauernbefreiung vom Ausgang des 18. bis über die Mitte des 19. Jhs.* Cologne, Germany: Böhlau, 1974.

Schrenck, Erich von. *Baltische Kirchengeschichte der Neuzeit.* Hannover-Döhren, Germany: H. v. Hirschheydt, 1988.

Valk, Ülo. *The Black Gentleman: Manifestations of the Devil in Estonian Folk Religion.* Helsinki, Finland: Suomalainen Tiedeakatemia, 2001.

Vööbus, Arthur. *The Martyrs of Estonia: The Suffering, Ordeal, and Annihilation of the Churches under the Russian Occupation.* Stockholm: Etse, 1984.

———. *Studies in the History of the Estonian People: With Reference to Aspects of Social Conditions, in Particular, the Religious and Spiritual life and the Educational Pursuit.* Stockholm: ETSE Papers of the Estonian Theological Society in Exile, 1969–1984.

Wagenknecht, Willy. *Die deutschen evangelischen Gemeinden.* Würzburg, Germany: Buchdruckerei R. Mayr, 1939.

12. Science

Engelbrecht, Jüri. "Development of Science in Estonia." *Towards a Baltic Europe: Annals of the European Academy of Sciences and Arts* 30, no. 10, 2000 (2001): 65–71.

Martinson, H. *Science Policy in Estonia.* Tallinn, Estonia: Estonian Science Foundation, 1992.

Prunskiençe, Kazimiera, and Elmar Altvater, eds. *East-West Scientific Co-operation: Science and Technology Policy of the Baltic States and International Cooperation.* Boston: Kluwer Academic Publishers, 1997.

Vihalemm, Rein. *Estonian Studies in the History and Philosophy of Science.* Dordrecht, The Netherlands: Kluwer Academic Publishers, 2001.

13. Swedish Estonians

Aman, Viktor, et al. *En bok om Estlands svenskar.* Stockholm: Kulturföreningen Svenska odlingens vänner, 1961.

Andersson, Olof. *Folkliga svenska koralmelodier från Gammalsvenskby och Estland.* Stockholm: Svenska kyrkans diakonistyrelses bokförlag, 1945.

Ekman, Mats. *En bygdeskald bland den gamla svenska folkstammen i Estland.* Göteborg, Sweden: Elanders boktr., 1924.

Hyrenius, Hannes. *Estlands svenskarna, demografiska studier.* Lund, Sweden: C. W. K. Gleerup, 1942.

Jakobsson, Svante. *Från fädernejorden till förfäders land: Estlandssvenskt bondfolks rymningar till Stockholm 1811–1834: motiv, frekvens, personliga konsekvenser.* Stockholm: Almqvist & Wiksell, 1976.

Jonsson, Stig. *Svenskar hos ester i öster.* Visby: Gutebröcker, 1989.

Loit, Aleksander, and Nils Tiberg. *Gammalsvenskbydokument.* Estlandssvenskarnas Folkliga Kultur 3. Skrifter utgivna av Kungl. Gustav Adolfs Akademien. Uppsala, Sweden: Lundequist, 1958.

Rosenqvist, Johan, ed. *Speglar i minnenas hus: estlandssvensk diktantologi.* Stockholm: Svenska odlingens vänner (SOV) and Svenska odlingens nya generation (SONG), 1990.

Steffensson, Jakob. *Livet på Runö: en berättelse om hur 300 människor levde på den lilla svenskön Runö i Rigaviken från 1920-talet fram till andra världskriget.* Stockholm: Seelig, 1976.

Söderbäck, Per. *Rågöborna.* Stockholm: P. A. Norstedt, 1940.

Tiberg, Nils. *Estlandssvenska husdjursnamn: Jämte en dialektuppsats: Husdjuren på Runö*. Uppsala, Sweden: Lundequistska bokh., 1972.

Wieselgren, Per. *Ortnamn och bebyggelse i Estland forna och hittillsvarande svenskbygder, Ostharrien med Nargö*. Uppsala, Sweden: Lundequistska bokhandeln, 1951.

14. Tallinn

Angermann, Norbert, and Wilhelm Lenz. *Reval: Handel und Wandel vom 13. bis zum 20 Jahrhundert*. Lüneburg, Germany: Institut Norddeutsches Kulturwerk, 1997.

Anting, Leida. *Firearms and Firearm Makers in Tallinn in the XIV–XVI Centuries*. Rochester, N.Y.: n.p., 1968.

Elias, Otto-Heinrich. *Reval in der Reformpolitik Katharinas II: die Statthalterschaftszeit 1783–1796*. Bonn-Bad Godesberg, Germany: Verlag Wissenschaftliches Archiv, c. 1978.

Etzold, Gottfried. *Seehandel und Kaufleute in Reval nach dem Frieden von Nystad bis zur Mitte des 18. Jahrhunderts*. Marburg/Lahn, Germany: J. G. Herder-Institut, 1975.

Feyerabend, Liselotte. *Die Rigaer und Revaler Familiennamen im 14. und 15. Jahrhundert: unter besonderer Berücksichtigung der Herkunft der Bürger*. Cologne, Germany: Böhlau, 1985.

Freytag, Hartmut, et al. *Der Totentanz der Marienkirche zu Lübeck und der Nikolaikirche in Reval (Tallinn): Edition, Kommentar, Interpretation*. Cologne, Germany: Böhlau, 1993.

Gierlich, Ernst. *Reval 1621 bis 1645: von der Eroberung Livlands durch Gustav Adolf bis zum Frieden*. Bonn, Germany: Kulturstiftung der Deutschen Vertriebenen, 1991.

Hartmann, Stefan. *Reval im nordischen Krieg*. Bonn-Bad Godesberg, Germany: Verlag Wissenschaftliches Archiv, 1973.

Hehn, Jürgen von, ed. *Reval und die baltischen Länder: Festschrift für Hellmuth Weiss zum 80. Geburtstag*. Marburg/Lahn, Germany: J.-G.-Herder-Inst.,1980.

Holst, Niels von. *Riga und Reval; ein Buch der Erinnerung*. Hameln, Germany: F. Seifert, 1952.

Johansen, Paul, and Heinz von Zur Mühlen. *Deutsch und Undeutsch im mittelalterlichen und frühneuzeitlichen Reval*. Cologne, Germany: Böhlau, 1973.

Kala, Tiina. *Lübeck Law and Tallinn*. Tallinn, Estonia: Tallinna Linnaarhiiv, 1998.

Pezold, Johann Dietrich von. *Reval 1670–1687*. Cologne, Germany: Böhlau, 1975.

Pullat, Raimo. *All Roads Lead to Tallinn: History of Old Tallinn*. Tallinn, Estonia: Estopol, c. 1998.

———. *Tallinn through the Ages*. Tallinn, Estonia: Perioodika, 1983.

Pullat, Raimo, and U. Mereste. *Über die Formierung der Tallinner Stadtbevölkerung im 18. Jahrhundert und die Rekonstruktion der Zeitreihen in der geschich-*

tlichen Demographie (anhand der Kirchenbücher). Cologne, Germany: Selbstverlag Forschungsinstitut für Sozial- und Wirtschaftsgeschichte an der Universität zu Köln, 1982.

Reval und die baltischen Länder. Festschrift für Hellmuth Weiss zum 80 Geburtstag. Marburg/Lahn, Germany: J. G. Herder-Institut, 1980.

Der Revaler Kodex des lübischen Rechts 1282 = Lübecki õiguse Tallinna koodeks 1282. Tallinn, Estonia: Tallinna Linnaarhiiv, 1998.

Soom, Arnold. *Der Handel Revals im siebzehnten Jahrhundert.* Wiesbaden, Germany: O. Harrassowitz, 1969.

———. *Die Zunfthandwerker in Reval im siebzehnten Jahrhundert.* Stockholm: Almqvist & Wiksell, 1971.

Tallinn, Linnaarhiiv. *Das Revaler Geleitsbuch, 1515–1626.* Tallinn, Estonia: 1939.

Taube, Arved, Freiherr von. *Reval, Tallinn: Hansestadt, Landeshauptstadt, Olympiastadt.* Düsseldorf and Kempten/Allgäu, Germany: Rau, 1979.

Thomson, Erik. *Geschichte der Domschule zu Reval, 1319–1939.* Würzburg, Germany: Holzner Verlag, 1969.

———. *Reval/Tallinn Porträt einer Ostseestadt.* Cologne, Germany: Rodenkirchen Liebig, 1979.

Vahemetsa, Aigar. *Tallinn, Autumn 1917.* Tallinn, Estonia: Perioodika, 1987.

Weinmann, Arno. *Reval 1646 bis 1672: vom Frieden von Brömsebro bis zum Beginn der selbständigen Regierung Karls XI.* Bonn, Germany: Kulturstiftung der Deutschen Vertriebenen, 1991.

Wolf, Thomas. *Tragfähigkeiten, Ladungen und Masse im Schiffsverkehr der Hanse: vornehmlich im Spiegel Revaler Quellen.* Cologne, Germany: Böhlau, 1986.

Zobel, Rein. *Walls and Towers of Tallinn.* Tallinn, Estonia: Estonian Encyclopaedia, 1996.

Zur Mühlen, Heinz von. *Reval vom 16. bis zum 18. Jahrhundert: Gestalten und Generationen eines Ratsgeschlechts.* Cologne, Germany: Böhlau, 1985.

IV. REFERENCES

1. Bibliographies and Genealogies

Arens, Ilmar. *Jurisprudence, Political Science, Sociology, Economy 1942–1976: A Bibliography.* Stockholm: Institutum litterarum estonicum, 1977.

Beare, Arlene. *A Guide to Jewish Genealogy in Latvia and Estonia,* vol. 3, *A Guide to Jewish Genealogy.* London: The Jewish Genealogical Society of Great Britain, 2001.

Blumfeldt, Evald, and Nigolas Loone. *Bibliotheca Estoniae historica, 1877–1917; Nachdruck mit einer Einführung neu herausgegeben von Paul Kaegbein.* Cologne, Germany: Böhlau, 1987.

Brennsohn, Isidorus. *Die Aerzte Estlands, vom Beginn der historischen Zeit bis zur*

Gegenwart; ein biographisches Lexikon. Nebsteiner historischen Einleitung über das Medizinalwesen Estlands. Riga, Latvia: n.p., 1922; Hannover-Döhren, Germany: H. v. Hirschheydt, 1972.

Hurt, Vambola. *Estonia: Philately & Postal History: Handbook, Catalogue = Estland: Philatelie & Postgeschichte, Handbuch.* Stockholm: Estonian Philatelic Society in Sweden, 1986; Old Tappan, N.J.: Estonian Philatelic Society in New York, 1986.

Kaelas, Aleksander. *Ortsnamen Estlands = Place Names in Estonia,* 2nd rev. ed. Stockholm: Estnischer Nationalfond, 1965.

Kändler, Tiit. *A Hundred Great Estonians of the 20th Century.* Tallinn, Estonia: Eesti Entsüklopeediakirjastus, 2002.

Kõks, Endel. *A Bibliography of Estonian Art and Artists Outside Estonia = Välis-Eesti kunstielu bibliograafia.* Stockholm: Välis-Eesti & EMP, 1984.

Mäelo, Meemo. *History—Archaeology, History, History of Art, Music, Religion, and Church 1945–1983: A Bibliography of Works Published by Estonian Scholars in Exile.* Stockholm: Institutum Litterarum Estonicum, 1985.

Maldonado, Sigrid Renate. *Estonian Experience and Roots: Ethnic Estonian Genealogy with Historical Perspective, Social Influences and Possible Family History Resources: An Aid or Guide to Those Wanting to Know Some Local History and to Search for their Estonian also Latvian Roots and to Professional Genealogists.* Fort Wayne, Ind.: As Was, 1996.

Maurer, Küllike. *Bibliographia iuridica estonica 1918–1940 = Eesti õigusbibliograafia = Legal Literature of Estonia.* Tallinn, Estonia: Eesti Rahvusraamatukogu, 1994.

Paucker, Julius. *Die Literatur der Geschichte Liv-, Ehst- und Curlands aus den Jahren 1836 bis 1847.* Hannover-Döhren, Germany: H. v. Hirschheydt, 1973.

Ränk, Aino. *A Bibliography of Works Published by Estonian Historians in Exile 1945–1969; History, Archaeology, History of Art, Music, the Church and Law.* Stockholm: Institutum Litterarum Estonicum, 1969.

———. *A Bibliography of Works Published by Estonian Scholars in Exile 1945–1975: Ethnology.* Stockholm: Estniska vetenskapliga inst., 1975.

Smith, Inese A., and Marita V. Grunts. *The Baltic States: Estonia, Latvia, Lithuania.* [Bibliography.] Santa Barbara, Calif.: Clio, 1993.

Webermann, Otto Alexander. *Studien zur volkstümlichen Aufklärung in Estland: Friedrich Gustav Arvelius (1753–1806).* Göttingen, Germany: Vandenhoeck & Ruprecht, 1978.

2. Periodicals in English

Baltic Defense Review. Biannual. 1999–. www.bdcol.ee/bdcol/publications.php?id=01

The Baltic Observer: News from Estonia, Latvia, and Lithuania. [microform] Riga, Latvia: Baltic News Ltd., 1992–1996.

The Baltic Review. Tallinn, Estonia. Quarterly. 1993–. www.tbr.ee
Baltic Studies Newsletter. Irregular. 1976–. www.balticstudies-aabs.lanet.lv
The Baltic Times: News from Estonia, Latvia, and Lithuania. Riga, Latvia. Weekly. 1996–.
Central European Review. Prague, Czech Republic. Fortnightly. 1999–. www.ce-review.org
Elm (Estonian literary magazine). Irregular. Tallinn, Estonia. Estonian Institute, 1996–. www.einst.ee/literary
Estonian Art. Estonian Institute. Irregular. 1997–. http://einst.ee/ea/
Folklore: Electronic Journal of Folklore. Institute of the Estonian Language & Estonian Folklore Archives. Quarterly. 1996–. http://haldjas.folklore.ee/folklore
Journal of Baltic Studies. Quarterly. 1971–. www.balticstudies-aabs.lanet.lv
Juridica International. Tartu, Estonia: Faculty of Law of the University of Tartu, 1996–. www.juridica.ee/index.php
Music in Estonia: Estonian Music Review. Tallinn: Estonian Music Council, 1997–.
Pro Ethnologica. Estonian National Museum. www.erm.ee/pro
Studies in Folklore and Popular Religion. Tartu, Estonia: Dept. of Estonian and Comparative Folklore, University of Tartu. 1996–.
Trames: A Journal of the Humanities and Social Sciences. Tallinn, Estonia. Quarterly. 1997–.

3. Internet Resources in English

3.1. Official Information

Baltic Defense College: www.bdcol.ee/bdcol/
Estonia and NATO: www.vm.ee/eng/nato
Estonian Embassies Web Pages: www.vm.ee/eng/kat_135/1425.html
Estonian Legal Translation Center: www.legaltext.ee/indexen.htm
Estonian Ministry of Foreign Affairs: www.vm.ee/eng
Estonian State Web Server: www.riik.ee
Government of Estonia: www.riik.ee/en/valitsus/
Internet Law Library—Estonia: www.lectlaw.com/inll/59.htm
President of Estonia: www.president.ee/eng/
Riigikogu—Parliament of Estonia: www.riigikogu.ee
Supreme Court of of Estonia: www.nc.ee/english/
United States CIA World Factbook—Estonia: www.cia.gov/cia/publications/factbook/geos/en.html

3.2. Parties and Elections

Estonian National Electoral Commission: www.vvk.ee/engindex.html
Estonian Political Parties and Organizations: www.politicalresources.net/estonia.htm

3.3. Economics and Statistics

Bank of Estonia: www.ee/epbe/index.html
Estonian Chamber of Commerce and Industry: www.koda.ee/e_index_en.html
Estonian Investment Agency: www.eia.ee/index_eng.php3
Statistical Office of Estonia: www.stat.ee
Tallinn Stock Exchange: www.hex.ee

3.4. European Union

Estonia and the European Union: www.vm.ee/eng/euro/
Estonian Ministry of Foreign Affairs EU Site: http://spunk.vm.ee/euro//english/
EU Law Portal: http://europa.eu.int/eur-lex/en/index.html
European Commission Enlargement Site—Estonia (complete EU documentation): http://europa.eu.int/comm/enlargement/estonia/index.htm

3.5. News Media

The Baltic Times: http://archives.baltictimes.com/www/Baltics Worldwide: www.balticsww.com
City Paper daily new on the Internet: www.balticsww.com/wkcrier/daily_news.htm
Radio Free Europe/Radio Liberty—Estonian Service: www.rferl.org/bd/es/index.html
Estonian Review (weekly review of Estonian news from the Ministry of Foreign Affairs): www.vm.ee/eng/kat_137/2411.html

3.6. Academic Institutions

Estonian Business School: www.ebs.ee
Estonian Educational and Research Network: www.eenet.ee/englishEENet/index.html
Estonian Science Foundation: www.etf.ee
Estonian Social Science Data Archive: http://psych.ut.ee/esta/
Institute of Baltic Studies: www.ibs.ee
Institute of the Estonian Language: www.eki.ee/index.html.en
Tallinn Pedagogical University: www.tpu.ee
Tallinn Technical University: www.ttu.ee
University of Tartu: www.ut.ee

3.7. Libraries

British Library—Estonian Collections: www.bl.uk/collections/easteuropean/estonian.html

Estonian Historical Archives: www.eha.ee
Estonian Libraries Network (ELNET): http://helios.nlib.ee/screens/mainmenu.html
Herder Institut, University of Marburg: www.uni-marburg.de/herder-institut/
Library of Congress's Selected Internet Resources on Estonia: www.loc.gov/rr/international/european/estonia/es.html
National Library of Estonia: www.nlib.ee/inglise/indexi.html
University of Helsinki Library: www.lib.helsinki.fi

3.8. Art and Culture

The Art Museum of Estonia: www.ekm.ee/english/
Estonian Art: www.einst.ee/Ea/
Estonian History Museum: www.eam.ee/index.html
Estonian National Museum: www.erm.ee

3.9. Cities' Websites

Narva Home Page: www.narva.ee
Pärnu Home Page: www.parnu.ee/in_english/index.html
Tallinn Home Page: www.tallinn.ee/eng
Tartu Home Page: www.tartu.ee
Viljandi Home Page: www.viljandi.ee

3.10. Search Engines

Delfi (Estonian and Russian only): www.delfi.ee
Estonia-Wide Web: www.ee/www/
NETI—Eesti Interneti Kataloog ja Otsingusüsteem (Estonian-only Internet catalogue): www.neti.ee/

3.11. Other Web Resources

Baltic Explorer: www.balticexplorer.com
Baltic Links: www.balticlinks.com
English-Estonian Dictionary: www.ibs.ee/dict/index.html
Estonia Country Guide: www.ciesin.ee/ESTCG/
Estonian Atlas: http://atlas.ibs.ee/
Estonian Institute's Estonian Information Page: www.einst.ee
Information about Estonia: muhu.www.ee
Maps of Estonia in the Perry-Castañeda Library Map Collection, University of Texas at Austin: www.lib.utexas.edu/maps/estonia.html
Web Encyclopaedia Estonica: www.estica.org

WWW Virtual Library—History Index: Estonia: www.ukans.edu/history/VL/europe/estonia.html

3.12. *Estonians Abroad*

Estonian American National Council: www.estosite.org/eng/
Estonian Central Council in Canada: www.ekn.ca/start.htm
Estonian National Congress in Sweden: www.rel.ee/eng/index.htm

About the Author

Toivo Miljan is professor of political science at Wilfrid Laurier University, Waterloo, Ontario, and adjunct professor of political economy, Swedish School of Economics and Business Administration, Helsinki, Finland. From 1990–92, he also served as adjunct professor and chargé a.i., chair of Estonian studies, University of Toronto. Earlier, in 1965–66, he served as research officer with the Royal Commission on Bilingualism and Biculturalism in Canada and wrote a two-volume report, *Bilingualism in Finland*, which provided guidance for developing the Canadian federal bilingualism program. Subsequently he also did research for the United Nations and spent 20 years studying and teaching third-world trade and financial policy relations. For five years from 1988, Professor Miljan closely followed developments in Estonia and the other Baltic states by frequent field trips. In 1993 he was appointed to a five-year term as founding director of the EuroFaculty by the Council of Baltic Sea States, and he was charged with restructuring the teaching and learning of law, economics, public administration, and political science at the University of Tartu in Estonia, the University of Latvia in Riga, and Vilnius University in Lithuania, the three national universities of the Baltic States, as well as the University of Kaliningrad in Russia.

Born in Tallinn, Estonia, in 1938, he received his early education in Stockholm, Sweden; his secondary education in Toronto, Ontario; and his B.A. and M.A. from the University of Toronto. He studied at the Faculty of Laws, University College, London, and was awarded his Ph.D. by the University of London. Professor Miljan is the author of *The Reluctant Europeans* (McGill-Queen's University Press, 1977), and editor of *Food and Agriculture in Global Perspective: Discussions in the Committee of the Whole of the United Nations* (Pergamon Press, 1980) and *The Political Economy of North-South*

Relations (Broadview Press, 1987). In 1998, the University of Latvia awarded him an Honorary Doctorate and the University of Tartu made him an Honorary Fellow. The president of Estonia decorated Professor Miljan in 2001 with the Order of the White Star V in recognition of his contribution in assisting Estonia to achieve and rebuild its independence.